THE LITERARY DIGEST
History of the World War

Compiled from Original and Contemporary
Sources: American, British, French,
German, and Others

BY

FRANCIS WHITING HALSEY

*Author of "The Old New York Frontier," Editor of "Great Epochs in
American History," "Seeing Europe with Famous Authors,"
"Balfour, Viviani, and Joffre, Their Speeches
in America," etc.*

IN TEN VOLUMES—ILLUSTRATED

VOLUME X

THE NAVAL BATTLES OFF HELGOLAND, SOUTH AMERICA, THE DOGGER BANK
AND JUTLAND—PERSONAL SKETCHES OF WAR LEADERS—THE PEACE
CONFERENCE IN PARIS, VERSAILLES, ST. GERMAIN, AND THE SIGN-
ING OF THE TREATY—THE PEACE TREATY IN THE UNITED
STATES SENATE—CHRONOLOGY AND INDEX

August, 1914—May, 1920

FUNK & WAGNALLS COMPANY
NEW YORK AND LONDON
1920

CONTENTS—VOLUME TEN

IN THE GERMAN COLONIES AND ON THE SEA—
Continued

PART III—BATTLES BETWEEN WARSHIPS AND THE WORK OF COMMERCE RAIDERS

PERSONAL SKETCHES, THE TREATY OF PEACE AND A CHRONOLOGY OF THE WAR

PART I—PERSONAL SKETCHES OF WAR LEADERS

CONTENTS—VOLUME TEN

ILLUSTRATIONS—VOLUME TEN

FULL PAGES

ILLUSTRATIONS—VOLUME TEN

TEXT ILLUSTRATIONS

ILLUSTRATIONS—VOLUME TEN

MAPS

FRANCIS WHITING HALSEY

INTRODUCTORY

FRANCIS WHITING HALSEY, the talented editor-author of this work, who died November 24, 1919, had practically completed the task that he had undertaken before he closed his eyes, so that the work of bringing the tenth and concluding volume down to date has involved very little additional labor.

His work has received a well-deserved meed of praise, which is reflected in the words of the Editor of The New York *Times:* —"This admirable account of the World War, intended primarily for general reading, will have its value for the historical student and for the seeker of source material because it preserves much vivid description of important scenes that might otherwise be lost and forgotten. The general reader will find its particular value in the fact that Mr. Halsey approached his task with a true perspective, and justly saw and accurately described the part taken by each nation involved in its due relation to the whole conflict and the final victory."

The tenth volume will be found to contain the history of the battles on the sea and of commerce raiders, a description of the work of the Peace Conference, sketches of fifty of the statesmen and military leaders, a summary of the League of Nations, and of the treaties of peace, and a chronology of events from the beginning of the war to the refusal of the United States Senate to ratify the Treaty of Versailles.

Born October 15, 1851, Francis Whiting Halsey was graduated from Cornell University in 1873. Two months after his graduation, he went to Binghamton, N. Y., where he edited *The Binghamton Times* for two years, and then obtained a position on the editorial staff of *The New York Tribune,* for which he served as foreign correspondent writing letters from the World's Fair in Paris, contributing book reviews as well as literary notes and articles until 1880, when he joined the staff of *The New York Times.* On this paper he worked for several years as foreign editor and critical reviewer, later becoming literary editor, succeeding in that post Charles DeKay on his appointment by President Cleveland as Consul-General to Berlin. When *The New York Times Saturday Book Review* was established in 1896, Halsey was appointed its editor, and conducted it on such a broad-minded plan that it made rapid advancement as a power in American literary life. Assiduous labor and painstaking care placed the *Saturday Book Review* on so high a plane that it soon became the mentor and guide of millions of readers, but in 1902 its editor resigned his post to become literary adviser to D. Appleton & Company. On the termination of this contract, he joined the staff of the Funk & Wagnalls Company in a similar capacity, and continued in this connection until his death.

With the passing of Francis W. Halsey a highly valued member of the editorial staff of *The Literary Digest* entered into rest. Well known both as author and editor, his literary work was supplemented by wider activities in the publishing enterprises of the Company of which he was literary adviser for many years.

Mr. Halsey was the author of a number of books chief among which may be mentioned his "An Old New York Frontier; Its Indian Wars, Pioneers, and Land Titles," which was an account of the early history of the head waters of the Susquehanna from Otsego Lake to the Pennsylvania line (1901). In 1878 he published "Two Months Abroad," and in 1895 he wrote an elaborate introduction for a volume of family history entitled "Thomas Halsey of Hertfordshire, England and Southampton, L. I." Other works from his pen were "Our Literary Deluge"; "The Pioneers of Unadilla Village"; an historical and biographical introduction to Mrs. Rowson's "Charlotte Temple"; an introduction to Richard Smith's "Tour of Four Great Rivers." In 1900 he wrote a memoir of his wife, "Virginia Isabel Forbes," to whom he was married in 1883, and who died in January, 1899.

As an editor, Mr. Halsey produced "American Authors and Their Homes"; "Authors of Our Day in Their Homes"; "Women Authors of Our Day in Their Homes"; "Of the

INTRODUCTION

Making of a Book"; "Great Epochs of American History Described by Famous Writers"; "Seeing Europe with Famous Authors"; "Balfour, Viviani, and Joffre, Their Speeches in America." Associated with Willam Jennings Bryan he produced "The World's Famous Orations" in ten volumes in 1906, and in the year following, in conjunction with Senator Henry Cabot Lodge, he published "The Best of the World's Classics."

Mr. Halsey's formative influence, his ability to steer clear of alluring sensationalism and precocity, pedantry, and staleness; his frankness and modesty, all served to establish him in the community long before his death as a man of sound literary judgment with a gift of being wholesome without being prudish, and well-read without being a prig—a man who loved his fellow men, one by nature temperate and generous, honest and faithful, who added to these attributes, wit, culture, and scholarship of that highest order which may be fittingly characterized as practical.

Of him and of the present work, George Douglas said in *The San Francisco Bulletin:*—"Twenty years from now Mr. Halsey's work will stand with no more needed than the addition of some necessary foot-notes as more and more of the truth is divulged. The main thing is to get intelligently interested in the war, interested in something more than its butchery tho that should be ever present in the mind. People who forget its horrors are apt to become as warped in their judgment as those who seem to have eliminated all consciousness of the fact that there was a war in which millions of men lost their lives, and who can not see that there will be other wars in the future unless something be done to prevent them when the horrors of the great struggle that has just passed are still fresh in the mind. Not a question concerning the war but is dealt with in these pages, and upon all there is the fullest information. Halsey writes as an American and an ally. He is fair, very fair, in dealing with the enemy; but he is just, as he understands justice. Yet he is not one of those historians who write for the purpose of maintaining national animosities."

To him it was a God-given privilege to live in those stirring times when men fought against the lust of dominion to vindicate the rights of small nations against the arrogant and overbearing might of perfidious powers; for, he had the faith of one who could look with fearless eyes beyond the tragedy of a world at war, and he gloried in the fact that he had lived to see the powers of Darkness put to flight and the Morning of a greater Freedom break.

F. H. V.

IN THE GERMAN COLONIES AND ON THE SEA

(Continued)

Part III
BATTLES BETWEEN WARSHIPS AND THE WORK OF COMMERCE-RAIDERS

VICE-ADMIRAL SIR DAVID BEATTY
Commander under Jellicoe of the British fleet in the Dogger Bank, Heligoland and Jutland battles. Beatty, in August, 1919, was made an Earl

BATTLES IN THE FIRST YEAR—HELIGOLAND, CORONEL, FALKLAND ISLANDS, DOGGER BANK, AND THE AFFAIR IN THE GULF OF RIGA

August 4, 1914—August, 1915

WHEN at 11 o'clock on the night of August 4, 1914, Great Britain declared war on Germany, the Admiralty flashed by wireless to the British fleet, throughout the world, this order: "Great Britain declares war on Germany. Capture or destroy the enemy." Then followed a flood of official orders and the following personal message from King George: "I have confidence that the British fleet will revive the old glories of the Navy. I am sure that the Navy will again shield Britain in this hour of trial. It will prove the bulwark of the empire." Sir John Jellicoe assumed supreme command of the home fleet, with the acting rank of Admiral. Daily thereafter it was expected that an engagement would be fought with the German fleet in the North Sea.

On August 7, Winston Churchill, First Lord of the Admiralty, declared as yet there had been no naval losses, except a small British cruiser, the *Amphion,* and the German mine-layer, *Königin Luise.* A flotilla of torpedo-boat destroyers accompanied by the *Amphion,* while patrolling the upper reaches of the English Channel, had found the *Königin Luise* laying mines, had pursued and sunk her, about fifty of her crew, which probably numbered 120 or 130 men, being saved by British destroyers. The *Amphion* continued to act as "scout," but in making her return journey was blown up by a mine. The use of mines in sea-warfare was then new.

Survivors of the *Amphion* said they had hardly left Harwich, when they were ordered to clear the decks for action, having sighted the *Königin Luise,* which refused to

3

stop after a shot was fired across her bows. Then destroyers, after a brief bombardment, surrounded and sank her. The German captain, revolver in hand, threatened his men when they prepared to surrender, refused to give himself up, and had to be taken by force. As the *Amphion* was returning to Harwich, the smoke of a big ship was seen on the horizon, and the *Amphion* gave chase, firing a warning shot as she drew near. The vessel proved to be only a Harwich boat, the *St. Petersburg,* which was carrying Prince Lichnowsky, the German Ambassador to Great Britain—afterward famous for his "Memorandum"—across the North Sea to the Hook of Holland on his way home to Germany. While continuing her journey to Harwich, the *Amphion* struck a sunken mine, gave two plunging jerks, followed by an explosion, which ripped her forepart, "shot up her funnels like arrows from a bow," lifted her guns into the air, and then she sank. Falling material struck several boats in the convoying flotilla and injured some of the men aboard them, while others were burned and scalded.

By the middle of August, the North Sea was said once more to be safe as a high-road of commerce, and Denmark was sending supplies to England. Shipping was passing between England and Scandinavian ports and British cruisers as well as converted merchantmen were on every sea. The ill-starred *Lus'tania* had arrived safely in Liverpool from New York, and the *Mauretania* was about to sail from Liverpool. All German and Austrian ships, which when the war began were away from home ports, had come under British attacks or been mewed up in neutral ports. More than half the ocean greyhounds of the Hamburg-American and Nord-Deutscher Lloyd liners were at their piers in New York, Boston, Pernambuco, Kiaochow, Shanghai, or Yokohoma, and to get home would have had to elude the British fleet. The magnitude of the German merchant marine thus "put out of business" was little understood, at least in this country. Its North Sea section in 1913 comprised 2,047 sailing ships of 416,559 gross tonnage, and 1,587 steamers with a gross tonnage of 4,174,186, every one of which became interned abroad or at home, save such as were at the bottom of the sea. The Baltic section numbered 583 vessels of 520,000 tons gross, and 361 sailing vessels aggregating 16,811 tons. The Kiel Canal in 1913 was used by 54,628 vessels, having a total register tonnage of 10,292,153; after the war began, the canal became little more than an anchorage for warships, and a thoroughfare for a few coasting and local steamers.[1]

The main German war-fleet was at Kiel, safe from attack unless it ventured out. Because of the Canal, it could move in either of two ways—eastward into the Baltic, or westward into the North Sea. The enlarging of this great waterway had been completed only a few months before war was declared. Only on July 1 had Kaiser Wilhelm pronounced

THE GERMAN MINE LAYER "KÖNIGIN LUISE"
One of the earliest naval incidents of the war was the sinking of this ship by the British *Amphion*

formally open the enlarged canal to which had been given his name. It had been made into one of the most important artificial waterways in the world, ten miles longer than the Panama Canal, and had been used by probably ten times as many vessels as passed through Suez. It was constructed, however, more for naval than for commercial purposes, since it gave to the German fleet a short cut from the North Sea to the Baltic, and compelled an enemy, seeking to move between the same points, to sail two hundred miles around Schleswig-Holstein and Denmark. Originally completed in

[1] "Statistisches Jahrbuch für das Deutsche Reich. Herausgegeben vom Kaiserlichen Statistischen Amte." 1915. (Berlin) Puttkammer u. Mühlbrecht.

1895, the rapid increase in the size of ships had soon made it inadequate for both mercantile and naval uses. Accordingly, new tide-locks of double the strength and breadth of the old, had been put in and the channel deepened from twenty-eight to forty-six feet. The new locks were probably the largest in the world; they had about 60 per cent. more water than the locks at Gatun. The *Vaterland* could be accommodated in the Kiel Canal. As to England's naval position at the outbreak of war, Mr. Churchill on September 27, made the following statement:[2]

"A great battle on sea has not yet been fought, but we enjoy as great command of the sea and as free use of sea-power as we should have after a decisive engagement. What is there, for instance, that we could do then that we are not doing now? German trade has ceased. German supplies have been largely strangled, but British trade, in all essentials, is going on uninterruptedly. Materials of industry and food for the people are entering the country daily in vast quantities at commercial prices. We are moving scores of men across all the oceans of the world. We started with a substantial naval preponderance, much more like 2 to 1 than 16 to 10. In the next twelve months we shall have twice as many battleships competing and three or four times as many cruisers as Germany, if the losses were even equal. Our position this time next year will be far stronger than it is to-day. You must remember that none of the ships built in my tenure of office, except the small cruiser *Arethusa,* has been commissioned, yet these are the most powerful and most expensive ships that have ever been built. They are the fruits of the greatest naval effort England ever made. We always regarded the first month of war as our most difficult and critical month from a naval point of view, and we have nothing to complain of in the way that the month has gone. We have made up our minds to win it if it costs the last sovereign and the last man in the British Empire."

Except for movements in the Kiel Canal, a portion of the Baltic, and in the estuary of the Elbe, the German main fleet was now tied up. Britain, meanwhile, had outlying squadrons available as follows: In China, one battleship, four cruisers, six smaller vessels, eight destroyers, four torpedo-boats, three submarines; in the East Indies, one

[2] To a writer in The *Giornale d'Italia* (Rome).

battleship, two cruisers, four smaller craft; at the Cape, three cruisers; in New Zealand, three cruisers and one sloop; on the West Coast of Africa, three sloops; on the West Coast of America, three sloops; on the East Coast of South America, one cruiser; in the Australian Navy, one battle-cruiser, three light cruisers, three destroyers and two submarines. The Fourth Cruiser Squadron consisting of five ships, was then on the point of returning from Mexico and the West Atlantic. In addition the British had available for defense and the destruction of commerce, a number of fast liners that had been put in commission under naval commanders and so had become ships of war flying the White Ensign. Many merchant steamers, at the request of their owners, had also been provided with guns, mounted astern, for defense in the event of being chased. Some eight or nine German cruisers were believed to be at sea, all efficient ships for commerce-destroying purposes, and several had high speed. How many German armed liners were out was a matter of conjecture and of much interest, inasmuch as merchant vessels were liable to seizure. Every cruiser became busy at once picking up prizes all over the world. Prize courts soon had work enough cut out to last for many weeks.

It was comparatively easy to blockade the German coast from Borkum near the mouth of the Ems, to Cuxhaven, where the Elbe pours its waters into the North Sea, but the task of bringing the German navy out to battle was difficult, chiefly because the Kiel Canal gave it a wide and deep waterway to a hiding-place in the Baltic. The topography of Denmark, moreover, was almost as great a safeguard to Germany as the canal. The German North Sea coast forms roughly a right angle. Fifty miles out from the great naval base of Wilhelmshaven lies the fortified island of Heligoland, formerly a British possession, and parted with in an evil hour by a shortsighted British statesman. The coast of which Heligoland was the vigilant sentinel has a length from Borkum to the mouth of the Elbe of about one hundred miles. Between the Ems and the principal naval base, Wilhelmshaven, on Jade Bay, is a broad peninsula through which runs the Ems-Jade Canal, navigable for destroyers.

Between Wilhelmshaven and Cuxhaven is a bay thirty miles in width, into which the Weser flows. Almost at the Weser's mouth in Bremerhaven, and forty miles up the river lies Bremen. On the Ems at Emden was a torpedo-boat station. Forty miles due north of Cuxhaven and guarding the mouth of the Elbe was another torpedo-base in Holstein at the mouth of the Eider. On the south side of the canal, between Brunsbuttel and Kudensee, was a new naval station that had cost $8,000,000 and had just been finished when the war began. There were abundant shelters for submarines and destroyers all the way from Borkum to the Eider, besides no fewer than three interior waterways giving timely passage when necessary. At Wilhelmshaven, Cuxhaven, and Kiel, the whole German fleet could lie at anchor in safety.

To dig out an enemy thus made secure in shelters had the look of a forlorn hope. He could not be dug out unless he was really ready to fight, for he could withdraw from North Sea waters through the Kiel Canal and so into the Baltic. It was obvious that, if the British wished to try fortunes in the Baltic, their fleet would have to be divided and that would be a perilous undertaking. To get to Kiel, British warships would have to traverse the Skagerrak, a deep body of water sixty miles wide, and the Kattegat, another body of water of about the same width, between Denmark and Sweden, and would then have to find their way through the channel of the Great Belt, which could easily be mined by the Germans, or dominated by their torpedo-boats. Even in the wide Kattegat, large warships would have to move cautiously, navigation being difficult. By using mines and submarines in these waters the Germans could obtain a tremendous, almost an insuperable, advantage. A British fleet might get as far as the eastern entrance of the Skagerrak without great risk, for the Skagerrak could not be mined, but beyond those waters every mile of the way could be made to bristle with hidden perils.

There seemed, therefore, nothing for the British Navy to do, but patrol the North Sea and blockade the German coast, and so be content with bottling up the German fleet. By this means, it could control all the Seven Seas and Ger-

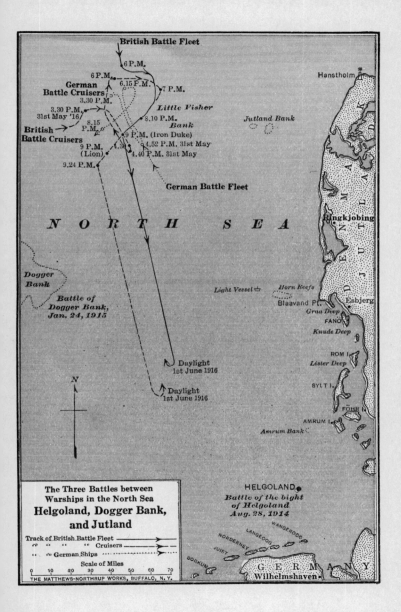

The Three Battles between
Warships in the North Sea
**Helgoland, Dogger Bank,
and Jutland**

mans could get little food or supplies from the world out-side. The fleet of Great Britain, thus controlling the fleet of Germany, provided a support on which all British opera-tions could depend. One of the reasons why the German Fleet refrained from leaving its North Sea shelters, was the fact that on Germany's right flank were the sea forces of Russia. Measured by modern standards, Russia's ships were not formidable, but Russia had a considerable number of cruisers and so had to be watched in the Baltic.

Such losses as the British suffered later, on the high seas, from the *Emden* in the Indian Ocean, and from the *Karls-ruhe* in the Atlantic, were small when compared with the services rendered to the Allies by British sea-power. Almost in a day the German flag was made to disappear from ocean waters, thousands of tons of shipping were captured and other ships made helpless in neutral ports. Hamburg and Bremen became as deserted as Savannah and Charleston were in the time of our Civil War. Because the Allies had control of the sea France was able to bring African troops to the battle-line and England her colonials and Indians. Because of this fact it also was possible to meet the Turkish attack on Egypt by a concentration of Australian, Indian, and Territorial troops brought through the Suez Canal. Some supplies still flowed into Germany from neutral stations— notably from Scandinavia, but in decreasing quantities. German industry suffered more and more from the blockade, and exports fell to the vanishing points. Meanwhile, France and England remained open to the commerce of the world. Purchases made in America were promptly taken to Europe —clothing, automobiles, arms, ammunition, all in vast quan-tities. Conditions such as these helped to bridge over the gap between German preparedness and Allied want of it.

After four weeks of waiting for German ships to come out of the Baltic into the North Sea, British naval com-manders went in search of them. On August 28, a battle-squadron of cruisers and destroyers, under command of Rear-Admiral Sir David Beatty, found and attacked a cruiser-squadron off Heligoland. In an eight-hour action, two of the German cruisers, the *Mainz* and the *Ariadne*, were sunk, a third was set on fire, and two destroyers were

sent to the bottom. The British losses were described as
"negligible." During August and September several other
German warships in different waters were sunk, chief among
them the *Kaiser Wilhelm der Grosse,* formerly a well-known
North-German Lloyd North Atlantic passenger-ship, which
was sunk by a British cruiser on August 27 off the west
coast of Africa. Another cruiser, the *Hela,* was sunk on
September 13. German ships, meanwhile, had inflicted a
good deal of damage on Russian commerce in the Baltic.
None of these conflicts was a great naval fight, but they
were sufficient to make the sea more safe for English, French
and neutral ships, thus permitting the transport of food-
supplies and troops, and practically suspending Germany's
oversea commerce, which meant the closing of many German factories and the throwing of German people out of
regular employment. As early as August 12, the British had
announced to port authorities that Atlantic lanes were again
open. At the same time, the British Home Fleet—sixty
vessels of war, against thirty in the German High Seas
Fleet—guarded the exit of the Kiel Canal.

Thrilling stories of the engagement off Heligoland were
told by men who took part in it. The engagement lasted
about eight hours, during which time a mist hung over the
contending fleets. The fighting was described as sharp and
terrible, the British losses light. Of the destroyers only
one afterward presented outward signs of having taken part
in a battle. The official British report said five German
craft were sunk. A non-commissioned officer of the *Fearless,* which in the thick of battle picked up many German
wounded, said the whole operation "took place in a thick
haze. When we opened fire, there was not a single search-
light playing on us. The Germans all seemed to be asleep.
The action was very hot while it lasted."

At 3.30 A.M. the *Fearless* and *Arethusa,* the latter vessel
the pioneer-ship of a new class and then less than three
days out of the builders' hands, escorted by some twenty
destroyers, advanced in a southwesterly direction at twenty
knots, on a course that would bring them to a point about
six miles south and three miles west of Heligoland. At 8
o'clock dim shadows became visible through the mist. These

THE SINKING OF THE "MAINZ" IN THE HELIGOLAND BATTLES
The photographs from which these pictures were made, were taken on board
British warships that had a part in the battle

were soon found to come from six German destroyers, and orders were given to engage them as soon as possible. At 8.30 A.M. fire was opened by the *Arethusa* and some of the destroyers; at 8.45 A.M. the course was so altered as to bring the other destroyers into the fight. At the same time were sighted three German cruisers of the same class as what are known in the British Navy as "Town" cruisers, of which, at the outbreak of the war, there were fifteen in the British Navy, all light cruisers ranging from 4,800 to 5,400 tons. After these ships got into action the fight became general. In the German fire, tho often well directed, many shots fell short and exploded on striking the water. Before 9.45 A.M. the British ship, the *Arethusa* came in for severe handling, and at 10 o'clock had to haul away temporarily, as only her foremost 6-inch gun was capable of continuing the fire. The British wondered at the time why, at this juncture, German cruisers did not close in and complete her destruction. For some reason unexplained they did not follow up what had been an undoubted success for them.

After 55 minutes of strenuous work, the British cruiser was able to steam into action again, and several German destroyers disappeared. The *Arethusa* continued to receive most of the fire. Altho shells damaged her feed-tank, and materially reduced her speed, she was able to continue the fight. It was now seen that two guns on one of the German cruisers were gone, also the mainmast, and that she was blazing amidships, but she continued to keep up a spirited fire from her foremast and after guns. So far the battle had been waged on the British side by light cruisers and destroyers. Out to seaward German submarines—the first use this was of submarines in a sea-battle—were attacking the squadron. The water being smooth, the submarines were detected, and Admiral Beatty, by maneuvering at high speed, had no difficulty in avoiding them. Meanwhile, all ears were strained to catch more distinctly certain ominous sounds of distant firing. Of this action Admiral Beatty said:

"At 12.15 *Fearless* and First Flotilla were sighted retiring west. At the same time the light-cruiser squadron was observed to be engaging an enemy ship ahead. They appeared to have her beaten. I then steered northeast to sound of firing ahead, and at 12.30 P.M.

THE GERMAN ADMIRAL COUNT VON SPEE

X.

sighted *Arethusa* and Third Flotilla retiring to the westward engaging a cruiser of the *Kolberg* class on our port bow. I steered to cut her off from Heligoland, and at 12.37 opened fire. At 12.42 the enemy turned to the northeast, and we chased at 27 knots. At 12.56 P.M. sighted and engaged a two-funnelled cruiser ahead. *Lion* fired two salvos at her, which took effect, and she disappeared into the mist burning furiously and in a sinking condition."

It would appear that only the *Lion* among the big ships actually fired, the remainder arriving in time only to see the German cruiser, which was the *Mainz*, lying on her beam ends with only a propeller and her starboard quarter showing, while a heap of wreckage marked the spot where the *Köln* had gone down. A dim ruddy glare in the haze showed where a third cruiser was drifting away, her hull a blazing furnace. A naval lieutenant, who took part in the battle, said, in a letter describing this the first notable naval battle of the war:

"We were getting nearer and nearer Heligoland. I expected every minute to find the forts on the island bombarding us. So the *Arethusa* presently drew off, after landing at least one good shell on the enemy. The enemy gave every bit as good as he got. We then reformed, but a strong destroyer belonging to the submarines got chased, and the *Arethusa* and *Fearless* went back to look after her; we presently heard a hot action astern. So the captain in command of the flotilla turned us around, and we went back to help, but they had driven the enemy off, and on our arrival told us to form up on the *Arethusa*.

"When we had partly formed and were very much bunched together, a fine target, suddenly out of the everywhere arrived five or six shells, not 150 yards away. We gazed whence they came, and again five or six stabs of fire pierced the mist, and we made out a four-funnelled cruiser of the *Breslau* class. Those five stabs were her guns going off. We waited fifteen seconds, and shots and the noise of guns arrived pretty well simultaneously, fifty yards away. Her next salvo went over us, and I personally ducked as they whirred overhead like a covey of fast partridges. You would suppose the captain had done this sort of thing all his life. He went full speed ahead at once at the first salvo, to string the bunch out and thus offer less target, and the commodore from the *Arethusa* made a signal to us to attack with torpedoes.

"So we swung round at right angles and charged full speed at the enemy, like a hussar-attack. We got away at the start magnificently and led the field, so all the enemy's firing was aimed at us for the next ten minutes. When we got so close that the débris of their shells fell on board we *altered* our course and so threw them out in their reckoning of our speed, and they had all their work to do over again. Humanly speaking, the captain, by twisting and turning at the psychological moment saved us; actually I feel that we were in God's keeping those days.

"After ten minutes we got near enough to fire our torpedo, and then turned back to the *Arethusa*. Next our follower arrived just where we had been and fired his torpedo, and, of course, the enemy fired at him instead of at us; what a blessed relief! After the destroyers came the *Fearless*, and she stayed on the scene. Soon we found that she was engaging a three-funneler, the *Mainz;* so off we started again, now for the *Mainz,* the situation being that the crippled *Arethusa* was too tubby to do anything but be defended by us, her children.

"The *Mainz* was immensely gallant. The last I saw of her, absolutely wrecked below and aloft, her whole midships a fuming inferno, she had one gun forward and one aft still spitting forth fury and defiance like a wildcat mad with wounds. Our own four-funnel friend recommenced at this juncture with a couple of salvos, but rather half-heartedly, and we really did not care a d——, for there, straight ahead of us, in lordly procession, like elephants walking through a pack of dogs, came the *Lion, Queen Mary, Invincible,* and *New Zealand,* our battle-cruisers, great and grim and uncouth as some antediluvian monsters. How solid they looked! How utterly earthquaking: We pointed out our latest aggressor to them, whom they could not see from where they were. They passed down the field of battle, with the little destroyers at their left, and destroyers on their right, and we went west, while they went east. Just a little later we heard the thunder of their guns for a space, and then all was silence, and we knew that was all."

Heligoland, off which this battle was fought, lies thirty miles from the German coast, and is probably the most strongly fortified small spot on the face of the earth. It is an island only one-fifth of a square mile in area, equipped with probably $10,000,000 worth of long-range guns, and was believed to be capable of sending to the bottom of the sea any hostile fleet venturing within fifteen miles of the range of its guns. Naval and military strategists had agreed that it was doubtful if all the navies in the world acting together

could batter Heligoland into submission. In a time of peace
it was the guardian of Germany's main artery of commerce,
the way to Hamburg, the sentry that protected German fishermen, but in this war it became the key to all the elaborate
German naval plans. Heligoland was a second Gibraltar. At
the time of this battle great cliffs in its sides had concrete
emplacements for hundreds of guns besides which just below
lay a German fleet. The English knew it was impossible
for their ships to pass Heligoland, the passage being defended by ten rows of contact-mines sunk at various depths.
Inside these were fleets of torpedo-boats and destroyers, all
placed ahead of the battle-fleet. On the island were 364
mounted guns, of which 142 were of the 42-centimeter disappearing type. Any British warship coming within sight
of Heligoland would have been speedily blown to pieces.
No ship could have withstood a salvo from a score of great
cannon, each capable of hurling a steel explosive-filled shell
weighing nearly a ton.

It was late on August 27, 1914, off the west coast of
Africa, that the *Kaiser Wilhelm der Grosse* was sunk
by the British cruiser *High Flyer*. This German merchant
cruiser, which was of 14,000 tons, and armed with ten four-
inch guns, had interfered with traffic between England and
the Cape for three weeks. She was one of the few German
armed auxiliary cruisers which succeeded in getting to sea
at the beginning of the war. Before she sank her survivors
were all landed. Formerly a regular liner plying between
New York and Bremen, she was built in 1897 at a cost of
between $3,000,000 and $4,000,000, was 626 feet long, of
66 feet beam, and 14,350 gross tonnage. She had an average
speed of 23 knots and was fitted to carry an armament of
eight 5.9 guns, four 4.7 guns, and fourteen machine-guns.
She was the first vessel to have suites de luxe, consisting of
parlor, bedroom, and bath, costing $1,000 for the passage.
The innovation proved a success, so that succeeding ships
also had sumptuous accommodations, which soon ran the
passage price up as high as $2,000 until a new limit was
reached with a rate of $5,000 for an imperial suite on the
Vaterland and *Imperator*. Soon after the war the *Kaiser
Wilhelm der Grosse* had taken the record for the eastbound

passage from the *Lucania,* of the Cunard Line, making the passage in five days and seventeen hours. She had a narrow escape from destruction in the Hoboken wharf fire of June, 1900. By being towed out into the Hudson she escaped serious injury. On August 9, 1910, Mayor Gaynor of New York was shot while on board this ship, just as he was starting for a vacation in Europe. In 1913 she was converted into a third-class steerage ship, her luxurious fittings being removed. She sailed on her last voyage from New York on July 21, 1914, and arrived at Bremen on July 28, the day Austria declared war against Serbia.

On September 14 occurred a duel between the *Carmania,* a British converted liner formerly a Cunarder running to New York, and a German ship of like nature and about equal force, named the *Cap Trafalgar.* The antagonists met off the east coast of South America, and had a stubborn fight. For an hour and three-quarters they exchanged hard knocks. The battle was something of a reminder of the old form of duels between ships at sea. The *Carmania* began the action at 9,000 yards, fire from both ships being maintained at various ranges, but never within 3,000 yards. British gunners made hits on the hull, at or near the waterline, while the German projectiles crashed into boats and upper works. The *Carmania* had nine men killed and twenty-six wounded; the German ship probably suffered greater losses. She was in flames before the action was half an hour in progress, and capsized before she sank. The men who survived got away in a collier.

On October 17, occurred the sinking by the British of four German destroyers known as *S*-115, *S*-117, *S*-118, and *S*-119. The official report said the British loss was one officer and four men wounded, and that thirty-one German survivors were made prisoners. The senior officer of the light cruiser *Undaunted* was Captain Cecil H. Fox who, on board the *Amphion,* had taken part in the first naval action of the war. His next adventure came when the *Amphion* was sent to the bottom by a mine. The explosion of the first mine knocked him insensible, but he recovered so as to be able to leave the ship three minutes before she went down under shock of a second explosion. He was afterward appointed to a new destroyer, the *Faulkner,* which had been under construction for Chile when war was declared. Only a few days before this action off the Dutch coast, Fox was transferred to the *Undaunted,* the second light cruiser of a new class, the first having been the *Arethusa.* The British destroyers were of the "L" class, parts of the 1911-1912 output, formidable vessels of 35-knot speed, armed with three 4-inch guns and four torpedo-tubes, in pairs, discharging 21-inch torpedoes. The German destroyers were older boats, carrying only two 24-pounder

THE GERMAN COMMERCE-RAIDER "EMDEN"
Sunk by the Australian warship *Sydney* off the Cocos Islands

guns, and not only slower, but there was no comparison between the accuracy of their shooting and that of the British craft. The destruction of the British cruiser *Hawke* by a German submarine had taken place on October 15. The sinking of four German destroyers two days afterward adjusted the balance as between the two navies, at least from the British point of view. The loss of life, being some 300 men in each case, was about the same, but the loss of an obsolescent cruiser like the *Hawke* was thought to be less serious to England than that of four destroyers to Germany.

When the German Admiral von Spee, with the German Pacific Squadron, left Kiaochow early in August, he had succeeded in collecting seven vessels from the China and Australian stations. One of these, the *Emden,* was detached for commerce-raiding in the Indian Ocean, while the light cruiser *Karlsruhe,* noted for its speed, was to become a privateer in the South Atlantic. Spee kept with him two armored cruisers, the *Gneisenau* and the *Scharnhorst,* and three light cruisers, the *Dresden, Leipzig,* and *Nürnberg,* the first two sister-ships, both launched in 1906, with a tonnage of 11,400 and a speed of at least 23 knots. They carried 6-inch armor, and mounted eight 8.2-inch, six 5.9-inch, and eighteen 21-pounder guns. The *Dresden* was a sister-ship of the *Emden*—3,540 tons with a speed of 24½ knots, and ten 4.1-inch guns. The *Nürnberg* was slightly smaller, 3,350 tons; her armament was the same, and her speed was about half a knot quicker. Smaller still was the *Leipzig,* 3,200 tons, with the same armament as the two others, and a speed of over 22 knots, but not shown on the map.

This squadron set itself to prey upon British commerce routes, remembering that the British Navy was short in cruisers of the class best fitted to patrol and guard the great trade highways. Admiral von Spee himself sailed for the western coast of South America, finding coaling and provisioning bases on the coast of Ecuador and Colombia, and in the Galapagos Islands. The duties of neutrals were either imperfectly understood or slackly observed by some of the South American States at the beginning of the war, and so the German admiral seems to have been permitted the use of wireless-stations which gave him valuable information as to the enemy's movements.

Early in August, a small British squadron had set sail to protect the southern trade routes thus menaced. It was commanded by Rear-Admiral Sir Christopher Cradock, a capable and popular sailor, who had served in the Soudan and at the relief of Peking, and had distinguished himself in the work of saving life at the wreck of the *Delhi.* He had in his squadron, when formed, a twelve-year-old battleship, the *Canopus,* two armored cruisers, the *Good Hope* and the *Monmouth,* the light cruiser *Glasgow,* and an armed liner, the *Otranto*. None of his vessels was very strong either in speed or armament. The *Canopus* belonged to a class which had been long obsolete. Her tonnage was 12,960, her speed 19 knots and her armament four 12-inch, twelve 6-inch, and ten 12-pounder guns, all of an old-fashioned pattern. Her armor belt was only six inches thick. The *Good Hope* was

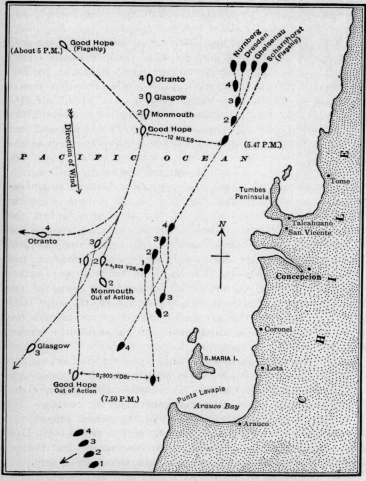

THE BATTLE OF CORONEL, OFF THE COAST OF CHILE

also twelve years old; her tonnage 14,100, her speed 23 knots, and her armament two 9.2-inch, sixteen 6-inch, and twelve 12-pounder guns. The *Monmouth* was a smaller vessel of 9,800 tons, with the same speed, and mounting fourteen 6-inch and eight 12-pounder guns. The *Glasgow*, which had been stationed on the southeast coast of America, was a much newer vessel, and had a speed of 25 knots. Her tonnage was 4,800 and her armament two 6-inch and ten 4-inch guns.

Admiral Cradock's squadron, after sweeping across the Atlantic, by the third week of October went into the Pacific, moving up the coast of Chile, on the lookout for Admiral von Spee. He went first to Coronel, then on to Valparaiso, and back to Coronel to send off cables. The *Glasgow*, to whose officers England owed the story of the fight, left Coronel at 9 o'clock on the morning of November 1, sailing north, and at about four o'clock in the afternoon sighted the enemy.

That Britannia was to have trouble in "ruling the waves" had already become evident, not only from exploits by German submarines in the North Sea, but by the commerce-destroying activities of the *Karlsruhe* in the Atlantic and the *Emden* in the Indian Ocean. But a still more serious blow to British naval prestige, and an impressive demonstration of German naval prowess now came with the defeat of Rear-Admiral Cradock's cruiser-squadron off Coronel by the German squadron under von Spee on the evening of that November day. The British, however, could still point to the fact that their real naval strength had as yet hardly been touched; it still remained about twice that of Germany, and it had been reinforced by the navies of France and Japan. But the immediate result of the Coronel engagement was that Great Britain for the time being had been swept from the South Pacific. Cargoes in British ships for the west coast of South America became practically uninsurable. The fact that the German squadron had the advantage in numbers, tonnage, guns, and speed, only emphasized Great Britain's mistake in allotting to an inadequate fleet the task of clearing the Pacific of German commerce-destroyers.

Tributes were paid to Spee's strategy in having secretly

ADMIRAL SIR CHRISTOPHER CRADOCK
Cradock commanded the British ships at the Battle of Coronel

gathered widely scattered German units, in estimating the probable movements of Admiral Cradock's fleet, and in striking under conditions apparently of his own choosing. According to his report, five German cruisers, the *Gneisenau, Scharnhorst, Nürnberg, Leipzig,* and *Dresden,* met and engaged four British ships, the *Good Hope, Monmouth, Glasgow,* and *Otranto,* "between six and seven o'clock in the evening, during a heavy rain and rough weather off Coronel." This dispatch, as telegraphed from Valparaiso, continued:

"The *Monmouth* was sunk and the *Good Hope,* after a great explosion on board, took fire. Her subsequent fate is unknown, owing to darkness having set in. The *Glasgow* and the *Otranto* also were damaged; the darkness prevented our obtaining knowledge of the extent of it. Our ships, the *Scharnhorst* and *Nürnberg,* were not damaged. The *Gneisenau* had six men wounded. The rest of our ships also were undamaged."

The *Monmouth* and the *Good Hope* brought the number of vessels lost by the British Navy since the beginning of the war to twenty. Germany's naval policy, unlike her policy in her land campaign, in which she struck at once with the full weight of her army, seemed to be one of slow attrition and minor engagements. It mattered not at Coronel that the Kaiser's ships were in a slight numerical superiority. The British had in their flagship, the *Good Hope,* a vessel 3,000 tons larger than the largest of the Germans and carrying two 9.2-inch guns, while the *Gneisenau* and *Scharnhorst* had none of heavier caliber than 8-2 inch, but sixteen guns of the latter size gave them the advantage. The fight took place in a hurricane, under conditions when it was supposed that British seamanship would tell. Yet the Germans got the range first, sank the *Monmouth* in thirty minutes, disabled the *Good Hope,* and drove the other two ships in flight into a neutral harbor. Thus a British squadron, which at the beginning of October had quitted the Atlantic and rounded Cape Horn in order to pick up one by one isolated German cruisers in the Pacific, was almost wiped out.

Of greater importance than the loss of the ships, or the plight of British trade on the west coast of South America, was the blow apparently given to British naval prestige. One had to search the annals of ocean warfare to find an exploit comparable to that of Spee. At the outbreak of the war, his five ships were scattered all over the Pacific. The *Gneisenau* and the *Scharnhorst* had shelled Tahiti on September 22, sinking a French gunboat; the *Leipzig* had coaled in San Francisco on August 17, and the *Dresden* was in Honolulu about the same time. There were several British, French, and Japanese warships in the Pacific, and yet, altho the *Leipzig, Dresden,* and *Nürnberg* were vessels of less than 3,600 tons, their concentration had not been prevented. They avoided their pursuers, and, despite the lack of naval bases, kept the seas, the *Leipzig* sinking rich prizes off the Peruvian coast late in September. By the aid of the wireless the German ships had been brought together in time to meet the fleet of Admiral Cradock, with some of that superiority which it is the aim of the naval strategist to obtain before entering a fleet action.

John Buchan [3] reconstructed something of the scene off Coronel. To the east was the land, with the snowy heights of the southern Andes fired by that day's evening glow. To the west "burned one of those flaming sunsets, which the Pacific knows, and silhouetted against its crimson and orange were the British ships, like woodcuts in a naval handbook." A high sea was running from the south, and half a gale was blowing. At first some twelve miles separated the two squadrons, but the distance rapidly shrank till at 6.18 P.M. the distance was eight miles. About 7 o'clock the squadrons were converging, and the leading German cruiser opened fire at seven miles. By this time the sun had gone down behind the horizon. A lemon after-glow made visible the British ships, while the Germans were shrouded in an inshore twilight. Presently the enemy got the range, and shell after shell hit the *Good Hope* and the *Monmouth,* while the bad light and the spray from the heavy seas made good gunnery for them almost impossible.

English disquietude over the naval situation was further deepened by the dropping of mines on steamer-lanes from Liverpool to the United States. The landing in Liverpool

---

[3] In "Nelson's History of the War."

of 1,417 men, comprising crews of merchantmen reported sunk in the Atlantic by the *Karlsruhe* further shook the early confidence of the British in their Navy. It was true that British cruisers had captured one and sunk two German raiders, but they were refitted merchantmen. The war was three months old before any itinerant German warships had been picked up. Britannia seemed to have found a foeman worthy of her steel. The eighteen vessels lost by her since the outbreak of the war indicated that the German policy of attrition had met with some success. That Great Britain's fleet was stronger in spite of this, not to mention the finishing and near completion of battleships, and the taking

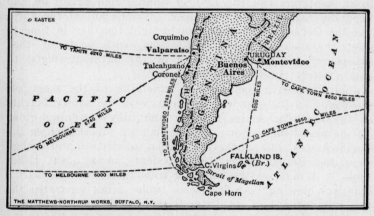

SOUTHERN SOUTH AMERICA, SHOWING THE RELATION OF THE
FALKLAND ISLANDS TO CORONEL

over of Turkish battleships and Brazilian monitors, was not to be overlooked. Her numerical superiority remained overwhelming, and could hardly be altered save by an unthinkable disaster in a great fleet action. But it could not be denied that the honors of the war for skill, daring, and courage in the face of great odds, appeared thus far on the side of her adversaries.

Owing to the superior range of the guns on the *Scharnhorst* and *Gneisenau,* the Germans had been able to open fire when six miles away. As the ships closed and the range came down to a distance of four miles, the British were able to reply, but by that time they were already seriously damaged. The Germans declared that the British fought heroically, but that their artillery was ineffective against the superior weight of metal that the Germans were able to pour from more modern guns on armored cruisers. A light German cruiser closed in on the British and gave the *Monmouth* her death-blow, as, crippled and in flames, she tried to escape.

The only satisfaction the British found in their defeat was that their little Pacific fleet had itself chosen to give battle to a stronger squadron and had not been overwhelmed until the last possible shot was fired at the enemy. Rear-Admiral Cradock lived up to his reputation as a follower of that naval school which believes the enemy should be engaged regardless of his superiority. It was he who brought about the action. The German squadron at first was disinclined to give battle. It was only when dusk came on and the light was in their favor that they engaged the British, who were three to their four, while the range of guns was also in favor of the Germans. The battleship *Canopus*, sent to reinforce Cradock, had not arrived in time, however, to keep the advantage on the British side, while the transport *Otranto* was of no value in a fight against armored ships.

That the Germans were able to sink or scatter a British squadron with only minor damage to their own ships and a casualty list of only six wounded, caused surprize. The *Monmouth* was lost with practically all her crew; the *Good Hope* was severely damaged and on fire when she escaped under cover of darkness, but she afterward went to the bottom, while the *Glasgow* and *Otranto* took refuge in a Chilean port. The *Scharnhorst, Gneisenau*, and *Nürnberg* were in the harbor of Valparaiso the next day coaling and provisioning in preparation for steaming away. They were expected to relieve the cruisers *Leipzig* and *Bremen*, which had the *Glasgow* and *Otranto* bottled up in the port of Talcahuano, eight miles northwest of Conception.

Opposed to an overwhelming preponderance of gunfire, both the *Good Hope* and the *Monmouth* were quickly in a blaze, and altho fighting with courage to the last, the two vessels went down with all on board. The *Glasgow* alone of the three British ships engaged escaped. At the long range at which the action took place, the light armament on both sides must have been all but useless. Weather conditions, moreover, were against a full employment of the lower batteries of the British cruisers. The marksmanship of the German gunners was of the best. From the small losses on

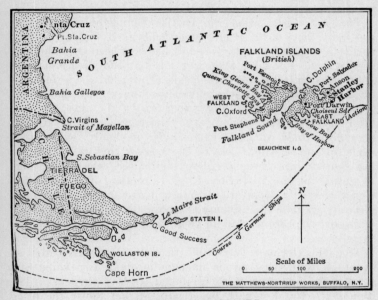

THE FALKLAND ISLANDS

The map shows how the large warships which the British had sent against the German fleet, were in waiting for them, screened by these islands, when the Germans came around into the Atlantic by way of Cape Horn

their side it appeared that they could have scarcely felt the effect of the British fire at all.

Altho the *Scharnhorst* and *Gneisenau* had been intended for bigger work than commerce-raiding, they had been a distinct menace to South American trade; but as far as known, neither of these large cruisers had ever attacked a British merchantship. The work of preying on commerce was left to smaller ships. The *Leipzig* in October sank the *Bankfields* off Peru, while bound from Eten for England with 6,000 tons of sugar, and the oil-tank steamer *Elsinore,* and early in November sank the *Vine Branch* off the Chilean coast while outward bound to Guayaquil. The *Dresden* sank the *Hyades* off Pernambuco on August 16, while the vessel was bound from the Plate for Holland with grain, and the *Holmwood,* on August 26, near Santa Maria, while on a voyage from South Wales for Bahia Blanca with coal. The *Nürnberg* cut the cable between Barnfield, British Columbia, and Fanning Island early in September.

The news from Coronel woke up the Admiralty to the necessity of dealing further with Spee. Lord Fisher had succeeded Prince Louis of Battenberg as First Sea Lord, and one of the earliest acts of his administration was the dispatch of Rear-Admiral Sir Frederick Doveton Sturdee, who had been Chief of the War Staff at the Admiralty, with a squadron to the South Atlantic, in which were included the *Invincible* and the *Inflexible,* both battle-cruisers. Great Britain had not long to wait for revenge.

On the morning of December 7 the British squadron arrived at Port Stanley, which lies at the eastern corner of the East Island of the Falkland group. The Falklands, with bare brown moors shining with quartz, prevailing mists, gray stone houses, and a population of Scotch shepherds, look like a group of the Orkneys, or Outer Hebrides set down in southern seas. Port Stanley is a deeply cut gulf leading to an inner harbor on the shores of which stands the little capital city of the group. From the lower shores on the south side one has from the deck of a vessel almost a sight of the outer sea. Off these islands the *Scharnhorst, Gneisenau, Nürnberg, Leipzig,* and *Dresden* were discovered at 7.30 in the morning. In the action that followed, the *Scharnhorst,* flying the flag of Admiral Spee, the *Gneisenau,* and the *Leipzig* were sunk, while the *Dresden* and the *Nürnberg* made off and were pursued. Two colliers were captured. The British casualties were few. Survivors were rescued from the *Gneisnau* and *Leipzig.*

The engagement was counted by the British a dual victory, since they not only sank three ships but outwitted the

THE ARMORED CRUISER "SCHARNHORST"

THE LIGHT CRUISER "LEIPZIG"

THE LIGHT CRUISER "NÜRNBERG"

THREE GERMAN VESSELS SUNK IN THE FALKLAND ISLANDS BATTLE

27

German intelligence department. Unknown to Spee a British squadron of feeble cruisers in the South Atlantic had been reinforced by two new and powerful battle-cruisers, the *Invincible* and the *Inflexible,* and elaborate pains had been taken, after a junction was effected, not to allow any hint of their presence to escape. When the British fleet arrived at Port Stanley, on December 7, the two larger vessels immediately sought concealment in the bay. The trap having been set, its victims were not long in sailing to attack. On the following day the German squadron appeared in the offing, accompanied by the converted merchantman *Prinz Eitel Friedrich,* afterward interned at Norfolk, Virginia, and which came to Port Stanley probably for the purpose of using it as a coaling station.

Seeing only the five British cruisers—none of them equal in fighting value to the German armored cruisers—and one old battleship on guard, the Germans promptly cleared for action. Closing in, they opened fire, to which the British cruisers replied. The action had become furious and apparently was evenly contested when, out through the narrow harbor entrance, came the long gray forms of the two great battle-cruisers, each with her eight 12-inch guns swung out for action. Spee, realizing the situation, made signal for his squadron to scatter. It was too late, however. The Germans had come far within British range. The *Scharnhorst* and the *Gneisenau* at once became targets for the British battle-cruisers, the light German ships being left to the smaller cruisers.

The *Invincible* received the brunt of the German fire. Both German cruisers fought desperately and had at least the satisfaction of getting home several broadsides on the *Invincible,* which, however, rattled vainly against her heavy armor. The *Scharnhorst* had won the gold medal for target practise in the Kaiser's navy in 1913. Her shooting in this, her last fight, justified her reputation. But one 12-inch British salvo after another battered the German ships to pieces, raking them from stem to stern, tearing away their light armor and opening up holes. It was not long before flames were licking about the upper works, first of the *Scharnhorst,* then of the *Gneisenau.* One after another their guns

VICE-ADMIRAL SIR FREDERICK STURDEE

Sturdee commanded the British ships which fought with the Germans at the Falkland Islands off the South American coast in 1915

became silent as the crews had been killed at their stations behind the guns. There was no hint of surrender, however. With their last guns still blazing defiance, the two German cruisers heeled slowly over and went down, with Admiral von Spee's flag on the *Scharnhorst* still flying.

An event of peculiar interest had already taken place at another point. This was a death-grapple between the *Leipzig* and the *Glasgow,* both survivors of the engagement off Coronel. This fight was not as unequal as was the one between the larger ships. On the *Glasgow* occurred most of the British casualties, comprising nine killed and four wounded in the fight. But the 6-inch guns of the *Glasgow* counted more than the 4-inch guns of the *Leipzig.* At the end of a two-hour action the German ship, on fire and sinking, hoisted the white flag. The *Glasgow* ceased firing and, running close to the sinking German ship, lowered her boats to save the remnants of the crew. Other British cruisers a little later came up to the *Nürnberg* whose captain refused to surrender. Completely outnumbered and outweighted she was speedily sent to the bottom. Her destruction became the salvation of the *Dresden* and *Prinz Eitel Friedrich,* because the British cruisers stopt to pick up survivors from the *Nürnberg,* giving a brief respite, which enabled them to get away. In the London *Times* the German fleet's gallant end was acknowledged as follows: "The battle off the Falkland Islands was declared to have redeemed modern warfare from a reproach. On both sides men fought with men; not machines with invisible machines. The human factor figured as surely as it did in the days of the *Bon Homme Richard* and the *Serapis*.[3a] Finally those who still like to see some of its ancient glory hang about war owe a debt to Sturdee and von Spee."

The German admiral fought as Cradock had fought; the German sailors died as Cradock's men had died. They went down with colors flying, and the crew, at the last lined up on the decks of the doomed ships, continued to resist after the vessels had become shambles. One captured officer reported that, before the end, his ship had no upper

[3a] A reference to the battle of John Paul Jones in the North Sea during the American Revolution.

deck left. Every man there had been killed, and one turret blown bodily overboard by a 12-inch lyddite shell. But in all this slaughter, which lasted for half a day, there was never a thought of surrender. "Spee and Cradock," said John Buchan, "lie beneath those Southern waters in the final concord of those who have looked unshaken upon death."

The victory was made complete two days later, when it became known that the *Nürnberg,* one of the two light German cruisers that escaped destruction in the first action, had been overtaken by Sturdee's squadron and sent to join her fellows, and by a despatch from Buenos Ayres indicat-

THE CRUISER "DRESDEN"

The *Dresden,* a sister-ship of the *Emden,* the commerce-raider, was in the Falkland Islands battle, but escaped from the action and was afterward bottled up

ing that the swift *Dresden,* the sole survivor of Spee's forces, had been bottled up. Sturdee in this battle had at least nine ships under his flag, including the battleships *Albemarle* and *Hindustan,* and the battle-cruisers *Lion, Indefatigable,* and *Indomitable.* That three battle-cruisers should have been detached from Admiral Beatty's division, after the service they performed in the fight of August 28 off Heligoland in the North Sea, was of itself a sufficient indication of the importance attached by the British Admiralty to the task of avenging Cradock's squadron and clearing the ocean of German ships. Any one of the three battle-cruisers, on sheer weight of metal, should have been more than a match for the German squadron.

It was not until January 24 that ships of the dreadnought class were first matched against others of the dreadnought class. On that date the most powerful German fleet that had ventured to sea since the war began was met and defeated at the Dogger Bank in the North Sea, by a British battle-cruiser squadron under Vice-Admiral Sir David Beatty, the victor of Heligoland. Surprized into an action which they had sought to avoid, the battle-cruisers *Derfflinger, Seydlitz,* and *Moltke,* the armored cruiser *Blücher* and several light cruisers, were hammered in a running fight of three hours and a half by the British battle-cruisers *Tiger, Lion, Princess Royal, New Zealand,* and *Indomitable,* assisted by a few light cruisers and destroyers. After the battle had covered more than 100 miles, at a speed never before known in naval warfare (a speed equal to the *Mauretania's*), and had carried the British to the fringe of mines guarding German naval bases, the German armored cruiser *Blücher,* shattered by the guns of the British *Lion,* went to the bottom and two German battle-cruisers were badly damaged. Other German ships regained protection from land forts, submarines, and mines.

On the *Blücher* probably more than 700 lives were lost. The casualties on the battle-cruisers that escaped may have been larger. Only 123 of the *Blücher's* complement of 885 officers and men were understood to have been rescued. The destruction of the *Blücher* was the hardest blow that had yet been suffered by the German Navy. She cost $6,750,000. No British ship was lost or seriously damaged. Admiral Beatty reported that only eleven men were wounded on his flagship. The *Lion* led the fight, as she did at Heligoland, when Sir David drove her at twenty-eight knots and got up in time to save a light cruiser and destroyer. One course only was open to the Germans when they encountered Beatty's squadron—to make for home with all possible speed—for they were hopelessly outclassed; the most they could expect to do was to get away without loss. The loss of the *Blücher* was a serious blow to them. She was built to offset the first of the British battle-cruisers, the *Indomitable,* which had taken part in this engagement, but had proved herself inferior to cruisers of the class she was supposed to rival. It was difficult to account for the circumstances that exposed the German squadron to this reverse, except on a supposition that a recent raid on Scarborough had created an excess of confidence among the Germans. All the ships that took part in the battle participated in the raid on Scarborough, with the exception of the *Blücher*.

The *Blücher*, a powerful pre-dreadnought, well protected, was the fifth German armored cruiser to be sent to the bottom. Of this type Germany now had left four out of the nine with which she began the war. Four of the five that were sunk were the newest, having been launched between 1904 and 1908. The four included all the known effective vessels of their class in German waters, with the exception of the *Von der Tann*, which was reported to have sustained injury. The most serious British damage was sustained by the *Lion*, Beatty's flagship, which had been instrumental in sinking the *Blücher*. She was hit once below the water-line and several of her forward compartments were flooded so that she had to take up a hawser from the *Indomitable* and be towed into port. The *Tiger, Princess Royal, New Zealand*, and the crippled *Lion* found port at Leith.

When the German fleet was overtaken in the fight, and the *Blücher* had fallen behind, with the other big ships racing to escape, the British cruisers went after the *Moltke*, the *Seydlitz* and the *Derfflinger*. As the *Lion* passed the *Blücher* she let go a salvo that shook the German boat from stem to stern. She then steamed on and left the *Princess Mary* to rake the *Blücher* with a broadside, while a few minutes later the flying *Tiger* repeated the attack, until the *Blücher* was completely disabled. "We were now closing in," said a British officer afterward, "as the *Blücher*, her speed failing, began to lag behind." Her nose "pointed home and she was struggling hard to get into shelter of the mine-field." But she "died game, pounding away with her stern guns to the last." She was afire afterward and was just struggling along when the end came. When sinking by the head she "let fly a salvo from the aft turrets." The *Arethusa* finished off the *Blücher* with a couple of torpedoes. There had come a time when the *Blücher* "wasn't worth any more heavy powder and shot; so word was passed to

THE "BLÜCHER" SUNK IN THE DOGGER BANK ACTION

THE GERMAN ARMORED CRUISER "MOLTKE"

BRITISH OFFICIAL PHOTO.   © UNDERWOOD & UNDERWOOD, N. Y.

THE GERMAN BATTLE CRUISER "SEYDLITZ"

The *Seydlitz* took part in both the Dogger Bank and the Jutland battles.
She was among the ships interned at Scapa Flow, where she was sunk by
Admiral von Reuter, along with the other German ships in June, 1919

GERMAN SHIPS IN THE DOGGER BANK BATTLE

us on the *Arethusa* to set to work with torpedoes"—so said one of the crew, who added:

"We could not miss her, for she was almost stationery. Our second torpedo went right into her amidships. She had a terrible

THE "KÖNIGSBERG"

The *Königsberg*, which had made raids on merchant ships, was finally bottled up at the mouth of a river in German East Africa, where escape became impossible

list even before this, and had thrown up the sponge. Her crew were game to the last. We saw 'em lining up at the taff-rail standing at attention. It was a thrilling moment. No man with any feelings could fail to admire such coolness. When we had launched our second and last torpedo we knew that the end would come quickly. We steamed within 200 yards. They would have met their deaths standing rigidly at attention had not warning been sent to them. Shipping up a megaphone one of our officers shouted to them in German. They understood and waved their caps, and after shouting a hurrah all took headers into the water. We threw overboard some hundreds of planks and they clung to them until our boats picked them up. To do this we had to dodge the bombs which two aeroplanes tried to drop on us. In the meantime our torpedoes had got home. The explosion had appalling results. Not a man of the crew would have survived it if they had remained standing at attention. The *Blücher* sank like a tin can filled with water."

In July the German cruiser *Königsberg*, which in the autumn had taken refuge from the British in the Rufiji River in German East Africa, was totally wrecked by British river monitors. The *Königsberg* was a vessel of 3,348 tons, and had a speed of 23 knots. She was a protected cruiser. Using Zanzibar harbor for a base, she had preyed on British merchantmen in the Indian Ocean since the beginning of the war. She had a complement of 296 officers and men, and was armed with ten 4.1-inch, eight 3-pound guns and two 17.7-inch torpedo-tubes. From August 8 until September 15, 1914, she had captured or sunk ten ships, mostly small trading craft, taking her prizes into the ports of German East Africa. On her return to Zanzibar on September 20, she surprized the British light cruiser *Pegasus,* which she disabled with a loss of twenty killed and eighty wounded. The *Pegasus* had returned from destroying the wireless-plant and floating-dock at Das-es-Salaam. The *Pegasus,* an old "P"-class cruiser of 2,000 tons, carrying eight 4-inch old-pattern guns, was no match for a German craft of 1907, altho she finally forced the latter to retire. The disabling of the *Pegasus* caused the British squadron to seek out the *Königsberg* and, on October 30, she was discovered hiding in shoal-water about six miles up the Rufiji River.

A German fleet consisting of nine of the older battleships, twelve cruisers, and a destroyer flotilla attempted, early in August, 1915, to force the southern channel which leads to the

PART OF THE CREW OF THE GERMAN RAIDER "KÖNIGSBERG," AS PHOTOGRAPHED AFTER HER DESTRUCTION

Gulf of Riga, but the attempt was for a time defeated, probably by Russian submarines and smaller craft. On August 16 it was renewed with determination, and the German fleet engaged the Russian at the mouths of both channels, but their attacks were again repulsed. Next day when a thick fog had settled over the water, the Germans were able to sweep the mines from the entrance, and the Russian light craft retired into the Gulf, while the larger units remained outside. In such weather a general action was impossible. When the Germans moved in they were apparently under an impression that the Russians had withdrawn from the Gulf altogether, and on the 19th began preparations for a landing at Pernau, a town in the Gulf unfortified but connected directly with Petrograd. Four large flat-bottomed barges laden with troops moved in shore, and on the 20th attempted to land. Conditions for this would be favorable only on the assumption that no Russian craft were near, for the shoal-water forbade ships to approach the shore. Here was a fine opportunity for Russian light craft, and quickly they seized it.

Meanwhile, the Russian fleet joined battle with the Germans, the heaviest fighting being in Mohn Sound, where retreating German vessels were caught by Russian destroyers. One old gunboat, the *Sivoutch*, engaged a German cruiser while escorting torpedo-craft. The action began at a range of about 1,200 yards. "The *Sivoutch*," said the Russian Admiralty report, "wrapt in flames, and on fire fore and aft, continued to answer shot for shot until she went down, having previously sunk an enemy torpedo-boat." This was the only serious Russian casualty. Eight German destroyers and two cruisers were either sunk or put out of action; a submarine was driven ashore and it seems probable that an auxiliary cruiser was destroyed. The accounts were conflicting, the Germans denying that they had had serious losses.

The Russian squadron maneuvered to intercept a retreat, and were attacked by German destroyers with gunfire and torpedoes, but none of the projectiles found their mark. The destroyers then retired before salvoes from the Russian guns. Half an hour from the beginning of the action, the German light cruiser *Augsburg* abandoned her slower consort, the *Albatross*, and made off to the south, the fog, which had by this time become dense, enabling her to escape. To save the *Albatross*, which was already showing signs of distress, the destroyers poured forth thick volumes of black smoke from their funnels, thus interposing a screen between the Russians and their quarry. About nine o'clock the foremast of the *Albatross* went by the board and clouds of steam rose from the mine-layer. At the same time, she began to list slightly to starboard. Describing several circles and hauling down her flag, the *Albatross* then made for the coast. As she was damaged and rapidly approached neutral waters, the Russians ceased fire, and shortly afterward she was seen to run ashore on the coast of Gotland behind the Ostergarn lighthouse.

The Russian squadron continued its course northward. About ten o'clock the smoke of several approaching ships was sighted to starboard. As the distance lessened, the vessels which were German were seen to consist of an armored cruiser of the *Roon* class, a light cruiser of the *Augsberg* class, and four destroyers. The Russians immediately joined battle, and half an hour later the German ships began to retreat southward, after having been accompanied by submarines which unsuccessfully attacked the Russians. The Russian battleship *Rurik,* bringing up the rear of the squadron, was ordered to attack, and in a quarter of an hour was engaged with the two cruisers. The fire of one weakened, as her four 8-inch guns were silenced one after the other, till only one replied, while flames, bursting from their decks, showed that fire had broken out on board. The two cruisers finally withdrew from the contest and disappeared rapidly in the fog, pursued by the *Rurik.* Toward the close of the action the *Rurik* was again attacked by a submarine, but beat off her assailant.

About this time, there were naval activities elsewere in the Baltic. The German battle-cruiser *Moltke,* a sister-ship of the *Goeben,* which took part in the raid on Scarborough, and was damaged in the battle of January 24, was torpedoed by a British submarine under Commander Noel Laurence. She was struck in the bows, and, altho she succeeded in escaping, she was put out of action for a time. The *Moltke* was of 23,000 tons displacement. Completed in 1911 at a cost of £2,200,000, she carried ten 11-inch guns, twelve 6-inch guns, twelve 24-pounders, and four torpedo-tubes. She was armed amidship with 11-inch Krupp steel. Her engines of

70,000 horse-power were designed to give a speed of 27 knots. Like the *Goeben,* she was supposed to embrace in her design the most recent inventions, German and others, for securing stability, immunity from fire, and a maximum of resistance to gunfire and torpedo attack. She was in the action against Admiral Beatty's squadron, which resulted in the sinking of the *Blücher.* The *Sivoutch* was a vessel of 960 tons and 12 knots. She carried a crew of 148. Her captain was Commander Tcherkasoff, who had made a record in the Japanese War at Port Arthur.

The purpose of the Germans in the Gulf of Riga was not only to obtain mastery in the Gulf, but to effect a landing at Pernau. If the plan had succeeded, the communications of Riga with Petrograd would have been cut, and a further advance on the capital facilitated. But it was necessary, first, to obtain command of the waters of the gulf. It was insufficient for the Germans to sweep a passage through mines and fixt defenses, provided the mobile defenses could not also be accounted for. That was where the German scheme failed. So long as the defenders were there in force every attempt at a disembarkation could be made only at great peril. Russian torpedo-craft and a gunboat flotilla, skilfully handled, made a landing of German soldiers hopeless. The affair was regarded as an illustration of the weakness of an attempt to carry out an invasion oversea, before control of land-communications had been obtained.

The most severe fighting appeared to have taken place in Mohn Sound, where the Russians lost the *Sivoutch.* Slow but well-armed for her size, the *Sivoutch* was a useful vessel, but the Russians had many more such gunboats. The Germans claimed to have sunk the *Koreets,* a sister-ship of the *Sivoutch.* The four remaining German battle-cruisers were the *Von der Tann, Seydlitz, Derfflinger,* and *Lutzow,* of three distinct types, the first-named being armed with eight 11-inch guns, the second with ten 11-inch, and the others with eight 12-inch. This news, coming to the Russians after their great retreat following the fall of Warsaw, was of much value in raising their spirits. Had the Pernau landing succeeded, and an advanced German base been established there, the successful Russian defense of the

Dwina would have been nullified and the retirement of their right must have been gravely compromised.

With the *Medilleh,* formerly the *Breslau,* reported sunk in action off the entrance to the Dardanelles late in January 1918, and the *Goeben* driven into the Straits and beached at Nagara halfway up to the Sea of Marmora, the Turkish Navy had been so reduced that it could not even send a squadron to sea. The German Admiral, Souchon, could command only a flotilla of small nondescript Turkish ships and a few destroyers and submarines. Turkey's losses at sea had included before this the battleship *Messudyeh* (10,000 tons), torpedoed by the British submarine *B*-11 in the Dardanelles; the battleship *Kheyr-ed-din* (9,000 tons), torpedoed by the British in the Sea of Marmora; the cruiser *Medjidieh* (3,300 tons), sunk by a Russian mine in the Gulf of Odessa; six small gunboats of which the British accounted for four and the Russians for two; two destroyers, the *Yadikar Millet* and the *Yar Hissar,* both torpedoed by British submarines; one torpedo-boat interned at Chios and another driven ashore on the Greek coast. In addition seven transports had been sunk and one, the *Rodosto* (6,000 tons), captured by a Russian submarine. The last eight months had seen the sinking also of minor warships, transports, and supply-vessels. Turkey had been planning a modern navy in 1913. On paper her complement was impressive, including 30,000 sailors and 9,000 marines. But, with the exception of the small cruisers *Medjidieh* and *Hamidiyeh,* there were no modern ships. Two dreadnoughts, the *Osman* (bought of Brazil) and the *Reshadieh,* were building in British yards when Germany began the war, and a third, the *Faith,* had been ordered. The *Goeben* and *Breslau* had, therefore, been a lucky acquisition for Turkey when they steamed into the Dardanelles in 1914. They gave the Turks the upper hand in the Black Sea.

The reported sinking of the *Breslau* and beaching of the *Goeben,* seemed the greatest triumph for the British sea forces for many months of weary waiting. Both were new in 1912; both were swift, altho they had deteriorated in Turkish waters; the *Goeben's* batteries of 11-inch guns had made her supreme in the Black Sea. Escaping from close quarters at Messina at the beginning of the war, the ships had sped to Turkey when they were sold to that country, but their German crews remained aboard. They did much to force Turkey into the war by attacking Russia.[4]

[4] Principal Sources: *The Review of Reviews*, The *Times*, New York; The *Morning Post* (London), The North German *Gazette*, The London *Times'* "History of the War," The *Evening News* (London), The *Berliner Tageblatt*, the Wolff Bureau, The *Standard* (London), Reuter dispatches, The *Economist* (London), "Nelson's History of the War" by John Buchan; The *Sun*, The *Evening Sun*, New York.

EXPLOITS BY THE EMDEN AND OTHERS ON THE HIGH SEAS AND ON THE ENGLISH COAST

August 1, 1914—March 5, 1916

RAIDS and captures by German commerce destroyers were reported from various seas soon after the war began. British merchant vessels had been exposed to these attacks everywhere. The *Emden,* commanded by Captain Karl von Müller, particularly distinguished herself. Being a vessel of only about 3,500 tons, but having a speed of 25 knots, she was quite fast enough to overhaul any British merchant steamer she was likely to encounter, and could easily have run away when necessary. Her exploits recalled to Europeans those of Robert Surcouf, a famous French privateersman of over a hundred years before, whose *Confiance,* his swiftest and rakiest craft, was generally heard of where least expected. After reaping a harvest of merchantmen, Surcouf's vessel unaccountably disappeared. The exploits of the *Emden* also recalled those of Raphael Semmes and the *Alabama* in our Civil War. A statement made by Captain John M. Kell, the executive officer of the *Alabama,* might almost have been written by the corresponding officer of the *Emden,* since it dealt with the *Alabama's* exploits in the same waters as those through which the *Emden* operated against about seventy British, Russian, French, and Japanese ships: "In a few weeks we had so paralyzed the enemy's commerce that their ships were absolutely locked up in port, and neutrals were doing all the carrying trade." The disguises which the *Emden* assumed on entering Penang were those which had frequently been assumed or resorted to by Captain Semmes, of the *Alabama,* and in every case were legitimate. The history of naval sailing days abounds in instances of ships that hoisted flags other than their own, in order to find out the nationality of another vessel, or to approach near some prize that might otherwise escape them.

IN THE GERMAN COLONIES AND ON THE SEA

The captain of the *Emden*, when finally captured, had been steadily at sea for forty-eight of ninety days; in the South China Sea, the Indian Ocean, and the Bay of Bengal; had nearly closed up the port of Calcutta for a couple of weeks, had fired on Madras, captured or sunk 22 merchant ships, and then, having been reported 200 miles south of Ceylon near the Equator, had doubled on his tracks and again crossed the Bay of Bengal. Several times he had recoaled and provisioned his ship from prizes and, barring the fouling of his ship's bottom, was in better shape when captured than when the war began, for his successes had greatly increased the morale of his crew. It was his invariable practise to sink prizes, reserving one in which to send crews and passengers into port. Indeed nothing else could be done, since he could not take them into any friendly port, nor could he cumber his own ship with captured crews. The *Emden* steamed one evening into Madras roads and shelled the outskirts of the town for half an hour, oil-tanks being set ablaze and two or three natives killed. Fort George returned the fire, probably without effect, and the *Emden* then retired. At the end of October, when in disguise by carrying an extra dummy funnel, and flying the Japanese colors, the *Emden* contrived to torpedo a small Russian cruiser and destroyer in the British harbor of Penang, but on November 10 she was caught at the Keeling or Cocos Islands, south of Sumatra, by the Australian cruiser *Sydney*, driven ashore and burned.

One of her greatest exploits was the one at Penang, which is in the Straits Settlement, and where, after a few brief hours in that busy harbor, she left death and destruction behind her. Penang lies on the western coast of the Malay Peninsula, just below the Siamese border, and is the shipping point of the Federated Malay States, where 65 per cent. of the world's tin is produced, as well as a great amount of rubber. The thing that made Penang a point of importance in the war was the fact that it was the last port of call for ships from China and Japan to Colombo and Europe, and it had been made more or less of a naval base by the English Government. It was probably for the purpose of crippling this base that the *Emden* made her raid on it.

Had she found Penang undefended, she could, at one blow, have embarrassed English cruisers patrolling those waters, and at the same time have caused a terrific loss to English commerce by sinking merchantmen at anchor in the harbor.

It was early in the morning that the *Emden,* with her dummy fourth funnel, and flying the British ensign, got past a French torpedo-boat, the *Mosquet,* which was on patrol duty outside, and entered the outer harbor of Penang, where, across the channel leading to the inner harbor, lay the Russian cruiser *Jemtchug.* Inside were French torpedo-

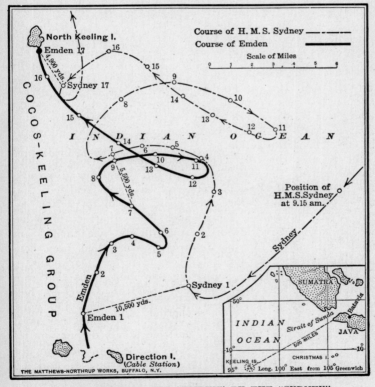

THE SINKING OF THE "EMDEN" BY THE "SYDNEY"

The Cocos, or Keeling, Islands, are in the Indian Ocean about 600 miles southwest of Sumatra. The *Sydney* was an Australian, not a British warship

boats and torpedo-boat destroyers, the torpedo-boats lying beside the long Government wharf, while the *D'Iberville* rode at anchor between two tramp steamers. At full speed the *Emden* steamed straight ahead for the *Jemtchug* in the inner harbor. In the semi-darkness the Russian ship took her for the British cruiser *Yarmouth,* which had been in and out of the harbor two or three times during the previous week and did not even "query" her. When less than 400 yards away, the *Emden* suddenly emptied her bow guns into the *Jemtchug,* and prest on at a terrific pace, with all the guns she could bring to bear in action. When she had come to within 250 yards of the Russian ship, she changed her course slightly, and as she passed the *Jemtchug,* poured two broadsides into her, as well as a torpedo, which entered the engine-room, but did comparatively little damage, however. The Russian cruiser, taken completely by surprize, was crippled. Her captain had been spending the night ashore, and as there was no one on board who seemed capable of acting energetically, she was defeated before the battle began. Such men as were on board finally manned her light guns and brought them into action.

In the meantime the *Emden* had got well inside the inner harbor among the merchant shipping. She now discovered the presence of French torpedo-boats and realized that, unless she got out before they could join in the action, her fate would be sealed, for at such close quarters torpedoes would have proved deadly. Accordingly, she turned and made once more for the *Jemtchug,* which had been bombarding her with shrapnel, but, owing to bad markmanship, had succeeded only in peppering merchant ships that were within range. As the *Emden* neared the *Jemtchug,* both ships were actually spitting fire. At less than 150 yards the *Emden* passed the Russian ship and torpedoed her amidship, striking the magazine. A tremendous detonation followed, paling into insignificance all the previous din in that harbor. A column of heavy black smoke rose and the *Jemtchug* sank in ten seconds.

The *Emden* then started for a point of safety, but sighted the torpedo-boat *Mosquet* coming in at top speed and immediately opened on her, causing her to turn. After a running fight of twenty minutes the *Mosquet,* hit by shells, sank rapidly. Here the chivalrous conduct of the *Emden's* captain, which had been many times in evidence throughout her career, was again shown. He stopt, regardless of danger, lowered his boats, and picked up the survivors of the *Mosquet* before steaming on his way. The English in Penang afterward said of him admiringly that he "played the game." Boats of all descriptions now started toward the place where the Russian cruiser was last seen, the water being covered with débris to which survivors were clinging. Their blood-stained and, for the most part, naked bodies, were enough to send shivers through the most cold-blooded observer. Out of a crew of 334 men, 142 were picked up wounded. Only 94 were found practically untouched, while 98 were "missing."

The French torpedo-boats and the *D'Iberville,* whose help the *Jemtchug* had had a right to expect, lay at the time in the harbor with fully ten minutes' warning that a hostile ship was approaching, and yet they allowed that ship to enter the harbor, and to turn and make her escape without so much as firing a shot—so reports definitely said. If they had gone into action, the *Emden* could hardly have escaped. The range was everything they could have wished for. The fact reported in explanation was that, altho it was a time of war, a large percentage of the officers of these ships had been allowed to remain ashore over night and not one of the

THE AUSTRALIAN WARSHIP "SYDNEY" THAT SANK THE "EMDEN"
The *Sydney* shown at her arrival in the Harbor of Colombo, having on board Captain von *Müller,* and others from the *Emden*

ships had steam up. Their decks were not even cleared for action. Two or three torpedoes from any one of them would have saved the day, but none was fired.

When the *Emden* first arrived off the Cocos Islands the wireless operator there had sent out the *"S O S"* call, and it was caught by the Australian cruiser *Sydney,* which soon arrived and engaged the *Emden.* The *Sydney* was a larger, faster and more modern vessel. With her 6-inch guns she was able to hit the *Emden* and keep out of range of her 4-inch guns. The *Emden* soon lost one of her masts and two of her funnels, and steering to shore grounded and was burned. The twenty-five or thirty British vessels captured by the *Emden* were valued, apart from their cargoes, at over $10,000,000.

This ended one of the most exciting adventure-cruises that war-history can supply. Violence and disaster had followed in the *Emden's* wake nearly every day of the three months of her war career, but in the code of war, there had been no cruelty, no treachery, nor any stain upon the honor of the ship, crew, or commander. Even the British press said Müller had made for himself and his vessel a name which any of his fellow wearers of the Iron Cross might envy. While the English rejoiced in the destruction of the *Emden,* no one failed to acknowledge admiration for Müller, or to commend the spirit of fair fighting exhibited in his attacks on British shipping. Müller was a native of Blackenberghe, Belgium, and at one time had been an officer in the employ of the Hansa line of steamers. Fast cruisers had been in search of the *Emden* for some time, British cruisers being aided by French, Russian, and Japanese vessels. Included in this work were the Australian warships *Melbourne* and *Sydney.*

The effect of the sinking of the *Emden* was better seen in London at Lloyd's perhaps than anywhere else in the world. She had for weeks caused deep and painful anxiety. But a dramatic scene now took place. The business of the day was in full swing, when suddenly above the hum the *Lutine* [5]

---

[5] The bell of H. M. S. *Lutine,* which was wrecked, with the loss of all hands, off Vlieland, in the Netherlands, October 9-10, 1799. The bell was recovered in salvage operations and sent to Lloyd's as a memorial.

bell rang out. Only on momentous occasions is this bell rung. Instantly business was now suspended as all turned toward the rostrum, from which it was known that some great news would be made public. An official crier mounted the steps and in the rolling tones for which he was famous, began: "Gentlemen, it is officially announced that the *Emden*———" That was as far as he was allowed to go. Cheer after cheer went forth. Hats and papers were thrown into the air. Again the *Lutine* bell was rung—to enjoin silence—and at last the message was completed— "the *Emden* has been destroyed." The shipping industry in the Indian Ocean was now relieved of the greater portion of its peril, and underwriters slept more comfortably.

Once located, the *Emden* had small chance of escape. She had a crew of 361 men, and was completed in 1909. The *Sydney*, of 5,400 tons and a speed of 24½ knots, was manned by 400 officers and men, and had been launched in 1912. The broadside of the *Emden* was only 175 pounds; that of the *Sydney* 500 pounds. Thus the disparity between the ships was almost as great as that between Cradock's squadron and Spee's in the action off the Chilean coast. Captain Müller had received command of the *Emden* two years before his capture, and after some years of service in the German Admiralty. He had a sense of humor, as was shown when he offered by wireless to the Indian Government to carry the mail from Calcutta to Rangoon, and when again he rang up one of his first victims to ask if anything had been seen of a German cruiser in the Bay of Bengal, only to be answered by the innocent captain of the vessel that such a thing did not exist. A few minutes later, and shortly before the *Emden* hove in sight, Müller's wireless rapped out in reply, "Oh, yes, it does; I am it."

More than five months after the destruction of the *Emden*, that is on April 29, fourteen survivors of the *Emden's* crew straggled into Damascus. Of thirty who had been sent ashore at Cocos to intercept the wireless, these fourteen were survivors. Standing on shore at Cocos they had seen the *Emden* fire on the *Sydney*, had witnessed the chase that followed, and then were compelled to see the *Emden* take flight while afire, only to go down on the rocks of another island fifteen miles away. With the *Emden* gone, these thirty men had no wish to be captured as their companions had been. Within a short time they were able to secrete themselves in a commandeered schooner called the *Eyashe*. Their numbers were increased by some forty others who managed to escape in small boats after the fight. In all, the survivors numbered seventy-five men and seven officers. The final, and perhaps most thrilling, stage in their wanderings, was their journey home across the desert where they were attacked by Bedouins and all but wiped out. This adventure was recounted by Dr. Emil Ludwig, a special correspondent [6] sent out to meet them when they should emerge from the desert. The facts were given to Dr. Ludwig by Lieutenant Captain von Mücke, the leader of the little party. Dr. Ludwig's narrative written at Damascus contains the following:

"Two months after our arrival at Hodeida we again put to sea. The Turkish Government placed at our disposal two *sambuks* (sailing ships) of about twenty-five tons, fifteen meters long and four meters wide. In fear of English spies, we sailed from Jebaua, ten miles north of Hodeida, on March 14, and at a considerable distance apart, so that both parties would not be lost if an English gun-boat found us. After adventures in which some of the men perished, others got to the first boat. Now we numbered, together with the Arabs, seventy in all on this little boat. We anchored before Konfida, and met Sami Bey, who was in the service of the Turkish Government and did good service as guide in the next two months. He was an active man, thoroughly familiar with the country. He procured for us a larger boat, of fifty-four tons, and with his wife sailed alongside on the little *sambuk*. For two days we sailed unmolested to Lith, when Sami Bey announced that three English ships were cruising about to intercept us. I now advised traveling over land, but we could travel only at night. When we slept or camped around a spring, we had only a tent for the sick. After two days' march from Jeddah, the Turkish Government, receiving news about us, sent us sixteen good camels.

"On the night of April 1, I was riding at the head of the column, when all our shooting implements were cleared for action, because danger existed of an attack by Bedouins, whom the English had bribed. When it began to grow a bit dark we were all tired, having been riding eighteen hours. Suddenly I saw a line flash up before me, and shots whizzed over our heads. The whole space around the desert hillock was occupied. We at once formed a fighting-line and rushed upon them with bayonets, whereupon they fled, but returned to the attack again from all sides. Several gendarmes who had been given to us as an escort were wounded; the machine-gun operator fell, killed by a shot through the heart; another was wounded; and Lieutenant Schmidt, in the rear-guard, was mortally wounded with bullets in his chest and abdomen.

"Suddenly the Bedouins waved white cloths, and the wife of the Sheik, to whom a part of our camels belonged, went over to negotiate with them. We quickly built a sort of wagon barricade, a circular camp of camel saddles, rice and coffee sacks, all of which we filled with sand. As we had no shovels, we had to dig with bayonets, plates and hands. The whole barricade had a diameter of about fifty meters. Behind it we dug trenches. As the camels inside had to lie down, they served very well as cover for the rear of the trenches. An inner wall was constructed, behind which we carried the sick. In the very center we buried two jars of water, to guard against thirst. In addition, we had ten petroleum cans full of water. All told there was a supply of water for four days. Late in the evening the wife came back after futile negotiations. She unveiled for the first and only time on this day of the skirmish, distributed cartridges, and conducted herself faultlessly. The number of the enemy was about 300, while we numbered fifty, with twenty-nine guns. We had to dig with our hands and bayonets a grave for one of our men, and to eliminate every trace above it in order to protect the body. Another companion was buried immediately after the skirmish. Both were buried silently, with all honors.

"The wounded had a hard time, as we had lost our medicine-chest in the wreck and had only little packages of bandages; but no probing instruments, no scissors. On the next day our men came up with thick tongues, feverish and crying 'Water! Water!' Each received a little cupful three times a day. Had our water supply been exhausted we would have had to sally forth from camp and fight our way through. Arabs simply cut the throats of camels that had been wounded, and then drank the yellow water contained in their stomachs. Those fellows could stand anything. At night we dragged out dead camels that had served as cover and been shot. Hyenas then came, hunting for dead camels. I shot one of them, taking it for an enemy.

"On the third day there were new negotiations. The Bedouins demanded arms no longer, but only money. The negotiations took place across the camp wall. When I declined, the Bedouin said:

'Beaucoup de combat' (Lots of fight). I replied, 'Please go to it!'
We had only a little ammunition left, and very little water. It
really looked as if we would soon be dispatched. The mood of the
men was dismal. Suddenly, about 10 o'clock in the morning, there
bobbed up in the north two riders on camels, waving white cloths.
Then there appeared, coming from the same direction, a long row of
about one hundred camel troops, who drew rapidly nearer, singing,
in a picturesque train. They were messengers and troops from
the Emir of Mekka.

"The wife, it appeared, had in the course of the first negotiations
dispatched an Arab boy to Jeddah. From that place the Governor
had telegraphed to the Emir. The latter at once sent the camel
troops with his two sons and his personal surgeon. The whole
Bedouin band now speedily disappeared. Our first act afterward
was a rush for water. Then we cleared up camp, but had to harness
the camels ourselves, for the drivers had fled at the beginning of
the skirmish. More than thirty camels were dead. Saddles did not
fit. These German sailors knew how to rig up schooners, but not
camels. Much baggage was left lying in the sand for lack of pack-
animals. Under protection of Turkish troops we now got to Jeddah,
where the authorities and populace received us well. From there we
proceeded in nineteen days, without mischance, by sailing boat to
Elwesh, and under abundant guard with Suleiman Pahsa, in a five-
day caravan-journey towrd El Ela, where we were seated at last
in a train and riding toward Germany. We shall get into the war
at last."

Details of another armed cruiser's exploits, the *Karlsruhe,*
in capturing British vessels during September and October,
1914, became public some weeks afterward. The Houlder liner,
La Rosarina, and the Yeoward liner, *Andorinha,* arrived in
the Mersey on November 3 from Teneriffe, bringing the
masters, officers, and crews of thirteen British vessels that
had been captured in the South Atlantic Ocean by the
Karlsruhe. With the exception of three, all were sunk.
The three spared were kept for the sake of the large amount
of coal they had on board and the oil and stores. In each
case the *Karlsruhe* followed the same procedure. Crews of
the captured vessels were first transported to two German
merchantmen, who accompanied her on her raiding expeditions, and then the doomed ships were sunk by heavy charges
of dynamite. The merchantmen carried their passengers
to Teneriffe, where they were cared for by the British

Consul until ships arrived to take them to Liverpool. With the publication in November 1916 of the war diary of Captain Lieutenant Aust, one of the surviving officers of the *Karlsruhe*, the mystery surrounding her fate was dispelled. According to Captain Aust's account, the *Karlsruhe* was blown up by an internal explosion on the evening of November 4, 1914, while a short distance off the northeast coast of South America. Her surviving officers and men, by sailing in one of her prizes, had succeeded in slipping through the British network of warships and reaching a Norwegian port on November 29. The *Karlsruhe* was at Havana at the outbreak of the war. Prior to that she had been on duty in

THE GERMAN CRUISER "KARLSRUHE"

The *Karlsruhe* was described by the Hamburger *Fremdenblatt* as "the terror of the Atlantic." She was reported to have been blown up by an internal explosion off the northeast coast of South America in November, 1914

Mexican waters. She took on coal and provisions at San Juan, Porto Rico, on August 9, 1914. Captain Lubinus understood that she had sunk seventeen ships between that date and her capture of the *Farne* on October. How many more she sent to the bottom between that time and her own sinking on November 4, was not known.

On January 28, 1915, the American schooner, *William P. Frye*, loaded with a cargo of wheat consigned to an English firm, was sunk by the German auxiliary cruiser *Prinz Eitel Friedrich*, and in a communication to the German Government the Government of the United States contended that the act was unwarranted by international law, as the cargo could be considered only conditional contraband, and there was no evidence that it was to be used for military purposes. The outcome was regarded as a victory for the American contention for the safety of innocent persons on the high seas. The agreement was reached at a time when grave issues had risen between Germany and the United States in consequence of the loss of many American lives in the sinking of passenger ships, of which the most notable was the *Lusitania,* in May 1915. The *Prinz Eitel Friedrich* and the *Crown Prince Wilhelm,* two German commerce destroyers, entered the harbor of Newport News in March 1915, after extended cruises in the Atlantic and Pacific oceans, during which a number of French and English vessels were destroyed. At first the commanders of both vessels indicated their intention of making necessary repairs and putting to sea again, but the presence of English war-vessels outside the harbor caused them to change their plans, and both vessels were eventually interned.

Late on the afternoon of November 2, 1914, eight warships sailed from the Elbe base—three battle-cruisers, the *Seydlitz,* the *Moltke,* and the *Von der Tann;* two armored cruisers, the *Blücher* and the *Yorck;* and three light cruisers, the *Kolberg,* the *Graudenz,* and the *Strassburg.* Except the *Yorck,* they were fast vessels, making at least 25 knots. The battle-cruisers carried 11-inch guns. Having cleared for action, they started for the coast of England, and early in the morning ran through the nets of a British fishing fleet eight miles east of Lowestoft. An old police boat, the *Halcyon,* was sighted, and received a few shots. About eight o'clock, when opposite Yarmouth, they proceeded to bombard the wireless-station and naval air-station from a distance of about ten miles. Their shells only plowed sands and disturbed the water. In a quarter of an hour they moved away, dropping many floating mines, which later in the day caused the loss of one submarine and two fishing-boats. The enterprise was unlucky, for on the road back the *Yorck* struck a mine and went to the bottom with most of her crew.

The cannonade caused a sensation in Yarmouth. It began soon after 7 o'clock and went on furiously for 20 minutes.

WARSHIP BATTLES AND RAIDS ON COMMERCE

Many who were asleep were awakened by reverberations, the clattering of windows and the shaking of houses. At the beach there was little to be seen. The haze of an autumn dawn hung over the sea. The ships that were firing were not visible to the gathering crowds, who could see only flash after flash on the horizon, followed by the dropping of shells in the sea and the leaping of great cascades. Men with glasses on the pier at the harbor-mouth were only able to distinguish one ship, a large four-funneled vessel, steaming close to the Cross Sands lightship, which lies about 10 miles off the coast, well outside the Yarmouth Roads. Some of the shells dropt within a mile or two of the shore; others came closer. Soon after the departure of the ships, several destroyers and submarines put out of Yarmouth into the North Sea. The submarines were in company, and during the morning's patrol work one of them came to grief. After striking a mine a few miles from the coast, she sank quickly. Only four survivors were picked up.

In the middle of December, while the Allies were strengthening their lines in France and Belgium, and while, in Poland, Germany was claiming the greatest victory of the war, and "a complete shattering of the Russian offensive," and while the eastern theater witnessed the torpedoing of the Turkish battleship *Messudyeh* in the Dardanelles by a British submarine which had dived under five rows of mines, a German cruiser flotilla eluded the British patrol fleet in

THE AUXILIARY CRUISER PRINCE EITEL FRIEDRICH
This is the ship that sank the *William P. Frye*, and was afterward interned at Newport News

the North Sea, bombarded three English towns, and made good its escape. While developments then taking place in France and Poland were major events, the feat of the submarine in the Dardanelles was perhaps the most daring exploit thus far in the war, but the interest of the British public and press was focused chiefly on the bombardment by German cruisers on Dcember 16 of Scarborough, Hartlepool, and Whitby. For the first time in centuries, English blood had been shed on English soil by a foreign foe. As a consequence of this event Englishmen now knew from experience that England was not immune from attacks; that the British Navy was not an impregnable fortress floating around the British Isles, and, that Great Britain would require in this war all her military resources of whatsoever kind and character.

But the event, it was thought, might be worth "a million recruits to Kitchener's army." An immediate sequel to the bombardments and the killing of more than a hundred innocent persons, two-thirds òf them women and children, was a general rush to the recruiting-offices. Prince von Bülow, the former German Chancellor, was quoted as saying this was "simply the prelude to what the German fleet would soon undertake and which might astound the world." The exploit probably produced a more profound impression on the English people than any other event of the war up to that time. Stories of English people, with familiar English names, dwelling in an every-day English town that was like hundreds of other towns, now torn to pieces by shrapnel, their homes burned, their women folk struck down in the streets, and their babies buried in burning wreckage, were declared to be "taking hold of the imagination of people as no tales of atrocity, fire, and sword in Belgium; as no shiploads of wounded soldiers and starving refugees, had been able to approach."

Nearly a year afterward a German naval officer [7] insisted that "before the cruisers had fired a shot the *Moltke* got a 6-inch shell from the forts, which struck the battle-cruiser and tore away officers' cabins in a lightly protected portion

[7] In an interview with Karl H. von Wiegand, correspondent of the United Press, as published in The *World* (New York).

© UNDERWOOD & UNDERWOOD, N. Y.

SCARBOROUGH, ONE OF THREE ENGLISH TOWNS BOMBARDED BY GERMAN WARSHIPS

It was contended by the Germans, in justification for this bombardment, that Scarborough was a fortified town, altho it had nothing about it resembling a fortress, except for an ancient castle that long since had been in ruins. Scarborough is a popular vacation resort

of the ship.'' He himself saw "a number of steel-patched holes, the result of that shell,'' which to him was "convincing proof that Hartlepool is not an open, undefended town, as widely heralded by the English.'' Englishmen familiar with Hartlepool still persisted that the only forts Hartlepool had were forts of sand built by children on the beach. As for Scarborough, it boasted only the ruins of an ancient castle, and after this attack lamented the more ruinous state in which that ancient relic found itself. There was not a single fortress-gun in or near the town. The Germans had attacked a half-awake seaside resort.

There were three attacking ships, apparently two cruisers and a smaller vessel which some observers thought was a destroyer. They sailed into the South Bay from the northeast, rounding Castle Hill at eight o'clock, and opened fire. Sailing across the bay in the direction of Cayton, they turned about and sailed back again, still firing. The bombardment lasted half an hour. It was difficult from conflicting estimates to decide how many shells were fired, but probably about 100. When they saw no danger to them was to be feared from Castle Hill, the ships gave all their attention to the town. People were killed in their beds and in the streets. Four were killed in one house by a shell which, missing the railway freight-yard, brought down half the side of a house. Four churches were struck and the town hall. The hospital in Friar's Entry escaped, but the building next to it was struck. One shell went through the boundary wall of the power station of the Scarborough electric-supply conduit.

The damage mostly in evidence was done on Castle Hill, where the old barracks—then unoccupied—had been razed. The Castle keep and the walls facing south were also damaged. Thrilling stories were told by fishermen who were at sea at the time. They said the German ships, when they came within two miles of the town, were flying the white ensign. One man saw four ships, and at first thought they were British patrol-ships. The crew of his boat were undeceived when they found themselves in an inferno of noise and smoke.

The bombardment of the Hartlepools caused a loss of

nearly 100 lives in the two boroughs, including 41 civilians and eight soldiers at Hartlepool, and 41 civilians at West Hartlepool. The old borough suffered much more severely than the newer districts of West Hartlepool. Hartlepool had scars, gashes and gaping wounds from one end to the other. The Germans seemed to have varied their fire to cover the widest possible area of workshops and human habitations. Hundreds of houses were seriously damaged, and hundreds more had their windows smashed. Terrible

UNDERWOOD & UNDERWOOD, N. Y.

REMAINS OF THE ANCIENT ABBEY OF WHITBY
Near Scarborough, England, after the bombardment

havoc was wrought along the sea front. The district lying behind the lighthouse was severely battered, but the battery on the front, that guards the entrance to the port, was not touched. Behind and beside it houses were unroofed and holes made in their walls. A whole terrace on the front escaped injury. A few yards behind it a residential square had on one side hardly a house left whole. Further in the rear, by the Rugby football field, was a long row of houses every one of which was extensively damaged. Half were no longer habitable. A violent earthquake could not have caused the same measure of ruin. Except as an example of "frightfulness," the visit to the Hartlepools was fruitless. Work was going on next day in workshops and at docks as usual, the port working normally, and merchant ships were steaming home through sea fogs just as if nothing had

THE BRITISH SHIP "APPAM"

happened. The hostile cruisers did nothing but sacrifice nearly a hundred lives of innocent non-combatants.

The cruisers steamed close into Whitby, and when about a mile off the port discharged shots into the town, which was undefended by artillery. It was estimated that 100 shots were fired. After the bombardment, they steamed out to sea and were soon lost to view. Two men were killed and houses and other property were damaged. Whitby Abbey, close to the signal station, was struck, as was the Abbey Lodge. News that the venerable ruins of Whitby had been damaged caused a feeling of anger, as deep in purpose as in resentment, to pass through England. These ruins, battered by the storms of many generations, stood still unconquered, perched high above the huddled beauty of the old port and the town near the edge of a cliff and on the right bank of the Esk. They stood almost alone, with the quaint old parish church of St. Mary between them and the town, at the head of a precipitous flight of 199 steps.

This German exploit occurred in waters associated in all

American minds with the famous victory of John Paul Jones with the *Bonhomme Richard*. What surprised most readers was the great daring and skill of the Germans in piloting vessels through British mine-fields and making off after a raid, which, as far as it went, was perfectly successful. That it was also perfectly aimless in a military sense seemed an inevitable conclusion. Berlin merely announced that a part of the High Seas Fleet had bombarded certain "fortified towns" on the east coast of England, but added that, "regarding the further course of its action, no information can be given." It was impossible to avoid associating these deeds with the advice of one of Germany's popular naval writers, published the day before the raid occurred. "We must see clearly," he wrote in the *Deutsche Tageszeitung*, "that, in order to fight with success, we are obliged to fight ruthlessly—ruthlessly in the proper meaning of the word, that is to say, without any regard whatever for any conceivable thing which lies outside the line leading to our final military goal. Our sole thought is devoted to

© UNDERWOOD & UNDERWOOD, N. Y.

THE MÖWE AFTER REACHING KIEL
The *Möwe* is the second vessel from the right

increasing vengeance by any and every means which can lead to victory."

Like a fantom, gliding over the sea, in which for days she had been supposed to be lost, the British passenger liner *Appam* of the West African trade, on February 1,

1916, slipt into Hampton Roads, in the gray of early morning, and dropt anchor there under the guns of Fortress Monroe. Over the liner flew the naval ensign of the Imperial German Government, and on her bridge walked Lieutenant Berge of the German Naval Reserve. A German prize crew of twenty-two men stood guard over the *Appam's* company of 429. As wonderful as any exploit of the *Emden* or other raiders, was the tale which those aboard the *Appam* had to tell of another strange small German raider, which was credited with having slipt out of Kiel through the British North Sea Fleet into the open Atlantic, and cruised for days in the paths of British and French vessels, six of which it captured before their prisoners were put aboard the *Appam.*

On March 5 official announcement was made that the *Appam's* unidentified raider had arrived home and was the *Möwe,* which had on board 199 prisoners and 1,000,000 marks in gold bars. Count von Dohna, the *Möwe's* commander, was awarded the Iron Cross of the First Class and members of the crew the Iron Cross of the Second Class. The *Möwe* had performed one of the most spectacular feats of the war by reaching a German North Sea port in safety. Wilhelmshaven had been patrolled with ceaseless vigilance by British warships. Through waters which had been blocked off in districts for patrol by different British units the *Möwe* had threaded her way to safety. She had reached the North Sea by going around Iceland.

Later in the war a disguised commerce-raider named *Crocodile* and five armed trawlers were sunk by British destroyers in Kattegat waters. The *Crocodile* was a new vessel, of nearly 1,000 tons, with a crew of 100 men, and had been disguised as a neutral merchantman, carrying a deck load of casks. The British destroyers rescued about thirty men. The rest of the crew were killed in the fight.[8]

[8] Principal Sources: The *Evening Post,* The *Times,* New York; the *Berliner Tageblatt; The Independent, The Literary Digest, New* York; The *Daily Mail* (London) ; The *Sun,* The *Journal of Commerce,* New York; The *Morning Post,* The *Standard,* The *Times,* The Manchester *Guardian,* London; The *World* (New York), "Nelson's History of the War" by John Buchan, the "New International Year Book" (1914-16).

THE GREAT BATTLE OFF JUTLAND
May 31, 1916

FOR almost twenty-two months, or from the day when the war began, the British public had looked forward without ceasing to a pitched battle between great ships at sea. Active command of the sea it was asserted could not be obtained, either by Great Britain or by Germany, until a fleet action had been fought by those powers and won by the strongest. The conditions in which the two navies had so long faced one another were not such, however, as had given promise to naval men of an early conflict on a large scale. The German flag had completely disappeared from the ocean, while the oversea traffic of the Allies had continued unmolested, save by submarines. British naval policy had in the main been directed to the destruction of German commerce and trade—that is to the enforcement of what, in all but name, was a blockade. So long as the Germans made no attempt to take to the sea in force, it was not easy to see how a decisive engagement could be brought about. Nevertheless, it was hoped that, as the blockade became more and more stringent, this condition, combined with others, would soon operate to force the Germans to risk a battle. For nearly two years the British Grand Fleet in the North Sea faced German bases and so had made secure the passage of Allied trade and troops unmolested. Campaigns for the possession of the German colonies had meanwhile been undertaken, and assistance rendered to Allied land forces in three continents without let or hindrance. The British fleet had also provided safeguards against an invasion of the British Islands, and had enforced what was almost strangulation of trade with Germany. Perils from mine and submarine menace had, however, always been present, and the call upon the vigilance of flotillas and fleets on patrol service remained unremitting. The principal base of the Grand Fleet was Scapa Flow in the Orkneys.

While a predominant position at sea had thus been maintained by Great Britain, there was in being, within a short distance of her shores, the second strongest fleet in the world, manned by courageous and competent officers and men. The Germans believed their methods of training, their guns and mechanical equipment, and the armament and armor supplied them by Krupp, were superior to those of their opponents. Given that they could choose their own time and place for action, they believed these advantages would more than compensate for their deficiency in numbers of men and ships. Yet when tried in the ordeal of battle, the higher standards of technique, according to British experts, would be found on the other side. Neither in nerve nor in *morale* were the staying powers of the Germans equal to those of their opponents, nor had they proved the better in tactical efficiency, scientific gunnery, or the handling of ships and machinery.

The event so anxiously expected, and which, altho not a complete victory, was sufficient to demonstrate the superiority of the British fleet and of British seamanship, occurred on May 31, 1916, when, for the first time, two modern warfleets came into a great conflict, and the superdreadnought was put to the test of battle. The action occurred in the North Sea off the coast of Jutland in an engagement which began on both sides with battle-cruisers, and ended with battleships. The battle-cruiser was a new type of vessel that aimed to combine the highest speed with the greatest gun-power. Naturally something had to be sacrificed in such ships, and so it was defensive armor that suffered. A battleship such as the British *Warspite* had a belt of 13½-inch armor, while a battle-cruiser such as the *Queen Mary,* a ship almost as large, had an armor of only 9 inches. Battle-cruisers usually carried eight guns of 12-inch caliber, as on the *Invincible,* and of 13½-inch, as on the *Queen Mary,* and could make 26 or more knots an hour. Their weakness was that they could not stand punishment as a regular battleship could. For safety the battle-cruiser depended mostly on its speed, which enabled it to keep its distance and pound an enemy at long range.

The battle was commonly referred to, in accounts printed afterward, as having had three phases. The first dated from 3.45 P.M., on May 31, when Admiral Beatty's battle-cruisers *Lion, Princess Royal, Queen Mary, Tiger, Inflexible, Indomitable, Invincible, Indefatigable,* and *New Zealand,* while on a southeasterly course, followed at about two miles distance by the four ships of the *Queen Elizabeth* type, sighted enemy light cruisers and shortly afterwards the head of a German battle-cruiser squadron, consisting of the new *Hindenburg,* the *Seydlitz, Derfflinger, Lützow, Moltke,* and possibly the *Salamis.* Beatty at once began firing at a range of about 20,000 yards, which was shortened to 16,000 yards as the fleets closed. The Germans could see the British distinctly silhoueted, or outlined, against a light yellow sky, while the Germans, covered by a haze, could be only indistinctly made out by British gunners. The vessels of the *Queen Elizabeth* type opened fire on one after another of the German ships, as they came within range and the German battle-cruisers turned to port drawing away to about 20,000 yards.

The second stage began at 4.40 P.M., when a destroyer screen appeared beyond the German battle-cruisers and the whole German High Seas Fleet could be seen approaching on the northwestern horizon in three divisions, coming to support their battle-cruisers. The German battle-cruisers now turned round 16 points and took station in front of the German battleships. Beatty, with his battle-cruisers and supporting battleships, thus had before him the whole German battle-fleet, and Admiral Jellicoe was some distance away. The opposing fleets were moving parallel to one another in opposite directions, and had it not been for a master maneuver on the part of Beatty, the British advance ships would have been cut off from Jellicoe's Grand Fleet. In order to avoid that disaster and at the same time prepare the way so that Jellicoe might envelop his adversary, Beatty immediately turned round 16 points so as to bring his ships parallel to the German battle-cruisers and facing in the same direction. Then he increased to full speed in order to get ahead of the Germans and take up a tactical position in advance of their line which he was able to do, owing to the superior speed of his battle-cruisers. Just before the turning-point was reached, the *Indefatigable* sank, probably from striking a mine, while the *Queen Mary* and *Invincible* were lost at the turning-point, where the High Seas Fleet had concentrated fire. A little earlier, as the German battle-cruisers were turning, the ships of the *Queen Elizabeth* type had in similar manner concentrated their fire on the turning-point and put out of action a new German ship, believed at the time to be the *Hindenburg*.

THE BATTLESHIP "HINDENBURG"

This ship was one of the latest of German dreadnoughts. She was in the battle of Jutland and, after the armistice, was surrendered off the Firth of Forth and taken into Scapa Flow, where she was afterward sunk by the Germans

Beatty had now got round and was headed away with the loss of three ships, and was racing parallel to the German battle-cruisers. The *Queen Elizabeth* followed behind, engaging the main High Seas Fleet.

The third phase began at 5 P.M. with the *Queen Elizabeth* turning short to port 16 points in order to follow Beatty. At this point the *Warspite* jammed her steering-gear, failed to get around, and drew the fire of six of the enemy, who closed in upon her. It was not surprizing that the Germans claimed her as a loss, since on paper she ought to have been lost, but as a matter of fact, altho repeatedly straddled by shell-fire with the water boiling up all around her, she was not seriously hit and was able to sink one of her opponents. Her captain in due course recovering control of the vessel, brought her around, so that she followed her consorts. In the meantime, the *Barham, Valiant* and *Malaya* had turned short to avoid the danger spot where the *Queen Mary* and *Inv'ncible* were lost, and for an hour while waiting for Jellicoe to arrive fought a delaying action against the High Seas fleet. The *Warspite* joined them about 5.15 o'clock. All four ships were so successfully maneuvered that no hits of a disabling character were received. They had a speed over their opponents of fully four knots, and so were able

THE GERMAN BATTLESHIP "HINDENBURG" AS SUNK AT SCAPA FLOW.

to draw away from part of the long line of German battle-ships, wh'ch almost filled up the horizon. At this time the *Queen Elizabeths* were steadily firing at the flashes of German guns at a range which varied from 12,000 to 15,000 yards, especially against those nearest them. The Germans being enveloped in a mist only smoke and flashes were visible.[9]

The vis'bility at 6.50 was not more than four miles. Soon after that the German ships were temporarily lost

[9] From a detailed account printed in The *Herald* (Glasgow) and cabled to The *Times* (New York).

sight of, but Beatty continued his course to the eastward until 7 o'clock, when he gradually altered to the south and west in order to regain touch with the Germans. He was in action twice again, and with battleships as well as battle-cruisers, at ranges of 15,000 to 10,000 yards. Each time his gunners "got home" on the retreating German vessels. On the last occasion the leading German ship, after being repeatedly hit by the *Lion,* turned away eight points, emitting high flames, with a heavy list to port, while the *Princess Royal* set fire to a three-funnelled battleship, and the *New Zealand* and *Indomitable* reported that a third ship hauled out of line, heeled over and was on fire. Then the mist enveloped them, and the battle-cruiser's part in the engagement ceased.

The concluding phase of the daylight engagement, that between the battle-squadrons, was a one-sided affair. As soon as Admiral Scheer saw the situation he turned to the south-ward, and, under cover of declining daylight, thickening mist, and smoke-clouds from his small craft, withdrew from the fight. Before he could get away, the three squadrons of the British battle-fleet in a single line had been hurled across his van. Under fire from 13.5-inch guns the German formation was shattered and the ships themselves severely mauled. The supreme moment, leading to the climax of the whole battle, was when Jellicoe brought his dreadnoughts at top speed into the *mêlée,* a situation which called for tactical skill, calm judgment, and instant decision. Flashes of guns were visible through the haze, but no ship could be distinguished. Even the position of the German battleships could not always be determined. So thick was the mist that great care was essential to prevent British ships from being mistaken for German ones. Conditions were unparalleled, but Jellicoe delivered a vigorous thrust which threw the Germans into confusion, and after this, all their tactics were of a nature to avoid further action. How they extricated themselves was not made clear. The fighting between big ships lasted intermittently for two hours more, and then developed into a chase, until under cover of darkness and the thickness of weather, Scheer escaped. It was not until the following day, after the whole large area covered by the fight had been thoroughly searched, without a trace of the Germans being seen, that the British Commander-in-Chief returned to his bases to refuel and refill his magazines. It was then officially stated that he was ready again to put to sea.

The loss of the *Indefatigable* was one of those catastrophic strokes of fortune made possible by the tremendous power locked up in modern ships of war. The ships on both sides had become vigorously engaged when suddenly a heavy explosion took place on the last ship of the British line

THE BLOWING UP OF THE "QUEEN MARY"

which was the cruiser *Indefatigable*. A black column of smoke shot upward 400 feet, hiding the ship, and when it cleared away a little later the ship had disappeared. Out of her 900 officers and men, only two survived. At 4.18, when the third ship in the German line was seen to be on fire, another misfortune befell the British squadron, the battle-cruiser *Queen Mary* being vitally hit, and, with a terrific explosion which appeared to blow her hull asunder, she disappeared. She had at least 1,000 people aboard, and only about a score were saved. In modern warfare seamen have to face perils that were unknown to their predecessors. In the old wars, ships were more often captured than sunk.

According to a Portsmouth correspondent,[10] the manner in which the *Warspite* fought the German battle-fleet, when she went to the rescue of the *Warrior*, formed one of the most thrilling stories of the battle. The *Warrior* lay helpless, her engines disabled, her magazines under water, and her crew unable to use guns. She was calmly waiting for the end when suddenly on the horizon the crew saw a huge ship coming, the fast and powerful *Warspite*, which Jellicoe, learning of the *Warrior's* peril, had sent ahead of the Grand Fleet to succor her. Helpless sailors on the *Warrior* greeted her with cheers as she threw herself between the imperilled ship and the German vessel. The first salvo from the *Warspite's* 15-inch batteries hit a German ship with full force, and she reeled and sank. The *Warspite* circled around the *Warrior*, drawing upon herself the fire of German ships and replying with vigor. After a shell had damaged her steering-gear, the *Warspite* held on, fighting alone the German ships. Four times in this manner the *Warspite* circled the *Warrior*, punishing the German ships with her great guns. No episode of the fight was more thrilling or spectacular than this. The cruiser, after putting one or more of the German cruisers out of action, had been battered and terribly injured, and was expecting the shells that would finish it when the *Warspite* appeared. An officer of the *Warrior* afterward said:

"The first shot from the *Warspite* lopped off the foremast of the leading enemy cruiser. The next overturned both the fore gun-turrets, and in five minutes the enemy vessel was ablaze from end to end, enveloped in a cloud of dense smoke. The second battle-cruiser, which had been concentrating her fire on the *Warspite*, turned to starboard, smoke belching from her funnels, and endeavored to pick up her main squadron. But it was not to be. Two shells from the *Warspite* blew every funnel she had to pieces. The third made a great rent in her stern. The fourth plowed up her deck

[10] In The *Times* (London).

THE "INDEFATIGABLE"

THE "LION," IN THE CENTER AS HIT, DESTROYERS ARE
ON THE LEFT

THE "WARRIOR"

and burst against the foremast, bringing it down. Two minutes afterward this vessel also was on fire and heeling over, with the *Warspite* still pounding her and ripping great gashes in her starboard side and bottom. The last we saw of her was nothing more than a broken hulk. The *Warrior* was towed for ten hours and then sank."

This, the greatest sea-battle of the war, and the most sanguinary engagement in naval history, was commonly described at the time in neutral circles as a draw. The contrary was not definitely accepted until the war was over and a confession came from Germany. With equal weight given to German and British claims at the time of the battle, Dutch papers, as neutral onlookers, made an estimate of the result as a "Pyrrhic victory" for England. The Amsterdam *Telegraaf* and the *Handelsblad* indorsed this view, but both argued that the battle had to be considered a British victory because the Germans had failed to accomplish what they set out to do, and the British blockade remained unbroken. "Nothing will be changed in this respect," said the *Telegraaf*, "even if the Germans make more hunger-sorties." To Great Britain the battle, however, was a "Pyrrhic victory" because the immense losses in ships and men could hardly have been surpassed in defeat. The Amsterdam *Tijd* said Spencer Churchill's "rats" had finally "come out of their hole and bitten Britannia badly."

The British claim was that the German losses were as great as, if not greater than, their own, and the claim, tho officially denied by German authorities, was reiterated more strongly after a German admission was made that certain losses had been concealed by Berlin for "military reasons." A belief was encouraged, and became generally prevalent, in Germany that British supremacy on the sea had been broken. The Munich *Neueste Nachrichten* said it was a catastrophic defeat for England and the beginning of "a new era in naval warfare," for it had "completely dissipated the idea that the British Navy was superior to all others." The *Leipzig Neueste Nachrichten* said "England's invincibility on the seas was broken," and the German fleet had "torn the venerable Trafalgar legend into shreds." In the Austrian capital, the *Neues Wiener Journal* added that "such a crushing defeat as the English suffered would place a doubt upon their whole supremacy on the seas and deal a decisive blow to their desire to continue that supremacy." The official *Norddeutsche Allgemeine Zeitung* was not quite so sanguine, but was supremely satisfied with the results:

"From the beginning of the war the officers and crews of our fleet longed for an opportunity to measure their strength against their chief enemy. They have been able to show on a great scale how well founded were the expectations which all Germany attached to their efficiency, heroism, and determination. The first great sea-battle has ably demonstrated the excellent quality of the German naval forces."

An official statement from Berlin on June 3 gave the total loss of the German High Sea forces as one battle-cruiser, one ship of the line of older construction, four small cruisers, and five torpedo-boats. The statement added that of these losses the battleship *Pommern* was launched in 1905. While the loss of the cruisers *Wiesbaden, Elbing, Frauenlob,* and five torpedo-boats had already been reported in official statements, "for military reasons," said the statement further, "we refrained until now from making public the loss of the battle-cruiser *Lützow* and the cruiser *Rostock*." These were declared to be all the losses sustained by the Germans. The losses of the British were again said in Berlin to have been heavier than had been admitted, including the dreadnought *Warspite,* the battle-cruiser *Princess Royal,* the cruiser *Birmingham,* and probably the dreadnought *Marlborough.* Berlin added that many official and semi-official reports from the British side had been spread abroad "in order to deny the greatness of the British defeat, and create an impression that the battle was a victory for British arms." Another Berlin statement from an "authoritative" source, on June 8, gave the respective strength of the two fleets at the high tide of battle, as follows: British—At least twenty-five dreadnoughts, six battle-cruisers, and at least four armored cruisers. German—Sixteen dreadnoughts, five battle-cruisers, six older German battleships, and no armored cruisers. In addition, "numerous light warships were engaged."

This Berlin statement contained the first mention of the loss of the cruiser *Rostock*. None of the British claims had included it. Final admission by Berlin of the loss of the *Lützow* and *Rostock* brought the total admitted German loss to twelve ships, 58,000 tons. Before the admission, it stood at 32,515 tons, as against admitted British losses of about 105,000 tons. The *Lützow* was a battle-cruiser of the *Derfflinger* type, of 28,000 tons displacement, length 718 feet and speed 30 knots. Her armament was eight 12-inch guns and twelve 5.9-inch guns. The *Rostock* was a small cruiser of the type of the famous sea-raider *Karlsruhe*. Her displacement was 4,822 tons, length 456 feet and speed 27 knots. Her chief armament was twelve 4.1-inch guns. She

THE "POMMERN"
Lost by the Germans in the Jutland battle

carried 373 officers and men. As the Germans had fought near home, they had a greater chance than the British of getting their damaged ships safe into home ports. They were only about 100 miles from the shelter of Heligoland, and probably less from the mine-fields in the neighborhood of the Bight, when the battle was finished, whereas Jellicoe's bases were 400 miles away.

Both the jubilation in Germany and the depression in Great Britain which greeted the first news of the sea-fight were materially modified in the light of later and fuller information, with the result that, while neither side admitted a defeat, neutral observers were inclined to agree that it was impossible for either side to claim a great victory. In first-class fighting ships the British admitted the loss of three battle-cruisers, and claimed to have sunk one German super-dreadnought and two or three battle-cruisers. The Germans admitted the loss of one battle-cruiser and one small battleship and claimed to have sunk two British super-dreadnoughts and four battle-cruisers. The Kaiser, addressing the sailors of the fleet at Wilhelmshaven nearly a week after the battle, announced that "the English fleet was beaten" and its "tyrannical supremacy shattered" and that the result "will cause fear to creep into the bones of the enemy." Enthusiastic German editors acclaimed the German ruler as "Admiral of the Atlantic," but the New

© KEYSTONE VIEW CO.

THE "DERFFLINGER" AS SUNK AT SCAPA FLOW

York *World* retorted that "an Admiral of the Atlantic Ocean who has not a single ship afloat on the Atlantic Ocean and can not get a ship there should have hesitated somewhat before assuming the title." If Great Britain's sea-power had been shattered, the same paper asked, "why were the North German-Lloyd and Hamburg-American ships rusting at their Hoboken docks?" "The German Navy," it concluded, "was still a navy in jail, which could assault its keeper now and then with great fury, but remained in jail nevertheless." Popular rejoicing in Germany would be succeeded by disillusionment, said the New York *Times,* when the people found "the hateful blockade no less rigorous, and food no more plentiful in Berlin." The *Evening World* summed up the results for the two nations as "materially a minor loss for England, but a serious moral setback; for Germany, a very costly matter, but a stimulating moral victory."

In England public opinion rallied quickly from the consternation caused by the first news of the loss of fourteen ships and thousands of brave sailors when the second report from the Admiralty claimed the result as a British victory. King George, in a message to Jellicoe, exprest regret that "the German High Seas Fleet, in spite of its heavy losses, was enabled by misty weather to evade the full consequences of the encounter," thereby "robbing us of the opportunity of gaining a decisive victory." It was nevertheless a "British victory," declared Admiral Lord Charles Beresford, retired, who summed up his version of the result as follows: "We lost cruisers which we can afford to lose; the Germans lost battleships which they can not afford to lose."

The British Admiralty, in a later statement, admitted the loss of fourteen ships, including three battle-cruisers, three cruisers, and eight destroyers, with a tonnage of about 114,000. As many of these went down with virtually all on board, the loss in personnel was admittedly heavy, available estimates placing it at about five thousand. The casualty list gave the names of 333 British officers killed, among them Rear Admirals Hood and Arbuthnot. The British ships admitted sunk were the *Queen Mary, Indefatigable,* and *Invincible,* battle-cruisers; the *Defense, Black Prince,* and *Warrior,* cruisers; the *Tipperary, Turbulent, Fortune, Sparrowhawk, Ardent, Nomad, Nestor,* and *Shark,* destroyers.

Against these Germany admitted the loss of eleven ships— the battle-cruiser *Lützow,* the battleship *Pommern,* the cruisers *Wiesbaden, Elbing, Frauenlob* and *Rostock,* and gave unnamed torpedo-boats—representing a total of 60,720 tons. Additional German losses claimed by the British were the super-dreadnought *Hindenburg,* the battle-cruisers *Derfflinger* and *Seydlitz,* two battle-cruisers of the *Kaiser* class, a light cruiser, five destroyers, and a submarine— which would have increased the German loss in tonnage by more than 100,000. The *Hindenburg, Derfflinger* and *Seydlitz* may have been seriously crippled, and even put out of action altogether, but they survived the battle, and were not sunk until the Germans themselves sunk them at Scapa Flow in June, 1919. An early unofficial estimate of the German loss in personnel was as follows: 800 dead, 1,400 wounded, 4,600 missing. Each side insisted that the other was concealing losses and each officially denied the charge. The British Admiralty stated positively that the *Warspite, Marlborough, Princess Royal,* and *Birmingham* were safe in British ports, with the *Acasta* and *Euryalus,* all of which the Germans claimed to have sunk, and that no English submarines took part in the battle, so that, if the German fleet sank a craft of this type, it must have been one of its own. What the naval situation remained was best revealed by examining the relative standing of the British and German fleets afterward, as compared with their standing at the outbreak of the war. On this point the New York *Evening Post* said:

"England began the war with 215,000 tons in battle-cruisers, against Germany's 208,000 tons. We have no data for adding anything to the British tonnage, and must subtract 63,000 tons lost last Wednesday, leaving a total of 152,000 tons. From the German side we must subtract the *Goeben,* of 23,000 tons, unavailable for North Sea fighting, and add probably four cruisers of 112,000 tons, giving a total of about 300,000 tons; so that in battle-cruisers Germany to-day is twice as strong as Great Britain.

"In older battleships Great Britain began with 556,000 tons and has lost 115,000 tons, and Germany began with 243,000 tons and has lost 13,000. In heavy cruisers Great Britain began with 450,000 tons and has lost 134,000 tons, and Germany began with 94,000 tons and has lost 64,000 tons. Thus in dreadnought strength the ratio remains the same as at the beginning of the war. In old battleships England's advantage has declined from 2¼ to 2, and in heavy cruisers it has increased from about five times the German strength to ten times. In battle-cruisers, on the other hand, it has apparently fallen from an equality with Germany to one-half."

As to what was the real object of the German fleet in going out, no definite information was obtained. The first official German report of the battle merely stated that it was engaged in "an enterprise directed to the northward" when the encounter occurred. The Paris *Temps* made the suggestion that this northward dash was aimed to cut off Russian communications at Archangel, which was now free of ice and was Russia's chief means of communication with the outside world. Another theory was that the Germans were deliberately seeking to join battle with Admiral Beatty's battle-cruiser fleet. Other views were that their objective was the British coast, or that the Germans were trying to turn some of their fast commerce-destroyers loose in the Atlantic. Whatever the German purpose, British commentators predicted that it "would be many a long day before the German fleet showed itself again in the North Sea" —a true prediction, as it never again came out except to surrender in 1918. As a result of this battle, said Mr. Balfour, first Lord of the Admiralty, "the German dream of an invasion of England has been dissipated."

In Great Britain the public was a long time in recovering from its astonishment at the manner in which the Admiralty had first announced the battle, which was in terms as if it were a complete British defeat. The London *Morning Post* afterward remarked: "We are a strange people. Our navy wins a great victory with incomparable strategic skill, faultless tactics, and magnificent fighting, and the Admiralty announces it a defeat." The British view that nothing had been changed by the battle was not admitted by their opponents. The Berlin correspondent of the Budapest *Az Ujsag* said:

"The old saying that the British fleet is invincible has been contradicted by the battle in the Skagerrak, where the mightiest fleet in the world suffered a terrible defeat, and with it the proud leviathans of the sea, each of them worth $40,000,000, wounded to death by the German torpedoes, sank to the bottom of the sea, taking with them the ancient glory of the British domination of the seas. The British fleet evaded the battle with German might on the sea as long as possible. Hiding in their bases, they never dared to come out whenever the German fleet went out to search for them. This time they were trapt, and had to give battle. The greatest blow at English prestige will open a new phase in the history of the word."

What was called "a gain in solidarity" was depicted by the

Hamburger Fremdenblatt in telling how the news was received in one of the remoter villages of northern Germany. Describing the celebration that followed, the *Fremdenblatt* said:

"There was not a man who did not have one or two glasses to drink to the health of our boys in blue. We have celebrated many victories, but never have I seen such unmixed joy among our soldiers as on that day. They speak of the Russians with a laugh, and to be transferred to the Eastern Front is regarded as a holiday. For the French they feel pity, even tho the French artillery 'shoots damned well.' But their eyes flash and their fists are clenched unconsciously when somebody speaks of the Britons. And now comes this glorious German victory on the element which the English thought to be their eternal heritage. That is something for our soldiers on the Verdun front. In quiet joy we welcomed the victories of our comrades over the Italians, and the constant advance of our infantry before Verdun was no surprize. But this unhoped-for victory of our sailors over haughty Albion we have celebrated like none before."

In discussing the political effect, Count Ernst zu Reventlow argued in the Berlin *Deutsche Tageszeitung* that those who favored an understanding with Great Britain, on the ground that Germany could never rival her in seapower, had been silenced. Before the war there was a small but influential party which favored a *rapprochement* with England and opposed the policy of naval expansion upon the grounds that Germany could never equal Britain on the sea, and that constant additions to the navy were a source of international irritation. Count zu Reventlow said that fallacy was now exposed:

"Great Britain's power and reputation, her political and economic life, have been based upon her navy, or, rather, her naval prestige. Great Britain, therefore, can not possibly acquiesce in her defeat, either for her own sake or for that of her Allies. The consequence is that the idea of an Anglo-German understanding is now relegated to limbo—a fact which we greet with a feeling of relief. The fight will now be continued with the utmost energy, and will necessarily lead to the employment of every possible weapon."

Notwithstanding all this bombast one fact stood out clearly —that control of the seas remained as securely British as it had ever been since the war began. The real questions were whether British transports were less safe than they were on May 30; whether the arrival of supplies and food in Great Britain had been in any way hampered; whether the seas were any nearer being open to German commerce; whether the blockade against Germany had been weakened. The answer to all was obvious, but a further question had to be answered. Admitting that the German fleet was still confessedly inferior to a full trial of strength for mastery of the seas, how many such exploits as that of May 31 would be necessary to reduce the British fleet to a point where Germans might be in a position to try-out full conclusions? The final evidence was that the British had not been as badly outwitted as had appeared from the first reports. Beatty's cruisers were not caught in a trap. Rather, he chose to take a great risk in the hope of winning a great victory. He failed in that, but he did not stumble into defeat.

That the battle was essentially inconclusive was admitted by Jellicoe in a later official report. He cheerfully and generously bore witness to the courage of his foe, in accordance with the best English tradition. The enemy "fought with the gallantry that was expected of him," said he. He particularly admired the conduct of a German light cruiser which passed down the British line firing from the only gun it was able to use. All this coming from Jellicoe, was the handsomer, in view of what must have been to him great disappointment that the naval part of the war could not have been ended that day, just because an evening mist and fading light robbed the British fleet of the complete success it had striven for. How the fog interfered was shown by Beatty's report which said that at 6.52 P.M. the British lost all sight of the enemy for 20 minutes and again at 7.45 for 35 minutes, while at 8.40 the Germans had disappeared. During intervals when they were sighted Beatty had to fire at a range of 15,000 yards, which was a far cry from the old days when, at the coming of darkness ships hauled off and watched each other as they lighted battle-lanterns before politely renewing the action at arms' length.

In the use of new devices, the most dramatic, said Jellicoe, was the launching of a seaplane from the British auxiliary *Engadine*. To identify four enemy cruisers, the aircraft flew at a height of only 900 feet within 3,000 yards of these vessels which fired with every gun that they carried. Twenty-two minutes after this plane arose the *Engadine* was receiving wireless reports from the observers flying above that terrific fire. Next in interest were the attacks of the de stroyer flotillas—raids in unison by these "cavalry of the seas" being attempted, without, however, producing decisive results. As they sought to torpedo German battle-cruisers, eight British destroyers ran into a flotilla of fifteen enemy destroyers and a light cruiser, with the result that the fiercest kind of action at close range took place. Jellicoe gave several instances of the sighting of submarines during the action, but their presence was denied by the Germans. They said the speed of the fleet was so great that no submarine could have kept up with it. As for Zeppelins, Jellicoe had nothing to say that bore out the early English reports that the Germans were helped by the presence of several of them. The Germans themselves—one eye-witness in particular—seemed positive that they were without this new type of fighting craft.

The general impression made by Admiral Jellicoe in the book he published in March, 1919,[11] was one of superior, farther-sighted preparation for a naval war on the part of the Germans. Their fire-control was better, especially at night; and their armor, projectiles, and shells more effective. Relatively, the British Navy had been unprepared. Jellicoe's volume showed how serious might have been the German menace had the Germans realized their opportunity in the earlier nine months of the war, but the book semed to be in the main an effort to explain why Jutland was not a decisive British victory. It aroused wonder as to why, if the British Grand Fleet was so inferior in destroyers, range-finding appliances, armor-piercing projectiles, direct-firing gear for secondary batteries, and searchlights, the Germans were

[11] "The Grand Fleet, 1914-1916" (George H. Doran Co.).

worsted, and why, under such advantageous conditions, should they have run home to their base under a rout.

Jellicoe, however, was thought to have made out a good reason for his decision not to fight a night battle. Pollen and other critics of his tactics had been contending that he should have continued fighting until darkness fell, and that his attack had not been sufficiently aggressive. Pollen insisted that the British fleet was torpedo-shy at Jutland, and Admiral Jellicoe admitted as much. A comparison of several capital ships of the two fleets showed that German constructors had put more faith than the British in torpedo tubes. Again, Jellicoe made a surprizing revelation in saying that the British were weaker than the Germans in destroyers. As to dreadnoughts, the Germans were supposed to be at a hopeless disadvantage, but Admiral Jellicoe presented a catalog of misfortunes to the British fleet to prove that its superiority on October 27, 1914, existed only on paper:

The *Ajax* had developed condenser defects. The *Iron Duke* had similar troubles. The *Orion* had to be sent to Greenock for examination of her turbine supports, which appeared to be defective. The *Conqueror* was at Devonport refitting, and the *New Zealand* was in dock at Cromarty. The *Erin* and *Agincourt*, having been newly commissioned, could not yet be regarded as efficient, so that the dreadnought fleet consisted only of seventeen effective battleships and five battle-cruisers. The German dreadnought fleet at the time comprised fifteen battleships and four battle-cruisers, with the *Blücher* in addition."

The chief impression made by Jellicoe's book was that he exalted German strength and minimized British. It was a fact, however, that at Jutland at least the gun-power of the British was superior and greatly so. Jellicoe's showing in general seemed to be that at Jutland the Germans had had a fine opportunity to wrest the mastery of the sea from Great Britain and had stupidly let it slip out of their hands.

All other naval fights in this war had been comparatively small affairs. Encounters had been exaggerated beyond measure by inexpert observers. When the unfortunate Cradock was defeated off Chili, the event was magnified into a disaster. It was apparent that the Germans off Jutland avoided a general fleet action and drew off when the main body of the British fleet came up. If there had been a victory for Germany—even a victory that Germany believed was hers—the action would undoubtedly have been followed up. Instead of doing that the German ships retired to port and stayed there. That the conduct of the German commander in his retirement was strategically sound was not doubted, but the act showed plainly how absurd it was for the Germans to talk of the battle as having been decisive for them in any sense. Some newspapers emphasized the loss of trained seamen as a most serious blow to the British navy. The highest estimate of casualties, however, did not go above 7,000 men, and there were at least 150,000 men left in the British service. The loss was therefore only a trifle over 4 per cent.

Compared with the force commanded by Admiral Jellicoe, the forces commanded by Alexander, or Cæsar, or Napoleon, or Nelson were puny, and even those of Togo and Rojesvensky were unimportant. Compared with this force indeed the aggregate land forces of both the Allies and the Teutons were inconsiderable because the total offensive power of one salvo from one of Jellicoe's battleships was greater than that of half a million muskets. The aggregate artillery-power of the twenty-four modern battleships that Admiral Jellicoe had in his main column at the battle of Jutland was greater than that of 10,000,000 infantry soldiers—and he moved these battleships at a speed of nearly twenty miles an hour. No other person ever commanded a force comparable in power with the force commanded at Jutland by Admiral Jellicoe.

The force was the concentration of at least 90 per cent. of the naval defensive power of the British Empire. It was opposed to the German High Seas Fleet, possessing an offensive power which, while inferior, was not greatly so. It was not so much inferior as to render impossible the defeat of the British fleet, by reason of superior strategy or tactics on the German side, or of accident, or of all combined, especially since the defensive armor of the Germans was the better. If the battle of Jutland had been a decisive victory for either side victory in the World War would have gone to the side that was the victor in this battle.

More appropriate than ever before now seemed the name *Jammerbugt* (Bay of Woe) which the Danes had given to waters that wash the sand-dunes of the northwestern coast of Jutland. With the black ribs of many ancient wrecks on this dangerous coast were now mingled ships and sailors from what were once two of the proudest battle-fleets that ever sailed the seas. Jutland, the continental portion of Denmark, comprises nearly two-thirds the area of that kingdom, but it has considerably less than half the total population. It compares with Vermont in size, but has a density of population three times as great. Its most striking physical characteristics are the fjords which cut into the sandy seaboard, particularly on the west coast. The highest point of land in Jutland, which is also the highest in the kingdom, is a 564-foot "eminence" on a line of low hills near the center of the peninsula. Jutland was the ancient home of the warlike Cimbri, a tribe which for twelve years kept Rome in a state of anxiety.

Two British destroyers on patrol-duty in the English Channel off Dover on the night of April 20, 1917, came upon a flotilla of six German destroyers and an encounter which promised to live in the history of naval engagements followed. Every gun aboard the combatants was kept sweeping the decks and tearing gaps in the sides of the opposing craft. One incident of the fight was that a British and a German destroyer became locked together and men fought furiously hand to hand. The British destroyers were the *Swift* and the *Broke*. Altho badly damaged they returned to port. The story of the engagement was an exciting and graphic tale of a boarding encounter with cutlasses and bayonets, recalling the days when wooden warships came together and men fought on the decks. The *Swift* and the *Broke* on night-patrol had been steaming on a westerly course when it was intensely dark but calm. The *Swift* sighted the enemy at 600 yards and the Germans instantly opened fire. The *Swift* replied and tried to ram the leading German destroyer. She missed ramming, but shot through the German line unscathed, and in turning torpedoed another boat. In the meantime the *Broke* had launched a torpedo at the second boat in the line, which hit the mark, and then opened fire, while the remaining German boats were stoking furiously for full speed. The *Broke's* commander swung round to port and rammed the third boat fair and square abreast the after-funnel. Locked together thus, the crews of the two boats fought a desperate hand-to-hand conflict.

Two other German destroyers attacked and poured a devastating fire on the *Broke,* whose foremost gun-crews were reduced from eighteen to six men. Midshipman Donald Gyles, altho wounded in the eye, kept all the foremost guns in action, he himself assisting the depleted crews to load. While he was thus employed a number of frenzied Germans swarmed up over the *Broke's* forecastle out of the rammed destroyer and, finding themselves amid the blinding flashes of the forecastle guns, swept aft in a shouting mob. The midshipman, amid the dead and wounded of his own gun-crews and half blinded by blood, met the onset single-handed with an automatic revolver. He was grappled by a German who tried to wrest the revolver away. Cutlasses and bayonets being among the British equipment in anticipation of such an event, the German was bayonetted. The remainder of the invaders, except two who feigned death, were driven over the side, two being made prisoners.

Two minutes after the ramming the *Broke* wrenched herself free from her sinking adversary and turned to ram the last of the three remaining German boats. She failed in this object, but in swinging around succeeded in hitting the boat's consort on the stem with a torpedo. Hotly engaged with these two fleeing destroyers, the *Broke* attempted to follow the *Swift* in the direction where she was last seen, but a shell struck the *Broke's* boiler-room, disabling her main engine.

The enemy then disappeared in the darkness. The *Broke,* altering her course, headed in the direction of a destroyer, which a few minutes later was seen to be heavily afire and whose crew, on sighting the British destroyer, sent up shouts for mercy. The *Broke* steered slowly toward the German regardless of the danger from a possible explosion of the magazines, and the German seamen redoubled their shouts of "Save! save!" and then unexpectedly opened fire. The

Broke being out of control, was unable to maneuver or extricate herself, but silenced the treachery with four rounds; and then, to insure her own safety, torpedoed the German amidships. Aside from the war on submarines, this was the last naval action of notable consequence, that occurred in the war.

Germany's naval losses as published in June, 1919, in the *Vossiche Zeitung* of Berlin, were declared to be complete and authoritative, and were so accepted in Washington. At the close of the year 1918 the number of destroyers supposed to have been lost by Germany was less than twenty, but the official report, as now printed in the Berlin newspaper, made the total forty-nine. Few of their big ships had been lost by the Germans. Only one battleship, the *Pommern* of 13,200 tons, had been sunk during the war, but one battle-cruiser of 26,000 tons, the *Lützow*, was lost—both went down in the sea fight off Jutland. The British had added to this list, but apparently only from observations of crippled ships which reached port afterward, having had a whole night, during which they were not molested, in which to stagger back to their base. In ships not of the first line of battle the Germans sustained considerable losses—six older armored cruisers, eight modern small cruisers of the latest design, and ten smaller cruisers of the old type, besides twenty large and forty-one small torpedo boats, nine auxiliary cruisers, of which the largest were the *Cap Trafalgar* of 20,000 tons, and the *Kaiser Wilhelm der Grosse* of 21,000 tons, twenty-eight mine-sweepers, and one hundred and twenty-two trawlers and patrol vessels. The number of warships of all kinds lost was 490. As Germany's naval warfare was for the most part defensive, aggressive only by stealth or when a raid was attempted, the conclusion had to be that the British, the most active of the Allies had been very much on the alert to attack the enemy when he showed himself. Germany's losses of men killed in the naval service were reported to have been 29,685, but 10,625 of these were marines, some of whom had served on land on the Western Front. When Great Britain announced in an Admiralty report of November 26, 1918, that her naval casualties had been 39,-766—officers killed or died of wounds 2,466, and men 30,895;

officers wounded, missing, or prisoners 1,042, and men 5,363—
it meant that these losses had all been incurred by the navy.
To this total were to be added 14,661 officers and men of
British merchant ships and fishing craft who lost their lives,
and 3,295 who were taken prisoners in the submarine warfare.

A GROUP OF GERMAN NAVAL OFFICERS

It seemed probable that the Germans killed in actual sea warfare were considerably less than one-half as many as the
British total.[12]

[12] Principal Sources: The London *Times'* "History of the War"; The *Herald,* The *Times,* The *Evening Post, The Literary Digest,* The *Tribune,* New
York; The *Times* (London); Associated Press reports; British and German
official reports, including that of Admiral Jellicoe, and Jellicoe's book, "The
Grand Fleet, 1914-1916" (George H. Doran Co.); also United Press dispatches.

PERSONAL SKETCHES
THE TREATY OF PEACE
AND A
CHRONOLOGY OF THE WAR

Part I

PERSONAL SKETCHES OF WAR LEADERS

MARSHAL FOCH INSPECTING A GERMAN FORT ON THE RHINE
AT MAINZ AFTER THE ARMISTICE
Above the stonework in the picture rises the colossal statue of "Germania"

MILITARY AND NAVAL LEADERS

(Arranged alphabetically as to surname)

SIR EDMUND ALLENBY, British Commander in Palestine and Syria

Allenby, the conqueror of Palestine and Syria, who ended his campaign at Aleppo, and then entered Constantinople, was one of those unpretentious Englishmen with quiet voice and manners, who at a meeting frequently fail to impress the unobservant and unthinking. With a touch of gentleness, he was a man of few words and long vision. Courteous and kindly he did not aim to shine in small talk. Men who never see below the surfaces of things did not recognize the tenacity and clearness of brain which marked him out only to such as have eyes to see. He was regarded with respect and almost reverence by Eastern peoples with whom he had been long associated, which was an indication of his character. He was fifty-seven when he completed his conquests in Asiatic Turkey.

As a boy he had been sent to Haileybury College. At Haileybury an important part of a boy's education consists in acquiring manners, upright conduct, and skill in outdoor sports—in other words, manliness. Under this system, unless a boy has great aptitude in that direction, mere bookish pursuits sometimes suffer. More precious than all else to the average English father and mother is the atmosphere of these schools, carefully adapted to turning out English gentlemen—not in the loose, but in the noble, sense of the word. At Haileybury Allenby was noted for high spirits and quickness of comprehension, but left no record of distinction in scholastic attainments, altho he did manifest an interest in literature which deepened and broadened as time went on. After he began his soldier's life with a commission in the Dragoons, he grew into a picture of the dashing cavalry officer, filled with zest for the picturesque career which the position opened up, but with a vein of seriousness not often found in young fellows from aristocratic circles in the British Army. Allenby had strong stuff in him, and meant to make good. He soon had opportunities of showing that he was no carpet knight.

When 23, Allenby was serving in the Bechuanaland expedition. Four years later he fought in Zululand, and became an adjutant.

In the South African war his cavalry tactics led to his being twice mentioned in dispatches from his Commander-in-Chief, and he was decorated. His big work began in the World War, when he went to France with the first British army, and helped resist the German rush on Paris. Outgunned, overwhelmed by numbers, deluged with high explosives, Allenby with that little army of less than two hundred thousand men, retreated stubbornly, helping to kill Germans, and yielding an awful tribute of death as it went back, step by step, from Mons. With cavalry acting as a screen, he helped British infantry to sell their lives at high price. Time and again he flung his command into positions, often deadly to many of his men, and his own life repeatedly in danger. As stated in the report of Sir John French, it was largely due to Allenby that one of the remnants of the British army was saved from destruction.

Allenby was afterward in the thick of fighting on the Western Front, where he had opportunities for distinction. In 1917, he commanded the right wing of the British in the battle of Arras, one of the most successful British actions fought until the offensive of 1918. His men carried an intricate network of trenches east of Arras, and fought their way along the Scarpe toward Douai. He was then transferred to Egypt, where he built up a careful plan for an advance through Palestine. As one of the original Kitchener generals he had been trained in the school of that organizer. In Egypt now he gave evidence of Kitchener's influence by a keen, long-sighted survey of the task before him. He made a request for additional forces, and refused to move until they came. Only when men, guns, and ammunition arrived in sufficient amount did he strike and then with terrific force.

Never was given a better illustration of the true character of the man than in his careful handling of the delicate situation when he entered Jerusalem and made a declaration to that mixed community which was a model of statesmanship on the part of a military commander. His proclamation, prepared in Arabic, Hebrew, English, French, Italian, Greek, and Russian, contained the following:

"Lest any of you be alarmed by reason of your experience at the hands of the enemy who has retired, I hereby inform you that it is my desire that every person should pursue his lawful business without fear of interruption. Furthermore, since your city is regarded with affection by the adherents of three of the great religions of mankind, and its soil has been consecrated by the prayers and pilgrimages of multitudes of devout people of these three religions for many centuries, therefore I make it known that every sacred building, monument, holy spot, shrine, traditional endowment, pious bequest or customary place of prayer of whatsoever form of the three religions will be maintained according to the existing customs and beliefs of those to whose faith they are sacred.''

Allenby placed guards over the holy places and gave Moslems special charge over buildings and sites precious to Moslem sentiment. On the day when he was to take formal possession of the city, he came, not on horseback in glittering display, but modestly on foot, approaching the shrine of his own belief. His staff and the civil officers, with attachés from America and other countries, entered on foot with him. His careful regard for all religious feeling, his steps to safeguard the interests of all peoples, were at once appreciated and his fame spread to the surrounding country until a legend grew up about him among Arabs, who regarded his conquest of Jerusalem as an inspired act because, in the name Allenby, they found an equivalent of the words "Allah Allah," meaning God and Prophet. For many generations there had been current among the Arabs and other tribes a prophesy that "He who shall save Jerusalem and exalt her among the nations will enter the city on foot, and his name will be God and Prophet."

The effect he produced in this proclamation undoubtedly helped him in all his military operations from that time onward. He left no stone unturned to fall in with the deeply seated sentiments of Eastern peoples. One of his first actions after entering Jerusalem was to ensure the return of the "Holy Scrolls," a parchment on which are inscribed the fundamental laws and which had been taken to Jaffa, thirty-five miles away, to prevent their falling into the hands of the Turks. Allenby presided at the gathering where they were formally returned. The grateful people gave him, as a memento of the occasion, a copy of the scrolls inclosed in a silver case.[1]

Allenby was the principal figure at the welcome of the American Red Cross Commission on July 4, when there were assembled representatives of the Allied nations and high dignitaries of the Roman Catholic Church, the Protestant, Moslem, Armenian, and other churches. On this occasion Dr. John H. Finley, State Superintendent of Education in New York, head of the Mission in Palestine, made a speech in which he said that America's contribution to the restoration of Palestine was only an intimation of how the people of America and those of all nations were eager to contribute their genius to the spiritual and physical encouragement of people in the Holy City. How Allenby prest on from Jerusalem step by step to the north, to Damascus and Beirut and thence—as

[1] Adapted from an article by Frank Dilnot in The *Times* (New York).

Foch was rounding out his victories in northern France, Picardy, Flanders, the Champagne, and the Argonne—how he reached Aleppo, and no doubt thought of Othello as having once been there, and how finally he entered Constantinople and there met Franchet d'Esperey who a few weeks before had forced Bulgaria to surrender—all this has been told elsewhere in this work as part of his military campaign against the Turk.

SIR WILLIAM RIDDELL BIRDWOOD, British General

As Commander of the Australian and New Zealand Army Corps from 1914 to 1918, Sir William Birdwood brought with him a wide knowledge of military affairs supported by a large experience in the field.

Entering the army as a lieutenant in the Fourth Battalion of the Royal Scotch Fusileers in 1883, he was transferred to the Twelfth Lancers in 1885, and to the Eleventh Bengal Lancers in 1886. In 1893 he served as adjutant on the Viceroy of India's Bodyguard. He went to Africa in 1899 as brigade major, serving as secretary to Lord Kitchener, Commander-in-Chief in South Africa in 1902. At the close of this campaign, Birdwood returned to India as quartermaster-general in 1912.

In the course of his military career he was several times wounded, and repeatedly mentioned in the dispatches. He served in command of the detached landing of the Australian and New Zealand Army Corps above Gaba Tepe at Gallipoli. Altho a strict disciplinarian as a commander in the field, he was much liked by his men who felt the magnetism of his personality and were always eager to carry out whatever orders were issued by him.[2]

TASKER HOWARD BLISS, Chief of Staff, United States Army

General Bliss was born at Lewisburg, Pa., December 31, 1853. He was graduated from the United States Military Academy in 1875, and in 1884 from the United States Artillery School with honors. His military career began as a second lieutenant in the First Artillery, June 16, 1875. Five years later he was promoted to first lieutenant, and in 1892 became the captain in the commissary of subsistence, rising to the rank of major in 1898, and of lieutenant-colonel as Chief Commissary of Subsistence of the Volunteers, 1898-1899. In 1902 he attained the rank of brigadier-general of the United States Army.

At the outbreak of the Spanish-American War, General Bliss was military attaché at the United States Legation at Madrid,

[2] Compiled from "Who's Who, 1918-1919" (London).

Spain. He served through the Porto Rican campaign in 1898, in which year he was appointed a member of the board of officers to select camp sites for United States troops in Cuba. From December, 1898, to May, 1902, he was Collector of Customs of the port of Havana and Chief of the Cuban Custom Service. He negotiated the treaty of reciprocity between Cuba and the United States, 1902, and 1903 was Commandant of the Army War College. During 1905 and 1906 he was in command of the Department of Luzon, P. I., and from 1906 to 1909 of the Department of Mindanao. From August, 1910, to June, 1911, he commanded the Department of California, and during the Mexican insurrection, March to June, 1911, was in charge of a provisional brigade on the Mexican border. From 1911 to 1913 he was commander of the Department of the East, and from 1913 to 1915, of the Southern Department Cavalry Division.

General Bliss was appointed a member of the General Staff of the United States Army and Assistant Chief of the Staff, 1915, and rose to the rank of Chief of the Staff, September 22, 1917. On October 6, 1917, he was confirmed Commanding General of the United States Army, and served as such throughout the Great War, being appointed a member of the Allied Conference in 1917, and also a member of the Supreme War Council in France, 1917-1918. He served also as Military Representative of the United States at the Peace Conference.[3]

ALEXIS A. BRUSILOFF, RUSSIAN GENERAL

Brusiloff, Russian commander from early in the war until after the final defeat in the summer of 1917, was sixty-four years old when the war began, but looked forty-five. He had long served Russia as a soldier, having taken part, as a captain and then as a major, in the Russo-Turkish conflict of 1877. He was described as one who lived by his nerves, and his sense of duty. Soldiers worshiped him, altho he never courted popularity, and talked to them seldom. When he did talk, it was with a matter-of-fact abruptness, but in his few words lay knowledge of the soldier's soul. He had skill in finding the direct road to a soldier's heart. His physical endurance at sixty-four was still amazing. One of the best cavalrymen in Europe, he could out-distance many younger horsemen. Whenever his automobile got stuck in black soil, he would continue his way on horseback, and when the going was impossible for horses, as in the Pinsk swamps, he would go on foot, jumping from clump of soil to clump of soil in places

[3] Compiled from "Who's Who, 1918-1919" and The *Times* (New York).

where water prevailed, and never showed fatigue. "How old values have been upset!" he once remarked to M. Breshkovsky of the Petrograd *Bourse Gazette*. "Take Skobeleff"—naming one of the most distinguished generals of the war of 1877. "Is it thinkable that an ostentatious, decorative general like that, galloping about at the front in a white uniform and on a white horse, should exist to-day? Possibly he would last a quarter of an hour. Should Germans fire a few volleys in that direction, nothing would have been left of the dashing horseman. In 1877 that splendid bravado had an object and meaning in his conduct—it was to serve as an inspiration to his troops. But now, when everything spectacular has disappeared from the surface, and been buried, Skobeleff would have been seen at best by about two regiments only."

Brusiloff was born in the Russian Caucasus, in a little semi-Oriental city named Kutais, about half-way between Poti, the Black Sea port, and the summit of Kazbek, which is some 3,000 feet higher than Mont Blanc. His father was a soldier and a general, trained, like so many Russians, in wars in the Caucasus. The Brusiloffs for generations had been distinguished in Russian military and political history. The general kept with care a curious packet of ancient documents, each of which conveyed the thanks of a sovereign of Russia to a member of his house. He went to school at Tiflis, in the Caucasus, and thereafter to a Russian military school where he distinguished himself. Back to the Caucasus he went afterward as a lieutenant of dragoons and entered thoroughly into the daring and adventurous life traditional with regiments quartered in the Caucasus, a life that Lermontoff and Tolstoy have depicted so well. Brusiloff had a heart for every adventure; but most of all, loved perilous boar and bear hunts in Caucasian forests. He earned a reputation as one of the best riders in that region, whether after hounds or in regimental steeplechase. In a sense that reputation determined his destiny.

When in the late spring of 1877 Alexander II declared war against Turkey, and sent armies southward to deliver Bulgaria from oppression, the Czar's brother, the Grand Duke Nicholas—father of the Grand Duke Nicholas of this war—was put in command of armies operating in European Turkey, while another brother, the Grand Duke Michael, commanded against the Turks in Asia, fighting southward toward Erzerum by way of Ardahan and Kara. While taking part in that war on a distant front, Brusiloff saw little or no actual fighting, but, after the war ended, when Grand Duke Nicholas the elder undertook to reorganize at Petrograd the Cavalry School for Officers, which had been founded by his uncle, Alexander I, he chose as head of the school Colonel

Vladimir Sukhomlinoff, and Sukhomlinoff chose as his right-hand man, Brusiloff. Thus transferred from the sunny south to the rather forbidding climate of Petrograd, Brusiloff was brought into close touch with the elder Grand Duke Nicholas and with his sons, who were deeply interested in the Cavalry School, as a place both for fine military training and for brilliant social functions.

Brusiloff rose steadily until he obtained command of a section of the Cavalry Guard, the *corps d'élite* of the Russian army. He developed the theory, then novel in Russia, that the training of an officer in time of peace should conform as closely as possible to the conditions of war, and so demanded from officers under him rigorous tests in horsemanship, including long cross-country rides at night and in bad weather. Remonstrances from the mothers of darling sons threatened with pneumonia and broken necks, were sometimes carried to Court and so made their way to the Emperor, who, at a Court function, would take Brusiloff to task, and Brusiloff would answer: "Very good, your Majesty, I will discontinue the rides if you will guarantee that the enemy will attack us only in sunshine."

During the Japanese war, as the single-track Siberian railroad could take east only one army corps a month, the bulk of the Russian European army never became involved, and so Brusiloff did not see service against Japan. He was one of a group of able, trusted commanders who were held in Europe for use in case any of Russia's neighbors to the west should take advantage of her Manchurian difficulties, as they did, three years later, when Austria annexed Bosnia and Herzegovina and Kaiser Wilhelm "stood beside his ally in shining armor." To that incident the present war was in large part directly due, for the act of Austria in thus turning the Berlin Treaty into a "scrap of paper" sank deep into many Russian minds, and among others, into the mind of Brusiloff, who thenceforth looked forward to war as inevitable.

Brusiloff learned how to execute great movements in warfare by knowledge and experience gained while associated with the Grand Duke Nicholas and from visits to grand maneuvers in France. The Grand Duke and Brusiloff both knew French battlefields and the war chiefs of France, and so understood the magnificent spirit and sense of equality that existed in French armies. Joffre returned some of these visits, and was present at a grand Russian maneuver as late as 1913. Brusiloff married early, but was early left a widower, and afterward married the second daughter of Madame Jelihovski, a well-known Russian novelist. The second Madame Brusiloff worked like a Trojan after the recent war began, particularly in hospital and Red Cross work. In 1916, when she visited her husband and brother at the front, she took from Moscow, Kieff, Odessa, and Vinnitza, four carloads of Easter gifts for soldiers. Brusiloff was then the head of a complete army officered by half a dozen generals.

He had done such fine work at Lublin before the war that he was transferred to Warsaw, then an advance post of the Russian army toward the west, where at that time, General Skalon was in command, while Rennenkampf was in command at Vilna, further north, facing East Prussia, Ruzsky being commander of the military district to the south, which faces Galicia, with headquarters at Kief. Of army centers, Warsaw was the most important. There Brusiloff had an opportunity to think in terms of armies, rather than corps, and to handle considerable bodies of troops. He had two desires unsatisfied, one for an independent command, another for a place close to the frontier. Warsaw, from a military point of view, was badly placed and essentially weak, threatened as it was from both East Prussia and Galicia.

Brusiloff, confident that war was coming, obtained a transfer to Vinnitza, southeast of Warsaw, in the province of Podolia, as Commander of the Twelfth Army Corps, his military standing making it certain that, if war broke out, he would be placed in command of an army which might consist of five or six corps. He was at Vinnitza, at the end of July, 1914, when the Czar began to mobilize his army in order to meet the already far advanced Austrian mobilization. A decisive battle was fought on this line in the opening days of September—before the battle of the Marne—and was won by the Russians, being the first great Allied success. Ruzski captured Lemberg, and Brusiloff at the same time captured Halicz, making Russian victory complete. The Austrian army alone never recovered. Only when stiffened by German troops did it ever afterward make any real headway against the Russians. Ruzski fought westward toward Krakow, the capital of Poland, while Brusiloff fought on a line running parallel, some seventy miles further south, being the extreme left wing of the Russian forces which, on the right, touched the Baltic. Przemysl was invested, but not assaulted, because the Russians were already suffering from lack of guns and shells. The Russian army instead swept forward, round the fortress, toward the Carpathians, locking up three Austrian army corps in Przemysl. A strong Austrian force, gathered in eastern Hungary, attempted to relieve the beleaguered garrison, but as it made its way through Lupka Pass, Brusiloff, with his base at Baligrad, met and smashed it, and Przemysl surrendered.

As Brusiloff was afterward fighting his way into the Carpathian passes, Mackensen gathered on the little Dunajec River, east of Krakow, a vast weight of guns and ammunition with which to carry out his famous drive. He did not try to push back the whole Russian line, but simply sawed at it at a single point; and, by threatening to cut it through, compelled the whole line to move backward, which it did, unbroken and undislocated. Brusiloff had to take his part in the general retreat, but never wholly relinquished Galicia. He remained, in fact, on enemy soil through the first twelve months of the war. In the spring of 1916 he began another campaign with a higher command, a far larger and more vigorous force, vastly greater supplies of guns and ammunition, riper experience, indomitable faith, and with the enthusiasm of a united nation behind him. But of Brusiloff's subsequent career details have already been given in an earlier part of this work.[4]

GENERAL COUNT LUIGI CADORNA, ITALIAN COMMANDER-IN-CHIEF

Seldom has a human face been more lined than that of Cadorna, whom the Paris *Gaulois,* as early as 1916, hailed as one of the great soldiers of the Latin world—the man who, when Italy declared war, went at once to the front as commander-in-chief of her forces and long led them to success, but only to fail in 1917 at Caporetto. Cadorna was a Count, but by no means as impecunious as Italian Counts sometimes have been. He was described in Italian dailies as of the offensive, rather than the defensive, school of strategy, with theories of the art of war in marked antithesis to those of Joffre. Cadorna was one of the highest living authorities on tactics, concerning which his ideas were Frederickian rather than Napoleonic. Frederick II strove first of all for homogeneity in his army, which was a unit before it was anything else, artillery, cavalry, and infantry welded together like links in a chain through a series of drills that made the whole force a simple instrument, responsive to the touch of the master. There could be no raw levies in such a body of men—regiments scraped together in a hurry after the fashion of some of the Napoleonic masses. Cadorna went back to the great days of Prussian militarism for his ideals. He could never wait patiently as Joffre did for the time to fight. He was swift and daring, a dealer of tactical blows, a contriver of strokes, to whom war was an art rather than a science.

Cadorna belonged to one of the most distinguished families in

---

[4] Adapted in the main from an article by Charles Johnson in The *Times* (New York). Mr. Johnson's wife is a sister of Brusiloff's wife.

Italy. His father, like an uncle of his, had served in the Piedmontese army during the war against Austria and won renown in those campaigns. General Raffaele Cadorna was in his day a tactician who informed the mind of his son with his Frederickian ideas. The son was the Italian Count in perfection. In him we had instead of the bluff good nature of Joffre, instead of the pious simplicity of the Grand Duke Nicholas, the slightly sophisticated good breeding of an Italian who was at home in the two worlds of Rome, the clerical and the political. He belonged, by right of birth and family tradition, to a circle in which a Pope's brother would have been distinguished. He had very little of the modern Roman in tastes and habits, but belonged rather to the rural aristocracy. He early won affectionate admiration by a genial simplicity beneath fine manners, that came, or seemed to come, from the heart. At sixty-five when the war began, he still danced beautifully.

Strive as it might to belittle Cadorna's prestige as a tactician, the Viennese press admitted that he had won a reputation greater among professional soldiers than among masses of Italians. His work on tactics had been translated into German by order of the Berlin General Staff. The book was unique because of the importance it attached to mobility in an army. He was not a soldier who could sit down in a trench and wait. He attached infinite importance to minute knowledge of topographical details and so came to know the frontier between Austria and Italy so well that he could have made a livelihood as a tourist's guide. He carried his passion for topographical detail to such a point that he thought Napoleon's years of success coincided with occasions when he was in a country familiar to him; the Russian campaign became a disaster because he was in an unknown land. The one thing in modern military Germany which was commendable to Cadorna was the insistence of her general staff on the acquisition of maps of every region in which the Kaiser's forces were ever likely to fight.

The seared visage of Cadorna, the slight stoop in his shoulder, his bleached-out aspect, seemed a result of the physical strain of a long and hard career. He had been almost everything in the shape of an officer that a man could be in the Italian army—a military cadet at Milan and Turin, a lieutenant through grades until at thirty-three he was at the head of a regiment. When little more than twenty-five he began to study German military history, which confirmed him in admiration of Frederick II as one of the few great captains of the world. War became for Italy a grand rush upon the foe. There could be little doubt that what

German papers said with reference to Cadorna was true—that his initiative was so fraught with recklessness, or perhaps one should say with daring, as to involve tremendous risks. On the other hand, Cadorna summed up in his nature a combination of qualities which was Italian instead of German. Cadorna's mind did not impel him to foresee every contingency so precisely that he arranged in advance• just what he would do in any event. He was too artistic, too subtle, not to leave something to the inspiration of the emergency itself. There was much in this reasoning that imprest the Parisian press, which gained from Cadorna a decided impression of genius.

He looked like a man of genius to the *Secolo,* which credited him with an amiable sympathy with anybody about anything. The Italians called that characteristic politeness of the heart, which all agreed that Cadorna had. He was an impressive figure at the royal palace in Rome on great reception days. The gold and the dark blue, red and white of the uniform of his rank brought out his face and form impressively. He wore a mustache finely waxed, and the Queen invariably gave him her hand to kiss, an honor of which she was not prodigal. Cadorna never adapted himself to the gastronomical habits of Roman society, which eats heavily at unusual hours. He rarely dined out, except in the years when he was stationed near Verona. He had a reputation in the service for severity to young officers who danced and dined to excess. He also set his face severely against the motor craze when it broke out among mere lieutenants and poorly paid captains. He made no secret of his belief that the enemy of efficiency in the army was social ambition, which he deemed only a shade better than gambling. His charm of manner and his sweetness of disposition enabled him to put down these and many similar weaknesses among his staff without manifesting the least bruskness. He indoctrinated them with his tactical conceptions and at the same time avoided even the appearance of being obsessed with them.

Cadorna made his home at different times in Naples, Genoa, Verona, and Ancona, manifesting in each the easy affability of the Italian aristocrat. Much was said in Italian character sketches of his social gifts. A brilliant talker, with an intuitive perception of the weak points, as well as the strong ones in people he met, Cadorna showed a fine hand in avoiding feuds between Clericals and Anticlericals, which tended to divide Rome. He was credited with the sort of faith that accompanies a temperament naturally artistic. His recreations reflected this artistic impulse, for he was fond of the opera, especially of Verdi's music, and admirers of d'Annunzio insisted that he was one of them. All agreed that his face was marked with anxieties and that the eyes showed fatigue.

Just as Joffre was practically unknown outside of France before the war began, so Italy's leader came upon the European field unheralded and unknown—especially to American readers. But in Italy he was already famous. He had long been regarded there as the army's hope, the one man who had the ability to revive its glory. An Italian writer characterized him by two words, "vivacity" and "calm," which described alike his career and his temperament. His quick mind had built up a storehouse of military knowledge; it judged keenly both inferiors and superiors, foresaw and planned long in advance, but always beneath a calm surface without the friction that comes of disordered haste. Maintaining his balance in the most trying circumstances, he refused to yield to the bludgeonings of hasty argument or prejudiced persuasion. He endeavored more and more to instil into the rather sluggish blood of the old Italian army, ideas of a new era. Every one in Italy knew in what condition the Italian army would find itself when Cadorna became its chief.

Cadorna's spirit became to the army a moral fulcrum. His person, bony but square of build, solid, full of vigor, that seemed to belie his age, quickly revealed his energy and simplicity. None of the trappings of pomp contributed to his prestige. One who had never seen him and who entered his office for the first time, had had no correct conception of how would appear the old gentleman soldier who, standing erect, would receive him in field uniform on which glistened the insignia of his rank. His thick mustache was white, his sparse, straight hair rose from a forehead lined by thought, his whole face marked with the wrinkles that the cares of life print there, but a verdant youth looked from out clear eyes. He was not, like Joffre, a silent man, but he never wasted words; he economized words as he did ammunition, saved them up to attain an object to which they would move straight as a cannon-shot. Often he was silent for a long time, and seemed distraught, but he was listening; and if, in the conversation, there came up an error to be destroyed, or a truth to be demonstrated, he would let go a telling sentence.

Cadorna was born in Pallanza on September 4, 1850, and was barely fifteen years of age when he entered a military academy, graduating as a sub-lieutenant in 1868. He was a full-fledged lieutenant in 1870, and received his captain's commission in an artillery regiment in 1875. Since 1892, when he got his colonelcy, he had been identified with the Bersaglieri, the "wide-awakes" of the Italian army. When he took command of the Tenth Regiment of the Bersaglieri, he started to improve it after his own mind, and brought it out in the grand maneuvers of 1895 in splendid form, practising in fact on the adversary forces that same type of outflanking and surrounding movement that worked so effectually on the Carso in 1917. The breaking out of war in 1914 found him a general waiting for command of an army in case of war.

When the terrible defeat at Caporetto occurred in October, 1917, he was the only commander in the Allied forces who had retained his position since the war began, without even as much as a hint of a breakdown, either in the confidence of his country, his king, his army, or the Allies. He was a deeply religious man. The particular characteristic of his mind was breadth of vision and a sweeping aside of minor issues, not to speak of petty details. He was above all practical and simple. The fundamental law of his thought was common sense. He had remarkable clearness in seeing things as they were, not as he might like them to be, or as he might object to their being. Cadorna had a boyish freedom of movement and gesture, interestingly contrasting with the whiteness of his hair and mustache. He had a clear, forceful voice, with a breezy sense of vitality, a distinctly attractive personality, and in general was a gentleman warrior. As a young lieutenant in 1870 he stood by his father in helping to secure Rome for Italy. As a mature leader of men, fighting from 1915 to 1917 to give Trieste to Rome, he still stood in the eyes of Italians as a representative of the fight of Latin civilization against barbaric German brutality. During the first three years of the war, he was probably the least known of all the Allied war chiefs, certainly the least photographed and least interviewed. In Italy there had been Counts of Cadorna for hundreds of years, but Cadorna's title became completely submerged in that of General. He was the acknowledged master of Italian armies and his rule was absolute. He had his critics, but he would say, "Whenever the country gets tired of me, I will quit. I refuse to stay a second longer than I am wanted. But while I am Generalissimo what I say goes."

Cadorna never bothered about critics. He lived a hermit's life in the war, never saw anybody except his King, his Chief of Staff and a few special officers. Prominent visitors to the Italian front got only a brief glimpse of him and then with the greatest difficulty. He lived in an old house and there did his work. He was a strict Catholic like the French General Castelnau, and had a private mass said every morning of his life.[5]

[5] Adapted from a compilation by Alexander Harvey in *Current Opinion;* based on articles in the *Gaulois* and *Temps* (Paris), *Stampa* (Turin), *Messaggero* and *Secolo* (Rome), *Corrier della Sera* (Milan), The *Eagle* (Brooklyn), The *Times* and *The Literary Digest* and an article by Luigi Barzini in "Current History of the War" of The *Times* (New York).

EDOUARD, MARQUIS DE CASTELNAU,
FRENCH GENERAL ON THE WESTERN FRONT

The Marquis de Castelnau, the aristocrat among generals in this war, had been a great pillar of the republic. In the last days of August and first of September, 1914, almost simultaneously with the battle of the Marne, the Germans had made a formidable attempt against a French army in Lorraine, when, impatient for a decision, they threw themselves against the Grand Couronné. Entire batteries were sacrificed in the customary German method, but the Grand Couronné stood firm. The French, to the extreme limit of endurance, fought until the Germans beat a retreat and Nancy was saved. Had Nancy fallen, the Marne probably would have been lost. The commander at the Grand Couronné, the soul of the resistance, was the Marquis de Castelnau.

Castelnau was somewhat short in stature, but well proportioned, with a bronzed complexion, and a frank, alert expression. The rough soil of the tablelands of Languedoc and Gascony that had produced Joffre and Foch, produced also Castelnau. His family had long been settled in that country, at the foot of hills. His father, a lawyer of ability, well known and greatly esteemed, for many years was mayor of St. Affrique. There were three sons, the oldest of whom entered the Polytechnic School and became an engineer; the second followed his father's profession; the third chose the profession of arms, Edouard de Castelnau. Born in 1851, in the same year as Joffre and Foch, he was sixty-four years old in the second year of the war, and the father of ten children, of whom two were killed early in the war, and a third in the French offensive in Champagne of September, 1915. Castelnau studied at the Jesuit College of his native town, and at the age of eighteen had passed into the military school of St. Cyr, where cavalry and infantry officers were trained.

When the Franco-German war broke out, young men at St. Cyr obtained commissions as second lieutenants, and thus Castelnau served in the whole of that campaign. Joffre and Foch also had experience in that war, but not as much as Castelnau had. The interval since then—a period of forty-four years—Castelnau had devoted to one single problem—to aid in fitting the French army for another conflict with its old enemy, which he knew to be inevitable. After the retreat from the Marne and the battle of the Aisne, the first effort made by the Germans was a turning movement against the French left wing, where violent engagements took place in the neighborhood of Peronne and Amiens. Castelnau, having led a single army in Lorraine to a brilliant success under conditions of the utmost difficulty, was promoted by Joffre to command groups of French armies. Later, in the French offensive in Champagne, he added a new achievement to his record. The heaviest fighting took place along the Souain-Sommepy road, north of Massiges. Near Souain was a division under command of Marchand, the French general who at Fashoda on the upper Nile had the memorable meeting with Kitchener. To reach the valley of Navarin, Marchand's men had to fight their way through two miles of German trenches, Castelnau's objective being the Bazancourt-Challerange railway, which ran behind German positions and was the main line of supply for their army. On the Butte de Tahure his forces reached within two miles of this railway. Had they actually reached it the Germans, under the Crown Prince and Heeringen, would have been forced back to the Aisne.

Not long afterward when Joffre was Commander-in-Chief of all the armies in France, Castelnau was Chief of his General Staff and so became the Generalissimo's right-hand man. When the Germans attacked Verdun, in February, 1916, Joffre at nine o'clock at night received a dispatch from the local commander recommending that the fortress be given up and that the French retire to the heights across the Meuse. Joffre seemed at first inclined to agree with the suggestion—at least on military grounds—but Castelnau argued against it, and it was agreed that Castelnau should go to Verdun and assume command. His trip to Verdun was a race, a sort of Sheridan's ride, and having looked the situation over, he telephoned to Joffre: "Send Pétain." Pétain went at once to Verdun, quietly and alone, followed by his army, mostly in motor-trucks. "They must not pass," said Castelnau. "They shall not pass," returned Pétain.

With the changes afterward made in the French Ministries, the office of Chief of Staff was abolished and Castelnau was sent to command in the southeast. When the armistice was signed it was known that Foch had been waiting to cut the Metz corridor and split the German armies; Castelnau was to turn loose great forces which he had collected around Nancy for an advance into Lorraine and Alsace. One of Castelnau's sons had already been killed in battle. While attending a council of war Castelnau received news of another son's death. Pausing for a few moments and recovering from his tears he said calmly, "Gentlemen, let us proceed." Observers agreed that no finer personality than Castelnau had come to the front in this war. In him was seen all that had been best in men of the old régime.

SIR ARTHUR WILLIAM CURRIE, CANADIAN MAJOR-GENERAL

Major-General Currie was born December 5, 1875, and commanded the First Canadian Division in the European War, 1914 to 1917. From 1917 to the close of the war, Currie was in command of the Canadian Corps, and entered Mons at the head of his troops, November 11, 1918.[6]

FRANCHET D'ESPEREY, ALLIED COMMANDING GENERAL IN THE BALKANS

D'Esperey, who late in the war succeeded Sarrail as Commander-in-Chief of the Allied armies in the Balkans, commanded there in the final victory over Bulgarian and Teutonic forces in the early autumn of 1918. Fortune had often smiled on him. He had been in the war from the beginning. In the fighting about Charleroi and Mons, he was the only Allied general who won what could have been called a victory. D'Esperey was in command of the Fifth French Army Corps, made up for the greater part of men from Lille and Flanders. On August 21 and 22, he was holding bridges on the Meuse at no great distance above Namur, but it was not until the evening of the 23d that his troops began to fight.

Several Allied corps, in an inferior position both as to numbers and equipment, had been forced back. It was left to d'Esperey to protect their right flank, and he achieved that task. Attacking Saxons who were pressing closely upon him, he threw them into disorder and in so furious an attack drove back to the Meuse a division which had crossed the river, that they could not withstand the assault. During the night of the 23d and all day on the 24th the Germans allowed the French to pass, not moving to interfere. D'Esperey had compelled Hausen, the German commander, and one of the most famous of the German generals, to pay a heavy price for his failure; Hausen lost his command. Had he made better plans the crossing of the river could at once have taken place. The delay became a contributory cause of the failure of the German army in the beginning of September; the German forces marching toward Paris had now to be grouped differently.

The operation brought promotion to d'Esperey. On the Marne he was the first to win laurels. He was holding the line north of Provins (the most southern point reached in France). He had the British on his left and Foch on his right. On the morning of September 6, when Joffre gave his famous order to attack, d'Esperey threw himself on the left wing of Kluck's army and the right of Bülow's, both of which were facing him, and forced

6 Compiled from "Who's Who, 1918-1919" (London).

a wedge between the two, taking Esternay at the point of the
bayonet, throwing into disorder everything in his advance, and on
the 8th entered Montmirail over German dead.

On the morning of the 9th, his aviation service signalled that
Kluck and Bülow were retreating. From that time all he had to
do was to push forward. He had been the first to make a real
breach in the German wall. D'Esperey now received command of
army groups, which meant that he occupied the same rank as
Foch, Castelnau, and Fayolle. His name thenceforth for three years
was associated with operations on the Somme, in the Champagne, and
on the Aisne, until June, 1918, when he received command of the
Allied armies in the Balkans. Eight weeks afterward he landed
in Saloniki, from which, as his base, he advanced to become the
victor of the Vardar, and the first Allied general to gain a notable
success in the Balkans, where so much blood had been shed and
where it almost seemed as if some evil genius had refused to
allow the Allies even one success.

So much good fortune was not the result of chance. D'Esperey
won his victories because he deserved them. He had learned the
secret of making the gods of war smile on him. He was a tremendous worker, and knew how to make others work. The Vardar
campaign was fought on the hardest, most difficult sector in the
war. It was a front where there were practically no roads, no
depots of equipment, and no heavy artillery. The position was
said by the Bulgarians to be impregnable—so much so that they
maintained only a handful of troops there. In eight weeks
d'Esperey built roads, installed depots, caused heavy artillery to
be placed in position, and organized a system of communications.
On September 14 he threw Senegalese and Colonial battalions
against the Bulgars, just as he had thrown regiments against the
Germans at Montmirail, and again he made a breach. Through
that breach he led Allied forces that for three years had been
marking time on that front.

D'Esperey not only knew how to deal with terrain and cannon,
he knew how to deal with men. He could make soldiers do anything, because he knew how to talk to them. He had the ready
word that wins the heart of a trooper, and it is with the heart,
as much as with muscle, that battles are won. For a long time
before the war d'Esperey was a commanding officer in Algeria,
that corner of Africa which gave glorious names to the French
army in this war—Gouraud, Mangin, Degoutte—and which had
been the cradle of the Foreign Legion.[7]

[7] Stephane Lauzanne, editor of *Le Matin* (Paris), in an article contributed
to The *Times* (New York).

GENERAL ARMANDO DIAZ, COMMANDER-IN-CHIEF OF THE ITALIAN ARMY

General Diaz was appointed Commander-in-Chief of the Italian armies, November 8, 1917, when General Cadorna was made Italian Military Representative at the Supreme War Council of the Allies. He was a Neapolitan by birth, and was fifty-six years old at the time of his appointment. He served with distinction as a colonel in the Libyan War.

Altho comparatively unknown outside of military circles when appointed, General Diaz had had a distinguished career. Educated at the Military College at Naples and at the Military Academy at Turin, he gained in reputation during the Abyssinian campaign, and added to it in the Libyan War, for the plan of campaign of which he was largely responsible.

After brilliant successes achieved on the Isonzo under his leadership as division commander (Twenty-third Army Corps operating on the Carso), Diaz received that promotion which ultimately led to his being made Commander-in-Chief. He was especially talented as an organizer and was a man of volcanic energy. His military experience embraced practically all branches of the service. He was secretary to three chiefs of the staff in succession, and for a time was in charge of a staff appointment where he achieved the reputation of being stern but impartial in his dealings. His character as a soldier was that of an inflexible disciplinarian who applied to himself the same rules as he enforced on others. In the daily routine of military life, evenly poised, and in the face of danger characteristically calm, General Diaz, tho southern born, had proved that self-control and calmness were not characteristics restricted to northern Italy as is commonly believed. Physically General Diaz was medium build, of dark complexion, with hair turning gray. He had a slight caste in the eye which among his fellow countrymen was held as a sign of good luck.[8]

GENERAL ERIC VON FALKENHAYN, CHIEF OF STAFF OF THE GERMAN ARMIES

In the early part of the war, when the Kaiser's plan for entering Paris in September, 1914, and reaching London from Paris by the end of October, had been frustrated, and the German armies forced to retreat, the Kaiser accepted the resignation of Moltke, Chief of the General Staff, who thus appeared as the scape-

[8] Compiled from The *Times* (New York).

goat in the German miscalculations, and appointed in his stead General Eric von Falkenhayn, one of the cleverest of Berlin courtier-soldiers. Cold, calculating, suave, and an intriguer, the scion of one of the oldest German houses, Falkenhayn had begun his career by winning the good will of the Kaiser's sons through a brother Eugene, who had been their tutor, mentor, and military governor in their boyhood. This, together with an intimate association afterward with Field-marshal Count von Waldersee, on whose staff he served in the allied march upon Pekin in 1900, and from knowing the American-born Countess von Waldersee, a favorite aunt of the Kaiserin, brought Falkenhayn into contact with the Kaiserin, and it was not long before he won favor. He had a gift for repartee, was mentally alert and resourceful. Various accomplishments and a readiness of speech finally commended him to the Emperor as particularly well qualified to take charge of the Department of War, and especially to champion the cause of the army in the Reichstag, after the public uproar created by the sabering at Zabern of a lame and unarmed cobbler by a young infantry officer.

As Chief of Staff, Falkenhayn reigned supreme at the Kaiser's headquarters, and acquired an extraordinary ascendency over his sovereign. On the profest ground of military exigencies he was disposed to keep at a distance from Imperial Headquarters not only the Chancellor, cabinet ministers, and various statesmen and foreign diplomats, but even the rulers of some of the sovereign States comprised in the German Empire. Owing much as he did to the Crown Prince, Falkenhayn, in 1916, yielding to solicitations such as had failed Hindenburg in the East, when he wanted reinforcements to take Riga, sent all his available troops to the heir apparent, and his mentor Count von Haeseler, in order that they might attempt the capture of Verdun, a scheme to which, however, he had become himself committed, believing it would be possible thus to open up a road to Paris. The Kaiser was afterward disposed to saddle Falkenhayn with blame, both for the successful renewal of the Russian offensive and for the Crown Prince's failure before Verdun, so that Falkenhayn might sooner have shared the fate of Moltke, had he not possest influence at Court. Verdun and Riga, however, had opened the Kaiser's eyes to the fact that Germany was confronted with ultimate defeat, owing to the greater resources of her foes in man-power, munitions, and money. The best Germany could now hope for was a draw. Owing to the extraordinary growth about this time of Hindenburg in popular favor, the Kaiser removed Falkenhayn, and put Hindenburg in his place as Chief of the General Staff.

Falkenhayn did not wholly disappear from public view, however, serving as he did afterward in Roumania and Asiatic Turkey.

Falkenhayn was in sharp contrast to Moltke. As age went among commanding German officers, he was young, while Moltke was over sixty-six. Temperament Moltke had not, but Falkenhayn did have it, being alive and energetic, a bundle of nerves, sometimes agreeable and sometimes irascible, intuitional and venturesome, while Moltke was placid and methodical, democratic, liberal-minded and cautious. The two were about as far apart as two Germans could be. Moltke, until the Marne battle, had never got into a real embarrassment in his life, while Falkenhayn, in peace times, had repeatedly been in situations from which only a genius, or a favorite of fortune, could have been extricated. Physically he bore a resemblance to the Japanese Chief of Staff, Kodana. He had the same alert eye, and winning smile, the same habit of asking interminable questions, and the robustness of youthful middle age. He was of middle height, and extremely slender, which was quite unusual for a German officer past fifty. He had been little with troops, but enough to conform to the regulations which required that no one designed for staff duty could entirely escape service in the field. He was a graduate of the War Academy, and before succeeding Moltke had been twice a Chief of Staff, altho never before a chief of the entire army. During 1909-10 he was Chief of Staff to the Sixteenth Army Corps, with headquarters at Metz, and previous to his appointment as Minister of War, was Chief of Staff to the Fourth Army Corps, with headquarters at Magdeburg.

Falkenhayn was an adequate representative of the German military caste. He embodied its ideals and traditions. The renascence of the German army after the failure of 1914 was commonly ascribed to Falkenhayn. He was a man whose ambitions were limited only by his power to achieve them. It was he who planned, and Mackensen who acted, in the great drive against the Russians in the summer of 1915. He was the strategist and Mackensen the tactician. For a Chief of Staff, he was dangerously temperamental, rushing as he did from extremes of pessimism to heights of optimism. In moments of anger he would raise his voice—a good powerful voice. When pleased, his whole countenance would seem to participate in the expression. While often ungracious he had in him much real good nature. When living at Metz he often seemed stiff and autocratic in public, but those who called at his modest home found him willing to grant favors and quite eager to make friends.[9]

[9] Compiled from an article in *Current Opinion,* by Alexander Harvey, and one in The *Times* (New York), by F. Cunliffe Owen.

FERDINAND FOCH, Marshal of France and Allied
Generalissimo

Some one given to aphorisms said that Joffre was made Chief
of Staff "because he seldom or never rode horseback," a remark
not so senseless as it might sound when one considered the
temperament of the French, and the fact that some man, given
to the spectacular, with elements of a conqueror in his nature,
had often exerted a tremendous influence over them, provided
that, combined with ability, he had a commanding personality,
such as Joffre did not have. Joffre did not ride on horseback—

THE ÉCOLE DE GUERRE IN PARIS
Here Marshal Foch was long the director of the school. Under him were
trained many French officers prominent or active in the war

or at least seldom did—and was not an impressive figure even on
the ground, so short and stout was his build; but there was another
general in France of such superb ability that Joffre himself had
termed him "the greatest strategist in Europe"—a man who had
real personal magnetism, and was a masterful rider of horses, in
fact "a man on horseback" of the type whom the French have
often honored—Ferdinand Foch. Foch was a soldier of equal
experience, of about the same age, and from the same part of
France as Joffre, and with Joffre had won the British Grand
Cross of the Order of the Bath. Before the war Foch's services

to France had been notable in the efforts he had made to develop the École de Guerre, of which he was long director, and especially in the organization of the great French "Krupps," that is, the Creusot arms and ammunition factory. Altho a strict disciplinarian, Foch was beloved of his men, whom he treated as human beings. Severe on shirkers, he was liberal in rewarding honest effort and real merit wherever he found them.

Like Napoleon, Foch was an artillery officer and born strategist, and like him applied to military science speed, decision, and unity of control. There was revived early in the war the story of Boulanger, who some thirty years before had held the same place that Foch held, as Director of the École de Guerre, and Boulanger came near making himself dictator of France. Only moderately elderly men can now remember him with his black charger, but in 1887 it looked very much as if France might turn once more to a "man on horseback," to lead her out of a quagmire of party politics and opportunism into which she had fallen. If Boulanger had been really the great man the French imagined he was, instead of a commonplace poseur who fled the country only to kill himself on the grave of an affinity, parliamentary government might have fallen before his sword and that black horse.

At the end of August, 1914, when the great Allied retreat was in progress in Belgium and Northern France, the Tenth French Division retreating in the direction of Reims, Foch one day after serving in Lorraine under Castelnau, was walking in front of the Hôtel de Ville in the market-place of Attigny, having just assumed command of a new army expressly created for him. Only a few days later the retreat ended and the battle of the Marne began. Near the end of the battle the Prussian Guard in a colossal effort smashed through Foch's right, and, wild with joy, began to celebrate. When Foch heard of the disaster he telegraphed to general headquarters a famous message: "My center gives way; my right recedes; the situation is excellent. I shall attack." Foch then gave his order to attack, with everything he cared about in this world at stake—Paris, France, his own reputation. It was a desperate maneuver, an historic moment, when all would be saved or lost. Having given the order to attack, Foch went alone for a walk on the outskirts of the little village where he had established his headquarters, awaiting the issue of that famous stroke at Le Fère Champenoise which was to prove decisive in the great conflict.

Foch had demanded a final and sudden effort of heroism from sorely tried troops. He had improvised a skilful maneuver. The Germans had driven themselves into the French as a wedge, until their front had the form of an elbow. Foch, having the genius to turn to advantage a position which appeared wholly favorable to the Germans, slipt one of his divisions abruptly from left to right in such way as to throw it suddenly on the German flank, a movement which took the Germans by surprize and made the battle a French victory. On a smaller scale, it was the same kind of maneuver that Joffre had used in throwing Maunoury's army against the flank of Kluck on the Ourcq, and in each case the result was a French success. The two maneuvers were deciding causes of the German retreat to the Aisne.

After the Aisne battle in the early days of October, Foch, who had been directing an army in the center of the Allied line, was transferred to the French left wing and given a far more important command, all French armies in the north being placed under his orders. Besides that he was accorded the delicate task of achieving complete unity of effort between French, British, and Belgian armies. Foch thus became virtually commander-in-chief of the troops which resisted the German onslaught in Flanders.

Foch was born in October, 1851, at Tarbes, in the south of France, the son of a civil servant, and an exact contemporary of Castelnau and Joffre—both of whom were born in the south of France. Tarbes lies not far from Pau and Lourdes in the foothills of the Pyrennes, and has long been famous for a breed of horses suitable for cavalry. In the mid-sixties Foch's father moved from Tarbes to Rodez, almost two hundred miles northeast of the old home. It was quite an uprooting. Tarbes was the ancestral country. The removal was due to the father's appointment as a paymaster at Rodez. Here the family found themselves in a new and quite different atmosphere. Soon afterward they went to Saint-Etienne, near Lyons, the father having been appointed a tax collector there. In 1869 Foch was sent to Metz, to attend the Jesuit College of Saint Clement, to which students came from many parts of Europe. He had been there only a year, winning a grand prize, when the Franco-Prussian war began and he enlisted for the duration of the war, but of this, his first war experience, there is little to relate. Foch was just one of a multitude of young men who rushed to the colors when France called for troops, and did what they could in a time of great confusion and disaster. Just at the time when his fall term should have begun at Saint Clement's, Metz was under siege by the Germans, its garrison and inhabitants suffering horribly from hunger and disease; Paris was surrounded; German headquarters had been established at Versailles; the imperial standard,

dear to Foch because of the great Napoleon, was lowered and a
white flag had been hoisted at Sedan, the Emperor with his army
in captivity. In what Foch suffered because of what he could
not do in helping to save France were laid the foundations of
what he afterward accomplished.

In the autumn of 1871 Foch took up military studies at the
École Polytechnique in the Latin Quarter of Paris. Paris was
then scarred and seared as the result of the German bombardment
and the fury of the Communards, which together destroyed nearly
two hundred and fifty public and other buildings. The government organized at Bordeaux had avoided the capital and gone to
Versailles, recently evacuated by the Germans. Among the two
hundred and odd students at the Polytechnic besides Foch was
Joffre, his junior by three months, who had entered the school in
1869, his studies interrupted by war, and now had come back to
resume them. After Joffre was graduated, in 1872, he went to
the School of Applied Artillery at Fontainebleau and Foch,
graduated about six months later, followed him to Fontainebleau
to get the same special training. Both were hard students, tre-
mendously in earnest, both heavy-hearted over the ruin of France,
and both hoping the day might come when they could serve her
and help restore what she had lost. But no one, indulging in the
wildest fantastic extravagances of youth, would ever have ventured to forecast a tithe of what these two afterward did for
France. When Foch reached the rank of lieutenant-colonel he
was appointed professor in strategy and general tactics at the
École de Guerre, and ten years later, after holding commands in
various armies, was made director of the school.

In daily life Foch was a man of few words, who spoke with
mathematical conciseness, his conversations vigorous and clear.
Calm and self-possest, he was conspicuous for qualities which the
English prize. He had close knowledge of the British Army, and
keen sense of the British temperament and character, which explained the influence he came to exert over most Englishmen who
came in contact with him, as well as the cohesion which existed
between French and British almost from the beginning of the
war. To Foch, as to Castelnau, the war early brought heavy
private sorrows, a son and son-in-law both being killed. Saying
little about his own grief, he gave an example to all Frenchmen
by redoubling his efforts for success in the war. Before his advancement, he had enjoyed among military experts a solid reputation as a teacher of the art of war. Even the *Militar-Wochen-
blatt*, organ of the German General Staff, ranked him high among
strategists. To Frenchmen in general, however, he was so much

a stranger when he made his fine stroke in the Marne battle, and when he took supreme command in the north, that Paris newspapers had to correct a serious misapprehension that prevailed as to his origin. Foch did have a German name, but he was not Teutonic, not even an Alsatian; his ancestors for generations had lived in the Basque country, the name a corruption of Foix. Foch's age in 1914 was given in an official bulletin as sixty-three, but his litheness, leanness and horsemanship suggested a man of forty.

Foch had sometimes been regarded lightly. Wilson also had been thought of as a mere "professor." Foch read over and over again the campaigns of Cæsar and Napoleon, and wrote books on war. No one dreamed that he would ever lead an armed world to victory any more than Germans dreamed that Hindenburg, "the old man of the lakes," would be their leader in a great war. As with Hindenburg, so with Foch; his active years in service were thought in 1914 to be over, since he as well as Hindenburg was not only old enough to have seen service in the war of 1870, but was troubled with rheumatism. Foch in the gun-factory at Creusot had often been seen in a workman's blouse. While there he made a favorable report on the "75" gun that did so much to hold the Germans back on the Marne and the Aisne, at Soissons and Verdun. He had been all his life out of touch with most things except army life. He was in temperament typically a Latin of the South. He had more qualities essentially Gallic than Joffre had, was given to daring strategical conceptions—such as are known in France as Napoleonic—believing that French genius lent itself to them, as Napoleon had also thought. Not that Foch was flamboyant, for he lived and acted simply. When a student at the Polytechnic School he ate black bread. His parents were thrifty in the French sense, and had brought him up simply. Abstemious habits, acquired in youth, kept him always thin and robbed him of a kind of social ease and self-confidence that many of his subordinates possest, among them d'Urbal and Maud'huy, who were his pupils at the War College. All Foch's students acquired from him a dramatic conception of war—which was to surprize an enemy by strategy and secrecy, to operate rapidly and with suddenness. He was credited with knowing the human element in the French army better than any man living, and weeded out shirkers remorselessly.

Foch had lived much alone, as his face and manner indicated. He had had no social career and little social experience except such as came from formal calls on garrison hostesses. He gave dinners, as he had to, about twice a year to his staff, but jesting was rare at these gatherings. "The French officer," Foch might remark when the soup came on, "should resolve to perish with glory." "Find out the weak point," he would perhaps say, when dessert was reached, "and deliver your blow there." Similar remarks dominated such conversation as Foch ever started at a banquet in some provincial town. "Suppose, General," an artillery-officer might venture to say, much to the horror of the staff, "suppose the enemy has no weak point?" "If the enemy has no weak point," Foch would answer, "make one," a retort that he would deliver in crushing class-room manner, accompanied with a flash of the eye and a characteristic cock of the chin. There was no staff officer in the French army under forty who was comfortable when he met Foch's piercing eye and uplifted chin, or who would risk becoming the victim of a Foch retort. He had been so long at the War College that almost every officer in the French army trained for twenty years had acquired the Foch stamp. While there he produced two notable works, "Principes de la Guerre" and "De la Conduite de la Guerre." "La Conduite de la Guerre" was a minute historical examination of the battles of 1870. "Nothing can replace the experience of war," wrote he, "except the history of war." "Les Principes de la Guerre" was less a speculation than a visualization of what modern war was destined to be.

Simplicity and directness marked his teachings, and indicated a perfection to which few could aspire. Anybody could see that the whole secret of strategy was to place superior forces before an enemy's weak point, but to see as Foch did on September 9 a gap between the Prussian Guard and the Saxon army on the Marne and be ready to bring up artillery to crush the Guard in the Saint-Gond marshes, that was an act of genius. He was represented as perturbed by the blaze of European fame into which he emerged after that battle. When Joffre said Foch was "the greatest strategist in Europe," he added that he was "the humblest." Foch had knowledge, energy, and experience, and could set souls afire as well as trenches. No sooner did he appear at the front than every commander received a visit from him. He cultivated no splendid isolation. He could call any colonel by name. Every corps commander without exception had attended his lectures. He took to the Napoleonic habit of first-hand contact with men in the ranks—not that of jovial comradeship, but a quiet, comprehending contact, in which even boots were inspected and food tested.

Clémenceau in a speech had once referred to a certain day as an "unforgettable day." It was a day in the war when Foch was virtually on the retired list. Foch was actually for a time without a command, but it appeared that he was engaged on "important duties," but during M. Painlevé's tenure of the War Office on May 15, 1917, Foch returned to service as Chief of the General Staff. The public had heard little of Foch in the year which preceded his appointment. The fact was he had met with a motor-car accident in June, 1916, or a short time before the opening of the battle of the Somme, for which he had been preparing from his headquarters near Amiens. He was, however, kept on the active list, altho about to reach the age limit of sixty-

UNDERWOOD & UNDERWOOD, N. Y.

MARSHAL FOCH AND GENERAL MANGIN (AT THE LEFT)
Inspecting fortifications on the Rhine during the Allied occupation

five, but by special decree, owing to his services in Lorraine in August, 1914, in the Battle of the Marne in September, and in command of the armies of the north from Compiègne to the sea after October 4, 1914. Foch in 1916 was dealing with various problems relating to inter-Allied action, but carried out the work in comparative obscurity, first at Senlis, then in eastern France where he had "important duties," which were the organization of defenses in the Jura in anticipation of a turning movement by the Germans through Switzerland and the framing of plans for Italy in case of an emergency arising from an Austrian offensive.

The formula of an Allied commander-in-chief had been mooted for a long time when Lloyd George, speaking in Paris in November, 1917, on his return from Italy, where Foch was helping to hold the Austro-Germans on the Piave, made public confession of his conversion to the idea, but national and personal susceptibilities were awakened by the suggestion in London and this compelled Lloyd George to defer action. President Wilson, at the Allied conference which followed shortly thereafter, at which he was represented by Colonel House, threw the weight of American prestige into the scale in favor of unity of command. Then came the supreme argument in its favor out of the mouths of German cannon thundering past Bapaume and Noyon toward Arras and Amiens. To that argument there was no answer, and especially after Pershing had placed all the American resources in France under French direction in his "all we have" message that will never be forgotten in France. Foch was soon proclaimed Allied Commander-in-Chief by agreement between Great Britain, France, and the United States. Great democracies, free partners in an enterprise of self-preservation and liberation, thus made one man their collective agent, to use supreme authority to the best of his ability, all their war resources being at his disposal against the German onslaught. By a happy coincidence, Foch was the man whose indomitable spirit and infinite resourcefulness years before had appealed so forcibly to Clemenceau during a previous premiership that he had appointed him head of the War College, a post for which Foch was not a candidate. Much of the brilliant work done by the French Army in this war was directly traceable to the spirit which Foch had instilled into it at the War College, and later on the field at the Marne, Ypres, and elsewhere.

Two great military figures, Joffre and Foch, reached almost simultaneously the topmost height of fame; Joffre the massive, the reflective, in whose speech one detected more readily than in that of Foch the accent of the mountaineer from the Spanish border, Foch being an embodiment of lightning thought in action. Master as he was of the theory in war, Foch was never fettered by it. His keen perception readily discerned the exception to the rule under right conditions. He did not play safe by avoiding risks, but determined which was the lesser risk and boldly took it. When asked to take command of the French offensive at the Somme in 1916—a command he did not take, owing to the accident already referred to—he inquired as to the number of guns that would be at his disposal, and when told exprest himself somewhat thus: "We will be able to make an advance upon a limited front and thus shall bend the German line, but can not expect to break it." His report in writing was in the hands of the Government before the attack began, and was confirmed to the letter by subsequent events. Foch knew what could be done and what could not be done. Just before the battle of Mons-Charleroi, when Sir John French felt doubtful of the advisability of accepting battle, the relations between the French and British were largely undefined, and it became necessary that French should be induced to fit the British into Joffre's plan, making his little army a virtual part of France's army. Foch went to see him. Never was tact in manner more perfectly combined with firmness in purpose. He won French over completely, and then hastened back to take his own command at the French center, where a few days later he was to fight and win, at La Fère Champenoise, the decisive phase of the Marne.

Foch's words were so few that he often made his meaning unmistakable without resort to speech by using a mere gesture, or by the way in which he bit the cigar he was forever smoking. At Foch's headquarters no fuss and feathers were seen. No orderlies galloped up on smoking steeds. No mud-splashed dispatch-riders arrived on snorting motorcycles. A single sentry stood at the gate. A graveled drive led to a plain oaken door in an unornamented red brick wall. At one of his headquarters there was an oak-paneled reception-hall about twenty feet square, in the center a billiard-table covered with brown linen, at one side an unpainted yellow-pine table, on which lay Kipling's "Jungle Book" in French. Across the hall were two doors, on one of which was pinned a piece of cardboard with the words *"Le Bureau du Général."* During a battle Foch would be found in a big room before a large scale map, pencil in hand and a telephone receiver at his ear, his staff in a semicircle behind him. There was perfect silence, the only movement his pencil on the map as he followed the battle and pondered details of the district where the fighting was in progress. One thought of Thomas at Chickamauga, of Grant in the Wilderness. There was something in Foch that was stedfast and something more that was relentless.

Foch was not tall, only five feet six inches in height. What you saw first were his eyes, his large, well-shaped head, his rather thin iron-gray hair, his broad, high forehead. Gray eyes, set wide apart, bored through you and smiled on you all at the same time. His nose was large, his mouth wide and straight, his chin massive. At his headquarters in November, 1918, there was a ceremony. General Pershing had come to present to him a decoration for Distinguished Service as conferred by the United States Government, a medal afterward presented also to Haig, Joffre, and

Pétain. A small company, composed of Staff Officers, had assembled on the garden side of the château. As the two leaders came round the corner, the contrast between them was interesting. Both had marked personal distinction, but were entirely different. Foch swung along with a sort of amble, what military men call "cavalryman's walk," with little to mark him as a military man. Save for his uniform he might have been taken for a lawyer or a doctor. As the two soldiers walked to a center between men of the staff and the guard of honor, a bugler sounded the salute known as the "Marshal's Flourish." Then Pershing, in French, spoke with soldierly force and dignity, his French, by diligent study and practise in France, having been built up on a foundation of West Point teaching and showing hardly a trace of accent. The Marshal in his response spoke longer than he had been known to speak before, his remarks extemporaneous, full of fire, driving points home with that emphasis on words and phrases which the French know so well how to bestow. After Pershing had pinned the medal on Foch's breast, they stood with their hands clasped as a trumpet sounded once more. In accepting the decoration Foch said:

"I will wear this medal with pleasure and pride. In days of triumph, as well as in the dark and critical hours, I shall never forget the tragical day last March when General Pershing put at my disposal without restriction all the resources of the American Army. The success won in the hard fighting by the American Army is the consequence of the excellent conception, command and organization of the American General Staff, and the irreducible will to win of the American troops. The name 'Meuse' may be inscribed proudly upon the American flag. I want to say to you that I shall never forget that tragic day when, stirred by a generous impulse, you came and placed at my disposition the entire resources of your army. To-day we have gained the greatest battle in history and saved the most sacred cause—the liberty of the world. An important part is due to the action undertaken and well carried through by the American Army upon the two banks of the Meuse. For the last two months the American Army has fought in a most difficult region a fierce and ceaseless battle. The complete success of this struggle is due to the fine qualities displayed by all. I do not forget the breadth and clearness of conception on the part of the generals, the method and ability on the part of the staffs, and the ceaseless energy and indomitable courage of the men; nor do I forget that, at the moment when this vital battle was being fought by your principal forces, American divisions were reinforcing the armies of their Allies on other fighting fronts where their conduct evoked the ardent admiration of us all. General, I thank you with all my heart for the aid you have brought us. For all time the words '*la Meuse*' may be borne with merited pride upon the standards of the American Army. I will keep in my heart the recollection of those great hours, often very difficult, but now crowned with glory, during which we fought together for liberty, justice and civilization.'' [10]

SIR JOHN (NOW VISCOUNT) FRENCH, BRITISH FIELD-MARSHAL, COMMANDER OF BRITISH ARMIES IN FRANCE AND BELGIUM

There were two outstanding British figures in active service at the beginning of the war, Lord Kitchener and Sir John French, their reputations high, but very dissimilar in character. That of Kitchener was as an organizer of war, that of French as a brilliant commander in the field. Kitchener's successes had come from the slow and patient labor of the engineer, such as a new railway driven through an Egyptian desert, or a system of block-houses constructed on the veldt; French's from fine daring exploits such as those by which he relieved Kimberley and helped to cut off Cronje's retreat at Koodoosrand Drift, east of Paardeberg, or the more definitely strategic skill with which for three months he held a much superior force in check at Colesberg.

From the point of view of experience in actual war it might have been assumed that the British started with an advantage in generalship. Only two countries had had large and recent acquaintance with war—Great Britain and Russia, but Russia's experience had served only to disclose the incapacity of her generals. No Russian reputations had survived the Russo-Japanese War. The only general engaged in that war who was given a considerable command in August, 1914, was Rennenkampf, but he disappeared after the first year of the war. The case was otherwise with the British, many of whose officers had seen fighting in various fields, and had achieved victory in most of them. But it might also have been doubted whether their experience of war had not been a loss rather than a gain, since it had tended to make them shape their methods in a great European conflict according to the teaching of their experience in colonial war, to assume that a continental war was different only in scale from the colonial wars in which they had learned their lessons; but it was not a difference in scale only, or even chiefly; it was a difference in character. Here on a colossal scale was a war that had no points of similarity with the rounding up of dervishes in a North African desert, or of Boer farmers on a South African veldt.

[10] Principal Sources: Maurice Leon in *The American Review of Reviews,* Clara E. Laughlin's "Foch the Man"; *The Literary Digest,* The *World,* The *Tribune,* New York; The *World* (London), The *Tribuna* (Rome), The *Saturday Review* (London); The *Temps, Figaro* and *Journal des Débats,* Paris; Associated Press dispatch.

Not without significance was the fact that, while the war in France for three months remained in a fluid state, the British achieved some success in it; that is to say, while the operations in 1914 bore some resemblance to others with which the British Army was familiar, that army proved its superior skill. Great Britain's original army, altho small, consisted of the most seasoned soldiers in Europe, and the demands made on generalship were demands with which that generalship was familiar. History may find in the part which the small British Army played in the retreat to the Marne one of the momentous single facts of the war. The Kaiser there flung the spear-head of his army at the British, and the attack virtually failed, despite its mass and impetus, not only because of the hard stuff of which the British Army was composed, but because in that phase of the war Sir John French, Sir Douglas Haig, and Sir Horace Smith-Dorrien showed themselves masters of certain kinds of craft in war. Apprenticeship at Colesberg in South Africa where French and Haig had served together, the one as commander, the other as chief of staff, had prepared them for such an emergency. It would be no extravagant claim to say that this played a real part in saving France in a moment of supreme crisis.

Hardly less momentous was the act of French which led him in the nick of time to transfer his army from the Aisne to Flanders. Here was an act of consummate daring, one which compelled him to spread out his line so thin that, as one might say, one could see rents in it. The risk was as great as any ever taken up by a general in the field; but it saved Calais, and much more than Calais. Few know how narrow that margin of safety was, how near at the end of ten days' struggle before Ypres the power of resistance had approached the exhaustion point; how in that moment it was the courage of French that inspired men and officers alike to "hold on" until aid came from Foch and the surging tide of the German attack was forced to fall back shattered and prone.

French, who had led the British Army into France in August, 1914, commanded it from Mons to the Marne, and from the Marne to the Aisne and the Yser. He retired after the battle of Loos in December, 1915. He was sixty-two years of age when the war began. With two exceptions, Roberts and Kitchener, he was probably the most striking military figure in England. An eventful career had led him to India, Africa, and Canada, and with brilliant results. In the Boer War he was the one British general who was uniformly successful. His soldiers were popularly supposed to have had no sleep. During the siege of Kimberley he was shut up in Ladysmith, with Boer lines ever circling closer when no retreat was possible for English troops even if they had sought it. If Kimberley, with its treasure of diamonds, was to be saved from the Boers, its beleaguered troops had to be relieved, and French apparently was the only man who could accomplish that feat. The Boers were then permitting trains to run out of Ladysmith in order to carry women and children to safe places. In one of these, by squeezing himself under the seat of a second-class carriage, French managed to make his escape. Once outside Boer lines, he made his way to the Cape when he was put in charge of about eight thousand cavalrymen. With horses dropping out about every mile, and stopping only long enough to annihilate any Boer force that was sent to impede their progress, these cavalrymen swept through the Free State, riding day and night until they reached Kimberley, which was just in time to save the place. Two days more would have seen its surrender.

French's family intended him for the Church but when he was fourteen he chose the Navy instead, and joined the *Britannia,* but he left the Navy for the Army in 1874. He commanded the Nineteenth Hussars from 1889 to 1893, rising steadily in rank until, in 1907, he was made Inspector-General of the Forces, and in 1913 Field-marshal. His once fair hair had now become gray, but his Irish blue eyes had not lost their sparkle. Devotion to long tramps kept down the extra pounds which his short, stocky figure had showed a tendency to put on. It had been said that South Africa, where French served so conspicuously, was the grave of military reputations, a saying older than the second Boer war, but it was that war which gave the saying the significance that attached to it afterward. Buller's failure, altho most conspicuous, was only typical of what had happened in earlier stages of the war. In later ones Roberts and Kitchener, tho more successful, can not be said to have added to their reputations in that field. There was, however, one exception to a depressing rule—one reputation which had found in South Africa not a grave but a birthplace. That was French, who went into the Boer war unknown, and emerged from it with the most secure reputation as a fighting general in the British Army. This was no reflection on Kitchener, whose success was that of an organizer of war rather than of a general in the field.

Until the Boer War brought the British Empire to a crisis, French had languished for lack of promotion. He was judged on the whole an unsafe man because of an apparently reckless gift for originality, and unsound because of the departures he had made from traditional military methods. The War Office disliked certain theories he had regarding the use of cavalry—for example, his suggestion to his men that they learn to fight on foot. He was passed over at a critical moment of his career by the Duke of Cambridge who could understand nothing about war unless Napoleon had endorsed it. Even his successes discredited him with the pedants of militarism, because those successes had been gained by means that were new and strange, and he had taken gamblers' chances. French's spirit, however, was not that of the gambler, but that of adventure itself. For this reason his boldness was never a bet on a proposition, but an intuitive perception of the chances that were in his favor. That was the impression French conveyed to Parisian journalists who strove afterward to explain him to the Boulevards. Anybody could see, remarked the *Figaro,* that French was essentially Irish. He had the merry Irish eye, the merry Irish laugh, even the Irish brogue. His gestures were quick, nervous, and eloquent. Not being a large man, French did not show his sixty-two years conspicuously. He shared the taste of the Duke of Wellington for cold meat, and was noted for a sweet tooth and a fondness for fiction. His favorite authors were French. He found satisfaction in the fact that his name itself was French, since his favorite authors, his favorite landscapes, and his favorite viands were all French. His success was the more enduring because it was won in a human and unpretentious way. He had not the grim aloofness of commanders like Wellington or Kitchener, nor did he cultivate Napoleonic arts. But he was hardly inferior to famous commanders in conveying one impression which is essential to all successful generals—an impression that he had in him the secret of victory. Without that an army goes into battle robbed of its most powerful asset. French did not convey this impression by enveloping himself in an atmosphere of remoteness and mystery, but by showing a sane, balanced, daylight-mind, firm in judgments, yet open to conviction; masterful, yet without the blemish of vanity or ambition; profoundly informed, yet free from the taint of the mere doctrinaire.

Cooperation among allies has always been a delicate and difficult operation. The relations of French and Joffre were therefore susceptible to strain and something like strain appears at times to have occurred. French was not only a field-marshal, and therefore at that time Joffre's superior in rank, but he had entered the war with a reputation established on the field of battle, while Joffre, his chief, had had no experience of war on a great scale. Nevertheless, the English commander gave the world an example of loyalty, not merely in deed and word, but in spirit.[11]

[11] Compiled from articles by A. C. Gardiner in The *Daily News* (London), Alexander Harvey in *Current Opinion* and from *The World's Work.*

JOSEPH SIMON GALLIENI, French General and Military Governor of Paris

Gallieni's death in the midst of the war, while not unexpected, for he had long been seriously ill, created a deep impression in France, where he had been idolized by the people, particularly the poor, and was regarded as the savior of Paris in those critical days of August and September, 1914. He died at Versailles after a painful illness that culminated in an operation for transfusion of the blood, which gave only momentary hope. On the morrow of the defeat of the British and French at Mons-Charleroi, Gallieni was made Military Governor of Paris and during the first fortnight that he held this office a turning-point occurred in modern history. Because of the magnitude of the issues at stake, millions of people in those two weeks suffered anguish day after day—a period crowded with private and public tragedies. No one who was then in Paris could ever forget his sensations, nor could he forget the slight, nervous, yet dominating figure of the man who, well knowing that the old circle of Paris forts was unequal to the task that seemed about to fall to them, boldly announced that he would defend the city to the last. Following was the proclamation Gallieni issued:

Army of Paris! Inhabitants of Paris!

The members of the Government of the Republic have left Paris, to give a new impetus to the national defense. I have received the order to defend Paris against the invader. This order I will carry out to the end.

GALLIENI.

The last few words of that manifesto became a popular French war cry, *"Jusqu'au bout."* Later he had a conversation with M. Millerand, the Minister of War. "I have come for your orders, Monsieur le Ministre," said he, as he entered. "If, unfortunately, the enemy should succeed in entering Paris, what am I to do?" To which Millerand replied: "Defend Paris quarter by quarter, house by house." "And if it becomes necessary to retire to the south side of the river?" asked Gallieni. "Then you will destroy the bridges," said the minister. "You can count on me," replied Gallieni, and the conversation ended. A witness of the scene compared Gallieni's manner to that of Rostopchin when he decided to burn Moscow rather than yield the city intact to Napoleon.

The French Government had removed to Bordeaux, and with it

had gone many foreigners, the idle rich, and a good many of the middle class. Parisians in general, however, remained with, and were faithful to, their Governor. Never before nor since had the city presented an air such as it did then and in ensuing months—an air of quiet dignity, of serene and spacious self-possession. Paris was not in a position to defend herself against a German flood. Modern artillery, if nothing else, had rendered her circle of forts little more than a nominal defense. As the public had known nothing of what was being done in preparation for a counterstroke on the Marne, the appointment of Gallieni came as a great relief. It meant a defense to the end. Every morning gangs of laborers left Paris in tourist motor char-à-bancs to work in throwing up trench-defenses. Countless indications showed that Gallieni was preparing to defend the city inch by inch. When finally Kluck swept down to the southeast, ignoring the capital and exposing his flank, Maunoury's army was hurried forward by every available means of transport until, on the Ourcq, it played a momentous part in winning the coming victory. All the organizing and administrative ability of Gallieni had been displayed in that flanking operation.

The circumstances in which Gallieni did so much to save Paris were capable of two interpretations. All military critics admitted that he saved the city, but some declared that if he had carried out Joffre's orders exactly he would have done more—he would have captured Kluck. Joffre, with "clairvoyant strategy," had foreseen that the German right would press on until it reached the outer fortifications of Paris and then would swing to the southeast in an attempt to encircle the city. He knew that German lines of communication could not at once supply the necessary men, nor the heavy guns, for a siege, and that in the interval he could capture Kluck's army. For this eventuality, he had caused Gallieni to prepare a picked body of fighting men—mostly colonials from Tunis—who at the critical moment were to deploy east of the capital in the direction of Châlons, thereby cutting off the Germans south of the line.

The Germans advanced exactly as Joffre had foreseen. They reached the outer fortifications on September 3, and then swung to the southeast, enveloping La Ferté, Sézanne, and Vitry on September 5. Next day Joffre sent an order to division commanders, "Prepare to advance," intending that they should stiffen their lines and await further orders. On that day Maunoury, who commanded the French left north of Paris, sent word to Gallieni that his positions were in jeopardy, and Gallieni, collecting every available motor-car in Paris, rushed all his reserve troops to

Maunoury's relief, and a fierce attack was made on Kluck's flank at the Ourcq. The French front in the southeast, feeling the pressure of the Germans weakening, not only "stiffened," but through the stroke delivered by Foch rolled the Germans back, and the later phase of the battle, which turned their retreat into a rout, was fought. Paris had been saved, but Kluck's army escaped.

During the first months of the war Gallieni, as the Military Governor of Paris, not only reconstructed the fortifications and prepared defenses for the city from aviation attacks, but as the city became a great clearing-house for wounded, troops, and supplies, it became his duty to facilitate all things pertaining to movements. In November, 1915, when the French Cabinet was reconstructed Gallieni became Minister of War, succeeding M. Millerand. Here his ability as an organizer and administrator was again shown. In February he took over the direction of the Department of Aviation, but shortly afterward was taken ill and compelled to resign on March 16. After that he remained ill in the Military Hospital at Versailles, and there he died.

Among many dramatic episodes in Gallieni's life was his defense in 1871, with Commandant Lambert, of the house called "Les Dernières Cartouches"—the Last Cartridges—which formed the subject of one of De Neuville's famous paintings. Gallieni was born, so to speak, with a knapsack in his cradle. He was a child of the Army, his father being an officer, and was sent to a school on a military foundation. Later he passed out of St. Cyr to a commission in the Army just as the Empire had become involved in war with Germany. The date of his appointment was the fatal July 15, 1870. He fought with General Faidherbe in one or two engagements in which the Colonial Infantry distinguished itself. Later, Faidherbe became his chief in the Sudan, and he grew to be remarkably like his distinguished chief in ways of thought and action. In Senegal and on the Niger he was known as a great colonial soldier and administrator. In Madagascar he conquered by persuasion as well as by force of arms. There was never a greater humanitarian engaged in the business of war. Not even Joffre, whom he resembled closely in origin and attainments, excelled him in a fine quality of heart allied to a fine quality of head. Like the Commander-in-Chief he was a southerner, having been born in a small town in the Pyrenees, and so in origin resembled Joffre, Foch, Pau, Castelnau, and Pétain. Like Joffre, Gallieni was a silent man. Summers spent in the Sudan and on the high plains of Madagascar sat lightly on him. Behind a "pince-nez" bridging a pointed nose in a rather gaunt face, he had a cold and penetrating eye. One deciphered energy in those features.

Gallieni's figure, tall and slim, was quite destitute of that corpulence which defined Joffre. He was "elegant," as the French say. A touch of the courtly characterized his every gesture. He spoke the language of the salon, liked flowers and poetry, looked discriminatingly at pictures through eye-glasses set gracefully upon a prominent nose. His eyes were blue, but with a suggestion of green, his voice ingratiating. His manners made one see why the French have so just a reputation for politeness. His was cool politeness, not curt, and yet suggested the man who was master of himself and others. Never was he seen unkempt, bedraggled, or ungroomed. His physical endurance was simply incompatible with the whiteness of his hair, the paleness of his face—which tropical suns had failed to tan—and the delicacy of his frame. He wore a uniform like a beau, acting, talking, and seeming the courtier. He looked like a carpet commander such as graced the palace of the "Sun King" on days of grand balls and diplomatic receptions.

The similarity between the career of Kitchener and that of Gallieni, both of whom rendered great services early in the war and died within a few weeks of each other, was often commented on. Each found himself an officer at an early age, struggling along ill-defined frontiers in Africa, coming into collision with Mohammedan despots, asserting a dubious sovereignty over uncharted oases, ascending mysterious rivers, attacking interior capitals against tremendous odds. Each passed in due time from Africa to Asia, but Kitchener emerged first in a blaze of glory when discovery of him by Lord Cromer marked him as an "arrival." Gallieni did not come into his own until he went to Tonkin. In the prime of life he came into collision with the Chinese, and acquired from the Chinese that "mandarin manner" which became so marked in his gestures and deportment, an ineffable ease of bearing in trying situations which would have left him unruffled when the house was afire.

Nothing could have been more characteristic of him than his refusal to go to Madagascar, unless he could be an absolute despot over the whole island. He made Madagascar a French "possession," until the name Gallieni became a household word among the French in that island. Functionaries from the Colonial Office went out to investigate him, only to return with enthusiasm for his personality. Characteristic of him was the enthusiasm he imparted to subordinates. In this respect he was a contrast to Kitchener who, on the whole, was not popular with the men with whom he had to work. Gallieni was of the accessible, smiling, indulgent type, ready enough to forward anyone's ambition, taking the day's work as an adventure. He was charming to the young and indulgent to the inexperienced. Kitchener buried himself in a back room, gave orders by indirection, and dined in solitary state.

Gallieni was fond of the theater, graceful as a dancer, read poetry, was swift and resourceful, and a dominating figure at a council of war, partly because of his "charm," also because of the subtlety and plausibility he showed in defending propositions. He thought Joffre too cautious. "You ought to be in Madagascar, General," said the stout commander to the thin one in 1915, after a discussion of some new conception he had outlined as the War Minister. "No, General," said Gallieni smilingly, "by this time I ought to be in Berlin." He had a pretty little home at La Gabelle, in a rolling French valley near Saint Raphael, where domestic bereavement had not escaped him. Distinguished as was his career, the financial results had been inadequate and he died poor. With him there passed away a fine servant of France whose career embraced three great periods of French history—the tragic moment of defeat in 1870, the Colonial renaissance, and the World War. His part in the war of 1870 was modest, but in the sorrows of that tragedy he acquired some of the patriotic fire from which rose into action the France of 1914. He showed the faith that was in him in the long years of service that he gave for building up and consolidating the French Colonial Empire in Africa.[12]

THE GERMAN CROWN PRINCE

Perhaps the most unattractive royal figure in Europe when the war began was the German Crown Prince, then thirty-two years old, his best-known intellectual accomplishment being a profound admiration for Napoleon. He believed thoroughly in rule by divine right for himself as well as for Napoleon. He once made a dramatic speech before the Reichstag, dissenting from a proposal by the Chancellor that a peaceful settlement could be made with France about Morocco. This at once made him a leader of the war-seeking element and incidentally got him into friction with his father. He was tall, slim, and impulsive, his full name Frederick-William-Victor-August-Ernst. Queen Victoria was not only his great-grandmother, but his godmother. He had completed a course of instruction at Ploen, and like his father and

[12] Compiled from an article by Alexander Harvey in *Current Opinion,* The *Times* (London) and from Associated Press correspondence.

grandfather, the Emperor Frederick, had studied at Bonn. Completing university studies in 1903, he entered upon a course of travel in many lands, and then, in order to get training for future responsibilities, was sent to the office of the Potsdam local administration, to the Prussian Ministry of the Interior, to the Admiralty, and to the Foreign Office. In 1905 he married the Duchess Cecelia of Mecklenburg-Schwerin. The Kaiser was quoted as having once said of him, "Well, William is no diplomat, I will admit; but I believe the fellow has marrow in his bones. He will turn out to be our Moltke yet."

The adage that no man is a hero to his valet was strikingly proved in the case of Friedrich Wilhelm of the House of Hohenzollern. After he fled to Holland, in November, 1918, to be interned there on a lonely island, as Napoleon had been on another island, the impressions of one Felix, a former servitor of his, were given in an interview with Edgar M. Moore, who also had known him from having played before him in Berlin as a professional banjoist. "If any one had formed a regiment for him in platoons," said Mr. Moore, "he couldn't by his own commands have done so much as march it down a perfectly straight street, let alone halting or turning it, had he found a stone wall at the end. He was railroaded through Bonn and the military colleges. He hated a uniform and wouldn't have one on when he could avoid it. What he liked best as to clothes was to lounge in English tweeds. At a first meeting you'd have taken him—his English was perfect, absolutely clean of accent—for an English squire from the countryside. He was what Americans used to call an Anglomaniac. He never dreamed of posing as a German warrior of blood and iron; he preferred to ape the English 'Johnny,' the kind of chap who used to hang around the stage-door of the Gaiety Theatre. When in Berlin you could always find him at night in one of two or three of the most expensive night-life cafés. He never ate very much for fear of losing his slim waist and I never knew of his taking enough to make him drunk. He had a favorite brand of whisky—an English brand, of course.

"After you had known him a while," Mr. Moore went on with his report of what the servitor had told him, "you would have realized that his mind was the mind of a rather dull boy of fourteen. I don't mean just mere silliness. I mean that this kind of thinking was as far as he could go. His ego, his vanity, was exactly of that boyish kind. He was like a bragging kid in the recess-yard. Felix, the valet, told me that what he liked to read was Nick Carter's books in German translations. You could buy

THE FORMER CROWN PRINCE WITH HIS DUTCH PLAYMATES

He is engaged in his familiar pastime of romping with Dutch children, accompanied by an aide or guardian, wearing sabots and the clothes of a Dutch fisherman

them in Berlin for ten pfennigs a number, at little notion shops. Fritz always had a stack of them on his dressing-table. Felix used to keep accounts for him. He had an income of $50,000 and when it gave out he would borrow where he could. Banks and money-lenders generally were shy of him, for they knew him; but of course the shops had to give him unlimited credit, so he would buy expensive jewelry, furs and things on credit, and then pawn or sell them for ready cash."

When Mr. Moore and his partners were summoned to play in private before the Crown Prince, the Prince would take part in the performance by playing a guitar. He could play a little and had a fair ear. "We kept down to him and covered him on his breaks. He could play in the keys of G, D, and F, but not in B-flat. He was always going to learn that, but he never did. 'Ragtime,' as he called me from our first meeting, he once said to me, 'how am I making out?' to which I said if anything ever went wrong with him in the princing business he could have a job with our band at any time. That tickled him to death, and whenever he afterward had us play anywhere, or came across us in one of the cafés, he would stand up and grin and call out to everybody, 'Ragtime says if I'm ever out of luck I can always get a job with the band.' And then he would guffaw.

"It wasn't long before I got to know well the Prince's valet, Felix Makadoff, whom a Russian once called 'the perfect valet.' He was a godsend to Fritz. About half his time was spent in covering some of Fritz's tracks, or getting him out of scrapes or raising money for him. Felix was the highest type of his class of servant. He had served the Grand Duke Boris of Russia and other notabilities, and knew the courts of Europe so well from the backstairs side that powerful diplomats would have given their stars for his opportunities. He spoke four languages and had had a first-rate education. Later Fritz quarreled with Felix and turned him off, after nearly twenty years of service without a pension and without so much as a letter of recommendation. That was Fritz all over. He didn't care for his position, his future responsibilities, his father and mother, or his wife, or his children, or anybody or anything but himself and his hobbies, principally his sports.

"According to Felix, the Kaiser used to send for him and try to draw him out about Fritz and what he was thinking and planning. Once Felix was shaving the Kaiser on the morning of the day of a race-meeting, when the Crown Prince had been entered to ride his own horse in a steeplechase over a dangerous course. The horse was young and mettlesome and the Prince's father and mother were panic-stricken that he should have taken such a risk. The Kaiser sent for Fritz while Felix was in the room and said, 'Your mother and I ask that you withdraw your entry.' 'Do you?' says Fritz. 'Well, I can't, that's all; my friends know I'm going to ride, and a fine fool I'd look, wouldn't I?' 'I forbid your riding,' said the Kaiser. Fritz didn't say anything, but just knocked the ash off his English cigaret. 'As your Emperor,' stormed the Kaiser, 'I command you to withdraw!' As Fritz went out he said, 'Command away!' over his shoulder. 'Emperor or no Emperor, I'm going to ride that race if I lose the crown!' And he did it, too.

"Nobody ever was able to discipline Fritz. He may have been sent away at times to fortresses. If he was, it made no impression. It wasn't that he was spoiled; it was natural; the thing was in him. He'd have his way, he'd do as he pleased, or die. Naturally the army men detested him. Their name for him was 'Cockney Fritz,' and they made no bones of it. He wouldn't smoke a German-made cigaret, altho you could get them as good as any in the world. His were made for him in London. So were his clothes and shoes, and everything else that could be made there. Felix came to any quantity of clothes through him. The last time I saw Felix he told me he had enough clothes saved up to last him the rest of his life. Fritz so loved England that he used to slip over there *incognito* a lot oftener than the public ever knew. He'd take Felix along and they'd see a big prize-fight or attend the Henley races, or some other sporting event. Then they'd do a show and London by lamplight and come home next day. Fritz used to say again and again that he'd love to live in England."

FIELD-MARSHAL VON HAESLER

When the war began the Crown Prince was entrusted with nominal command of the army which invaded France by crossing Luxemburg and reaching France at Longwy. It was his command that made the long and fruitless assault on Verdun in 1916. Only in a titular sense was he the director of these assaults. The operations were in reality under control of Marshal von Haesler, one of the oldest commanders in the German army, if not the oldest, his age variously stated at from sixty-eight to seventy-nine, reference books not agreeing as to the date of his birth. He was old enough, however, to have been in the war against Denmark in 1864. Haesler's rotund form and the severity of his facial expression combined to make him one of the "figures" in militarist Germany. "The old guardian of the Moselle," Germans often called him. It was Haesler's business to advise the Crown Prince. All agreed that the Crown Prince needed him and that he took the advice offered. Gossip said Haesler was the most abstemious war-horse in the empire. For fifty years he had risen every morning at five to drink a glass of milk and swallow two raw eggs. At two in the afternoon he ate a small piece of steak and a cup of broth. Characteristic of him was an anecdote that included Prince Henry, the Kaiser's brother. At an annual maneuver Prince Henry had been asked to come to Haesler at eight in the evening. When he arrived, he had to wait until nine, and then found that he and all Haesler's guests were to sit down to a glass of water and an apple. "This," said the old man, "is set before you as a practical lesson in war conditions, when absolute necessities only can be obtained and appetites, like baggage, must be restricted." "His Highness alone," added the General, "having a special claim, may eat two apples and drink two glasses of water."

In his capacity of inspector, Haesler for years was the terror of German soldiers. If he was to inspect a garrison at some place, such as Morhange, he would board a train that did not stop there, and then, just before getting to Morhange, would have the train halted under an emergency signal he had ordered. Fined as he would be for having stopt a train, he would pay the conductor the regular amount of a hundred marks and then rush off to the barracks. On returning to Berlin he would insist on repayment of his hundred marks, turning the administration upside down until he got the money. Haesler was known to think a long time before spending a mark. In the war he sometimes wore a suit of clothes that he had bought thirty years before and a hat that his father wore in another century. Candor was his least liked trait and Emperor William had as much reason as any one to be aware of it.

Soldiers, according to Haesler, should eat very little. Eating he regarded as a bad habit. "March a lot, eat a little, and shoot all the time," was his motto. He made his own corps a model of efficiency, knowing none of the caste distinctions common among Prussians, and yet maintaining an admirable discipline. His personal ascendancy was absolute, a circumstance the more remarkable because of deformity and invalidism. Once in the saddle he seemed a part of the horse. He was indulgent to men in the ranks, but severe with his staff. Thus he reversed an order usual among Prussian military magnates, being considerate to inferiors, grim to equals, and merciless to superiors, not excepting the Emperor himself, whose "conceptions" he sometimes openly laughed at in conference with the general staff. Not many years before the war, he once ordered maneuvers near the town of Siereck, where many lines of trenches had been dug, and a blue corps was on the defensive theoretically for a whole week living on dry bread. On going his rounds, Haesler saw an improvised table, made from a plank and four sticks, around which several officers sat on boxes, eating sausage. "Do you gentlemen think you are in a lady's boudoir?" roared Haesler, as he forced his horse against and over the table. "The Sixteenth Army Corps is not a school of domestic manners," he added; "it is an institution that teaches trench life." Not daring to offer an apology, the offending officers, when the old man disappeared over the brow of a hill, were said to have vented their feelings in a single untranslatable word: *Heiligkreuzkanonenbombengranathageldonnerwetterelementnocheinmal!*"

Between this old man and the one-time heir to the imperial throne there long existed warm affection. Alone among marshals, Haesler took seriously the conception attributed to the Crown Prince that Verdun was the true German objective in 1914. Stories were current of the fury with which he had received the decision of the General Staff in August, 1914, to make the rush toward Paris through Belgium. The road to Paris, he believed, lay through Verdun. On the basis of a common purpose before Verdun he and the young Prince were in firm alliance. The long and futile drive of 1916 was believed to be an expression of the very soul of Haesler. The grimness of the fray, its implacable continuity, its steady hail of projectiles, its stern unyielding advance, its disdain of all cost as well as the enthusiasm of the attack—these manifested the mood of Haesler in war. In great contrast as a man to the Crown Prince who was gentle, smiling, boyish, and gay, Haesler's devotion to the Prince illustrated the familiar attraction of opposites. Haesler never read a book, except the manual, and his favorite relaxation was the society of horses.[13]

SIR DOUGLAS HAIG, British Field-Marshal and Commander of British Armies in France and Belgium; Now an Earl

For Sir Douglas Haig the utmost that could have been claimed in 1915 was that, of the men in the running for Field-Marshal French's place when French retired, he alone had survived among British generals as a thinkable substitute. Sir Ian Hamilton's

[13] Adapted from an article by Alexander Harvey in *Current Opinion;* based on others in the *Gaulois, Matin* and *Figaro* (Paris), and The *Sun* and *The Literary Digest* (New York).

reputation had been eclipsed by the tragic episode of the Dardanelles. Sir Horace Smith-Dorrien, whose handling of the Second Army Corps in the retreat to the Marne was a brilliant feature of that exploit, had been removed to a home command and then sent to German East Africa as the result of a collision of temperament, as well as of opinion, with his staff. Sir William Robertson, Chief of the General Staff, was felt to be more adapted to the work of initiating strategy than for executive command in the field. Thus no one really challenged the claim of Haig. He had been regarded as something of a favorite of fortune since his career had been one of unusual advancement. Exceptionally late in entering the army—he had not only taken a public-school course, but had gone to Oxford—it was not until 1885 that he joined the Seventh Hussars, and even then his career as a soldier was threatened by the refusal of the medical board to admit him to the Staff College on the ground that he was color-blind, a decision overruled by the Duke of Cambridge, then commander-in-chief.

Haig first saw active service in the Nile Expedition in which he was present at the battles of Atbara and Khartoum. In the South African War he was French's right-hand man, serving as chief of staff in operations about Colesberg which prepared the way for Lord Roberts's advance. He continued his association with French in the work of the cavalry division when that advance began, and became ultimately deputy-assistant adjutant-general. After the South African War he went to the War Office as director of military training, was then appointed chief of the general staff in India, and in 1911, while still under fifty, was called to take the coveted Aldershot command. There was an undercurrent of complaint in the service at his rapid progress. Suggestions were not wanting that court influences had been at work in his favor, suggestions which had root in the fact that he had married the Hon. Dorothy Vivian, who had been maid of honor to Queen Alexandra. Personal contact with him, however, and a study of his career disabused most candid minds of the idea that Haig's progress had been a matter of mere social good fortune.[14]

In the World War Haig was active from the outset, engaged in what was, or might become, intensive fighting, and often of the most desperate character. Few soldiers in history had been exposed to greater strain than he endured and triumphed over during four years and three months of war. About all that had been known of him, however, outside France, was that his name had

[14] A. G. Gardiner in *The Century Magazine*.

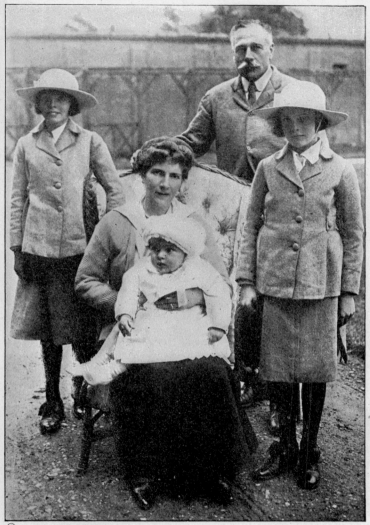

FIELD-MARSHAL SIR DOUGLAS HAIG
At home with his family at Eastcott, Surrey, England, after the war closed.
Haig, in August, 1919, was made an Earl

figured a good deal in headlines. "D. Haig" was the simple way in which he signed his name. "We have all passed through many dark days," he said in an address to his troops after the successful and decisive offensive of October 8, 1918. "Please God these never will return." One of those dark days was April 12, 1918, when the British army was fighting for its life in the Ypres sector, but always indomitably. That was the occasion when Haig issued his famous "back to the wall" order, in which he also said, with a simplicity having something of the sublime in it:

"Many among us now are tired. To those I would say that victory will belong to the side which holds out the longest. The French Army is moving rapidly and in great force to our support. There is no other course open to us but to fight it out. Every position must be held to the last man. There must be no retirement."

With Sir Horace Smith-Dorrien, his fellow corps commander, Haig more than once saved the British Army during its retreat from Mons. Major Ernest W. Hamilton, historian of that retreat, has said that "one hundred Victoria Crosses were earned for every one that was given." One-third of Britain's little army of that time now sleep their long sleep in France. Smith-Dorrien, whose health broke down under the strain, and Haig, the man of iron, vied with each other in fighting rear-guard actions until flesh and blood could endure no more. The escape of remnants of certain British brigades bordered on the miraculous. "We shall have to hold on here for a while if we all die for it," said Haig on one desperate occasion. The first battle of Ypres, in 1914, was as touch-and-go a business as anything experienced in the retreat from Mons. The Seventh Division, which was 12,000 strong when it left England, lost 336 officers out of 400, and 9,664 men. On the darkest day, when all seemed lost, down the Menin road galloped Haig and his small escort of the Seventeenth Lancers, shells falling thick about them. He had gone for no other reason than to encourage his faltering troops, a general's place being behind the line. On the battle of the Somme, in 1916, which he fought with tried as well as with green troops, Haig's fame will perhaps rest most securely. No fiercer long battle was ever fought. On the Somme the enemy had to be pried out of one Gibraltar after another; driven from one Plevna after another, but the British, under Haig, moved relentlessly forward; their losses some 500,000, German losses much greater. If Haig ever showed a trace of the tremendous strain, nobody made mention of the fact.

This Scottish gentleman, son of John Haig of Ramornie, in Fifeshire, who in this war at one time commanded 2,000,000

British and Colonial troops, was in the prime of life at fifty-seven, tall, lithe, well knit, a consummate horseman, fair of complexion, blue of eye, in manner gracious, reserved, and kindly. "I have rarely seen a masculine face so handsome and yet so strong," said one who tried to interview him. He shunned publicity. He was a knight of the prized Order of the Thistle. Modest and indifferent to fame, Haig was among the great commanders whom the war brought to the front. The impression he created in an interview was unlike the traditional conception of the man of war, and yet his bearing, gallant and soldierly, conveyed an impression of a man master of himself and of his task.

He was young-looking even for his years, a suggestion due, not only to rapid movements made by a stalwart frame, but more definitely to his smooth, untroubled face, which in profile slanted forward from a retreating brow to the nose and a big, strong chin. Seen in front, the face was square and massive, the mouth broad and decisive, the blue-gray eyes calm and direct. In his speech and manner there was no trace of the "rough-hewn" soldier. He suggested Oxford more than the barrack-room. One felt that he would be charming and reassuring at the bedside as a visiting rector or physician. Mingled gravity and gentleness were the note of his bearing and his conversation. One could not resist the frankness and courtesy seen in his direct but kindly glance. He won confidence by sincerity and candor, was tolerant of a contrary opinion, listened with respect to anything that deserved respect. In the midst of his staff, his mastery was obvious without being demonstrative. He had the art of the judge who encouraged counsel to enlighten him, but reserves right of judgment.

In a report on the retreat from Mons, French spoke of "the skilful manner in which Haig extricated his corps from an exceptionally difficult position in the darkness of the night," while at the Aisne "the action of the First Corps under the direction and command of Haig was of so skilful, bold, and decisive a character, that he gained positions which alone enabled me to maintain my position for more than three weeks of very severe fighting on the north bank of the river." In reporting on the first battle of Ypres, French gave the chief honors to Haig: "Throughout this trying period, aided by his divisional commanders and his brigade commanders," he "held the line with marvelous tenacity and undaunted courage." "Words fail me," added French, "to express the admiration I feel for their conduct, or my sense of the incalculable service they have rendered." When the first forward movement was attempted at Neuve Chappelle, and the First Army Corps went southward for the task, to Haig was committed the executive command in the field. It was an ill-fated venture, despite an apparent success, but its failure was attributed mainly to an insufficiency of artillery preparation. French declared that in this engagement "the energy and vigor with which Haig handled his command showed him to be a leader of great ability and power."

Haig's record revealed many of the qualities of great generalship, caution in preparing his stroke, ingenuity in extricating himself from difficulties, constancy of mind, a temperament of confidence, power of commanding the affections, as well as the obedience, of subordinates, resolution and impetus in action. There was no other personality in the British General Staff for whom possession of so many essentials of command could have been claimed. No one knew more about the hairbreadth escapes the first seven British divisions had in the retreat to the Marne, nor was any one better qualified to tell the story of the German failure to destroy the British contingents in the critical battle around Ypres in the autumn of 1914. Haig said in one of his reports that "the margin with which the German onrush of 1914 was stemmed was so narrow, and the subsequent struggle was so severe that the word 'miraculous' is hardly too strong a term to describe the recovery and ultimate victory of the Allies." In this statement he had in mind the wonderful survival of remnants of the British army and its slender reinforcements when the Kaiser made his drive for the sea after the Marne. Foch and Haig must often have talked about the German failure and wondered why the Kaiser, who went to Roulers to witness a *débâcle* of the Allies, could have come so close to success and then missed it. At Ypres a division under Rawlinson was reduced to about 400 officers and men. From Mons to the stand at Ypres, the British army lost one-third of its complement in killed.

No soldier of recent times had paid more attention to certain aspects of our Civil War. Haig thought the Confederate "Jeb" Stuart the supreme cavalry genius of the nineteenth century. When commanding at Aldershot he imprest the lesson of Stuart's career upon his own staff. His personality had something in common with that of "Stonewall" Jackson. Like the Confederate leader, he had a marked strain of evangelical piety, a serious style of speech and a touch of the pale student. He was somber like Jackson, rather than dashing in the fashion of Stuart. Haig made apt citations from the Scriptures. His intellect was Scotch and metaphysical, his favorite poet Burns.

Looking somewhat taller than he was, owing to the slimness of his build, Haig suggested the military hero of whom young ladies love to read. He was graceful in every movement, yet masculine in the strength stamped upon him by a life of activity. His complexion was swarthy, tanned by African and Indian suns, yet the bluish gray in large, limpid eyes, that flashed under gray brows, betrayed his northern extraction. His hair was grizzled, like his mustache, but he had an oddly youthful appearance and features finely chiseled. The salient feature was a strong and shapely chin. A lean, brown hand clasped that chin in moments of reflection. His voice, in which few words were spoken, was low, modulated to the atmosphere of the drawing-room, yet commanding and decisive. He moved quickly, but his gestures were few. His figure was clean-cut, his cheek smooth and darkened by years of close shaving, his bearing erect and his walk straight and rapid.

Haig's career was typical of younger sons in a wealthy and aristocratic British family. English and Scotch were blended in him. His early ambitions were literary and his career at Oxford was distinguished from that point of view; but a decline in the family fortunes made a definite career important. Skill as a rider indicated cavalry as his goal. For a long time he was thrown constantly with Kitchener, discussing plans of campaign in Egypt, sharing with him the hardships of the drive through the desert when he would take the liberty now and then of making suggestions, always palatable to Kitchener. The relation of the two continued delightful. The fact that Haig not only got on with so cold and distant a man as the Sirdar, but thawed him into cordiality, was cited as proof of his charm. Kitchener succumbed to it and saw that the efficient Scot was mentioned in dispatches and rewarded with promotion.

Haig did not swear, or gamble, or dance all night at revels, or affect the dress uniform of his rank. His asceticism was understood and recognized. He had the Presbyterian temperament. His quartermaster one day asked him during the Colesberg operations if, in a brush with the Boers, he had lost anything. "Yes," confest Haig solemnly, "my Bible!" Not once did his countenance relax as he gazed at the grinning faces around him. He attended Presbyterian services when they were held at the front, and in a certain passion for theology suggested Gladstone. In Berlin he profoundly imprest members of the German Staff when he studied there several years before the war. In Paris his name was a familiar one long before the war. He had followed French maneuvers in the Champagne and elsewhere in the capacity of British military attaché.

Of all the Allied commanders Haig at the end of the war was the oldest in point of service as a chief and was perhaps the youngest in years. He came to supreme command when the new

British Army had just begun to reach France, and the real organization for victory was still to be made. In the great Somme campaign of 1916 the British Army, under his direction, learned its business in war, a costly lesson, and in learning which mistakes were made, but at the end of that campaign the British Army believed itself superior to the German; really felt that it had "learned its job." Next year at Arras a real achievement was won for Vimy Ridge was a genuine military triumph. The blow he dealt in Flanders in the autumn of 1917, altho it started with a great success at Messines, began too late for final success. Men talked of it as they had talked about Grant's campaign from the Rapidan to Cold Harbor. It was a terribly costly campaign that had not brought immediate success, and then within a few months Russia collapsed.

Next spring Ludendorff's great drive went west into Picardy, and Haig was driven back. Foch assumed command of all the Allied armies, and some men said Haig should go home, but he was permitted to stay, and after that came, on August 8, a British victory which sent the Germans far back from Amiens, and from which Ludendorff dated a German belief—even the Kaiser's belief—that the war could no longer be won by Germany. Following the success of August 8, came the blow under Horne, which broke a portion of the Hindenburg line, and then Haig's success of October 8—one of the great achievements of the war—which definitely smashed the Hindenburg line and began the last phase of the war, with the rapid collapse of German resistance. The achievement of the British Army, when it forced its way from the outskirts of Amiens to Mons, between August 8 and November 11, 1918, was one of the finest things in military history. One could not yet know how much Foch did, or how much Haig did, but under Foch's supreme command the British Army, rallying from terrific losses and heavy defeat in March and April, smashed its way forward over innumerable obstacles. It was clear that if Haig had not loyally cooperated with Foch, victory would not have been possible. However brilliant the strategy of Foch, if it had not been intelligently and efficiently interpreted by Haig, no such success could have followed.

Therefore, if the great glory was to Foch, as in our Civil War it was to Grant, Haig deserved the praise which the North gave to Sherman, and which France gave to Pétain. That the British might yet rank Haig with Wellington and Marlborough seemed not unlikely. By comparison Haig's task was gigantic; he had taken a huge British volunteer army when it was little more than a mob and fashioned out of it an effective instrument; he suffered severe defeats and severer disappointments, but ultimately he led that army to complete victory. His problems were different and more difficult than those of Joffre or Pétain, who had armies already at their hands, organized for contemporary continental warfare and provided with staffs trained in the tasks set for them. Two-thirds of Haig's work was constructive work and it had to be done in the heat of battle and under the stress of great campaigns. But in the face of all obstacles he brought a victorious British army back to Mons on November 11. His achievement promised to grow rather than diminish with the passing of time.[15]

FIELD-MARSHAL PAUL VON HINDENBURG, Chief of Staff
of the German Armies

When on the night of August 29, 1914, it was announced that German troops under the commanding general von Hindenburg, after three days of fighting, had defeated the Russian Narew army, consisting of five army corps and three cavalry divisions, near Tannenberg in East Prussia, and was pursuing the Russians across the frontier, many persons, including Germans, were asking who Hindenburg was, only to learn that he had formerly been a commanding general, but had been retired and until now had been living a quiet life in Hanover. It was no more true of Byron than of Hindenburg that he "awoke one morning and found himself famous." He had long been known favorably in higher army circles, and among civilians in towns where he had held appointments he was remembered as an agreeable man, with a reputation for military capacity, but the great masses throughout Germany still asked: Who is Hindenburg? Hindenburg himself explained his sudden call to army service in the following statement:

"A few weeks ago I was living on my pension at Hanover. Of course, I tendered my service immediately after the war broke out, but since then I had heard nothing for three weeks. The waiting seemed endless, and I had given up all hope of being reinstated, when suddenly came a dispatch informing me that His Majesty had given me command of the Eastern Army. I had time only to get together the most necessary articles of clothing and have my old uniform put in condition for service."

Late that night—it was August 22—an extra train bore Hindenburg out of Hanover, and on the following afternoon he ar-

[15] Compiled from articles by A. G. Gardiner in *The Century Magazine,* by Alexander Harvey in *Current Opinion,* and in The *Tribune* (New York) and The *Morning Post* (London).

rived at the Russian front. He already knew intimately the military features of the East Prussian country, and was not long in fixing upon a plan of battle; in fact, only three days after he arrived he was engaged in battle. Germans called this battle Tannenberg, not because the village of that name had figured in any marked way in the fighting, for it was miles away from the scene of it. The name was chosen for the sentimental reason that Tannenberg was the name of another famous battle in German annals, but fought five hundred years before and of unhappy memory, because at Tannenberg the old Teutonic Knights had been crushingly defeated by the Poles.

Hindenburg's victory took on unheard-of proportions. Never had so many prisoners been taken in an open engagement; the stroke eclipsed in one sense Sedan, for the battleground was four-fold greater. According to first reports, the prisoners numbered 30,000, but the number rose steadily for several days and finally exceeded 90,000. A few days later Hindenburg defeated and drove across the frontier another Russian army and took 30,000 prisoners more; at least so said Berlin. Hindenburg was quoted as saying that 80,000 Russians had been killed or drowned in the Masurian Lakes. In any previous war these losses—had the figures been correct—would have meant irreparable defeat for the country that suffered them, a complete breakdown of its military position. That they did not mean this in the present case was attributed not only to German exaggeration, but to the un-paralleled numbers that Russia had brought into the field, to the vastness of the theater of war, and to the difficulty Germany would have in moving troops further east in midwinter.

Hindenburg's full name was Paul Ludwig Hand, Anton von Beneckendorff und von Hindenburg, that is, he was twice en-nobled. The Beneckendorffs, while belonging to the lower German aristocracy, were among the most ancient of Prussian families. His name Hindenburg was of recent origin. His great-grandfather was a Beneckendorff, who in order to comply with the wish of a great-uncle had obtained in 1799 the legal right to add Hinden-burg to his own name. The great uncle, who was the last of the Hindenburgs, had bequeathed his landed estates to his young kins-man, with a wish that he add the Hindenburg name to his own. In the lapse of time the Hindenburg half became much better known than the Beneckendorff half, until the field-marshal got the habit of signing himself simply "Von Hindenburg."

After a few years in a private school Hindenburg was sent to a cadet school at Wahlstatt, in Silesia, where Blücher had his headquarters during the battle of Katzbach. His windows at the school looked out over the field of that battle. When the Danish war broke out in 1864, he was a pupil at a military school in Berlin, but not quite old enough to go into the war. His turn did not come until two years later, with the outbreak of war with Austria, when he was eighteen and a half years old. At the battle of Königgratz (Sadowa), a bullet penetrated the eagle of his helmet, grazing his head and leaving him prostrate. That helmet was kept ever afterward and adorned the walls of his workroom in Hanover, having been preserved by his parents as a sacred relic, with an appropriate Bible verse attached to the eagle. In the Franco-Prussian war, in the fighting about Metz, he was in the storming of St. Privat, where two German battalions were reduced to one-fifth* of their strength, and nearly three-fourths of the officers were killed. He also fought at Sedan and was before Paris during the siege.

In the forty years that followed, Hindenburg pursued with diligence his military education, rising from one post to another and broadening his grasp of problems. In 1881-83 he was at Königsberg as staff-officer to a division, and there began his studies of the Masurian Lake region. Appointments took him to widely separated parts of the empire, and carried him through the most varied range of military work. Besides being a staff-officer, he rose through various grades until he reached the rank of commanding general in 1903—the summit of a German general's hopes in times of peace. In 1911, when sixty-four years old, but still in strength and vigor, he resigned. Not the least important of his appointments had come in 1886, when he was assigned to a post on the General Staff and made a professor in the War Academy where he lectured for seven years on applied tactics, and gave much attention to the Masurian Lake region where he had worked out a theoretical battle.

Whenever one got a view of Hindenburg's inner life during his active military career, it was that of a man absorbed in his profession, taking a serious view of all work, and ever occupied with the possible tasks that the future might bring. "When we had free evenings at the Hindenburg house," said a woman friend of the family, who had seen much of him when he was in command of a regiment in a country town, "he would often sit pondering over maps spread out before him on a table, marking movements of troops, directing armies, fighting imaginary battles." He often said it was the dream of his life to lead an army corps against an enemy. When his only son was an infant, he once tossed him up and said: "Boy, I am already rejoicing at the thought of seeing you with me around the bivouac fires in a war with Russia." It was his habit ever to keep this boy's mind occupied with military thoughts, to accustom him to military language. In taking walks across country with his children he would keep the boy playing at soldier, addressing him as "Herr Lieutenant," and ordering him to carry out evolutions with imaginary troops.

It was Hindenburg's aim in war to keep ever on the offensive. Grant himself did not strike an enemy with greater vehemence and persistence. Like Grant again, he had the habit of shifting the blow to another point once he became convinced that the obstacles in his immediate front were too great for him. But Hindenburg was favored by railways as Grant was not. Never before had railways played so important a part in war. He probably employed them more extensively and with better effect than any other commander had ever done. Railways enabled him effectively to follow Napoleon's strategy of massing superior forces at given points and bursting suddenly upon an unsuspecting enemy. In planning battles he showed a marked preference for flanking movements and boldness and skill in carrying them out. He took care not to be outflanked himself while trying to reach around an enemy's wings. By an unrelenting pursuit he sought to win the greatest possible advantage. He was not satisfied with merely defeating the enemy, but strove to crush him completely.

In early life Hindenburg painted so well in water-colors, as to give promise of a career as an artist. On the walls of his little home at Hanover hung reproductions of the Sistine Madonna and an antique head of Juno, as foils to portraits of the old Emperor William, Frederick III as Crown Prince, Bismarck, Moltke, and the last Emperor. Other pictures—paintings, copperplate-engravings, lithographs—gave a flavor of olden times to the small rooms. The furniture was of antique patterns, and not a few heirlooms spoke of his love for his family. He was a religious man. Not Cromwell or Stonewall Jackson was more firmly convinced of being an instrument in the hands of God. The optimistic fatalism begotten of this faith—just as with those two great commanders—was an important element in his military success. His creed was of a more orthodox type than that which was generally prevalent in Germany; his religion of the oldest, simplest kind. When great crowds gathered to give him an ovation after Tannenberg, he merely halted his automobile, rose from his seat, pointed upward, and said, "Thank Him up there!" and rode away.

Hindenburg made few demands upon the many servants placed at his disposal at headquarters; his meals were of almost puritanical simplicity, consisting nearly always of one meat course cooked with vegetables, and ending with a cheap grade of cheese. Even when princely personages were guests at headquarters, his only indulgence was a glass of champagne. His office door was marked only with the word "Chief," written with chalk. Hindenburg was six feet tall, with a commanding figure, and carried himself with ease and dignity. He had a deep chest, broad shoulders, and a short and thick neck. The chin and lower jaws were massive, giving the face a squarish appearance. The mouth, with the corners of the lips drawn sharply down, exprest firmness, the effect heightened by the mustache, which was allowed to grow out on the cheeks beyond the corners of the lips. His blue eyes were deep-set, frank and penetrating, and had a tendency to close when he was talking or smiling. His forehead was fairly high and somewhat flat, still surmounted by a good shock of hair, which was nearly white and kept close-cropped. Standing erect it completed an expression of energy and strength given by his countenance. His voice was a deep, rich bass. Among his comrades he was regarded as a companionable man when off duty, but he never learned to play cards. His sister found it impossible even to teach him "sixty-six," the simplest of German games. Avoiding cards, he also never gambled, thus escaping temptations that have proved the undoing of many a young German officer. For hunting he had a great liking. The walls of his cottage at Hanover were decorated with the antlers of stags shot by his rifle.

The title of "Old Man of the Swamp" became Hindenburg's as long ago as when he was an instructor in the War Academy in Berlin, and was bestowed upon him by common consent of brother officers, who had suffered from his apparently mad enthusiasm for the Masurian swamp section. He knew every square inch of territory from Königsberg to Tannenberg, and he fought innumerable battles on paper-maps of that region before it became his duty to fight his first great battle in the swamps themselves. The impression he gave was one of bigness, both mental and physical. Simply drest in field-gray, wearing only the order *Pour le Mérite*, bestowed upon him by the Emperor for the Russian drive of 1914, he had the directness and simplicity of great men. He was wholly without ostentation, and easier to engage in conversation than many a younger officer. He ate simply and worked hard. Dinner at headquarters consisted of soup and one course, around an undecorated table with ten officers.

In sham engagements he had fought again and again the battle of the Masurian Lakes when he would insist upon cannon being pulled through the muddiest parts of the district and when they became mired fast always seemed pleased. After several days he would bring his exhausted soldiers, horses and muddy guns back to Königsberg where officers would tell each other how "mad" the old man was. Then came the war, when the Russians got into East Prussia so much sooner than the German commanders ever supposed they could, and the small army the Germans had there was almost annihilated. Then the Emperor went to Moltke and demanded another general. Moltke named one man after another and at each name the Emperor shook his head. "Is there any one else you can recommend?" he asked. "Von Hindenburg," replied Moltke. "He is not to be thought of," declared the Emperor. While the Emperor was turning the problem over in his mind, and delay could continue no longer, he finally sent a message to Moltke, "Appoint von Hindenburg."

His early successes gained for him among army men the reputation of being their foremost military strategist. Before the war he had never appeared in the War Office without a portfolio of maps of the lake region. In the Reichstag it was once proposed that the lakes be filled up and the reclaimed ground given over to farming. When Hindenburg heard of the proposition, he caught the first train for Berlin and with his bundle of maps, hastened to the Kaiser, to whom he talked strategy and defense at the lake and for a half hour until the Kaiser, a little wearied, stopt him. "Keep your lakes!" said he. "I promise you they shall not be filled in."

He became in the war the most popular man in Germany. Several degrees were conferred on him by the University of Königsberg— a degree of divinity, because he had taught the youth of East Prussia that "the God of Battle still lived"; a degree of philosophy, because he had "brilliantly demonstrated to Königsberg Kant's thesis of the categorical imperative"; a degree of law, because of "prompt body execution upon the defaulting Russians"; and a degree of medicine, because of "the successful amputation of the Cossack canker from the vital organs of the German nation." Of a huge wooden statue of him in Berlin and the countless number of nails driven into it as a privilege paid for, all the world has heard.[16]

[16] Principal Sources: An article by William C. Dreher in *The Atlantic Monthly*, one by Edward Lylle Fox in the *Wildman Syndicate* and one in The *Times* (New York).

PERSONAL SKETCHES OF WAR LEADERS

SIR SAM HUGHES, Canadian Lieutenant-General

Born in Darlington County, Durham, Ontario, January 8, 1853, Sam Hughes was the son of John Hughes of Tyrone, Ireland, and Caroline Laughlin, of Scotch-Irish-Huguenot descent. He was educated in the Toronto Model and Normal Schools and Toronto University. He started life as an instructor, being lecturer in the English language, literature, and history in the Collegiate Institution, Toronto, a post which he held until 1885. Then he entered into journalism, editing *The Lindsay Warder* until 1897. In 1891 the post of Deputy Minister of Militia was offered to him but declined.

As Lieutenant-Commander of the Forty-fifth Canadian Battalion, he participated in the Queen's Jubilee celebration in 1897, and had long urged upon the Canadian military authorities the desirability of offering military assistance to the British Empire in imperial wars. At the outbreak of the Egyptian and Sudanese risings, the Afghan Frontier War, and the South African War, he personally offered to raise Canadian corps to aid the Motherland.

General Hughes served in the South African War, 1899 to 1900, being mentioned in the dispatches several times. He participated in the European war in France, 1914 to 1915, having raised Canadian contingents in support of the cause of the Allies, 1914-1916. Sir Wilfred Laurier, characterizing General Hughes, said of him: "He has done more in his day and generation for the upbuilding of the militia in Canada and the empire than any other living man." [17]

BARON FISHER, British First Sea Lord

The recall of John Arbuthnot Fisher—Lord Fisher—from retirement late in 1914, to take the place of Prince Louis of Battenberg as First Sea Lord of the British Admiralty, caused a sigh of relief from the decks of British fleets, wherever they might be. Officers and men who personally disliked Fisher, as a hard-hearted, harder-tongued disciplinarian, had every confidence in his professional skill and far-sighted strategy. They knew, far better than politicians could hope to know, that it was to him Great Britain owed the remarkable readiness for action which her Navy displayed when grim-visaged war burst into the midst of that

[17] Compiled from "Canadian Men and Women of the Time" and "Who's Who, 1918-1919" (London).

147

peaceful early summer of 1914. In the Navy Fisher was known simply as "Jackie," with hatred or admiration exprest in the tone of voice employed in enunciating the word. He had been the First Sea Lord before—in fact, for seven years from 1904 to 1910; before that he was Second Sea Lord for two years, and before that had served at the Admiralty as Director of Naval Ordnance, as Controller of the Navy, and as a Lord of the Admiralty.

As Sir John Fisher he had been one of the principal naval advisers of three sovereigns of England—George, Edward, and Victoria. To him credit was largely due for the eradication of an "old fogyism" which had been sapping the heart out of Britain's sea-service in the latter part of the nineteenth century. One of his most conspicuous successes was in stopping the issue of boarding-pikes to dreadnoughts. He was no respecter of persons, having risen to the rank of Naval Commander-in-Chief and Admiral of the Fleet by dint of sheer personal capacity, hard work, and all-round ability.

Sir John was seventy-three years old when the war began—another of the old men who became active in the World War—but he was in splendid health and capable of more work than many men his junior. He had entered the Navy as a lad of thirteen, which was in time to have seen service in the Crimean War. In 1860 he was made a lieutenant, and served in the Chinese expedition, participating in the attack on the Canton and Peiho forts. At Alexandria, as captain of the *Inflexible*, he took a prominent part in the bombardment. After the Egyptians were driven from the fortifications, he was made commander of a police force of bluejackets organized to bring order out of anarchy, and gave in that capacity an illustration of ruthless severity. With an iron hand he supprest looting. He shot culprits without fear or favor. Men and officers of the fleet, caught red-handed, even his own friends, were placed under arrest and punished. His great reputation in the Navy rested more on administrative ability than accomplishments at sea, altho it would be unfair to emphasize this to the point of seeming to indicate that he was not a blue-water sailor. He was an able naval strategist, and had done splendid work on fleet commands. But the great reforms he achieved, and the accomplishments which won him a peerage and the confidence of his countrymen, were gained in bureaus of the Admiralty.

From 1899 to 1902 Lord Fisher, then Commander-in-Chief of the Mediterranean fleet, conducted a campaign intended to educate bigwigs at the Admiralty as to the real needs of a modern fleet. He threw a bomb into the midst of their peaceful conclaves by demanding one day to know what new ships, and how many men, could be spared in the event of war developing with certain European powers. Such a contingency would be met when it arrived, said their Lordships of the Admiralty, but this did not satisfy Fisher, who, in one sense with subtlety, in another with brutality—which was his distinguishing characteristic, and perhaps the real reason for his remarkable success in accomplishing what he set out to do—drew to their attention certain existing conditions which, to say the least, as he presented them, were sinister. Fisher scared their Lordships with the statements he made. They took his comments so much to heart that they went out to Malta to make personal inspection of the things he complained of, and returned to England convinced that Fisher knew what he was talking about. At the Admiralty House in Valetta he had talked to them bluffly, frankly, instructively.

It was not until 1903, when he made a speech at a dinner of the Royal Academy, that he became really known to the British public. Few before then had any knowledge of his existence. At this dinner St. John Brodrick, Secretary of State for War, preceded Fisher as a speaker. Fisher had come in his capacity as Second War Lord, to answer to a toast "To the Navy!" Brodrick, after speaking somewhat boastfully of the army, and of certain reorganizations he had affected, casually made a slighting reference to the Navy, which gave Fisher his opportunity when he got on his feet a few moments later. Looking straight at Brodrick he launched at him this satire:

"The great fact which I come to is that we are all realizing—we of the Navy and the Admiralty are realizing—that on the British Navy rests the British Empire. Nothing else is of any use without it, not even the Army. We are different from Continental nations. No soldier of ours can go anywhere unless a sailor carried him there on his back."

All Britain loved Fisher after that and in 1903 he was made Commander-in-Chief at Portsmouth, and in 1904 First Sea Lord. The many reforms he put through were principally in the way of concentrating the Navy's effective strength, and modernizing fire-control, supply, and battle-tactics. Britain's whole modern system of naval strategy and tactics was afterward remodeled or altered after a plan conceived by him, and in the 1909 birthday honors he was created first Baron Fisher of Kilverstone. Fisher became celebrated for a definition he once gave of war:

"The humanizing of war! You might as well talk of humanizing hell! When a silly ass got up at the Hague Conference and talked about the amenities of civilized warfare, putting your prisoners' feet in hot water and giving them gruel, my reply, I regret to say, was considered unfit for publication. As if war could be civilized! If I am in charge when war breaks out, I shall issue as my commands: 'The essence of war is violence. Moderation in war is imbecility. Hit first, hit hard, hit all the time, hit everywhere!' Humane warfare! When you wring the neck of a chicken all you think about is wringing it quickly. You don't give the chicken intervals for rest and refreshment.''

Fisher came to leadership with a definite purpose. With an overmastering idea of making the British Navy instantly prepared for war, he stamped with heavy sea-boots on everything and everybody that interfered with that supreme purpose. He tore to pieces red tape that had been accumulating for centuries. Men, ships, guns, methods, plans, ideas fell into a dust heap at a stroke from his strong arm. Before 1904, Great Britain, despite deceptive appearances, had had no efficient fighting navy. It had several huge armadas scattered all over the seven seas, but, so far as constituting effective protection to the empire, they were huge delusions. In this war Britain's Navy, under command of Fisher and one of his favorite pupils, Sir John Jellicoe, found itself able to strangle to death the German Empire. What Fisher had struggled for, through five tempestuous years, was exactly the thing that happened in the early days of August, 1914. An overwhelming naval force was in instant readiness for war, and was concentrated exactly at the spot where most needed. Had it not been for Fisher and Jellicoe, it may safely be said that this would not have happened.

In 1904 this British admiral, then not widely known outside the service, short of stature, with a round head, round eyes, stubby nose, with hair like a scrubbing-brush, and a profile that, from forehead to chin, stuck out from his face like the prow of a ship—entered Whitehall virtually as commander-in-chief. Had any other man than Fisher taken this post at that moment, no one can say what might have been the position of Great Britain at the outbreak of war. "There never was such a plucky little beggar," said a friend, recalling Fisher as a midshipman in the Crimean War; "quick as a monkey, keen as a needle, hard as nails. He would do anything and go anywhere, and didn't know what fear was." Fisher's soul, filled with the highest enthusiasm for the Navy, constantly revolted at shiftlessness and laxity. Backward he knew that Navy to be, but he had studied its history, he loved its achievements, and he had his aspirations for its future. Fisher's favorite quotation was Admiral Mahan's picturesque description of Nelson's work in thwarting Napoleon: "Nelson's far-distant, storm-beaten ships, upon which the Grand Army had never looked, stood between that army and dominion of the world."

When the Government called Fisher to Whitehall as First Sea Lord, Mr. Balfour, then Prime Minister, and one of Fisher's most enthusiastic converts, gave him practically a free hand. When Fisher began to upset things, many Englishmen exprest horrified amazement. Critics shouted "autocrat!" but Fisher quietly answered that the British Navy "was not a republic." The organization of the Admiralty had been so changed as to give him practically absolute control. He was placed at the head of several important committees and most officers of importance were ordered to report to him. A life spent in carefully thinking about plans for the safety of the empire began now to flower into definite acts. The system "that had stood the test of centuries" went to pieces almost in a day. Britain's lame duck ships in foreign waters began to limp home; many were broken up where they stood, and dozens were sold at auction. "By one courageous stroke of the pen," said Premier Balfour in a public speech, "150 vessels disappeared from the British fleet." This and other changes that followed, he insisted, represented the greatest naval reform since Napoleon's day. Crews were brought back to England and placed on seaworthy ships that were lying tied to docks, with the result that England, for the first time, had an efficient reserve fleet equipped with crews. These vessels, instead of needing three months to prepare for war, could now be sent to sea in two or three days.

At the same time Fisher, in view of the changed political situation, abolished certain fleets that had been roaming about more or less aimlessly for years. There had been fleets in the North Atlantic and South Pacific. He abolished these and joined their effective vessels to new fleets established nearer home. The North Sea, instead of the Mediterranean, now became the headquarters of the most powerful British squadron. A new fleet, of twelve battleships and six armored cruisers, was stationed there based on home ports. Then Fisher organized a Mediterranean fleet, with eight battleships, based on Malta. He created an entirely new battle-squadron, of eight battleships and six armored cruisers, which he called the Atlantic fleet, based on Gibraltar. This was known as the "pivot fleet." With the help of wireless telegraphy it could swing at a moment's notice and join either the Channel fleet or the fleet stationed in the Mediterranean.

For British naval preparedness, the real test came with the sudden outbreak of war in 1914. The Kaiser did not find the British ships scattered all over the world, many unfit for service of any kind. He found a huge armada stationed literally at his front door, blocking his own egress. Fisher had made other preparations. He had handed gunnery-work over to Sir Percy Scott and Sir John Jellicoe, with results that became apparent in every naval engagement of the war. He engaged in another scrapping performance, compared with which that of 1904 was trifling. When Fisher launched a dreadnought, in 1906, it was apparent that he was a radical indeed. This vessel virtually "scrapped" the whole British Navy. England's old-fashioned fleet had never had such a preponderance over other navies as in 1906, when Fisher, by his new building program, relegated it to the pigeon-hole.[18] On July 10, 1920, having lived to see his beloved navy do its part in the war, Lord Fisher died in London in his eightieth year.

SIR JOHN (NOW VISCOUNT) JELLICOE, ADMIRAL OF THE BRITISH FLEET

Admiral Sir John Jellicoe, now Viscount Jellicoe, who commanded England's Home Fleet and so was responsible for the coast-line of Great Britain and Ireland, was physically a small man—one of the smallest in the British Navy. But his intrepidity was as great as his inches were few, and he was a man of the Fisher type. In his younger days he was a famous boxer, football-player, and all-round athlete. He had seen plenty of fighting before battles were fought in this war in the North Sea. As a sub-lieutenant he was present at the bombardment of Alexandria, and afterward took part in the battle of Tel-el-Kebir as an officer of the Naval Brigade. Jellicoe was ill in the latter fight, suffering from Malta fever. He was on board the *Victoria* when that ship was rammed by the *Camperdown,* and sent to the bottom of the Mediterranean off the coast of Syria, carrying with her Admiral Sir John Tryon and more than 600 officers and men. Jellicoe escaped miraculously. He was forced into the water when his temperature from fever was over 103, but was fished out at the normal, 98, and so cured of his illness. Jellicoe was badly wounded in the attempt to relieve the foreign legations at Peking fourteen years before the World War began. He was then serving on the staff of Admiral of the Fleet Sir Edward Seymour, and received a Boxer bullet through one of his lungs but recovered. Jellicoe was regarded in the British and foreign navies as more responsible than any other officer for progress made in

[18] Compiled from an article in The *Evening Post* (New York), and one in *The World's Work* by William Corbin.

naval gunnery. He raised the percentage of hits from forty-two a hundred rounds to over eighty while Director of Naval Ordnance at the Admiralty.

Immediately after the outbreak of the World War Jellicoe was appointed commander of the Grand Fleet guarding the North Sea. Under his orders the battle of Jutland was fought. This put the German battleship fleet not only to flight, but out of business for the remainder of the war. Afterward he became First Sea Lord of the Admiralty, and on the completion of his term was raised to the peerage as Viscount Jellicoe. Son of a naval officer, he had married the daughter of a rich man, Sir Charles Cayzex, principal owner of the Clan Line of steamships. At Sir Charles's death Lady Jellicoe inherited a fortune. She gave birth to a son, after having two daughters already in their teens. The christening of the youngster, for whom King George and Queen Mary acted as sponsors, was made the occasion of a remarkable demonstration of affectionate remembrance on the part of the officers and men of the Grand Fleet. It took the form of an immense gold cup with an inscription to the effect that it was given to the child with good wishes for its future by the officers and men who had had the privilege of serving under his father.[18a]

JOSEPH JACQUES CÉSAIRE JOFFRE, MARSHAL OF FRANCE

When the war began, barely a year had passed since the name of Joseph Joffre as chief of the French General Staff first became familiar in Europe. Joffre had toiled in a long obscurity from the rank of second lieutenant at eighteen to the post of commander-in-chief at sixty without impressing his personality on the French, but when in September, 1914, he won the battle of the Marne, all the world outside of Germany talked of Joffre, and when in October, 1914, he removed five generals from high commands on the ground of incompetence, the sensation in Paris was tremendous. A man of less iron will than Joffre, one not so sure of the technicalities of his calling, or less capable of imparting their significance to an astounded Minister of War, would then and there probably have gone into collapse in an official sense, but Joffre had won at the Marne and now won at the War Office. Joffre's manner was the kind and unaffected manner, but his will was comparable to tempered blades which bend exquisitely at the swordsman's thrust, only to resume a rigidity worthy of Toledo steel.

All personal descriptions made much of Joffre's deep blue eyes,

[18a] The New York *Evening Post* and *The World's Work.*

his pugnacity of chin, the bushiness of his whitened brows and the heaviness of his ear. It was a countenance typical of the south of France whence he came, a country in which he was never quite liked in some circles, because of his intense republicanism, his indifference to the old nobility, his disregard of traditional military etiquette. He had the temperament of the Pyrenees, with an intensity prone to assert itself beneath correctness of form and manner. His nostril, which quivered readily betrayed a quick temper, seemingly under control, and yet too impetuous to conceal itself from an expert in human nature. He had bursts of epigrammatic frankness which won enemies and explained in some degree the slowness of his rise.

Joffre was sixty before the world ever really heard of him. In his late teens, in the war of 1870, he had been an officer commanding a battery of artillery during the siege of Paris. In 1885 he was sent to Indo-China, and later to the French Sudan. Now and again in official dispatches from North Africa his name had emerged, as in 1894 when he led a force that occupied Timbuktu, after Colonel Bonnier's column had been massacred there, and again as head of affairs in Madagascar when that island still had a Queen. He had gone from one French possession to another, organizing native troops, administering provinces, testing artillery, equipping fortresses, buried in details, yet never the slave of them. He rose slowly through military grades, was always diligent, judicious, explosive, and burly, but remained unknown, even in France, until he had donned a black uniform coat, with three bronze stars on his sleeve, and a cross on his breast that marked a military magnate of the highest rank.

Joffre was something more than a soldier of high professional integrity; he was a first-class military scientist in whom were sustained the high traditions of the French engineering corps. His organizing genius had placed him on a level with men like Vauban, Lazare, and Carnot. Nevertheless the monarchical element in French society disliked Joffre, and was chagrined when he was placed in command over General Pau, who was their favorite. Something like a feud lay behind the circumstances that kept Joffre for years from becoming a captain, and withheld from him the badge of the Legion of Honor until he had gone through a Tonkin campaign. It took Joffre nine years of hard service in the French Sudan to attain the rank of lieutenant-colonel. In 1897 he was made colonel and it was not until eight years later (1905) that he obtained the epaulets of a brigadier-general.

From a grandmother Joffre derived his Gascon qualities—the fire in his eye, the swiftness of his gestures, the sharp stamp of his foot. A great-grandfather had come from Picardy, where handsome men are reared. No one was ever more French, not French of the restless, energetic kind that paces hurriedly to and fro in head-quarters, but the kind that possesses and suggests repose. He had a full, healthy face, a fresh, vigorous voice, teeth that showed slightly when he talked, a mustache that moved up and down, a chin that quivered. There was no suggestion of self-importance about him. Subordinates came to see him and went away after little ceremony. But his calm, slow manner could flash into rapid and energetic action whenever a suggestion was refused; he seemed literally to wipe it out of existence with one move of his hand. At the same time his face could light up with a delighted, almost in-fantile, smile when an idea was presented that found a welcome in his brain. Then came an eager handshake, a slap on the back, and a word of praise for any one who had suggested the right thing at the right time. Noticeable, too, was the facility with which Joffre could handle a dozen subordinates in as many minutes, listening to each affably, grasping the question in a trice and meeting the situa-tion with one quiet word. There was never a hint of hurry. He was a general to whom supreme command was a matter of transact-ing business and not a thing of state and ceremony.

Until the war began, Joffre dwelt in a large, airy house on a beautiful street in a Parisian suburb, his household comprising a wife and daughters. His private life differed little from that of the average Parisian with a social position to maintain in the world's gayest capital. Like the soldier born, he rose early, and was served at breakfast by an orderly while he read dispatches. Then he went off through the Bois, sometimes on horseback, as early as six. One day each week he would walk ten miles to keep in condition. He prided himself on cleaning his own sword, and saddling his own horse, nor would he touch, when with troops on maneuvers, any food except army-rations served in the field. He could not sleep comfortably in a feather bed, so rigidly had he adhered to the rude conditions prescribed for French soldiers on active duty. His chief source of physical discontent was his burly figure; much good-humored banter was indulged in at his expense on account of it.

It had been remarked that Joffre was of the school of Napoleon. Nothing, however, could have been further from methods employed in the wars of Napoleon than those displayed in the great battles on the Marne, the Aisne, and in the north. In themselves they pre-sented nothing like the tactical interest of those older campaigns. For this the aeroplane was mainly responsible, because from it everything could be seen and from it nothing could be hidden. The aeroplane could look behind a screen of cavalry that masked an enemy's front; it could see troops on the march, or carried in trains, could note the number of army corps massed on the other side of the battle-line, the proportion of the different arms, and all other details of a vast fighting machine. The art of war had been robbed of that element of surprize which afforded Napoleon his best opportunities to display his genius. Napoleon's aim was to discover the weak spot in an enemy's lines, and, having discovered it, to hurl upon it all the forces at his command. Success depended upon the speed and sureness with which a great blow was struck. A coup of that sort was no longer possible; a maneuver on the one side was now met instantly by one on the other. War consisted of a series of parallel movements. Two armies turned about each other like boxers in the preliminary phases of a fight, and then pivoted clumsily to catch each other at a disadvantage. In this war that was practically all the art that was left, the rest a ding-dong of resistance, of marching and counter-marching. War now was more like playing bridge with an opponent looking over one's shoulder. No longer was it possible to revive Napoleon's canter on a white horse along the line on the eve of a battle. Joffre could not canter over the hundreds of miles from Dunkirk to Belfort before breakfast when beginning a battle that would last a week.

All conditions of warfare had changed, and with them the mentality and methods of the commanders. Joffre was rarely seen on horseback. He had much the same figure as the Corsican had late in life, was heavy, short and stout, and he gave an impression of power. Joffre spent a part of each day in a long, low, rapid motorcar visiting the lines. It was impossible for him to visit all points—much had to be left to corps commanders after the general plan had been settled. This robbed him of personal contact with his troops. He was more or less unknown to them; he probably had to show papers to sentries. He could wear out two chauffeurs a day in his rush from point to point.

In the formation of the general staff Joffre brought together the best military brains in France, and coordinated and controlled their efforts. He exorcised politics, that bane of the French Army. A Republican and Freemason, he was surrounded by men who were Catholics in religion, some of them disposed to cavil at the Constitution; but this made no difference in his appreciation of them. His chief confidence was given to Foch, Pétain, and Castelnau, regardless of his and their school of politics. The result of his firmness and singleness of purpose was that he commanded a great fighting machine, from which every other consideration than efficiency had been obliterated. Joffre's headquarters, the nervecenter from which were moved more than 2,000,000 men, was for many months in a village school-house seventy miles behind the firing-line. Observers permitted to see it found a startling contrast between its tranquility and simplicity and the intense action going on near the trenches. Neither cannon, machine-guns, nor rifles could be seen or heard. Joffre in that school-house coordinated his information and arrived at his decisions, not only far from the disturbance of actual conflict, but in the depth of a peaceful country district. An air of actual repose surrounded the place, but life was intense within. A single sentinel paced in front of the school-house. Except for a few forester guards, there were no other soldiers at the house or in the village. These guards were youngish men on Joffre's staff, who had been picked for their talents from among the 50,000 officers in the French Army. Gendarmes watched the road of approach. It was impossible to enter except by pass, either from the chief of Joffre's staff, or from one of the few persons in the military administration who had been duly authorized to sign a pass.

The headquarters of a commanding general used to be distinguished by orderlies and horses in front; his rank could be reasonably well determined by their number. Now it was the number of motor-cars that told his rank. Long, high-powered runners were usually lined up in the playground before Joffre's little school-house. With no tooting of horns, cars came and went, quietly and swiftly. When Joffre went to the headquarters of an army, he went in an automobile fitted to serve as an office. A writing-desk that could be let down from one end had convenient devices for docketing papers. A special map, the scale of which was 1-1,000, showed every road, canal, railway, bridle-path, bridge, clump of trees, hill, valley, river, creek, and swamp in the Western war-zone.

When a battle was about to begin, troops were distributed along a 50-, or perhaps a 200-mile line, with Germans facing them. At headquarters a bell would ring saying the Germans were attacking, say, General Durand's division in superior numbers, and that the general needed reinforcements. The staff officer who took this information would then hurry to where say, General Bertholet was sleeping, the general having just dozed off for perhaps the first sleep he had had in thirty-six hours. That general, soon wide awake, would jump to the floor, still wearing his pajamas, the only garment he had worn in several days and, knowing his map as he did his own face, he would locate Durand's division. Ten miles back of it were quartered reserves. "Order General Blanc," he would command, "to reinforce Durand at once with 10,000 men, four batteries of 75-millimeter artillery, ten machine-guns and three squadrons of cavalry. Tell Blanc to transport his troops in autobuses." Within two minutes General Blanc would have received the order, and within five more he would be executing it. Durand, meanwhile, had been informed that help was coming. Every time a bridge was blown up or a pontoon was thrown across a stream or a food convoy was shifted, Bertholet would leap from his chair, or his bed, and change the pins. The war map at headquarters had to be kept posted up to the minute.

After twenty-one months of responsibility in the conduct of the war, during which he had been on duty an average of seventeen hours a day, and had traveled more than 70,000 miles in a motor-car, Joffre did not seem to have aged a bit; there was not the slightest betrayal of fatigue in his countenance, his step, or his mind. For the school-house he afterward substituted a quiet villa surrounded by a pretty garden where, in a spacious room on the ground floor, was a billiard-table covered with maps with other maps on the walls. Each morning on sitting down at his work-table, Joffre found a single sheet of paper on which was noted the latest news of the situation. After a hasty glance at it, he would listen to reports from his staff, rapidly comment upon them, and give concise orders. Matters of consequence would be submitted to him by members of his staff, or would be submitted by him to them. Questions of organization were disposed of—the troops required at different points, the movements by rail, the sanitary service and the arrangements for reinforcements, all of which were decided upon to the smallest detail.

Three hours were often given to reports and orders. Joffre would then rise from his desk and put on his cap, which was the signal for his departure from headquarters to visit some one of the armies at the front. Three powerful motor-cars were already standing in front of the villa. As he passed out, an officer would push into his hand a time-table and the itinerary of the day's journey, as arranged and approved by him the evening before and from which no divergence was to be made. The hours he spent in speeding over the country became hours of comparative rest, which he improved to read in more detail long reports that had not required earlier attention, but which he wanted to understand from beginning to end. His car was known to every one in the army from a tri-colored fanion with gold-fringed cravat which it carried. He always arrived at a place without ceremony and proceeded immediately and simply to the business in hand. He preferred to be unnoticed on these trips, insisting that they in no way partook of the forms and ceremony that attached to reviews, but, instinctively, when he passed, sentinels and soldiers presented arms and reddened with pleasurable emotion because they had had an opportunity of honoring the General-in-Chief. Of all generals who conferred decorations, none did it with such apparent feeling as Joffre. After pinning a cross upon a soldier's breast, whether the simplest trooper, the blackest Senegalese rifleman, or an officer, he kissed him heartily on both cheeks, never satisfied with a semblance of an embrace.

Joffre's tour of inspection was generally finished about five in the afternoon. Back to headquarters he would go for an annoying part of the day's work—questions of displacement, promotion, retirement, recompenses for officers, and citations of soldiers, besides questions relating to arms, material, ammunition supplies, and the sanitary department. The reserve supplies of shells for cannon of different caliber was a matter of such momentous importance that Joffre left these details to no one else; he kept the figures in his head and could give the exact reserve stock of ammunition on hand. He was described by some of his generals as the safety-valve of the army. While he was the directing intelligence of the great machine, he was at the same time a source of relief for the overcharged minds of subordinates who, under certain contingencies, were over-concerned with matters of secondary importance. To such men, surprized by an unlooked for development, and imprest by a complication that seemed decisive and perhaps irremediable, a simple observation from Joffre would often reduce the exaggerated incident to its proper proportions.

Near Perpignan, on the eastern Pyrenees border, lies Rivesaltes, the birthplace of Joffre. It is a country in which, farther west, Foch was born. From the south of France also came Castelnau and Pau, and in an earlier age Henry of Navarre. The house where Joffre first saw the light stands in an unpretentious street, the Rue des Oranges, where women sit out of doors while children play about their knees. Strangers could easily get permission to enter the birthplace with its double doors and knocker that gave it an almost patrician air, but all was simple within. The downstairs room was an ante-chamber without light and contained the stairs. On mounting, one discovered a bedroom with bed in an alcove alongside a small window looking out upon a court. In that alcove Joffre was born.

In this small house Joffre père had been the proud possessor of eleven children, of whom three survived, the general, a future excise official, and a daughter. The elder Joffre's modest circumstances as a working cooper, owning a little land, did not enable him to raise with ease his large family, and in consequence Joseph, the Marshal, was confided to an uncle whose interest was stimulated by a school report of the boy's great ability in mathematics. After a year's preparation (instead of the habitual two), the lad was able to enter the École Polytechnique in Paris twelve months younger than was usual with boys.

At Rivesaltes, after 1914, people were ready enough to talk of their illustrious son, of his goodness of heart, and his utter simplicity. Whenever he had been there in later life they would tell how in his country home on the banks of the Alps he would often go himself and make purchases in the market. "Ah! he was a wonderful boy, a phenomenon!" some old inhabitant would say. "He would fight the other lads, in order to be left at peace to work at mathematics!" Joffre's light-colored complexion and his taciturnity made a French Minister of War once ask questions as to his origin. "You are from Lorraine, *mon Général?* No! Then perhaps you are Flemish, or Norman?" *"Non plus,"* Joffre would say. The Minister would look puzzled until Joffre had said simply, *"Je suis Catalan,"* a description that told volumes.[19]

HORATIO HERBERT, EARL KITCHENER, British Field Marshal

"K. of K.," Kitchener of Khartoum, the most widely celebrated of British soldiers of his period, with the single exception of his old chief, "Bobs" (Lord Roberts), and whose tragic death off the Orkney Islands near the end of the second year of the war all England mourned, was born in the service in 1850, the eldest son of Lieutenant-Colonel H. H. Kitchener, of the Thirteenth Dragoons. Fifty years before the war, on the borders of Normandy and Brittany in the quaint old town of Dinan—the birthplace of DuGuesclin, where the warrior's heart is still kept in the little Church of St. Sauveur—Kitchener was living as a lanky English lad, often teased by French boys who, as they followed him, cried out *"V'la l'Angliche!"* an age-old taunt that fisherfolk had had a habit of flinging in the face of the traditional enemy of France across the "Silver Streak." Young Kitchener was wont to do battle with his enemies under the medieval ramparts of Dinan, and as his tormentors were many, he often reached home with his clothes torn, and the Kitcheners were not rich in clothes.

Of pure English stock Kitchener's father, on half pay, had married the daughter of an old Huguenot family, a Miss Chevallier of Suffolk, and had three children, all boys, of whom the eldest, Horatio Herbert, was born at Ballylongford, in Ireland, while his father's regiment was stationed there. Horatio Herbert got what learning

[19] Compiled from The *Nouveau Larousse Illustré Supplement* (Paris); also from an article by Alexander Harvey in *Current Opinion,* and from The *Times* (London) and The *Evening Sun* (New York).

he could in County Kerry, then attended a school at Villeneuve, in France, and with what coaching his father could give him, managed in 1868 to pass the entrance examinations for the Royal Military Academy at Woolwich. He was in Dinan, waiting to learn the result of his final examinations when, in 1870, Louis Napoleon surrendered at Sedan and the French Government of National Defense led by Gambetta called Chanzy from Algiers and gave him command of the Army of the Loire. In the great wave of war-feeling that ensued young Kitchener found himself swept into the ranks of the French Mobiles, and after his British commission arrived, enlisted as a sub-lieutenant of Royal Engineers. Despite the protests of his father who feared the wrath of the British War Office, young Kitchener took the field as a French soldier to fight in the ranks where he learned a lesson that stood him in good stead years afterward in the Sudan and in South Africa, which was—that in modern warfare valor is worth nothing if not backed by a thorough organization.

In that terrible winter campaign of 1870-71, in France, Kitchener saw miles of freight-cars stalled when already loaded with needed war material; soldiers freezing for lack of overcoats that were stored in plenty half a mile away, with no one to release them, and starving for food that was rotting because there was lack of machinery for its distribution. His first campaign ended rather ingloriously in a balloon ascent, in which, his clothes getting wet, he caught cold. Three months after he had left Dinan as a soldier of France, Kitchener found himself back under his father's roof and in bed near death with pleurisy. In 1871, with the Franco-Prussian war ended, he joined the British Engineers and for three years worked at Chatham and Aldershot. He was then detached to work in a semi-civil capacity on the Palestine Survey and passed four years measuring land and learning the ways and speech of the people. In Palestine, as afterward in Cyrus and Egypt, he adapted himself to the ways of natives, came to understand the secret workings of their minds, and acquired not only their language but their intonation in speech, until he could live among Arabs almost as safe from detection as Kipling's "Kim" could live in the crowded streets of Lahore.

When England acquired Cyprus in 1878 Kitchener was placed in charge of its exploration. The maps and reports he sent to London were models. In 1880 he was made British Vice-Consul at Erzerum. After the bombardment of Alexandria in 1883, when England had to reorganize the Egyptian army, Kitchener's professional opportunity arrived when he was one of twenty-six men chosen to raise in Egypt a force of 6,000 men for defense of the country, and attached to the Egyptian Intelligence Department, where he was told to "lick the cavalry into shape." Kitchener found the Egyptian fellah like a bicycle—incapable of standing alone, but very useful in the hands of a skilled master. In ten weeks after the arrival of his first raw recruits, he had 5,600 men who could go through ceremonial parade movements like British guards in Hyde Park, and do it with precision.

Kitchener served in Egypt for fourteen years. He was with the Gordon Relief Expedition in 1884 and stayed in the country till the hero of Khartoum was avenged and a cathedral raised over the spot where he had fallen. Severely wounded at Handoub by a bullet that shattered his jaw and buried itself in his neck, he was invalided back to England, but in 1888 returned to head the First Brigade of Sudanese troops at Toski, where he led the final charge. After serving as Governor-General of the Red Sea Littoral and Commandant of Suakim, he was made Chief of Police at Cairo, and, on Lord Cromer's recommendation, in 1892 was promoted to be Sirdar, altho he was then only Colonel. Four years later Kitchener began the reconquest of the Sudan and in the Dongola expedition won the rank of Major-General.

Next year he started out to avenge Gordon's death. His first step was to plan a railroad from Cairo to Khartoum which from Halfa to Abu Hamed would have to cross 230 miles of sand. Experts scoffed at his idea. In that dry country the entire carrying capacity of a train they said would have to be taken up by the water-supply alone necessary for the locomotive. But Kitchener started his road and as he built it he bored in the sand until, just where he needed it, he struck water. The road was finished in 1897. In the following year Kitchener won the battle of the Atbara, and caught up with the Mahdi's forces at Omdurman, which sealed the Khalifa's doom, and avenged Gordon. He cut off the dervishes' retreat, and as they were huddled in a hollow around their standards, played on them with machine-guns, killing about 15,000, and thus wiped out the last trace of Mahdism. The Mahdi's tomb, the great shrine of the dervishes, Kitchener demolished and so scattered the mummy contained therein that no part of it could ever be found and used as a focus of future trouble. Kitchener had given peace to Egypt and was created Baron Kitchener of Khartoum, with the Grand Cross of the Order of the Bath, the thanks of Parliament, and $150,000—the Kaiser telegraphing his congratulations.

Only two weeks after Omdurman, Kitchener's forces, on an historic occasion memorable in all stories of the World War, met at Fashoda the French officer, Marchand, with eight other French officers and 120 Sudanese tirailleurs. After negotiations ending in the final withdrawal of the French from Fashoda, the whole of the Sudan was in the hands of England, and Kitchener began to build it up. His powers of organization led to the creation there of a new civilization. Within a year the Boer war broke out, with British disasters at Stormberg, Magersfontein, and Colenso. Lord Roberts was sent out and Kitchener, still Sirdar of the Egyptian Army, promoted to be Lieutenant-General and made Roberts' Chief of Staff. He arrived in Cape Town in January, 1900, and in November, after Roberts left for England, took supreme command.

Kitchener built across the Transvaal a line of blockhouses con-

KITCHENER IN A TRENCH IN GALLIPOLI
During this visit, made late in 1915, Kitchener was frequently within a few yards of Turkish trenches. The withdrawal from Gallipoli was a consequence of Kitchener's observations. He is standing at the extreme left

nected by wires charged with electricity; put sixty mobile columns into the field, and had all women, children and non-combatants taken off farms and placed in concentration camps. By a slow process the Boers were worn down, and in May, 1902, the long struggle ended. It was Kitchener's work—not the work of a dashing soldier, or a brilliant tactician, but the work of a plodding, methodical traffic superintendent with an organization in which nothing was left to chance. Kitchener had trained himself to regard war as an industry.

To him it meant raising, clothing, arming, feeding, and caring for men, and placing them in positions where they could not lose, and placing the enemy in positions where they could not win. An actual battle he looked upon as a necessary, but noisy and rather vulgar, affair. When he fought a battle, however, it was without feeling for the safety of any one. He was personally responsible for the frontal attack at Paardeberg, the bloodiest in the South African War. For this new service Kitchener was made a viscount, advanced to the rank of general "for distinguished service," and given the thanks of Parliament with $250,000, and the Order of Merit.

No sooner was peace signed with the Boers than Kitchener was sent as Commander-in-Chief to India where, in seven years, he revolutionized the army and freed it from red tape. He put an instant end to polo-playing and whisky-and-soda drinking in garrison life, made every one work, and thanked no one for working. Just as in South Africa he had sent back to England more than 400 officers as "useless," so he weeded out incompetents in India. Failures were treated with unbending severity, whether committed by men in high or low places. He never played favorites and never permitted an excuse to prevail. The rank and file loved Kitchener. Women were greatly attracted to him but he never married. There seemed to him an element of chance in matrimony, and no one could imagine Kitchener leaving anything to chance. This tall, handsome man was no woman-hater, however, and yet he did not carry his heart upon his sleeve, being the most undemonstrative of men, unreadable, still-faced, iron-jawed and wordless, with hard gray eyes that looked over other men's heads, and told of a soul of steel fortified by great physical strength. Over a six-foot two inches frame his muscles were stretched like wire rope. At sixty-four he was lithe and wiry. Altho his bearing was dignified and cold, he could display at times the agility of a cat. In an accident in India, where other men might have lost their lives, he escaped with only a broken leg.

After leaving India with the rank of Field-Marshal, Kitchener succeeded the Duke of Connaught as Commander-in-Chief and High Commissioner in the Mediterranean, and made a tour of England's colonies to organize fighting forces. On his way from Australia he visited Japan and the United States, returning to England in 1910. When the war began his latest service had been in Egypt, where he went to continue Lord Cromer's work and succeeded in restoring the fellah to the land. With a grant of $15,000,000 from the British Government, he created a great cotton-raising industry which so changed economic conditions along the Nile that a nationalist movement which had threatened to create trouble almost died out. When the war broke out, Kitchener was in England, having been called there for promotion to an earldom. The Prime Minister at once made the new earl Secretary of State for War. His first question when he went to the War Office was, "Is there a bed here?" When told there was none, he replied, "Get one." At the War Office Kitchener slept only five hours out of twenty-four, leaving his post each morning at 1 o'clock and returning before 9.

Kitchener was one of the first men in Europe to forecast a long war. His announcement, made within a fortnight of his appointment as Secretary for War, that the war would be of three years' duration, came as a shock to people all over the world who had been led to believe that in six months everything would be over except the shouting. He at once set to work to recruit 5,000,000 men, known afterward as "Kitchener's armies." As he seldom did any talking, he was called inarticulate; but Kitchener could talk when he wished, his words curt in the manner of a soldier. A remark from a cockney non-commissioned officer became current, "'E's no talker; not 'im. 'E's hall steel and hice." That was Kitchener—all steel and ice!

The decision of the Government to entrust Kitchener with supreme direction of the war was received in England with unanimous approval. As the war advanced, Great Britain's deficiencies, particularly in artillery ammunition, became apparent, and Kitchener was subjected to severe criticism, led by Lord Northcliffe of the London *Times,* who charged him with responsibility for failure to foresee an extraordinary demand for heavy shells. As a result there was formed a Ministry of Munitions with David Lloyd George at its head, and Kitchener's responsibilities were further lessened by the appointment of General Sir William Robertson as Chief of the Imperial Staff. Notwithstanding criticisms his great accomplishments during the war were recognized universally. Foremost among them was his creation from England's untrained manhood of a huge army. At the beginning of the war Great Britain had only a few hundred thousand trained men. When Kitchener died more than 5,000,000 had been enrolled in various branches of the service.

The trip in which Kitchener lost his life (he was on his way to Russia) was not the first time he had ventured to cross the seas during the war. He went to France at an early stage of hostilities, and later, while British troops were hanging on to Gallipoli, went to the Near East. Landing at Kum Kale, he visited first-line trenches, surveyed positions, and, as the British troops were withdrawn from the peninsula a few months afterward, was believed to have reported back the inadvisability of attempting to press operations on the peninsula to a successful conclusion. Before he sailed for Russia, the last heard of him in England was that he had been to Westminster Palace to be questioned by members of the House of Commons, who were not satisfied with the conduct of the war.

In the first weeks of the war occurred a famous hoax. A body of Russian soldiers, said to number 100,000 men or more, was reported to have circled around from Archangel, landed in Scottish ports, and been shipped through at night to reinforce the British in France. The scheme of sending them in this way to the Western Front was declared to have originated with Kitchener. The myth spread rapidly through the United Kingdom, with any number of witnesses to swear they had seen and talked in England with the Russians in their native language. For a long period the reports were not denied and belief in them deepened. Months afterward a British officer declared that the story had been given out for the purpose of impressing German commanders in Belgium and northern France and so to keep them in fear of a surprize either in the rear or on the western flank. Perhaps the ruse accomplished a purpose. Dread of Russians coming to France did become real among the German staff, and may have accounted to some extent, at least psychologically, for the retreat of Kluck from Paris. Kitchener was said to have caused a hundred transports laden with sundry goods to be sent from Scottish ports to Archangel, and in order to give further color to the hoax, had insured them in Holland, where the Germans would be sure to hear of it. When British troops were moved from various points in Scotland and the north of England to Channel ports, he had directed that the blinds of the trains should be lowered so as to arouse popular curiosity and speculation—in fact, to encourage the belief that these soldiers were Russians.[20]

ALEXANDER VON KLUCK, German Field-Marshal

Kluck was one of the few military men in history—Xenophon was another—who won fame by a successful retreat. In that famous swoop of his on Paris, in August and September, 1914, he became for a time the foremost figure in world news—almost the only commander of whom men heard—but before the year ended he was relieved of his command and soon was heard of no more outside of Germany. In 1871 Kluck was a sub-lieutenant, his regiment stationed just outside Paris, where it waited until the first few millions of the billion dollar indemnity were paid by France to Germany, and then, in accordance with Bismarck's iron-bound agreement, marched with his regiment back twenty miles toward Germany, and there waited on French soil until another portion was paid. Months later, when

[20] Compiled from an article by Henry N. Hall in *The World* (New York), from Associated Press correspondence and from The *Evening Post* (New York).

the second portion was paid, his regiment marched back another twenty miles. This was Kluck's first retreat from Paris, but it took longer than the second, for it occupied a year and a half. Kluck in 1914 had been put in the position of greatest danger, because he was regarded by the High Command as their ablest officer in the field.

Eminent soldiers have almost always been silent men—Grant and Lee, Kitchener and Joffre, and now Kluck. A story told in Berlin illustrated this quality. He had just been appointed Inspector-General of three army corps, a position which made him practically suzerain over a quarter of a million men. Some learned society, numbering among its members leading men, requested him to address them on the duties of his position. Kluck replied with a courteous declination. He had twice been a professor in military schools, and of course had spoken before professional soldiers concerning their duties, but that was different from speaking about his own duties to a learned society. Soon afterward the society secured from the Emperor himself an intimation to Kluck that he might appear before it; Kluck now had to go. His address was, perhaps, the shortest of the kind on record. "Gentlemen," said he, "it is the duty of a soldier to obey. That is why I have come here and am speaking to you. Thank you." Kluck then took his seat.

He was plain Kluck without the "von" for fifty years. When making him a colonel, the Emperor placed "von" before his name, which if not quite befitting a man in command of a regiment, was better adapted to one who had married a Baroness. Kluck was the son of a minor Government official, and had entered the army in 1865, when nineteen years old. In the war against Austria he was a sub-lieutenant in the campaign directed against the southern German States, Bavaria and Württemberg. In 1870 he served in all the operations about Metz, and at Colomby Neuilly gained the Iron Cross, without which a German officer would feel that he had lived in vain. During the year and a half he spent on French soil, following the treaty of peace, he had ample opportunity to become acquainted with the topography of the country over which he so desperately contested the French advance in the battle of the Marne.

In his own person, Kluck conveyed a sense of fatherhood to his soldiers. He was not as formal and silent as many commanders. He had a stout figure that inspired confidence. Because of his ability to "get under the hide," as it were, of the common soldier, he was advanced in 1881 to the post of teacher in a school for non-commissioned officers. Here he was so successful that in the following year he received a similar appointment at another non-commissioned officer's school. He held these positions while only a captain in rank. In 1887 he was made a major and taught in a school at

Neubreisach. Next year he took command of a battalion of infantry, was made a lieutenant-colonel of a regiment in 1893 and colonel in 1896. He was then stationed in Berlin, an unusual honor for an officer who had never been to the War Academy, and who had never served on the General Staff. His advancement was due to sterling qualities and real ability. In 1898 Kluck was put in command of Fusileer Regiment No. 34, and 1889 in command of the Twenty-third Infantry Brigade. In 1902 he became a lieutenant-general, in 1906 a general, and in the following year was placed in command of the Fifth Army Corps. In 1913 he was made an inspector-general, and was still on the active list when war was declared, altho then sixty-eight years old.

No hesitation was shown in placing him in command of the army that was to advance through Belgium to the gates of Paris. It was popularly understood that the Emperor's orders to Kluck had been to "take Paris or die." There was, however, no sound military reason for taking Paris, until the larger part of the French Army had been destroyed or captured. Kluck made a wonderful dash, a gigantic stab, as it were, at the French capital, but he missed his mark. One's balance might easily have been lost in that heroic dash. For days it was alternately hoped and feared that he might fail in his purpose and that he might not. He got away by the simple expedient of attacking as he retreated. He struck and fell back; and again he struck and fell back. When the French followed, they found him fully emplaced, with his flank on the Oise and facing a forest north of Compiègne, while his front was along the north bank of the Aisne, a river deep and unfordable. He was now in positions with which he had been familiar for forty-three years, in intrenchments previously prepared, and from which the French and British heroically battled in vain for over a month to dislodge him. After the Battle of the Aisne, Kluck, now sixty-nine years old, was retired. He had been made a field-marshal but the world heard of him no more.[21]

GENERAL ERIC LUDENDORFF, German Grand Quarter-Master-General

One's first impression of Ludendorff was that of a man with a large, rounded forehead denuded of hair, with eyes of profound blue, searching keenly. A blond mustache ran along thin lips. As a whole his face reflected an alert intelligence. His mentality contrasted strongly with that of Hindenburg, who had a heavy mass and ponderous look. Ludendorff's corpulence was large considering

[21] Adapted from an article by Richard Barry in The *Times* (New York).

his medium height, but he conveyed an impression of an energetic man, who felt entirely sure of himself and was in full physical and intellectual vigor. Henri Carre,[22] who knew him, declared at the zenith of Ludendorff's success that he was no abler man than Foch and that he had yet to display the same artistry. By nature he was indefatigable, endowed with a supple mind, rich in expedients devised on the spur of the moment—a quality precious to the elder Moltke. He was a real soldier because he had imagination and ideas. All his qualities were accentuated by cool energy. He had a tenacious will and a strong soul.

As German commanders went, he was young, not much past fifty when the war began, and was born in the province of Posen, April 9, 1865. His rise had been so meteoric that ordinary reference-books in Germany failed to note its steps. He had the good luck to possess a far-seeing and wealthy parent of Prussian stock, who got him at seventeen into the Ploen Cadet School, from which he emerged as a sub-lieutenant in an infantry regiment at Wesel. Later he turned up as a lieutenant of marines at Kiel and then got into the grenadiers. From the War College he emerged at thirty with the rank of captain. How he got into the Great General Staff at Berlin in view of his comparatively mediocre origin, was not clear, but he went through the grades successfully, and proved himself an officer of the General Staff type, bred in the Moltke school and a creditable pupil of Schlieffen. When he was forty-seven, he took command of the Fusileers at Düsseldorf and not long after was at Strassburg as major-general of infantry. With the latter force he went into the grand mobilization in July and August, 1914.

In the siege of Liége, in August, 1914, Ludendorff happened to be on the spot when a major-general at the head of the leading brigade was struck by a bullet. Ludendorff assumed command in his place, led the brigade forward and became the first man to break into the fortified towns. This commended him to the Kaiser, who bestowed upon him the *Pour le Mérite,* founded by Frederick II, and attached him to the Headquarters Staff. When General von Prittwitz in the same month of August, while commanding in the east, retreated from the advancing hosts of Russia and allowed them to overrun East Prussia and Posen, penetrating to .Silesia and threatening Breslau and Berlin, Ludendorff took advantage of his presence in the immediate entourage of the Kaiser to recall to the latter's mind the almost forgotten "Old Man of the Lakes," and his hobby, the eastern defense against Russia. The Kaiser took up the idea and sent Ludendorff off by special train to fetch Hindenburg from his retirement in Hanover to assume supreme command of the

[22] A writer for *L'Illustration* (Paris).

Eastern Front, where, in a series of battles in the lakes, he managed to compel the Russians, hampered as they were at the time by lack of arms and munitions, to evacuate not only Prussian territory but the westernmost portion of Russian Poland.

Under these circumstances Ludendorff became chief of staff to Hindenburg.[23] Next year the two redeemed their native land from other pressing perils by the conquest of Poland and Galicia. Afterward, in consequence of the Brusiloff offensive, which for a time caused the German defense to halt, Hindenburg, still "doubled" with Ludendorff, received command of the Austro-Germans in the Eastern theater, and before many days replaced, as Chief of Staff, Falkenhayn—on whom was cast the blame for the Verdun check. With Hindenburg Chief of the General Staff, Ludendorff became his right-hand man, as general of infantry, exercising the functions of a Chief General Quartermaster. From that time until March, 1918, the two men "ticked like two clocks."

The whole German press was jubilant over the appointment of Hindenburg. "An immense delight," said one paper, "reigns everywhere in the Fatherland. Our new Blücher retains at his side our new Gneisenau. Ludendorff remains with Hindenburg." The Kaiser had really assented to the eclipse of his own imperial star by the rise of the twin constellation of Hindenburg-Ludendorff. The Field-marshal, free from jealousy or full of gratitude, permitted the personality of his right-hand man to grow constantly more decisive and conspicuous, and the collaboration of Hindenburg and Ludendorff became most intimate. One acted as the brain, the other as the right hand. One represented the young and active element, the fecund brain with "ideas," the other the mass which brought the weight to bear. Decisions seemed to have been taken in common, but they were for the most part inspired by Ludendorff. In the enormous machine one was the motor, the other the source of power. Ludendorff had the true directing mind. Force was eminently his characteristic. He was fond of saying that the strong man "does not talk of danger, but of the way to avoid it. A strong will creates its own destiny." He held that there was no such thing as fatality or destiny. There was only "the will of the strong man."

The character of Ludendorff was hard, cruel, and pitiless, in accordance with the dominant ideal of Prussians in high command. He was the most determined supporter of continued submarine warfare, and insisted upon constant aerial bombardments of open and unfortified towns. "By killing the women and children," he was quoted as saying, "we destroy future mothers and the ultimate defenders of their land; the future forces upon which the enemy de-

[23] F. Cunliffe Owen in The *Times* (New York).

pends." He was sly and affected, not above telling newspapers that the lives of German soldiers were more precious than some blackened ruin of a town that France had wanted preserved, and yet he was notoriously the most sanguinary of feeders of cannon with "fodder," never hesitating to pile high the plains of the Somme with German dead. He attached great importance to "morale" and no press agent had more skill. He kept in touch with journalists night and day, held regular receptions for his friends, the reporters, and was often quoted. He inspired a school of military experts who could keep on proving that Germany was invincible. He was a master of propaganda and used fairy-tales without scruple. He invented a system of heralding every German offensive far in advance, as "according to plan," arguing that the effect upon enemy "morale" would be tremendous. Ludendorff sought less a strategical surprize than a tactical one. An organizer of experience and ability, he excelled in preparation.

To German intellectuals of certain types Hindenburg presented a model of material beauty, if not brute force, in conformity with the Germanic ideal, and Ludendorff was a superior type of cerebral beauty, or incarnated strength of thought. Compared to the Field-Marshal, the Lieutenant-General seemed, however, of another culture and of a more refined essence. Ludendorff was a methodical spirit with a brain gifted with a remarkable sense of organization—a quality of which Germans were proud. He possest rare faculties of assimilation, and a prodigious power for work, and was more a master of himself than Hindenburg, who was subject to terrible outbursts of anger which sometimes made those about him tremble. Ludendorff, with greater coldness in his cruelty, was neither less hard nor less implacable. He was supposed to have conceived and ordered the deportation in masses of the Belgian civil population during the winter of 1917.

Nominally the Kaiser remained *"Ober Feldherr des Deutschen Reiches"* with his pompous title of Supreme War Lord, but the effective direction passed eventually into the hands of the Hindenburg-Ludendorff team. More than ever closely allied as "the War Twins," their names appeared in all mentions of the High Command. As the Emperor consented to efface himself before Hindenburg, so the latter slowly permitted the growth of the influence and fame of his clever lieutenant, Ludendorff, whose personality asserted itself more and more. Hindenburg had succeeded Falkenhayn, and so had Ludendorff replaced Freytag-Loringhoven, who attracted attention, in September, 1917, by the publication of a volume which created a sensation, "The Consequences of the World War," wherein he discust the reasons for the loss of the war by Germany; a strange book from a man who had occupied such high posts and was familiar with the secrets of the German General Staff. The book was supprest in Germany, but published in London and New York.

Official accounts of German military operations were often loquacious, and sometimes surpassingly false. Ludendorff, for the sake of explaining away facts, employed arguments that were rarely ingenious, and were mostly clumsy. Sometimes he would invent out of whole cloth an Allied attack that had been victoriously repulsed; at others he would pretend to discover that the plan of his adversary was to advance ten kilometers, when they had advanced only five, the difference being put down to the account of profits and losses for the German General Staff. When an Allied attack created a retirement of the German line which it was not possible to dissimulate, Ludendorff was not embarrassed, but would declare it to have been "a voluntary retirement to better positions, an elastic recoil from which the counter offensive will jump with a new bound, a feint meant to draw the enemy into a trap." With supreme skill he could describe territory he was forced to abandon as a "zone of subterranean dugouts, the possession of which lost its tactical value." All that happened, whether favorable or not, was "according to plan." Every engagement was represented as a German victory, with comments on "German courage," "the spirit of the German offensive," and "Prussian ardor." His masterpiece was put forth in August, 1918, when he had been driven out of the Marne salient and said "the enemy eluded us." Ludendorff became a master of the art of explaining away failures. His contrivances were of unheard-of clumsiness, but the German brain, strictly disciplined, accepted them and pretended to be satisfied with them. Until July 18, 1918, he kept this method going with some success. He kept trying it during his retreat from the Marne, but few of the wise were any longer deceived by him, even in Germany.

In the summer of 1918, in order to keep up the morale in the ranks of the army, Ludendorff hit upon the creation of a corps of *"Wohlfahrts Offizieren,"* or welfare officers, whose duty it was to answer queries from soldiers in the barracks. All kinds of military questions were answered. His purpose was to attract attention to news favorable to Germany and to convince fighters of the necessity of the war going on until it achieved the complete triumph of Germany. This propaganda was followed up, not only in the interior, but in the trenches, by a distribution of tracts, pamphlets, booklets, and posters proclaiming the superiority of a Hindenburg peace over a so-called peace of the Scheidemann and Erzberger type. Forced to busy themselves with the internal affairs of the nation, it was not surprizing to see Hindenburg and Ludendorff playing at certain moments an active political rôle, for example, in the great interior crisis of March, 1917, when Ludendorff came out energetically against Bethmann-Hollweg, reproaching him for lack of firmness and for moderation in military aims.

One could understand the place which Ludendorff held in the estimation of powerful German leaders when one remembered that even Bismarck had not been beyond the reach of imperial disfavor. The military party was incarnated in these two heads, and consolidated itself more and more as the sovereign power in Germany. Ludendorff, in particular, because of extraordinary activity in military, moral, and political domains, obtained a growing influence until his fame rose to that of Hindenburg. While the old Field-Marshal could wrap himself up in popular worship, the intellectual element appreciated Ludendorff still more, but both enjoyed the unlimited confidence of Germans. That Ludendorff should have succeeded in handling the sword as well as the dagger; that he should have used all the means, even the most barbarous, as well as the most criminal; that he should have cleverly utilized all the poisoned weapons of the German arsenal, treachery, corruption and lies, indicated a cunning spirit, fertile in resources, but they placed an indelible blot on his reputation as captain that could never be forgotten. If he struck powerful blows at the Entente, he nevertheless did not accomplish those truly great achievements which imprint on a man the mark of genius. If he won successes for a time it was almost invariably against weaker enemies and never by superiority of talent against an equal.

The Western theater of operations brought to Hindenburg and Ludendorff a series of uninterrupted checks and defeats after August, 1916, which was the date of their supreme command in that field of the war. If the team appeared formidable, it was not through genius and greatness, but by force, energy, and cruelty, much more incarnated in the vigorous maturity of Ludendorff than in the heavy senility of Hindenburg. Without doubt the two men, as representing in German eyes good servants of the empire, would have their place in a German Pantheon, but the battles engraved on their monuments would recall no more than mediocre victories over weaker foes—Belgians, Serbians, Russians, Roumanians—compared with those shining Entente names, the Marne, Verdun, the Somme, the Hindenburg Line, and the Argonne, which, when the war was over, were already blazing in golden letters on the shields of Joffre, Foch, Pétain, Haig, and Pershing.[24]

[24] Henri Carré in *L'Illustration* and *La Revue* (Paris) and F. Cunliffe Owen in The *Times* (New York).

AUGUST VON MACKENSEN, German Field-Marshal

It was often said that this was "an old man's war." The truth of the assertion was proved beyond doubt when only the ages of leading commanders and some statesmen were considered. While millions of very young men were paying the price of war with fatal illness, wounds, and sudden death, the men who were directing the sacrifice, who were determining just how many hundreds or thousands should be sacrificed, were nearly all middle-aged and some were really old men. Joffre, when the war began, was well over sixty, Kitchener and French were also over sixty, Hindenburg was sixty-seven, and Italy's leader, Cadorna, was seventy. Of the two German generals in command of the Austro-German forces that swept through Galicia in 1915, Linsingen was sixty-five and Mackensen sixty-four. Elderly and old men performed deeds in this war that would imprint their names indelibly on history. Oldest of them all was Clémenceau, seventy-six.

After the battle of Tannenberg, Mackensen won a place in German annals that for at least two years equalled Hindenburg's. He had made his way from obscurity with no help save his own ability. His career, as well as Hindenburg's, Joffre's, and Foch's, began in the Franco-Prussian War when he was a plain one-year volunteer, the son of a Saxon country squire. Ordered with a small detachment of hussars to make a reconnaissance in the direction of Wörth, where one of the great battles of the war was fought, he found that a bridge across a river, giving access to the village, had been destroyed. Only the supports were standing, but he managed to crawl from one support to another and so crept stealthily into the village and got the information needed, but he found the village filled with Zouaves, who opened fire on him. With great difficulty he got back within German lines.

Recklessness in youth gave place in the mature Mackensen to an imperturable calm. He was called "sphinx-like," because of his aversion to unnecessary conversation. He never discust a plan until it was distinctly outlined in his own mind. Then he was willing to listen to comment and criticism, and would make any changes that subordinates convinced him were necessary. Mackensen was one of the few German officers who had not graduated from the War College, and yet he was recognized as one of the greatest strategists in the army, a master of organization and concentration. Many stories were told of his democratic demeanor. During the Lodz campaign against Russia he issued strict orders to outposts to allow nobody to pass, except with a special permit signed by himself. One day he and several staff officers were inspecting outposts, when a Bavarian trooper, disregarding the coat of arms on the automobile in which Mackensen rode, stopt his party at a rifle's point because they could not show passports. Officers with Mackensen in vain told the sentry that he was delaying the commander-in-chief. Mackensen said nothing, except to send for the commander of the outpost, who, on arriving, ordered the sentry to let him pass. A few days later the Bavarian trooper, by express direction of Mackensen, was made a sergeant. These and similar actions endeared him to soldiers. The word of the "old man" was law, his judgment infallible. During the early stages of the fight around Lodz he was repulsed with great losses, but his soldiers never murmured. "It's part of the old man's plan," they said, and went cheerfully on with the battle.

After the Dunajec and the great drive into Russia that followed in the summer of 1915, Mackensen received a monster petition from the German people expressing their gratitude to the "Liberator of East Prussia"—a term they had applied to Hindenburg the year before, after Tannenberg. Mackensen had received many honors, including degrees from two universities. With it all he remained a simple, hard-working soldier. The hussars with whom he had served in 1870 remained his first love. He usually wore their uniform, and his first Iron Cross, won as a hussar scout, was pinned to it. Mackensen as head of German and Austrian armies, in the drive of 1915, smashed through the Russian lines on the Dunajec with extraordinary swiftness, crumpled them up and sent them headlong backward with armies that had been surging over the Carpathians threatening the Hungarian plain. He pursued them relentlessly to the San, crossed in a tempest of artillery-fire, wrested from them the fortress of Przemysl (two months after it had been taken from Austria), and threatened Lemberg, which had been the first fruit of the Russian onslaught of 1914. Looked at from any angle, Mackensen's achievement was tremendous. It will live alongside other audacious and brilliantly successful military feats. Just as the sudden rise of other men in this war had made people in 1914 ask, "Who is Joffre?" or "Who is Hindenburg?" so they had asked, "Who is this man Mackensen? What has he ever done before?"

When Hindenburg hurled his legions upon Russians covering Lodz at the end of 1914, Mackensen was his right-hand officer. He drove into the heart of the battlefield, got himself surrounded by Russians, and was close to annihilation, when he rallied his men and cut a pathway through with bayonets, not only saving his army but seriously shattering the Russian forces. He had "escaped from the trap and taken the trap with him," somebody said. The lion's share of the glory went to Hindenburg; but there was plenty of it left for

Mackensen. He was often called the hero of Lodz as well as of Galicia.

Mackensen was born on December 6, 1849, at Haus-Leipnitz, near Schmiedeberg, in Saxony. Before his twentieth birthday he was serving with the colors in the Second Hussar Body-Guards, already famous in German annals. When the Franco-German war began he went to the front with his regiment in the humble capacity of *"Vice Wachtmeister."* After marching to Paris with the German armies and seeing William of Prussia crowned German Emperor at Versailles, he entered upon the long years of peace that ensued by going to the University of Halle, and did not return to the army until 1873, when he joined his hussar regiment again. Later he was made adjutant of the First Cavalry Brigade and stationed at Königsberg. In 1892 he wrote a history of the Hussar Body-Guards for the celebration of the 150th anniversary of the regiment, in which he recounted their exploits in the Franco-German and other wars.

Of all the great reputations made by the war, that which had the greatest *réclame* was probably the least important—Hindenburg's, altho his victory in the Masurian Lakes was for the time one of the few decisive incidents of the war; it was a victory in a complete and real sense, and due entirely to superior generalship. On ground that he knew thoroughly Hindenburg had maneuvered Samsonov's army into swamps and achieved the most sensational victory of the war, at once revered as the savior of his country, until in the popular imagination he overshadowed every other figure and had the whole nation at his feet. Great as the achievement was, it was not as great, however, as the public estimate of it made it seem. It was inflated in importance by the East Prussian panic that had preceded it. Those who followed campaigns with expert knowledge and examined battles in detail held Mackensen in higher regard than Hindenburg.

Like Hindenburg he had been ignored at the beginning of the war. His troubles with the Crown Prince had culminated early in 1914 in a request that either he or the Prince be removed from Danzig. The result was that Mackensen remained and the Prince was recalled. Then the war broke out, and the Prince was placed in command of an army in the West, while Mackensen was left to cool his heels in the East doing obscure tasks. Not until some months passed did he emerge, as second in command to Hindenburg on the Russian front. His first achievement was his skilful extrication of his army from envelopment east of Lodz. After that every task of critical importance in the East was committed to Mackensen's hands. His smashing blow on the Dunajec opened sensationally a new and formidable phase of the war. The operations that followed, by which the Russian left was forced back to the Privet marshes, revealed a grim power not inferior to Hindenburg's and a constructive subtlety which Hindenburg had never shown. His campaign in Serbia was on a smaller scale, but here again his strategy was of a fresh and original character that commanded the respect of students of war.

No campaigns in the war were studied by military experts with more attention than those of Mackensen. Unlike Hindenburg, he was silent, almost morose, a characteristic popularly attributed to the loss of a much-beloved wife, but in reality his manner was the natural habit of a singularly absorbed and self-contained man. His brevity of speech was the expression of a ruthless temper. In the severity of the demands he made on all who came under his will, as well as in his cold and concentrated silence, he was reminiscent of Kitchener. Miracles were performed by soldiers and civilians during his advances, not because of affection for him, but because of fear.[25]

PEYTON CONWAY MARCH, Chief of Staff, United States Army

General March was born December 27, 1864, at Easton, Pa. He was graduated from the United States Military Academy in 1888, and from the Artillery School at Fort Monroe in 1898. He was in command of the Astor Battery during the Spanish-American War, 1898, and of the American forces in action at Tilad Pass, Luzon, P. I., December 2, 1899, during which engagement General Gregorio del Pilar was killed. During this expedition General March received the surrender of General Venancio Concepcion, chief of the staff to Aguinaldo.

March was appointed Military and Civil Governor of the district of Lepanto-Bontoc and the southern half of Ilocus Sur in 1900, and the province of Abra till February, 1901. He then served as Commissary-General of Prisoners until June 30, 1901. He was appointed member of the General Staff, 1903-1907, and Military Attaché with the Japanese Army in the Russo-Japanese War, 1904. As Army Artillery Commander of the American Expeditionary Force, he went to France in 1917, and was appointed Acting Chief of the Staff of the United States Army, February, 1918.

General March has been cited several times for distinguished gallantry in action from 1898 to 1902. He was promoted to rank of major-general January 4, 1918, and on his return from France asked for modification of the censorship that then prevailed. He

[25] Compiled from articles in The *Public Ledger* (Philadelphia), The *Times* and The *Tribune* (New York) and one in *The Atlantic Monthly* by A. C. Gardiner.

assumed his duties as Chief of the Staff March 4, and allayed the alarm in the United States that followed the battle of Picardy in March, 1918, pointing out that there was really little cause for it. He was nominated to the rank of General May 20, 1918, and the nomination was confirmed by the Senate May 24. On June 22, 1918, in an interview with newspaper men, he announced that 900,000 American troops were in Europe and that 100,000 more were being transported weekly. Whether in active service or in office, General Peyton March had shown himself to be eminently capable as an organizer and commanding officer.[26]

SIR STANLEY MAUDE, British General in Mesopotamia

More than a year after Maude recovered Kut-el-Amara, captured Bagdad, and then suddenly died in Mesopotamia, Lloyd George rose in the House of Commons and told how he had "died a victim of his own inbred courtesy." Maude was visiting a plague-stricken area at the invitation of its inhabitants who wished to thank him for many kindnesses and he knew the peril so well that he "forbade any soldier of his escort to eat or drink during the visit." But when the ceremonial cup was offered to Maude, as a part of the welcoming festivity, "he ran the risk himself rather than hurt the susceptibilities of people who had asked him to come. There was cholera in that cup, and he died in a few days." Maude, said Lloyd George, would be remembered as one of "the great figures of this war." While he did not know what destiny was in store for the land Maude had conquered, he was certain that "the whole course of its history will be changed for the better as a result of his victory and rule." He would always be cherished by its inhabitants as "the gentlest conqueror who ever entered a city's gates." The House of Commons then voted £25,000 to Maude's widow.

Bagdad was a long way from Belgium, and it was much easier to form an idea of Haig or Pétain, because we had seen so many photographs of them, and read so many stories about them; but in Maude England had a general about whom a legend soon grew up very like the one about Kitchener. The Kitchener comparison suggested itself because of the striking parallel between the Bagdad campaign and Kitchener's Nile campaign to Omdurman and Khartoum. As Kitchener had been, so Maude was faced by the problem of advancing into a desert along a river which had to furnish his line of communication. Maude had to create transport, hospitals, housing, sanitation, and water-supply. He was obliged to rely for munitions and supplies on bases far overseas, with the additional menace of a

[26] Compiled from "Who's Who, 1918-1919" and The *Times* (New York).

hostile sea-power. He had to contend with an alien climate in which white troops could work only in the cool months of the year.

Maude's story was that of a six months' offensive campaign which resulted in the recapture of Kut-el-Amara and the taking of Bagdad, the reestablishment of British prestige in the East, and the defeat of the German threat toward India. Before he advanced a foot he had to have every contingency provided for, and every precaution taken against failure. He had the strength of the man who is sure of himself, the ability to bide his time, to keep his own counsel, to drive men unmercifully, and yet to inspire all about him with his own indomitable spirit. The Tommies adored him. He was a silent man with a face clean-cut and strong. He drove his staff terribly, and when an officer made a blunder he gave punishment. At the same time his men had implicit confidence in him.

Maude reached the British base in Mesopotamia, sixty miles up the Shatt-el-Arab, the stream formed by the junction of the Tigris and the Euphrates, in August, 1916. From then until December 13 he devoted himself entirely to the work of organizing the campaign he had in mind. During his preparations Maude left only a few troops on the fighting-line just below Kut, where the Turks held the apparently impregnable Sunniyatt position, between the left bank of the Tigris and a small lake. The British Army had been reinforced until it was much larger than the army under Townshend that had tried unsuccessfully to get to Bagdad. Including coolies, transport, commissariat, base troops, boatmen, and other units behind the line, the Mesopotamian Expeditionary Force, as it was called, must have numbered 300,000 men. Of fighting troops he had four complete divisions and part of three others. Townshend's force was almost inconsiderable compared with this.

Maude did not rest with the recapture of Kut. He followed up the Turks by land and water. The greatest fighters in his army who had been marching up the right bank of the Tigris arrived in the suburb of Bagdad in the early morning of March 11. Among the troops in this division were battalions of the Black Watch, Seaforths, and Leicesters. The Seventh Division claimed that they entered Bagdad first, but the Lancashire battalions of the Thirteenth Division said they had entered at the same time or earlier from the south. The British casualties in the whole campaign were about 30,000. The only flag found flying in Bagdad was an American one, and the American Consul, Oscar Heiser, was about the only check to the lawlessness that prevailed during the evacuation. The British kept on after reaching Bagdad, and by May 1 were fighting about 100 miles north of the city, 32 miles above Samara. Not long after this achievement Maude came to his untimely end.

SKETCHES, PEACE TREATY, CHRONOLOGY

GENERAL VON MOLTKE, Chief of Staff of the German Armies

Moltke, being chief of staff at the time, had the disposition and direction of the German forces at the outbreak of the war, but after several months was displaced and a little more than a year afterward was in his grave. He was four years older than his French antagonist, Joffre, and looked what he was, a typical product of German militarism, his face like a mask, rigid, formal, official. He was known as a "Kaiserman," that is to say, he was, and for many years had been, a favorite, holding his position by a combination of favor and ability—altho rumor had several times declared that his star at court had grown dim and only the Kaiser's inability to find a suitable successor had kept him where he was. When his uncle, the famous Field-Marshal, died in 1891, he became aide-de-camp to the Kaiser and had been Chief of the General Staff of the army since February, 1904.

The younger Moltke did not show himself a great military genius. Many believed him less able than others in the German Army, among them von der Goltz. His promotion as Chief of Staff caused a good deal of unfavorable comment, which, however, disappeared with time after he had given evidence of being able to do an extraordinary amount of work. Probably he owed his capture of "the blue ribbon" more to possession of a great name than to eminent military abilities. It well might have flattered the Kaiser's martial pride to have another Moltke at the head of his army, but many writers felt that really able soldiers had been displaced in order to make room for him. Altho he had Bismarckian bulk, he was never genuinely popular with army officers because of an alleged softness in his nature. German martinets preferred a man with square head and bulldog physiognomy, such as Hindenburg possest, that idol of East Prussia, who once said he had never wasted an hour on light literature and ascribed his prowess to the fact that his mind had never been poisoned by anything so corrosive as poetry and romance.

The dismissal of Moltke, which was officially announced early in November, 1914, produced a significant effect on Berlin. Nobody believed he had left his post on account of ill-health, as the authorities declared. There had been a rupture between him and the Kaiser. His illness, perhaps, was not wholly a myth, but the true reason for his dismissal probably lay in court intrigues and disputes, including a desire by the Crown Prince to act on his own initiative, and to the autocratic ways of the Kaiser. Recent failures in theaters of war had contributed in no small degree to the Kaiser's decision. Moltke died of heart disease or apoplexy during a service of mourning in the Reichstag for von der Goltz.

F. W. Wile, writing in the London *Daily Mail,* said he could testify to the literal accuracy of a piece of history which identified Moltke with a military clique in Berlin which on August 1, 1914, induced the Kaiser to abandon all his remaining doubts as to the wisdom of declaring war. On the afternoon of that fateful Saturday, Moltke's wife paid a visit to a certain home in Berlin "in a state of irrepressible excitement." "Ach! what a day I've been through," she said to Mr. Wile's informant. "My husband came home just before I left, almost the first I've seen him in three days and nights. He threw himself on a couch, a complete physical wreck, and said he had finally accomplished the hardest task of his life. He had helped to induce the Kaiser to sign the mobilization order."

During the fall of 1914 there had been repeated announcements of Moltke's illness, and it was said that he had been removed. These reports proved for the time false, but in December he actually retired, failing health having prevented him from returning to the front. Falkenhayn was appointed in his place in the following January. Moltke was born in Mecklenburg-Schwerin, and at the outbreak of war was in his sixty-seventh year. He had served as adjutant to his distinguished uncle from 1881 until the old man's death. While the Field-Marshal was being taken to his grave, Emperor William had informed the younger Moltke that he had decided to elevate him to the rank of personal aide-de-camp, and in that position he had served for five years. Moltke also held regimental and divisional commands in the Guards, and in 1914, when the Emperor created the position of Quartermaster-General on the General Staff, a place that formerly had been filled only in war time, he designated Moltke for the post. Two years later he succeeded Count Von Schlieffen as Chief of the General Staff.

Moltke's career up to that time had therefore been exceptional. As a young man during the Franco-Prussian war he had won an Iron Cross, and in 1902 was made a Lieutenant-General. When appointed to succeed Schlieffen, men in the army and in civil life said he owed the prize primarily to the Emperor's passion for the picturesque, to a desire to have the magic name of Moltke at the head of the army. Moltke was often called "Count," but that title, conferred on his uncle in 1870, on the day Metz fell, was inherited by his elder brother, General Count Wilhelm von Moltke, and had ceased with his death a few years before the war began. Moltke, after his fall, still retained the confidence of the German people. When first appointed to the post they had distrusted and ridiculed him, but the vigorous way in which he put through revolutionary ideas about "preparedness" forced them to change their minds. The rapidity and smoothness of the German mobilization at the beginning of the war was largely credited to him. He was held responsible, however, for the retreat of Kluck's army from before Paris, altho many believed the blame should have been laid elsewhere. A cloud of mystery pervaded the question as to why the German army retired as it did.[27]

THE GRAND DUKE NICHOLAS, COMMANDER-IN-CHIEF OF THE RUSSIAN ARMIES

Altho he was nearing his sixtieth year when the war began, and suffering from a reaction against him in the mind of the Czar and his court, the Grand Duke Nicholas was a logical necessity. Russia really had to entrust her destinies to him and nobly did he justify his command in those first years of the war, even after he was relieved of his command and sent to the Caucasus, there to startle the world by taking Erzerum and Trebizond. He was the one man of genius in the Russian royal family. He manifested military genius, not only in the boldness of his strategy and the success with which he realized his aims, but in a subtle influence called personality. He had the piety of genius, its reverence and mystical tendencies, its energy, and its decision of character. Russian reserve, as reflected in official communications, was seen in this Grand Duke, but in spite of that he permitted journalists to follow his armies with a freedom at which the French and British stood amazed. He was audacious in decision and rapid in thought.

Behind the Grand Duke were years of the hardest work. He had spent his young manhood in comparative poverty on remote frontiers, where he had acquired a mastery of his profession on its technical side such as made him the finest cavalry officer in Europe. He had never been the slave of vodka or of ballet-dancers. His piety was no less striking than his lofty stature. Those who studied him at close range saw a Grand Duke tinged with that western culture which was dear to a certain type of Russian. In temperament he was conspicuously a Slav, for he had the fatalism, poetic melancholy and characteristic spirituality of his race. He always distrusted the tendency of his countrymen to adopt western manners and methods in society as things remote from the spirit of the Russian race. His idea always was that Holy Russia embodied a genius capable of developing best along lines of her own, spontaneously, organically, without the adventitious aid of outside culture. This attitude explained his reputation as a reactionary.

[27] Based on articles in *The World's Work* and The *Times* (New York).

Nothing could have been more humanly conspicuous than the Grand Duke as he strode at his gigantic height among throngs of worshippers at St. Isaac's, in Petrograd. His vein of mysticism made his religion the most emotional thing about him. He would stand like a man in a dream before the model of the holy sepulcher in that vast edifice. His sternly fanatical type of faith found expression in the campaigns he directed, which was done as if he were engaged in a crusade. The singing of hymns as troops went into battle, the carrying of images in camp and strict observances of feasts as well as fasts, were all due to him. He resembled Cromwell in admiration for the soldier who prayed.

Infinite gossip was circulated in newspapers regarding the relations between him and the Czar. Obscurity and disgrace seemed at times to threaten him. He would be missed from Tsarskoe Selo for weeks, and then in a trice would return and regain favor. When his wealthy wife died in Moscow he contracted a somewhat hasty second union with one of the daughters of Nicholas, the King of Montenegro, who was a Slav to the marrow, physically big, famed for a somewhat odalisque type of beauty, all imagination and fire, no thinker, but intuitive, subtle, wedded to weird superstitions, and even given to seeing ghosts. The shadow over her life was her failure to give birth to a child. To the influence of this new Grand Duchess over the Czarina was ascribed the rise of Nicholas to supremacy in the councils of Nicholas II. But for her he might have been sent into permanent exile, and yet he was the one great man in the Imperial family.

He was a soldier of the intellectual, executive type, capable of infusing his personality into a whole staff until it burned with energy. He inspired a devotion that did not shrink from death, had the magnetism of Ney, compelled confidence by the example of efficiency that he set, by his knowledge of his profession and his incorruptible nature. No financial scandal ever affected the repute of the Grand Duke—not even in a court notorious for corruption. He was most Russian in his comradeship with the men whom he commanded. This took the form of a spontaneous display of affection, a spiritual understanding, a unity like that of primitive Christians. Only a Slav could commune with Slavs on such a basis. The soul of the Grand Duke was simple, like a child's, sympathetic, capable of revealing itself without shame. In Petrograd, shortly after the Russian-Japanese War, Sir Ian Hamilton was watching the arrivals at a ceremonial occasion, he being there as a distinguished British general, when suddenly he ejaculated, "By Jove, who's that?" pointing to a towering figure, at least six feet four in height, with close-cropped black hair shot through with gray, short, pointed Vandyke beard, keen eyes, extraordinary length of limb, but lean and graceful, with exceptional ease and power of movement—a magnificent figure. It was the Grand Duke.

The Grand Duke was born the year after the Crimean War and so was fifty-seven in October, 1914. His grandfather was the son of Czar Nicholas I. Altho his military career had attracted little attention outside of Russia, largely because he had concentrated wholeheartedly on each task as he met it, his supreme command was the logical result of a consistent rise through all ranks. It was not because, but almost in spite of, his imperial blood. His rise began under his father, also a Grand Duke Nicholas, who commanded the Russian Army of the Danube in the Turkish War of 1877-78. The younger Nicholas was then about twenty-one, a junior officer of a hussar regiment, the uniform of which he took pride in wearing, when on the staff of General Radetzky. For gallantry in action at the Shipka Pass and the siege of Plevna, he was decorated. He was a fine horseman, hunted keenly, and gave the Czar instructions in military riding. His seat was quite peculiar to himself. His legs were enormously long and yet, whether for power or comfort, he rode with what for him were short stirrups. He sat back in the saddle and almost slouched, his feet stretched far forward, his knees sagging outward. The result was not easily described, but it was distinctly individual. In appearance he was the embodiment, on a gigantic scale, of a certain dashing type inseparably associated in the popular mind with heroic cavalry leaders.

None of the imperial family was assigned to high command in the Japanese War, which was the reason given for the Grand Duke Nicholas having stayed in Petrograd. But when the war was over, it found in the person of the Grand Duke one of the keenest minds in Russia as a student of its lessons. He was made President of the Council of Defense in 1905, and next year took command of the military district of Petrograd, which included not only the great garrison of the capital, but forces in Finland and in the vast stretch of territory northeastward to Archangel, the premier military district of Russia. Until 1906 he was known only as a cavalryman. He had been the only member of the imperial family to adopt a military profession as his chief purpose, with the possible exception of the Grand Duke Sergius, who became an artillery expert.

When he relaxed none could be more charming than Nicholas. He made it a practise to dine frequently at mess with his officers. Like many Russians he spoke several languages, including English. His position as the Czar's cousin and the dominant military figure in the imperial family relieved him of the political intrigues and jealousies which had nullified the genius of Kuropatkin in the

Japanese War. Personal and physical ascendency, coupled with solid expert knowledge, had free play.[28]

GENERAL JOHN J. PERSHING, COMMANDER OF THE UNITED STATES ARMIES IN FRANCE

In Linn County, Missouri, where he was born fifty-eight years before 1918, John Joseph Pershing, General in command of American troops to France, came to be revered something as the memory of Ulysses S. Grant has been revered in Clermont County, Ohio. No one from Laclede, Pershing's early home, or from any part of Linn County, so far as the Kansas City *Star* was able to discover, had ever done anything suggesting world fame or even national fame, except John Pershing. Pershing did enough in one and a half years mightily to flatter Laclede, and to prove that a soldier, if not a prophet, was not without honor in his own county. When Pershing took his examination for West Point, competing with others for an appointment by the Congressman from that district, the whole country came near losing him as a soldier, for he was only one point ahead of the next man, who was Higginbotham. A wrong answer to one question would have sent the other man to West Point and Pershing would have gone off in despair to become a lawyer, having had, as second choice, a predisposition for the legal profession. ✓ Firmness, discretion, dash, mastery of detail, comprehensive breadth of vision, patience and relentless determination were among the somewhat contradictory qualities accredited to Pershing. From the outset he had a quiet way of acquiring distinction and saying little or nothing about it. He won the highest honor West Point could confer when, twenty-six years old, he was graduated in 1886 as senior cadet captain. No mere "grind" or military athlete could have hoped to gain that honor. It betokened scholarly excellence and soldierly distinction, a sound and well-trained mind, in a body expert in management of arms and horses, and, above all, self-control, suggesting ability to command others. He left the academy for a more rigid training-school in the Southwest, where he plunged into the campaign against Geronimo and his Apaches, as a second lieutenant in the Sixth Cavalry, and in August, 1887, when scarcely a year from school, won special commendation from General Miles for "marching his troop with pack train over rough country, 140 miles in forty-six hours, and bringing in every man and animal in good condition." While at Fort Wingate, in 1889, with ten

[28] Adapted from an article compiled by Alexander Harvey for *Current Opinion*, from the *Gaulois* and *Figaro* (Paris), the *Tribune* and *Avanti* (Rome), the *Carriere* (Milan), *Truth* (London), and from an article by Basil Miles in *The World's Work*.

troopers he rescued a mixed group of cowboys and horse thieves when besieged by a hundred Zunis, and arrested the horse thieves after he had rescued them, all without firing a shot. By General Carr he was "highly commended for discretion"—not a common quality in a young man with a body as tough and powerful as his horse's and a demonstrated liking for rough-and-tumble work. In the Sioux wars of the early nineties, because of his knowledge of Indian fighting, he commanded scouts, and in the Cree campaign of 1896 again won "special recommendation for judgment and discretion."

Pershing's Western training now ended, but it left him to the end of his days a man of the southwest, silent, with frank, unprying eyes that looked men through, a gentle voice, chary of words, laughing but seldom, smiling a slow, quiet smile more of the eyes than the lips, and gifted with incisive turns of speech. The sobriquet "Black Jack" Pershing by which he was known among the rank and file was the result of his first promotion in 1895 when he was appointed to a colored troop—the Tenth Cavalry—a crack negro command that won fame at San Juan. This nickname stuck to him ever afterward.

Having made a thorough study of tactics, Pershing became known as one of the best strategists in the army. After his Indian campaign he was assigned to West Point as instructor and when war with Spain was declared, applied for and received command of the old Tenth Regiment which was among the first to be sent to Cuba, where he distinguished himself in the field. At El Caney Pershing was promoted for gallantry to the rank of captain. In 1901 he was chosen by General Chaffee, commanding in the Philippines, to cope with the oldest of all the difficulties Spain had left us and one she had always shirked. In the hills of western Mindanao, some thirty miles from the sea, lay Lanao, and around it were fierce, uncivilized Mohammedan Malays, industrious, frugal, murderous fanatics, who loved a fight, and whose simple creed made the killing of Christians a virtue. From a distance of several thousand miles the job did not sound big, but a more difficult task had seldom been given to an officer of the regular army. Pershing undertook the work with a smile. He had a picked lot of regulars under him, every man of whom he could trust.

Pershing found the Moros had mobilized in the crater of an extinct volcano called Bud Dajo, on the island of Jolo. To drive them out had been a task which the army had long contemplated. Pershing told his men the Moros would have to come out of the crater, if it took ten years to accomplish the job. There were 600 of them—every one a Mohammedan fanatic. Without Bud Dajo securely in

PART OF PERSHING'S ARMY HALTING ON THE MOSELLE AFTER LEAVING TRÈVES

On the hillside are seen some of the many vineyards for which the Moselle is famous. At Trèves Pershing established his headquarters

American control, the Moro problem could not be solved. With a thousand men, half of them Pershing's trusted troopers and the others picked Filipino scouts, the campaign began. Troops and scouts had to proceed through miles of dense jungle, opposed at every yard by Moros. But Pershing kept on, and finally fought his way to the foot of the mountain. His jungle-fighters then cut a trail around the mountain, and, fortifying themselves from attack from above, began the siege. Having formed a cordon around the mountain, they watched for the first sign of Moros leaving the crater. In their retreat to the crater the Moros had been so hotly pursued that they were unable to take with them supplies for a long stand. Pershing knew this and so he waited. After a time small detachments of Moros tried to gain the open by dashes through the American cordon, but every dash was frustrated, the fanatics rushing forth to certain death. On Christmas day, 1911, the 400 Moros who still held the crater did something a Moro seldom had done; they marched down the mountainside and surrendered. A few, however, got into the jungle, but regulars pursued them, and in the end they paid the penalty of their daring. Pershing then set about the task of completing the subjugation of the other Moros, and accomplished it when he won the battle of Bagsag, where they made a last stand.

Pershing now returned to Washington to serve in that city for awhile on the General Staff. He afterward went to Tokio as military attaché, first at the embassy and afterward with the army of Kuroki during the Russo-Japanese War. On September 26, 1906, he had a spectacular promotion which jumped him over 862 officers to the rank of Brigadier-General, and was again sent to the Philippines to command the department of Mindanao and Jolo. Later he served as Governor of the Moros and after eight years went to the Presidio in San Francisco where he took command of the Eighth Brigade. Four months later he was transferred with his troops to the Mexican border, where he had two years of routine patrol duty—time far from wasted, however, as was shown when as commander of the punitive expedition against Villa he marched into Mexico. The story of that march told why Pershing, in inside circles, came to be spoken of sometimes as the American Kitchener, the organizer and administrator, and why his later success as commander of the American forces in France gave occasion for no surprize in army circles where he was best known. What the battle-front in France might hold for him was at first a sealed book; but those who knew him best said he would come back either a national hero or with his body wrapt in the national flag.

How Pershing was recalled from Mexico soon after the United

States entered the World War, how he arrived in Washington to seat himself unnoticed at a desk in the War Department, and how he sailed away with a small force unknown to the public until he landed in England, unfolds the immediate steps to Pershing's entry into the great conflict in northern France. Colonel Roosevelt on one occasion when President addrest Congress on promotions in the Army and Navy. Promotions usually went by seniority and the army caste was jealous of the tradition. Roosevelt wanted the seniority rule abridged, and specifically mentioned Pershing as a gallant officer who had been held back by a tradition that worked him harm, as it often did to men who should have been advanced. In the gallery during the reading of this message was Frances Warren, daughter of United States Senator Warren of Wyoming. She followed the message closely, and when leaving the Capitol declared she would like to meet the officer who had merited such commendation. Less than two years afterward the soldier and the senator's daughter were married. Grim tragedy afterward entered into Pershing's married life when his wife and three children were burned to death in their home. Only one, Warren, his five-year-old son, was rescued. Lean but rugged, six feet and better, Pershing typified the ideal cavalry officer. He had been hardened by field service physically and broadened in executive work by service on difficult posts. He cared little for swivel-chairs and desks, but doted on boots and saddles.[29]

HENRI PHILIPPE PÉTAIN, Marshal of France

By promoting Pétain after the armistice to the rank of Marshal of France, which had already been conferred on Joffre and Foch, the French Government merely performed a duty which, not performed, would have awakened surprize, and even criticism, in the whole Entente world. The defender of Verdun had earned the right to a distinction already bestowed upon the victors of the first and second Marne. Foch, Joffre, and Pétain were the French soldiers who became most preeminent in this war. Before Verdun, Pétain had earned a solid military reputation. His offensive in the Champagne in 1915 was the first considerable victory of the Allies after the initiative had passed to them. It had only local results and was in no sense decisive, but it yielded more than 25,000 prisoners, more than a hundred guns and brought to Paris and London the first sense of victory. Verdun, however, had been the great achievement of Pétain. A situation as critical as that which confronted Foch

---

[29] Adapted from a compilation by Alexander Harvey in *Current Opinion*, based on articles in The *Star* (Kansas City), *The World* (New York), and The *Public Ledger* (Philadelphia).

confronted Pétain in the last days of February, 1916. Within a few days after he reached Verdun his army had accepted as their watchword, "They shall not pass"—an old Garibaldian cry which they had made their own. Pétain's strategy was to sell the Germans such parcels of ground as he could spare, at tremendous cost to them, and meanwhile to wait for the great new British Army in the north to get ready on the Somme for its first offensive of real magnitude. Verdun became the graveyard of German hopes. Nothing in French history is finer than its story. Pétain was the soul as well as the brains of that epic.

After Verdun the politicians chose a lieutenant of Pétain's instead of Pétain himself, to replace Joffre, who had grown old and weary. It was an unfortunate choice, and Nivelle's failure at the Aisne in April and May, 1917, for the moment shook the morale of the French army as well as that of the French nation. After that Pétain was chosen to reorganize the army and restore confidence. He transformed the situation in such fashion that, in a few months, the army was able to win a new victory at Verdun and Pétain obtained a shining success at the Aisne by taking Fort Malmaison. He suffered afterward from the rapid growth of the reputation of Foch. That the Allied commander-in-chief was the greater soldier will probably be the judgment of history, but that he owed much to the loyal and competent aid of Pétain was unmistakable. They worked in complete harmony at all times and this was a tribute to the patriotism of each. Not one of the three Marshals created in this war could have been suspected of the smallest selfish ambition. Magnificent as were their achievements, those of the civilian and republican, Georges Clémenceau, probably were as great. Without Clémenceau not even Foch could have saved France and brought about the German capitulation in the forest near Senlis.

Pétain's appointment as Marshal of France was made just as he was marching with his army into Metz. It was characteristic of the stern, grave way in which France entered into the war that she should have appointed no Marshal at its outbreak. The Marshal's baton was there waiting for some one, but it had first to be won by some extraordinary achievement. It had not been so in other times. Napoleon III fairly encumbered the French army with Marshals, appointed for no great services, and there was an additional drop of bitterness in the French cup of defeat in 1870, in the fact that the men who were so easily surrounded, played with, and beaten by the Germans, were all Marshals of France. It was a Marshal who surrendered Metz, and a Marshal who commanded the army which surrendered at Sedan. France then learned her lesson. She determined in this war to make no man a Marshal unless he compelled her to do so, and three men had now compelled her. Joffre did not get his baton until he had retired from leadership and his fame was forever secure. Pétain did not get his until he had marched into Metz at the end of the war. In Foch's case France was hurried into giving him a Marshalship while yet there was a chance of defeat; because he had been made Generalissimo he had to have the highest rank. This stern rule had made the title of Marshal of France the most glorious in the military world; there was now no other that touched it. The three men were not merely worthy of being in a class with the first Napoleon's Marshals, but surpassed them, for there was some poor timber in that generally glorious list, some names that are now almost unremembered while no Frenchman will ever forget the names of Joffre, Foch, and Pétain.

Pétain was Commander-in-Chief of the French armies, as Haig was of the British, Cadorna and Diaz of the Italian, and Pershing of the American. Properly speaking, Foch had not been a French General at all since he became Generalissimo. He was the commander of all the Allied armies, and responsible, not to France, but to the Allied War Council at Versailles. He was the General of the Allies, as Pétain, Haig, Pershing, Cadorna, and Diaz were the generals respectively of the French, British, American, and Italian armies. Some time before this, ill-advised admirers of Pétain had demanded a Marshal's baton for him for his superb direction of the French armies, but they were quietly put aside. Afterward they were glad because now Pétain had received the compliment of getting his "Well done" at the end of a series of victorious campaigns, and at the moment when he was performing the physical act of restoring Metz to France—Metz, which had been surrendered basely by one of the lesser Napoleon's marshals nearly fifty years before.[30]

Pétain when the war broke out was preoccupied with training officers. Altho fifty-nine years old in 1916, his mental and physical vigor made him appear younger. His brigade in making the long retreat from Charleroi to the Marne in 1914 had repeatedly harassed the enemy with savage ferocity. Just before the battle of the Marne he was promoted to command a division and later was chosen to command an army corps at Arras. Carency, a masterpiece of German defensive work, considered impregnable, but taken in 1915 by Pétain, was a brilliant local victory. In September, 1915, he served with distinction under Castelnau in Champagne. The war had found Pétain a retired colonel, noted for strategic ability. It was Joffre who made him a brigadier-general. In September, 1914, he was a general of division and passed rapidly on to army corps commander

[30] The *Times* (New York).

and army commander. The Allied offensive in Artois and the success won in Champagne owed much to Pétain.

In December, 1917, when Joffre was made a Marshal of France and the question of his successor at the front arose, Pétain seemed destined to have the post. He was then in command of the armies of the center, comprising the front between Soissons and Verdun, but apparently Pétain's adherence to the principle of having absolute field command, independent of political interference, stood in the way of his selection, and the appointment went to Nivelle. How much power Pétain insisted on wielding, and whether it included command of all the Allied armies and the economic dictatorship of France, was not disclosed, but his later appointment to supreme command was not looked on by those who knew Pétain as indicating that he had made a surrender of this principle.

Pétain was a soldier's soldier who did not care for politics and politicians. Tall, broad-shouldered, virile, and blue-eyed, he was a man of few words, cold energy and iron will, and his calm demeanor covered resources of power and determination. His stonelike expression frequently relaxed into a rather whimsical smile, and, on occasion, he could speak with a warmth of eloquence which, devoid of all fine phrasing, nevertheless carried his every word straight to the heart. His *poilus* adored him despite his uncompromising firmness; he was fair in his judgments and he knew just how to mingle with his men. By his mere presence and tact he calmed all the agitation which followed the offensive of April, 1917, the causes of which are well known to-day and could easily be guessed then. His record as a thorough reorganizer included much work in rebuilding the French forces. Inexorable in discipline, going to the length of meting out the death sentence, he at the same time was held in the highest esteem by the rank and file for brilliant military qualities. Soldiers followed him devotedly and the people of France had great faith in him. One of the finest things said by any commander in the war was said by Pétain. When a French army, in 1918, was about to occupy German soil, he warned the *poilu* against reprisals. "So act," said he, "that the enemy will not know which to admire more, your heroism in battle, or your conduct in victory."

WILLIAM S. SIMS, ADMIRAL OF THE UNITED STATES NAVY

It was said of Admiral Sims that, much as the quiet order of Admiral Dewey at Manila "You may fire when you are ready, Gridley," had gone into history, so probably would stand some words of Sims, who, on arrival at Queenstown in the early summer of 1917 with a fleet of American destroyers, when asked by the British commander how soon he would be ready for duty, replied calmly: "We can start at once." The high place which Sims acquired with the British was strikingly emphasized soon afterward when the Admiralty transferred to him chief command of the Allied naval forces in Irish waters during an absence of the ranking British Admiral. That responsibility was an important one, for it meant protecting the big liners that were plying between America and Great Britain.

Sims had sometimes been called *"L'enfant terrible* of the American Navy." He was outspoken, had a way of breaking through red tape and "speaking out in meeting"—at least when he thought criticism would be of benefit to the Navy. At a formal dinner in London, in 1910, Sims declared that, if England should get into the war which then seemed imminent, the Navy of the United States would be found fighting beside the Navy of Great Britain, his exact words as reported being: "If ever the time comes when the British Empire is menaced by an external foe, she can count on every dollar, every ship, and every drop of blood of her kindred across the sea!" After this sentiment had reached the Kaiser, Germany promptly entered a protest to Washington. The President disavowed the country's sympathy with the statement, and Sims was reprimanded. Sims had himself achieved his advancement in the Navy despite all the traditional handicaps. By hard work and unflagging zeal, he had demonstrated his capability and his capacity for taking the initiative. He knew fully the military value of personality and popularity. Possessing personality in marked degree he was in that sense akin to Admiral Sir David Beatty, of whom a British sailor exclaimed after the battle of Jutland, "Confidence in David? Why, we'd go to hell for David!"

Sims failed grievously when as a boy he sought admission to Annapolis, but this did not dishearten him; it only made him determined not to be refused again, and so he set to work to master the subjects in which he had been most deficient. Once more he presented himself and was accepted. Devotion to duty, uncommon fearlessness and an ambition to see our Navy the best in the world, were leading characteristics of his. Sims had a thorough knowledge of the service and the courage to impress his opinions upon those in authority, even when this might be unpleasant business. He was a Pennsylvanian, but born in Canada. His father, A. W. Sims, had married a Canadian woman, who lived at Port Hope, Ontario, and there William was born October 15, 1858. He spent his boyhood in Canada, and then his father moved back to Pennsylvania. There were three boys in the family, and when William was seventeen, his father was offered a place for one of them at Annapolis. The others did not care to go and so William had his chance for a naval career. "It is not saying too much to credit Sims with having pulled the Navy by its own boot-straps high out of a rut in which it once seemed in a fair way to remain," said a writer in the New York *Sun*. In that way Sims's career ran somewhat alongside of Lord Fisher's. Improvement in gunnery had always been one of his main hobbies. Another was efficiency, with promotion by merit and not by years of service. He was typically cosmopolitan. Probably no man in the American Navy had known intimately so many ranking officers in European fleets. He was well-known in the naval circles of London, Paris, and Petrograd, and everywhere welcomed because of his personality and his professional attainments.[30a]

ALFRED VON TIRPITZ, GRAND ADMIRAL OF THE GERMAN FLEET

Germans had their own word for Tirpitz; he was "Tirpitz the Eternal," which freely interpreted meant that among numerous qualities he possest one that was rare in German cabinets; he was the one minister who displayed tenacity in holding his job. No German since Bismarck had held public office so long. The Kaiser had had an endless succession of chancellors, foreign ministers, war ministers and colonial secretaries; but "Tirpitz the Eternal," until he was suddenly displaced early in 1916 on the submarine issue, apparently had a life tenure. With the adoption of unrestricted submarine warfare in February, 1917, however, he returned to power and on him was placed the chief responsibility for the colossal crimes with which that warfare thereafter was carried on. Things that lay on the surface did not really produce this war—neither the ultimatum to Serbia nor hurried mobilizations, nor the invasion of Belgium. Back of all these stood in succession a long series of events which as deeply affecting national interests, ambitions, and fears, had changed national policies and popular psychology. One fact that probably had most to do in changing the whole morale of the German people within a few years was the German navy, and that meant Tirpitz. He was more than a sailor, politician or administrator; he was a statesman who, for good or ill, fundamentally directed the course of European history.

No longer ago than 1890 Lord Salisbury for lands in Africa had given Heligoland back to the Kaiser—that same Heligoland which in the World War served so effectively as a German naval base. The explanation was simple enough; in 1890 the German Empire had no fighting fleet. For many years afterward Great Britain still unallied with any other Power, could glory in her "splendid isolation." For a generation Russia, silently meditating the over-

[30a] Adapted from an article in *The Literary Digest*.

throw of British power in the East, had been playing the part in the British outlook that Germany came to play in later years. In 1898 England and France had been almost on the verge of war over Fashoda. In the nineties the tie that bound Great Britain to her colonies, and especially to Canada, Australia, and New Zealand, was slighter than it had been in years, but within fewer than ten years these conditions had so changed that instead of being splendidly isolated, England found herself splendidly allied. France and Russia, hereditary enemies, had become earnest friends and were now England's friends and the colonies and mother country found themselves reunited in a happy family.

The man chiefly responsible for this change was Tirpitz and his famous "preamble," which as put into the naval law of 1900, formed a new basis for the future history of Europe. "Germany must have a fleet of such strength," the preamble read, "that a war, even against the mightiest naval Power, would threaten the supremacy of that Power." No nation had ever before announced a national policy in such challenging fashion. Germany had declared her purpose to build a navy so strong that it could destroy the navy of Great Britain. Hence came a change in British foreign policy, an abandonment of "isolation," and that series of alliances, ententes, understandings, and good feeling, that ultimately left Germany and her Austrian ally with no friend in Europe except the Turk. Despite official explanations, magazine articles, and interviews, Englishmen saw only one purpose in a steadily increasing German sea-power which in case of war was to isolate Great Britain and ferry a German army across the Channel. So long as Great Britain remained the greatest naval Power and Germany the greatest military Power, there had been no possibility of conflict. Germany's army and Britain's navy both served similar national ends; each protected the nation from obvious dangers, but neither could fight the other. As the elder Moltke was the directing genius of German militarism, so Tirpitz started Germany on the path of navalism which was to become the Kaiser's absorbing passion. In looking for the real inspiration of the German fleet one had, however, to go beyond Tirpitz and the Kaiser. The inspiring mind was not a German but an American; a man who wrote a book which, soon after its appearance, became the Kaiser's inseparable companion—Admiral Mahan and his "The Influence of Sea Power in History." "I have not read your book," said the Kaiser on meeting Mahan. "I have devoured it!"

Tirpitz's origin, altho very respectable, was comparatively bourgeois; his father was a lawyer and judge in Frankfort-on-the-Oder. Tirpitz was born in the Mark of Brandenburg, more than one hundred miles from the sea. He grew up a somewhat rawboned, ungainly, loutish boy, not especially marked for talent, distinguished only by a certain force of character and fixt determination. To his father he presented something of a problem and when only sixteen was placed on board one of several frigates which composed the Prussian navy and at that time served chiefly as havens for the younger sons of impecunious Prussian noblemen. In after years youthful aristocrats were often pained at Tirpitz's habit of advancing sons of tradesmen over their heads and would run to the Kaiser for consolation. "You'll have to get along with him as well as you can," the Emperor would say, "That's what I have to do." Once a ball-room favorite was discussing with Tirpitz his chances of naval promotion. "You have very white hands for a man who hopes to command a cruiser," was all the comfort he received. Another candidate for advancement discovered that, in the eyes of Tirpitz, he had one insuperable disqualification: he was a splendid dancer. "The fact that you waltz so divinely," said the Grand Admiral, "proves that you have no sea-legs. Sailors in the German navy can not waltz their way to the bridge. Go learn the hornpipe." He never regarded social graces as desirable attributes for men who expected to fight battles at sea, and always frowned upon the practise of using warships in foreign ports for balls and receptions.

His talents so stood upon the surface—initiative, industry, knowledge, commanding personality, the evidence which he gave, in every act and work, of a capacious brain—that his career became one success after another. He was a lieutenant at twenty; a lieutenant-commander at twenty-five and twenty years after entering the navy was flying the pennant of a rear-admiral. He first attracted the attention of the Kaiser by reorganizing the German torpedo fleet. He was also instrumental in establishing the German outpost of Kiaochow which was directly under his jurisdiction as Minister of Marine. With his forked beard, large, round face, huge bulk, he incarnated physically the sea-god Neptune. With a genuine sailor he could easily unbend. He could roar out a sailor's ditty with the best of them. His business and his relaxations were all nautical and he had one favorite topic of conversation—the disgraceful inadequacy of the Kaiser's fleet and the necessity of placing German sea-power on a plane with its military strength. If he had one enthusiasm, it was the British Navy; he admired its history, traditions and great achievements. Nelson, Drake, Hawkins, and other great sea-rovers had been the guiding influences of his life. When he came to the United States with Prince Henry in 1902, American naval officers found him a delightful and congenial comrade as well as a wide-awake observer.

The task enjoined upon him by the Kaiser was a definite one; to create an effective German fleet. Public opinion, and public opinion only, as he manipulated it, created the German fleet. Before he was admiral, or a naval statesman, Tirpitz became a press-agent—probably the most successful in the world; certainly the one who operated on the largest scale. America never organized a press bureau that could compare with Tirpitz's. His Navy League—started in 1898—was the parent of all similar organizations. We now have a Navy League of our own, but, with some thousands of members, a pigmy compared with the one Germany had with nearly a million and a half members. While Tirpitz organized his *Flotten-verein* Prince Henry was placed at its head, purely for the purpose of being the main instrument in a "campaign of education." Tirpitz sought to teach the German people why they needed a navy, what kind they needed, and how they could get it. The league had branches not only in every province, city, town, village, and hamlet in the empire, but in every part of the world where Germans lived. Even England—the country against which the German navy was aimed—had branches of the German Navy League, and it had thousands of loyal and contributing members in the United States. It poured forth an unending stream of naval information, in the shape of newspaper articles, interviews, pamphlets, and lithographs; it had motion-picture shows and lecturers who visited the remotest villages. It even introduced its propaganda into public schools. As a result the most benighted Pomeranian peasant who had hardly known that salt water existed and had never imagined what a warship was, began to discuss glibly the relative values of destroyers and light cruisers and to debate the possibilities of dreadnoughts and submarines. The German navy, almost as much as the army, began to figure as a bulwark of the empire.

Besides the Navy League, Tirpitz organized a regular press bureau. These agencies, always active, displayed particular liveliness when legislation was pending. He organized special excursion trips from the interior to the seaboard, at extremely low rates, so that the every-day German farmer and workman, with his wife and babies, might have an opportunity to see the Kaiser's battleships, inspect big guns, and so feel himself a part of a machine he had helped to pay for. In our own country we have had no "accelerator" who could rank with Tirpitz. When the Reichstag met and took under consideration naval estimates, they found they had a new master; back of Tirpitz were the "folks at home." He was not only a great press agent, but a finished wire-puller and button-holer. He did not stiffly remain aloof and request the Reichstag to do certain things, but went among its members with an ingratiating smile and a quiet voice, making individual appeals. He cultivated members, joked with them, told them funny stories, made them his friends. His six feet of bulk, his grizzled forked beard, his rotund, weather-beaten face moved among them with the adroitness of an American lobbyist.

Clad in the full uniform of his rank as he appeared before the budget committee there were few figures so compelling. Tirpitz loved to answer questions, especially when they were irritating ones; "heckling" was his meat and drink. Without a memorandum or a navy register he could instantaneously give details of practically everything pertaining to naval construction. He knew not only the German navy, but every navy in the world; could rattle off the naval appropriations made by other countries for a dozen years back, and tell how they had been spent. To all inquiries he responded in a modulated voice, never becoming excited, never attempting to bulldoze any one, but always displaying a mild persistence that invariably triumphed.

A British view of his work came from Mr. Balfour in a speech that almost stunned the people of England. "For the first time in modern history," said Mr. Balfour, "there is bordering upon the North Sea, upon our own waters, the waters that bathe our own shores, a great Power that has the capacity, and looks as if it had the will, to compete with us in point of actual numbers of battleships." With England it had been no longer a matter of maintaining the two-power standard; it was a question of maintaining a one-power standard. This speech was made in 1909—the year in which England awoke to learn that the German fleet, at the existing rate of construction, would, in a couple of years, be more powerful than Great Britain's. Tirpitz was building so rapidly, and apparently so secretly, that Britain's naval power was threatened with extinction. There was something humorous in the idea of building battleships clandestinely; ordinarily nothing would seem more difficult to conceal; yet this, according to Mr. Balfour and Premier Asquith, was what Tirpitz was doing. In 1909 a German naval law stipulated laying down four capital ships; besides these, said Mr. Asquith, Germany was laying down four not on the program. Never, said the London *Times,* had the world witnessed such a complete, deliberate preparation for war on a gigantic scale. There was no longer any possibility of ignoring Germany's objective.

Prussia throughout its history had always struck in the dark, and always aimed, by secret preparation, to take an enemy unawares. As Frederick II had struck at Austria and ravished Silesia, as Bismarck had struck at France and taken Alsace-Lorraine, so Wilhelm II was craftily preparing to make a sudden onslaught on England. Tirpitz had labored only a little more than ten years and here was the fruition of his work. In 1909 the wisest of living English statesmen had warned the country that the German navy, in two years, would be in a position to give battle to English ships with more than even chances of success. The thing that had so changed the outlook was an English development—the dreadnought.

Fundamentally, dreadnought-building represented a contest of wits between the two greatest naval minds of the day—Sir John Fisher and Tirpitz. For several years the two had been conducting a new kind of long-range duel, concretely exprest in new battleships, destroyers, cruisers, and other fighting craft. Tirpitz, in his rapid program, had already caused great changes in British naval policy. For one thing he had forced Sir John to withdraw his big ships from the Mediterranean and concentrate them in the North Sea, thus making the British Empire dependent on France for its highway to India. German money was pouring into the navy so fast, the ships were being launched so rapidly, and popular enthusiasm in Germany was increasing at such a pace, that Sir John was nonplussed. What possible way to meet and to destroy for all time this growing German menace? A ship, designed several years before for the American Navy, but never built, presented itself as the solution.

This was a huge affair, displacing 18,000 tons—the biggest ships before 1905 had displaced about 15,000—and distinguished by the fact that its armament consisted chiefly of big guns. Such a ship could sail faster, shoot farther, and have greater destructive power than any other then afloat. "If I start building a fleet of this type"— we can imagine Sir John reasoning to himself—"Germany will have to retire from the contest. The cost is appalling—three or four times that of the prevailing style in battleships—and Germany, being a much poorer country than England, will not be able to raise the cash. Again, Germany built the Kiel Canal for strategic purposes— as a commercial enterprise it was a failure—so that she could keep her fleet at will either in the Baltic or the North Sea; but this new ship is too big to go through the canal; so Germany will not build it. Anyway, even if she wills, she can't do it. There is not a shipyard in Germany that has a slip big enough to build such a vessel, and the navy has no docks big enough to hold one. Here, therefore, is the one way of snuffing out this presumptuous young sea power— and this without anything resembling a war."

Such was the philosophy back of the dreadnought. Apparently it destroyed at a stroke the strong navy that Tirpitz had laboriously built up on conventional lines, but Tirpitz saw the situation in another light. It really furnished him the great opportunity he had been seeking. The dreadnought was the most colossal instance of miscalculation that naval history records. It was true that, as Sir John had foreseen, it made obsolete the German navy, but it made obsolete the British Navy as well. After it was launched, the first-line battle strength of all navies would be measured by dreadnoughts and by dreadnoughts alone. This meant that, in the race for naval supremacy, every nation would start on even terms. England had had such a great lead that, had the *status quo* been preserved, Germany could never have caught up with her but when England voluntarily pigeon-holed her whole fleet, she lost this enormous handicap.

Tirpitz sprang at this opportunity with all the rapidity of genius. The Navy League and the press bureau found a new inspiration; the new navy of dreadnoughts became the staple of conversation. When the Reichstag met, huge naval estimates were presented, and Tirpitz made another of his historic appearances before the budget committee and the Reichstag passed an amendment to the naval law, providing for a naval program of thirty-eight dreadnoughts and twenty cruisers. In 1908 the Reichstag amended its program so that an ultimate German navy of fifty-eight dreadnoughts became Tirpitz's answer to Sir John's challenge and an appropriation of $50,-000,000 for rebuilding the Kiel Canal, so that these ships could pass through was promptly voted. Sir John had asserted that Germany, in 1906, hadn't a single slip big enough to build a dreadnought; three years later she had seventeen. Tirpitz had called together all the biggest shipbuilders and told them to prepare to build these warships.

Such an enormous spurt followed in shipping equipment as the world had never seen before. Mr. Asquith informed a bewildered Parliament that one firm had manufactured the complete armament of eight battleships in a single year. Until the dreadnought period no country had been able to build ships as rapidly as England, but in 1909 there was no question that German yards could turn out as many ships a year as the English; the only debatable point was whether they could not build more.

Every morning at seven Tirpitz could be found at his desk in the Leipzigstrasse, going over plans, receiving contracts, driving bargains. In the work of construction and finance he also shone. He felt so sure of his success in the Reichstag that he virtually awarded contracts before the money had been voted. To all English excitement he turned a smiling and deprecating face. He denied that Germany was secretly building ships. "The purpose of the German fleet," he said, "is to preserve peace for Germany—even against the strongest opponent at sea."

A half century of service more strenuous than that of any sailor since Nelson seemed to have affected Tirpitz slightly. His bony frame and the deliberate movements of his legs and arms made the old man seem heavier and bigger than he actually was. The heartiness of his mode of salutation, even when he met a stranger, and the unflinching gaze of his eyes, together with a frankness of speech bordering at times on indiscretion, received their due from British newspapers, which confest that Tirpitz was really a fine old pirate. His smile was irresistible. When he could carry his point in no other way, he would smile at you. He was, however, fundamentally a hot-tempered creature, ready with a heated retort upon occasion, but he was capable of ineffable benignity in persuasive moods.

One saw Tirpitz at his best when the naval committee of the Reichstag, hesitating over some huge appropriation, was listening to him. The deputies before him might be grotesquely ignorant of the sea, they might represent any form of radicalism and might have no social standing whatever, but never, for that reason, would Tirpitz abate a jot of his geniality. Nor would he crush a stupid objection with the sarcasm of an expert. He simply would beam—beam irresistibly—while elucidating with paternal benevolence the mysteries of naval strategy to a dolt. This was all unlike the traditional Prussian mode of handling men at popular assemblies. Tirpitz suggested less the courtier and the diplomatist than the kind father laboring over a stupid son. Many an hour had he sat with Reichstag deputies, maps and plans spread out before him, explaining in a low, guttural voice the significance of scout-cruisers and the importance of torpedoes. He had the expert's knowledge of his subject; but, unlike the average expert, he could impart what he knew lucidly, and make the theme entrancing.

The social gifts for which Tirpitz was famous—felicity in anecdote, hospitable spirit, eagerness to win a place in the heart of a guest—promoted his ambition to make the fleet invincible. His capacity to develop the submarine was not more remarkable than his aptitude for the genial arts that make converts. His object was ever to win over the young. A youthful deputy in the Reichstag was always made much of when shown over a dreadnought. In dealing with journalists, Tirpitz was no less winning. There was no haughtiness, no official manner, no secrets with him. One could not get away from him without a cigar, an embrace, and a pressing invitation to come again. All this was a great change from days when journalists had had doors slammed in their faces in Berlin. Even visiting London journalists were welcome, Tirpitz benevolently protesting with uplifted hands that there could be no possible enmity between the fleets of the Kaiser and those of the King.

The genius of Tirpitz was primarily that of the engineer. At least such was the verdict of many well-informed journalists who had studied the man. All agreed in high estimates of his statesmanship, his instinctive diplomacy, masterful disposition, and temperamental geniality. Beyond these traits, or underlying them, was a genius for engineering that had made his extraordinary career possible. He had the highest form of imaginative constructiveness—that of the mathematician. His was the Euclidian mind which went in a straight line to his object, never losing sight of it. He did not lose himself in unbounded vistas after the manner of many Germans. His characteristics were not those of the sailor in the British sense. He thought in terms of the torpedo; how that projectile could be aimed, its range, its possibilities, and its limitation. Such details absorbed him and hence his concentration upon the submarine.[31]

[31] Principal Sources: Largely an article by James Middleton in *The World's Work*, but in part based on a compilation by Alexander Harvey in *Current Opinion*, and on articles in The *Spectator* and The *Daily Mail* (London), *Vossische Zeitung* (Berlin), *Neue Freie Presse* (Vienna) and *Figaro* and *Gaulois* (Paris).

II

RULERS AND STATESMEN

ALBERT, KING OF THE BELGIANS

The world at large had known little about Albert when, on August 4, he sent to King George of Great Britain his "supreme appeal to the diplomatic intervention of your Majesty's Government to safeguard the integrity of Belgium." Albert's appeal was the factor which finally impelled Great Britain to cast her lot with France and Russia, but he had already refused to permit German troops to take a short cut through his country on their way to France. "Blood and iron" made much history in Belgium after the "scrap of paper" was torn up. The Belgians suffered as no other people had suffered in modern times. They fought a good fight against overwhelming odds. Their country was overrun, their fields were laid waste, towns and cities were destroyed, and thousands of humble peasants made destitute and hungry. Albert himself was driven from three capitals—Brussels, Antwerp, Ostend—to seek refuge in France with the remnant of his shattered army.

Albert, a king without a kingdom, was then thirty-nine years old. When he ascended the throne, on December 23, 1909, in succession to his uncle, King Leopold II, of unsavory memory, he looked for prosperous and peaceful days for his people. He had no military aim to achieve; he believed his country was secure because of the Treaty of London. His individual tastes ran to peaceful pursuits; his chief desire being to help the Belgians, an industrious people, to achieve greater prosperity. He had already trained himself in statecraft, and by doing so had won confidence. Not until the death of his elder brother, Prince Baodoin, in 1891, did he realize that he might some day be called upon to rule over the Belgians. He was then sixteen years old. In 1898 he came to the United States to see its engineering and electrical wonders, and to study educational methods, particularly those relating to industrial training. He traveled over the country, saw the oil fields of Pennsylvania, the steel works of Pittsburgh, visited large manufacturing cities in Massachusetts, and made a tour of the railroad centers of the West with James J. Hill as his guide. He dodged social events as much as possible, altho he met many men responsible for American industrial development, and dined at the White House.

One day he spent at Harvard, where he watched crew squads and inspected dormitories and historic buildings. A Harvard graduate recalled how one day the Prince was ushered into his room in old Stoughton Hall by President Eliot, who said to him and his roommate: "Young gentlemen, this is the Crown Prince of Belgium." "I saw," said the Harvard man afterward, "a tall, pale-faced, angular, and rather awkward youth—he was only about twenty-three then. An army officer in uniform and a court physician trailed along behind. The Prince held his silk hat stiffly in hand and stept forward. His hand-shake was hearty and vigorous. 'I am glad to meet you,' he said. 'It is a pleasure to see your quarters, and it is very good of you to admit us.' He spoke good English, with scarcely a trace of accent. The Prince spied a group picture of some college girls, and examined it carefully. 'You have some very beautiful women in America,' he said, with a smile. 'I have often heard them praised, and now I am learning that it is all justified.' "

When he became king, Albert was the only European monarch who had been in personal contact with the industrial life of America. One of the problems that King Albert had to tackle was the Kongo, the rich and extensive African colony which Leopold controlled and exploited personally as a business venture. The Kongo atrocities had long been a blot on the white man's civilization, and the whole world demanded better treatment for the negroes in Belgium's possessions. King Albert was well equipped to formulate a humane policy. Some years before, contrary to the wishes of King Leopold, he had visited the Kongo country and observed the condition of the natives. He thus applied first-hand knowledge in working out reforms, and if all the abuses were not remedied, a more intelligent and humane policy was enforced under his guidance.

Albert maintained a reputation for clean living. He kept himself apart from his uncle. His married life had been a happy one with his consort, Queen Elizabeth, daughter of Duke Charles Theodore of Bavaria. Queen Elizabeth was an accomplished woman, a registered physician, a graduate of Leipzig, and had a sound knowledge of art, literature, and music. The King admitted that she taught him to appreciate art and literature, two things that were banished from the Belgian court during the reign of Leopold. After the marriage of Albert and Elizabeth in 1900, they made a tour of Europe and the Far East, traveling only with one maid and courier. Three children have been born to them—Phillip, the Crown Prince; Prince Charles, and Princess Marie. Both the King, whose mother was a Hohenzollern, and the Queen severed many blood ties in defying the German Kaiser.

War did not have to reveal the true King Albert to the Belgians, but it did reveal him to the outside world. Long before the war crisis the people of Belgium had seen their king in mines with a pick and shovel, on railroads driving an engine, and in factories, in which he exploited a mechanical gift for which he was remarkable from boyhood. He afforded the anomalous spectacle of an intellectual sovereign ruling a not particularly thoughtful people, a grave monarch in a normally gay realm. His stern devotion to sociology, his dreams of a paradise on earth for workers in mine and mart, brought upon him some criticism. Even his genius, mathematical and mechanical, seemed alien to his environment, for Brussels before her tragedy was the gayest of capitals, and her sovereign in his splendid palace was sometimes a riddle to his people. They were more accustomed to Leopold.

One had to go back to the Homeric age for an ideal illustration of all that Albert, in the capacity of King, came to signify to the Belgians. He was the comrade as well as the sovereign of his soldiers. The Homeric virtues of courage, endurance, and strength equipped him for the Homeric life he was to lead, charging the foe in the forefront of battle, lying by night in a circle of his soldiers, listening to tales of war. He was the commander-in-chief of his people, their judge and their representative before the world. Like an Homeric prince he helped in the building of trenches and acted as his own charioteer, or chauffeur. His sway was absolute because founded on the example of heroism that he set. His people loved him because he lived their life. Glimpses of King Albert in the trenches revealed him in a soiled uniform, eating warmed-up soup, sharing his match with a soldier from whom he received a cigaret, or affording first aid to the injured.

Albert's cheek-bones tended to prominence, and his voice was rough and heavy. The tall figure lost flesh during the war and his complexion was no longer ruddy. Early in the war there was a slight limp in his walk, for a wound in the foot received at Antwerp was slow to heal. His presence with his men was so much a matter of course that he expected no attention after a swift salute from a soldier to whom he spoke. The etiquette of peace was gone. Belgians no longer stood when in the King's presence. His rank was quite forgotten as he held a torch while engineers repaired a break in a gun-carriage, or lathered his face for him to shave himself without a mirror. Albert was knocked down by a wounded horse during the retreat from Antwerp, and, as his car had been commandeered for ambulance purposes, he walked into France surrounded by thousands of troops as ragged and hungry as himself.

King Albert before the war ran over to London frequently, walking up the Strand in London with no evidence of his rank about him. He and his consort would put up at a plain little hotel of an exclusive kind and visit the theater as ordinary persons. Albert was often fortunate enough to pass through throngs unnoticed except for his height. It was related of a dealer in motor-cars in London that he had dealt personally with King Albert, selling him two automobiles, and even going with him to luncheon without suspecting that his customer was a European sovereign. One day in making a purchase in London, in reply to the usual question, he stated that his name was Albert. "Albert what?" queried the salesperson. "King," said his Majesty. In due time the purchase arrived, addrest to "Albert King, Esquire."

The courage of Leopold defied the public opinion of Europe in Kongo affairs, but the courage of Albert enabled him to lead a national forlorn hope to a high consummation. The tragedy in which Leopold played the conspicuous part was that of the Kongo; the tragedy of which Albert was the central figure glorified him in the eyes of mankind. His personality was a lesson since it taught that men become great, not through possessing great qualities, but through the use to which those qualities are put.[32]

HERBERT HENRY ASQUITH, PRIME MINISTER OF GREAT BRITAIN

While reasonably approachable, Mr. Asquith was sometimes a hard person to see. He was an exceptional public man in that, while far from courting publicity, he by nature and habit shunned the limelight. His most implacable enemy would never have suggested that he was anything of an actor. Even when he entered a room he did not feel called upon to act the part of Prime Minister. He was strong, healthy, and British, his hair almost white, but his face youthful, discounting his age by ten years. He was a reserved man, and might have been taken for a shy professor of Greek as he bowed, not without geniality, and walked quietly to a place in a room. But he was a different person in the House of Commons, where he never made a bad speech, altho at times he had "tough cases." Whenever he spoke he disclosed his feeling for good English by a rare choice of words, and a style that easily and clearly made its points. Nothing but thorough scholarship and long training in public speaking could have produced addresses so eloquent. His career at school and at Oxford had been strewn with classical prizes. In debate he overshadowed at Oxford all others of his day. He would talk with such simplicity of some British disaster as to make the event all the more dramatic. In that way he talked in 1914 of the

[32] Adapted from an article by Alexander Harvey in *Current Opinion* and based on articles in The *Tribune* (New York), *Figaro* (Paris), The *Standard* (London), and from an article by "W. B. H." in The *Evening Post* (New York).

loss of three warships—the cruisers *Aboukir, Cressy,* and *Hogue*— 12,000-ton boats. As he made that announcement of the first disaster to the British Navy in this war one thought primarily of his serenity. Not in the slightest degree was he flustered, and yet he was not indifferent. One knew intuitively how deeply he was moved, but he did not unmask his emotion. His poise was admirable— nothing about revenge, and no boasting.

Mr. Asquith was called to the bar at Lincoln's Inn in June, 1876. After success before the Parnell Commission, he became Queen's Counsel and gradually concentrated on appellate work before the House of Lords and the Privy Council. He was earning, perhaps, £15,000 a year when he became Prime Minister. When the English bar celebrated in him the elevation of one of its members to the premiership, Sir Edward Clarke said that "for thirty years he had preserved an untarnished shield." Mr. Asquith was born in Yorkshire of Puritan stock sixty-two years before the war began. He never took his business home with him, notwithstanding his home as Premier was also his place of business. The Chief Executive of the British Government was both officially and privately domiciled in a house of dull-brown brick which, from the outside at least, would be considered unworthy any Cabinet officer's dignity in the United States. Within doors, however, it was delightful.

Even on great occasions Mr. Asquith seldom allowed himself more than half an hour for a speech. Twenty minutes would usually suffice him even when he had something historic to reveal, but everything essential had been said. Serenity of temper, reserve of language, an absence of everything that was personal, made him the ideal spokesman of a government. One would search in vain throughout his speeches for a word that was violent and provocative. Slowly, steadily, without passion as without haste, he conducted debates day after day, week after week. Tories might yell and fume, even break out in riotous disorder, but Mr. Asquith would proceed on his way with deadly precision and relentlessness, tranquil, self-contained, and unmoved.

With his rise to supremacy not so much of station as of intellectual mastery, there came a subtle change in his personality. No man had been more misunderstood. No man lent himself so much to misunderstanding. He was an Englishman to his finger-tips, and a Yorkshireman, and had more than the usual reserve of his countrymen, but reserve has often been the mask for shyness and shyness lends itself to misunderstanding. Even if he wanted to, Mr. Asquith was incapable of making advances—especially to those who misunderstood him. He was of the type to whom power gravitates. In a crowd he would sit in silence, but his personality would impress all with his distinction even tho no one knew who he was. No living statesman eschewed the trappings of greatness more sedulously. Even his clothes lacked suggestion of distinction; he affected the quiet black sack coat and the gray trousers that were the vogue in his youth. He had not modified the habits of a lifetime to the extent of keeping a valet. Unlike the modern man, he used the telephone very little and his motor-car rides were never for pleasure. His taste in literature reflected his mind. He read philosophy and economics rather than poetry and fiction. The deeds of great explorers always interested him. He never concealed his lack of sympathy for "feminism" in its extreme contemporary form. His Utopia would be a man's world; but the men would be high-minded, chivalrous, and above all efficient.

His was a quiet and sheltered youth giving no indication of future renown. There remained in him much of the English middle-class mind. His soul was shadowed by Yorkshire hard common sense. While he had a wide acquaintance with literature he seemed to belong distinctly to the Victorians. This left him at times disconcertingly old-fashioned, not only as to literary likings but as to political ideals. He preferred the Victorian novelists, Charles Reade and Wilkie Collins, to writers of contemporary fiction. Few English politicians had read so much American literature, but what he read had the Victorian flavor—Poe, Hawthorne, Lowell, Longfellow, and Emerson. He came from a rather long line of Yorkshire nonconformist ancestors, men and women who were dissenters from the established church and lived by the Scriptures, but he was devoted to the theater and made no concealment of his fondness for cards. He was prejudiced against peers and claims of noble birth, resenting superiority not founded on natural gifts. His aristocracy would be one of talent.

"Asquith is the one pupil of mine," said Jowett who was proud of him, "for whom I most confidently predict success in life." Jowett made another remark which showed how well he understood his pupil: "Asquith will get on—he is so direct." His capacity to get at facts and to state them with lucidity was equalled only by his integrity in disclosing them. He made his big hit when he appeared before the Parnell Commission. The prestige of that effect had not worn away when Gladstone, delighted with his first speech before the Commons, offered to make Asquith Home Secretary, which was then a great post. Those historic trouble-makers, Home Rule for Ireland and Welsh Church Disestablishment, both under him received the royal assent—Home Rule after twenty-eight years of effort, and Disestablishment first introduced by Mr. Asquith under Gladstone, now after twenty years of waiting. These two momentous reforms could not have been made law but for the Parliamentary Act, Asquith's own measure, that abolished the veto of the House of Lords, and thus freed the democratic institutions of England of the last strain of feudalism. He was the first Minister of Great Britain to recognize the right of every man and woman in the country to live in comfort when too infirm to earn a living, for he secured old-age pensions for the poor.

Eminent fairness, or a desire to be eminently fair, characterized all his comments on the war. Not only in public remarks was this true, but in private conversation. Everything he said was in the best of temper and marked by unvarying moderation. There was no note of infallibility in his statements, or his arguments, nothing to the effect that England could do no wrong. In his view Great Britain was at war, in 1914, to vindicate the sanctity of treaty obligations and of what was properly called the public law of Europe; to assert and to enforce the independence of free states, relatively small and weak, against the violence of the strong; and to withstand, in the interests not only of their own empire, but of civilization at large, the arrogant claim of a single Power to dominate the development of Europe.[33]

THEOBALD VON BETHMANN-HOLLWEG, Chancellor of the German Empire

Strolling with his hands behind his back along the unpretentious Wilhelmstrasse in Berlin, and pausing in a characteristic manner as if he had suddenly remembered something, Bethmann-Hollweg, Chancellor when the war began, and destined to his principal place in history as the author of the "scrap of paper" phrase, remained for more than two years as impressively unimpressive to journalists in Berlin as he had seemed to be to the German people when Emperor William suddenly made him Chancellor, in succession to Prince von Bülow. He was a lonely, as well as a distinguished, figure, whose gigantic height was accentuated by a black overcoat and high silk hat. His bowed head, with its Saxon nose, was seldom lifted up toward the unassuming fronts of the buildings he passed in his daily walk to the imperial palace. On his way he would sometimes drop into a bookstore to finger the latest issues from the press, paying most attention to works of philosophy—not commentaries on Nietzsche and Schopenhauer, but studies in the manner of Hermann Turck, the latest thinker under discussion in Germany. Bethmann-Hollweg was essentially a Christian in his outlook upon life, a man remote from materialism, a simple nature in a complex age.

[33] Adapted from an article by Alexander Harvey in *Current Opinion* and from one by H. B. Needham in *The Saturday Evening Post* (Philadelphia).

What especially amazed a journalist in conversing with him was the recklessness of candor with which he would discuss anything. Continental Europeans in high office were as a rule discreet—overwhelmingly discreet—but the Chancellor would discuss anything with no reserve at all—the war, the Emperor William, the future of the Pope, Göthe, Belgium, or what you like. This was no mere policy. It was just his way. A certain artlessness of manner and slowness of utterance that suggested one who thinks aloud, heightened the effect of his uncalculated indiscretions. Now and then when he would forget a detail he did not summon a lackey in uniform, as Prince von Bülow would have done, but went himself in search of a paper he wished to lay before the visitor. Everything he said and did was done with characteristic gravity. There were no sweet smiles after the Bülow manner, no epigrams, no airs.

Prussian in origin, Prussian by birth, and most Prussian of all by education, a classmate of the Kaiser at Bonn, Bethmann-Hollweg revealed, neither in manner nor in mode of life, qualities best known to men as Prussian. He represented a survival from an age that glorified Göthe and Schiller and imbibed Kant and Fichte. His simplicity in eating and drinking—his favorite beverage being light beer and his favorite edible cold sausage—suggested the humble professor. He loomed above most men when afoot in Berlin streets, carrying a parcel of books in his hand, instead of riding in the vehicle of his office. For luncheon a table was reserved for him in a quiet little restaurant that never was fashionable and, despite his regular coming, never would be. When accosted he seemed to come out of a brown study into a world he had altogether forgotten. His simplicity was that of one who never considered his own personality, his own interests, or the effect upon his fortunes of whatever he did or said.

Never in his career had he exemplified this trait so completely as in the course of his famous speech in the Reichstag on the invasion of Belgium. When he spoke of "a wrong" his country would be doing, he gave no thought at all to what his enemies might make of the admission. One trait only was shared by him with his brilliant predecessor Bülow—a love of the arts. He surrounded himself with books, pictures, and musical instruments, and had a preference for Verdi over Wagner. Apparently if he had any favorite composer it was Beethoven. He delighted, too, in Brahms. His discriminating taste in pictures revealed itself in a preference for Jan Vermeer, at a time when that Dutch artist had not been recognized except by a few. His supreme resource was his private library, a great sunny room lined from floor to ceiling with well-stocked shelves. The place showed at once that it was the working library of a scholar.

His taste was not for the elegant in literature. One encountered no such author as Merimée, in whom Bülow delighted, nor Carducci, whom the Prince deemed Europe's first modern poet. Bethmann-Hollweg read Kant, whose "Critique of Pure Reason" he placed beside anything from Aristotle or Plato. He was like Gladstone in devotion to theology, and, like the British statesman, gave much attention to classical literature.

In a remote village of Brandenburg he was born nearly sixty years before the war began, and he had the melancholy temperament of Brandenburgers, the characteristic grave eye and the fervent Christian piety. The Kaiser himself was sometimes called a Brandenburger by which it was implied that he was more prayerful more addicted to theology than the average Prussian. Bethmann-Hollweg was given to the economies of his type, which carefully saves pieces of string for future use, and eats sparingly. He was likewise careful of his clothes, which he wore long after they had ceased to be fashionable. Such thrift was ascribed in part to his comparative poverty for one in his class; but, had he been very rich, he could not have thrown off the habits of a lifetime. These tendencies were inherited from a Frankfort merchant who founded the family early in the last century and was noted for ability to accumulate money.

A more eminently respectable figure than Bethmann-Hollweg on his way to church—which he never missed on Sunday—it would have been hard to conceive. He had a pleasing voice and never shrank from the sound of it when hymns were sung. Members of the little congregation had known him for years. Nothing was thought of the fact that, in flat defiance of all precedent, he slipt into a rear seat and made way readily for any one who afterward came in. Now and then in leaving church he would forget his umbrella, whereupon some little boy would run after him with it. Sometimes he would accept an invitation from the pastor to lunch, and off the pair would go on foot side by side, immersed in theology or philosophy, to some humble street in Berlin, from which the Chancellor would return, still afoot, swinging his long arms, stretching his long legs, a highly respectable gentleman, colliding occasionally with a pedestrian, or menaced by the whip of an impatient driver, or yelled at by a chauffeur. The compelling and original fact about the German Imperial Chancellor of 1914 was his unimportant and inconsequential aspect. The nation which "aroused the world to arms and filled the ears of men with strange new cries, as it revived Napoleonisms and Cæsarisms, confronted the world with a simple-minded Herr Doctor, carrying a shabby umbrella, when you expected to see a Bismarck."

That unassuming personality did not reflect insignificance. He was essentially a man strong in principle and action, unable to be a mere instrument in the hands of others. Those who knew the court of Berlin at first hand were sure of his moral ascendency over the Kaiser. There existed between them, not only a strong tie of affection dating from Bonn, but a bond based on a perception by the younger man of the heroic moral traits of the elder. There was no sycophancy in the Imperial Chancellor, no yielding of conviction to expediency. The fact that so strong a nature was chosen for so exalted a dignity refuted the charge that William II would endure no criticism. Bethmann-Hollweg was succeeded in his office by a succession of brief-tenured men—Michaelis, Hertling, Prince Max—but none of these are names that will survive in histories of this war, as will Bethmann-Hollweg's and his "scrap of paper." [34]

SIR ROBERT LAIRD BORDEN, Premier of Canada

A descendant of Samuel Borden, surveyor, who went to Falmouth, Nova Scotia, from the American colonies in 1760, Sir Robert Borden was styled the ablest parliamentarian in Canadian public life, one whose whole attitude stood for everything that was best in the life of the Dominion. The *Canadian Law Journal* described him as having "a wide and accurate knowledge, fertile of resource, firm of purpose, and a manner that has won for him the friendship and the confidence of all men well posted on public affairs." Such was the man who was elected leader of the Conservative Party in the Canadian House of Commons upon the resignation of Sir Charles Tupper in February, 1901.

Before entering into politics Sir Robert Borden was an extensive practitioner in law, both in the Supreme Court of Nova Scotia and the Supreme Court of the Dominion. As a master of the political situation in Canada, and as one best qualified to speak of its resources, Sir Robert Borden was summoned by the Government of Great Britain to attend a meeting of the British Cabinet held July 14, 1915. He was the first overseas minister to receive such a summons and represented the Canadian Dominion at the Imperial War Cabinet in 1917 and at the Imperial War Conference in 1918. He was born at Grand Pré, June 26, 1854, and has been Premier of the Dominion of Canada since 1911. As a representative of one of the larger Dominions beyond the seas, Sir Robert Borden proved an able representative of his country, and a man of whom Canada had good reason to be proud. [35]

[34] Adapted from an article compiled by Alexander Harvey for *Current Opinion* from the *Figaro, Temps,* and *Gaulois* (Paris).

[35] Compiled from "Canadian Men and Women of the Time" and "Who's Who, 1918-1919" (London).

PERSONAL SKETCHES OF WAR LEADERS

LOUIS BOTHA, Premier of the Union of South Africa

Louis Botha was born at Greytown, Natal, in 1863. He was a member of the first Volksraad of the South African Republic, and served as field cornet at the beginning of the Anglo-Boer War.

As Commander-in-Chief of the Boer forces he succeeded General Joubert, being in command at the battle of Colenso, and during the remainder of the war. In the interests of his country he visited England in 1902, 1907, and 1911.

He was elected Premier of the Transvaal 1907-1910, and as Honorary General of the British Army commanded the Union forces in Southwest Africa from 1914 to 1915, during which time he succeeded in defeating the Germans and received their surrender, as already stated in the body of this work.[36]

ARISTIDE BRIAND, Premier of France

A resemblance to Lloyd George was discernible in Briand, who during the war was at the head of the French Cabinet briefly, but for the third time. The resemblance did not include similarity in tactics as used by the British Minister in his labor difficulties and by Briand when faced with a great railway strike. Briand's method of calling all railway employees to the colors, and thus exposing a persistent striker to charges of insubordination and breach of military discipline if he refused, became instantly efficacious; but it earned for him adverse criticism and suspicion that did much to limit his official career afterward.

Briand had spent fifteen years in a sort of nomadic life, as barrister, journalist, trade-unionist orator, political organizer, and general secretary to the French Socialist party. The clients he cared for most were proletárian victims of economic conditions, whose gratitude was his reward. "Gentlemen of the jury," he was once heard to exclaim, "in defending my client I am defending myself." His popularity with the common people was widespread. They regarded him in France, as fellow workers in England regarded Lloyd George—not as a proud and unsympathetic political officer, but as one of them. They called him *"notre Aristide."* When he spoke they listened, for he spoke directly to them.

To oratorical gifts Briand owed much of his rapid, tho long-delayed, rise to public prominence. As a boy he delighted in attending public meetings for the purpose of hearing speakers. With a school-fellow—afterward a bootmaker at Saint-Nazaire, proud of a

---

[36] Compiled from "Who's Who, 1918-1919" (London).

Premier's friendship—he used to go assiduously to a Catholic church to profit by the eloquence of the preacher. On his entry into Clémenceau's first Cabinet, an Englishman wrote of Briand's voice: "A penetrating voice, audible in its lowest tones at the remotest corner of the chamber. It is what Carlyle would have called a 'downy voice, a caressing voice, a coaxy voice;' since Gambetta's, the most seductive heard in the Palais Bourbon."

Briand was somewhat tall for a Frenchman and had a slight stoop. His black, straight hair was brushed straight back from a square, massive forehead. His face had usually a somewhat melancholy expression from which dark eyes looked out with a tranquil, searching gaze. Workmen of Saint-Etienne knew his genial, frank, unassuming manner, and would say "Our Aristide is like ourselves." No living statesman had such genius in disclosing himself intimately to his countrymen. That accounted for the swiftness of his rise, his unexampled success in life. He long dwelt in a cheap flat on one of the back streets of Montmartre. No one was ever more human. Some writers attributed this to a peasant origin; but he was of the bourgeoisie. His father had become comfortably situated after success in business at Nantes, and no difficulty was found in educating Aristide for the bar. He had from his early youth what the French call flux of words. He thought of becoming a novelist, of the school of Balzac, whose works he devoured when young. He had the literary gift, but he was without the literary temperament. A man of words, he was likewise a man of action, a combination unusual in France.

Rare ability and exceptional opportunities did not alone account for Briand. He acted always on the theory of "nothing venture, nothing gain." He would risk his whole career upon a single throw, as every one noticed when he faced trade-unions in the railway strike and terminated a great political crisis. It was essentially characteristic of him that he employed reckless chauffeurs. He was in many collisions. The French like that sort of thing. Oratory alone did not make him politically, altho he was perhaps the most daring orator in France. With more imagination than Viviani, and more earnestness than Clémenceau, he had besides inexpressibly graceful gestures. He never pounded the tribune, but walked toward it naturally. This detail meant much to French deputies. Many a speech in France has been wrecked by an epigram, launched in malice as a speaker proceeded from his seat to the fatal tribune. Briand took the trip naturally. Altho his speeches were compelling, because his voice sent them home, they read like a poet's prose.

He was noted for capacity to sleep like Napoleon, anywhere. It was a survival from his journalist days, when he wrote about economic crimes for the more radical papers, and exposed the financial irregularities of deputies. He nibbled rather than ate, and looked over a newspaper while doing so. His luncheon was often brought in to him at the ministry from neighboring restaurants. A waiter once returned to find his food untouched. "I declare," said Briand, looking up with astonishment, "I thought I had eaten it." [37]

GEORGES CLÉMENCEAU, Premier of France

Little was left unsaid during the war of the public and private life of Clémenceau, his energy, notwithstanding his age, his good humor, animated rejoinders, and general "tiger" characteristics. He was much praised for his admirable spirit, his nervy and solid good sense during the most critical months of the war as head of the French Government. Beyond all the sympathetic traits that made him so popular, he remained one of the greatest characters in contemporaneous Europe, and one of the greatest leaders of men. He belonged to a line that had come down from the Revolution. Philosopher, writer, man of science, orator, author, he testified through his entire public career to the fact that ideas guide the world, drawing men and their interests in their train. The war had been an immense economic conflict, since it was in the name of democracy, justice, and liberty that the world rose to win it. It was for these three magic words, democracy, justice and liberty, that Clémenceau had fought all his life, in untiring opposition to everything that could limit their sway or dull their glow. Of all political heads of the Third Republic he was the one who had exercised the greatest influence on the present generation and had most vigorously directed the people of his country toward democracy.

Impartial history will some day perhaps tell what struggles Clémenceau had to undergo in the Inter-Allied Councils, as well as at the head of the French Government, in order to make certain ideas and solutions prevail—such as unity of command in the appointment of Foch as Generalissimo. It will relate what fatiguing physical effort was exacted from him in uninterrupted visits to the front, questioning soldiers and exhorting commanders, exposing himself to first-line fire; doing this in spite of all advice to spare himself; simply to fill his rôle as a chief, and knowing the immense power of personal example—the embodiment to all eyes of the spirit of duty. For half a century he had battled in the van of democracy, when in 1917 he assumed the reins of political power resolved to make an

[37] Adapted from an article in The *Evening Public Ledger* (Philadelphia), and from a compilation by Alexander Harvey in *Current Opinion*, based on articles in The *Daily News* and The *Daily Chronicle* (London), and the *Matin*, *Humanite*, *Gaulois*, and the *Journal des Débats* (Paris).

end of the war and recover the lost provinces. No public man ever realized a like destiny—none ever knew such consecration to a life-time of effort. All his former life had predestined Clémenceau to the great rôle he played in the war. He seemed ordained by fate to meet Wilson. The two were worthy of standing face to face and deliberating as to democracy's future.

When Clémenceau in 1917 was again called to be Prime Minister, France turned to "a wrecker of Cabinets" in her hour of need, to a man once described as having "torn, clawed and bitten his way to power." His enemies had been legion, but now the nation chose Clémenceau to lead her Government. No one had ever doubted his patriotism. His every act of construction, or destruction, had been in the interest of what he considered the welfare of France. He had wielded his power with a fearless pen in his newspaper, *L'Homme Libre* (*The Free Man*). His paper was suspended once early in the war because he refused to suppress certain passages in an article. He met the condition by changing the name of the paper to *L'Homme Enchâiné* (*The Chained Man*). Afterward the paper reappeared under its old title. While Clémenceau was in office as Prime Minister his name appeared on his newspaper only as "founder," instead of as "political director" as before. He would not write for it while in office.

Clémenceau was no longer a young man—he was seventy-six in 1917, but his powers were unimpaired. A friend once asked him how many ministries he had overturned, and he replied pleasantly that he was quite unable to recall the number. Some of the titles he won during his long career besides "wrecker of Cabinets" was the "Stormy Petrel of French Politics," the "Red Indian," the "King-Maker" and the "Tiger," the latter of which clung to him. Having married an American girl, at one time his pupil during his exile in America, an epithet applied to him by his opponents was the "Yankee School-teacher."

The storms that attended his career began early. His father was imprisoned by Napoleon III, at the time of the *coup d'état* that destroyed the Second Republic. The son was thus a child of Revolution. It was characteristic of him that he supported General Boulanger, as long as he believed him to be working in the interests of the Republic, but when the "Man on Horseback" began to scheme for the return of the Bourbons, Clémenceau rose up and drove him from power. Before he was twenty he was arrested for shouting on the streets of Paris, in the midst of a celebration of one of the imperial anniversaries, *"Vive la Republique!"* Having served his term in jail be became practically an exile and came to America. Between 1865 and 1869 he lived in New York near Washington

Square, and in Stamford, Conn. Having been educated as a physician he started in practise on West Twelfth Street, New York. Before he left France he had made the acquaintance of Marshall, the artist, who made famous portraits of Washington and Lincoln. By invitation from Marshall he had come to New York.

His father had been a physician before him. Generations of his family had followed the medical profession, but he was not successful like the others of his line as a doctor of medicine. The chief reason was said to be that he was not deeply interested in that calling. Even as a student in Paris he had found time to inform himself on political questions and to contribute controversial papers to reviews. In New York he gravitated naturally toward the study of social and political conditions and drew his income, not so much from the practise of his profession, as from letters about things in America which he sent to papers at home. His first impression of Americans was that they had "no general ideas and no good coffee." Failing to build up a medical practise, and his funds running low, Clémenceau obtained a position as teacher of French language and literature in a young ladies' seminary in Stamford, Conn. The future celebrity appears in after years to have looked back on Stamford with real pleasure. He once told how he had "accompanied young ladies on walks and pleasant and easy rides along charming wooded roads that lined the smiling shores of Long Island Sound." He added that in those "happy and light-hearted years" at Stamford his temperament "became strengthened and refined." It was during one of his "charming horseback rides" that he ventured to propose to one of the young American "misses"—Mary Plummer, of Springfield, Mass., whom he afterward married. Returning to France in 1870, Clémenceau's natural inclinations led him into politics.

During the Franco-Prussian War and the siege of Paris, Clémenceau was Mayor of Montmartre. One of his duties during the siege was to see that 150,000 men were properly fed, and another to look after thousands of refugees. In this work he became responsible for large amounts of money. Foreseeing that accusations against any one's honesty might be made in such trying times, he engaged an expert accountant to "check-up" and make public his use of every sou of public funds. Next year he was elected to the General Assembly, and opposed the treaty of peace with Germany. From 1871 to 1875 he was a member of the Paris Municipal Council, of which he became President, and in 1876 was elected member from Montmartre in the Chamber of Deputies, where he became leader of the Radicals. From the outset of his career in the French Parliament he was the bitter opponent of the Royalists, and soon became known for eloquence and independence of action. He was independent even in his radicalism, and followed no leader but himself. Some men called him "an undisciplined vandal" who was making a reputation as an upsetter of other men's careers. His political power was increased by his journalistic activities. In 1880 he founded *La Justice,* a daily paper with which he destroyed the Broglie administration, overthrew Boulanger, caused the fall of Jules Grévy and Jules Ferry and wrecked the position of M. de Freycinet at least three times.

Clémenceau's policy was a consistent but radical Republicanism; he stood for a realization of what the Revolution had hoped for and dreamed of. He was opposed to the alliance with Russia, determined that his country should not be joined in close friendship with a despotic power, unceasingly upheld the complete separation of Church and State, and urged the development of French resources. In 1893 Clémenceau's career apparently was wrecked when, during the Panama scandals, he was accused of dishonesty, but he met every charge and beat down attacks in the Chamber. His constituents, however, deserted him, and so he dropt out of politics. It was nine years before he was again officially in public life. For that period he was a man of letters, instead of a politician, a reckless duelist, and a hounder of his foes. As a philosopher and litterateur, who wrote exquisite prose, a lover of nature and a friend of humankind, he flourished again. Among his writings were a book on the philosophy of nature, "Great Pan"; a novel of social life, "The Strongest"; a play of which the scene was laid in China, and some notable criticisms. He returned afterward to journalism, his old paper having gone down in the wreck of his political career. When the Dreyfus affair was stirring all France, a new journal called *L'Aurore,* edited by Clémenceau, made its appearance. It was devoted to proving Dreyfus innocent. Clémenceau thus got back into the active world of French affairs. Because of Clémenceau's tireless defense of Dreyfus, Zola published in his paper his scathing denunciation of conditions, *"J'Accuse."*

In 1902 the same constituency that had forsaken Clémenceau in his hour of trial returned him to the Senate, and in the spring of 1906 he was appointed to public office as Minister of the Interior. In November of the same year he became Premier. Three years later his old enemy, Delcassé, overthrew his ministry, but his power was not broken, for he kept his place in the Senate. In 1912 he overthrew Caillaux's Ministry and 1913 wrecked Briand's Cabinet. When the war began he was in the Viviani Ministry. Clémenceau's patriotism was widely recognized. He never hesitated in the midst of the stress of war to argue, criticize, and actually to attack where he believed a need for opposition existed.

PERSONAL SKETCHES OF WAR LEADERS

In the late autumn of 1918, after Clémenceau had been Prime Minister a little more than a year and the war had been won, it was possible to measure his achievement. He came to office when the army had failed on the Aisne and for the first and only time was shaken in morale. A monstrous defeatist campaign had begun in France. A break on the home-front and then on the firing-line was forecast. Not willingly did France turn to Clémenceau. His strength all men recognized, but his strength and his weakness alike terrified his contemporaries. If his eloquence in his newspaper had again and again roused the nation, his long political struggles had made enemies and his destructive course over half a century had left him with few political friends and a host of enemies. "Briand will fail and go," Caillaux had said in Rome in 1917. "There may be another, and then will come Clémenceau, who will try and fail, and then— then I will come." The whole game had been set for Caillaux to come and make peace with Germany; then Clémenceau came and Caillaux languished behind the bars. Ere long the armies of France were in Strasbourg and Metz.

The first task of Clémenceau was to restore the home-front. After terrible sacrifices for more than three years, with the Russian revolution destroying the Entente's Eastern Ally, and a new invasion in sight, France faced a crisis which had only two solutions—collapse, or the discovery of a great leader. Without leadership nothing more was possible. Then almost in an hour the atmosphere cleared. Backed by Clémenceau, Pétain reorganized the army; single-handed, Clémenceau wrestled with weaklings. To every protest, every feeble whine, he responded: *"Je fais la guerre."* Did men ask him questions, did they make motions in the Chamber, did they seek to trap and entangle him, his answer, ever clearer and clearer, was the same, "I make war," and he would add, "Victory is to the side which endures to the last quarter of an hour."

Clémenceau faced hostile critics in the Chamber with the dust and mud of battlefields on his clothes; left the tribune to reappear at the front, as scornful of personal danger as he was impatient of intrigue. Armies knew him better than did the politicians. When the German line broke before Amiens, in 1918, he was promptly on the scene and took back to Paris the first authentic news that the German flood had been checked. So, too, in Flanders when Haig's army stood with its "back to the wall." As he returned from Bethune, he announced in Paris, "The skies are already brightening." "There was a time," Clémenceau once said, "when I despaired of my countrymen. I believed France was finished, but now—now, look about for yourself. I have not one word to say." That was in the Verdun time of 1916 when Clémenceau had been daily thundering forth that,

"The Germans are at Noyon," His confidence in his countrymen was immeasurable; but his impatience at mistakes, at lack of courage, at blindness beyond restraint for three years, grew more and more vocal.

When ruin was in sight France had turned to Clémenceau, as the Allies, spurred by his urgings, afterward turned to Foch. France once more became the corner-stone of the Alliance, the foundation on which victory could be built, and Clémenceau was the embodiment of France. Before the end those who had opposed him shrank from challenging a man whose voice had become the voice of their country. In defeat he made the nation believe victory was possible, and when victory came it seemed only the logical conclusion of his leadership. This war produced more great generals than brilliant statesmen, and the achievement of one general, Ferdinand Foch, was a far-shining triumph, which would endure through all history; yet without Clémenceau, Foch might have failed, and when France came to decide to whom she most owed her "lost provinces" she might name this man of seventy-seven who, in the national legislation of 1871 had forbade the cession, and now had redeemed the loss. It had been a wonderful career and a wonderful old man was Clémenceau.[37a]

THÉOPHILE DELCASSÉ, FOREIGN MINISTER OF FRANCE

Altho Delcassé during the war was still living but not in the public eye, his career in the French Foreign Office before the war had an intimate relation to the world conflict. Writers like Morton Fullerton went so far as to say that, while various reasons were found for the failure of the German advance through Belgium and northern France to the Marne, and while the first stumbling-block to the Germans was the resistance of Belgium, that was not so real a thing, counting all the late years, as the remarkable personality, the shrewd and agile brain, of Delcassé. He it was who undid the work of Bismarck by making possible an alliance between Great Britain and France.

One morning in France the work of Delcassé was particularly brought to Mr. Fullerton's attention. He had spent that morning with the French Minister to Belgium, and in leaving was suddenly arrested by a musical note alien to French music. It was the sound of a bagpipe accompanying the march of invisible men. Soon there swung round, out of a side street into an avenue skirting the sea, a column of the new khaki-clad army of Great Britain, followed by an officer on horseback, with a score of terriers, fox and Scotch,

---

[37a] Principal Sources: The *Tribune*, The *Times* (New York), Alexander Harvey in *Current Opinion*, and Henri-Martin Barzun in *The Review of Reviews*.

yelping up and down the line. Regiments soon filled the avenues. Seaward were seen brown French battleships riding at anchor. From marching men came forth the song, "It's a long, long way to Tipperary." Five thousand British lads had just landed on French soil, and were going to trenches in Flanders. At Mr. Fullerton's elbow, there in Havre, stood a Belgian deputy and a French Foreign official. Turning to the Frenchman the Belgian said, "That's the work of your Delcassé." Later in the day Mr. Fullerton had an audience with a Belgian Minister, when the talk associated itself instantly with that landing scene. "Your Excellency," said Mr. Fullerton, "Belgium has saved Europe, to which the Minister replied: "It is not Belgium that has saved Europe. The savior of Europe is M. Delcassé."

For many months, if not a full year, before war actually began, Delcassé had been one of the quietest of 580 members of the French Chamber of Deputies. No one knew what he thought of the situation, and no one took much trouble to find out. Meanwhile events continued to take the road that led directly to the cataclysm. This alert little statesman, no taller than Napoleon, was always seen in his seat, playing an almost silent part in the Parliamentary game, a model of party discipline. Men heard his staccato step in the lobby, noted the directness of his glance through eye-glasses, his frank and unembarrassed manner, his readiness to listen and his reticence in reply. All signs betokened the same energy, straightforwardness of purpose, absence of academic priggishness, but the presence of diplomatic and statesmanlike composure that had enabled him to secure for France those far-reaching diplomatic victories that altered the balance of power in the European system. But now with grim resolution he held his peace. Not even in the press were seen words of his counseling his countrymen. No interview restored him to the limelight. Some thought him dead. Beyond the Vosges, the Alps, and the Pyrenees, and across the Channel, his figure, however, was still to close observers one of few still visible to the naked eye. To foreigners Delcassé personified a regenerated France. All competent observers knew that his apparent political burial was only an optical illusion, that before long he or his work would rise again, to incarnate a new national hope.

This confidence was well founded. It is not every man who earns the reputation of being "the man who undid the work of Bismarck" and "encircled" the Germans. Bismarck's plan had been remarkably simple; to involve France with Italy in Tunis, and with England on the Kongo, in Madagascar, and elsewhere, and so to keep all three nations in a fractious state, unfriendly toward one another and dependent on Germany's sympathy for strength. He made his plan work well and stood by watching his neighbors weakening themselves for his ultimate benefit. All things had gone on well, up to the very point where France and Great Britain would fall out and come to blows, and then, in the person of Delcassé, the stumbling-block appeared.

Great Britain and France had been fatefully and logically brought to an issue in an African desert, where the swords of Kitchener and Marchand had been upraised. It was Delcassé who dared to give the French commander at Fashoda an order to stay his blow and return the weapon to its scabbard. Delcassé had himself, as Minister for the Colonies in an earlier time, been among the most responsible of French statesmen who directed a policy against British colonial ambitions. With Hanotaux, who as Foreign Minister had the responsibility, he pursued a policy of colonial expansion originally conceived years before by Jules Ferry, and helped to wrest from Great Britain coveted strips of African soil, and Pacific islands. When the event of Fashoda occurred, no one better than he understood the full extent of French humiliation. As Hanotaux's usefulness ended, Delcassé was chosen to succeed him and direct the destinies of France.

Two roads then lay before France. One led to Berlin and was the road that had been followed for more than twenty years—but it carried the French people further and further away from Alsace and Lorraine, and had now brought them face to face with disaster at Fashoda. The other road, utterly untried, a strange new path through an undiscovered country, led to London. It was now seen that one furthen step on the road to Berlin would lead to war with Great Britain, and Delcassé did not hesitate but chose the path of peace with Great Britain. It had suddenly dawned on him that France and Great Britain had long been playing into Germany's hands. Fashoda was their Damascus road. With this knowledge came a quick decision. France and Great Britain should compose their differences. So believed Delcassé, and he proceeded to make overtures for a settlement of all Franco-British difficulties.

The Fashoda incident of 1898 threatened actual war, and Germany with open arms was ready to make friends with France, but Delcassé, instead, humiliated himself before Great Britain. The English Ambassador who had called to present to France an ultimatum fumbled in Delcassé's presence at his frock-coat pocket preliminary to getting a piece of paper. "Do not undc that button," said Delcassé—so at least the story ran. "I must not see that paper. It is a threat, and if I see it France must fight. Matters will arrange themselves." So was sown the first seed for the *entente cordiale*, an indispensable seed for France in the World War. The *entente cordiale* was afterward built up through private informal conferences in Paris and elsewhere between King Edward VII and Delcassé. The French Ambassador in London and Sir Edward Grey, the Foreign Minister, meanwhile practically stept aside.

Had there been in 1914 no formal declaration of war between France and Germany, the appointment by Viviani of Delcassé, as Minister of War, would have been sufficient, for Delcassé had been like a flare of scarlet to the Teutonic bull. As recently as January, 1913, Germany had virtually ordered his dismissal from the French Cabinet. Delcassé was a little man, of stocky peasant build, whose hair seemed always in disarray, whose brilliant neckties served only to emphasize a muddy complexion, and whose ill-fitting clothes looked as if they might have been bought at the Shop of the Three Balls. He had a face as hard and as strong as marble. Pity, compassion, even the emotion of hatred, seemed unknown to it. He was a Frenchman who had nothing of French volubility. He was a peasant who had the exquisite manners of a prince—when he wished to employ them. When standing beside his wife he was overshadowed by a tall lady of ample proportions, splendidly gowned as befitting the widow of a millionaire, who looked down upon her second spouse with pride, effacing herself before him so completely that the little man seemed to stand alone and to fill the room.[38]

ENVER PASHA, THE WAR-MINISTER OF TURKEY

For his connection with the Armenian massacres, of which he was everywhere accepted as the chief instigator, Enver's name became probably the most execrated of all names familiar in men's minds during the war. However men might differ about the judicial arraignment of the Kaiser for war-crimes, there was little difference of opinion as to the propriety of trying the chief personages connected with Turkish atrocities. These, besides Enver, were Talaat Bey and Djemel Pasha, but it was Enver who was most responsible, not only for the Armenian massacres but for a proposal that Allied civilians, in 1915, be sent to the bombardment area in Gallipoli as a "reprisal." The apportionment of blame among Talaat, Enver, and the Germans, called for thorough and exact inquiry. For nothing did the world demand a more rigorous meting out of just punishment. Enver was the real head of the Turkish Government, actual control being in his hands and those of Talaat and Djemel. Together they had caused the massacre of perhaps a million Armenians, Syrians, and Greeks—Enver the brains of the crime, the others the brutal directors of its execution. Henry Morgenthau, American

[38] Adapted from articles in *The World's Work* and The *World* (New York).

Ambassador to Turkey during a part of the war, described Enver thus: "His nature had a remorselessness, a lack of pity, a cold-blooded determination, of which his clean-cut, handsome face, his small but sturdy figure, and his pleasing manners gave no indication." When defeat and disgrace came he and Talaat fled, after having first robbed the Turkish treasury of a hundred and more millions of dollars.

Advices in May, 1919, that Talaat had been found among Caucasian Tatars added a new and satisfactory page to the life-history of a man who first saw the light in the household of a Stamboul "layer-out" of corpses. Embezzlement was the least crime with which Enver could have been charged because Turkish authorities could have indicted him for assassinations of public men and army officers. Not long afterward the Turks, by court-martial, condemned him to death. He was then supposed to be in Germany. The same sentence was passed on Talaat and Djemel. Concerning "the 1,800,-000 Armenians who were in the Ottoman Empire two years ago," said Mr. Balfour in a message to America in February, 1917, "1,200,-000 have been either massacred or deported." Enver was a forceful man and for a magnetic personality stood alone among the Turks. In any other country besides Turkey—in England, Germany, or the United States—he could scarcely have failed to have a career of some kind, good or bad.

Enver was the evil genius who, by conspiring with the German Ambassador, had brought Turkey into the war at a time when her people were opposed to intervention. He was a tool of Germany and betrayed his country. From the time when Great Britain and France allowed Italy to move in Tripoli, Enver had stood definitely committed to cooperation with Germany, in Turkey's domestic and international affairs. Having received his military training in Berlin, he admired the German military system, and in all ways promoted German interests. His capacity for leadership had made him at thirty a military dictator. At that age most Europeans would not attain to captaincies. He had deep faith in the soundness of the things for which he stood. His early plans and dreams were all to one end—the regeneration of Turkey. Of his swordsmanship, his fluency as a linguist, the almost ascetic simplicity of his life, his strange compound of the mystic and criminal in action; his way of exercising influence and authority, often at the expense of discipline, and quite out of proportion to his official or military rank—much has been written by those who knew him well.

Before the war Lewis R. Freeman discerned that he was small in stature, but remarkably well set up, strikingly handsome, and with an indefinable, but compelling, magnetism, which made itself felt through a curtain of dignified reserve. At a casual meeting this reserve, with a certain detachment of manner, would impress one as a dominating trait, and such was Mr. Freeman's feeling until a chance remark regarding the way in which the Arabs of Mesopotamia and Syria had clamored to be led to Tripoli against Italy and how several had even worked their way to Aleppo, brought a warm flush of color to his cheeks and a glint of moisture to his eyes. "Ah, my brave Arabs!" he cried affectionately. "If I could only gather them in from all their desert ways, and arm them properly."

"The plans of all the Powers," said Enver to Mr. Freeman, in that interview before the World War began, "have always been entirely selfish as far as Turkey was concerned. For years Russia coveted Constantinople, to say nothing of the rest of Turkey along the Black Sea and south of the Caucasus, and the British endeavored to keep us just strong enough to prevent Russia from realizing these ambitions. Finally came the Kaiser with his scheme of a chain of German-controlled States from the Baltic to the Persian Gulf, and for the success of this plan a strong, not a weak, Turkey was *sine qua non*. Russia would wipe us off the map, England would keep us weak, but Germany would make us strong. All selfish motives on face of them, no doubt, but—can you wonder what alternative was the least repugnant to us Turks, especially to us Young Turks who have done our best to avoid being enmeshed in the nets of British and Russian diplomacy and intrigue which have held helpless our predecessors? I think I will not need to say more to answer your question as to why it was that Germany obtained the Bagdad railway concession, why the Hedjaz line was built by Germans, and why the Germans are recasting our military establishment." [39]

"Do you care to speak of your so-called Turkish reform program?" Mr. Freeman asked him in a final question, warned by Sheiks and officers gathering under the flap of a reception tent that a conference with Enver was about to be held. Enver hesitated for a moment, and then, his eyes lighting with the enthusiasm kindled by a project which in those days was the one nearest his heart, rose to his feet and spoke briefly and to the point, meanwhile grasping Mr. Freeman's hand in a grip of farewell:

"Real Turkish unification is my dearest wish, and any international political arrangement which will leave me a free hand to work for that, I will subscribe to. Turkey contains a great many Christians, as well as Mohammedans. The latter I would regenerate from within, not from without. The West has little that we need, save battleships and shrapnels, and if it would leave us alone we would not need even these. Nor can the Occident give us anything better to follow than the precepts of

[39] In a *Review of Reviews* article.

the Koran. For us Mohammedans, I would purify the old faith, not bring in a new one,—there are close to a score of them, as you know. But for our Christian peoples, I would let them follow their own faith in peace and security, something they have not always been able to do in the past. I would offer them everything that England, or Greece, or France could,—more than Russia ever would,—and by this means I would make them Turkish subjects in fact as well as in name. Great Britain, a Christian power, has made good subjects of the Mohammedans in India; why shall not Turkey, a Mohammedan power, make good subjects of the Christians in the Ottoman Empire? A real Turkish nation is my dream—a nation able at last to stand upon its own legs.''

Enver was only thirty-two years old when the World War began. He was of Ottoman descent, by which was meant that he was one of the eight or nine million Mussulmans in whom the blood of the original Turkish conquerors had received, in the course of centuries, a strong Albanian, Slav, and Greek tincture. Thus he was not a pure Turk such as was Osman Pasha, the hero of Plevna. He justified the proverb "as strong as a Turk," and was as healthy and tough as he was vigorous, and extremely handsome. An illustration of his powers of endurance was found when he headed the expedition for the recapture, in 1913, of Adrianople, riding fifteen hours on end and fighting a couple of hours after that for possession of the town, all the while suffering from a severe attack of appendicitis. Operated upon for this complaint a month later, he was up and doing again in a week. Born strong and healthy, he had always led a hygienic life—active, regular, and free from indulgences, so much so that he had never touched alcohol, following in this one of the prescriptions of Islamism. Neither did he smoke or drink coffee.[40]

KING FERDINAND OF BULGARIA

Only the German Emperor was more often sketched from an intimate point of view late in the war, than Ferdinand of Bulgaria. Cartoonists familiarized frequenters of cafés and beer-halls with a gigantic nose, a portly frame, an impressive height and statuesque repose. There were studies of him from the psychological standpoint also and estimates of his moral nature. And yet this so-called superman of the Balkans remained something of a mystery. His enemies seemed all in the Allied camp. He was said to be at once an artist and a grand-seigneur, consummately skilled in knowledge of human nature, especially on its weaker side, with gifts of ingratiation, but which he rarely deigned to exercise, a man of many moods and many stratagems, a botanist and a bird-stuffer, a disciple of

[40] Compiled from an article by Lewis R. Freeman in the *Review of Reviews* and one by A. Rustem Bey in *The World's Work.*

Machiavelli, the incarnation of a hero for a moving-picture melodrama. Power came to him because of his personal sway over men. It was said of the Bulgarian Czar that he ruled men, bending them to his will subtly, by the exercise of something beyond and above charm. He cast spells.

All that was mysterious in Ferdinand could be understood by reference to his dream of being crowned in Constantinople. He was a man of genius fretting and fuming behind the iron bars of a parochial cage. His traits and tendencies were what might be expected from one who must work with and conciliate and manage intellectual inferiors. He was the lion who assumed, now the manners of the lamb, now the hide of the ass. He was a man to whom modern science had unfolded its mysteries. He had been a frequenter in the recent past of the laboratories of the Sorbonne, an admirer of Berthelot, a diligent reader of the mathematician Poincaré. He had his superstitions, too. When still in his cradle his mother received an assurance from some gypsy that he would sit on the throne of a Cæsar. He still studied signs in the heavens and did not disdain the lore of those who cast horoscopes. At his birth major constellations were in the ascendant, above the horizon. The English explained his career by his genius for intrigue and the windings of a devious nature.

The mother of Ferdinand was Clementine, daughter of the French King, Louis Philippe, one of the ablest women of her day, in whom his own fascination was foreshadowed. She had the same imperial "pose"—a majestic wave of the right hand and arm—which delighted cartoonists who used it to make much capital out of her son. He had her voice, which was loud and pleasing, "flexible as that of a Bernhardt," and he had as well that genius of hers for conversation of which much was made by writers of memoirs of the period. Ferdinand was rated one of the best talkers in Europe; a witty raconteur, an exhilarating companion. All these things came to him from his mother, together, it was hinted, with a capacity for concealing his true self, which was feminine rather than masculine. Ferdinand got shrewdness as well as charm from his mother. She it was who revealed to him the mysteries of a statecraft such as he learned to practise. She was determined that her best-beloved boy should be something more than "one of the hapless group of unemployed Highnesses," that he should not lead a futile life as a mere officer in the Austro-Hungarian army. She meant that he should be a king, and gave him one bit of advice to which he adhered—to conceal rather than to reveal the extent of his powers.

Nothing, however, could have seemed more extravagant in the last quarter of the nineteenth century than that Ferdinand should be summoned to rule a State. There were no thrones unoccupied and the old world was tranquil. Then suddenly Alexander, Prince of Bulgaria, was kidnapped, the land was without a head, and Ferdinand had the audacity to offer himself for the place. He took a secret trip down the Danube and on one occasion slept in a farmer's wagon to escape the knife of an assassin. Chaotic Bulgaria was under the sway of Stambouloff, a rude, rough man, reared in the inn his father had kept and who roared with laughter at the cultivation, fine manners, perfumes and pedigree in which Ferdinand delighted; but in no long time Stambouloff fell completely under his spell, despite all their quarrels. Ferdinand began as a figurehead and ended as an absolute ruler.

His success was attributed to the essentially constructive activities of his mind. He built things up, organized and brought them together, always knew what he wanted, was positive, affirmative and ready with a plan. Relatively to other Balkan States, the school system of Bulgaria was efficient, and Ferdinand stood behind it at every stage. His scientific interests were reflected in it. He was remarkably receptive to new ideas, recognized ability wherever he saw it and never hesitated to advance a man of merit however humble in origin. Bulgaria came to have a long list of men whom Ferdinand had "discovered." If some farmer's boy showed an intelligent interest in the stars, he might be singled out as a possible Tycho Brahe, destined to shed luster on science in Bulgaria. Should a country bumpkin reveal oratorical gifts of an unusual order, he was welcomed at court, complimented by the sovereign and listened to with profound respect. Nobody, in short, in Bulgaria could manifest capacity without attracting Ferdinand. The somewhat ostentatious catholicity of his culture was partly calculated for effect upon the Bulgarians, whom he sought to civilize, refine, and educate, and so he popularized chemistry as well as the dinner-fork. Nor was he above saying a good word from time to time in behalf of wearing gloves, against which plain Bulgarians were inclined to protest.

The most serious charge against Ferdinand in his sovereign capacity concerned finance. If what some of the French and British dailies said was true, he had accumulated great wealth by methods likely to land an ordinary capitalist in the penitentiary. He never profest morality in the conventional sense. The life of Ferdinand was once described as a combination of the industry of Faraday, the energy of Bluebeard and the activities of Gil Blas, traits and tendencies of all being blended in the mosaic of his character.[41]

[41] Adapted from an article by Alexander Harvey in *Current Opinion*, based on articles in the *Journal des Débats*, *Temps*, and *Gaulo·* (Paris). The *Daily Mail* (London), the *Neue Freie Presse* (Vienna), and the *Vossische Zeitung* (Berlin).

PERSONAL SKETCHES OF WAR LEADERS

FRANCIS JOSEPH, Emperor of Austria

It was the Government of Francis Joseph of the house of Hapsburg, backed by the Government of William of the house of Hohenzollern, which launched in July, 1914, that fatal and brutal document, the ultimatum to Serbia, which precipitated the World War. Francis Joseph died at 86, two and a half years afterward, having had the longest active reign known to the history of kings and emperors. A likable man was Francis Joseph—very likable personally—in spite of the gross anachronism that his form of government presented to the modern world—a purely medieval autocracy, of which he was the soul and head.

The end of his long reign recalled a curse which the Countess Karolyi, nearly seventy years before, had passed upon him. The Countess had a son who was executed by Austria-Hungary for complicity in the Kossuth revolt in 1848. In her grief she called on heaven to blast the young emperor's happiness, "to exterminate his family, to strike him through those whom he loved, to wreck his life and ruin his children." Signally complete was the fulfilment of this curse, or prophecy. Almost from first to last, the reign of Francis Joseph was marked by political disasters, domestic misfortunes, and acute tragedies such as recalled the doom that fell upon the ancient and legendary house of Atreus, of which Homer sang and tragedians spoke their lines. There was the execution of his brother Maximilian, whom Louis Napoleon tried to maintain on the throne of Mexico; then came the assassination, in broad daylight in Geneva, of his wife, the Empress Elizabeth, and the mysterious suicide, in circumstances pointing clearly to a great scandal, of his only son and heir, Rudolph. A brother disappeared from Vienna suddenly, and wandered to many distant parts of the earth under the name of John Orth. A sister-in-law was burned so badly that she died from her injuries. Three attempts were made on his own life. Last of all came the assassination of his nephew and heir, with his consort, at Serajevo, in June, 1914.

Francis Joseph's reign, in spite of a few notable successes, had been marked by political ill-fortune quite as tragic. As it had opened with revolution and civil war, so in the years before he reached middle life, Austria lost her Italian provinces, including states ruled by members of the Emperor's own family—Venice, Lombardy, Parma, Modena, and Tuskany. Austria had also lost to Prussia her supremacy among the German states. His reign finally closed amid the appalling ruin foreshadowed for Austria, as a result of the World War. Since his accession to the throne as a boy of eighteen, when he found his country in the throes of revolution, he had lived on full of years and sorrows, until he saw it in a crisis destined to end in its extinction as a Great Power.

When it was said that his reign had been the longest active reign in history, account was taken of the fact that, while Louis XIV was King of France for seventy-two years, the early part of his reign took place in years when he was a minor, so that, as an active monarch, Francis Joseph exceeded the record left by Louis XIV. The reign of George III came within eight years of being as long as Francis Joseph's, but George III, near the end of his life, was virtually insane, and a regency had been necessary. Queen Victoria came closer than did her grandfather, but her reign was four years shorter than Francis Joseph's. Born August 18, 1830, Francis Joseph was a son of Archduke Francis, and a grandson of the Emperor Francis, who was then reigning. The Emperor Francis, as the father of Marie Louise, was Napoleon's father-in-law. From 1835 to 1848 Francis Joseph's uncle, Ferdinand, occupied the Austrian throne, but was exiled from his capital during the revolution of 1848, and then abdicated. Ferdinand being childless, a brother would have succeeded him, but the brother was unwilling to take the responsibility of being Emperor in a time of revolution, and thus Francis Joseph, as the next heir, ascended the throne, after having been thoroughly and religiously trained by his mother, and having had five months of military training in the Italian War. Much respect for the kingly prerogative and little for popular rights or constitutional government had been acquired in his youth.

Before Francis Joseph became Emperor Vienna had been practically pacified, but the revolt in Hungary under Kossuth and Gorgei was not crusht until afterward, when help was obtained from a Russian army that descended into Hungary through the Carpathian passes. Francis Joseph, in spite of all his errors, due to the autocratic principles fundamental in his political faith, was no mere figurehead. His hand had been the deciding factor in everything that could have been called a crisis in Austria. He had ability as a conciliator, a faculty for which he had much need in an empire so polyglot as his own. Of the thirty million people over whom he ruled, less than one-third were Germans. Of the twenty-one millions in Hungary, of which country he was king, fewer than one-half were Magyars. Austria-Hungary, unlike most States in every part of the world, had not grown organically through expansion under natural racial laws, but was a collection of discordant, unrelated States, which, through financial and matrimonial arrangements, military aggression and other compelling occurrences, had gradually come into the hands of the Hapsburgs. Some one had wisely said that "if Austria-Hungary had not existed as a State, it would have been necessary to create her." Francis Joseph bore the title of Emperor of Austria, Apostolic King of Hungary, King of Bohemia, Dalmatia, Croatia, Slavonia, Galicia, Lodo, Meria, and Ellyria. He was also an archduke of Austria, a grand duke of Tuskany, Krakow, and Lorraine.

But with all these distinctions the greatest—on paper at least—that had elsewhere existed since Napoleon's time, his reign, as already seen, was marked by a succession of disasters, public and private. Last and most tragic of all was the outcome of the World War. Before the promulgation of the ultimatum to Serbia, the kingdom of Francis Joseph had embraced 240,900 square miles; it was territorially the second largest in Europe, Russia being the largest, and had over 50,000,000 inhabitants. After peace was signed with the Entente Allies, all that remained of Francis Joseph's Austro-Hungarian empire was its kernel—that is, Teutonic Austria, whose area was something under 50,000 square miles, and whose population was under 10,000,000. In other words, an empire that had been territorially larger than France or Germany, and that had contained 10,000,000 more people than France, was left with a territory about equal to that of New York State, and a population somewhat less than New York's.[42]

KING GEORGE V, of Great Britain

King George, whose title is King of Great Britain and Ireland and of Dominions Beyond the Seas, Emperor of India, was the second son of King Edward VII, born at Marlborough House, in London, June 3, 1865. He entered the Navy in 1877, studied at Greenwich, became a lieutenant in 1885, a captain in 1893, a rear-admiral in 1901, and vice-admiral in 1903. After the death of his elder brother, Albert Victor, Duke of Clarence, in 1892, he was made Duke of York, and in 1893 married Princess Victoria Mary of Teck, who had previously been engaged to Albert Victor. Four sons and one daughter were born to him and Queen Mary, the eldest, Edward, Prince of Wales, in 1894. Upon the accession to the throne of his father, Edward VII, in 1901, Prince George received the title of Prince of Wales and Duke of Cornwall, and made a journey around the world, in the course of which he visited the British colonies. On his return to England in November he was formally created Prince of Wales and in 1905-06 made a tour of India. His father dying in 1910, he succeeded to the throne as George V, his wife having the name of Queen Mary. They were crowned in Westminster Abbey

[42] Compiled from articles in The New York *Tribune, The Literary Digest,* and the "Encyclopedia Britannica."

June 22, 1911. In December of that year they visited India and in February, 1912, returned to England.

In the glare of war King George was revealed as a truly democratic and human personality. In camps and hospitals "over there" as well as in England he was often seen and always had a kind word of cheer for every one. He spent his days in "doing his bit" like a soldier. If Thackeray had been alive his pen might have added to his "Four Georges" a new chapter, in which he would have told how the Fifth George with his Queen ate buckwheat-cakes in an American canteen in London. Brief and tactful was the way of their coming to that canteen. "The King and Queen," said a message one day, "desire to call at the Eagle Hut and will be there in a few minutes." Unannounced they drove up, King George in a snug uniform, carrying his familiar stick; Queen Mary, a size larger, motherly, wholesome, simple in dress and manner, and looking as might almost any Englishwoman who was the mother of four well-brought-up boys and one girl. From the entrance they climbed a flight of steps into a hall where soldiers and sailors, British, Canadians, and Americans, were playing games, writing letters, singing camp-songs and feeling quite at home in a congenial atmosphere; a free-and-easy place of many sounds and much laughter, of liberty and equality. King George and Queen Mary went in as ordinary visitors who wished to disturb no one, but to mingle with others and be friendly without ceremony. They exprest a wish to eat an American dish and then sat down at one of the big tables covered with oilcloth. "Buckwheat-cakes is the best thing we have," said the host, a little flustered by the visit. And buckwheat-cakes it was, with New England maple-syrup. King George and Queen Mary voted the unfamiliar griddle-cakes delicious, went the rounds of kitchens and dormitories, and departed like people who had had a good time.

The King liked to talk with Tommy Atkins, and so acquired the habit of being simple and hospitable to plain fighting men. He was heart and soul in the war all day long. While he had a preference for the Navy, in which he had been brought up, he was careful never to show it. In the Navy he had learned equality and how to be a plain man. Probably he never felt quite like a traditional king after he assumed the crown. "Pat" O'Brien, the aviator who escaped from German captivity and wrote a popular book about it, found King George, to whom by request he told the story of his adventures, one of the most democratic men he had ever met. O'Brien talked with him for an hour and a quarter and after the first few minutes said he never felt more at ease in his life.[42a] King George was fifty-one years old in 1916. He was one of the best wing-shots in Eng-

[42a] The *Times* (New York).

land, an expert navigator, an authority on men-of-war, and domestic in his tastes, but he disliked classical music, preferring instead sprightly melodies. He had a large collection of babies' photographs and had made a collection of postage stamps. He often went to see people in humble neighborhoods and carried sincere messages of good-will to them. He was in such close contact with the English people that he had destroyed an old belief that a king lives in an atmosphere of exclusion and mystery. He had visited scores of hospitals, fac-tories, schools, homes for the aged, industrial homes, and labor forums, going about like an ordinary citizen. The feeling of friend-ship for him was everywhere so deep that it was not thought neces-sary to keep a close guard over him. He missed no opportunity of making official visits to American soldiers and sailors and of saying pleasant things to them.

By simplicity and sincerity King George won his way to the hearts of his countrymen just as effectively as did his father in a more diplomatic way. Admittedly he had not the social gifts of his father, the fluency of language, or the marvelous memory for faces, but he had the same happy knack of saying the right thing at the right time and in the right place, and thereby made a multitude of friends. No nation ever had a more popular king. Bred a sailor, he is as much at home on the quarter-deck of a dreadnought as in a royal drawing-room; there was nothing about a man-of-war that he did not know. The King and Queen were both domestic in their tastes, their family life distinguished by simplicity no less than by happiness, until the war came to disturb its peace. Early rising prevailed. Pipes were blown by a royal piper at Buckingham Palace or Windsor Castle at 8 A.M. to waken all sleepers and be a signal that every one must be ready for 9 o'clock breakfast. After breakfast business for the day began. When at home the King devoted most of his time to affairs of state. Much depended upon the program, as arranged, the day's time carefully mapped out. While the King was engaged with state affairs, the Queen was busy elsewhere. She was an indefatigable worker, with never an idle moment, and dis-tinguished for wanting to know the why and wherefore of everything in which she was interested.[43]

SIR EDWARD (NOW VISCOUNT) GREY, British Foreign Minister

That hatred of England, to which Germany during the war gave expression through song and scornful phrases, was vented with most fury in early days on the personality of Sir Edward Grey, afterward

[43] Compiled from "Who's Who"; The *Times* and The *Herald* (New York).

Viscount Grey, whose untiring efforts to avoid war, through a conference of the Powers, gave him fame that will last while men read of the war's origins. And yet this British Foreign Minister, who was evolved in the radical conditions which for ten years governed Great Britain under Asquith, incarnated to all Berlin certain qualities of greed, duplicity, and lust for world dominion, that made Albion perfidious in German eyes. To the *Kreuz-Zeitung* Sir Edward seemed subtle and sly. He had plotted for years the desolation of the world. This war, according to the *Vossiche Zeitung* ("Auntie Voss") became the hour of his triumph. He was a far more sinister figure in diplomacy than Macchiavelli had been, if we were to believe the *Norddeutsche Allgemeine Zeitung*. He had a genius for duplicity, lived aloof from the world, and was a cold and calculating instrument of that British policy which had made the destruction of Germany a cult, if not a religion. Sir Edward found his eulogists, however, and they were not confined to newspapers printed in London. As a "guardian angel of peace," the Milan *Corriere della Sera* lauded him. If the late King Edward VII had made himself "the peace-maker," he might well have thanked Sir Edward for it, but Sir Edward was the world's most self-effacing diplomatist. Sir Edward's bright fame among the diplomats concerned in the war seems secure enough. Moreover, it is likely to grow, as time passes and men still study the causes of the great catastrophe in human affairs, which he strove so whole-heartedly, and yet vainly, to avoid.

Few members of the Commons rose to speak so seldom as Grey. Political foes suspected him of a purpose to keep back from Parliament all control of foreign relations. In the radical camp, hostile voices were raised against what they regarded as his peculiarly personal mode of conducting diplomatic world affairs. It was affirmed that he was by temperament too aristocratic to be a Cabinet Minister in a democratic State. He was in fact far from that ideal type of Cabinet official dreamed of by the doctrinaries of radicalism. No irresponsible sentimentalist was he, and never a dangerous visionary. Radicals generally contemplated with dismay his supremacy at the Foreign Office. They objected to him because he was not romantic, because he never dramatized in a speech, or shed tears for Balkan woes. He would not spend his time in retailing to the Commons—especially to young and inexperienced members—the contents of ciphered dispatches that had come in. He declined to transform Parliament into a Jacobin club for the betrayal of the secrets of a great empire. Journalists grew horrified at his discretion.

Refusing to listen to extreme radicals, Sir Edward often heard them yelling at his heels. He simply smiled and ignored them. In truth it was only by a sort of political accident that so great a man

234

found himself in such insignificant company. He was the most conservative of the combination of Social Revolutionists who, in 1914, made up the ministry in London, and certainly the least democratic. He came from a magnificent stock of Whig nobility, now almost barren, and so was one of the few active survivors of a splendid class the essential characteristics of which he embodied in urbanity of manner, clearness of vision, poise, moderation in tone and temper. It was a stroke of good fortune for the Liberal party when it returned to power in 1906 that it was able to entrust the direction of Great Britain's foreign policy to this young member, then only forty-two, who, during the South African war, had separated himself from his party and avowed himself an Imperialist. He had Liberalism, however, but it was enlightened, tempered by knowledge of life and respect for the British spirit.

Sir Edward had been in the British public service thirty years. He was Under Secretary of State in Gladstone's last cabinet. The striking fact about him was that Englishmen of both parties had placed in his hands the fate of the nation with implicit confidence in the honesty and frankness of his public actions. He was not a diplomat in the old sense of the word. He had no tricks or wiles. He was straightforward. With all the cards on the table he conducted foreign affairs in much the same way as ordinary business is conducted. He could have had the least possible hand in the intrigues, compacts, plots, and stratagems of an old-time diplomatic game. As far as the situation would permit, he endeavored to realize for Great Britain the American policy of "friendship with all, entangling alliances with none." In the House of Commons, before war actually began, he made it clear that Great Britain was under no agreement or contract to fight for France or Russia. Sir Edward's policy of not meddling with other nations and provoking their hostility seemed well repaid when the long expected war arrived and found Great Britain with many allies and Germany almost isolated.

He had from the beginning disbelieved a notion, common in European chancellories, that lying for the good of his country was a necessary gift for a diplomatist. He could no more lie in public affairs than lie in private ones. When he did not wish to speak, no amount of House of Commons questioning or pressure could make him do so, but when he did speak he spoke the truth. Cold and reserved, with a low and restrained speech, he was a typical Englishman, a pure Anglo-Saxon. When it fell to his lot to announce war with Germany to the House of Commons he did it in the same even tones that he would have employed in opening a bazaar. There was no passion in his voice, there were no declamatory gestures, no attempt to play for a theatrical climax. He was simply doing that which belonged necessarily to his office, and, however extraordinary the occasion, he remained calm and even complacent, as if the act were part of a routine that had to be gone through.[44]

COLONEL EDWARD M. HOUSE, ONE OF THE AMERICAN DELEGATES TO THE PEACE CONFERENCE

If the average American citizen had been asked in 1917 what he knew about Colonel House he would have been apt to reply: "House? E. M. House? Why he's—he's President Wilson's friend and adviser," but after saying that much it is doubtful if many could have told whether Colonel House came from New York or Texas; whether he was a lawyer, a business man, a man of leisure, or a plain politician. Without intending it, Colonel House, who during the war was the President's personal observer of affairs in Europe, his representative on the War-Mission, and afterward a member of the American peace delegation, had been very much a man of mystery in his own country. He did not represent the Government by virtue of any office; he was seeking neither place, power, nor political preferment. While he was acting almost as an ambassador or a minister, he had neither a portfolio nor credentials. The Boston *Transcript* called him the President's *alter ego;* the St. Louis *Dispatch* described him as "rather an amazing person, a sort of embodied Intelligence, uninfluenced by traceable motives, and undisturbed by discoverable prejudices." Curiously enough, the American people as a whole seemed to share from the first the President's confidence in him.

As far back as 1912, when Woodrow Wilson was Governor of New Jersey, some letters passed between him and this mysterious Texan. Whether Colonel House or Mr. Wilson wrote the first letter is not recorded, but the fact stands out above all else that in 1912 Colonel House was scarcely known outside the Lone Star State, but by February, 1913, his name had appeared in practically every newspaper in the country and he had not held any political office; nor was he talked of for one. Colonel House had become celebrated because he was the closest political friend of Woodrow Wilson. He had probably been asked to make suggestions in regard to Mr. Wilson's Cabinet and as to scores of other matters we know not of, nor will ever know, but he had got nothing for himself out of all this service, except the satisfaction of honestly believing that he was serving his country and his party.

[44] Adapted from a compilation by Alexander Harvey in *Current Opinion* from German and Italian newspapers, and from articles in *The World's Work* and The *World* (New York).

Colonel House was sixty years old on the 26th of July, 1918, the son of a successful Texas banker and born in Houston, but he had made his home in Austin before he came to New York. His father had sent him to the Hopkins Grammar School, in New Haven, and then to Cornell University, where he was graduated in 1881. In the same year he married Miss Loulie Hunter, of Austin. He has two daughters, both of whom are married. He inherited some money, but made the larger part of his fortune himself through investments, agricultural and others, and had been a director in banks and railroads, but only in those in which he could take an active part. Aside from banking and railroad investments he made money from farms and ranches. No one knew the extent of his wealth, but it was not great as fortunes go. All sorts of guesses had been made about it, a favorite guess being $2,000,000. In any case he had reached a point where he did not care to make any more money, having already more than he could use. There was enough for his children and he saw no reason to struggle for more. He kept a business office in Austin in one small room, with an old-fashioned, flat-topped desk that had seen better days, a few filing-cases, some chairs and a small, old-fashioned safe. His reticence amounted almost to bashfulness. When he was working successfully for the nomination of Mr. Wilson in 1912, newspaper men flocked to see him and he made the following statement:

"To a man such as I am, publicity is not only annoying, but injurious. I am not seeking anything for myself, and I am not seeking anything for anybody else; I am simply trying to do the best I can for the measures I favor. I am for measures, not men. To say that I have been able to accomplish anything, would only be to draw upon me attention which would be most distasteful. I am not working for any influence that might be obtained, or favors that might be granted; I am just a plain citizen, and am determined to remain one."

Naturally it was something of a jolt to a great many veteran politicians to find that this unknown Texan had suddenly got into President Wilson's confidence. To Democratic leaders it was in fact a rude jolt. Hardly a hundred politicians in Texas knew House well enough to speak to him, but in 1916 there was not a politician of any weight, influence, or importance but knew who he was and what he could do. Without question he could have been a member of President Wilson's cabinet—but he wouldn't accept any such place. If Colonel House has achieved nothing else in national politics, he has purified the conduct of campaigns and set an example of clever strategy and resourceful leadership rather than blind expenditure of millions. He has demonstrated that a party can win in national elections without wholesale debauchery simply by placing issues squarely before the voters. He illustrated, with sensational success, the shift in the political center of the country from east to west and the increasing weight which must be attached to the march of progressive doctrines in the West. Best of all, he had taken the Democratic party out of the solid South and made a really representative party, controlling States in every section of the Union. Some of his political maxims were these:

"What is bad morally is bad politically. Politics ought to be as honest as business. I haven't any use for bribery in politics. I have never paid a cent to a newspaper or a man in any of my campaigns. Personally, I never handle a cent of money. I have always made that the first stipulation in consenting to participate in any campaign. I will not collect funds or account for them, but I insist on knowing what is done with the money. Even when I went to Europe with the War Mission, I asked the State Department to send along an expert accountant to keep track of disbursements. I will not bother with money in connection with public work. It is bad enough having to manage your own pecuniary affairs.

"I wouldn't promise a man an office in return for his political support, no matter what might be the exigency of the situation. It is bad business, practically as well as morally. It is likely to create ill-feeling in other men when it becomes known. Politics, when you come right down to it, is largely a question of organization." [45]

GOTTLIEB VON JAGOW, German Foreign Minister

Journalists, familiar with the traits and temperaments of heads of the German Foreign Office, were disposed to cite Jagow as of the type most representative of the Emperor William. He had had the good luck to be one of his Majesty's college-mates and William II had never been disillusioned on the subject of college chums, but loved them still. He could take them out of poverty and obscurity into high offices. Each of those whom he so favored was a sort of romantic person; each had charm, perfection of manners, intimacy with current ideas. Jagow was the sweetest of dilettantes, a maker of compelling conversation, an impeccable waltzer, felicitous in quotations. No one could help loving him, dilettante tho he was. In him the fine flower of the Prussian species was in bloom, but one hardly expected to find him at the head of a great imperial foreign office.

Jagow was once the German Ambassador in Rome. Italian dailies applied to him their most complimentary word, "sympathetic." He

---

[45] Principal Sources: *The Literary Digest* and Arthur D. Howden Smith's "The Real Colonel House" (George H. Doran Company).

was not tall, nor in manner commanding, but he conveyed an impression of power. He knew how to dress, could carry a lady's train and could send flowers and bonbons impartially. For a bachelor he managed difficulties of etiquette with nicety, offending no one. It was characteristic of him that the very flower in his buttonhole had symbolical significance. He never sported the Austrian color among Garibaldians, or carried a yellow bloom into the Quirinal when a quarrel with the Vatican had become acute. He was among the first in Germany to take to the fashion of having creases in the trousers, but he did not follow the example of the Crown Prince in affecting English sartorial styles. Italians greatly admired his well-kept hands and nails and the expressiveness of his eyes. The moment he entered

U. S. OFFICIAL PHOTO.

STATESMEN WHO WERE SOMETIMES KNOWN DURING THE PEACE CONFERENCE AS "THE BIG FOUR"

Left to right—Premier Lloyd George, Premier Orlando, Premier Clémenceau, President Wilson. The picture represents the four men standing at the doorway of President Wilson's house in Paris

a ballroom, or a conference, he darted swift glances everywhere, as if to take in the general situation.

His dispatches from Rome were so intimate and personal, that each had to be laid personally before Emperor William, who was curious about Italy. Jagow displayed rare genius in characterizations of men who swayed the destinies of Italy and in estimates of national and international situations. He could read Giolitti like a book and took the measure of Sonnino, Salandra and San Giuliano accurately. This was Jagow's strong point. He never showed much grasp of principles, but human nature could not elude him. He had the reputation of understanding women—a most important thing in a diplomatist at the court of Victor Emmanuel III.

Jagow was not of the blood and iron breed, nor was he a hearty drinker and eater like Bismarck, nor dour and implacable like the older Moltke. He was the poetical, Hamlet-like Prussian, sweet of manner, and could conceal incredible sophistication beneath an aspect of ineffable simplicity. The English might say that the dreaming and soulful Prussian passed away when William II became a warlord, but it was not so. That type survived in Jagow, who might have stept out of Göthe's "Wilhelm Meister," so romantic was he, so susceptible to beauty. Jagow, unlike Bethmann-Hollweg, had not read the philosophers. His mind had the bent of Bülow's, who loved Merimée, Carducci, Dante, and the art of Siena. While Bülow was epigrammatic and witty, Jagow was a good listener. He made no epigrams and his enemies denied that he could make them, whereas Bülow scarcely opened his mouth "without there flew a trope." Jagow understood you. His smile was not that of amusement, but that of comprehension, and he let you lead. One could not grow intimate with him without thinking of the warning that the Prussian is a *"faux bonhomme"*—a sophisticated person, that is to say, knowing things well while manifesting all the artlessness of a child.

Generations of Jagows had served Kings of Prussia. They hailed from that Mark of Brandenburg of which William II always made so much in his orations. The family was aristocratic to the finger-tips, but no consciousness of that was apparent in the manner of Jagow in his relations to the lower-born Helferichs and Dernburgs, or even with Socialists. He knew that a modern period had come in German annals and the aristocracy of finance, boasting Ballins and Gwinners, had to be tolerated, side by side with the aristocracy of the sword and old paternal acres. For popular opinion, such as the Reichstag gave a voice and all that sort of thing, he had disdainful shrugs of the shoulders. Not even Bismarck attached more importance to the work of journalists. He was accused in Paris papers of being the organizer of a German press campaign. He deemed it a perfectly legitimate thing to feed the public as from a spoon with ready-made views of imperial policy, or things that people "must think officially."

Imagine a quiet, well-contained little man, well groomed, carrying a cane, wearing spats, arriving at the Wilhelmstrasse at ten in the morning. Jagow, the foreign minister of the German Empire, was that man. He had a small, carefully groomed mustache on a long upper lip. In winter he wore a long overcoat carefully brushed. Patent leather boots shone resplendently below. Once inside, valets helped him off with his hat and overcoat, and secretaries placed documents on his desk. He was accustomed to the world's ways and to the ways of lackeys, could be sympathetic to former German ministers, former German secretaries of embassy, former German attachés who came to pour into his receptive ear their several complaints and disillusions. They formed a melancholy procession to his office, those whilom diplomatists whom Emperor William had told to seek other careers. Their faces were long and their tales dolorous, but Jagow had smiles for them, and the flower at his buttonhole was not fresher than his face. Every complaining caller departed from him soothed and sustained.

Recreation in the ordinary sense seemed to have been denied him, his constitution never having been sufficiently robust. His four years as ambassador in Italy built him up wonderfully and Rome saw him go with real regret. Never was a diner out, at least in the German diplomatic corps, so abstemious. His principal exercise was walking. Like Bülow, he took an occasional fancy to animal pets, but he was not followed everywhere by a little dog after the fashion of at least one former imperial chancellor. Jagow took to flowers, music, poetry, and pictures. He was too good a courtier to run counter to Emperor William's well-known taste in art. For that reason it was hinted with some malice that one never found the Foreign Minister at an exhibition of secessionists in art, but he would halt in ecstasy before some battle-picture of a school dear to William II. Had he not sprung from a long line of Prussian Junkers he might have become an artist of distinction, or at any rate a brilliant student of the arts.[46]

[46] Adapted from a compilation by Alexander Harvey in *Current Opinion*, based on Irving S. Wile's "Men About the Kaiser" and articles in the *Figaro* and *Gaulois* (Paris) and the *Tribune* and *Giornale* (Rome).

ALEXANDER FEODOROVITCH KERENSKY, Premier of
Russia

Kerensky was born in 1882. He was a Socialist of the moderate type and in the Provincial Government set up the revolution of March, 1917, he first served as Minister of Justice and later as Minister of War. Kerensky, in the crisis that followed within a few months, seemed to some observers destined to become Russia's Washington rather than its Napoleon—guiding it through stormy seas into a haven of peaceful democracy, rather than distorting its democracy into an ultimate imperialism. In a sense Kerensky's voice had been the first resounding voice of the revolution. After listening to the Czar's edict dissolving the Duma, it was he who rose in his place and said: "We will not go, we will stay here," and they stayed. So staying, the Duma accomplished the first act of the revolution—it was an act destined to be as historic as the refusal of the States General of France to disperse at the command of Louis XVI. Kerensky again gave evidence of possessing the instinct of leadership when, on the first day of July, 1917, having gone to the front, he called on his soldiers to charge the German trenches, declaring that if they failed to do so he would make the assault alone. In that act he sounded the note of personal appeal, the cry of individual valor that was needed by an army that had been disintegrated by German intrigue and had become hesitant and vacillating in its conception of duty. With a roar and a rush his troops responded and Russia once more seemed a factor in the war. It was a stroke such as Napoleon in his youth more than once used with revolutionary soldiers, notably at the bridge of Lodi.

Physically frail—a fine soul in a sorely racked body—Kerensky became the most interesting figure in the war drama at that time. Kerensky was born in Tashkend, Turkestan, in Asiatic Russia, of pure Russian blood, his parents not rich. He studied in Moscow and was educated to be a lawyer. In childhood he had seen the sufferings of Siberian exiles which ever afterward affected his views of political questions. He began his work as a lawyer by defending "political criminals," men who had now become the real revolutionists of Russia. During the uprising of 1905 he became a speaker among the working classes and continued to defend Jews and political criminals against the old régime, often without taking money for his work. Elected to the Fourth Duma from Saratoff on the Volga, he became a leader of the Trudoviki, or Labor group, winning wider popularity. When at the beginning of the war Grand Duke Nicholas Nikolaivitch— not the warrior Grand Duke Nicholas, but another—accused the

Jews of being traitors, Kerensky made a fearless speech against him in the Duma. Two weeks before the revolution Minister Protopopoff had been planning to send him to Siberia; papers revealing the plan afterward came into his hands. He had often been pursued by spies of the old régime.

A young man in the early thirties, neither tall nor short, his figure characterized by a stoop that came from much poring over books, brown hair brushed straight up, the forehead lined and seamed, a sharp nose and chin, quick, restless, steel-gray eyes, lips comprest with a very obvious decision—such was the personal impression Kerensky gave. He wore a black or gray sack-suit even on formal occasions. In his face was a peering expression that indicated near-sightedness. His hands often wandered restlessly to a pencil in his waistcoat pocket as he talked. It was not easy for him to sit still. In the middle of a conversation he would leap out of his chair and pace restlessly to and fro. As he talked, nervously and in a low tone, it was not easy to understand upon what his great reputation as an orator was based. One had to hear him in the Duma, or when he confronted a Labor group, to comprehend that. In his earnestness he would sometimes advance close to an interlocutor and seize the lapel of his coat while talking. Anything but a dandy in his dress, his boots often sadly needed polish.

Kerensky's pleadings in local courts were made in a theatrical manner. He would fold his arms and glare in disconcerting fashion at an opposing witness, or at a judge who ventured to correct him, or at a lawyer with whom he was battling. That stare in the Duma had prodigious effects. He would swiftly launch a torrent of words, and yet each was distinct and telling. He would fold his arms and gaze about in a tense, strained, alert fashion when a pin could be heard to fall and then he would fire a shot—an epigram it might be, or a charge of turpitude, or a crushing citation of what Peter the Great had said, or what Pushkin said, and a sensation would ensue. Kerensky was most at home at a workingmen's meeting in Petrograd or Moscow. One thought of Marat. He had the same passion for the mob, the unfed sons of toil. His perfect sincerity made him the idol of labor-unions. He risked imprisonment by scorning openly a favorite device of the old bureaucracy—drafting men and exiling them to remote places upon a plea of administrative necessity. Protopopoff, the incarnation of bureaucracy, who once secured a decree against Kerensky, did not dare thus to banish him.

Kerensky had striking resourcefulness in denunciation. He had called his predecessor at the Ministry of Justice "a crocodile without tears," had said Stürmer spoke Russian "with a Hohenzollern accent," and coined the phrase that there are two kinds of democracy—

"the kind the people want and the kind the people get." Interrupted in the Duma by a remark that socialism was a dream, Kerensky retorted: "Yes, and capitalism is a nightmare." This readiness of tongue helped him to hold his own in that most turbulent of organizations in Petrograd, the Soviet or Council of Workers' and Soldiers' delegates. It was his influence at the Council that led to the adoption of the red flag as an emblem of the triumph of the people over autocracy. Others had favored a modification of the old Muscovite standard, but Kerensky would hear only of a red flag, use of which had been forbidden in many a bureaucratic rescript.

Kerensky had an intuitive realization of crowd psychology. He could leap on a table at a moment's notice and gain attention when he made some happy remark that put every one in a good humor. He knew how to bring forward a practical suggestion at the right time, or how to wave his arm dramatically in a crisis and then shout "Follow me!" He loved an uproar, but could quiet crowds with a word. There was a touch in him of Camille Desmoulins, the journalist leader of the French Revolution. There were times when by great effort he could shout almost with the lung power of Danton. And yet his influence was in the main on the side of moderation. He kept a restraining hand on radical leaders in the Workers' and Soldier's Council.

In his waiting-room in Petrograd might sometimes have been seen a dozen dingy civilians and some soldiers sitting on rickety chairs around the wall, the room quiet, the visitors wearing that distant, meditative expression that seemed to have settled like a common mask upon the people of Petrograd since they had caught a glimpse of primitive Russia at the outbreak of the revolution. The double doors that led into his inner office would open suddenly, and then one would see "a man of middle height, with close-clipt brown hair, flashing eyes and a sullen mouth," who surveyed his callers, and when he saw the soldiers, cried out abruptly in a rough voice, "Come on, comrades," whereupon they arose, shook hands, and went inside. Fifteen minutes later the doors would open again, and the soldiers would emerge smiling.

Kerensky had learned revolutionary enthusiasm from France and stability from Great Britain, but he was a Russian first and last, and left no doubt in the minds of French and British that Russia "would henceforth endeavor to manage her own destiny." He had apparently "swung Russia away from license toward restraint; from oratory toward action; from a temporary autocracy of workmen and soldiers toward general tolerance." He once said that an autocracy of workmen or an autocracy of soldiers "is as bad as an autocracy of aristocrats," and Russia "should have no aristocracies.

PERSONAL SKETCHES OF WAR LEADERS

Each man should be a free citizen, with as much respect for his neighbor's rights and prerogatives as for his own." As compromise was the essence of government in England, so compromise became the essence of Kerensky's method and it was compromise that eventually led to his fall and flight.

Kerensky's proclamation of a republic in Russia, on September 17, without waiting for a Constitutional Convention, showed once more how at that time he was the genius, as well as the leader, of the Revolution. The restraint he had exercised upon violence, the success with which he had met the intrigues of domestic reactionaries and foreign foes, the ability with which he had inspired and led a demoralized army, the comparative ease with which he had put down the Korniloff rebellion, and the boldness with which he presented to his countrymen the vision of a Russian republic, filled the world with a new hope that, so far as it was ever possible for one man to shape the destiny of a nation, Kerensky had been raised up for that task. Such Kerensky seemed, for many weeks, to all the world, none dreaming of his precipitate fall, the rise of the Bolsheviki and the frightful excesses that ensued under its dominance.[47]

DAVID LLOYD GEORGE, Premier of Great Britain

Of Lloyd George's birth in Manchester, England, and his boyhood in Llanystymdwy, Wales; of his early loss of his father; of the uncle who, in humble circumstances, nobly promoted his education; of his rise as a lawyer and his activities as a member of Parliament in promoting the uplift of the common people, readers had read much before the war. Early in the war, as Chancellor of the Exchequer, wider fame came to him and then fame still wider as Minister of Munitions. Finally he reached the topmost round of the politicians' ladder as Prime Minister of Great Britain, and dauntlessly saw the war through to victory and peace. " 'E's the bloke wot they gets to do wot no other bloke can't, or else is 'fraid to," was the way Lewis R. Freeman [48] said he once heard a Cockney "publicist," in an informal debate in Hyde Park, London, characterize Lloyd George.

Lloyd George had fine ability and high courage. His were tasks that lack of "grasp" or of nerve has made other British statesmen unfit to perform. The salient facts of the "shell muddle" after Neuve Chapelle, and of how a special "Ministry of Munitions" was created to cope with the difficulties arising out of it, formed early in

[47] Adapted from an article compiled by Alexander Harvey for *Current Opinion* from The *Daily Chronicle* (London), *Temps* and *Humanite* (Paris), and from articles in The *Evening Post*, The *Sun* and The *World* (New York).
[48] In an article in *The Review of Reviews* (London).

1915 a notable incident of the war. That fatal shortage of high-explosive shells which caused the British such frightful loss in their attempted offensive, and which became responsible for great changes in the war on both the Eastern and the Western Fronts, had been clearly foreseen by Lloyd George, as a consequence of a visit he made to the fighting-line in October, 1914. He was then Chancellor of the Exchequer. Army officials, impatient of civilian interference, turned a deaf ear to his earnest warnings. Pinning their faith to shrapnel, they had laid the train that led to disaster. Repulsed by those who should have been vitally interested in what he had to reveal, Lloyd George then resolved to bend every effort to bring the truth home to the British Government and the British people. The alarm note rang clear through a speech he made at Bangor, Wales, in February, 1915, the keynote of which was thus exprest:

"This is an engineer's war, and it will be won or lost by the efforts or shortcomings of engineers. We need men, but we need arms more than men, and delay in producing them is full of peril to the country. We must appeal for the cooperation of employers, workmen, and the general public; the three must act and endure together, or we delay and may imperil victory. We ought to requisition the aid of every man who can handle metal."

Lloyd George already had great prestige in England, but the grave import of his utterance did not at once strike home in any quarter where it could take effect. While the Ordnance Department was striving to increase the munition output, it made the fatal error of placing full dependence on a time-hallowed system of obtaining supplies from armament firms and sub-contractors who, even under normal conditions, could not turn out anything approaching an adequate supply. With railways and ports congested with transport work, and with trans-oceanic shipping facilities greatly reduced—at times raw material was two months in going from New York to Birmingham, and six weeks from Liverpool to London—a breakdown became almost complete. One firm that had contracted to deliver 1,000,000 shells had ready only a pitiful 10,000; another that contracted for 500,000 delivered 45,000. To make matters worse, many of the shells that became available were not of a character best suited to the work in hand. Tenders from responsible American firms were ignored.

As a consequence the long-heralded "spring drive" of 1915 got no farther than a few lines of German trenches, and these were won at a cost in lives unparalleled in previous warfare. A really considerable French advance, the ultimate success of which was largely dependent on British cooperation, was almost stultified by a British

LLOYD GEORGE AND THE PRINCE OF WALES
After a luncheon at the House of Commons

failure, and the Germans, now made safe for an indefinite period against an offensive on the Western Front, turned on the Russians, who at that time were almost ready to go through the Carpathian passes to the plains of Hungary—and so started their great eastward drive under Mackensen after the Dunajec battle. With McKenna amply equipped to fill Lloyd George's portfolio as Chancellor of the Exchequer, it was natural that the head of the new department, the Minister of Munitions, should be the Cabinet Minister who had foreseen the necessity of its formation almost since the outbreak of war. So it came about that the little Welshman with the sunniest of smiles, kindliest of eyes, warmest of hand-clasps, and love of his fellow men in his heart, bent his energy and his talent for organization to the task of building up for England a war-supply machine which, in the fulness of time, would rival that of Germany.

How this miracle was accomplished the public at the time did not know. The machine for it was a compact of units assembled from the ends of the United Kingdom. It started with a minimum of "lost motion," because its parts were selected with judgment and it ran true as day followed day as a consequence of being "oiled" by the tact and persuasiveness of the chief engineer, who set to work laying out the whole country into districts, each under its own committee of management. This body in each case consisted of heads of local manufacturing firms, assisted by a technical expert. In each district a bureau was established for giving advice and direction to factories in its own area. The engineers of this bureau decided such questions as the kind of work the existing machinery of any given factory was best fitted to perform with a minimum of alteration; the character and quantity of the new machinery needed; the competency of any factory to handle adequately a given order; and such advances of money as any factory was justified in demanding for war-work extensions. Through the reports of committees in each district the Ministry had an intelligence system which enabled it to anticipate and prevent congestion of orders in one district, or a shortage of orders in another. England, through its Ministry of Munitions, was now applying ordinary business methods to war-supply.

By a system of district control, a heterogeneous lot of labor was kept track of and sent where it would do the most good. Indeed, the handling of the laborer—both as a man and as a workman—as Lloyd George realized at the outset, was the crux of the whole problem. The most unskilled and unschooled of volunteers—everybody from noble dames and university professors to costermongers and girls from the sweatshops of Houndsditch and Petticoat Lane— were included among the thousands who took up this work of patriotism. They had to work side by side with the most highly trained machinists. In inducing trades unions to concede this and other of their bitterly-fought-for privileges, Lloyd George was credited with one of the cleverest strokes in his career. Concessions from the unions included an agreement not to strike while on war work, and to suspend restrictive regulations limiting outputs for a given time. Nothing approaching so amicable an understanding between capital and labor, or between government and labor, ever before occurred in British industrial history.

But discontent broke out, and the deliberate charge was made that the Government was doing little or nothing to limit the abnormal "war profits" of the employers, and that these were, therefore, waxing fat at the expense of the working-man. Men were being robbed, these malcontents declared, and they challenged Lloyd George or any one else in the Government, to prove the contrary. The Minister of Munitions, recognizing the threat as well as the tactical possibilities of the occasion, snatched the gauntlet with eager hand. There was no time to prepare a set speech. But here was a chance to relieve himself of a burden of facts. He took a train to Bristol where was assembled a Labor Congress and at once addrest representatives of British labor as one man ·addresses another, words straight from his heart. He began his speech by telling delegates to that congress that they represented the most powerful force in the life of the country. "With you," said he, "victory is assured; without you, our cause is lost." Recalling to their minds a resolution they had passed a few days previously, pledging themselves to assist the Government in carrying on the war, he told them that he was there to take them at their word. To the charge that the Government had not kept its promise to intercept "war profits," he replied by showing how the state had taken control of practically all the engineering works of the country and was appropriating profits and employing them in the prosecution of the war. Simply but convincingly he showed that the Government was carrying out completely both the letter and the spirit of its promises:

''We have set up sixteen national arsenals and are constructing eleven more. We require, in order to run those—the old and the new—and to equip works which are at present engaged on turning out the equipment of war, 80,000 more skilled men, but we require in addition to that 200,000 unskilled men and women. At present you have only got 15 per cent. of the machines which you could use for the turning out of rifles, cannon and shells working night-shifts. If you could get plenty of labor to make these machines go night and day—ah, just think of the lives that could be saved! We are not trying to displace skilled workmen by unskilled. We have not enough skilled workmen to

go round. There is a good deal of work being done by skilled workmen now, highly skilled men of years' training, which can just as
easily be done by those who have only a few days' training. We want
to turn the unskilled on to work which these can do just as well as
the highly skilled, so as to reserve the highly skilled for work which
they alone can do. Take shell-making, for instance. Instead of putting skilled people to that work, what we would like to do would be
to put on, say, ten or eleven unskilled men or women to one skilled
man to look after them.''

The speaker then went from the explanatory, and the defensive,
to a swift offensive that swept his hearers off their feet:

''The reports we get from our own offices, the War Office and the
Munitions Department, show that if we had a suspension during the
war of those customs which keep down the output, we could increase it
in some places 30 per cent., in other places 200 per cent. Between 30
and 200 per cent.—well, I will hardly need to tell you that makes the
difference between victory and defeat in the quantity you could turn
out and place at the disposal of our armies.''

Adding instance to instance, piling proof on proof, he went on to
show how persistence in these very trades-union practises which the
men had undertaken to suspend had been hampering the munitions
supply at every turn. He rose to a dramatic climax in pointing
out the shame of their having interfered with Belgian workmen:

''The Belgian workman has several reasons for putting his back into
his work. But whenever he has worked his best he has always been
warned that he was breaking some trades-union custom. He has been
invited to desist, and he does not understand it. His home has been
destroyed, his native land has been ravaged, Belgian women have been
dishonored, Belgian liberties have been trampled under foot; and Belgian workmen can not understand entering into any conspiracy to keep
down the output of rifles and guns and shells to drive the oppressor
from the land which he is trampling under foot. I do say that if there
is any man who wants to dawdle while his country is in need of him,
do let him have the decency at least not to appeal to Belgian workmen
not to avenge the dishonor of their country.''

The head of many a British workman was bowed in shame after
these words had been spoken; not one but lifted up cheers when the
Minister of Munitions, with a fervent appeal for help and cooperation, brought his speech to a close and rushed off to board the train
waiting to take him back to London. From Belfast to Birmingham,
from the Clyde to the Thames, British labor writhed under the lash
that had been laid along its back. Then fine manliness asserted
itself. British labor began to put its house in order. Delegations

from all classes hurried to London and sundry conferences were held at the Ministry of Munitions. Finally, on the 18th of September, 1915, a fresh undertaking on the part of labor was announced, by which the workmen agreed to "cut out the frills and get down to brass tacks." There have been more finished oratorical efforts in English history than Lloyd George's speech, but there is serious doubt if one was ever fraught with greater import.

Lloyd George could usually be seen—often on a few moments' notice—by any one whom his secretary deemed warranted in having the privilege. But he would not be interviewed for publication, nor send a "message to the public," or undertake to answer any written questions summitted. Mr. Freeman, whose article [48a] is summarized here, related how on the day after that famous Bristol speech, he chanced to be lunching at a political club near the Houses of Parliament, with a technical expert of the Munitions Department, when Lloyd George, another Cabinet Minister, and a couple of M.P.'s were at a near-by table. "Lloyd George doesn't know me from Adam," said Mr. Freeman's friend, "but I can not miss the chance of congratulating him on his great speech." Stepping to the other table, he extended his hand, with a word of explanation as to who he was. Lloyd George, who had been accepting without rising a running fire of felicitations, was on his feet in an instant.

"You're C—— of the B—— E—— Company, I know," said he. "You came from South Africa at your own expense and have been working in the Munitions Department at a fraction of your regular salary. You have been in the hospital for a month with chronic dysentery, and have only been back at your desk for a week. It's a shame I haven't even sent word to tell you and the other chaps with you who have come from the ends of the earth to help us, how deeply we appreciate your sacrifices and services. I don't know what we should have done without you all. By the way, isn't there a young American explosive expert from Johannesburg working with you—a chemical engineer named Q——, I think it is? Please tell him how especially fine I think it is that he should have joined us to 'do his bit.' I'm going to get around to see you all before long." "By Jove!" ejaculated Mr. Freeman's friend, as he rejoined him at the table; "I was so taken aback that I quite forgot to congratulate him on his labor speech. Think of his having such a line as that on our work!"

As Chancellor of the Exchequer Lloyd George saw his country through the chaos of the first months of the war when the pillars of the financial world were shaking to their foundations. As Minister of Munitions he found the way out of another chaos no less

48a In *The Review of Reviews.*

baffling and then came his splendid career as Prime Minister, of which the record is writ large in histories of this war.

Before the war ended a sort of legend had grown up around the name and fame of Lloyd George, who was described by Isaac F. Marcosson, in the *World's Work*, as "the most picturesque and challenging figure of the English-speaking race." Only one man—Theodore Roosevelt—rivaled him for this plural distinction. Reducing the wizard to a formula, Mr. Marcosson described him as "50 per cent. Roosevelt," in the virility and forcefulness of his character, "15 per cent. Bryan," in the purely oratorical phase of his make-up, the rest "canny Celt opportunism." It was with Roosevelt that the happiest comparison could be made. Lloyd George was the British Roosevelt, the Imperial Rough Rider, the minor distinction between them being that the head of the British Government, instead of flourishing a "big stick," employed a compelling voice. Each was more of an institution than a mere man; each dramatized himself in everything he did; each had a genius for the benevolent assimilation of idea with fact. One could trust Lloyd George as one could Roosevelt to know all about the man who came to see him, whether he were statesman, author, explorer, or plain captain of industry. That was one of the reasons why he maintained his political hold. He also had Roosevelt's striking gift of phrase-making, altho he did not share the American's love of letter-writing. There was a tradition that the way in which to get a written reply out of him was to enclose two addrest and stamped postal cards, one bearing the word "Yes," and the other "No." Like Roosevelt, Lloyd George was past master in the art of effective publicity. Each projected upon the public the fire and magnetism of a dynamic personality and each had been the terror of the corporate evil-doer.[49] Roosevelt had one distinct advantage over him in that he was a deeper student and had wider learning. On the other hand, Roosevelt was no match for the eloquent Welshman in oratory. The stage "lost a star when Lloyd George went into politics."

So wrote Mr. Marcosson, but the Rev. Charles F. Aked went further and maintained that Lloyd George was one of the foremost orators of all time. Dr. Aked once spoke from the same London platform with him, when he was not and never had been a member of the British Government. Five thousand persons had gathered at what was to be a Liberal demonstration. Dr. Aked described the meeting, Lloyd George being then a comparatively obscure member of Parliament:

"He was suffering from a bad attack of stage-fright—or thought he

[49] In *Everybody's Magazine.*

was. He profest the utmost misery when waiting for the meeting to begin. He asked if I ever suffered the same unutterable wretchedness before facing an audience, and added, 'I feel as if I were in the condemned cell waiting to be led out to be hanged. There (pointing to the Chairman) is the Governor of the jail, and (to me) there is the Chaplain. And I don't know whether I would not sooner be led out to the gallows.' I really think his speech that night was the greatest of his amazing career. He was not eloquent, but eloquence, not passionate but pure and living passion. When he reached the 'grand style' as he often did—or did in those years—there was something weirdly coercive in the physical qualities of his voice, something uncanny, defying analysis, indescribable. It seemed to us as we came away that nothing finer could ever have fallen from human lips than his peroration about the streams gathering in his own Welsh mountains until a torrent swept through the valleys, and, of course, he meant this to illustrate the gathering floods of righteous sentiment which were to sweep privilege and obstruction and all the rest of it into oblivion. Commonplace? Familiar stuff for perorations? Quite so; but the thrill and the leap and the gladness and the glory in it were—superhuman.''

MARIE ADELAIDE, THE FORMER GRAND DUCHESS OF LUXEMBURG

Marie Adelaide in a military sense was not an ally of Germany, but in a moral sense she was commonly so regarded in Entente councils. Journalists were baffled again and again in their efforts to see her inside her palace in Luxemburg where she was the most interesting of all German prisoners of war, for such, as a matter of fact, she was. Germany, however, denied that she was a prisoner. She was an independent and reigning sovereign of a neutral nation, they said, rather than a prisoner or an ally of the King of Prussia. She was, however, to all appearance devoted to the cause of the Fatherland. Only twenty years of age, she was for four years surrounded in her capital by guards of honor, virtually her jailers, against whom she sometimes fumed. London and Paris dailies described an interview during the war between her and Emperor William, in which she declined to be seated during the conference, and so forced the Emperor to stand, for even a Hohenzollern might not take a chair in the palace of an independent sovereign until he had been invited to do so.

So profound was the mystery that surrounded her destiny before the war that for months she could have been called maid, wife, or widow—which she was none could tell. For months her betrothal to Prince Henry of Bavaria had delighted the Pontifical Court, since both were fervently Roman Catholic and Luxemburg had been ravaged by Anticlerical queries. As to what had become of the supposed Bavarian consort inspired fantastic rumors. The German

Emperor figured in one story as the heavy villain of the piece. He had menaced the Grand Duchess with his displeasure unless she espoused one of his own sons. A secret marriage, a compulsory divorce, a solemn betrothal and partings in grief and tears, all had their place in stories of this the most sentimental matrimonial complication of the war. She could not, as a Catholic, secure a divorce, and a new marriage into which she might have entered would have been void from the start. There were many eligible royal bridegrooms among German princes, many among Balkan princes, while in Russia the Grand Duke Constantine was twenty-six, to say nothing of six other Grand Dukes on the list, all wealthy. The Grand Duchess of Luxemburg would not have lacked suitors could they have gained access to her presence and had she been really marriageable.

The Grand Duchess and her five younger sisters were of a much more ancient branch of the house of Orange-Nassau than that to which the Queen of the Netherlands belonged. She had been received with much enthusiasm in Luxemburg when, on the attainment of her legal majority, she headed a glittering procession to the legislative palace and there vowed fidelity to the national constitution. She was accompanied by her august Portuguese mother, the Infanta Marie Anne of Braganza, from whom the Grand Duchess inherited her piety; by her sisters, by her venerable grandmother, by the Grand Duke and Grand Duchess of Baden, devoted relatives always, and by the Prince Alois of Loewenstein, to say nothing of a brilliant suite. Majesty was in every gesture with which the Grand Duchess ascended the steps of the throne and announced to the brave assemblage that she had assumed her proper rank among the sovereigns of the world, ruling a nation free and independent.

A diplomatist on a mission in Luxemburg edified the Parisian press with impressions of her spirit in what he called her "captivity." Her trim young figure was shrouded in black and her eyes showed traces of weeping. She had given up horseback-riding, but occasional glimpses obtained of her in the park by the curious who passed sentries suggested that she was in fairly good health and able to enjoy the fresh air; but the smiles were gone from her face. Her own functionaries had been removed by the German officers during the war, and their places given to Prussians, with whom she would hold no communications.

She had the long oval face characteristic of the princesses of the house of Orange in the elder branch, and blushed with almost no provocation at all. Her hair was the fine silky sort, not over-abundant, and rebellious to the brush. Her full red lips manifested a wealth of temperament. Her figure was slender and girlish, with a gait that revealed a proficient dancer. In addition to being born royal she was born "chic." One evidence of this was the ease with which she had her hair done without regard to fashion, the result being harmonious with her type. She was of the sanguine and statuesque type, conventional and inclined to seriousness. This made her seem every inch a queen along traditional lines. She exacted perfect deference from every personage in her suite, both official and personal, being especially sensitive if her independent sovereignty was not clearly apprehended. "I am a reigning Queen!" she would say. The fact that she was "chic" in aspect imparted to her deportment on occasions of disputed etiquette the majesty that she asserted. But Marie lost her grand ducal throne soon after the war —after she and Pershing, side by side, had reviewed the American Army that passed through Luxemburg on its way to the Rhine at Coblenz. That was perhaps the last day on which she felt that her tiny throne was really hers.[59]

CZAR NICHOLAS II, of RUSSIA

When Nicholas II came to the Russian throne he showed himself an idealist, and made passionate efforts for universal peace. Strange indeed was it that he should have lost his throne in a revolution, and lost his life ignominiously at the hands of his own people. For a time the cause of peace had been associated largely with his name. An absolute monarch had been the champion of a cause that was dearest of all to democrats and liberals. He had become the colleague of men like Stead and Carnegie. Despite all that seemed to militate against him, many people kept their faith in Nicholas as a man who was sincere in his peace endeavors. The most touching example was perhaps W. T. Stead who, with many others, saw in the Czar, the granter of the Duma, a new Peter the Great, or a God-chosen monarch, leading his nation through the most difficult and hazardous ways of national evolution. They held that it had been comparatively easy for Alexander II to give liberty to the serfs, but that it needed a determined and sincere man of genius to cope with the difficulties which liberalism would lead to in Russia. But it was always to be remembered that no Russian monarch previous to Nicholas II had ever had to face one hundred millions of peasants and working-men recently made free.

Nicholas had survived his indulgence of his passions for peace, his unfortunate war with Japan and the wild revolutionary era that followed, but was sometimes almost laughed at behind his face.

[59] Adapted from an article by Alexander Harvey in *Current Opinion*, based on articles in the *Journal des Débats, Croix, Libre Parole,* and *Matin* (Paris), The *Times* (London) and the *Vossische Zeitung* (Berlin).

Moreover, thousands of soldiers had to be lined up on a railway-track whenever he made a journey to Petrograd because he did not dare to stir from his palace except with an army to guard him. Before going to the third city of his empire, he had first to have several thousand people arrested as suspicious characters. In many parts of Russia he did not dare show himself even under such precautions. One remembered how at Kief a Jewish police agent once managed to get into a theater and only at the last moment changed his mind and shot Stolypin instead of Nicholas. Some revolutionaries said the Czar did not count; he was not a commanding figure, and his survival would help their cause more than could his death. They meant that by his folly he had shown more clearly than they could show by propaganda that the day of Czars was over and that it was better for mankind to dispense with Czars altogether.

Nicholas had outlived an earlier accusation of insincerity and an early unpopularity. He had given the lie to much that had been said against him. His character was shown in a courageous attack he made on a corrupt police system which had sold itself in part to the revolutionary party. The police system in Russia was in some respects more powerful than the Czar. It could almost always procure the assassination of its persecutors.

Later in his reign Nicholas entered upon a more peaceful, but less easy, problem of giving land to peasants, of settling them on small holdings, and finally by issuing his extraordinary manifesto against drunkenness in 1914, when several hundred thousand vodka shops were closed. He also gave amnesty to revolutionary exiles, permitting Maxim Gorky, among others, to return to Russia unharmed, and next came his proclamation extending a brother's hand toward Poland, and another permitting religious pilgrimages to Russian shrines in order to pray for Russia, and still another for complete abolition by Imperial Ukase of the sale of vodka, first for a month, then for the duration of the war, and then by promise, for ever.

When hostilities began in 1914 great crowds in Moscow and Petrograd carried his portrait while singing "God save the Czar," and cheering with indescribable enthusiasm. After that Nicholas went about his kingdom unguarded and without hesitation, and to the front to become an inspiration to his soldiers. He visited Roman Catholic and Polish Vilna where he saluted emblems of Catholicism and Polish nationalism. That he might appear in the uniform worn in Russia by a common soldier, he asked that a complete soldiers suit be sent to him, with boots, rifle, and full kit, and so put off his royal clothes, shouldered kit and gun and walked in them on his estate in Livadia. He was photographed thus attired and allowed the photograph to be reproduced for common sale and distribution among soldiers.

Nicholas was a simple man. Inheriting the awful power of his ancestors, and coming to a tragic end in 1917, he thus liked to spend a day as a common soldier in the trenches. Such action resounded through Russia and won hearts all over the non-German world. But necessarily he remained to peasants something unearthly, a giant, a demigod. They were not influenced by his democratic acts, and probably did not understand them. Strange indeed was the fate that overwhelmed him, recalling in more ways than one the fate of Louis XVI of France.

Nicholas II was born on May 18, 1868, and succeeded his father, Alexander III, on November 1, 1894. He was married to Princess Alix of Hesse-Darmstadt November 26, 1894, the betrothal having been announced by the German Emperor.[51]

VITTORIO EMANUELE ORLANDO, Italian Premier

The effect of the Italian defeat in October, 1917, brought about the consolidation of the national spirit and the appointment of Vittorio Orlando, an energetic representative of the Italian people, as Premier. As a statesman he was acknowledged to be the most subtle in Italy, and during his term of office as Minister of the Interior in earlier Cabinets, he was the cause of three crises, the last of which placed him in the premiership. Orlando's career as a publicist began as a Sicilian lawyer and as a deputy from Palermo. From 1903 to 1905 he served as Minister of Education and became known to Americans through negotiations concerning the excavations at Herculaneum. From 1907 to 1909 he served as Minister of Justice, and from 1914 to 1917 was a member of the War Cabinet under Salandra. Perhaps no statesman in any country had been as bitterly assailed as Orlando, yet he long survived criticism. In December, 1917, he sent a message to the American people welcoming them in the fight against the common foe, and at the opening of Parliament in April, 1918, announced that the right wing of the Allied armies in France was in charge of Italian troops.

As representative of Italy, he attended the Supreme War Council at Versailles, and in an interview given at that time announced the Italian check to the German offensive. He was always enthusiastic in his praise of the work of the American Red Cross in Italy and at the adjournment of Parliament eulogized King Victor Emanuel and the Italian army. In June he received congratulations from Lloyd

[51] Adapted from an article by Stephen Graham in The *Morning Post* (London), with additions.

George on the success of the Italian Piave drive, and told the Italian Lower Chamber that the battle was won. He was among those who refused to consider the Austrian peace terms, which caused the subject to be brought up in the Chamber of Deputies, and a few days later announced to the Italian people the news of the retreat of the Austrians across the Piave.

He was a stern advocate of the strict policy of arrest and internment of enemy aliens, and the confiscation of their property. He was

among the first to welcome the Czecho-Slavs unit on the Italian front, and to congratulate it for the valor it displayed. Late in November, 1918, he attended a plenary peace conference in London, and a few days later conferred with President Wilson in Paris over the Italian peace claims. He was appointed member of the commission to draft the complete plan for the League of Nations in January, 1919, having indorsed this plan as set forth by President Wilson at the plenary session where he spoke on the League of Nations' constitution. He was one of the opponents of the article for the abolition of conscription, but subsequently cabled President Wilson that the Italian people acclaimed the League of Nations.

PREMIER ORLANDO

Before the Italian Chamber in March he stated that Italy had agreed to a policy of compromise in conjunction with Italian and Jugo-Slav claims on the eastern coast of the Adriatic. Before the peace treaty was signed, however, his position became insecure and he resigned his office. Orlando had been a leading figure in the Peace Conference, ranking next after Clémenceau, President Wilson and Lloyd George, who with Orlando made up what was called the "big four." Italian discontent over the proposed giving of Fiume to the Jugo-Slavs then undermined his former great popularity.[52]

[52] Compiled from an article in the New York *Times*.

KING PETER OF SERBIA

King Peter was the second man in this war to become a "king without a country." Serbia was as clean swept as Belgium was, altho the sweeping took place more than a year later. Peter at that time was seventy-one years old and physically infirm. As men read of his wanderings about his doomed country, of his flight from it, followed by a nation of fugitives, his condition attained something of a Lear-like majesty. He said he was no longer a king, he was "only a soldier," but it was as an indomitable soldier and an inspired figure that he still ruled Serbia. All through his career, from gaining the Cross of the Legion of Honor in the Foreign Legion against the Prussians in 1871, through service in the Bosnian outbreak against Turkey, down to the World War, the soldier predominated in Peter.

When late in December, 1914, a second Austrian invasion swept over his country, an old man might have been seen with a remnant of the Serbian army hobbling along on a stick. It was Peter Karageorgevitch, who five months before had surrendered his throne to a Regent, because he was himself too old and infirm to discharge royal duties, even in time of peace. But now, after making an electrifying speech, he had dropt his stick, caught up a rifle, and fired at the advancing Austrians, after which his troops fired also and with enthusiasm until twelve days later there was no Austrian left on Serbian soil, and Peter entered his recaptured capital at the head of his army.

With the aid of Germans and Bulgarians, Austria nearly a year later made a third invasion of Serbia when the three powers conquered the little country. Peter, in this invasion, fought in the uniform of a private soldier, and so feeble was he at times that he had to be supported on his horse by two men alongside him. But he was still able to inspire troops with fiery speeches and a dauntless courage. The end of the struggle soon came with his army dispersed and his enemies storming across Serbian soil to Montenegro. With his army the old man fled across the mountains and finally across the sea. He was still King of Serbia, but there was no Serbia to be king of. He found his way to Greece, sad but ever dauntless, still wearing his gray-brown Serbian uniform with blue cavalry collar, cavalry breeches, and a general's red stripe. Aided by a cane he could walk with something of jauntiness in his figure. Peter had "an eagle face, with hooked nose, a bristling white mustache and white imperial, short clipt iron-gray hair, and brown, almost unseeing eyes." Peasants, when he passed, reverently bared their heads, which both pleased and saddened him. "They have great hearts, sir, these

KING PETER LEADING HIS PEOPLE IN THEIR RETREAT OVER THE MOUNTAINS

people," he would say. "They are like the people of America—plain people, as I, too, am a plain man." [53]

RAYMOND POINCARÉ, President of the French Republic

Raymond Poincaré was called a strong man and all Europe was pleased with his election as President of France not long before the war began. His general aims were to discourage Cabinet disruptions, fifty-two of which had taken place in forty-eight years. He had been Minister of Public Instruction in M. Dupuy's first Cabinet, and was so much of a scholar and so charming a speaker that his Government had often asked him to deliver ceremonial orations. These were sure to contain a fund of knowledge and a delightful delicacy of touch that would charm an audience. Poincaré was a sturdily built man, a little over middle height, with closely cut beard and eyes that scrutinized even a stranger with interest. When the war began he had to talk to Europe, and even Asia and America, instead of delivering panegyrics at monuments to dead celebrities. He had done well in a democracy where to raise one's head above the shoulders of a dead level was often to invite the hurling of half a brick. Altho well-known in France for nearly a quarter of a century he had entered upon a larger fame a short time before the war.

M. Poincaré was born in 1860. His father was an inspector of roads and bridges—a modest civil appointment—but he was able to send Raymond to a public school from which he passed to the College at Nancy. He was called to the bar in 1880, and two years later took his degree as Doctor of Laws. Making a specialty of pleading in commercial affairs, he was doing well in the courts when his aspirations turned to politics, and he joined the staff of political writers, first on *Le Voltaire*, and afterward on *La République Française*. In 1886 he became principal clerk at the Ministry of Agriculture. The following year saw him elected deputy at the early age of twenty-seven, which made him the "baby" of the Chamber. He proved himself a hard worker, and was appointed secretary of several important commissions. Not until he had made a forceful declaration on the Morocco Treaty had he secured a reputation which, with ability to back it up, secured his election to the presidency.

His election was regarded as the choice not only of the College of Electors, made up of the Senate and the Chamber, and known as the National Assembly, an old revolutionary title, but the choice of the whole people. It was soon predicted that he would become the greatest President since Gambetta. His versatility as an author and

[53] Based on an article in *The Literary Digest*.

art connoisseur placed him high in the esteem of his countrymen. His clear-sightedness was only equalled by the fearless energy with which he carried out his views. His devotion to the public service was proved by the fact that he had abandoned a lucrative practise at the bar for public life. It was with cordial approbation that the press generally received his acceptance of the highest office in the Republic. Perhaps the most striking feature of the election was the fact that the only two candidates who did not retire in the course of the ballotings—M. Poincaré and M. Ribot—were on the same side in politics; both were Republicans, that is, Conservatives, as regards the form of the French government, or what Gambetta had represented. They were neither Socialist-Radical nor Radical-Socialist. So well did their ideas agree that before the election they met and exchanged political views with the utmost accord. Such were Poincaré's intellectual gifts that he had already become one of the "Immortals" at the French Academy.

It used to be said that the King of England reigns, but does not govern, that the President of the United States rules but does not reign, and that a French President neither rules nor reigns. The interest generally taken in the election when Poincaré was chosen President showed that the French were not content with that kind of President, and that through representatives in the National Assembly, they had put at the head of the State a strong man able to employ the great prerogatives with which he was entrusted. Poincaré, as President of the Council, was called "the strongest Prime Minister in Europe," and such appeared to be the unanimous opinion of the Paris press. "It seems," said the *Matin*, "that democracy, if often forgetful, has now found its memory." Calmette, the editor of the *Figaro*, who was killed by Madame Caillaux because of his criticism of her husband, exclaimed in glowing terms of eulogy that "another era will begin with him. He will preside over the difficult destinies of our country with an authority and experience which none save Ribot could have equalled." Calmette especially emphasized the view that the foreign and colonial policy of France would now keep "the high standard of success of which patriotic Frenchmen have felt so proud." All this was said before the war. That Poincaré justified the prophets all through the war and at the Peace Conference, none would afterward have questioned. Americans found in his address at the opening of the Conference an example of that finished ceremonial discourse for which he had been famous in France long before he was made President.[54]

[54] Adapted from an article by Ernest W. Smith in The *Daily News* (London) and one in *The Literary Digest*.

PERSONAL SKETCHES OF WAR LEADERS

ANTONIO SALANDRA, Prime Minister, and BARON SONNINO, Foreign Minister, of Italy

Salandra, the man who had to act, and Sonnino, the man who thought —thus did the newspapers of Continental Europe explain the political leaders who in 1915, emerging from the wreck of Giolitti's cabinet and his career, took Italy into the war. Not so many months before Giolitti had seemed unassailable in his post as Prime Minister, supported as he was by the great majority evoked from an election in the previous autumn. It had been the practise of the Piedmont statesmen to find relaxation every three years from office by a voluntary retirement, while, as the London *Morning Post* explained, "a caretaker looked after the affairs of the nation until such time as it might please the master to order his faithful majority to prepare the way for his return to the Palazzo Braschi." Accordingly, after having obtained confirmation of his Libyan policy by a tremendous vote of confidence, he made the defection of a handful of radicals anxious for democratic legislation an excuse for resigning, at the same time seeming certain that he could come back. As Baron Sonnino refused to form a cabinet in the face of the almost unbroken Giolittian majority, Signor Salandra, a former lieutenant of the Baron's—the latter being leader of the constitutional opposition —had accepted the post of Premier in March, 1914. For thirteen years and a month the Italian kingdom had been ruled by Giolitti. Yet it would be safe to say, as the London *Times* actually did say, that outside of his own country his personality was almost unknown.

Salandra was called by the *Secolo* of Rome the most plausible, as well as the most persuasive, talker in Italy, while to Sonnino it referred as the austerely reticent financier, the grim economist. Salandra said things, Sonnino thought them out. Salandra wielded a pen, having for years held responsible posts on important organs of Italian opinion. Sonnino studied facts and figures, digested statistics, framed his ideas elliptically, and was an expert on themes so dry and recondite in themselves, like the tax rate, for instance, that one had to be a specialist to appreciate him. Salandra gave himself freely with that exquisite courtesy which belongs to the well-bred Italian. Sonnino was reserved, unsmiling, hard to know. Salandra was afire with enthusiasm, but Sonnino—whose Utopia was a land wherein everybody's expenditure and income exactly balanced—was an effective extinguisher of ardors, zeals, and crusades.

Baron Sonnino—who had become foreign minister when San Giuliano died—was affirmed in the Paris *Temps* to be a complete stranger to the petty arts of the corridor or of the "pharmacy," as Roman slang denominated the corridor as contrasted with the actual chambers of debate wherein majorities were made or marred. His very high principles, added the London *Post,* long his admirer, involved a lack of flexibility; he could not be all things to all men, especially if those men were deputies or influential constituents, "grand electors," as the Italians say. When in office—and Sonnino had held all manner of posts, including that of Premier, the latter briefly—Sonnino once refused a place to a man who was recommended by his mother because he did not wish to be suspected of favoritism. His non-Italian blood—his father was an Italian Jew and his mother of Scottish origin—might account for the fact that he was no orator. His speeches, which he had the disconcerting habit of reading from a manuscript, were admirable as specimens of form and logic, but they sent younger deputies out into the corridor while the more elderly went unabashedly to sleep. On such occasions the Foreign Minister would look unexpectedly up and coldly ask that the slumberers be aroused by the proper officer. Now and then he had sergeants-at-arms posted at doors to prevent the egress of deputies while he was speaking. "I propose," he once said severely to his colleagues in the chamber, "to put a little knowledge of the state of the revenue into your heads, whether you feel interested or not."

Everybody had the profoundest respect for Sidney Sonnino and even the strongest Giolittian organ, like the *Tribuna,* exprest satisfaction that so British a type should have had so long and so successful a career in Italian politics. Nevertheless there was general regret that so strong a character should be such a slave of facts, to which he was addicted, said the *Stampa,* "like a mandarin to opium." He inspired no personal animosity at all, a rare thing in Rome, and except at the time when, outside the Cabinet, he supported the second reactionary ministry of General Pelloux, the mass of Italians trusted him absolutely. He had no propensity to intrigue, no talent for what the Romans call combinations. His iron-gray hair, large, mild, steel-blue eyes and rounded build rendered him, in the plain cutaway coat he affected, genial in aspect. He had a remarkably good voice, as the *Tribuna* observed, for such a remarkably bad speaker. Despite his intimate connection with national projects of finance, he remained a poor man. To Sonnino credit was due, as finance minister in the last century, for having laid the foundation of his country's stability from the revenue standpoint. He inaugurated the era of budget surpluses. He lived abstemiously himself. When not in Rome he vegetated in a villa not far from Florence, listened to Verdi's music and studied statistics. Grand opera and tables of figures engrossed him. Social problems, such as the condition of southern Italy and old-age pensions, formed the themes of his occasional contributions to contemporary literature.

Not that he was without experience in diplomacy, for he spent some years as secretary of Italian legations at Madrid, Vienna, Berlin, and Paris.

Salandra was in one respect, said a journalist who knew him well —the Roman correspondent of the London *Post*—unique among Italian Prime Ministers; he alone of the unified kingdom's twenty heads of past ministries was a native of the continental south. "There has been until lately a Piedmontese prejudice that only Piedmontese, or at least northerners, should hold the first place in Italian politics." Cavour and Signor Giolitti—"who, tho not a Cavour, lived at a place of that name"—were born in Piedmont. It was not until 1887 that the insular south had its first Premier in the Sicilian Crispi, an example followed in 1891 by the Sicilian Marchese Di Rudini; but not until 1914 did the continental south see one of her sons at the head of a ministry in the person of the Apulian Salandra. Like the poet Horace, adds this authority, Salandra hailed from the land of plains and noble churches. There ran in his veins the blood of those strong-armed Norman adventurers who captured the last Byzantine possession in the Italian peninsula. But Salandra, altho bold like the Norman, was cool and without hauteur. He was born at Troja, "the hottest town in Italy," six years after the birth of Sonnino in Florence. He was bald, with "wings" of hair on each side of his head turned gray, but he was an Italian of the emotional type, ready in gesture without going to the length of mere gesticulation. He looked the beau, just as Sonnino looked the "grave and reverend signor." His was the romantic attitude to life, just as Sonnino shrank from adventure. As a student Salandra sat at the feet of Francesco de Sanctis and had lectured first in the University of Naples and then in that of Rome, his subject being the law. He revealed very early his rare aptitude for handling his native tongue poetically, musically, without rioting in an excess of metaphor and declamation.

On becoming Prime Minister, Salandra had to sever his connection with the *Giornale d'Italia*, the "leaders" in which often reflected his shining gifts as a master of Italian prose and his insight into the subtler phases of finance. Salandra loved to handle topics like a tariff schedule from the intimate point of view, bringing out the number of new hats a young woman could buy in the spring if one rate prevailed, and what canes a man must deny himself should the exigencies of revenue extinguish a favored class of importers. He discovered all sorts of victims of unjust fiscal measures, from the young lady in overtaxed flounces to the disconsolate widower whose mourning made a mockery of the dead by turning brown through the use of substitute dyes. Everywhere and always he manifested this poetizing tendency, said the *Tribuna*, this fondness for shadows by moonlight, this aversion to the broad light of day.

The world found Salandra, in 1914, declaring first for neutrality and then proclaiming, as he put it, a "sacred egoism." In the end the forthrightness of Sonnino prevailed and Giolitti was left discredited in his private library, musing over his favorite dramatic authors. The authors loved by Salandra were dramatic, too, and he read much poetry, besides assisting his wife, Donna Maria Salandra, in prominent philanthropies. She and he were conspicuous in relief work when the earthquake ravaged Calabria and both rejoiced in the fact that their sons were old enough to go to the front. Sonnino was responsible for the entry of Italy into the struggle, according to Roman newspapers, for Salandra, unless impelled by a stronger will, would still have been hesitating, still poetizing, still making fine phrases and perfect gestures. On an eventful day long afterward Salandra lost his majority, and Orlando came to the helm. But Sonnino remained.[55]

GENERAL JAN CHRISTIAAN SMUTS, Minister of Defense in the Union of South Africa

Born in 1870, the son of J. A. Smuts, educated at Victoria College, Stellenbosch, General Smuts began public life as a lawyer. He practised at the Cape Town bar at Johannesburg in 1896, was State Attorney of the South African Republic in 1898, and served during the Boer War, being given supreme command of the Republican forces in Cape Colony in 1901. In 1907 General Smuts was elected Colonial Secretary of the Transvaal, and shortly after the outbreak of the World War was placed in command of the British East African expedition against the Germans, which he conducted with complete success during 1916-1917, when he was summoned to serve on the Imperial War Cabinet as special South African representative, a post which he held until the close of the war.[56]

ELEUTHERIOS VENIZELOS, Premier of Greece

An astonishing national revival had taken place in Greece between 1909 and 1912. Observers agreed that Venizelos was primarily responsible for it, all of which and much more was necessary to an understanding of him. The Turkish war of 1897 had apparently

[55] From an article by Alexander Harvey in *Current Opinion*, based on articles in The *Morning Post* and The *Times* (London), the *Temps* (Paris), *Tribuna* and the *Giornale d'Italia* (Rome).

[56] Compiled from "Who's Who, 1918-1919" (London).

done nothing completely to rouse the Greek nation. Meaningless squabbles by corrupt politicians had grown fierce, party life more and more a sordid struggle for place, until every branch of the administration was honeycombed with corruption, the army degenerating, if not disintegrating. The foreign policy was conducted with a combination of bombast and inaptitude which had drawn from Turkey a stinging rebuff to which Hellas had to bow. Popular fury over this humiliation led to an uprising in the army which, under the title of the "Military League," ousted the Government and took control.

To the Western world an army revolt meant jingo militarism, and the gloomiest prophecies prevailed. Greece was likened to a Central American republic and mourned as past redemption. Hellas was facing the supreme crisis of her destiny, in such an inextricable tangle that it seemed as if the sword alone could cut the Gordian knot. The remedy was an heroic one, which would either kill or cure, and would certainly kill if the cure were long delayed. Fortunately the head of the Military League was the man for the hour. This was Venizelos, born on the island of Crete, in 1864, of an ancient family, which according to rumor, came from the medieval Dukes of Athens, but really came from Sparta. Equipped with a good education gained in Greece and Switzerland, Venizelos plunged into the maelstrom of Cretan politics and became recognized as the strong man of the island both in peace and war. It was with a high reputation that he arrived in Athens toward the close of 1909 after being invited, not only by the Military League, but by the veteran politician Dragoumis, the least compromised figure in Greek parliamentary life at that time.

Most significant was the hold soon acquired by Venizelos over the Greek people. Athenians found themselves confronted with an iron will unshaken by the shoutings of mobs. He told them the truth, told it in fewest possible words and frequently with unpalatability. They had their choice of bowing to his decisions or getting rid of him. He was the incarnation of all that Young Greece had longed to be. Cretan deputies, Venizelos' own folk, tried by actual force to make their way into the National Assembly. It had been the dream of every Hellene, notably of Venizelos himself, that Cretans should sit there. But at the moment it meant a Turkish war and defiance of the will of Europe. Venizelos, therefore, drew up a cordon of troops about the House, repulsed the Cretans and deported them, and Athens applauded him. For nearly three years thereafter Greece dropt out of sight, the great world engrossed in international crises and local turmoils.

In the autumn of 1912 the Balkan tempest broke. That Bulgaria would do well everybody agreed, but concerning Greece many had serious doubts. A few weeks later forebodings were dispelled. Three short years of Venizelos had resulted in a new Greece. French and English experts had done their work there well. Hellenic forces had been transformed alike in spirit and performance. In both Balkan wars the Greek armies showed workmanlike efficiency and reaped successes. Astonished at these events, the world asked an explanation, and when Greece answered, "Venizelos," all eyes were turned on this new man. At the London Conference of 1913 his diplomatic insight won golden opinions from all observers, while, at the Bucharest Conference at the close of the Second Balkan War, he displayed a statesmanlike moderation which, if acted upon, might have resulted in better Greco-Bulgarian relations. During the Greco-Turkish crisis which threatened the Near East with a fresh conflagration during the early part of 1914, Venizelos showed a happy combination of tact and firmness which ended by averting a clash. Scarcely had this storm-cloud been dissipated than the tempest of the World War broke over Europe and presently spread to the Near East, with Turkey's entrance into the struggle at the beginning of November, 1914. Problems which Venizelos had fondly believed to have been adjusted rose quivering again for solution. The little Balkan peoples, exhausted as they were by their recent conflicts, saw their destinies flung into this new and far greater boiling caldron.

A great Anglo-French fleet, the mightiest armada of modern times, attacked the Dardanelles, which was touching the very heart of the Eastern question. If the Straits were forced and Constantinople should fall, the whole vast Ottoman heritage would lie at the feet of the Allies, to be disposed of at their good will and pleasure. Things looked well for the Allies during those February days, when the Dardanelles forts seemed to crumble beneath dreadnought shells, with Russia's hosts breasting the Carpathian crests and looking down upon the plains of Hungary. However menacing Russia might be to a realization of Hellenic aspirations, fear of the Muscovite and anxiety over Constantinople were in most Greek hearts counteracted by sympathy from the other Allied Powers. To France and Great Britain Greece was bound by many ties of sympathy and gratitude. These two nations had been the prime architects of Greek national existence and had always shown themselves her friends. Germany had proved herself well disposed to Greece, but Austria had long coveted as the goal of her eastern "Drang," Saloniki, which was the apple of a Greek's eye, while Turkey, their hereditary foe, menaced Hellenism all through Asia Minor. Bulgaria, burning for revenge since the Balkan wars, and inconsolable over loss of Macedonia, stood in close relations to the Teutonic Powers and to the Ottoman Empire.

As February went by, it became increasingly clear that the Allied armada could not batter a way through the Dardanelles; that an army was needed to supplement the work of the dreadnoughts and to consolidate their gains. Allied troops, however, were none too plenty in the Levant and could ill be spared from the battlefields of western Europe. Accordingly, Allied diplomacy cast about to remedy this defect by bringing new recruits to their banner. Greece seemed the most likely possibility. Next door to the scene of action, bitterly hostile to Turkey and well disposed toward England and France, her sympathies were primed by self-interest. The whole Ægean shore of Asia Minor was thickly peopled by Greeks eager to follow their island neighbors into union with the Hellenic Kingdom. Such was the bait held out to Greece by Allied diplomacy, and Venizelos promptly accepted it on principle, offering Greek armies for the Dardanelles campaign, in return for an Allied promise of a broad slice of Asia Minor stretching from a point just south of the Dardanelles athwart Asia Minor to the southern coast on the Mediterranean. This area would have doubled the size of the existing Kingdom of Greece. Under good government it could ultimately support several million inhabitants.

The prospect for Greek patriots was intoxicating, but open to two serious objections. The first was the attitude of Bulgaria. As a result of the Second Balkan War, Greece and Serbia had seized Macedonia and divided it between them, and Macedonia was to Bulgaria the sum of all her hopes. For it she fought in the Balkan Wars. Deprived of it she nursed an unappeasable grief. Venizelos approached Bulgaria and was informed that Bulgaria would remain neutral if Serbia would cede most of her Macedonian conquests and Greece certain rich Ægean coast districts, Kavala, Drama, and Serres, which stretched eastward and cut off the Bulgarian hinterland from the sea. This was a price far above what Greece was willing to pay, and Venizelos attempted a compromise, but Bulgaria absolutely refused to consider his terms. Greece itself pronounced emphatically against any Macedonian cessions to Bulgaria. Faced later by sharp differences of opinion as to Asia Minor, King Constantine summoned a Royal Council, and the council decided against Venizelos, who thereupon resigned. Events in Greece under Venizelos from this time forward have been already set forth in Volume VIII of this work in chapters on Greece and the Balkan States in the World War.

An English correspondent in Greece said Venizelos looked more like an Italian of Piedmont than a Greek islander. In fact, many foreign journalists doubted his Greek descent. His blue eyes, his surprising coolness, his absolute self-control, his ability to overcome and conceal emotions, his extraordinary will-power, his stedfastness of purpose, and his unswerving adherence to the object attained, were not generally characteristic of the Greeks of to-day, and yet Venizelos was a genuine Greek. His ancestors were living in Hellas when the Venetian Admiral Francesco Morosini bombarded and destroyed the Parthenon (about the middle of the seventeenth century). The name was originally Byzantine. The family had gone to Pylos, on the fertile western coast of the Peloponnesus, having been compensated by the Venetian Republic with a generous gift of land for the part they took in the efforts of Athens to cooperate against the Turks. From Pylos they moved to Crevatas, near Sparta, and then to the island of Crete, whence Venizelos in 1910 was invited by the Military League to assume the leadership in the revolution. Venizelos had himself in Crete taken an active part in uprisings against the Turk. He was a dreamer of dreams, his optimism as boundless as was his ability to transform dreams into realities. His hopes and his dreams were, however, interwoven with pure calculation. He was a kind of prophet and never had believed a Balkan confederacy was a hopeless impossibility.[57]

RENÉ VIVIANI, Premier of France

In America it is sometimes as difficult to dislodge a Cabinet officer as it is in France to retain one. The French form of government makes the Cabinet, as to its members, responsible to Parliament for official acts performed by the President of France. This for a new Premier makes the problems of forming a Cabinet and getting a Parliament to indorse it, a task sufficient to daunt many aspirants for that great political honor. René Viviani for a second time had the task, his first having been a failure; but his successor's Cabinet soon failed, and Viviani took up the task. Parliament then approved his selection by a generous majority vote, in spite of the fact that the list was practically identical with a list M. Ribot had just before submitted. The personality of Viviani, rather than the men whom he chose, brought him success where others had failed. What that personality was America had an opportunity to learn, in 1917, when Viviani came to this country with Joffre. A fine thing it was seen to be.

When the war began Viviani was Premier, and in his fifty-second year, or about the age of most active leaders in French politics. He was born in Algiers, where a new France of mixed race had sprung up since Algiers became a French colony. After law studies in

[57] Adapted, in the main, from articles by T. Lothrop Stoddard and Miltiades Christophides in *The Review of Reviews* (New York).

PERSONAL SKETCHES OF WAR LEADERS

Paris, he was enrolled in the Algerian bar, but with his great ability he soon gravitated toward Paris, where in 1889 he was made secretary of the Paris bar, an honorable position from which other chiefs of the Republic, including Gambetta, had made their start in public life. Four years later he was elected to Parliament, and he had held his seat ever afterward, with the exception of a four-year term in another office. In 1906, when he made his reappearance in Parliament, Clémenceau, then Premier, made him Minister of Labor. He held over in the later Briand Government until the end of 1910, when he was made Minister of Public Instruction.

Viviani, therefore, had had ample experience in public life when the war began and found him Premier. Unlike Briand and Millerand, who like him were Independent Socialists, he had not been a group leader. Perhaps his kind of independence had sometimes stood in the way of his success. He had never bent to the discipline of the United Socialists under Jaurès, whom he did not follow otherwise than to give recognition to him as leader. He was equally his own man under Briand and Clémenceau. Personally and professionally he was an old friend of President Poincaré, tho standing at the other end in politics. This became an advantage to him in a political crisis, for it eased the personal relations which existed between him and the President.

As a speaker Viviani ranked high. Joffre when here told us he was the best orator in France. But he was a little too academic to have the same popularity as Jaurès. Viviani as Premier made answer for France to the German ultimatum in August, 1914. "France must consult her own interests," said he. He was essentially an artist; he knew the work of almost every living French painter of any prominence. No poet gained renown in France without some gracious word from him, uttered when the poet was striving for recognition. He was essentially a man of taste, a discerning critic, and a perfect magician in the use of words. He had attracted, perhaps, more attention than any recent statesman in France because of his intellectual gifts. He had a fine presence, flashing eyes and a voice that was described as "a kaleidoscope of sound, changing effects in every new combination." At one moment it was soft with pathos, at another poetic and musical, and it could flow with martial energy.[58]

[58] Compiled from articles in *The Literary Digest,* The *Evening Post,* The *Tribune,* The *Times* and *The Review of Reviews* (New York).

SKETCHES, PEACE TREATY, CHRONOLOGY

WILLIAM II, THE FORMER GERMAN EMPEROR

At the outbreak of the war friends of William of Hohenzollern, who when the war ended had become the most humiliated, if not the most hated man, of his generation, insisted that he was naturally a peaceful man, altho he had grown up in a tradition of war. His avocations, such as yachting at Kiel, digging for antiquities at Corfu, and building museums, clearly were not the occupations of a man wholly given over to martial deeds. The development of his country, his gifts to universities, his courtesy to American and other yachtsmen at Kiel, all seemed to show a recognition of the high value of peaceful pursuits. Germany had had other rulers who were, perhaps, as energetic as he, but none with such varied interests. Every one who had been at a regatta at Kiel recalled his cordial way, and how he took defeats like a sportsman and victories like a gentleman. Yachting was not a passing fad with him. Year after year he had built boats and induced his subjects to do likewise. Men who had been on his yacht noted how little "style" he put on, how he enjoyed the sudden excitement and accidents due to wet decks and gusty breezes.

It was, perhaps, at Forfu that he showed most clearly how well he liked the pursuits of peace. There, week after week, each spring for several years, he had lived above the town in a villa built for the Empress Elizabeth of Austria, or in his private steamship, the *Hohenzollern*. The usual sleepiness of Corfu suffered a change when the Kaiser got there. He was accompanied by no pomp, only the necessary staff and one or more famous scholars. Of the latter one was Dr. Dorpfeld, architect and excavator, with whom he enjoyed getting up in the morning by six and going to the site of a Greek temple, where excavations were made. He not only went early but often stayed till the workmen went home, his excitement when anything was turned up delightful to see.

Miss Anna Topham, an English woman, serving some years as governess to the Kaiser's only daughter, who afterward became the Duchess of Brunswick, and thus had had an opportunity for observing the Kaiser under pleasant circumstances, wrote a book about him, "Memoirs of the Kaiser's Court," which was published before there had been any threat of war. She had not been long in the imperial family when she discovered that the Emperor was not always "playing the part of the frowning imperial personage of fierce mustaches, corrugated brow, and continually clenched mailed fist"—that he frequently "receded from this warlike attitude and became an ordinary, humorous, domestic 'papa.'"

The presence of the Emperor at some of his numerous residences, however, would make a great difference in the atmosphere of the place. "A certain vitality, and still more a certain amount of strain, became visible," said Miss Topham. "Everybody was to be ready to do anything and go anywhere at a moment's notice—to be always in the appropriate costume for walking, riding, or driving. It was altogether a strenuous existence for the entourage, that had always, so to speak, to be mobilized for active service, which was probably just what the Emperor wished. From early morning till night there was hardly a moment of respite from duty."

The Kaiser's six sons and his favorite child, his daughter, were always in his mind. He had a chivalrous way in making his wife

ACHILLEION, THE FORMER KAISER'S PALACE AT CORFU

the leading personage on State occasions. He led a simple household life, in spite of the splendor of his surroundings. Professor Münstenberg of Harvard recalled having seen the Empress in a magnificent evening-gown, wearing long chains of superb pearls, sitting down at the Emperor's side after dinner to do crochet work for a Christmas bazar, while talk between the two and their guests flitted hither and thither. The Kaiser was fond of long walks, rode horseback often and went hunting. Whenever State affairs permitted it, he took an outing. A multitude of topics were familiar to him, in science and art, branches of technique and practical life, movements in social reform and religion. He had one of the rarest of qualities, the ability to meet every one in his own field, such as Theodore Roosevelt had. After a Congress of Arts and Sciences during the St. Louis World's Fair, which was attended by more than a hundred leading European scholars of all scientific denominations, the international party went to Washington, where Professor Münstenberg had the honor of introducing each to the President, who received them in the East Room, where he talked with philologists about philology, with naturalists about natural science, with historians about history, with geographers about geography, and with lawyers about law.

Six years later Professor Münstenberg came to believe that the Kaiser in that art could outdo Roosevelt. It was at the hundredth anniversary of Berlin University to which the scholarly masterspirits of the world had come as delegates. After a great banquet in the gala halls of the Berlin castle, the Emperor received the foreign scholars personally, and Professor Münstenberg happened to stand quite close to him. He found it an intellectual delight to watch the versatility with which he met every man with a mention of his particular subject. The feat became the more fascinating because he addrest every one in his own language, speaking especially French and English with almost the same ease as German.

Caricatures made him appear a pompous man, who talked in a medieval and mystical way about divine rights which had lifted him above mankind. In reality, according to Professor Münstenberg, he was genial and thoroughly human. He would never stoop to undignified behavior, would never play the Emperor in shirt-sleeves; and in informal talk would stick to a certain formality when he spoke about royal persons. He did not in friendly anterooms appear to think himself a human being above others, but it was different with the office which had come to him by inheritance. That was treated as if it had been God-given. The crown to him was of divine grace, just as the wedding ring was of divine grace. A king was more than a citizen; he became the bearer of an office. This exprest the view which not only the Emperor had of himself, but which practically every German had of the meaning of royalty.

After the war had been some months in progress, observers noticed that the Kaiser's hair had become quite white, his face drawn and care-worn, his manner abrupt and lacking the ceremonial calm that once was shown. He was trying to carry the weight of the war upon his own shoulders; no detail was too trifling to escape his attention, and he was working twenty hours a day. The Kaiser was constantly at the front with his sons. He was in Berlin seldom. As the German troops moved forward in the west he made his camp in deserted French châteaux or in a portable house. Each day he was in his automobile at daybreak and it was common for him to do 200 miles a day along trenches. Always he had with him tobacco and cigarets for his "children," as he frequently called his soldiers in little talks when the machine halted. His interest in their comfort, his presence on the field, his devotion to the fatherland, early in the war inspired in soldiers something that approached veneration. His face in those days never lost gravity of expression. He never indulged in humorous sallies.

William II was fifty-nine years old on January 27, 1918. Altho one of his arms was withered, he had been a great out-of-doors man, and after a weak childhood grew into a strong and rugged man. What was called a typical day at the front was thus described by an eye-witness early in October, 1914: [59]

"Rid yourself, first of all, of the idea that the Emperor is a heroic figure. He is a man not exactly of small stature, but he is distinctly below the average height and rather fat, so that he is more like a typical German beer drinker and sausage eater than a knightly cavalier. Moreover, his left arm is about ten inches shorter than the right arm and partially paralyzed. This deformity strikes the eye unpleasantly, tho one can not withhold a certain admiration for the energy which enabled the Kaiser to become a good shot and a passable rider in spite of this tremendous handicap.

"On this particular occasion the Kaiser had been sleeping in a French château, but not without elaborate precautions against a surprize attack. The château was fortified against aerial attacks. Sacks were piled on the roof and a protective shield of metal network was erected. Whenever the Kaiser moves his quarters a small army of military engineers precedes him to carry out these defensive measures before his arrival. Around the château were men of his special body-guard, a detachment was outside of his bedroom door, another in the hall, another at the front door, and two more detachments were in the rooms immediately above and beneath his own room. Three unbroken lines of sentries surrounded the house, a whole battalion of infantry and several squadrons of cavalry were encamped in the parks. This was some twenty miles from the front, and the château was connected by field-telegraph with the headquarters of the nearest army, so that any sudden retreat of the German legions should not place the Supreme War Lord in danger.

"Soon after sunrise the Kaiser emerged from the château and greeted his soldiers with his customary 'Good morning, soldiers,' to which all of them in the immediate vicinity replied in unison: 'Good morning, Your Majesty.' A motor-car was in readiness and he was whirled swiftly toward the front, while the troops which had guarded him stood rigidly at attention. Ten drummers of the body-guard beat their drums

[59] The account was printed in The *Herald* (New York).

by way of salute. The imperial standard was conveyed in the second motor-car and the officers of the imperial suite followed in others. The cavalry of the body-guard preceded the monarch to the place where he left the motor-car to mount his horse.

"Then followed a spectacular progress from point to point in the rear of the fighting-line—at a safe distance to the rear, I may add, because the Supreme War Lord must not be exposed to stray bullets or shrapnel. Large bodies of reserves had bivouacked in those parts and fresh troops were marching up from the direction of the frontier. The Kaiser halted and addrest a fervently patriotic oration to one regiment and another to the second regiment as he rode from place to place. During the morning he delivered no less than nine speeches, all bombastic and excessively martial in tone. Lunch was taken in the open air at a table in front of a certain General's tent. Wine and food commandeered from the residence of a French country gentleman supplied the Kaiser with a splendidly luxurious meal prepared by his own cook and served by his flunkeys in gorgeously striped uniforms. None of the pomp of the imperial court was abandoned at the front. More visits to the troops and more speeches in the afternoon and back by automobile to the château for dinner. At no moment during the day had the Kaiser been within range of the enemy's fire.''

THE KAISER'S SISTER, THE FORMER QUEEN SOPHIA OF GREECE, IN A PRUSSIAN GRENADIER UNIFORM

The Kaiser had as a war talisman—it availed him little, however, as events proved —a four-leafed sprig of clover, prest, dried and tucked away in a pocketbook under his gray great-coat. Long after the beginning of the war he had carried it next his breast, where hope of victory beat. About this talisman had been woven a pretty story which formed a new romance in the life of the Hohenzollerns. It had been plucked by childish hands in 1870. Tho it had become in 1914 a mere wisp of memories, Empress, war-lords, soldiers and people all said it would bring victory to the Kaiser, just as it had brought victory to his grandfather at Sedan. It appeared that the little daughter of an old court official, named Louis Schneider, during the campaign of July, 1870, had plucked in a garden this piece of clover and been allowed to present it to the old King Wilhelm, who thereafter kept it in his note-book. After months had passed, when German troops were marching back in triumph to Berlin, one day along the route little Miss Schneider and her father were summoned into the presence of the newly made Emperor. "Here is your piece of clover," said Kaiser Wilhelm, as he opened the leaves of his note-book. "It has won me victory; it has brought me luck. I give it back to you, my child, and I hope it will bring you luck, too." The aged monarch then walked to a mirror, cut off one of his white locks of hair, and handed it with the clover leaf to Miss Schneider.

Years passed and Miss Schneider presented the precious clover leaf to the daughter of a Countess as a baptismal gift. Again years passed until it was August, 1914, and the German Empress in Berlin one day received in audience the Countess, now a widow, and her daughter, who carried in her hand the talisman of 1870, and asked if she might give it to the Emperor. "His Majesty is very busy," said the Empress, "but I will take your talisman and will give it to His Majesty with your best wishes," adding that she hoped it would be as powerful now in bringing victory as it had been for the Emperor's grandfather forty-four years before.

Late in the war the Kaiser one day after tea in Berlin, when the Empress and her ladies had retired, spoke in turn to the men present commonplace phrases enough, about the weather, new books, and the efficiency of the German railway system, and seemed to be making an effort to keep off the delicate topic of the war, when one of the party exprest admiration for the discipline and unanimity of the German people, and he said:

"That is the impression most foreigners should get, even hostile foreigners. I suppose for one thing the contrast between Germany as depicted by our enemies—Germany restive, war-tired, and half-famished —and the united, enthusiastic, still prosperous country when actually seen, would cause them a great deal of astonishment. The British theory that I am responsible for the war has got a great hold on the English people. It is curious how this theory seems to fascinate all my enemies. Yet the people who accuse me of having caused the war are the very people who previously testified to my earnestness for peace. I do not envy the man who had the responsibility for this war upon his conscience. I at least am not that man. I think history will clear me of that charge, altho I do not suppose that history will hold me faultless. In a sense every civilized man in Europe must have a share in the responsibility for this war, and the higher his position the larger his responsibility. I admit that, and yet claim that I acted throughout in good faith, and strove hard for peace, even tho war was inevitable. Why do neutrals always talk about German militarism and never about Russian despotism, the French craving for revenge, English treachery?

I think the next generation will strike a juster balance in apportioning blame.'' [60]

Men who read this statement at that time recalled after the war a remark made by Dr. Muehlon, the Krupp director, that in July, 1914, the Kaiser could have prevented the war, if only he had raised his hand once to Austria—that is, if he had simply said "No" to the Austrian proposal to make war on Serbia. It was recalled, also, that, in the barbarous conduct of the war, by submarines, Zeppelins, poison-gas, devastation and deportations, the responsibility had in the main been the Kaiser's, for they were unlawful war processes which he might have stopt, but so far as known, never attempted to stop.

One respect in which the war modified his character was that, late in the conflict, he did not assert his authority or his position in the old-time autocratic way. This was revealed plainly in his treatment of members of the Great General Staff. An occasional interference with a general plan was ventured, but only after due deliberation with the Imperial Chancellor, and members of the Bundesrath. In council he had become a listener rather than a talker, prone to defer to the judgment of others, but conscious at all times, perhaps, that his knowledge of the art of war was intuitive rather than scientific. Berlin inclined at times to a suspicion that the ordeal of war had tinged his disposition with meekness and humility, altho by no means with a diminished sense of his importance as the divinely appointed leader of the German people.

Until the war began the Kaiser had kept his consort somewhat in the background. In the course of his long reign she had been almost a cipher except for her sovereignty in the domestic sphere. There she reigned supreme, prescribing, it was said, even the thickness of the socks worn by the Emperor, forbidding strong cigars and concocting a peculiar broth, or beef soup, which was his diet when his throat became sensitive. During the war for the first time he was seen thrusting the Empress forward, as if he had revised his theory that she was unlucky. In this sorrowful period, the Empress, said an Italian journalist who saw her at Vienna, had the same wonderful blue eyes that had captivated William when, as a girl of twenty-two, he first saw her in a hammock at Primkenau, her father's castle in Silesia, and called her "a rosebud." Her eyes were very large, rather dark for so pronounced a blonde, stedfast and clear, with a full pupil. It had been said that she was able "to speak all the languages of Europe just with her eyes." She cast the spell of her fascination upon the young Austro-Hungarian Empress-Queen Zita, despite the difference in their ages, and was emphatically a woman's woman,

[60] Berlin letter to The *Daily News* (London).

KAISER AND KAISERIN IN OTHER DAYS
Their carriage has halted on their way to a reception in the
Guildhall in London

feminine, gracious in her smile, low-voiced, using two pretty hands in effective gestures as she conversed earnestly on topics of a personal nature.

She was not an "intellectual," altho she delighted in some such scholar as John P. Mahaffy with his inexhaustible fund of Irish anecdotes. Mahaffy told stories with inimitable drollery to an admiring circle at the palace, after which the Empress herself would serve him with tea. Her conception of entertaining was to supply guests with food and drink; nor did she disdain explanations of the merits of her kitchen. She was reported the best cook in Germany, and a very good nurse. Nor was she above such cares as the heat of her consort's morning bath, which she prepared for him at the palace as well as at a country seat, where she had her own particular brood of chickens, milked a cow and pursued other vocations upon which are based claims to being a farmer's wife. She had a passion for needlework, which she could gratify, however, only when she was living in the country. She was a great stickler for church attendance. No tenant on her country estate would risk her displeasure by not appearing in his place for divine worship. With a chapel on the estate the Kaiserin was as likely as not to appear early in the village church to look about her as worshipers trooped in and make pointed inquiries after the services about the health of the absentees.

These essentially feminine traits in his consort were not always palatable to William. She was not sufficiently imperial. He would have liked her to be more of a spectacle, to assume something of the grandeur of a Theodora, the majesty of a Zenobia, and the inspiring deportment of a Maria Theresa. His idea of feminine royalty was the famous Queen Louise of Prussia, whose career he knew by heart. The Kaiserin had been brought up in a German country mansion, the seat of the house of Schleswig-Holstein-Augustenburg, leading there the simple life of a German Marguerite, visiting the sick on her father's estate, doing a little needlework, watering flowers and reading books prescribed by the chaplain. She never in her life wore a pair of silk stockings until the day of her wedding. She was a wife and mother before she knew anything about lawn-tennis. Her diversions were horseback-riding, croquet, and archery, but she never was a good dancer. She had the indiscretion, not long after her marriage, to be caught asleep while the Emperor's mother was reading from a philosophical book aloud to the circle at Potsdam.

In the first years of this union, William soon thrust his wife into the background and she was long absorbed in the cares of a prolific maternity. At the time of the birth of her seventh child, the Princess Victoria Louise, her one daughter, afterward Duchess of Brunswick, she seemed to have become old. Her hair was already gray, altho she was only thirty-four. Her only official recognition in the military life of her husband's empire was comprised in her rank as colonel of a hussar regiment with the black eagle, which was conspicuously worn when she went on horseback at the head of her troops in a uniform that was not in the least becoming to her Gretchen type of beauty. If the worst came to the worst she could have lived well on her own fortune. It was quite large, and, according to the Paris *Temps,* very wisely invested in securities of dividend-paying American railroads. The silk industry of the United States also yielded her a comfortable revenue as she had put money into large American mills.[61]

[61] Adapted from an article by Alexander Harvey in *Current Opinion,* one by Herbert Bayard Swope in The *Herald* (New York), and a Berlin letter to The *Daily News* (London).

THE FORMER GERMAN EMPRESS ENTERING THE GATEWAY
OF AMERONGEN, IN 1919
In the distance is seen the Castle. At the gate stands one of the
military guards of the grounds

WOODROW WILSON, President of the United States

Perhaps the Entente Allies could in time have defeated Germany with the United States remaining neutral. After the signing of the armistice it was revealed as a certainty that British sea-power was slowly strangling Germany to death, that Germany was starving as the Confederacy starved under the resistless pressure of the Northern blockade; that the battle of Jutland, proclaimed to the German people as a great German victory, was in reality the death blow to German hopes. So it was possible that the Entente might have won alone, provided it could have held out long enough, but without the material assistance of the United States, her men and money and abundant resources, her inventive genius and adaptability, the task would have been far longer and far harder and the ruin of Europe would have been in every sense greater. Moreover, without the co-operation of the United States Army and Navy, the ships that rose from American shipyards, the food that America denied herself so that the Entente nations might be fed, Europe would not have been able to end the war in 1918. Then the problem would have been, could the Entente hold out for a 1919 campaign?

The chief work performed by President Wilson probably was not seen in concentrating the strength of his country on the common cause, so much as in finally investing the war with a wider scope of moral grandeur. The United States might still have coined the ultimate victory into profit, by territorial or other gains, but these were not her motives. The long record of history affords few samples of a nation going into a great war, knowing that it would be compelled to make great sacrifices in lives and fortunes and asking no reward except the privilege of doing service for a cause vital to her national life, the cause of freedom. In history there is nothing quite parallel to the action of this country when, on April 6, 1917, it took up the challenge Germany had flung down. Almost from the first day of the war President Wilson had preached from the text of duty and service, for the high privilege of championing the rights of mankind. When war first broke out, however, he had tried to play the part of mediator, and his offer was declined. Many Americans condemned him for counseling neutrality and continuing in that state.

But, looking back afterward, many could see how, in some sense, it was fortunate that the United States did not take up arms in 1914, but that more than two years and a half elapsed before she began to play her part. Had the United States declared war in 1914, or in the early months of 1915, when the costly and tragic experiences of England and France had still to be learned, it seems more than doubtful if Congress could have been induced to impose on the country the

PRESIDENT AND MRS. WILSON LUNCHING WITH ALBERT, KING OF THE BELGIANS, IN 1919

President Wilson's visit to Belgium, the last of his visits to European countries, was made just before he sailed for home after signing the Peace Treaty. The scene of this luncheon is the devastated forest of. Houthoulst, protection from the sun and from falling caterpillars having been secured by a piece of striped canvas. At the extreme left of the table is Miss Margaret Wilson, next to whom is King Albert. The President follows, with his cap on, and then comes Mrs. Wilson. Opposite them are Brand Whitlock, Rear-Admiral Grayson, and others

selective draft; but even if Congress had done so, America, like England and France, would have had to pay the dear price of ignorance. American armies, insufficiently trained, insufficiently equipped, knowing little or nothing of the art of modern war, would have been thrown into that furnace of death to be slaughtered as the British and French were slaughtered; bravely they would have had to face machine-guns, their bravery futile.

But in 1918, when America had marshaled her legions, the technical superiority of Germany was no longer feared. The advantage Germany had at the beginning, because she alone of all nations was prepared, had definitely passed. Even more than that gain was the spiritual strength gained by the delay. What Mr. Wilson said in his appeal for neutrality in August, 1914, and what he said in his address to Congress on April 2, 1917, he had said scores of times in the intervening months, and was to say again and again between the time when America declared war and Germany, broken and defeated, signed the armistice. On all these occasions he had preached the moral side of the war. The duty imposed upon the United States was to uphold democracy against autocracy, to champion small and weak nations, to be the means whereby justice should be done to the weak as well as the strong.

The great purpose Mr. Wilson had in view was not always understood in his own country. Nor was this surprising. Men's blood boiled in the Eastern States in 1915 (but not yet in the Western) when they heard of the crime of the *Lusitania,* and in their leaping passion were ready to fight to avenge the crime; but to fight for a thing so abstract as international morality, to be the champion of peoples with whom they had no intimate relations, of whose existence almost they were unaware, simply to spread the gospel of altruism, stirred no great emotion in 1914, 1915, or even in 1916. And yet in time Mr. Wilson stirred emotion as no man had done in our day, and as few men had in the long struggle between liberty and absolutism. Men will always fight with the gallantry of their blood in defense of their country, or to avenge old and deep-seated wrongs, but they will fight more desperately and die more gladly for a great and vital principle, once they fully understand it. That extraordinary trait in human nature is due, perhaps, to the fact that in every man there is planted some divine spark; in every man, even the most material, there is a touch of the mystic, to which some great spiritual cause, the meaning of which may be only dimly revealed, makes a powerful appeal. Americans of learning and men illiterate, from great cities and remote rural communities, even from isolated mountain homes, became in this war thrilled and uplifted at the thought of being crusaders to carry the banner of freedom three thousand miles across great waters.

Across those waters there flowed in 1917 and 1918 not only the 2,000,000 troops that were to complete the final undoing of Germany, but an invisible force of bright and great thoughts spreading and gathering force until they engulfed the continent. In places and lands where democracy had had no meaning, men asked what that force was which had induced a great nation to take up arms; what that new religion which had so inspired Americans to great sac-

THE BIRTHPLACE OF PRESIDENT WILSON'S MOTHER, IN CARLISLE, ENGLAND

rifice and complete devotion. Once that spiritual force was unloosed, the example became infectious.[62]

It was in 1807 that a County Down Scotch-Irish youth named James Wilson landed in Philadelphia, got work there as a printer, that old craft of adventurers and wanderers, with small purses stuffed with hope—the craft of Horace Greeley and Ben Franklin. He married an Ulster girl, who had "come over" in the same emigrant ship, thrived as a printer and become an editor in Pittsburgh, whence his son, after learning the same trade, went to college and became a Presbyterian minister, after the fashion of many Ulsterites, and in 1855 was pastor of a church in Staunton, Virginia, where, sixty-two years before the day on which that son was staying at Buckingham Palace with the King of England, that son was born, one who, by whatever gifts of will, of genius, of destiny, of energy, of industry, of ambition, of fortune's smiles, had become, in 1917-1919 the pillar

[62] A. Maurice Low in *The Review of Reviews* (New York).

of the hopes of many peoples and perhaps "the foremost man of all this world."

Woodrow Wilson was born a professor. His early academic environment seemed to have bespoken for him not more than the subdued but far-spreading influence of a teacher, or the head of a college or university. It was like a story from fairyland, his sudden rise and his fitness for high posts and duties. Not till he had led a peaceful people to war and filled them with the ardor of his own conviction, not until his long patience, unyielding courage, large perception of essentials and general principles, the passion and power of his speech, had filled the world with his fame, did any one begin to take Wilson's proper measure. There were flaws enough to pick in him, and the bitterness of censure, not infrequently well founded, had been equal to the fervor of the praise bestowed on him. But this, at least, no one denied him, that before he reached man's grand climacteric, he had reached that of world fame. More applauded, more illustrious, more powerful, he could never be; nor could he inspire any more sympathetic interest, or kindle any wider attention in the world, than on that birthday anniversary in Buckingham Palace, or that day two weeks afterward when he was made a citizen of Rome on the Capitoline hill-top. His position among leaders of democracy was unique; the plenitude of his fame startled all observers. This grandson of an emigrant had returned, in 1918, the "pillar of a people's hope, the center of a world's desire," and on Sunday, December 29, went to Carlisle, there to receive the freedom of the city and worship in his grandfather's church.[63]

Tardy as they had been in recognition of Mr. Wilson as a man of genius, European papers in Allied countries, after his re-election in 1916, more than made amends for earlier criticism by now ascribing to him rare gifts. From the liberal *Daily News,* in London, which saw in him a supreme master of statecraft, to the *Tribuna* in Rome, which had to go back to Cavour for his parallel, there came an admiring chorus. Extreme ideas prevailed as to the seclusion in which he loved to live. The Paris *Rappel* compared his solitude to that of a monk. Others made comparisons with great ecclesiastical statesmen of the Middle Ages. German dailies conceded his ability, but inclined to present him as artful, crafty, and hypocritical. The Berlin *Kreuz-Zeitung* deemed him an altogether sinister figure, devious in methods, subtle in policy, and lacking scruple. He had not hesitated, in the opinion of the *Frankfurter Zeitung,* to play the part of tool for the British. He was born a trickster, who had succeeded Sir Edward Grey as the world's arch-demon.

The complete revolution that took place in Entente estimates after

[63] The *Times* (New York).

PRESIDENT WILSON AND CARDINAL MERCIER
The two are standing at the entrance to the Cardinal's house in Malines

X.

1916 was based on considerations set forth elaborately in the London *Daily News*. His ability to lead struck that journal as amazing. There had been no one in Europe to compare with him since Gladstone, altho the traits and temperaments of the two were as the poles asunder. Mr. Wilson showed in his acts a comprehension of politics on the scientific side which living statesmen of the European countries had conspicuously lacked. In him, said the *Tribuna* of Rome, Germans in the Wilhelmstrasse had met their match; they found they now had a scholarly recluse to overreach. This man of fine phrase, this dealer in terms so spontaneous and unforced that he seemed to do his thinking aloud, this idealist and democrat, could understand an Austria ruled by the Metternich method as easily as he could divine a Prussian Junker. No American before him, no American at any rate in a place of power, had comprehended Europe as anything but a great and remote generality, but Wilson made distinctions, differentiated essences, penetrated combinations, moved with the art of some class diplomatist working with Bourbons. He was Florentine in the tactfulness of his approach, Roman in his scope, French in his politeness, British in his forthrightness and yet American in his daring, his freedom from the trammels of traditions. He mingled with intellectual inferiors without despising them and he could be sarcastic without cruelty. If Europe had been slow in getting the measure of him, she saw him now more accurately than did many of his countrymen.

Europe's first impressions in 1915 and 1916 were based on criticisms of Wilson emanating to a great extent from his own countrymen. Involved in a struggle for world-power, Europe did not distinguish at first the voice of mere partizan detraction from that of the competent critic. There had spread over the old world the legend of a mincing pedant, writing meaningless notes. He had the old Roman *suaviter in modo* coming a long way before the *fortiter in re*. The Jagows, Bethmann-Hollwegs, and Zimmermanns failed to realize the determination of character that was following them up, step by step, until they found themselves suddenly caught in a trap and baffled. European statesmen who had criticized him might have imitated him with advantage to themselves—his coolness under extreme provocation, his self-restraint, his ability to control events, his self-effacement, a man who had not taken the center of the world's stage like a man rushing up on horseback. Germans strove to make it appear that he was consumed by his own vanity and sought to thrust himself forward as a peacemaker, but not once had a trace of egotism shown itself in his attitude.

In histories of this war, affirmed the *Hamburger Nachrichten*, its sinister figure, its evil genius, would be discerned in the grandson of an emigrant, Woodrow Wilson. Germany was convinced that he was doublefaced—and she said so.[64] The change in later German views, say in the early winter of 1918-1919, was surprizing. When he was on his way to France the German press commented frequently on his journey, and the probable influence he would have on the peace terms. At one time slandered and maligned as hypocritical, he was looked upon now by the German newspapers as a peace apostle and the one person from whom the Germans could expect justice. His "fourteen points" were discust as meaning something for Germany and he was going to Europe in order to insist that his principles there set forth, and as Germany interpreted them, should be carried out. The *Lokal Anzeiger,* however, remarked that if he wished to put his demands through, he would have to act energetically and with all his personal force at the preliminary conference, "for his ideals had already been thrown in the dust by the armistice conditions and continued to be thrown in the dust at Spa." The Cologne *Volkszeitung* had learned, from an authoritative source, that "in spite of many difficulties which the Allies had imposed, Wilson intended to insist that Germany should have colonies in Africa." Like many others, that paper tried to prove that, while he would not play a leading rôle in the Peace Conference, he and the other American delegates, if they had an honest desire to do so, "could put through many of his ideas for a just peace." His idea of a league of nations, however, "would be poisoned, if the German nation were treated as an object of exploitation." As for Germany having "guilt for the war on her conscience," the whole German nation, said that paper, "denies the accusation."

Congress during the war bestowed upon President Wilson powers and functions wider than those possest by any ruling monarch—wider even than those Lincoln had. He was empowered to commandeer ships and shipyards, take over industrial establishments and operate them, construct a great merchant marine, send millions of Americans to the trenches in France, provide officers for an aviation service that was to expend $640,000,000, and administer the food-supply of an entire nation. He had to shut himself in and allow many matters which might engage him in times of peace to be handled by assistants.

For the first time in the country's history the exterior of the White House indicated the seclusion in which the President lived. In the daytime a policeman stood guard at every gate. When night came, soldiers with loaded guns and bayonets took places about fifty paces apart on the sidewalks surrounding the grounds. Soldiers had strict orders to make every one move on. There was no loitering about the White House after sundown. The police guard about the President

[64] Adapted from an article by Alexander Harvey in *Current Opinion.*

when out riding was doubled. Two motor-cycle policemen clad in khaki joined his automobile the moment it swung out of the grounds and followed within five feet to and from the golf links or wherever else it might go, while in a large automobile twenty to thirty feet to the rear were half a dozen secret-service men. After international affairs began to absorb the President's attention, there was little direct communication with newspaper correspondents. Their former semi-weekly conferences with him had to be abandoned after the submarine crisis became acute, because the President could not have answered half the questions that would have been asked, and Tumulty became the source of White House news. Night and day he was asked about

ALEXANDRA, DOWAGER QUEEN OF
GREAT BRITAIN

MARGHERITA, DOWAGER QUEEN
OF ITALY

Two Queen mothers on whom President Wilson called while in Europe in 1918

matters of international and domestic moment. Sometimes he was privileged to talk, but at other times he could impart no information.[65]

Mr. Wilson included promptness among the highest of minor virtues. He once scolded a delegation from the New Jersey legislature for being two minutes late for an appointment with him when he was Governor. One of his secretaries in Washington declared there never had been in Washington a man who was "so marvelously punctual day in and day out." He was not only punctual himself, but required punctuality from others. When he first went to Washington, senators and members of the House began to follow the old

[65] The *Sun* (New York).

system of taking as much of a President's time as they cared to, but were soon astonished to find that the thing could not be done with Mr. Wilson. Unless the matters on which they called under appointment were of unusual importance, each conference was expected to last not more than three to five minutes. At the end of the allotted time the President would rise to his feet and say: "Now you may be sure that this will be looked into." After each caller departed the President—who was so expert a stenographer that a page from his note-book was as clean-cut as a piece of engraving—made a shorthand note of the call and the business. At the end of each day he went through the note-book, gave directions or dictated letters, and thus ended the work for that day.

Breakfast was strictly a fixt feast at the White House, beginning at eight o'clock promptly. He did not scorn the saving of minutes and so was never five minutes late to breakfast. At 8.55—not "about nine" or "when I finish breakfast," but at 8.55 his personal secretary was expected to be ready to take down answers to important letters received the day before. At ten he was at his desk in his private office and for half an hour such routine as could be was disposed of. Then came the appointments, each cut down to a minimum. After luncheon he was ready to meet tourists—this was the case before the war—or to hold a conference with some member of the Cabinet, or with a foreign diplomat. After that came his recreation. Dinner was at seven, "and so to bed"—invariably between ten and midnight. He had on his desk four accurately arranged piles of documents and could say to a secretary: "Go over to my study desk. The paper we want you will find in the pile nearest my seat on the right-hand end. It is the fifth from the top." Always when he went after it, the secretary would find the paper exactly where the President said it was. He did things for himself, such as filing important papers with his own hands in a filing-case back of his chair. When he had finished using a pen, he would take a piece of chamois-skin from a drawer, wipe his pen clean and return the chamois-skin and pen to their places. He was so exact that he could tell whether anybody had moved anything on his desk during his absence.[66]

In his troubled days at Princeton, when he was President, one charge against him was that he so shut himself up in his home-life that he did not know men and the ways of men. In this charge there was truth, to the extent that Mr. Wilson's own fireside was always dearer to him than the thronged marts of casual contacts. He never felt so completely himself as when he had gathered with wife and daughters and a few chosen friends around the fireside, and allowed his spirit to move whither it listeth. He was no superman, but

[66] James Hay, Jr., in *The American Magazine.*

human to the core. One of his most obvious qualities in his home life was an incorrigible playfulness. Graver people sometimes thought he was too much that way, for he would joke in the midst of serious discussions. His fund of anecdote, his gleeful delight in nonsense rimes, his atrocities in punmaking (an inheritance from his father, from whom he derived many traits), all these things were pronounced in him, together with character-humor, the knack of giving word-portrayals of people in incongruous settings. Altho the tenderest of men, he was the least sentimental. When the war began the foundations of his own life were crumbling under him. It was just as the war opened that his first wife died. "I can not help thinking," he said, "that perhaps she was taken so that she might be spared the spectacle of this awful calamity." His relatives knew after her death that he was the loneliest man in the world. One of them wrote afterward of "the lonely figure walking down the long hallway at the White House, his hair much whitened in a few months." [67]

ALFRED ZIMMERMANN, German Foreign Minister

Not because he was a great figure during the World War does Zimmermann have a place among these sketches, but because he, more than any other, in a brief term of office, dealt the last stroke that was needed to consolidate American sentiment in favor of declaring war on Germany. When the sinking of the *Lusitania* and its civilian passengers aroused widespread sentiment for war among American people in the East, the Middle and Far West were indifferent. If rich Easterners chose to sail on British ships, it was their risk, said many in the West, and not the risk of all the American people. But when Zimmermann's note proposing to Mexico the invasion of the Southwest, with a view to conquering American States formerly Mexican territory, and asking Mexico to secure aid from Japan, the cost to be paid by Germany, people beyond the Allegheny and the Mississippi began really to see red.

No photograph had ever done justice to the strong, scarred face of Alfred Zimmermann, because, as the Paris *Figaro* said, the countenance of the Chief of the Foreign Office in Berlin, after Jagow left it, had an expressiveness too baffling for the camera. The blue eyes, the somewhat carroty hue of hair and mustache, the pallor of face, the traces of sword-slashes on his cheek, left over from university days, gave no more clue to the soul of the man within than did photographs in Berlin shop-windows. In an almost literal sense of the phrase, Zimmermann talked with his face. His features reflected every conceivable change. With ease he could look

[67] Stockton Axson in The *Public Ledger* (Philadelphia).

gay, yet in another second his eyes could flash an exquisite anger and the lines upon his brow could show an embarrassing accentuation, but a smile would arrive at the climax of his fury. His laugh was a masterpiece—ringing, clear, hearty, and revealing well-kept teeth, notwithstanding his fifty-seven years, and conveying an impression of spontaneity, of true mirth. His real vocation would have been histrionic cinematography. There was no artist in the "movies" whose countenance lent itself to the purposes of the film with a versatility so irresistible. Ordinary photographs in illustrated papers robbed him of his due, for his soul was that of a chameleon.

The lack of the particle "von" should not have led one to an inference that Zimmermann was not well born. On his mother's side he had relatives among the nobility of Bavaria, and the hereditary wealth of the family went back five generations. So far was he from being self-made that he went to the University at Breslau and to Berlin for the prosecution of severe studies in history, economics, law and literature. But to the diplomatic service he was a rank outsider. He had climbed the ladder of promotion by way of the consular service, having been a commercial expert. He was alien to the exquisite school of Jagow, his knowledge being not primarily of waltzing, or of dining, or of that human nature to which the Machiavellis and Metternichs had appealed. Zimmermann knew all about the importation of hides from Argentina, and could make a happy guess of the number of tons of tea there were in warehouses in Moscow. This afforded a hint of the avenue along which he had traveled, said the Rome *Tribuna,* a correspondent of which, like many other journalists, knew him well. He was an economist rather than a business man, one of the creators of practical economics in the new and German sense of that term. To him more than to any other living individual was the Berlin exporter indebted for the "science" behind his invasion of world markets. Zimmermann's exhaustive and learned works on the relations between commerce and diplomacy were German classics. Yet he was neither a pedant, a cosmopolite, a mere business man, nor a bureaucrat.

Ever since his first connection with the Foreign Department, of which he was for a time head, he had studied the characteristics of people among whom he was thrown—Chinese, Russians, Finns, Bulgars. Long scrutiny of human nature accounted for the ease with which he got acquainted with others. He was not long a stranger to any one, and no one remained long a stranger to him. He could meet no living human being without discovering mutual acquaintances. He had a positive genius for the discovery, at a first encounter, of intimate themes which gave to the talk a personal touch of the friendliest kind. He would go out of his way to be amiable to young attachés who arrived in Berlin from South America only to be snubbed by aristocratic secretaries at European legations. By his unconventional ways he abated the glory of the Master of Ceremonies at the court of Berlin, who was happy in many decorations and liked to invest the reception of a new ambassador with endless ceremonial. He defied etiquette and tradition by inviting unofficial personages into his sacred private office at the Wilhelmstrasse. The one respect in which he did not seem modern was in his correspondence. He dictated nothing to a stenographer. He was one of the few Germans in exalted posts who could use a typewriter himself and upon which he condescended to tap even in the Wilhelmstrasse.[68]

[68] Adapted from an article by Alexander Harvey in *Current Opinion*.

1. Obverse of design

2. Reverse (Figs 1 and 2 designed by J. E. Fraser)

3. Victory medal for domestic service

4. Foreign service, not in battle

5. Photograph of the original clay model of the Victory Button, A. A. Weinman, Sculptor

6. Battle service, also showing defensive sector bar

THE AMERICAN VICTORY MEDAL

PERSONAL SKETCHES
THE TREATY OF PEACE
AND A
CHRONOLOGY OF THE WAR

Part II
THE CONFERENCE AND THE SIGNING
OF THE TREATY

PREMIER CLÉMENCEAU ADDRESSING THE GERMAN DELEGATES AT VERSAILLES

The delegates have just arrived and taken their seats directly opposite Clémenceau at the extreme left-hand table shown in the picture

I

THE CONFERENCE OF THE ENTENTE IN PARIS

January 18, 1919—April 30, 1919

ON the Quai d'Orsay in Paris on January 18 the curtain rose on the first scene in the final act of the World War drama. This was the formal assembling of the Peace Conference,[1] in the famous Clock Hall of the Foreign Office. At the head of the council table was the gilded chair of the President of France, M. Poincaré. When all the chairs had been occupied some Indian princes in turbans gave to the scene its only distinctive costumes. It was an assemblage of the leading statesmen of the Entente world, German delegates not being present. At the head of the horseshoe were representatives of Great Britain and the United States; on the outside of the left-hand table representatives of British Colonies, whose recognition had been one of the significant acts of the conference, Australia coming first, Canada next, and India last. After the British Colonials came the Japanese. Inside both tables sat smaller nations, Cuba and America's ward, Haiti, included. Serbians sat alongside the newest nation of all, the Czecho-Slovaks; while French, Italians, Belgians, Roumanians and Brazilians sat on the outside of the right-hand table.

The United States, Great Britain, France, Italy, and Japan each had five delegates; the British Dominions and India two delegates respectively for Australia, Canada, South Africa, and India, including the Native States; one for New Zealand, and one for Newfoundland. Belgium, Serbia, and Brazil had each three delegates; China, Greece, Poland, Portugal, the Czecho-Slovak Republic, Roumania, two each; Siam, Cuba, Guatemala, Haiti, Honduras, Liberia, Nicaragua, and Panama one each. Montenegro was to have had one, but the designation of this delegate was not to be made until the political situation in that country where King Nicholas had been deposed, had been stabilized. The apportionment as to Great Britain was not considered so much as giving preponderance to her and her colonies, as giving her colonies separate representation "according

---

[1] The term "conference," as applied to a gathering of national delegates to negotiate terms of peace, has for some years been supplanting the term "congress," as used for the Vienna, Berlin, and other famous gatherings. There is no essential difference in the technical meaning of the two words as used for this purpose.

to their activities in the war." It had been the American view that it was preferable to give British colonies a direct voice, instead of one through the mother country, the interests of Canada and Newfoundland being regarded much the same as those of the United States. The five colonial members, with Brazil's three, gave to American countries an aggregate of eleven members of the Conference. The representation given to Jugo-Slavia was not at first decided upon, but it was expected that the Croats and Slovenes would be represented on about the same basis as the Serbians.

Brazil owed her special treatment largely to her historic position as a former empire combined with her population of more than 20,-000,000. These facts worked strongly against placing her secondary to nations much less populous. Another explanation of the allowance of three delegates to Brazil was that, while Greece had two and Portugal one, Brazil had not only given valuable services in the war by affording naval protection against German raiders on South Atlantic trade routes and the east coast of South America, but that she virtually had represented the South American continent in the ranks of the belligerents. Support of Brazil's claims was a part of America's plan to cultivate the closest relations with South American countries. This large representation of Pan-Americans and British colonies robbed the conference of any preponderating European character it might otherwise have had. Thus international politics would not be dominated as in former years by Europe.

The voice of the New World was to have an important part in deciding the terms of peace, which in spirit and purpose were to be quite unlike any previous peace terms in the history of nations. Ten out of twenty-five representatives were from non-European States and five more represented States whose future largely lay elsewhere than in Europe. Two big factors in the conference were to be the British Empire and Pan-America. Assuming that the League of Nations would have a similar organization, with separate recognition of the British colonies, the British Empire and Pan-America would be the largest factors in it, the two forces, as British statesmen saw it, which, by cooperating, could keep the peace of the world. The strong representation of Powers free from traditionary European ideas of a "balance of power" promised at once a profound influence on the Conference.[2] The number of sovereign States represented at the Conference in Paris was thirty-one. Germany, Austria, Turkey, and Bulgaria made the total number of belligerents concerned in the war thirty-five.

Standing between President Wilson and Mr. Balfour, Foreign

[2] Paris dispatch from Clinton W. Gilbert to The *Evening Public Ledger* (Philadelphia).

Minister of Great Britain, and facing the delegates, President Poincaré opened the Conference, which was preliminary to the meeting in Versailles where the treaty would eventually be signed and bear the name of that historic city. In the name of France, as host, President Poincaré exprest a solemn hope that its labors would end in removing forever from the world the menace of aggression by armed force. He made a long and admirable address in the course of which he said:

"This very day forty-eight years ago, on the 18th of January, 1871, the German Empire was proclaimed by an army of invasion in the Château at Versailles. It was consecrated by the theft of two French provinces. It was thus a violation from its origin and, by the fault of its founders, it was born in injustice. It has ended in oblivion. You are assembled in order to repair the evil that has been done and to prevent a recurrence of it. You hold in your hands the future of the world. I leave you gentlemen to your grave deliberations and declare the Conference of Paris open."

All eyes were then fixt on President Wilson who, in felicitous terms proposed, as the first business of the conference, that Premier Clémenceau be made permanent chairman. In his speech accepting the offer M. Clémenceau, having in mind the traditional difficulties

FRENCH OFFICIAL PHOTO.

THE CLOCK HALL AT THE FOREIGN OFFICE IN PARIS
Here the Peace Conference met until it held sittings in Versailles

that attend negotiations of peace treaties, remarked that, as the members of the Conference had come together as friends, so as friends they should disperse after their labors. After other preliminary formalities the Conference adjourned. On January 28, when the first plenary session of the Conference was held, it was addrest by President Wilson who, with great earnestness declared: "We are not here alone as representatives of Governments, but as representatives of peoples, and in the settlement we make we need to satisfy, not the opinions of governments, but the opinion of mankind." "Select classes of men no longer direct the affairs of the world," said he; "the fortunes of the world are now in the hands of the plain people." The war had swept away old foundations by which small coteries had "used mankind as pawns in a game." Nothing but emancipation from the old system could now accomplish real peace. He had recently seen in the streets of Paris American soldiers who had come to France, not alone for war, but as "crusaders in a great cause." "I, like them," he added, "must be a crusader, whatever it costs to accomplish that end."

Resolutions were passed at this session providing that a League of Nations be created as an integral part of the general treaty of peace, that a commission be named to draft a complete plan and that the League "should be open to every civilized nation which can be relied on to promote its objects," a provision under which it was to be a matter for future determination by the Great Powers to say when Germany had sufficiently retrieved herself in the eyes of the world to be entitled to admission. A commission composed of two representatives from each of the five Great Powers and five representatives to be elected by the other Powers, was to be appointed to inquire and report upon the following questions:

First, "The responsibility of the authors of the war"; second, "The facts as to breaches of the laws and customs of war committed by the forces of the German Empire and their allies on land, on sea and in the air during the present war"; third, "The degree of responsibility for these offenses attaching to particular members of the enemy's forces, including members of the general staffs and other individuals, however highly placed"; fourth, "The constitution and procedure of a tribunal appropriate to the trial of these offenses." The commission was also to examine and report: First, "On the amount of reparation which the enemy countries ought to pay"; second, "On what they are capable of paying," and third, "On the method, form and time within which payment should be made." Of the commission to draft the complete League of Nations plan President Wilson and Colonel House were made the representatives of the United States. The other delegates to the Conference from the

United States were Secretary of State Lansing, Henry White and Gen. Tasker H. Bliss. Special advisers to the delegation in large numbers went over with them, including Admiral Benson, who was Naval Adviser. Admiral Benson had been active during the war as Chief of Naval Operations. Before we declared war he had been occupied in putting the Navy in a fit condition for war. In 1917 he was in London with Colonel House, attending important conferences, and in October, 1918, acted as an adviser in the preparation of the armistice terms.

Indications soon came to the surface that the assembled statesmen had somewhat definite opinions—that each group, in fact, had formed plans of its own. Naturally, all did not hold the same views; they had not formed the same plans. But it had always been the business of statesmen to reach international agreements through well-considered conciliation. Peace conferences notoriously had led to differences. Czar Alexander in 1815 was continually threatening to withdraw from the Congress of Vienna; he scolded the Emperor of Austria and as to Metternich demanded that he be reproved and curbed. The course of Castlereagh who represented England was often objected to, and some titled personages were glad when he went home, while upon Hardenberg, Stein, and Humboldt who came from Prussia, many dark glances were cast because of the arrogance shown in their demands for the annexation of the greater part of Saxony. Vials of wrath were continually poured upon the head of Talleyrand, but Talleyrand at last triumphed over all his associates.

It was recalled again that during the Conference in Paris, 1898, which was to end our war with Spain, the Spanish Commissioners at one time packed their trunks, declaring they would return to Madrid, but the United States soothed their agitation by agreeing to give Spain $20,000,000—not, however, in payment for the Philippines, but to oil the creaking machinery of the negotiations. Count Witte at Portsmouth, in 1905, after the Russo-Japanese War, knowing that Japan could not long continue the war, and that she must have peace, as a part of his tactics made the familiar threats of "I won't play," and thereby won such points for Russia that the final treaty was looked upon as a triumph for Russia rather than for Japan.

On February 14 President Wilson laid before a plenary session of the Conference the completed plan for the League of Nations, and on behalf of the Conference invited the fullest criticism of the work he had been so largely instrumental in devising. He read the draft of the constitution, over which he and his associate committeemen had worked for three weeks, and in submitting it to the session said it came with the unanimous indorsement of fourteen nations engaged in its compilation. He was followed by seven speakers, all collaborators in the task, and all pledging their Governments to earnest support of the undertaking. Mr. Wilson made the longest speech he had delivered since his arrival in France, being on his feet forty-five minutes. He confined himself to an elucidation of specific subjects, instead of entering into further arguments as to general principles, and left that night at 10 o'clock for Brest to sail next day for home, but soon to return, several thousand American soldiers going with him to America on the same ship, the *George Washington*. He carried with him the League plan which was regarded as the greatest triumph of his career and an epochal development in world history.

Another "lucky thirteen" had turned up for Mr. Wilson. The final touches of the draft of the constitution for the League were made on February 13. There were twenty-six articles in the League constitution, or twice thirteen. "Lucky thirteen" had long been running through Mr. Wilson's life. There are thirteen letters in his name; he landed in Brest to attend the Peace Conference on December 13; thirteen played an important part in the inaugural plans of 1913, thirteen Governors being in line in the procession to the Capitol, militias from thirteen States being represented, and thirteen educational institutions. The marriage of one of his daughters was the thirteenth such ceremony that had taken place in the White House, and the names of both bride and bridegroom contained thirteen letters. President Wilson had observed early in his life that thirteen even then had been his lucky number, pointing out several instances where the number had figured in what to him was an important event.

Late in February the world was horrified by news that three shots had been fired at Premier Clémenceau as he was leaving his home in the morning to attend a committee meeting. One of them entered a lung but within a few days he was able to be out, after much international anxiety. His own story of the attack as he told it afterward was as follows:

"Yesterday, when I was passing that spot in the corner of the Boulevard Delessert, I remarked a strange silhouetted figure upon the pavement, showing that some one examining me attentively. The silhouette was that of a rather evil-looking man. I said to myself, 'Hello, that fellow is up to no good.' This morning at the same spot I perceived the same silhouette and immediately thought, 'Why, that's my friend of yesterday.' I hadn't time to continue the reflection, for the individual's arm was raised, revolver in hand, and he fired at the door of the automobile and hit the window. I didn't reflect that there were perhaps other bullets in the revolver, and as soon as the first shot was fired I leaned forward to look out. Other shots followed rapidly, one after another, and I felt a sharp pain low down the back of my neck. The pain was so intense that I could not help crying out. I realized perfectly that I had been hit. What followed passed with lightning rapidity. The orderly seated beside the chauffeur on the front of the automobile had at the first shot pulled his revolver out of his pocket. The chauffeur at the same time put on speed and got us out of range. My adversaries are really poor shots. They are exceedingly clumsy. Am I not a good prophet? Do I not arrange things

© PRESS ILLUSTRATING SERVICE.

THE MURAT MANSION, CALLED BY THE FRENCH "THE MAISON BLANCHE"

Here lived President and Mrs. Wilson during their first stay in Paris

ahead? I had arranged to have no meeting of the conference to-day so that I could get a little rest. Well, I've got it.''

Discussion in the Supreme Council, or Council of Ten, which included two representatives from Great Britain, France, Italy, Japan, and the United States, turned to the form of the future government of territory freed from enemy rule. The Conference accepted a plan of mandataries for colonies and backward nations. On March 26, Mr. Wilson having returned to Paris, the Council of Ten, in order to speed up the work, was broken up into two bodies, a Council of Four and a Council of Foreign Ministers. The Council of Four was composed of Premiers Orlando, Clémenceau and Lloyd George, and President Wilson. On April 14 the reparation demands to be made on Gremany were announced, and on April 16 the Germans were invited to send delegates to receive the treaty.

With the German treaty near completion the question of Italy's claims in the Adriatic came to the front. On April 23 President Wilson issued a statement that Fiume should not belong to Italy. The Italian delegation, keenly dissatisfied, announced their intention of leaving Paris, and on April 24, Premier Orlando started for Rome. Hardly had he departed when the vanguard of the German delegation reached Versailles, on April 25, to be followed on April 30 by the principal delegates. Previously the Germans had exprest an intention of sending "messengers" to receive the treaty, but finally were compelled to send delegates with full powers to act. In the absence of the Italian delegates the Conference on April 28 adopted the revised covenant of the League of Nations. Geneva was selected as the seat of the League, and Sir Eric Drummond, of Great Britain, was made first Secretary-General. On April 30 the Council of Three (Clémenceau, Lloyd George and Wilson) reached an agreement on the question of Shantung which gave territory to the Japanese who were to turn it over later to the Chinese. Premier Orlando was then absent in Italy, but he and the other Italian delegates returned to Paris in time to be present at the handing of the peace treaty to the Germans, apparently in a more satisfied frame of mind.[3]

[3] Principal Sources: The *Times,* The *World,* The *Evening Post* (New York), The *Evening Public Ledger* (Philadelphia), American Press and United Press dispatches.

II

THE PEACE TERMS DELIVERED TO THE GERMAN
DELEGATES AT VERSAILLES

April 25, 1919—May 7, 1919

WHEN the Peace Conference was near the end of its labors in Paris the terms in general became known and public interest turned to the meeting now to be held in Versailles. There the plenipotentiaries of Germany would for the first time meet the representatives of the Entente Nations and of the United States and the treaty would be presented to them for their signatures.

It was a symbol of the blending of an old order with a new that the same day should have witnessed the arrival of the German delegates at Versailles, and the ratification, in plenary conference in Paris, of the covenant of the League. Helpless Germany preparing to accept a peace of just punishment in the same stage-setting as that which had seen the apotheosis of German power forty-eight years before, was one of the scenes from which the ancient world derived its belief in Nemesis and in which the world at all times has discerned the giddy spin of the wheel of fortune. The conqueror conquered, the mighty ones humbled—in that there was nothing new. What was new was that the idea of ultimate reconciliation should have run parallel with the idea of retribution.

If one were to compile a list of seven historic spots in the world, as a companion set to the Seven Wonders of antiquity, the Palace of Versailles would have a place among them. There Great Britain first recognized the independence of the United States; there the Third Estate, called into life again after sleeping for a century or more, formed a national assembly and gave birth to the French Revolution; there Bismarck had William I crowned the German Emperor, while Paris was still under siege, and there representatives of the civilized world had now come not only to make peace with "the madman of Europe," but to sign a document that might rank in history with the Magna Charta or the Declaration of Independence.

Nor was this mammoth palace, which once could cover 10,000 persons, merely a historic shrine of epochal ceremonies. It seemed still to vibrate with echoes of human dramas more vivid and enthralling than any stage piece that Molière had shown there to dis-

tract the blasé Louis XIV and his dazzling court. There the unhappy Vallière, the vainglorious Montespan and the austere Main-
tenon successively had loved, infatuated and exploited, the magnificent
Louis; there, too, the brilliant Pompadour and the seductive du
Barry had shone among a galaxy of mistresses, and there some 10,000
half-drunken men and women from Paris had broken through the
gates and sent the weakling, Louis XVI, in flight to the Tuileries.

Louis XIV planned his residence on so grandiose a scale that
the leveling of the land, the building of a road to Paris and the
construction of an aqueduct had engaged 30,000 men for years. That
Gallery of Mirrors, literally the *"galerie des glaces,"* what scenes
had they not reflected! They had housed the Louis who proclaimed
himself "the state," with his diamond-embroidered coat and red-
heeled slippers four inches high; had sheltered his bloated successor
whose most satisfying exercise was to fry pancakes for his mistress's
breakfast; had looked on the irresolute Louis XVI, fated for disaster,
and the tragic figure of Marie Antoinette, she who "could bow to
ten persons with one movement, giving, with her head and eyes, the
recognition due to each one," and finally bowed to the headsman's
blade in the Place de la Concorde.

HÔTEL DES RÉSERVOIRS, WHERE THE GERMAN DELEGATES
WERE HOUSED AT VERSAILLES

German official couriers, in advance of the German delegation, arrived at Versailles on April 25, having traveled by special train from Creil, near Compiègne, and were received by Colonel Henri and other French officials, and by them taken to the Hôtel des Réservoirs. It was remarked sarcastically in Paris that the German delegation, according to the time schedule current in Berlin when the German armies started their swing through Belgium toward Paris, in 1914, had arrived "seventeen hundred days late." At Versailles the couriers were inclosed in a sort of huge gilded cage, not only for the purpose of keeping them in, but to keep the press and the public out. Once the German delegates reached the quarters reserved for them in the same hotel on May 1, they also found themselves restrained from passing beyond the barriers set up until the day when the final signature of the treaty should have taken place in the Gallery of Mirrors of the great Versailles Palace. In an annex of the hotel, formerly the residence of the Marquise de Pompadour, the delegates were housed. Use of this building had been determined by its situation, which was only a few hundred yards below the great palace. Behind trees on the further side of a lake was visible the roof of the Trianon Palace Hotel—formerly a Capuchin Monastery—where the first meeting between the Germans and the Entente statesmen would take place.

A trellis-work barrier eight feet high had been run from the junction of the Réservoir annex with the hotel proper, straight across the park to the rear of the Trianon Palace Hotel, thus forming, with the right-hand boundary of the park, a big "cage" about 100 yards wide and 300 long, within whose limits the Germans could walk about at liberty and obviate the humiliating conditions implied in a military escort. The only soldiers in evidence throughout this barrier were sentries at the locked gate of the park, at the Trianon Palace Hotel, and in passages connecting the annex with the main hotel. No one was allowed to pass them, no matter what his rank, unless he was the bearer of a special permit signed by the officer in charge. Passage otherwise was confined to hotel servants conveying food from the central kitchen.

The first official meeting with the Germans took place on May 1, when credentials were exchanged. A week later, in the spacious dining-hall of the Hôtel Trianon, the Peace Conference was installed at three long tables, arranged in horseshoe form and covered with the traditional green cloth of diplomacy. At one end of the room at a table about thirty-five feet long, sat representatives of the Great Powers, with President Poincaré and Premier Clémenceau in the center. Marshal Foch was the only man at a table who was not a plenipotentiary. Another who found himself a center of attention for a moment was, however, a delegate—Paderewski, representing Poland, with long hair and rather bizarre dress. All the Allied and other plenipotentiaries had been seated and were waiting for the appearance of the Germans, when the noted pianist's tall figure came rapidly through the doorway. Not an eye missed his rather confused progress to his place on the inside of the hollow square formed by the tables.

The whole scene had a setting that suggested peace, the room bright and cheery, and made more so by sunshine that came through great windows on three sides. Through these windows trees were seen in all the beauty of spring foliage, while flowers were growing profusely in the adjoining grounds, giving plenty of color to the background. The day was mellow in its warmth and suggested June rather than May. Nothing was there to bring to the minds of the German delegation the destruction their armed forces had wrought elsewhere in the fair land to which they had come in the humble rôle of representatives of a vanquished nation. The great dining-hall, fifty by seventy feet, was wholly free from any suggestion of French decorations. Walls, ceiling, and fluted columns were all white with no touch of color anywhere. Above hung four enormous chandeliers. Along the tables were blotters and paper for each delegate, and before the blotters squatty ink-bottles and ordinary pencils and pen-holders. The scene had none of the pomp and glitter of earlier peace gatherings—no display of court and military uniforms such as marked the congresses of Berlin and Vienna. It appeared to gain in impressiveness by these very circumstances.

When the German representatives arrived at the Trianon in automobiles throngs were near, but they stood mute as French orderlies opened automobile doors, and French and British officers conducted the Germans into the palace. Allied officers on the steps at the main entrance either saluted perfunctorily or turned their faces away. While the Entente delegates already inside were being seated, Clémenceau and President Wilson were observed engaged in conversation. After five minutes of waiting, Colonel Henri, the French liaison-officer, appeared at the door to herald the approach of the German delegation. An instant later a French functionary appeared wearing the glittering chain of his office, and announced in a loud voice: "Messieurs, the German delegates." Count von Brockdorff-Rantzau then slowly entered with gloves in his hand, and conspicuously undiplomatic in appearance. Neither he nor his associates looked to right or left. Nor did they pause, but moved with dignified steps to the places reserved for them. After a moment's hesitation all the Allied delegates and their secretariat personnel arose and stood courteously while the Germans were being seated, showing only a trace of nervousness and acting as if they were taking part in deliberations on equal terms with their adversaries.

At 2.20 o'clock attendants had brought in huge armfuls of the printed conditions of peace and distributed them, one copy to each delegate, as they went around the hollow rectangle. To the Germans a copy was not delivered until 3.17, while a translation was being made of Premier Clémenceau's introductory speech, in which, as President of the Congress, he declared the session opened and explained to the Germans the conditions of the meeting that was taking place with them. There were to be no oral discussions; the Germans were to submit within fifteen days, and in writing, any observations they had to make. He then read aloud the headings of the treaty and made a suggestion that within a few days the Germans should be ready to present their observations in writing. Clémenceau concluded with the inquiry, "Has any one observations to make?" whereupon Count von Brockdorff-Rantzau raised his hand. "Count von Brockdorff-Rantzau has the floor," said Clémenceau.

The head of the German delegation wore big horn spectacles and did not rise as Clémenceau had done in making his speech—indeed, as all the delegates had done when the Germans came in—but read his speech while he remained sitting. This apparent discourtesy to his adversaries was explained by the Count's friends as due to his physical condition, but he had offered no excuse or explanation for his conduct. As he spoke his guttural German repeatedly gave emphasis to particular phrases or words, as, for instance, when he declared that the admission by Germany of her sole guilt for the war would have been "a lie," or when he forbade the Allies to complain of "cruelty and murder" in view of the suffering and death German civilians had experienced under the blockade as continued since the armistice was signed. The interpreter of the Count's speech, in giving an English version, made the most of his opportunities, both in voice and selection of words. The Count's bold and unrepentant declarations as translated gave rise to a murmur of indignation throughout the chamber. As he proceeded with an increasing attitude of decision in his manner, the bodies of the other Germans perceptibly stiffened and with folded arms they sat stern and silent. Only Clémenceau and Wilson appeared unconcerned, the latter leaning back in his chair, with his hands in his pockets. On concluding his speech, Count von Brockdorff-Rantzau replaced his spectacles in their case, spread his hands on the table, and took an attitude of waiting. Clémenceau immediately rose and in two sentences brought the proceedings to a close. Brockdorff-Rantzau had accused the Allied nations of having murdered in cold blood, since the armistice became effective, hundreds of thousands of in-

GERMANY'S OCCUPIED TERRITORY

Under the conditions of the Treaty of Peace, Germany's Rhine Province, including what is known as the Palatinate, will be evacuated by Allied and American troops in three installments—the portion in the north marked 1 in five years, Part 2 in ten years, Part 3 in fifteen years

nocent German people. Many eyes were at once turned by this statement to Clémenceau, who seemed disturbed. Some thought he intended to interrupt the speaker with a show of resentment, but he let the stricture pass, and a sigh of relief went around the room.

Germany's European area by the treaty laid before the German delegates was reduced one-sixth, and it might be reduced one-fifth if the proposed plebiscites in the Saar Valley, Schleswig, and East Prussia should go against her. The area absolutely alienated totaled 34,437 square miles, that subject to plebiscites, 9,310 square miles. This reduction looked more serious than it was. In an economic and military sense Germany was only slightly crippled by her territorial losses, since the parts amputated were on the outer fringes of her domain. Excepting the small area of the Saar Valley and the Briey mineral region in Lorraine, no important industrial districts were alienated. Most of the territory marked for cession was inhabited by disaffected populations whom Germany had been unable to assimilate. Alsace-Lorraine, North Schleswig, and Posen had been liabilities for her as well as assets.

The greatest shrinkage occurred in the east, where a small fraction of Silesia (subject to a plebiscite), nearly all of Posen, and nearly all of West Prussia west of the Vistula were to be surrendered to Poland. Danzig was to be internationalized, a strip about Memel to be yielded and West Prussia, east of the Vistula, and the southern third of East Prussia to be disposed of by referendums. This part of Prussia was agricultural and economically stagnant. It had been of great value, however, as a base of operations in case of war with Russia. Now that Poland had been interposed as a buffer State and Russia had ceased to be a great power, Germany would no longer have need for a strong eastern military frontier, even if the Allies had allowed her to retain her old character as a militarist State. With all these cessions of territory, plebiscite sections included, Germany lost only about 7,000,000 inhabitants—one-tenth of her population—most of them strongly anti-German in blood and sentiment. Her losses, both in area and in population, would have been more than covered if the Peace Conference had left the door open for a union between Germany and what was left of Austria.

Under the treaty the great German General Staff was abolished and the army reduced for a time to 200,000 men, but eventually to 100,000, including 4,000 officers. These two requirements alone sufficed to tell the story of the limitation of military strength imposed upon Germany. She would not now be able to disturb the peace of Europe in our time, and perhaps never again. With her people released from the burden of taxation to keep up a great army and navy, her military system shattered, her military caste deprived of its arrogant power and dispersed, German statesmen could indulge no more in dreams of world empire. The old order had passed. A new order had come in which would be devoted to peace and industry, for great reparation costs had to be paid, and Germany had to qualify by good works and self-discipline to re-enter the family of nations and acquire their respect.

In 1912 the handbook of the German army gave the number of available trained and untrained men in the country as 9,898,000, made up as follows: Trained rank and file, including reserve and Landwehr, 3,302,000; trained Landsturm, 623,000; one-year volunteers, 85,000; non-commissioned officers of peace establishment, 92,000; total trained, 4,102,000; in addition, partially trained Ersatz reserve, 113,000, and untrained Ersatz reserve and Landsturm, 5,683,000. During the war Germany actually had placed 10,000,000 men in the field, altho her peace establishment was only 769,938 non-commissioned officers and men and 36,088 officers. The great expansion that had been brought about was not a meeting of an emergency in the sense in which the term is used in democratic countries. Under the German Constitution of 1871 every man able to bear arms was counted as a soldier, and all were under orders from the Emperor, who had power to declare war. The Treaty of Peace by a stroke of the pen had reduced the German army eventually to 100,000, or 1 per cent. of the enormous force which Germany had organized, trained and put into the field during the war.

No opportunity was left to the German Government to create a large army by stealth and double dealing. Interallied commissions of control, with authority to establish headquarters at Berlin, were to be kept on the watch against the manufacture of munitions, except in quantities sufficient for small land and sea services; the importation of arms and all war material was forbidden; nor could Germany manufacture munitions for foreign Governments; she was to have no dirigibles, and no airplanes except 100 machines which were to be retained until October 1, in order to search for submarine mines. Finally, conscription was abolished. As far as human ken could search the future, Germany was to become impotent to make war even on the smallest nation contiguous to her territory. She had been stricken from the list of land and sea powers, and made powerless to resist the sentence that had been passed upon her. There was nothing ahead for her but hard work, self-denial, and rigid economy, which was punishment for her misdeeds, but her submission might prove to her a blessing in disguise.

Against the German peril the world was apparently made safe. Loss of her navy in itself became a vital guaranty of good behavior, for altho she might have millions of men in the field her coasts would be open to invasion by Powers whose full command of the sea she would be in no position to question. Her navy was reduced to six battleships, six light cruisers, twelve torpedo-boats and no submarines. The world noted with deep satisfaction how time had brought its revenges, since it was on the anniversary of the murderous attack upon the *Lusitania* that the Germans there in Versailles learned of this sharp limitation to their sea power.

Germany forfeited much territory that had been the spoils of former wars and forays. Most important of all was Alsace and Lorraine, which were returned to France under conditions that forced Germany to admit the crime of seizing them. She yielded much to Poland, and there were small cessions to Belgium. Because of her destruction of French coal-mines, she had to give up the Saar Valley to France with the right to work Saar mines. Ancient French dominion over this territory was recognized by the provision made for a plebiscite after fifteen years to determine whether the populations preferred a continuance of commission government under the League of Nations, union with France, or union with Germany. Germany's colonies, near and remote, those outposts of her trade and military power which she had established at great cost and governed with brutality, she surrendered altogether. Many of them were committed into the keeping of the League of Nations for later determination. Her rights in the Shantung Province of China, including railroads, mines, and all her property there, she ceded to Japan, but by assurances, not included in the treaty, Japan promised to restore the province to China.

The eighth section of the treaty would long engage the attention of men who held to the wholesome belief that sin unatoned for offered a bad example. The atonement here exacted was heavy to a degree that would have transcended all German powers of imagination five years before. Germany acknowledged that she was responsible for all the loss and damage inflicted on the Allied and Associated Governments and their nationals; and she engaged to make reparation by money payments for all damages caused to civilians under seven categories embracing acts of war and acts contrary to the laws of war. She was to pay within two years twenty billion marks in gold, goods, ships, or other specified terms of payment, her total obligations to be determined by a Committee of Inquiry and made known to her not later than May 1, 1921. In acknowledgment of this debt she was required to issue gold bonds to the amount of twenty billion marks, payable not later than May 1, 1921, and forty billion marks between 1921 and 1926, with interest at 5 per cent.; besides undertaking to deliver gold bonds to the amount of forty billion marks under further terms to be fixt by the committee. While it was intimated that the grand total of damages assessed might exceed her ability to pay, the sums demanded, whatever they might be, would become a charge upon all her revenues with priority over the service or payment of any domestic loan. Some small part of Germany's pre-war debt would be assumed by the Governments to which she ceded territory, but Alsace and Lorraine were an exception to this rule, France not to take over any part of the German debt, since Germany had treated her in that way when she seized upon these provinces in 1871.

Germany's admission that the war was a crime and that she bore the responsibility for it was made complete by her assent to the purpose of the Allied Powers to put William Hohenzollern on trial, not under criminal law, but "for a supreme offense against international morality and the sanctity of treaties." The surrender of the former Emperor was to be "requested" of Holland and a tribunal was to be made up of one judge from each of the five great Powers which would try him. Moreover, Germany was to hand over for trial by military tribunal "persons accused of committing acts in violation of the laws and customs of war." For many years to come the hunting down of the trails of these criminals promised to engage the world's attention.

Other points in the treaty were these: Germany to renounce all her territorial and political rights outside of Europe; Germany to recognize the total independence of German Austria, Czecho-Slovakia and Poland; all German forts for fifty kilometers east of the Rhine to be razed; all Heligoland fortifications to be demolished and the Kiel Canal to be open to all nations; Germany to revert to pre-war "most favored nations" tariffs without discrimination; Germany to accept highly detailed provisions for the internationalization of roads and rivers; Germany to pay shipping damages, ton for ton; Germany to devote her resources to rebuilding the devastated regions; Germany to accept the League of Nations in principle but without immediate membership in the League; Germany to cede to Belgium 382 square miles of territory between Luxemburg and Holland; all Hohenzollern property in Alsace-Lorraine to go to France without payment; France to gain possession of the Saar coal-mines regardless of the result of a future plebiscite; Germany to accept abrogation of the Brest-Litovsk treaty; Germany to permit the formation of no militaristic societies; the German army to be demobilized within two months after peace was signed; the Allies to retain German hostages until persons accused of war crimes were surrendered; Germany to lease to Czecho-Slovakia wharfage in Hamburg and Stettin for ninety-nine years; the Rhine to be placed under control of an Allied-German commission; parts of the Elbe, Oder, Danube, and

Nieman rivers to be internationalized. In the matter of Entente claims for damages it was said that the American part reached about $1,000,000,000 and that claims growing out of losses inflicted by German submarines reached $600,000,000.

It was a terrible punishment that the German people and their mad rulers had brought upon themselves. Not only was their military power to be destroyed, but the military spirit would be crusht

THE GERMAN DELEGATES LEAVING THE GRAND TRIANON
AFTER RECEIVING THE PEACE TERMS
Count Brockdorff-Rantzau, the head of the delegation, is seen at the point
marked "X," on the wall

out of them by the stern but necessary conditions imposed. How great would be their moral and spiritual suffering we could not know, for the world had its doubts about the German conscience. The material hurt could more accurately be measured. They had become one of the world's greatest commercial nations, their trade was rapidly expanding, they had established commercial strongholds all over the world, and their merchant fleets were giving England cause for deep concern. Now they were cribbed within their own frontiers, their ships gone, their foreign trade had vanished and they were condemned to half a century of remitting toil to repay the loss they had caused and repair the ruin they had wrought. Could Germany live under these conditions? All the world could see that they were terribly severe. But the world knew, too, that they were just. They seemed even lenient compared with the terms a victorious Germany would have imposed upon an enslaved world had she won the war.

After the meeting, the German delegates were first to leave the Trianon. Before they appeared at the outer door, the military guard of the palace had been withdrawn so as to avoid giving any semblance of military honors. Brockdorff-Rantzau and Landsberg came out first, and then the others. The whole party were speedily shown into automobiles, which left under a British and French escort, moving through crowded streets, where the silence was absolute and oppressive.[4]

[4] Principal Sources: Associated Press dispatches; The *Evening Post,* The *Times,* The *World,* The *Wall Street Journal,* New York; "Bulletins" of the National Geographic Society.

III

GERMAN PROTESTS AGAINST THE TREATY AND ENTENTE REPLIES—OUR FIFTH, OR "VICTORY" LOAN

COUNT VON BROCKDORFF-RANTZAU, before leaving Germany for Versailles, had declared that Germany would stick to the Fourteen Points of President Wilson's speech of January, 1918, meaning by that to her own interpretation of them. When the German delegation arrived in Versailles it was to the accompaniment of loud German protests against signing any "hard peace." After the Entente terms were made known to the German delegates, Brockdorff-Rantzau, in an extended protest, argued for one thing, that, as the present German Government was not responsible for the war, it should not be punished for the acts of an overthrown predecessor Government. To this Clémenceau quietly replied that Germany "did not act upon the principle she now contends for, either in 1871, as regards France after the proclamation of the Republic, nor in 1917 in regard to Russia after the revolution which abolished the Czarist régime."

"This is the devil's work!" was the comment of Mathias Erzberger, head of the German Armistice Commission, after he learned what the terms were. Germany, he said, was to be left "with less freedom than Egypt had." "It condemns us to death," added Erzberger. "Not to sign would mean the same thing, most likely; but if we are to go under, let us go quickly at least." If Germany was to be denied even that privilege, "then the consequences would be upon the heads of those who made the promises which they never intended to keep, even with the new Germany, and who have therefore brought us to this desert of hopelessness in which we look around in vain for an oasis where springs the well of humanity."

Erzberger's pleadings that a "well of humanity" should be provided for men who had ravaged Belgium and northern France evoked little except scorn from the Entente. Men recalled what were the terms that Erzberger had been in favor of imposing upon the Allies if Germany had been victorious, as set forth in a memorandum written by him late in 1914, and made public on April 20, 1919, as coming from the private secretary of Kurt Eisner, the former

Bavarian Premier, who had just been assassinated. Erzberger declared:

"Germany must have sovereignty, not only over Belgium, but over the French coast from Dunkirk to Boulogne, and possession of the Channel Islands. She must also take the mines in French Lorraine and create an African German Empire by annexing the Belgian and French Kongos, British Nigeria, Dahomey, and the French West Coast.

"In fixing indemnities, the actual capacity of a State at the moment should not be considered. Besides a large immediate payment, annual instalments spread over a long period, should be arranged. France could be helped in making them by decreasing her budget of naval and military appropriations, the reductions imposed in the peace treaty being such as would enable her to send substantial sums to Germany.

"Indemnities should provide for the repayment of the full costs of the war and the damages of the war, notably in East Prussia; the redemp-

MATHIAS ERZBERGER

demption of all of Germany's public debt and the creation of a vast fund for incapacitated soldiers."

Mathias Erzberger's plea for humanity was not unlike many pleas that came out of Germany at this time. Declaring that the terms of peace contemplated the "physical, moral, and intellectual paralysis" of the German people and that Germans had been "hypnotized" by statements made by President Wilson, President Ebert exclaimed: "When in the course of 2,000 years was ever a peace offered to a defeated people which so completely contemplated their physical, moral, and intellectual paralysis as do the terms enunciated at Versailles?" Before the Reichstag the Chancellor of the Republic, Scheidemann, made a long speech of violent protests with threats of not signing the treaty. Scheidemann was not taken seriously, being too well known as a public man of a type familiar in all States, the type that has an instinct for floating on eddies of opinion. When the war was launched Scheidemann's public record required him to oppose it, but all Germany was then shouting for the lustful adventure, and so he adopted the view that the Teuton had been attacked by the Slav, and when Belgium was invaded, accepted the fable that Belgium in her conduct had been non-neutral. When Petrograd, after the revolution, became temporarily pro-Ally, and the future looked dark for Germany, he had been selected by the Kaiser to manage at Stockholm a proposed peace conference. When the Germans, through Lenine and Trotzky, became masters of Russia and the Brest-Litovsk treaty was written, Scheidemann became silent and remained so until the German military offensive in the West was wrecked. Scheidemann seemed a man possest of no real convictions that prevented him from accommodating his views to the demands of any new hour.

Hugo Haase, leader of the Independent Socialists, announced his flat refusal to form a government of Independents which would sign the Versailles treaty, which caused a great sensation in political circles, but it was regarded as further proof of Haase's astuteness. The Independent Socialist Party, as *Die Freiheit* remarked, "did not dream of taking blame for the World War and the terrible consequences from the shoulders of those responsible for existing conditions in Germany—the Scheidemanns and Erzbergers, the Clericals, and Democrats, who had zealously aided the late Government's war policy, had granted all credits, and by their attitude had prevented an early termination of the war." "Let them settle the bankrupt estate themselves," added *Die Freiheit*.

In Berlin a Government statement was issued and cabled to Entente countries declaring that the treaty would not be signed by Germany. It was a statement evidently intended for the most part for American consumption, having been furnished especially to the Associated Press for circulation here, but was filled with the most amazing misconceptions of American public opinion. It assumed that "the American press" considered the treaty too hard on Germany and so the appeal was addrest "to all America, to every individual," all of whom were asked to see to it that Germany's "claims" were fulfilled—these claims being such as worked out to Germany's advantage under Wilson's Fourteen Points. The assertion was made that, in the peace terms proposed, there was "not one single trace left of President Wilson's program." The overdoing of protest in this statement rather disgusted than persuaded clear-eyed Americans. They said, in the first place, that Germany had not come into court with clean hands. She was loudly proclaiming that the peace terms meant her "economic destruction" and yet she was the same Germany whose intellectual élite—including 352 university professors—had united on June 20, 1915, in petitioning the German Chancellor to make sure that France was "enfeebled politically and economically, without any consideration," and to insist upon levying on the French "a heavy war indemnity without any mercy." These and other proclamations of Germany's ruthless war intentions made it difficult to listen to pleas for leniency as made to people who had been her victims.

For the Germans now to pretend that the peace terms violated their "juristic right" under the Fourteen Points could not bear the weight of facts. Only a few of the Fourteen Points directly bore on the treaty now offered to Germany. She complained that she had received no assurance of the freedom of the seas, a point that had been expressly reserved by the Allies, with the assent of our Government, before the armistice was signed. Similarly it had been stipulated, with Germany's full knowledge, that German "reparation" should go beyond the apparent implication of President Wilson's phrase about "restoring" Belgium and invaded France. Those two points, therefore, were at once thrown out of court. Point 6 related to Russia; Points 9, 10, 11, and 12 concerned Italy and Austria, the Balkans and Turkey, and did not touch the German situation at all. In reality only seven of the Fourteen Points had to do with the German "claims," and these could not bear examination to Germany's advantage. Take her loss of territory. All but a minute fraction of it was distinctly contemplated by Points 8 and 12, providing for the restoration of Alsace-Lorraine and the setting up of "an independent Polish State" with "free and secure access to the sea." Having agreed to this in advance, Germany's mouth was closed. As for the Saar Valley, it figured merely as part of the reparation in coal due to France from Germany, for what Germany had done with Lens, the area to be temporarily under control of the League of Nations. The creation of that League was promised in Point 14, and Germany could not say that the promise had not been kept.

There remained only three points, all of which had to do with trade relations, disarmament, and the colonies. Concerning the latter, President Wilson was abundantly able to maintain that the arrangement of mandataries for the temporary administration of the former German colonies was in compliance with his principle of consulting "the interests of the populations concerned" as well as those of "the Government whose title is to be determined." As for disarmament, that of Germany was provided for in the treaty; that of other nations was to be undertaken under the League. While "equality of trade conditions" was not definitely assured to Germany by the treaty, assurance was repeatedly given that Germany's "industrial requirements" would be met. The German Government's statement had asked Americans to "place the Fourteen Points opposite the peace terms." If this had been done no fair-minded man could have come to anything but one conclusion, which was that, in

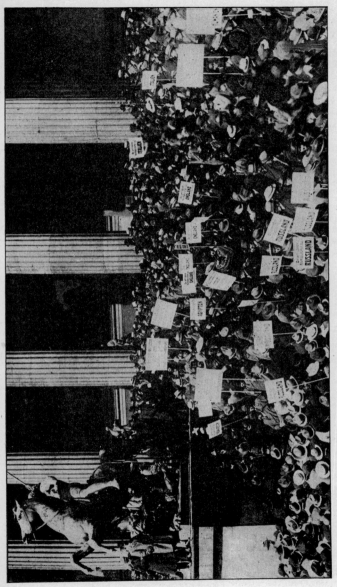

A BERLIN MEETING OPPOSING THE PEACE TERMS

Dr. Frederick Naumann, author of "Mittel-Europa," a much discust Pan-Germanish book, is addressing a crowd of Germans who, before the war, had lived in foreign countries

the matter of her claim, Germany had not a leg to stand on. Mr. Wilson, as if making a reply to the German claims as to his Fourteen Points, was quoted on June 6 as saying:[5]

> "I am convinced that our treaty projects violates none of my principles. If I held a contrary opinion I would not hesitate to confess it, and would endeavor to correct the error. The treaty as drawn up, however, entirely conforms with my fourteen points."

Following are the Fourteen Points as Wilson stated them in his speech in January, 1918:

1. Open Covenants of Peace openly arrived at, after which there shall be no private international understandings of any kind, but diplomacy shall proceed always frankly and in the public view.

2. Absolute freedom of navigation upon the seas outside territorial waters alike in peace and in war, except as the seas may be closed in whole or in part by international action for the enforcement of international covenants.

3. The removal, so far as possible, of all economic barriers and the establishment of an equality of trade conditions among all the nations consenting to the peace and associating themselves for its maintenance.

4. Adequate guaranties given and taken that national armaments will be reduced to the lowest point consistent with domestic safety.

5. A free, open-minded, and absolutely impartial adjustment of all Colonial claims based upon a strict observance of the principle that in determining all such questions of sovereignty the interests of the populations concerned must have equal weight with the equitable claims of the Government whose title is to be determined.

6. The evacuation of *all* Russian territory and such a settlement of all questions affecting Russia as will secure the best and freest cooperation of the other nations of the world in obtaining for her an unhampered and unembarrassed opportunity for the independent determination of her own political development and national policy and assure her of a sincere welcome into the society of free nations under institutions of her own choosing.

7. Belgium must be evacuated and restored without any attempt to limit the sovereignty which she enjoys in common with all other free nations. Without this healing act the whole structure and validity of international law is forever impaired.

8. All French territory should be freed and the invaded portions restored, and the wrong done to France by Prussia in 1871 in the matter of Alsace-Lorraine, which has unsettled the peace of the world for nearly fifty years, should be righted in order that peace may once more be made secure in the interest of all.

9. A readjustment of the frontiers of Italy should be effected along clearly recognizable lines of nationality.

[5] In the *Matin* (Paris).

10. The peoples of Austria-Hungary, whose place among the nations we wish to see safeguarded and assured, should be accorded the first opportunity of autonomous development.

11. Roumania, Serbia, and Montenegro should be evacuated, occupied territories restored, Serbia accorded free and secure access to the sea, and the relations of the several Balkan States to one another determined by friendly counsel along historically established lines of allegiance and nationality; and international guaranties of the political and economic independence and territorial integrity of the several Balkan States should be entered into.

12. The Turkish portions of the present Ottoman Empire should be assured a secure sovereignty, but the other nationalities which are now under Turkish rule should be assured an undoubted security of life, and an absolutely unmolested opportunity of autonomous development, and the Dardanelles should be permanently opened as a free passage to the ships and commerce of all nations under international guaranties.

13. An independent Polish State should be erected, which should include the territories inhabited by undisputably Polish populations, which should be assured a free and secure access to the sea.

14. An Association of Nations affording guaranties of political and territorial independence for all States.

Over and above the German maneuvering it was impossible to deny that there was something genuine in the indignant and moaning protests uttered by so many German people. They were acting like men suddenly confronted with something not only startling and charged with despair, but utterly unprecedented, out of the order of nature, incredible, monstrous—something they could not understand as a result of the war because they could not yet believe that they had actually lost the war. That state of mind was a necessary consequence of the German state of mind that had prevailed five years before. Her people had for two generations been drugged with false teachings and we now saw how the poison had impaired the whole mental and moral make-up of the country.

Taught to consider themselves not only invincible and destined to world-mastery, but also as the flower of civilization, and the chosen of the Almighty, the Germans could not in a few months come to believe it possible that they had been beaten and that in going forth with the sword to conquer the world they had been in danger of *niedergang*. Now that *niedergang* had come they refused to accept it. They who had believed themselves at the apex of civilization, were about to fall into an abyss. Hence their tears and wails. A people that four years before had been displaying what the Greeks called *hubris*—meaning a defiance of the gods destined to lead to condign punishment—was showing itself hysterical and mean-spirited in disaster; the two frames of mind went together with perfect naturalness.

Besides Erzberger's declaration late in 1914, of the peace that

Germany sought to impose on the Entente, another and much later illuminating illustration as to what Germany would have done had the war been won by her had appeared in a statement made on July 1, 1918 (just two weeks before Germany's definite defeat began), by Count von Roon, a leader in the Prussian House of Nobles. Roon rejected all idea of an armistice that was already being whispered about, until Germany had become sure of the annexation by her of Belgium and the Channel coast as far as Calais, of certain annexations on the eastern frontier of France and the restitution of all her colonies. Great Britain was expected to cede to Germany certain naval and coaling stations and her war-fleet, and to restore Egypt and the Suez Canal to Turkey. King Constantine was to be replaced on the throne of Greece, Austria and Bulgaria were to divide Serbia and Montenegro, and Great Britain, France, and the United States were to pay all of Germany's war-costs and an indemnity of not less than $45,000,000,000. France and Belgium meanwhile were to remain occupied by German armies at Entente expense until these conditions were fulfilled. So held Roon in the face of German defeat.

The world had long been forced to confess that it was at a disadvantage in endeavoring to understand or guess the motives of German policy. Principle, precedent, and custom were no guides, for the Germans disregarded them all. Once more was conjecture baffled in an effort to find any basis whatever for a demand now set up by the German peace delegates that, as an offset to the reparation demands of the Allies, Germany should receive, or be credited with, 12,850,000,000 marks, or some $3,200,000,000, for damages inflicted upon her by the Allied blockade. As a blockade is a lawful operation of war, this demand for credit to offset part of her reparation payment of 100,000,000,000 marks was about as thinkable a proposal as would have been another for damages because the United States had entered the war and sent 2,000,000 troops to France. Each would have had about the same basis in law and reason.

The bones of Reims now lay bleaching in the sun. The wreck of the martyred city lay as the war left it. The stark skeleton of its noble cathedral showed its tortured towers making the appeal of one in agony. Its wide avenues had tree-stumps bordered with ruin in various degrees. The wreckage of a million German shells filled the eye on all sides. The streets in some places had been swept clear of débris. Otherwise all was as war had left it. Only fourteen houses out of 14,000 in the city had not been hit. Through that scene of desolation sightseers prowled in spic-and-span automobiles, giving an incongruous touch. Near a fence built around the cathedral old Frenchmen sold souvenirs. Where in Germany was the power

**CHANCELLOR SCHEIDEMANN DENOUNCING SEVERELY THE TERMS
OF PEACE OFFERED TO GERMANY**

He is standing in front of the Reichstag building in Berlin. Scheidemann
resigned soon afterward, having in his speech committed himself too deeply
against the terms to change his attitude so soon again

that could restore Reims Cathedral? From what part of Germany could come a master to restore the noble avenues of trees, the blasted stumps of which marked the lack of them? What German architect could rebuild dainty mansions that had lined the roadways to the west? Could Ger-

FREDERICK EBERT
First President of the German Republic, who was formerly a saddler

city of homes and
stroyed?

Since the war
however, had come
a German here and
ing to understand
Zukunft, for ex-
Witting raised a
had been the matter
mind, as exhibited
While public men,
t a r y commanders
for bitter blame, he
ten that they had
German teaching
asked how had been
strange German
had brought the
answer he gave was
deliberately p u t
with modern ideas.
essentially that of
pletely misconceiv-
upon her by her
tion, she had been
bition to outstrip
thought of herself
Empire." In this
"like spoiled chil-
themselves into im-
ings," passing from
defeating violence
force had added
outlook had never
spirit of human-

many remake the
beauty she had de-

something n e w ,
into the attitude of
there who was try-
his countrymen. In
ample, Richard
question as to what
with the German
in its war policies.
diplomats, and mili-
had been coming in
said it was forgot-
been products of
and training. He
f o r m e d "this
mentality" w h i c h
empire to ruin? The
that Germany had
herself out of touch
Her spirit had been
"a parvenu." "Com-
ing the tasks laid
geographical posi-
crazed with an am-
E n g l a n d, and
as another Roman
spirit G e r m a n s,
dren, had thrown
possible undertak-
one form of self-
to another, and to
lies. The German
taken in "the real
ity"; hence her fall.

Germans, when they appealed to the sympathy and even to the "conscience" of the world, seemed totally unaware that they had forfeited all standing-ground for making such an appeal. After setting the world aghast at their unscrupulousness and brutality, they appeared to expect the world to shed tears of commiseration over their unhappy fate. The truth was that the Germans could not now speak of justice, or pity, or human kindness without provoking a feeling of nausea in those among Entente people who heard them. They even had the obtuseness to refer to Belgium as an example which Germany would follow; as the Belgians had heroically resisted brutal force, so now they said the Germans would. Thus, to remind the Entente of their own crimes while asking that Entente for clemency, was about the last disclosure of the inability of the Germans to see a fact as it was, or to read the minds of others. Germany was beaten and powerless, and had to agree to the treaty, and undertake to carry out its terms, looking for such amelioration as it was possible to secure by good behavior now or later; otherwise she would bring upon herself a still worse fate. Harden in *Die Zukunft* recalled the behavior of victorious Germany in 1871 and the heavy yoke that Bismarck placed on France:

"In 1871, at the time of the peace pourparlers, Jules Favre, annoyed, slightly raised his voice. Bismarck then began to speak in German, altho he was perfectly aware that Favre did not know a word of German. When asked what attitude Germany would adopt in case of a French refusal to sign the treaty, Bismarck replied: 'We will continue to occupy the forts. The armistice is not likely to be prolonged, and then we will lock up Paris more tightly than before. Our measures will prove efficient when the French feel the pangs of hunger; in the meantime we will ask for their arms and their guns. Let them cry if they like; they will at last realize how ridiculous it is to make formidable threats, which it is impossible to carry out against a victorious enemy.''

The Germans were still laboring under the gravest of all their disadvantages, which was lack of confidence anywhere outside Germany in their public faith and public purposes. The re-establishment of that confidence was the most difficult of all their tasks, far more difficult than the payment of reparation. The greatest German loss was not loss of men, of money, or of political prestige; it was the most considerable of all human losses—the moral loss, and Prussianized Germany promised for some generations to stagger under that load as a ponderous liability. New men in millions to take the place of the dead and maimed would be born and reared in Germany, and an industrious people would, in time, bring prosperous days to the fatherland; but generations could not wipe out the moral stain imprinted upon it by her ruthless devotion to the sword. In another age, perhaps centuries hence, some new Motley, in impassioned pages, would revive for an unremembering world the wrongs of Belgium and northern France, with William II taking the place of Philip II and Ludendorff that of the Duke of Alva.

Nobody could deny that the terms of peace were severe to the point of harshness, and that in certain instances, such as the seizure of the German cables and the exclusion, at least for a time, of Germany from the League of Nations, they might seem unjust. Yet this severity was applauded, and this seeming injustice excused, because nobody was convinced that there had been any real change of heart in the German people; they regretted the war only because they lost it. They were paying for all the political duplicity that they had so ardently defended for five years, from the invasion of Belgium to the treaty of Brest-Litovsk. Had they kept faith even in the matter of Russia, that alone would have given them some of the standing in court that was now universally denied them. In the hour of her extremity, Germany's official protests against the severity of the peace terms therefore fell on deaf ears. The world regarded them as only another form of the German propaganda with which everybody had become familiar. Nobody was quite sure whether the German Government at heart regarded the provisions of the treaty as impossible of fulfilment, or whether this was not a new example of German *camouflage*. Therein lay the real tragedy of Germany. A great nation had waged war in such manner that it had become an object of universal distrust, and even when its autocracy was swept away, that distrust still ran through the Entente world at flood-tide. Men took it for granted that German diplomacy was again playing its old game with loaded dice, and all efforts on the part of German officials to excite sympathy with their cause were fruitless because nobody believed in their sincerity. The German mark, which had recovered to forty-seven francs per hundred, fell on the publication of the peace terms to thirty-seven, and all shades of bonds connected with German enterprises dropt proportionately in price. By September the mark was worth less than four cents in gold.

The German reply and counter-proposals to the conditions of peace laid down to them at Versailles on May 7 were made public on June 15 in a note covering 119 pages. The Germans maintained that the Allied and Associated Powers had forsaken the peace of justice to which they solemnly pledged themselves in the armistice negotiations and had offered a peace of might, in which all the principles quoted from the speeches of statesmen among the Allied and Associated Powers had been violated. Germany demanded immediate admission to the League of Nations in part fulfilment of the spirit of the armistice agreement and as necessary for the acceptance of the proposed military, naval, and air terms. Germany profest to be wholly unable to accept the Reparations Commission set up by the Allies as involving an infringement of her sovereignty, but proposed a cooperative German commission to work alongside it. She accepted responsibility only for civilian losses in occupied Belgium and France and agreed to a maximum payment of 100,000,000,000 marks, provided the other terms as to colonies, overseas trade, and territories were accepted as she proposed. She refused to sanction the trial of the former Kaiser or to accede to his extradition from Holland, on the ground that no German could be brought before a foreign court without established law or legal basis. Similarly, she could not agree to extradite other Germans accused of violations of the laws and customs of war. Instead, she proposed a court of neutrals to judge the fact of crime, punishment to remain with the court.

A letter covering the Entente's reply to this plea from Ger-

THE WEIMAR THEATER

Here met the German National Assembly after leaving Berlin in the winter of 1918-1919. The statue is of Göthe and Schiller in bronze

many for what she called "a peace of justice," was signed by M. Clémenceau, President of the Peace Conference, and addrest to Count von Brockdorff-Rantzau, President of the German delegation. It contained the following passages that were widely praised in Entente circles at the time:

"The Allied and Associated Powers feel it necessary to begin their reply by a clear statement of the judgment of the world, which has been forged by practically the whole of civilized mankind. In the view of the Allied and Associated Powers the war which began on the 1st of August, 1914, was the greatest crime against humanity and the freedom of the peoples that any nation calling itself civilized has ever consciously committed. For many years the rulers of Germany, true to the Prussian tradition, strove for a position of dominance in Europe. They were not satisfied with that growing prosperity and influence to which Germany was entitled, and which all other nations were willing to accord her, or the society of a free and equal position.

"They required that they should be able to dictate and tyrannize over a subservient Europe, as they dictated and tyrannized over a subservient Germany. In order to attain their ends they used every channel through which to educate their own subjects in the doctrine that might was right in international affairs. They never ceased to expand German armaments by land and sea, and to propagate the falsehood that it was necessary because Germany's neighbors were jealous of her prosperity and power. She sought to sow hostility and suspicion instead of friendship between nations.

"They developed a system of espionage and intrigue through which they were enabled to stir up international rebellion and unrest, and even to make secret offensive preparations within the territory of their neighbors, whereby they might, when the moment came, strike them down with greater certainty and ease. They kept Europe in a ferment by threats of violence, and when they found that their neighbors were resolved to resist their arrogant will they determined to assert their predominance in Europe by force.

"As soon as their preparations were complete, they encouraged a subservient ally to declare war on Serbia at forty-eight hours' notice, a war involving the control of the Balkans, which they knew could not be localized and which was bound to unchain a general war. In order to make doubly sure, they refused every attempt at conciliation and conference until it was too late and the world war was inevitable for which they had plotted, and for which alone among the nations they were adequately prepared.

"Germany's responsibility, however, is not confined to having planned and started the war. She is no less responsible for the savage and inhuman manner in which it was conducted. Altho Germany was herself a guarantor of Belgium, the rulers of Germany violated their solemn promise to respect the neutrality of this unoffending people. Not content with this, they deliberately carried out a series of promiscuous shootings and burnings with the sole object of terrifying the inhabitants into submission by the very frightfulness of their action.

"They were the first to use poisonous gas, notwithstanding the appalling suffering it entailed. They began the bombing and long-distance shelling of towns for no military object, but solely for the purpose of reducing the morale of their opponents by striking at their women and children. They commenced the submarine campaign, with its piratical challenge to international law and its destruction of great numbers of innocent passengers and sailors in mid-ocean, far from succor, at the mercy of the winds and waves, and the yet more ruthless submarine crews. They drove thousands of men and women and children with brutal savagery into slavery in foreign lands. They allowed barbarities to be practised against their prisoners of war from which the most uncivilized people would have recoiled.

"The conduct of Germany is almost unexampled in human history. The terrible responsibility which lies at her doors can be seen in the fact that not less than 7,000,000 dead lie buried in Europe, while more than 20,000,000 others carry upon them the evidence of wounds and suffering, because Germany saw fit to gratify her lust for tyranny by a resort to war. The Allied and Associated Powers believe that they will be false to those who have given their all to save the freedom of the world if they consent to treat the war on any other basis than as a crime against humanity and right. Not to do justice to all concerned would only leave the world open to fresh calamities. If the German people themselves, or any other nation, are to be deterred from following the footsteps of Prussia; if mankind is to be lifted out of the belief that war for selfish ends is legitimate to any State; if the old era is to be left behind, and nations as well as individuals are to be brought beneath the reign of law, even if there is to be early reconciliation and appeasement, it will be because those responsible for concluding the war have had the courage to see that justice is not deflected for the sake of a convenient peace.

"It is said that the German revolution ought to make a difference, and that the German people are not responsible for the policy of the rulers whom they have thrown from power. The Allied and Associated Powers recognize and welcome the change. It represents great hope for peace and a new European order in the future, but it can not affect the settlement of the war itself.

"The German revolution was stayed until the German armies had been defeated in the field and all hope of profiting by a war of conquest had vanished. Throughout the war, as before the war, the German people and their representatives supported the war, voted the credits, subscribed to the war loans, obeyed every order, however savage, of their Government. They shared the responsibility for the policy of their Government, for at any moment, had they willed it, they could have reversed it.

"Had that policy succeeded they would have acclaimed it with the same enthusiasm with which they welcomed the outbreak of the war. They can not now pretend, having changed their rulers after the war was lost, that it is justice that they should escape the consequences of their deeds. The Allied and Associated Powers, therefore, believe that the peace they have proposed is fundamentally a peace of justice. They are no less certain that it is a peace of right on the terms agreed."

In the reply itself it was stated that the Powers could not "entrust the trial of those responsible for the war to those who have been their accomplices." The tribunals for the trial would represent the deliberate judgment of the greater part of the civilized world,

and there could be no question of admitting the right of jurisdiction of representatives of countries which took no part in the
war. The Allies, it was declared, would stand by the verdict of history for the impartiality and justice with which the accused would
be tried. The accused would be insured full rights to defense and
the judgment of the tribunal would have the most solemn judicial
character. The demand for the trial of the Kaiser, regardless of
what its results might be, was in part based on other grounds than
those commonly urged. There was more to the matter than the bare
question of whether the Hohenzollern was to be punished. The world
needed the fullest inquiry into the exact circumstances surrounding
the decision of the German Government to launch the war. Much had
been revealed—enough to warrant general conclusions—but many
details were covered and others had been contradicted. The best way
to obtain them was to try the Kaiser who was the center of information. At his trial the truth could be extracted concerning what went
on in Berlin in July, 1914, for the truth existed in documents and
witnesses, altho unwilling, could be induced to tell what they knew.
Particularly was this desirable for its possible effect on the German
people. To charges, deductions, arguments, general probabilities,
they had thus far been blind, but their eyes might be opened when a
narrative was made concrete and so another effort to open them was at
least worth making.

In conclusion, the Allied and Associated Powers said "they must
make it clear that this letter and the memorandum attached constitute their last word." They believed the treaty as drafted was
"not only a just settlement of the war, but that it provided the basis
upon which the peoples of Europe can live together in friendship
and equality." It was frankly "not based upon a general condona-
tion of the events of the 1914-1918 period. It would not be a peace
of justice if it were. But it represented a sincere and deliberate attempt to establish that "reign of law based upon the consent of the
governed and the organized opinion of mankind" which President
Wilson in 1918 had declared to be the Entente purpose for further
prosecution of the war.

After a brief reference to a long memorandum from the German
delegation in which it was sought to show that, in the pre-war crisis
Germany tried to induce moderation on the part of Austria, the
reply stated that there was nothing in the memorandum to shake
conviction that the immediate cause of the war "was the decision,
deliberately taken by those responsible for the German policy in
Berlin and their confederates in Vienna and Budapest to impose a
solution of a European question upon the nations of Europe by a

threat of war, and, if the other members of the concert refused this dictation, by war itself, instantly declared." Moreover, as to Germany:

"It supported the rejection, without consideration, of the extraordinary concessions made by Serbia in response to the insolent and intolerable demands of the Austro-Hungarian Government. It supported the mobilization of the Austro-Hungarian Army and the initiation of hostilities, and steadily rejected every proposal for conference, conciliation, or mediation, altho it knew that once mobilization and military action were undertaken by any of the Great Powers it inevitably compelled a response from all the rest, and so hourly reduced the chances.

"The German Government would now throw the blame for the failure of the attempts to procure peace on the mobilization of the Russian Army. They ignore that this was the immediate and necessary consequence of the mobilization of the Austrian Army and the declaration of war on Serbia—both authorized by Germany. These were the fatal acts by which the decision was taken out of the hands of statesmen and control transferred to the military. It is on the German statesmen that equally rests the responsibility for the hasty declaration of war on Russia when Austria herself was apparently hesitating, and for the declaration of war on France.

"So great was the haste of the German Government that when no plausible reason could be found allegations were invented, the complete falsity of which had long ago been demonstrated. The German delegation now admits that the German Government 'did not take the trouble to verify' reported facts which they published as justifying them in a declaration of war. After receiving what the German delegation has to say in self-defense, the Allied and Associated Powers are satisfied that the series of events which caused the outbreak of the war was deliberately plotted and executed by those who wielded supreme power in Vienna, Budapest and Berlin.

"The history of the critical days of July, 1914, however, is not the sole ground upon which the Allied and Associated Powers consider that the responsibility of Germany for the war must be tried. The outbreak of the war was no sudden decision taken in a difficult crisis; it was the logical outcome of a policy which had been pursued for decades by Germany under the inspiration of the Prussian system.

"It is said that Germany developed her armaments in order to save herself from Russian aggression. Yet it is a significant fact that no sooner was Russia defeated by Japan in the Far East than the German Government immediately redoubled its attempts to increase its armaments and to domineer over its neighbors under the threat of war. To them the collapse of Russia was not an occasion to try to reduce armaments and bring peace to the world in concert with the Western powers. It was an opportunity to extend their own power."

The changes finally made by the Entente delegates in the treaty were numerous, tho not radical, and included: A plebiscite for

Upper Silesia, with guaranties of coal from that region; frontier rectifications in West Prussia; the omission of the third zone from the Schleswig plebiscite; a temporary increase of the permitted strength of the German army from 100,000 to 200,000; a declaration of intention to submit within a month of the treaty's signature a list of those accused of violation of the laws and customs of war; an offer to cooperate with a German Commission on Reparations and to receive suggestions for discharging the obligation; certain detailed modifications in the financial, economic, and ports and waterways clauses, including the abolition of the proposed Kiel Canal Commission; assurance to Germany of membership in the League of Nations in the early future if she fulfils her obligations.

Berlin newspapers reappeared after the final Entente reply was made public with such headlines as "The Death Sentence" and "The Entente's Ultimatum" in their largest type, and extending across first pages. One paper called it "the blackest day in the history of the world." Count zu Reventlow, in the *Deutsche Tageszeitung* called Clémenceau's letter "a document of shameless lies." The German people should never forget this "most infamous example of refined lying and robbing." Next day the Berlin *Vorwärts* declared that "extortionate pressure renders signature of the peace treaty worthless. We must never forget it is only a scrap of paper. Treaties based on violence can keep their validity only so long as force exists. Do not lose hope. The resurrection day comes."

News on June 20 of the retirement of Scheidemann as Chancellor and of the reforming of a coalition German Government came as no surprise in Peace Conference circles, as it had been known for some time that Scheidemann, Brockdorff-Rantzau, and several other Cabinet members had become so thoroughly committed by past utterances to refusal to sign the treaty that a new Cabinet would have to be installed before the treaty could be signed and new delegates sent to Versailles, unless the treaty were modified again materially. On June 22 the German Government formally communicated to Versailles its intention to sign the treaty unconditionally in a note written by Haniel von Haimhausen, who said:

"It appears to the government of the German Republic, in consternation at the last communication of the Allied and Associated Governments, that these Governments have decided to wrest from Germany by force acceptance of the peace conditions, even those, which, without presenting any material significance, aim at divesting the German people of their honor. No act of violence can touch the honor of the German people. The German people, after frightful suffering in these last years, have no means of defending themselves by external action. Yielding to superior force, and without renouncing in the meantime its own

GÖTHE AND SCHILLER IN WEIMAR

The upper picture shows the house Göthe lived in, the lower one the
house that was Schiller's home

view of the unheard-of injustice of the peace conditions, the government of the German Republic declares that it is ready to accept and sign the peace conditions imposed.''

Contemporary with this declaration of acceptance of the terms and willingness to sign the treaty was the sinking of the German warships interned at Scapa Flow, an act accepted as an illustration of one of the problems which the Allied Powers would have to face in the execution of the treaty. That problem was the German mind. The incident imprest one less as an act of open treachery or piracy than as an example of the extraordinary mingling of stupidity and super-subtlety, and exaggerated legalism, of "rights" and "necessities" with which the world had had to deal since Bethmann-Hollweg's speech at the beginning of the war. If the Germans had sunk their warships before the armistice, or before the supreme humiliation of surrender, the act would have been human and understandable. But to have waited until the "expiration" of the armistice, as the German rear-admiral, and then to sink the ships during a sort of constructive recess, when there was no armistice and there was yet no peace, and therefore when the ships had presumably reverted to their former owners—that act was German. Such incidents would recur; and it would be for the Allies to decide in each case whether Germany was violating the treaty with forethought, or whether she was only fulfilling the treaty according to the laws of German thought.

Soon the Entente Powers had another example of the difficulties that awaited them in dealing with the Germans. On June 24 a delegation of officers from the cavalry of the guard, "gentlemen" representing the best families of Prussia, seized French flags captured by Germans in the war of 1870 and since kept in a museum in Berlin, but which by the treaty Germans now had said they would sign were to be restored to France, and had already been packed for shipment. These German "gentlemen" took the flags to a place before the statue of Frederick the Great, in Berlin, soaked them in gasoline, and burned them while a crowd stood by cheering wildly. The burning of the flags was the result of a scheme matured a week before, and the act was openly executed under the eyes of police guards, and almost within the shadow of the imperial palace.

The Allied and Associated Powers declared to Germany that they had taken note of these signal acts of bad faith, and that when the investigations into all the circumstances had been completed, they would exact the necessary reparation. Any repetition of acts like those would "have a very unfortunate effect upon the future operation of the treaty which the Germans are about to sign." They had complained that Germany's admission to the League of Nations might be too long deferred, but "how could Germany put forward such claims if she encourages or permits deliberate violations of her written engagements?"

While the world had been waiting somewhat wearily for the Germans to sign the treaty in spite of their protests and the various notes received from her delegates in Versailles, Secretary Glass of the United States Treasury on May 26 announced that approximately 12,000,000 persons had bought Victory Loan bonds—our fifth great loan. Subscriptions to the loan amounted to $5,249,908,300, which was an oversubscription of $749,908,300. Nearly 60 per cent. of the loan, or $2,663,154,850, had been taken by those who subscribed for not in excess of $10,000 each. Subscriptions by districts, after allowing for allocation of credit from one district to another, were as follows:

District	Quota	Subscription	P. C.
New York	$1,350,000,000	$1,762,684,900	130.55
Chicago	652,500,000	772,046,550	118.32
Boston	375,000,000	425,159,950	113.38
Philadelphia	375,000,000	422,756,100	112.73
Minneapolis	157,500,000	176,114,850	111.82
Cleveland	450,000,000	496,750,650	110.39
St. Louis	195,000,000	210,431,950	107.91
Richmond	210,000,000	225,146,850	107.21
San Francisco	301,500,000	319,120,800	105.84
Kansas City	195,000,000	197,989,100	101.53
Atlanta	144,000,000	143,032,050	99.34
Dallas	94,500,000	87,504,250	92.60
Treasury	....	11,140,300	....
Grand Total	$4,500,000,000	$5,249,908,300	114.66

The actual figures of the subscription fittingly completed a very remarkable chapter in American finance. Within two years, the Government had asked for $18,500,000,000 in its war loans; a sum exceeding all the borrowings of the British or German Governments since August, 1914, and three times as large as the war loans of any European belligerent in any two-year period. As against this aggregate of $18,500,000,000 asked for by our own Government, our people had offered us no less than $24,068,000,000. Our earlier war loans, for which two and three billion dollars had been asked by the Treasury, were oversubscribed in amounts ranging from 38 per cent. in the Third Loan to 51¾ per cent. in the First. With the very much larger applications of the Fourth Loan and the Fifth, it was natural that the ratio of oversubscription should be smaller. Yet the six-billion-dollar loan of October, 1918, was oversubscribed by $989,000,000, or 16½ per cent., and the official statement in May, 1919, of the count of subscriptions for the Victory Loan showed applications of $5,249,908,300 for the $4,500,000,000 total, or an over-subscription of almost exactly 16⅝ per cent. Taking all our five war loans together, the American people had applied for 28 per cent. more than the Treasury had asked for. Considering the immense amount involved, it was safe to say that no such exhibition of investment power had ever been witnessed in financial history.

The outstanding fact was that a great oversubscription had been made for a loan offered after the war was over, when the heaviest of war-taxes were being paid, when troops were coming home, when canvassers could no longer reckon on the white heat of patriotic fervor, and when people were turning from the concentration of all their energies on war finance and war production to the ·financial and industrial tasks of peace. Most curious was it, as an example of the workings of the German mind, that one Herr Schweibuser should have made, on May 14 of this year in the *Tageblatt* of Berlin, under the heading, "Failure of the American War Loan," the following extraordinary statement:

"According to reports from New York, it has been extremely difficult to obtain the necessary subscriptions to the most recent war loan, which amounted to $4,500,000. Last Thursday, with only five days more open for the receipt of subscriptions, 45 per cent. of the total had not been subscribed. Most desperate expedients have been resorted to in order to avoid a failure of the loan. The City of New York was supposed to subscribe $1,000,000 (sic). Thus far only one-third thereof has been subscribed." [6]

[6] Principal Sources: The *Evening Post*, The *Times*, New York; the *Matin* (Paris), The *Wall Street Journal* (New York), Associated Press dispatches; *The Literary Digest*, The *Tribune*, The *World*, *The Outlook*, New York.

IV

BISMARCK AND THIERS AT VERSAILLES IN 1871

PEOPLE in Entente countries from time to time had betrayed much impatience over the delay in completing the negotiations. But the time taken was not exceptional. Other peace negotiations had taken months, and more than one took years. The greatest example of prolonged negotiations were those which resulted in the Peace of Westphalia, closing the Thirty Years' War. The definite movement for peace in that war began twelve years before its actual conclusion. Not until nine o'clock on October 24, 1648—twelve years after the negotiations began—was the peace signed and then the town "was given over to dances, ballets, entertainments, conviviality, and intemperance." Hostilities in the war of the American Revolution were at an end when General Cornwallis surrendered on October 19, 1781, but the definite treaty of peace was not signed in Paris until September 3, 1783—one year, ten months and fourteen days later. The settlement of the American War, as the English call the war we call the War of 1812, required five months, and on several occasions the negotiations at Ghent were almost broken off before the treaty was signed on December 24, 1814. Hostilities continued in the interval; in fact, fourteen days after the treaty was signed the greatest land battle of the war was fought at New Orleans. Napoleon abdicated at Fontainebleau on April 4, 1814, but the final signing of the peace negotiations at Vienna did not occur until June 9, 1815, or a year, two months and five days after the abdication.

An exception to an almost general rule as to a long duration in war settlements was found in the peace negotiations in 1871 between Germany and France by Bismarck and Thiers. The armistice was signed on January 28, the final treaty, called the Treaty of Frankfort, being signed on May 10 and ratified on May 23. Thiers himself has given the world in his "Memoirs," a detailed account of his interview with Bismarck as to Germany's terms. The account calls for republication here, alike for the complete transformation that had now occurred in Franco-German relations, and for the light it sheds on the German character when flushed with complete victory, in contrast to the German character as revealed in the negotiations of May and June, 1919. Thiers had gone to Versailles from Bordeaux, where the French National Assembly, recently elected, had made him

339

the executive head of the State Government, really President of France, altho not having the title. He describes how he was received by Bismarck in a room where, on the mantel, were standing two bottles that were acting as candlesticks. He writes:

"I trembled to broach the question of the conditions of peace; however, it had to be done. 'Let us come now to the great question,' said I to the Count.

"He replied: 'I do not wish to jockey you, it would be unbecoming. I might speak of Europe, as they do on your side, and demand in her name that you should give back Savoy and Nice to their rightful owners. I will do nothing of this kind, and will only speak to you of Germany and France. I already asked you for Alsace and certain parts of Lorraine. I will give you back Nancy, altho the Minister for War wants to keep it; but we shall keep Metz for our own security. All the rest of French Lorraine will remain yours.'

"Count Bismarck looked at me to guess what I was thinking. Mastering my emotion, I answered coldly: 'You had only spoken of the German portion of Lorraine.'

"'Certainly,' said he, 'but we must have Metz; we must have it for our own safety.'

"'Go on,' I said, wishing to know the whole extent of his exactions before I should answer.

"Count Bismarck then opened the question of money. 'When I saw you in November,' he said, 'I mentioned a sum to you. That can not now be the same figure, for since then we have suffered and spent enormously. I had asked you for four milliards: to-day we must have six.'

"'Six milliards!' I exclaimed; 'but no one in the whole world could find them. It was the soldiers who suggested these figures to you; it was no financier.' The cold, determined, even scornful tone of my reply put Bismarck out of countenance. He listened without saying a word, and I added, 'but you are not to think I admit your demands: Alsace, Metz, a French city, six milliards, all that—it is out of the question! We will discuss these terms, and to discuss we must have time; let us extend the armistice.'

"If I had uttered a word implying an absolute refusal of any cession of territory, it would have meant immediate rupture, war, disaster on disaster. I confined myself, therefore, to refraining from accepting the claims put forward, at the same time without giving the idea that I rejected them. 'I will not jockey any more than you,' I said finally, 'but I shall let you know my terms . . . and then, if you demand impossibilities, I shall withdraw and leave you to govern France.' With these words in his ears Count Bismarck left me to go to the King to ask for an extension of the armistice. It was granted until midnight on Sunday."

Another meeting took place the next day, of which Thiers records:

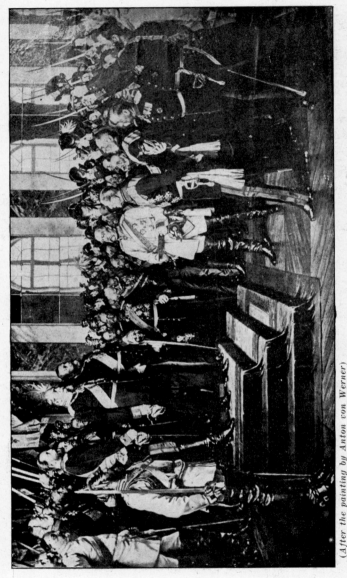

(After the painting by Anton von Werner)

BISMARCK IN THE HALL OF MIRRORS AT VERSAILLES IN 1870 PROCLAIMING KING WILLIAM
OF PRUSSIA THE GERMAN EMPEROR

See opposite page for picture of Clémenceau in the same place, in 1919, asking the German Peace
Delegates to sign the Treaty

x.

PREMIER CLÉMENCEAU IN THE HALL OF MIRRORS AT VERSAILLES IN 1919 ASKING THE GERMAN
DELEGATES TO COME FORWARD AND SIGN THE PEACE TREATY

See opposite page for picture of Bismarck proclaiming, in the same place, in 1870, the German Empire

x.

"The day was stormy. We left generalities; and the necessity of arriving precisely at facts gave rise to hot discussion. Count Bismarck then, with some signs of embarrassment, began to remind me of the sum of six milliards mentioned the previous day, and described it as very modest, since, he said, the mere cost of the war came to four milliards.

"I showed him that this was utterly impossible; that in France, where expenditure was all the time heavier than in Prussia, the cost of the war in itself only came to about two milliards, which we found enormous; and that if this year we were faced with a deficit of three milliards, it was because to the two milliards cost of the war there must be added at least a milliard for bridges, broken-down tunnels, roads to be repaired, necessary indemnities, railway transports, and finally, the loss of at least one-third of the year's taxes; that in no case could it be brought up to four milliards; with six milliards there would be at least three milliards of profit for Prussia, which would turn the war indemnity into a mere financial speculation.

"Count Bismarck replied that the war had cost more in Prussia than in France, because they had had to bring everything from Germany. I replied that we also had immense transport operations, and that besides, the Prussians had seized on all the resources of our soil, and what they had taken possession of on the spot was ample equivalent for all the cost of their transport.

"The Count seemed to set particular store by the money. He declared, with some temper, that the figures on which the indemnity had been calculated came to him from Prussia; that on this occasion he was only a mouthpiece, etc.; and that he could not settle anything before telegraphing to Berlin. It was agreed then that he should telegraph, and that when he received the answer from Berlin, he would send special envoys to treat with me on this point. This incident terminated our interview."

Then came a third meeting at which Jules Favre, the French Foreign Minister, was present. Thiers says:

"We set out, M. Jules Favre and myself, in a very uneasy mind. We were determined to present a kind of ultimatum, to hold fast to it, and to make an end, since the armistice expired at midnight on Sunday. We found Count Bismarck very ill, but sufficiently calm, to all appearances. Coming back to the question of territory, we spoke of Metz before everything else, Metz, the city that was French *par excellence*.

"Count Bismarck told us that he considered it highly impolitic to drive France to despair, and that he had opposed Count Roon's project of seizing two-thirds of Lorraine, that we were to lose only a very small fraction of it, but that there was no possibility of leaving Metz to us. 'In Germany,' he said, 'they accuse me of losing the battles Count Moltke has won. Do not ask me for impossibilities.'

"It was evident that the decision on this head was irrevocably fixt, and that we must reserve our energies to save the eastern frontier.

We next went on to the question of the money. I feared that Count Bismarck might take his stand upon his sum total of six milliards, and refuse to abandon it. He told us, calmly enough, that he had telegraphed to Berlin, that they had again insisted afresh on the amount of expenditure incurred, on the widows and orphans whose pensions we were expected to pay, on the maintenance of the prisoners, on the necessity of giving the southern States their share; but in the end that they had stopt at a total of five milliards, from which they would make no deduction. I perceived that on this point a rupture would probably be the result of discussion. Count Bismarck was inflexible.

"Upon the question of Belfort, I entered upon a struggle that I shall remember as long as I live. Belfort is the eastern frontier; in fact, if the Prussian troops were to come by Verdun and Metz, the South German troops would always come by Belfort, especially if the neutrality of Switzerland were violated. I spoke, then, of Belfort. Count Bismarck said at once that this fortress was in Alsace, and that it was decided that the whole of Alsace should be transferred to Germany. Throughout two hours, now with menaces, now with entreaties, I declared that I would never let Belfort go.

" 'No,' I cried, 'I will never surrender both Metz and Belfort. You mean to ruin France in her finances, ruin her on her frontiers! Well, take her, administer the country, levy the taxes! We shall retire, and you will have to govern her in the eyes of the whole of Europe, if Europe permits.'

"I was desperate. Count Bismarck, taking my hands, said to me: ' Believe me, I have done all I could; but as for leaving you part of Alsace, it is quite impossible.'

" 'I sign this very instant,' I rejoined, 'if you give me Belfort. If not, nothing! nothing, but the last extremities, whatever they may be.'

"Beaten, exhausted, Count Bismarck then said to me: 'If you will, I shall make an effort with the King; but I do not believe it will succeed.'

"Immediately he wrote two letters, which he dispatched, one to the King, the other to Count Moltke. 'I ask Moltke,' said he, 'for we must get him on our side; without him we shall obtain nothing.'

" Half an hour passed. Every sound of footsteps in the ante-chamber made our hearts leap. At length the door opens. We are told that the King is out of doors, and that Count Moltke is not at his house. The King will not come back until four o'clock. No one knows when Moltke will return. We decide to wait, for to go away without having settled the question would be to lose.

"Count Bismarck leaves us to go to dinner, and we pass an hour, M. Jules Favre and I, in inexpressible anxiety. Count Bismarck appears again. The King has come back, but does not wish to decide without having seen Count Moltke. Count Moltke arrives. Count Bismarck leaves us to go and talk with him. Their conversation seems very long to us. Count Bismarck returns, satisfaction in his face.

" 'Moltke is on our side,' said he; 'he will turn the King.' A fresh wait of three-quarters of an hour. Count Bismarck goes to find out what Count Moltke reports. After a long talk with him he at length comes back, and, his hand on the key of the door, he says to us: 'I have an alternative to propose to you. Which will you have, Belfort or the abandonment of our entry into Paris?'

"I do not hesitate for a moment, and with a look to M. Jules Favre, who divines my feeling and shares it: 'Belfort! Belfort!' I cried. The entry of the Germans into Paris must needs be a cruel blow to our pride, a danger to us who hold the reins of government; but—our country before everything!

"Count Bismarck rejoins Count Moltke, and at length brings us the definite concession of Belfort, on conditions that we will give up four little villages on the confines of Lorraine, where eight or ten thousand Prussians are buried. We respect this religious regard of the monarch for his soldiers. We had left Paris at eleven in the forenoon; we leave Versailles at half-past nine at night, having saved Belfort for France. From ten o'clock until midnight we hold a sitting of the Commission. We relate everything to them, and receive their thanks for our efforts."

V

THE SIGNING AT VERSAILLES OF THE TREATY
WITH GERMANY

June 28, 1919

ON June 28 Germany and the Allied and Associated Powers signed at Versailles the Peace Treaty. This event took place in the same hall—the Hall of Mirrors—in which the Germans had humbled the French forty-nine years before, and was the formal ending of a state of war lasting only thirty-seven days short of five years. The day was the fifth anniversary of the murder of the Archduke Francis Ferdinand at Serajevo, which had been the occasion for the brutal ultimatum to Serbia, as delivered by Austria, backed by Germany, and which precipitated the war.

Many persons have been familiar with a sort of official painting of the Versailles ceremony of December, 1870, when William I was proclaimed German Emperor, in which the central figure was not the old King and newly made Emperor, but the big and burly Bismarck, in the white uniform of a Prussian Cuirassier, holding a polished steel helmet and wearing a clanking saber at his side, his legs in great jackboots reaching half way up his thighs, standing forward near the front of the dais and reading the document which announced to the world that the King of Prussia had taken to himself the title of German Emperor. It was the great moment in Bismarck's life, marking as it did with pomp and circumstance, the triumph of his policy of blood and iron and the accomplished fact of the unity of Germany, which had been his goal. Bismarck had planned and precipitated three wars to bring that unity about, and in the third of them, France, the hereditary enemy of Germany, had now been crusht. Meanwhile, the old jealousies of the German States had disappeared in the pride which the common victory aroused in all of them, and the supremacy of Prussia became established beyond further question.

It was strange to think of that assemblage as taking place in the midst of war, within four miles of German front-line trenches at St. Cloud, and within five miles of the guns of Mount Valerien, where France had her heaviest artillery, for the war was still going on. Colors and standards from German regiments then besieging

344

Paris had been brought in to give to the scene a background of gold and silk, that was reproduced again and again as the reflection in one mirror was repeated in another across the hall. In front of the colors were grouped on the dais the princes of the German States, headed by the Crown Prince Frederick—"Unser Fritz." In the center stood the old King, and on the floor in front of him were Bismarck, Moltke, and Roon, the triumvirate who had brought to pass the event which was being consummated. Flanking the dais on either side were two gigantic troopers, living monuments of the Prussian ideal. In the body of the great hall was a mass of officers representing the armies of the German States. Bismarck left the Hall of Mirrors that day a proud and satisfied man, little dreaming that his intoxicating draught of victory and empire would go to the heads of his Prussians, and by making them drunk with power and lust of territory would bring them back forty-nine years afterward to the same room, in an overwhelming defeat.

The ceremony of June 28, 1919, was a very different affair. There were more black coats than there were uniforms; there were few ribbons and stars, and there were no gigantic troopers. The artist who should paint the second picture—for we might assume that the great and historic scene would be duly recorded on canvas—would not have so easy a task as his German predecessor had had. Neither Lloyd George, President Wilson, nor M. Clémenceau had cut a figure to rival, or even suggest, Bismarck in his jackboots. Foch, however, in horizon blue, might perhaps have challenged comparison with Moltke.[7] By noon that day, eleven regiments of French cavalry and infantry had taken positions along the approaches to the palace, while within the court on either side solid lines of infantry in horizon blue had been drawn up at attention. Hours before the time set for the ceremony an endless stream of automobiles had begun to move out of Paris, up the cannon-lined hill of the Champs Élysées, past the Arc de Triomphe, and out through the Bois de Boulogne, carrying plenipotentiaries, officials, and guests, the thoroughfares having been kept clean by pickets, dragoons, and mounted gendarmes. Thousands of Parisians meanwhile were packing regular and special trains upon lines leading to Versailles and contending with residents of the town itself for places in the park where the playing fountains would mark the end of the ceremony.

Long before the ceremony began a line of gendarmes had been thrown across the approaches, the Court of Honor had been cleared of captured guns and three regiments of infantry and five of cavalry had gone on duty. Republican Guards, in gala uniform and

[7] London dispatch from Gen. Sir Frederick Maurice to The *Times* (New York).

forming the guard of honor, were stationed on the grand staircase, by which the plenipotentiaries were to enter the hall. The Place d'Armes was a lake of white faces, dappled everywhere by the bright colors of flags and fringed with the horizon blue of troops whose bayonets shone like flames as the sun peeped at moments from behind heavy clouds. Above were airplanes—a dozen or more—which wheeled and curvetted. There could have been found no nobler setting for the great ceremony.

Up the triumphal passage, between the two wings of the palace, the representatives of the victorious nations passed in flag-decked limousines—a hundred or two hundred cars, one after another, without intermission and taking fifty minutes to pass. Midway down the courtyard was seen the big bronze statue of Louis XIV on horseback, and along its sides the statues of the Princes and Marshals, Admirals and Generals who had made Louis the *Grande Monarque* of France. Just inside the gates was General Bricker, commander of the Sixth Cavalry Division, sitting on a splendid chestnut, hardly less immobile than the bronze Sun King, save when he flashed his sword to salute some guest especially distinguished.[8] It was impossible to say what the day meant to the people of Versailles. To them, more than to the rest of France, it was the wiping out of an ancient stain, which they had felt more deeply than any other French community. At the entrance to the crowded dining-hall of the Hôtel des Réservoirs was seen an old aunt of the proprietor standing and looking about with eager eyes, reminiscent of the event of forty-nine years before. "I saw them die here," she said, "and now this—thank God I have lived to see it!"

The delegates after traversing the Bois de Boulogne and the park of St. Cloud, where once had stood the favorite residence of Napoleon, entered Versailles by the Avenue de Paris, a boulevard almost 100 yards wide leading directly to the main entrance of the château. Beyond the enclosure reserved for the general public they passed between stands erected for members of the Senate and the Chamber of Deputies and then reached the doorway through which the Paris mob of 1789, a momentous day in the French Revolution, broke into the château, massacred the Swiss guards and compelled Louis XVI and Queen Marie Antoinette to return to Paris. To reach the Hall of Mirrors they traversed the state apartments once occupied by the monarch and his queen.

One of the earliest to arrive was Marshal Foch, amid a torrent of cheering which broke out even louder a few minutes later when Premier Clémenceau—for once with a smile on the Tiger's face—was seen through the windows of a French military car. To both, as

[8] Versailles dispatch from Walter Duranty to The *Times* (New York).

OUR PEACE DELEGATES AT VERSAILLES

From left to right: Col. E. M. House, Secretary Lansing, President Wilson, Henry White, Gen. Tasker H. Bliss

347

to the other chiefs, including President Wilson, General Pershing, and Lloyd George, troops paid the honor of presenting arms from every point around the courtyard. After them came other diplomats and soldiers, including Princes of India in gorgeous turbans, Japanese in immaculate Western dress, Admirals, Arabs, and a thousand and one picturesque uniforms of the French, British and Colonial armies. Amid terrific enthusiasm a whole wagon-load of doughboys, themselves yelling "their heads off," drove up the sacred Area of Victory, swung around the Louis XIV statue, and went out by a side gateway, where other automobiles had gone after depositing their passengers. Ten minutes later a camion laden with British Tommies arrived and they, too, had a most cordial reception.

All the diplomats who attended the ceremony wore conventional civilian clothes. There was marked lack of gold lace and pageantry, with few uniforms suggesting the Middle Ages, or any later monarchical age, whose traditions and practises had been so sternly condemned in the great, seal-covered documents now to be signed. Only selected members of the Guard were there, resplendent in red-plumed silver helmets and red, white and blue uniforms. Notable among the persons who attended were five Senators who had participated in the campaign of 1870. Marshal Pétain came accompanied by six French generals. A group of Allied generals, including Pershing, wore the scarlet sash of the Legion of Honor. The ceremony had been planned to be austere, as befitting the purposes and sufferings of nearly five years. The lack of impressiveness and picturesqueness of color, of which many spectators, who had expected a magnificent State pageant, complained, had been a matter of pure design.

When the program for the ceremony was shown to the German delegation, Herr von Haimhausen, of the delegation, went to Colonel Henri, the French liaison officer, and said:

"We can not admit that the German delegates should enter the hall by a different door from Entente delegates; nor that military honors should be withheld. Had we known before that there would be such arrangements, delegates would not have come."

After a conference with the French Foreign Ministry, it was decided, as a compromise, to render military honors to the Germans as they left the building—but not as they entered it. Otherwise the program as originally arranged was not changed. The Germans had a separate route of entry through the park, and reached the marble stairway through the ground floor. Dr. Müller, German Secretary for Foreign Affairs, and Dr. Bell, Colonial Secretary, when shown into the hall, quietly took their seats. The Entente delegates did not rise. The Germans manifested none of the uneasiness which Count von Brockdorff-Rantzau, head of the first German peace delegation, had displayed when handed the treaty early in May. There was heard just the beginning of a murmur when the Germans appeared, but it was so quickly hushed as to recall an incident in the battle of Santiago, when Captain Philip of the *Texas* restrained his men from cheering because the Spaniards were dying, only the words seemed now to be, "Don't cheer, boys; they're signing." The actual ceremony was far shorter than had been expected, in view of the number of signatures that were to be appended to the treaty, ending as it did a bare forty-nine minutes after the hour set for the opening. Clémenceau, as President of the Conference, had risen and said:

"The session is open. The Allied and Associated Powers on one side and the German reich on the other side have come to an agreement on the conditions of peace. The text has been completed, drafted, and the President of the Conference has stated in writing that the text that is about to be signed now is identical with the 200 copies that have been delivered to the German delegation. The signatures will be given now, and they amount to a solemn undertaking faithfully and loyally to execute the conditions embodied by this treaty of peace. I now request the delegates of the German reich to sign the treaty."

Dr. Herman Müller and Johannes Bell, the German signatories, first affixt their names. President Wilson, first of the Allied delegates, signed a minute later, and then the others. The ceremony ended so quickly and quietly that it was scarcely realized that it could be over when Clémenceau rose unremarked, and in a voice almost lost amid the confusion and hum of conversation, declared the conference closed, and asked the Allied and Associated Delegates to remain in their places for a few minutes—the purpose being to permit the German plenipotentiaries first to leave the building before a general exodus began. No one rose as the Germans filed out, accompanied by their secretaries and interpreters, just as all the plenipotentiaries had kept their seats when Dr. Müller and Dr. Bell entered the hall. This was regarded as an answer to the action of Count von Brockdorff-Rantzau at the first meeting with the Entente at the Conference, in reading his speech while seated and making no excuses for doing so, but even more it was assumed to have been inspired by the German attitude toward acceptance of the peace and by the violation of its terms in the sinking of the ships at Scapa Flow and burning the French flags in Berlin. The stillest three minutes ever lived through were those in which the German delegates signed the treaty.

The most dramatic moment of the day at Versailles came unexpectedly and spontaneously at the conclusion of the ceremony, when Clémenceau, Wilson, and Lloyd George descended from the Hall of Mirrors to the terrace at the rear of the palace, where were massed thousands of spectators. A most remarkable demonstration ensued. With cries of *"Vive Clémenceau!" "Vive Wilson!" "Vive Lloyd George!"* dense crowds of struggling and cheering masses surrounded the three men from all parts of the spacious enclosure. These, the three most eminent civilians of the war period, were literally caught in the living stream which flowed across that great space, until they became themselves hardly more than parts of it. Soldiers and body-guards struggled vainly to clear a way for them. People jostled and pushed, all the while cheering madly, while the great fountains played. Probably the least concerned for their personal safety were the three men. They went forward smilingly, as the crowd willed, bowing in response to the ovation, and here and there reaching out to shake an insistent hand as they passed on their way to the fountains. No more picturesque setting could have been selected for the formal end of the great five-year drama. The return of the three men to the palace became a repetition of their outward journey.[9]

Some of the Berlin papers of the next day, in announcing the signing of the treaty, appeared in black borders, with captions such as "Germany's Fate Sealed," "Peace and Annihilation." The *Tageszeitung,* in closing an editorial article, said: "Clémenceau, Lloyd George, and Wilson and their accessories have sown dragons' teeth of eternal enmity." The whole German press wrote in a strain of melancholy pessimism. Evangelical churches arranged to observe Sunday, July 6, as a day of mourning when church bells were to sound a hymn of mourning.

On July 9th, by a vote of 208 to 115, the German National Assembly ratified the Treaty, 99 deputies abstaining from voting. Germany thus became the first Power to ratify it. Argentina, however, by a unanimous vote in her Senate on July 6th, had been the first nation to enter the League. Not having been a belligerent in the war—altho she had severed relations with Germany and had seized German ships—Argentina could not sign the Peace Treaty itself. Germans who had been near the guns of the Allied armies on the Rhine had been anxious enough to see the Treaty signed and ratified, but in other parts of Germany many were still unable to understand that Germany had been defeated; they still needed some tangible demonstration that they had failed in what they tried to do. It was hard for them to understand what had happened, with their territory still undamaged, while parts of France, Serbia and Poland had been converted into barren deserts. It was not yet certain to such minds that Germany had actually lost the war. Nor could they understand why they were short of food, much less why they failed to command the world's respect

[9] Associated Press dispatches.

and sympathy. The *Tageblatt* of Berlin exprest a German view when it said of the Treaty: "Despite the fact that it was written on parchment, it remains a scrap of paper." There were, however, men in Germany who knew the real truth as to the war, and a few who acknowledged it, but it promised to be a long time before the whole German people realized that their nation had been treated with some magnanimity and lenity—that the terms imposed upon them were mild and conciliatory, compared with what Germany would have imposed on the Entente had she as unmistakably won the war.

After all the impatience which the public in most countries had shown over the time taken by the Peace Conference for its work, it was interesting to recall now that the Conference did not formally begin its work until January 18, but that, in spite of the enormous bulk of the treaty as finally submitted, and the multiplicity of its detail, the gigantic task had been accomplished by May 7, that is, in about fifteen weeks, and that seven weeks later the Germans had signed the great document.

The signing of the German treaty was in itself one of the most impressive events in human history; moreover, the document was unique, not only in the manner of its negotiation, the volume of its contents, and the extent of its application, but in its character and purposes. It was not an agreement for the bondage of any nation, but one for the freedom of all nations. It had not been worked out in secrecy, or in what had been regarded as "confidence," but had been made in the open light, with freedom of discussion, and practically complete publicity during the whole process. Another unexampled incident of that June day was the brevity and simplicity of the sitting at which the signatures were attached in solemn and impressive silence, and the instant publicity that was given to the signing, accompanied in this country by a message from President Wilson to his "fellow countrymen," received nearly four hours before the sun's rays could make a journey from Paris to Washington.[10]

[10] The *Journal of Commerce* (New York).

VI

THE SETTLEMENT WITH AUSTRIA, TURKEY, AND BULGARIA

May 14, 1919—May 27, 1920

THE Austrian peace delegation arrived at St. Germain-en-Laye on May 14. The delegation was headed by Karl Renner, the Chancellor, who appeared in the doorway of the railway-car at St. Germain hat in hand, with a contagious smile that put the French reception committee quickly at its ease. He was a plump, round-faced man with a black beard and a bald head, eyes shining brightly behind a pair of gold-rimmed spectacles. A notable feature of the reception was the absence of the Germans from Versailles. They had requested permission to greet the Austrians, but received a refusal. The Austrian delegates were taken under military escort to villas overlooking the valley of the Seine, but lacking the high fences and the sentries who were so much in evidence in Versailles.

The ceremony of presenting the peace terms to the Austrian delegates took place in the ancient château, once a castle of kings, now a natural history museum, where children of French workmen may roam at will, gazing at prehistoric stone implements, stuffed birds and pictures of extinct animals. Altho the hall used was the one devoted to specimens of the cave-man age, the tone of the whole meeting was modern. The time set for it was noon. President Wilson arrived fifteen minutes late, having come over from Paris by the long road through Versailles to avoid the rush of traffic on the more direct route from Paris to St. Germain. On the way his automobile had had a blowout, and so he had set the dignitaries wondering what was keeping him. The most punctiliously punctual of men had kept waiting an assemblage of high plenipotentiaries from the Entente Powers. While the waiting went on, Paderewski was seen tearing a card into fine bits; Balfour was counting the great oak rafters of the ceiling; Venizelos was gazing at a map of France dotted with red squares showing the location of prehistoric places in the battle zone of France, in which cave-men had dwelt; Orlando was busy writing; the Serbian, Jugo-Slavic and the Czecho-Slovakian plenipotentiaries seemed fascinated like children in watching the scene and reflecting that in a few minutes their former masters, now the beaten Austrians, would be coming in to learn their tragic fate.

Dr. Renner led his colleagues into the room and took the middle chair. All the Allied delegates, at a signal from Clémenceau, stood in recognition of their presence. Then the French Premier, addressing them as representatives of the "Austrian Republic," spoke for not more than two minutes.[11] Dr. Renner delivered his response in French, and emphasized in the beginning that he and his colleagues represented a republic; that the ancient Hapsburg monarchy had ceased to exist on November 1, 1918; that from its ruins new nations had come, one of which he represented. "We are before you," he said, "as one of the parts of the vanquished empire."

Austria, by the treaty, was required to recognize the independence of Hungary, Czecho-Slovakia, and the Serbo-Croate-Slovene State, besides ceding other territories which, previously in union with her, composed the dual monarchy of Austria-Hungary with its population of more than 50,000,000. Austria agreed to accept the League of Nations covenant and the labor charter, to renounce all her extra-European rights, demobilize her naval and aerial forces, admit the right of trial by the Allied and Associated Powers of her nationals guilty of violating the laws and customs of war, and accept certain detailed provisions similar to those of the German treaty as to economic relations and freedom of transit.

Few events in history have had the dramatic significance of that scene at St. Germain. The Austrian delegates had come as representatives, not of a great power famous in history, but as one of the smallest of nations. When Dr. Karl Renner stood in that assembly, he spoke on behalf of only seven million people addressing the representatives of several hundred million; and among the people to whose mercy he appealed were the Serbians. Thus began the last act of the play on which the curtain had risen five years before, when the name Austria was commonly used to designate one of the most powerful and most arrogant empires in the world. It was Austria that found in the murder of the heir to her throne a pretext to crush her small neighbor Serbia; and, as if to increase the terror which her aggression had produced, she brought to bear upon those who would oppose her the military might of a powerful neighbor, the German Empire. Like many another criminal, she had become the dupe of her own intrigue.

There was something in Austria, however, that saved her from the opprobrium and contempt from which Germany suffered. There was something in her delegates of suavity and humaneness, which had always distinguished Austrians from their northern German cousins, and had made them, even when arrogant and intriguing, likable. Austria had played the part of bandit more than once, but she had

[11] Paris dispatch from Charles A. Seldon to The *Times* (New York).

not been a thug, like Prussia. It was characteristic of Germans that when Count Brockdorff-Rantzau replied, he remained seated, but the Austrian spokesman, Dr. Renner, stood as Clémenceau had done. It was a small thing, but a sure indication of the difference between the Prussian and the Austrian.[12]

The new Austria was smaller than her Czecho-Slovak and Jugo-Slav neighbors, and could offer no menace to them, still less to Italy, if left to do it alone. French opposition to any union of Austria with Germany—provided for in the treaty—probably had controlled the conference in making that provision. Care was taken that German Austria should have no army which could appear as a useful reinforcement to her neighbor in case of a new war. A clause in the German treaty obligated Germany to respect the independence of Austria as "inalienable, except by consent of the League of Nations." In this provision the way was left open for an ultimate reunion of Austria with the rest of the German States, if the Germans ever give any indications of having become trustworthy.

The Austrian Empire proper had at the beginning of the war an area of nearly 116,000 square miles, with a population of nearly 30,000,000. What now remained as Austria had an area of 32,000 square miles, with a population of not much more than seven millions. Of Austria's lost kingdoms, crownlands and provinces, Bohemia, Moravia and a portion of Silesia had become component parts of the Czech republic; Galicia and the greater part of Silesia had become Polish; nearly one-half of the Tyrol and all of Istria had been added to Italy; portions of Carinthia and Styria, with all of Bosnia-Herzegovina and Carniola, had gone to the Jugo-Slav kingdom; Bukowina to Roumania, and Dalmatia had been lost to Italy or Jugo-Slavia, or to both. The new Austria emerged as a State with an area slightly less than that of Portugal and much less than that of New York State, and with a population larger than Portugal's only by a million and a half. Not even the fate which awaited Hungary, through a reduction by about one-half her area and population, was as tragic as the judgment which had come on that ancient empire of Central Europe.

Left entirely to herself, the new Austria could hardly have survived. Even an area of 30,000-odd square miles overstated the resources of a country which was more than half mountain-land. A population of seven millions could not furnish the economic background for a city like Vienna with a population of more than two millions. Necessity therefore pointed in the near future to the restoration of economic bonds with some of the States with which Austria had formerly lived in political union. The terri-

[12] *The Outlook* and *The Literary Digest* (New York).

tories lost to Poland and Jugo-Slavia would be too closely assimilated to their new allegiance to make such an economic reunion feasible, but there still remained the new Czech State and reduced Hungary, both of whom still had need of Austria. Out of the ruins of the Hapsburg monarchy, therefore, the world might see emerge an economic group consisting of Austria, Czecho-Slovakia and Hungary, with an aggregate population of thirty millions. Beyond that was the further possibility of a Danubian Confederation comprising in addition Jugo-Slavia and Roumania, with an aggregate population surpassing that of the extinct Hapsburg monarchy. Upon such a confederation, at least in an economic sense, Entente opinion seemed inclined at the time to look with favor, as a means, for one thing, of weaning Austria away from a reunion with Germany toward which she might otherwise be compelled, but was forbidden to move by the terms of the treaty.[13]

Chancellor Karl Renner, head of the Austrian peace delegation, affixt his signature to the treaty on September 10th. His cheerful acceptance of it, after having frankly denounced it as impossible of acceptance, and the dignified good nature which he displayed throughout the ordeal, when he alone faced the Peace Conference and signed the document, excited the admiration of all the Allied delegates. A feeling of friendliness among Austria's former enemies was inspired by Dr. Renner's sportsmanlike conduct, and it augured well for Austria and was generally commented upon as giving assurance that Vienna, with its two millions of people, and four millions in the remaining parts of old Austria, which comprised the new Austrian Republic, might reasonably expect some amelioration of the treaty terms in the near future, if Austria should make an honest effort to live up to them. After the ceremony of signing was over, Dr. Renner, in the course of an interview, said:

"Austria can not hate. It always respects the man with whom it has to fight. We are the conquered. Yet, misfortune has given us liberty; freed us from the yoke of a dynasty whence for three generations no man of worth has sprung; freed us from bonds with nations which were never in understanding with us, nor with themselves."

The Council of Ten of the Peace Conference received the Turkish Peace Mission in the Clock Hall of the Quai d'Orsay on June 17. 1919. The Turkish delegates, headed by Damad Ferid Pasha, wore conventional morning clothes and fezes. The meeting, which was secret, lasted an hour. M. Clémenceau reminded the Turkish delegates that the audience had been granted at their request so that

[13] The *Evening Post* (New York).

they might state their case. He added that upon receipt of the Grand Vizier's memorandum the Council would make a reply. The enemy status of the mission was emphasized by its entering and departing through different doors from those used by the members of the Council. The conference was held only for the purpose of learning Turkey's position. The Grand Vizier pleaded that the Turkish people were not to blame for the war. He urged that the empire be permitted to remain intact in both Europe and Asia, and promised to submit a memorandum to the Council on Friday. He said his country had been committed through secret agreements with the former German Emperor, against the wishes of the Turkish people, by the Committee of Union and Progress. He added that a German admiral actually declared Turkey in a state of war. He exonerated the Sultan from all responsibility for the war and urged that he be permitted to remain in Constantinople, saying that Asia Minor had been reduced to a desert by the war.

For the third time a group of delegates, representing a people spotlessly innocent, appeared before the Peace Conference to maintain that wicked and unscrupulous persons had pushed them into the war when they were looking the other way. After the Germans and Austrians had come the Turks. Neither the Sultan nor his people had had anything to do with going to war; it was all due to a secret agreement between the Kaiser and the Committee of Union and Progress, supported by the naval guns of Admiral von Souchon. So the present Grand Vizier submitted an extraordinary appeal for mercy. It would be only fair to allow the Turkish Empire to remain intact—above all, to let the Sultan keep Constantinople, since "Asia Minor had been reduced to a desert by the war." It was true that the Russians had got into one corner of Asia Minor, and a few French and British troops had camped for a few weeks on the Asiatic side of the Dardanelles, but otherwise, no troops had been in Asia Minor, except Germans and Turks. The Turkish delegates did not explain who reduced Armenia to a desert; who massacred thousands of Greeks and deported hundreds of thousands more; nor, as yet, had they offered any plausible reason why the Turks did not awake to the enormity of the conspiracy between their leaders and the Germans until Allenby had annihilated their armies, and Germany was plainly falling to ruin. That Turkey's entry into the war was due to a conspiracy between Enver and his group and the Germans was true enough, but the conscience of the Turk did not seem to have been affronted by the plot. Instead it gave him a chance to indulge in his national sport of killing Christians. In reply to the Turkish petition, Premier Clémenceau, in a note to the Sultan's chief representative, said:

AUSTRIAN PEACE DELEGATES LEAVING THE
ST. GERMAIN CHÂTEAU

The head of the delegation, Chancellor Karl Renner, is walking in the center,
with two other delegates, each wearing a silk hat

"The Council is anxious not to enter into unnecessary controversy, or to inflict needless pain on your Excellency and the delegates who accompany you. It wishes well to the Turkish people and admires their excellent qualities. But it can not admit that among those qualities are to be counted capacity to rule over alien races. The experiment has been tried too long and too often for there to be the least doubt as to its result.

"There is no case to be found, either in Europe or Asia or Africa, in which the establishment of Turkish rule in any country has not been followed by a diminution of material prosperity and a fall in the level of culture. Nor is there any case to be found where the withdrawal of Turkish rule has not been followed by a growth in material prosperity and a rise in the level of culture. Neither among the Christians of Europe nor among the Moslems of Syria, Arabia, and Africa has the Turk done other than destroy wherever he has conquered. Never has he shown himself able to develop in peace what he has won by war. Not in this direction do his talents lie."

On May 11th, 1920, Tewfik Pasha and three associates received the Peace Treaty in the Clock Room of the Quai d'Orsay. The plenipotentiaries in costume would have been hard to distinguish from so many Frenchmen, but tho they displayed every evidence of dejection they accepted without outward emotion the document which was conceded in Paris "to contain more elements of trouble than does the German pact." The entire ceremony, including a short speech by Premier Millerand, blaming Turkey for prolonging the war, did not last more than a few moments.

By the terms of the Treaty provisions were made for the Dardanelles as well as the straits of the Sea of Marmora and of the Bosporus to be placed in control of an allied commission composed of Great Britain, France, Japan, Greece and Rumania. All of these waterways were to be open for free navigation both in time of peace and in time of war. If the United States so determined, she might become a member of the commission, tho it was evident that it would be difficult for her to do so without also becoming a member of the League of Nations, seeing that, in the event of hostile acts on the part of Turkey, no movement unless directed by the council of the League could be made against her.

It was also provided by the Treaty that Russia and Bulgaria, when they had been admitted to membership of the League of Nations, might become members of the commission of control. The Turks were to recognize the independence of Armenia, and all questions concerning the Turko-Armenia frontier, Erzerum, Trebizond, Van, and Bitlis, as well as Armenia's access to the sea, were to be submitted to the arbitration of the President of the United States. Constantinople, altho ostensibly remaining under the sovereignty of the Sultan, was to be occupied permanently by a small force of Allied troops, while the boundries of Mesopotamia, Palestine, and Syria were to be finally established by special commissions.

The Treaty was bitterly attacked by the French press. It was insisted that President Wilson's principles had been studiously avoided, and it was openly hinted that the agreement of France to many of its terms was only obtained because of her desire to secure the aid of Mr. Lloyd-George in pressing the terms of the German Treaty.[14]

Finally, after many protestations, the Turkish delegates signed the Treaty at Sèvres on August 10, 1920.

The Peace Treaty with Bulgaria was handed to the Bulgarian plenipotentiaries by the Supreme Council of the Conference on September 19, 1919, at the Foreign Office in Paris. In the terms the question of permitting Bulgaria to have an outlet on the sea through western Thrace was left for future determination by the Allied Governments. It was stipulated, however, that, whatever solution was adopted by the Allies, an "economic" outlet to the Ægean would be guaranteed to Bulgaria. The Powers reserved the right to return all or part of the territory in Thrace to Bulgaria, to transfer part of it to Greece, to incorporate the remainder with eastern Thrace, as an international State, or to make any other solution they chose of the Thracian question. The matter of permitting Bulgaria to have a pathway to the Ægean had been one of the grave questions that disturbed the serenity of the Peace Conference. President Wilson had urged this concession, contending that if an outlet to the sea was denied a foundation for future wars might be laid. If the Allies, in framing the treaty for Bulgaria, had thought only of the efforts and sacrifices which that little nation had imposed upon them in the war, the terms might well have been made of the harshest. Had Bulgaria remained on their side, or been neutral, the subjugation and ruin of Serbia in 1915 would not have occurred, and the tragic-comedy of Greece under Constantine would have been avoided. More than that, with Bulgaria standing aside, developments of the highest importance would have come in Turkey. Even Constantinople might have fallen, the Straits might have been opened, and Russia might not have been longer cut off from the fellowship of the western Allies.

To what extent Bulgaria made atonement for all this by her surrender, in September, 1918, thus giving evidence of the collapse of the Quadruple Alliance, it would be hard to say, altho she did not give up until the outcome of the war in France had virtually been decided. She did show the way, however, and on

[14] The *Sun and New York Herald.*

ethnic grounds she had strong claims to some portion of Thrace, and a denial of her rights would have left open the Balkan sore from which so much ill had come to Europe. Bulgaria had a heavy price to pay, in any case. She was to reduce her army to 20,000 men, surrender her warships and submarines, recognize the independence of Jugo-Slavia, cede western Thrace to the Allies for future determination, compensate Serbia for coal taken from her, modify her frontier at four points in favor of Serbia, and pay $450,000,000 in gold as reparation for damages, the payments to be extended over some thirty years.

WHERE THE AUSTRIAN DELEGATES STAYED AT
ST. GERMAIN-EN-LAYE

VII

THE PROLONGED CONTROVERSY IN AMERICA OVER THE
TREATY WITH GERMANY—THE PROPOSED ALLIANCE
WITH FRANCE—WILSON'S AND PERSHING'S GREAT
WELCOMES HOME—FAILURE OF THE UNITED
STATES SENATE TO RATIFY THE TREATY

February, 1919—May 27, 1920

A S IN December, 1918, there had been severe, and even acrimoni-
ous, criticism of the President for going to Paris as head of
the American delegation—this, however, had died quietly away
within a few weeks after he sailed, influenced in part, no doubt, by
his wonderful reception and the series of honors conferred upon him
in London, Paris, Rome, Milan, and Turin—so in February, 1919,
criticism flared up, and this time more severe than ever. The League
of Nations covenant had then been adopted by the Conference in
Paris and President Wilson had come home bringing it with him.
Leaders in criticism in the United States Senate were Senators
Lodge, Knox, Johnson, Poindexter, and Borah. The President, in
spite of it, had cabled inviting these and other Senators to dine
with him at the White House as soon as he arrived, the invitation
being accepted by all except Senator Borah, who, in speeches before
the President's arrival and afterward, in several parts of the country, took vigorous and impassioned ground against the League.
Within a few days after the President's dinner, Senator Lodge and
others spoke in the Senate against the League covenant, as adopted
by the Conference, and Senator Knox was quoted as saying he
would "strike out the enacting clause." The proposed arrangement,
said Senator Knox, "would divide the world into two great armed
camps," it would "breed wars," and it "would leave us bound and
helpless." Senator Lodge, who was soon to be the majority leader
in the Senate, condemned the League as a movement away from
George Washington "toward the other end of the line at which
stands the sinister figure of Trotzky, the champion of internationalism." Senator Lodge criticized also the phraseology of the
covenant and said there was serious danger that the nations signing
it "would quarrel about the meaning of the various articles before
a twelve-month had passed."

The criticism as summed up in the first few weeks, seemed to call
mainly for three modifications in the League covenant—first, guaran-

ties for the perpetuity of the Monroe Doctrine; second, declarations that would give the United States exclusive control over its own internal and domestic affairs; third, such limitations as would make it possible for the United States to withdraw from the League, in the event of this being necessary or desirable. Republican Senators to the number of thirty-seven, about this time, signed a round-robin in which they declared that the League covenant in the form in which it then stood should not be adopted by the United States, and called upon the Conference to conclude peace with Germany before giving further consideration to the League. This was thought to threaten final defeat of the League, since a two-thirds vote of the Senate was necessary for its ratification. Former President Taft, who soon afterward had been active in support of a League, appeared at the Metropolitan Opera House in New York on the platform with President Wilson, where besides giving his support to the League, he welcomed such constructive criticism as Senator Lodge and others had to offer. President Wilson sailed for France again the next day, and soon after arriving secured from the Conference certain modifications of the covenant that had been suggested in America, including the exemption of the Monroe Doctrine from being affected by it. It was afterward pointed out by *The Quarterly Review* of London that, so far as it was aware, the Monroe Doctrine had never before been recognized by any power except the United States, and that as recognition of it had now been obtained in the Treaty of Peace "the control of the United States over the new world was thereby assured."

© MOFFETT, CHICAGO.

FORMER PRESIDENT WILLIAM H. TAFT

While President Wilson had won in Paris a victory through the successful adoption of the League, his Republican opponents had now scored a success in the changes made. The President had been checked, but so had the embarrassing tactics of Senators been defeated. Notable at this time—indeed it had been notable from the beginning of the discussion of a League of Nations and so continued until the treaty was signed—was the active support of the League given in speeches in many parts of the country by former President

Taft. So cordial and free from partizanship was Taft's support that men thought more and more of him as the proper Republican candidate for President at the next election. What many sensible folk cared for most was the fact that a satisfactory and workable League had been agreed upon, and that a great endeavor to organize the world for peace had been crowned with success.

As to what had been the cause of the intense hostility to President Wilson that had seemed to increase ever since the Peace Conference began its sessions, many explanations were offered by psychologists and other observers wishing to be impartial. Probably a small group had opposed the League covenant, as supported by him, from little more than partizan motives, but a still larger group had sincerely distrusted it because they disliked the responsibilities and surrender of sovereignty which it might impose upon the United States. The great body of the American people believed in at least the principle of a League, and that a League was necessary in order to maintain international peace and justice. Of this body one-half probably supported the Paris plan because of the President; but the other half supported its principle in spite of him. It was from the latter large group, which included thousands of patriotic and intelligent citizens, that criticism and distrust mainly came. The underlying causes, as the *Outlook* saw them, were at least four in number. First, were the President's words and deeds during the period of our neutrality in 1915 and 1916, when he had been opposed to action which would have made the country better prepared for resisting Germany when war became inevitable, and had uttered such phrases as "Too proud to fight." This group did not, and could not, be neutral in thought; they did not believe that the aims of the belligerents on both sides were similar; they had a profound interest in and real convictions as to causes and responsibilities in the war; and, after the sinking of the *Lusitania,* were not "too proud to fight." While the President and his Administration had performed a great feat in organizing and transporting an army of two million men to Europe, some of the failures of the Administration at home were thought to have been lamentable, if not inexcusable, owing to the President's refusal, either to accept criticism or to associate with himself men of the highest efficiency and governmental skill. His "Too Proud to Fight" speech was perhaps the most criticized of all his utterances, but his real meaning in the speech was sometimes, and in fact, immediately after its delivery, universally, distorted. He did not say directly that this country was too proud to fight. What he did say was this—in a speech on March 10, 1915, made three days after the *Lusitania* was sunk, to a group of newly naturalized citizens in Philadelphia:

"There is such a thing as a man being too proud to fight. There is such a thing as a nation being so right that it does not need to convince others by force that it is right."

Before he went to France, moreover, that is in November, 1918, the President, in an appeal unprecedented in the history of the country, had assumed to ask Americans to vote the Democratic ticket, the result being that the country not only resented the request, but elected a Republican Congress. If this had happened in England, Lloyd George would have ceased automatically to be Prime Minister; but our system of government was such that the President remained our Chief Executive for his elected term, even after the country had registered its disapproval of him. At the Paris conference before he came home the first time President Wilson had set himself against criticism of details and proposals for amendments of the plan for a League and had done it in such a manner as to rouse resentment in the Senate, which, under our Constitution, is a part of the treaty-making power; that is, the Senate must ratify a treaty, altho it does not participate in negotiating one. The President had cabled from Paris, before he returned for his February visit, requesting Congress to refrain from discussion of the League and it was then supposed that he would discuss it himself when he arrived, but he did not do so, except in general terms, and did not relieve the natural anxiety of many people and of Senators and Representatives by dissipating, as many thought he might have done, the validity of criticisms that had been publicly made of certain details of the plan. Not only did he decline to take the Senate into his confidence, but pursued a policy and adopted methods which seemed to indicate lack of confidence in, if not respect for, the power and judgment of the Senate. So that, in addition to some party feeling and considerably more honest patriotism in criticism, we had, at least in the Senate, wounded pride as a cause of criticism, and no differences are deeper than those into which wounded pride enters.

When afterward the terms of the Peace Treaty were made publicly known, in an abstract given out by the Conference, including the modifications made in response to American criticism, the resentment did not cease. In fact, it was further increased when true and complete copies of the treaty, a document of more than 70,000 words, were known to have been received in New York, and to be in possession of New York bankers, while no one in the Senate had been furnished with a copy. An investigation was called for and witnesses were summoned, among them former Senator Root, who disclosed to the Senate the fact that a copy had been in his possession in New York, as received from Mr. Henry P. Davison of the house of J. P. Morgan and Company, Mr. Davison having received it from his partner, Thomas W. Lamont, who was attached to the American delegation to the Paris Conference in an advisory capacity on economics, while Mr. Davison had been at the head of the Red Cross in Europe. Mr. Lamont had passed this copy on to Mr. Davison, Mr. Davison in turn had passed it on to Mr. Root, and Mr. Root had shown it to Senator Lodge. When asked if it had not been the duty of President Wilson to keep the Senate informed as to negotiations taking place at the Conference, Mr. Root replied that it had not. He thought, however, that it would have been better had Mr. Wilson furnished the Senate with information from time to time. Mr. Root also wrote a letter setting forth what he thought the Senate ought to do with the treaty and the League. It was too late, he said, to separate one from the other, but he thought a ratification of the treaty by the Senate should include certain reservations. There was in the covenant "a great deal of very high value, which the world ought not to lose," but he was disappointed that nothing had been done to provide for "strengthening a system of arbitration, or judicial decisions upon questions of legal right." In addition, he complained that nothing had been done "toward providing for the revision or development of international law."

As a sort of climax to the spirit of criticism, which continued with the same intensity after Germany had signed the treaty, there was introduced in the United States Senate in May, by Senator Knox of Pennsylvania, a resolution to divorce the League of Nations covenant from the Peace Treaty, but even in Republican quarters this movement fell far short of unanimous and enthusiastic approbation. The Senators who organized this attack upon the League "will find that they have wholly misjudged the temper of the American people," declared the Republican Los Angeles *Times,* which proclaimed its conviction that "if the covenant were submitted to a national referendum it would carry by a three-to-one vote," and direct Republican opposition "would be tantamount to party suicide." "If Senators Lodge, Borah, and Knox and their handful of rabid anti-Wilson allies on the other side of the Chamber imagine for a moment that they are laying sound foundations for an appeal to the country they are going to have an unpleasant awakening," said the Independent Republican Philadelphia *Public Ledger.* The same paper deplored "the mischief" these Senators were doing and "the obstacles they were deliberately creating to the work of the Peace Conference." Even the New York *Tribune,* a leading Republican paper, which had been a frank and persistent critic of the League covenant and which believed that the covenant and the peace treaty should not have been combined in the first place, doubted the value of the Knox resolution, and suggested instead ratification of the treaty "with reservations." Other newspapers, some of them Republican, approved of the resolution, but with reservations—a few without them.

Senator Borah had declared that if the League were submitted to a referendum vote—as he knew that it could not be—it would be voted down, but Chairman Cummings, of the Democratic National Committee, exprest a belief that between 80 and 90 per cent. of the people were heartily in favor of it. Many tests of public sentiment had been made and they all pointed one way—in favor of making an honest and thorough trial of the League. All business men's associations that had gone on record had been in favor of it and so had labor organizations; every labor organization that had taken action at all had endorsed it. The same was true of churches. Formal resolutions in support of the League had been adopted by the Presbyterian General Assembly, by the Methodists, the Baptists, and the Unitarians. Every church organization that had exprest itself on the subject had at this time exprest itself in favor of it.

There was no doubt, however, that Mr. Wilson while in Europe had suffered in his own country some loss of former prestige; this as a loss was partly personal and partly political. The high repute in which his authority was held at the signing of the armistice had been grievously diminished, and while this might not be wholly his fault, the fact was undeniable. A slight reaction in his favor came in May and June by the excess of abuse that was indulged in in the Senate, but it remained true that in coming home he had to face the fact that he had lost something of his former hold upon his fellow-citizens. People felt that he had been too headstrong, too intolerant, too oracular; they thought him secretive, out of touch with the trend of popular feeling and of Congressional temper, and this at a time when a policy of good understandings and of conciliation had been obvious wisdom.

The voices of Republican newspapers, however, especially in the West, by July were beginning to rise in more anxious protest than before, against all attempt to commit the Republican party to a policy of opposition to the League. Many people recognized that Mr. Wilson had labored whole-heartedly and unselfishly to make America a potent influence for good and the world safe from war. Controversy over his work had arisen largely through misunderstandings, deepened it might be by more than a trace of partizan feeling. It was, therefore, gratifying to learn that the President, on arriving home again on July 9, was at once to hold a conference with the Senate and that the Senate had decided to hold the conference in open session. The President had not been bound by constitutional precept, or by precedent, to consult with the Senate during the earlier stages of the negotiations in France; nor was he bound at all until the treaty had been signed. But had he consulted the Senate as if he were bound, it would have been an act of manifest wisdom. In that way he might have spared himself much embarrassment and the country a great part, if not all, of the division in counsel which had arisen. In Washington Mr. Wilson was President of the United States. At Paris and Versailles he was practically our Prime Minister and as such it was his first duty to see to it that his majority in Congress was secure. It made no vital difference to Mr. Wilson as President that he had lost his majority at the November elections in 1918; but this loss had made a great deal of difference to him in the performance of his ministerial duties in Paris. Many held that he would have been well advised had he taken into his confidence some of the leading members of the Senate, Republican and Democratic alike, before his first departure for Paris, and it would have been well, also, had he renewed that interchange of views from time to time as the negotiations proceeded. But that was not Mr. Wilson's way. As he once said of himself, he had "a single-track mind," or, as an old saying might have put it, he "could not trot in double harness."

When Mr. Wilson arrived in New York on July 8, he was welcomed as no home-coming American had ever before been welcomed to these shores. All New York and many representatives of other communities went forth on land and water to greet him, bands playing, flags flying, and cannon roaring in deafening salutes from harbor forts and warships. Sirens, bells, and steam-whistles all along the waterfront added to the din, making one long, continuous outburst of welcome all the way from the entrance to the harbor at Ambrose Channel to Hoboken, where the President and his party landed. He had received at sea a naval welcome. An escort of five great dreadnoughts and forty of the finest destroyers of the Atlantic fleet escorted his ship, the *George Washington,* into home waters. Twenty miles beyond Sandy Hook the dreadnoughts fired the Presidential salute of twenty-one guns, while above circled a squadron of ten seaplanes from the Rockaway Naval Air Station, later joined by an American "blimp," which sailed along just above the mast-tips of the *George Washington* for more than ten miles. The whole made a marine picture which for impressiveness was rivaled only by the home-coming of the American dreadnoughts that had served in the Grand Fleet under Rodman and Beatty, and the great spectacle of 1916, when the entire Atlantic fleet, as then organized, had assembled for Presidential review in the Hudson.

Escorted up Fifth Avenue on a perfect summer afternoon, President Wilson was greeted by great throngs all the way. At Carnegie Hall he made a brief and unprepared speech, in closing which he said "when the long reckoning comes men may look back upon this generation of America and say: 'They were true to the vision which they saw at their birth.'" He reached Washington just before midnight and had a wonderful reception there at that hour. More than 10,000 persons had assembled on the plaza in front of the station. As he rode through the crowd in his automobile there was great cheering all around him. Never in recent years had any other President received such a welcome and especially at so late an hour. Not only were the crowds greater, they were more demonstrative in their greeting, and there was no mistaking the sincerity of their cheers. Altogether this reception in his own country recalled those which Europe had given to the President in December, or those which we, in May and June, 1917, gave to Balfour, Viviani and Joffre.

Soon after this, the President transmitted to the Senate a proposed special treaty with France by which the United States agreed for a limited period to assist in defending France against German aggression should it be found necessary. The President urged its ratification not alone on the ground of our historic obligations to France, but because of special conditions in Europe which would continue until the organization of the League of Nations had been completed. It was an arrangement he said, "not independent of the League of Nations, but under it." Announcing that Great Britain had volunteered the same promise to France, he interpreted the agreement as follows:

"Two Governments, who wish to be members of the League of Nations, ask leave of the Council of the League to be permitted to go to the assistance of a friend whose situation has been found to be one of peculiar peril without awaiting the advice of the League to act."

This arrangement with France was based on the main Treaty of Peace, and was designed as a supplement to it. Its chief purpose was to "assure immediately to France appropriate security and protection." France, it was maintained, had been unable to free herself of her historic dread of Germany. Thousands of living Frenchmen had twice seen their land ravaged by invading German hosts, until fear of Germany had entered into the blood of two generations who had lived under that fear and who, even now in victory, were haunted by it until they felt deeply the necessity of freeing coming generations from a new, prolonged and acute apprehension. The proposed treaty was described as esentially "a work of superabundant precaution," which would relieve France of her historic and justified fears. Doubtless this supplementary treaty had been an added inducement to the French delegates to agree to the covenant of the League of Nations, which they believed might otherwise prove inadequate to give them the swift and certain protection they desired.

Knowing of the existence of such a treaty, Germany it was believed, would not dream of attacking France again. In fact, if the Kaiser and his Chancellor had been certain in July, 1914, that England would have gone to the help of France they would not have forced the war. President Wilson had not publicly committed himself to do anything more with this treaty than to "submit" it to the Senate. In his message submitting it to the Senate the President said:

"We are bound to France by ties of friendship which we have always regarded, and shall always regard, as peculiarly sacred. She assisted us to win our freedom as a nation. It is seriously to be doubted whether we could have won it without her gallant and timely aid. We have recently had the privilege of assisting in driving enemies, who were also enemies of the world, from her soil, but that does not pay our debt to her. Nothing can pay such a debt. She now desires that we should promise to lend our great force to keep her safe against the Power she has had most reason to fear."

The instrument assured to France adequate protection against any aggression from Germany during "the years immediately ahead of us"—in other words, not permanently. It was provided in Article III that the treaty should continue in force "until, on the application of one of the parties to it, the Council (of the League of Nations), acting if need be by a majority, agrees that the League itself affords sufficient protection." Until the League could be fully established and in position to make good its guaranties, France asked that she be relieved of the burden and the anxiety of organizing and maintaining a state of defense against danger on her eastern frontier. Upon her had fallen the chief burden, the greatest waste and losses of the war. Our interest in the guaranty was not altogether one of sentiment, for a fresh assault upon France would have again endangered the peace of the world and our own peace as well.

France had lost 1,500,000 men in the war, her wounded numbered 2,800,000, and some 1,700,000 Frenchmen were still "subnormal." She had suffered from a high death-rate among the civilian population in invaded districts and her birth-rate, already discouragingly low when the war began, fell further while the war was going on. In spite of the restoration to her of the people of Alsace-Lorraine, the diminution in her population had been almost 3,000,000. At the same time the Germans had ruined her industrial establishments in the north and east; her plants and railways had been worn to the utmost; in ten departments agriculture had been practically destroyed. Before the war France grew 33 per cent. more wheat than she required at home. Now she was growing 4,000,000 tons less than she needed for domestic consumption; grew, in fact, only about one-half of what she needed. In 1914 the French debt was 34,000,-000,000 francs; April 30, 1919, it was 180,000,000,000 francs. Deducting advances to her allies, her debt was some 175,000,000,000. Such damage reparation payments as were to be made by Germany would come to her for some years only in driblets altho ultimately she would receive a great sum yet to be estimated in its totality. Since the armistice was signed, resilient, thrifty, indomitable France had nobly begun her work of recovery. Some 60,000 of the 550,-000 houses wrecked by shellfire had been rebuilt; nearly two-thirds of the railway mileage destroyed had been repaired; nearly half of the canal mileage made useless by the Germans had been restored; and of 1,160 destroyed plants, 588 had been put into operation again. Of the devasted region of 4,500,000 acres, about 1,000,000 acres had been given back to the farmers and 500,000 were ready to plant, more than 6,000 miles of barbed wire having been removed from them. All this was not due merely to the fruitful activity of experts and the Government, but to the French peasant who had been getting his wood and stone, building up room by room a new house, going to work even more steadily and passionately than before on the fields he loved.[15]

From correspondence published late in July it became apparent that former President Taft and Charles E. Hughes were seeking in common a basis upon which Republican members of the Senate could vote for a prompt ratification of the treaty with Germany and the covenant. Mr. Taft recognized the political situation in the Senate by attributing much of the opposition to the treaty to the "very serious mistakes of policy committed by Mr. Wilson," and in particular the partizan character of his Administration, his appeal for support on partizan grounds, and his emphasis on partizan and personal elements in negotiating the treaty, but Mr. Taft reiterated that he was nevertheless "strongly in favor of ratifying the treaty as it is." He believed that any defects in the structure of the League could be remedied by amendment after the plan had been put into operation, but suggested certain reservations in the hope that they might satisfy "the genuine objections of the Republican friends of the League." His proposed reservations allowed the United States to withdraw unconditionally at the end of ten years; made it impossible for self-governing colonies, or dominions, to be represented on the Council of the League at the same time with the mother country; left each nation free to decide declarations of war in accordance with its own constitutional procedure; stated that subjects like immigration and the tariff were domestic questions, not to be controlled by the League; and reserved the Monroe Doctrine to be

[15] The *Times* (New York).

administered by the United States. Mr. Hughes believed certain reservations could be made which would not impair the covenant and therefore should not be objected to by the other contracting parties. Mr. Taft did not believe that reservations were necessary, but, as they were unobjectionable, he had proposed them as a means of compromise to secure ratification. Mr. Hughes, however, regarded reservations as necessary, in order that in establishing the League "we should not make a false start."

On August 12 Senator Lodge made a carefully prepared speech on the floor of the Senate in which he pointed out what he believed to be the dangers to this country of adopting the covenant. It was assumed that Senator Lodge would vote for the ratification of the treaty, including the League plan, provided reservations like those which he proposed were adopted, but it was apparent that he accepted the possibility of reservations only as a compromise, and that if the possible failure of the Peace Treaty were not involved, he would prefer to reject completely the League of Nations. Mr. Lodge's fundamental objection to the League was that it involved a hard and fast alliance with European nations and that in that respect it was an analogy to the Holy Alliance of the early part of the last century, which was "hostile and dangerous to human freedom." Mr. Lodge concluded his eloquent address with an appeal for vigorous nationalism:

"You may call me selfish, if you will, conservative or reactionary, or use any other harsh adjective you see fit to apply, but an American I was born, an American I have remained all my life. I can never be anything else but an American, and I must think of the United States first, and when I think of the United States first in an arrangement like this I am thinking of what is best for the world, for if the United States fails the best hopes of mankind fail with it. I have never had but one allegiance—I can not divide it now. I have loved but one flag, and I can not share that devotion and give affection to the mongrel banner invented for a league. Internationalism, illustrated by the Bolshevik, and by the men to whom all countries are alike, provided they can make money out of them, is to me repulsive. National I must remain, and in that way, I, like all other Americans, can render the amplest service to the world."

The Senate's moral obligation speedily to ratify the Peace Treaty, including the League covenant, was emphasized in a notable statement on August 19 made by President Wilson at the White House to the Senate Committee on Foreign Relations. The statement was looked upon as being made as much to the general public as to the Senators present, the entire interview being staged with a view to the completest publicity. Everything that the President felt able to tell the Senators became next day the property of all readers of newspapers. Mr. Wilson's formal statement emphasized the moral duty of speedy ratification, while his answers to questions put by Senators were full of references to our moral obligations under the League covenant. He gave specific examples of industries suffering because of the prolonged uncertainty about peace. He spoke of the copper-mines of Montana, Arizona and Alaska being kept open "only at a great cost and loss"; of the zinc-mines of Missouri, Tennessee, and Wisconsin "being operated at about one-half their capacity"; of the lead of Idaho, Illinois, and Missouri reaching "only a portion of its former market"; of the "immediate need for cotton-belting and also for lubricating oil which can not be met, all because the channels of trade are barred by war when there is no war." The same condition existed regarding raw cotton. In fact, "there is hardly a single raw material, a single important foodstuff, a single class of manufactured goods which is not in the same class." Our full, normal, profitable production was waiting upon peace. Mr. Wilson continued:

"Our military plans, of course, wait upon it. We can not intelligently or wisely decide how large a naval or military force we shall maintain, or what our policy with regard to military training is to be until we have peace not only, but also till we know how peace is to be sustained, whether by the arms of single nations or by the concert of all the great peoples. And there is more than that difficulty involved. The vast surplus properties of the Army include, not food and clothing merely, whose sale will affect normal production, but great manufacturing establishments also which should be restored to their former uses, great stores of machine tools, and all sorts of merchandise which must lie idle until peace and military policy are definitely determined. By the same token, there can be no properly studied national budget until then."

Two days later, in response to a question which had been submitted to him by a Senator, President Wilson said, with all the emphasis of which he was capable, that the consummation of peace depended solely upon the Senate's action. He believed that he himself had no power to declare the existence of peace by a proclamation, nor would he under any circumstances issue such a proclamation. His conversation with Senators in the East Room of the White House had lasted more than three hours.

What a Paris journal called "the first break in the Peace Treaty," occurred over what was known as the Shantung provision, which the Senate Foreign Relations Committee decided to amend by substituting "China" for "Japan" in the paragraph disposing of the German privileges in the Shantung province. This decision was the first of a series of amendments which were being planned by the Committee to be submitted to a vote of the Senate. On October 16, by a vote of 55 to 35 the Lodge amendments to the Treaty, providing for restoring Germany's former economic privileges on the Shantung Peninsula to China rather than to Japan, as the Treaty had provided, were defeated in the Senate. The expected had happened to a proposed action that would have something in which the other many Powers who had signed the Treaty could not have acquiesced. Few Americans at any time had fully approved of the arrangement made in the Treaty, but the method proposed in the Senate was not generally regarded as one by which the situation could have been improved. Defeat for the amendment had long been foreseen. It was what the great majority of the country had demanded. The vote gave a clear indication that other attempts to make material changes in the treaty would meet the same fate. The nation had for weeks wanted the matter of ratification disposed of as soon as possible. Article X, however, was the heart of the controversy in Washington. By the beginning of September it was the point toward which the battle, after beginning on a far-flung front, had steadily narrowed down. As one side or the other yielded on essential issues involved in this article, victory seemed to incline. Article X provided that the League should undertake to protect each and all of the members against wars of conquest and aggression.

The battle seemed to many observers to have been waged, not so much for the safeguarding of American interests, as for safeguarding the *amour propre* of the Senate majority. For this the President had supplied the provocation when he omitted to give adequate representation in the peace work at Paris to the Senate majority and to the Republican party. By that action he had seriously offended personal susceptibilities and so had aroused partizan anxiety. Republicans saw that the record of their party might suffer, both in the immediate and the more distant future, if it should appear that they had had no share in shaping the terms of the treaty. Hence their insistence on amendments and reservations for acceptance by the other Powers, so that the record would stand that the Peace Conference had been compelled to recognize the power of the Senate majority. The Republican party would then have had a share in making peace. On September 10th the treaty as submitted to the Senate by President Wilson on July 10th was reported to the Senate from the Foreign Relations Committee with thirty-eight amendments and four reservations as proposed by the majority of the committee. Senator Lodge expected the treaty to be under debate for at least five weeks.

Contemporary with the report of the treaty to the Senate was the home-coming of General John J. Pershing. There are some occasions which can be compared to no others, in ancient history or in modern, and the arrival in New York, on September 8th, of the Commander-in-Chief of the American Expeditionary Forces, was one of them. No other American Commander-in-Chief had ever before come home after leading troops to victory on battlefields in Europe, and the fine, full ceremonies were events without precedent. There seemed some excuse, in fact, for that impulsive woman who broke the closely guarded ranks of tip-toeing watchers in City Hall Park and planted one firm kiss upon the conquering General's sun-browned cheek as he was stepping forward toward Mayor Hylan for his greetings. Pershing was going the way all heroes go on arriving in New York—up the City Hall steps—but never had just this kind of hero gone that way before or been received in that way. The General only shrugged a shoulder at the so truly personal tribute.

Pershing took his home-coming simply and quietly, altho it was plain to see that he was moved and had deep joy at being home again. Only once did he seem really perturbed. That was when Warren, his thirteen-year-old son, to whom he had entrusted his commission as full General, got lost in the crowd around City Hall Park and Pershing looked around in sudden dismay. When he spied his son again he was heard to call out, "Have you got that commission? Well—hang on to it!" Never had a General of the United States Army been created under more impressive circumstances. Secretary Baker, when Pershing reached the foot of the gang-plank, stood ready with the commission as authorized by Congress. He held it in his hand in welcoming Pershing, and after greetings in behalf of President Wilson presented it in the President's name. The General turned it over immediately to Warren, who had been the first to break the news to him of his elevation to full generalship, waking him that morning in order to give him a wireless message. Pershing was the fourth of our army men to be made a full general, the others being Grant, Sherman, and Sheridan.

Pershing's arrival signalized and symbolized the end of an epic in American adventure. Of the two million of armed men whom we had sent across the seas, only an inconsiderable number remained waiting in France for homeward ships; a still smaller fraction were in permanent quarters on the Rhine. The country had seen men of the drafted National Army, men of the National Guard, and men of the Regular Army come home ship-load after ship-load, and had seen great parades in great cities in honor of them. Now it welcomed the leader who, in May, 1917, had set sail for Europe with a mere corporal's guard. Pershing returned in the anniversary week of the battle of St. Mihiel and came on the *Leviathan*, once the Hamburg-American ship *Vaterland*. The conjunction vividly recalled the nature and history of our effort in a great cause.

Our battle history, except for a few preliminary experiences in Lorraine and at Cantigny, extended only from June 1, 1918, when we challenged the Germans around Château-Thierry, to November 11, or fewer than five and a half months. In a war of fifty-one and a half months this seemed only an episode, or a "splendid fragment," as the London *Times* called it, but it brought the climax and decision of the war. Concerning that there was no longer any notable difference of opinion. The few doubters could be referred to Ludendorff's own memoirs then in course of publication. Our armies, however, had had the benefit of nearly three years of Allied error and education and thus our effort came into play with a minimum of wastage. Our difficulty was the fact of our fresh and enormous strength. At the end of the war we were fully equal in battle strength to France or Great Britain. The temptation to start in and show Foch and Haig how to win the war might have presented itself to a commander-in-chief less sane than Pershing, who had behind him a virtually limitless store of men and boundless material resources. That temptation either never asserted itself, or was loyally overcome by Pershing. Legend, to be sure, spoke of how he had gone to Foch and protested violently against a continuance of the latter's Fabian policy, but against that picturesque incident we had Foch's moving acknowledgment of how Pershing went to him in the darkest moment of the campaign of 1918 and put the American Army and resources into his hands—in fact, "all that we have." With this offer probably came an intimation from Pershing that perhaps the American divisions were readier for use than Foch had thought. In any case, the lesson of Cantigny and Château-Thierry was not lost on Foch.

It was a smiling Pershing who leaned far out over a bandstand and railing and threw kisses into the rapturous faces of school-girls who, on September 8, after the formalities at the City Hall, gathered to welcome him in Central Park. The stern disciplinarian, the reticent commander of armies, seemed to have quite vanished before the waving of fifty thousand tiny American flags and the lusty cheers that came from leather-lunged schoolboys. Pershing for five minutes became a laughing, hat-swinging, hand-waving hero, just the kind of hero youngsters remember with a warm glow in their hearts for the rest of their lives. Pershing listened to a chorus of children producing a mingled accent of Italian, Russian,

Polish, Irish and all other nationalities that had sent their children to be trained in American citizenship in our schools. As he listened his lips tightened and his eyes grew soft, and he bent over and kissed the flag which stood beside him.

The more formal Victory Parade in Pershing's honor, on September 10, when the First Division with full equipment was led by him down Fifth Avenue, was the climax of processional shows celebrating the achievements of the American Army in France. There would be other parades in which Pershing would take part— welcomes to him soon followed in Philadelphia and Washington— but there would be no parade to match this one, because Pershing had then landed straight from the scene of his successes, with laurels fresh upon him, and the division that he led was his favorite division, of whose record in the war he was exceedingly proud. New York saw in this welcome the last chapter in its history of great military spectacles growing out of the war.

Altogether, more than 25,000 fighting men were in line. It was a vast throng that turned out, many deep, from 107th Street south to Washington Square. The applause was continuous, hearty and manifestly genuine. Here and there the chimes of church bells put an edge of sweetness on the shouting. Bells less musical, wooden "crickets," and improvised instruments of discord, converted the plaudits into a great popular demonstration. Now and then, from great office buildings, showers of confetti, long trailing paper streamers and clouds of paper snow helped forward the general gaiety. A group of army airplanes came to Manhattan as a special aerial escort, and flew low over the park and up and down the avenue, at times disappearing from the ken of watchers, only to come roaring back again over their heads. The whole route was gay and colorful with flags and bunting.

Most picturesque of all was the way in which Pershing, members of his staff, officers and men of lesser rank and the long line of marchers, were pelted with flowers. At times Pershing rode and men marched over stretches of asphalt carpeted with laurel. At others, roses and simpler flowers rained down about Pershing and were marched over by his men. Some enthusiast, high above Pershing, would toss down a single blossom at him; perhaps to fall almost at his feet, perhaps to drop far behind him. Even where crowds were least dense, Pershing was kept at almost continual salute by tributes volleyed from both sides of the avenue. His 23,000 men in line were cheered by 1,600,000, or perhaps 2,000,000, spectators in a four-hour parade. Cardinal Mercier of Belgium, who had just landed in New York, viewed the parade from a seat in front of a Knights of Columbus stand at St. Patrick's Cathedral at Fifth Avenue and Fifty-first Street. When Pershing reached the Cathedral he dismounted from his horse to shake hands with the famous Belgian priest. More than 1,600 guests gathered that night at the Waldorf for a dinner given in honor of Pershing. The guests crowded the big main ballroom, overflowed into the Astor Galleries, the Myrtle Room, the Waldorf Apartments, and the Rose Room, and even filled the Green Room and main foyer. So great was the throng that the hotel management had to detail large numbers of men to guide guests to proper places.

General Pershing, in receiving in person the thanks of Congress a few days later, presented a manly and attractive figure, seemingly unconscious of the eminence he had won as a soldier. His manner was so simple that it should have disarmed any critics who affected to see in him a champion of militarism. With his work well done in the field, he seemed now an average American in his point of view; a man of the people, and as much a democrat as Champ Clark who in a speech claimed him as a sample of the "sort of man Missouri grows when in her most prodigal moods."

© PAUL THOMPSON.

PART OF A COLORED REGIMENT BACK FROM FRANCE

These men were of the former Fifteenth New York, and are shown aboard ship on their return home in February, 1919. In September, 1918, this regiment captured 250 machine-guns and 400 prisoners

Pershing's genial good nature and sense of humor came to the surface when he stood there the cynosure of all eyes at a joint session of Congress, the galleries crowded. The remarks he made, while they had a certain eloquence because of their sincerity, were generous in giving credit to Americans of all classes and conditions who had played their part in the war, at home as well as "over there." In what he said of the army he had led there was a touching spirit of affection and loyalty. Vainglory and boastfulness were foreign to this stalwart soldier. It had no doubt been an ordeal greater than a battle for Pershing, while standing before Congress, to hear his praises sounded and afterward to express his thanks, but the occasion resulted in another victory for him.[16]

Cardinal Mercier was formally welcomed to New York on September 17th. After a day spent in receiving an almost continuous ovation from the public, he stood at night in the grand ballroom of the Waldorf Hotel with head bowed and hands clasped as tho in prayer, his shoulders draped with an American flag, while from 700 men and women of different creeds he received one of the most remarkable demonstrations ever accorded to a guest in that room. Representatives of the Catholic, Protestant and of other faiths were there, one in their desire to express their appreciation of his heroism. Later, in other cities enthusiastic welcomes were accorded him. Universities in several states conferred degrees on him; in fact, every possible honor was bestowed by the American people on the hero-priest, one of the outstanding figures of the war.

On October 4th, Albert, King of the Belgians, and Queen Elizabeth his wife arrived in New York. Laying aside their incognito and appearing as sovereigns, they became the guests of the city, and New York took them to its heart. The tribute began when the royal party in the morning, after making a cruise through the harbor stept ashore at the Battery, and reached its climax in the afternoon when 30,000 children gave them a great welcome in Central Park. It continued elsewhere as they were whirled in motors through avenues and side streets. After a day of unceasing receptions, and the King had learned of the seriousness of the President's condition, he announced that he would cancel all engagements for the next day, except those in Boston, and one on Monday, the 6th, in Buffalo, whence he would proceed to the Pacific Coast.

While the whole Entente world was waiting with ill-concealed impatience for the American ratification of the treaty, a League of Nations had actually been showing how it could operate, the Paris

16 The *Times* (New York).

Conference having intervened to bring about peace between Prague and Warsaw, that is, between Bohemia and Poland, and again had intervened to bring Roumania to her senses as to aggressions committed against coveted territory in Hungary. The disciplining process had taken some time but the essential thing was that the Peace Conference had been able to call Bucharest to order. In so doing Paris had virtually put the machinery of the League of Nations into motion. A truculent government, even if the government of an Allied people, had been warned that it must not endanger the uncompleted structure of peace.

Another example of what the League might do was shown when Gabriele D'Annunzio, the Italian poet, on September 15th, supported by a force of Arditti, went to Fiume and proclaimed a union of the city with Italy. Fiume thus became plunged into a state of anarchy. British and French troops left the city, lowering their flags at D'Annunzio's request. The touch of the swashbuckling days of long ago was what appealed most to American observers in this "conquest" of Fiume by D'Annunzio; this, rather than any possible political consequences that might follow upon so unauthorized a raid. At first news of the success of his coup D'Annunzio was variously classed with d'Artagnan, Coeur de Lion, and Garibaldi. Second thoughts made it evident to many that the exploit was a conclusive argument either for or against a League of Nations, as best suited the views of this or that person, revealing to some that the League had proved itself futile and to others that it was a necessity. D'Annunzio's personality and record as a patriot aroused very general sympathy. He had been aroused from a state of lethargy by the outbreak of the war and from the first had devoted himself whole-heartedly to bringing Italy into the conflict. Time and again he had led an air squadron in long raids over the Austrian base at Pola and over other Austrian cities, while during a terrible hand-to-hand struggle with the Austrians on the Carso, he had rushed among his comrades, inspiring them with fiery words. He had been wounded several times and once was reported dead.

There had been no real justification, however, for including Fiume, or any part of the Adriatic coast south of Fiume, within the boundries of the Italian Kingdom. Fiume, by situation and by all the circumstances of its development, was not an Italian, but an international port, serving countries to the east and north of the gulf of the same name and so it had been declared to be by the Peace Treaty. By the application of the principle of self-determination Fiume might be Italian provided the unit which should be allowed to decide its fate were regarded as simply the town and district of Fiume which, since 1868, had enjoyed autonomy under Budapest, and in which, according to the last census, there were 24,200 Italians and 15,600 Jugo-Slavs. But Fiume could not be separated (for international and economic, as distinct from purely administrative purposes) from its large Croat suburb of Sussak; and, if the two were treated as a whole, the 24,800 Italians would be found in a minority, against 27,000 Jugo-Slavs. Moreover, in order to establish a continuous land connection between Fiume and Italy, it would be necessary for the latter to annex at least 100,000 Slavs in excess of those who would fall to her under the treaty and, of course, incidentally to ignore self-determination for a Slav majority. With these facts before him President Wilson had insisted that Fiume should be an international part and could not with justice be subordinate to any one sovereignty.[17]

It was not necessary in the case of D'Annunzio to consider how much in his exploit was pure passion and how much a desire, unconscious perhaps, to supply a parallel to Garibaldi's conquest of Sicily on his own initiative in behalf of unredeemed Italy, because the parallel could be prolonged to his disadvantage, for, when Garibaldi, in 1862, with a volunteer army, marched on Rome, Victor Emanuel, fearful of foreign intervention, actually sent an Italian army against him and the old lion was defeated and taken prisoner. Patriotism, even in Garibaldi's case, had to be tamed. Premier Nitti by September 17th denounced D'Annunzio's *coup d'etat*, and the adoption of a firm policy in dealing with the situation was endorsed by King Victor Emmanuel who exprest a wish, however, that there be no bloodshed.

By September 19th D'Annunzio's army had increased to over 11,000, including 1,600 volunteers from Trieste, and Fiume was ablaze with flags, her streets filled with marching soldiers and her air vibrant with the confidence felt by men who, under the command of D'Annunzio, had marched into the city and were able firmly to hold it. Soldiers were to be seen everywhere. Motor-trucks lurched through the streets carrying armed men from one point to another, and hundreds of troops could be seen at any hour marching with the greatest precision and the strictest military discipline. To the detached observer, Italy had made great gains from the war. Her inveterate enemy, Austria-Hungary, to which, through fear, she had been bound by the Triple Alliance, had passed away, and her land boundries had been so arranged as to guarantee the almost absolute military security of Italy. The Adriatic had become virtually an Italian lake and practically all her *terra irredenta* had been recovered. But these gains appeared, to Italy, relatively small when compared with the territorial rewards of Great Britain

[17] The *Journal of Commerce* (New York).

and France. The Italians had not secured any great territorial gains; they were not to have a favored position in the division of the German indemnity, and they had no mandates in any of the former German colonies.

Fiume has a splendid harbor upon the development of which the Hungarian Government had spent millions. The docking facilities are of the most modern kind. Ships can tie up at the docks of Fiume and their cargoes can be stored in warehouses at terminals equal to those controlled by the Bush Terminal Company in Brooklyn. The city had every reason to look forward with confidence to a great commercial future. It is well built, with notable streets and some imposing public buildings. It has always been truly Italian in its atmosphere; its architecture is Italian; its mode of outdoor life has been such as one finds in Italy; most of its stores and banks are Italian, tho the best and largest before the war were kept by Austrian Jews, and most hotel-keepers and tradesmen spoke German. But it was absurd to attempt to separate Fiume from the neighboring Slavonic city, Sussak, for administrative purposes. The stream that divided them is scarcely wider than the Bronx river. A great number of the population of Sussak simply reside there and work in Fiume; Sussak bears the same relation to Fiume that Brooklyn bears to Manhattan. Surrounding hills hem in the two communities as a unit apart from the hinterland.[18]

D'Annunzio's dash was represented by some defenders of it as merely an idealistic demonstration of Italian brotherhood; that is, there was nothing imperialistic about it; no desire to entrench Italy militarily on the eastern shore of the Adriatic. It was just "a dramatic clasping of an Italian population to the heart of Italy." But if this were true as far as the seizure of Fiume was concerned, it obviously could not be true of the reported seizures by Italians of other towns that were unquestionably under Jugo-Slavic control, nor of incursions into Dalmatia and a threatened restoration to the throne of the King of Montenegro. The bad impression made on the outside world by these exploits was unmistakable. Italy obviously could not afford to place herself in the position of defying the authority of the Peace Conference, or of risking the bringing on of another war. It was clear, therefore, that eventually she would have to give heed to decisions come to in Paris. Italian brotherhood, and the unredeemed soil of Italy were stirring words with which to make an appeal, but they could not be utilized to camouflage grasping designs and a wanton attempt to hazard the peace of Europe.[19]

One of the Dalmatian towns involved in the incursion was

[18] Stephen P. Duggan in the *Times* (New York).
[19] The *Evening Post* (New York).

Trau, a seaport, inhabited partly by Italians and partly by Jugo-Slavs in a region which had belonged to Austria, but had been lost to her by the Peace Treaty, and which the Conference was expected to allot to Jugo-Slavia. Under the armistice terms, Entente forces had for months been patrolling the Adriatic, acting as trustees, until definite disposition could be made of Dalmatia. Trau happened to be in a neighborhood which was assigned to the American Navy for the maintenance of order. A group of Italians of the D'Annunzio faction having seized the town, Serbian troops from Spalato, Diocletian's old town, and only a few miles distant, which D'Annunzio had threatened to capture, had undertaken to 'drive the Italians out. If they had succeeded in doing this, a war which had been impending ever since the exploit at Fiume probably would have been precipitated. American sailors and marines were landed there. They persuaded the Italians to withdraw and induced the Serbs to return to Spalato, so that instead of making war the Americans averted it.[20]

By the end of September the Italian Chamber of Deputies, by a unanimous vote, passed a resolution demanding the annexation of Fiume, so that the Government at Rome in effect seemed to have indorsed D'Annunzio's enterprise. Italy's action thus brought the protracted dispute to a head. It was a dispute which had been active ever since President Wilson on April 23rd issued a statement opposing the assignment of Fiume to Italy. Orlando, at that time had quitted Paris and gone home to ask for a national mandate on the annexation question, which he got at once; but he failed to move the Council of Three in Paris and, because of this failure, his Cabinet fell and Nitti replaced him. Tittoni, the Foreign Minister, then without success took up the task of winning over the Council to a recognition of Italy's contention. As a sequel, D'Annunzio occupied Fiume with his Italian volunteers and so played Garibaldi's rôle in the Liberation period.[21]

Information reached Washington on October 10th that the Italian Government had agreed to the creation of a buffer state, comprising Fiume and the adjacent coastal territory southward to Breccia, as a solution of the Adriatic problem. The approval of the plan was conditional on the protection of Italian interests in the proposed state by the adoption of Italian methods of legal procedure, and the confirmation of Italy's title to the former district of Fiume in the interior and along the coast to the westward. This was regarded by the Italians as absolutely necessary, as a strategic measure to insure the safety of Pola and other Italian Adriatic cities. Probably no nation was more surprized than the

[20] The *Times* (New York).
[21] The *Tribune* (New York).

Italians themselves when D'Annunzio, in the course of the war, had displayed such military aptitude. His skill and heroism had made him one of the most popular figures among soldiers. Early in October he was showing ability in another field, that of diplomacy, as evidenced in a message to the Croats. His message, written in Croation, said:

"The Adriatic is a Latin sea, on which the Slavs have full right to a free economic outlet for their commerce. Italy is glad not only to concede, but to assure and protect with her military and civil forces, the liberty of such an outlet for all races in the hinterland. Therefore, Italians and Slavs have an urgent common interest to prevent other nations from controlling a sea which does not belong to them, thus disturbing prosperity and concord. Italy is resolved to defend her annexation of Fiume against any one, but at the same time is ready to assure you sincere and ample guaranties of free transit and the development of your commercial traffic through the port. Recognize the rights of Italy, so that Italy can recognize yours, and all misunderstandings will be dissipated. Long live Italian Fiume! Long live the Adriatic really free! Long live Italo-Slav peace, herald of common prosperity!"

Still another example of such work as a league might perform was given when the Supreme Council on September 27th decided to send to the German Government, through Marshal Foch, a note demanding under drastic penalties for non-compliance, the evacuation of Lithuania by German troops a considerable force of whom still remained there. Germany was told that her provisioning at home would be stopt and the financial arrangement she had requested would be held up if Lithuania were not evacuated. After having tried, without success, other methods to secure compliance from Germany with the terms laid down in the armistice, which had been signed more than ten months before, the Peace Conference was about to try with Germany the "American way"—that is, to use the economic weapons which had long been favored by the American delegation. It was said that with 100,000 troops, of various nationalities, General von der Goltz had become the real lord of the Baltic and that he might within a few days declare himself independent of the German Government. His immediate purpose seemed to be, first to overthrow the Russian Bolshevist Government, and then to establish cordial relations between the new Russia and Germany, and so lead to German domination of the Baltic provinces.

Weeks passed, however, and Germany failed to secure an evacuation by her troops. On the contrary, Riga by October 11th, had been attacked by Germans acting with anti-Red Russians, and the Letts under this pressure had abandoned their city.

An advance guard of German troops soon took possession of

Riga, and others, under von der Goltz with Russians, attacked the Letts thirty kilometers from Riga and occupied Shlotsk, 'the attack being repulsed. This German aggression was regarded in some quarters as the beginning of a new German attempt for supremacy in Europe by that Prussian landholding aristocracy which was still dominated by medieval ideas of aristocratic militarism. Von der Goltz's army was officered by the sort of men who had made Germany hated the world over, and was fighting in the interest chiefly of the land-owning nobility of the Baltic coast. Von der Goltz was cooperating with an organization calling itself "the West Russian Government," which appeared to represent nothing more than Baltic German Barons, the most reactionary class in old Russia, men who had furnished or inspired most of the traitors who had betrayed the Russian armies to Germany in the early years of the war. Von der Goltz, a few days after the attack on Riga, transferred his command in the Baltic region to General von Eberhardt, and was expected to arrive in Berlin soon after. The German Government had been deliberating on the latest note of the Entente with regard to the Baltic situation under which complete stoppage of provisions to the insubordinate troops in the Baltic lands had been ordered. All passenger traffic to the Baltic was to be stopt and only empty trains permitted to go there to fetch troops home.

Early in September was begun, so to speak, "an appeal to Cæsar," by President Wilson and by the chief opponents of the League covenant, through speaking trips across the continent and back. The appeal was made chiefly to the West and far West, the President's route being through the Middle West, the Rocky Mountain States, and the Pacific Coast States. The fact that Mr. Wilson was to speak in three different California cities—San Francisco, Los Angeles, and San Diego—seemed proof of his anxiety to relieve any misunderstanding that may have been created in California as to the effect of the Shantung grant on the Japanese problem along the Pacific coast. When he reached Spokane President Wilson made a notable statement in declaring that he was not averse to reservations of interpretation, but objected strongly to putting them in the ratification clause which would mean resubmission of the treaty, because, if textual changes were made in it, or if the resolution of ratification was qualified, the document would have to be resubmitted to the German Assembly; "that," he remarked, "goes against my digestion." He said further on this point:

"We can not honorably put anything in that treaty which Germany has signed and ratified without Germany's consent, whereas it is perfectly feasible, my fellow countrymen, if we put interpretations upon that treaty, which its language clearly warrants, to notify the other Governments of the world that we do understand the treaty in that sense. It is perfectly feasible to do so and perfectly honorable to do that, because, mark you, nothing can be done under this treaty through the instrumentality of the Council of the League of Nations except by unanimous vote. The vote of the United States will always be necessary, and it is perfectly legitimate for the United States to notify the other Governments beforehand that its vote in the Council of the League of Nations will be based upon such and such understanding of the provisions of the treaty.''

Two days after the President made this speech a written appeal for ratification without delay and without amendments to the treaty with Germany was submitted to every member of the Senate by 250 leading Americans, Republicans as well as Democrats, in a nonpartizan effort to bring about prompt action by the Senate. The address was signed by former President Taft, former Attorney-General Wickersham, President Lowell of Harvard, Judge George Gray of Delaware, President Gompers of the American Federation of Labor, Luther Burbank, Lyman Abbott, John Burroughs, Alton B. Parker, Oscar S. Straus, Jacob H. Schiff, Henry P. Davison, and others including Governors, former Governors and Senators. Men signing this petition lived in forty States of the Union, some of them of national reputation. The appeal declared that the "world is being put in imminent peril of new wars by the lapse of each day." Delay in the Senate by postponing ratification "in this uncertain period of neither peace nor war, has resulted in indecision and doubt, has bred strife, and quickened the cupidity of those who sell the daily necessities of life and the fears of those whose daily wage no longer fills the daily market basket." "The American people," the Senate was told, "can not after a victorious war, permit its Government to petition Germany for its consent to changes in the treaty."

Opinion in the country was much divided as to the proper steps to be taken by the Senate. On the one hand many saw, in the refusal to accept the Treaty without reservations, merely a vindictive desire to embarrass the President, while by others it was pointed out that from the entry of the United States into the war, the President had received the whole-hearted support of the Republican party and that the same patriotic feeling was governing the Senate.

Another impetus, leading perhaps to an earlier ratification than had seemed likely, was given early in September by Herbert C. Hoover, in an interview with the press on his arrival from Europe where he had been continuing his notable and beneficent labors as the American Food Administrator. Mr. Hoover in effect reminded

Senators of the ruined cities and villages of France and Belgium which, under the terms of the treaty Germany was to restore, but neither the gold nor the labor for this work could be had until the treaty was ratified. While Senators were disputing over the future world attitude of America, the bodies of dead Europeans still lay unburied in the cellars of their homes, and survivors in the devastated regions were eating the bread of charity. Some 35,000,000 people were spread over a devastated, famine-stricken country, persecuted on one side by a German army in Silesia, and on the other by Bolsheviki over a front of 1,500 miles. Germans by terrorism were trying to force a vote for German government in Silesia, where lay the coal field of Central Europe. Coal mining in consequence was disorganized and railways, at least in eastern and southern Poland, were obliged to suspend service for want of fuel. Since rolling stock could not be divided between the Central European States as the Peace Treaty provided, traffic in Poland, Czecho-Slovakia and Lithuania continued to be greatly impeded. Poland was still without a port, except through German territory, and part of East Prussia was being stript of its harvest by the Germans, who were anticipating the annexation of that section under the treaty. Entente intervention was not possible until the Peace Treaty was signed. With the existence of all these conditions it was impossible for Poland to arrange foreign loans. Unable to provide raw material, her textile mills remained idle and her people were in rags. There was no hope in Poland of rehabilitating economic life and assuring the political independence of Poland and other states until peace was formally declared. This condition was typical of fifteen States in Europe, whose whole economic and political life was in a state of suspension that in many particulars was more disastrous than war itself had been. Seventy-five million people were living on Government unemployment doles.

At a dinner given in New York in his honor, Mr. Hoover said the war's end found Europe facing a famine the like of which had not been known since the ending of the Thirty Years' War. Throughout everything it seemed as if chaos had taken the reins, and over it all hung the menace of Bolshevism and anarchy. There was only one hope for Europe: that was the American people. It was in response to this appeal that President Wilson had intervened a second time in Europe; this time to rehabilitate her economic life. This service had been accomplished at no mean national sacrifice. From the armistice to the harvest of 1919, there had been furnished to Europe over $2,250,000,000 worth of supplies, the majority of which had been given freely upon the undertaking of the assisted

Governments of repayment at some future date. There had been no demand of special security; no political or economic privileges had been sought. The American people, by this second intervention, "had saved civilization."

On September 26 the President was stricken with illness at Wichita, Kansas, and was compelled to abandon his tour. For sometime he had shown by an increasing irritability the effect of the severe strain that he had been subjected to, yet he persisted in his effort to convert the country to his views concerning the Peace Treaty. Finally, however, the collapse came and, at the order of Doctor Grayson, the President's personal physician, all engagements for the future were cancelled and Mr. Wilson returned to Washington, arriving at the White House on September 29.

Dr. Grayson announced that the President was suffering from nervous exhaustion and that while his condition was "not alarming" "he would be obliged to rest for a considerable time."

This sudden collapse gave rise to many alarming rumors, which the guarded bulletins from the sick-room did not tend to quell, and called forth from friend and foe alike genuine expressions of sympathy. So disturbing were the reports that the suggestion was made in Congress that the Vice-President should assume the duties of the President, as provided in Section One, Article Two of the Constitution. In face of the assurances from the physicians of the ultimate recovery of the President, however, this step was not taken.

Consequently, for several months the country was to all intents and purposes devoid of an executive head, and many matters of extreme importance were necessarily held in abeyance. It is true that the members of the Cabinet met on several occasions at the request of the Secretary of State, Mr. Lansing, but these meetings were necessarily of an informal nature and the government of the country was, none the less, at a standstill.

An unfortunate result of the President's illness was the inability of Viscount Grey, the newly appointed Ambassador from Great Britain, to present his credentials. Viscount Grey, who arrived in this country on September 26, returned to England on December 30 without having had an interview with President Wilson.

The utterances of the President in Cheyenne, Denver, and Pueblo, generally accepted as threats to withdraw the Treaty of Peace in case of the adoption by the Senate of specific amendments, gave the debate a stimulus too strong to allow of any actual truce between contending factions. In fact, it was generally recognized that the President's positive stand had brought the differences between himself and the Republican Senators to an unmistakable issue. This issue was crystallized by the chairman of the Republican National Committee into the phrase "Internationalism *vs.* Nationalism."

In Denver and again at Pueblo the President stated that he would declare the Peace Treaty rejected if the Senate adopted, in its present form, the proposed reservation of the majority of the Foreign Relations Committee to Article X of the League Covenant. He was variously quoted as saying:

"The negotiation of treaties rests with the Executive of the United States. When the Senate has acted, it will be for me to determine whether its action constitutes an adoption or a rejection. . . .

"Qualified adoption is not adoption. It is perfectly legitimate by a multiplicity of words to make the obvious more obvious, but qualifying means asking special privileges for the United States. We can not ask that. We must go in or stay out.

"We go in on equal terms or we don't go in at all."

White House officials in the Presidential party "permitted it to become known" that the proposed reservation which the President would regard as rejecting the Treaty, if adopted, was that quoted by him at Salt Lake City as one that he had been informed had been agreed on by several Republican leaders in the Senate. This "proposed form of reservation," which the President intimated would "cut out the heart of this Covenant," he cited as follows:

"The United States assumes no obligation under the provisions of Article X to preserve the territorial integrity or political independence of any other country or to interfere in controversies between other nations, whether members of the League or not, or to employ military and naval forces of the United States under any article for any purpose unless in any particular case that Congress, which under the Constitution has the sole power to declare war or authorize the employment of military and naval forces of the United States, shall by act or joint resolution so declare.

On November 19 the Senate rejected, by an overwhelming vote, the peace treaty. This had been presented by Senator Lodge, coupled with the following resolutions of ratification:

Resolved (two-thirds of the Senators present concurring therein), That the Senate advice and consent to the ratification of the treaty of peace with Germany concluded at Versailles on the twenty-eighth day of June, 1919, subject to the following reservations and understandings, which are hereby made a part and condition of this resolution of ratification, which ratification is not to take effect or bind the United States until the said reservations and understandings adopted by the Senate have been accepted by an exchange of notes as a part and a condition of this resolution of ratification by at least three of the four principal allied and associated powers, to wit, Great Britain, France, Italy, and Japan:

1. The United States so understands and construes Article 1 that in case of notice of withdrawal from the League of Nations, as provided in said article, the United States shall be the sole judge as to whether all its international obligations and all its obligations under the said covenant have been fulfilled, and notice of withdrawal by the United States may be given by a concurrent resolution of the Congress of the United States.

2. The United States assumes no obligation to preserve the territorial integrity or political independence of any other country or to interfere in controversies between nations—whether members of the League or not—under the provisions of Article 10, or to employ the military or naval forces of the United States under any article of the treaty for any purpose, unless in any particular case the Congress, which, under the Constitution has the sole power to declare war or authorize the employment of the military or naval forces of the United States, shall by act or joint resolution so provide.

3. No mandate shall be accepted by the United States under Article 22, Part 1, or any other provision of the treaty of peace with Germany, except by action of the Congress of the United States.

4. The United States reserves to itself exclusively the right to decide what questions are within its domestic jurisdiction and declares that all domestic and political questions relating wholly or in part to its internal affairs, including immigration, labor, coastwise traffic, the tariff, commerce, the suppression of traffic in women and children, and in opium and other dangerous drugs, and all other domestic questions, are solely within the jurisdiction of the United States and are not under this treaty to be submitted in any way either to arbitration or to the consideration of the Council or of the Assembly of the League of Nations, or any agency thereof, or to the decision or recommendation of any other power.

5. The United States will not submit to arbitration or to inquiry by the Assembly or by the Council of the League of Nations, provided for in said treaty of peace, any questions which in the judgment of the United States depend upon or relate to its long-established policy, commonly known as the Monroe Doctrine; said doctrine is to be interpreted by the United States alone and is hereby declared to be wholly outside the jurisdiction of said League of Nations and entirely unaffected by any provision contained in the said treaty of peace with Germany.

6. The United States withholds its assent to Articles 156, 157, and 158, and reserves full liberty of action with respect to any controversy which may arise under said articles between the Republic of China and the Empire of Japan.

7. The Congress of the United States will provide by law for the appointment of the representatives of the United States in the Assembly and the Council of the League of Nations, and may in its discretion provide for the participation of the United States in

any commission, committee, tribunal, court, council, or conference, or in the selection of any members thereof and for the appointment of members of said commisions, committees, tribunals, courts, councils, or conferences, or any other representatives under the treaty of peace, or in carrying out its provisions, and until such participation and appointment have been so provided for and the powers and duties of such representatives have been defined by law, no person shall represent the United States under either said League of Nations or the treaty of peace wth Germany, or be authorized to perform any act for or on behalf of the United States thereunder, and no citizen of the United States shall be selected or appointed as a member of said commisions, committees, tribunals, courts, councils, or conferences except with the approval of the Senate of the United States.

8. The United States understands that the Reparation Commission will regulate or interfere with exports from the United States to Germany, or from Germany to the United States, only when the United States by act or joint resolution of Congress approves such regulation or interference.

9. The United States shall not be obligated to contribute to any expenses of the League of Nations or of the secretariat, or of any commission, or committee, or conference or other agency, organized under the League of Nations or under the treaty or for the purpose of carrying out the treaty provisions, unless and until an appropriation of funds available for such expenses shall have been made by the Congress of the United States.

10. If the United States shall at any time adopt any plan for the limitation of armaments proposed by the Council of the League of Nations, under the provisions of Article 8, it reserves the right to increase such armaments without the consent of the Council whenever the United States is threatened with invasion or engaged in war.

11. The United States reserves the right to permit, in its discretion, the nationals of a covenant-breaking State, as defined in Article 16 of the covenant of the League of Nations, residing within the United States or in countries other than that violating said Article 16, to continue their commercial, financial, and personal relations with the nationals of the United States.

12. Nothing in Articles 296, 297, or in any of the annexes thereto or in any other article, section, or annex of the treaty of peace with Germany shall, as against citizens of the United States, be taken to mean any confirmation, ratification, or approval of any act otherwise illegal or in contravention of the right of citizens of the United States.

13. The United States withholds its assent to Part XIII (Articles 387 to 427, inclusive) unless Congress by act or joint resolution shall hereafter make provision for representation in the organization established by said Part XIII, and in such event the participation of the United States will be governed and conditioned by the provisions of such act or joint resolution.

14. The United States assumes no obligation to be bound by any

election, decision, report, or finding of the council or assembly in which any member of the League and its self-governing dominions, colonies, or parts of empire, in the aggregate have cast more than one vote, and assumes no obligation to be bound by any decision, report, or finding of the council or assembly arising out of any dispute between the United States and any member of the League if such member, or any self-governing dominion, colony, empire, or part of the empire united with it politically has voted.

Jubilation reigned in some quarters when this emphatic rejection came as a sensational climax to one of the most bitterly fought political battles in our history. By the opponents of the Administration and its peace-making policy it was hailed as an "American victory."

The attitude of those "mild reservationists" who had been looked upon to effect a compromise "ratification with reservations," but who finally voted for the Lodge program and against straight ratification, was indicated by these words of Senator Kellogg (Rep., Minn.):

"The people of the United States are generous. We are willing to join a League of Nations to insure a world peace, but we are not willing to give up the control of our domestic questions; we are not willing to pledge this nation to go to war and to send its sons abroad without the judgment of the American people, which must be exprest through their Congress."

But those who had expected much from the League were saddened at "the end of a dream," and by the conviction that our allies were left without the directing hand of America to keep them out of the maze of intrigue in which Europe was at war's edge for centuries.[22]

Now that the Treaty, if not dead, was in a state of suspended animation, as far as this country was concerned, until the opening of the next session of Congress, there was at once evinced by the spokesmen of both sides a desire to shift the responsibility for its rejection. On the one side such expressions as "assassinated by Republican Senators," "the United States Senate under the bankrupt leadership of Senator Henry Cabot Lodge has killed the Peace Treaty," were heard, and the statement was made that it was a work of blind partizan recklessness done in callous disregard of the need and the suffering of nations.[23]

But Republican papers, including dailies of all shades of friendliness and hostility to the League of Nations joined in laying the responsibility for the failure of the Treaty at the President's own door, in effect charging him with "infanticide." It was said that this country and the world are familiar with the record of how the

[22] The *Commercial* (New York).
[23] The *Times* (New York).

President refused to take counsel; of how he arrived in Europe without a plan; of how he adopted the theory, now an admitted blunder, of uniting in one instrument the distinct problems of settling one war and of creating safeguards for future peace; of how he boasted he had so cunningly arranged matters that the covenant could not have separate consideration and that the Senate must accept a covenant secretly written or not have peace at all; of how he revealed his ambition to be the sole treaty-making power, whereas the Constitution provides he shall have partners; of how in one breath he has conceded the just basis of the demand for reservations and in the next has said he would not accept them.[24]

Apart from the foregoing partizan expression it was felt by many that statesmanship had been lacking on both sides, and the conviction was hopefully exprest that the Senate's rejection was not final or that the ratification would not be very long delayed. It was hoped that before Congress met again in December the basis might be reached.

That the Allies intended to go on without American cooperation was shown by the fact that the day after the United States Senate rejected the Treaty, the Supreme Council at Paris decided that the nations which have already accepted the Treaty would exchange formal ratifications in time for the pact to become effective on December 1.

The Prince of Wales, who had been making an extended tour through Canada, arrived in Washington on November 11 as a guest of the nation. The royal special train was received by a guard of honor of Marines, and the Prince was welcomed by Vice-President Marshall, General Pershing, Viscount Grey, General March, and other prominent men. During his stay in Washington the Prince visited President Wilson at the White House and exprest his gratification at Mr. Wilson's improvement in health. On November 19 he went to New York, landed at the Battery and proceeded up Broadway to the City Hall where he was welcomed by Secretary of State Hugo and the Mayor. During his stay in New York he visited West Point and was a guest at a dinner given by the Pilgrims of the United States. He was most cordially received by the public wherever he went and it was remarked after his departure on H.M.S. *Renown* on November 22 that "he was the most successful ambassador that Great Britain had ever sent to this country."

The practical dismissal of Mr. Lansing the Secretary of State, by President Wilson on February 13, 1920, startled the United States and Europe.

The correspondence which culminated in the President's acceptance

[24] The *Tribune* (New York).

of Secretary Lansing's resignation "to take effect at once" began with a note from the President dated February 7, asking if it was true "that during my illness you have frequently called the heads of the executive departments of the Government into conference," and affirming that "under our constitutional law and practise, as developed hitherto, no one but the President has the right to summon the heads of the executive departments into conference, and no one but the President and the Congress has the right to ask their views or the views of any one of them on any public question." Mr. Lansing replied that, being denied communication with the President, he had frequently "requested the heads of the executive departments to meet for informal conference." His note continued:

"I can assure you that it never for a moment entered my mind that I was acting unconstitutionally or contrary to your wishes, and there certainly was no intention on my part to assume powers and exercise the functions which under the Constitution are exclusively confided to the President.

"During these troublous times, when many difficult and vexatious questions have arisen and when in the circumstances I have been deprived of your guidance and direction, it has been my constant endeavor to carry out your policies as I understood them and to act in all matters as I believed you would wish me to act.

"If, however, you think that I have failed in my loyalty to you, and if you no longer have confidence in me and prefer to have another conduct our foreign affairs, I am, of course, ready, Mr. President, to relieve you of any embarrassment by placing my resignation in your hands."

The President replied that Mr. Lansing's explanations did not justify his "assumption of Presidential authority," and that the Secretary's resignation would relieve him of embarrassment, adding:

"While we were still in Paris, I felt, and have felt increasingly ever since that you accepted my guidance and direction on questions with regard to which I had to instruct you only with increasing reluctance, and since my return to Washington I have been struck by the number of matters in which you have apparently tried to forestall my judgment by formulating action and merely asking my approval when it was impossible for me to form an independent judgment because I had not had an opportunity to examine the circumstances with any degree of independence."

Mr. Lansing, denying that he "sought to usurp Presidential authority," and expressing the belief that he would have been derelict in his duty if he had failed to act as he did, handed in his resignation "with a sense of profound relief."

President Wilson issued on January 12, 1920, a call for the first meeting of the Council of the League of Nations to convene at Paris on January 16. In accordance with this summons the League was formally launched on that date with representatives of Great Britain, France, Italy, Japan, Belgium, Spain, Greece, Portugal and Brazil in attendance.

On March 19, after more than eight months of discussion, the Senate returned unratified to the President the Treaty that the Peace Conference had worked nearly half a year to frame. While some papers joined in frank rejoicing over the Treaty's rejection, a majority of the press, like a majority of the Senate (but not the necessary two-thirds majority), seemed to desire ratification with reservations that would interpret but not stultify. The question arose as to who was to blame for thwarting the will of the public. Some regarded President Wilson himself as responsible, others declared that the Republican Senators were the real culprits, while some divided the blame.

In reply to criticism of the Senate for failure to ratify the Treaty Senator Lodge replied:

"Reservations were placed upon the Treaty which a decisive majority of the Senate felt were necessary for the protection of the independence, the sovereignty, and the peace of the United States. The President's followers in the Senate under his direction refused to ratify the Treaty with those reservations.

"The Treaty can be ratified with those reservations, but not without them, and it is for the President to determine whether he is ready to accept them in order that the Treaty may be ratified."

On the other hand it was said that heretofore Senators had ratified and rejected treaties, but that the grave offense that the Senate under the leadership of Henry Cabot Lodge had committed was in making a treaty of peace a partizan issue.[25]

More important than the assessment of the blame, however, was the consideration of what was next to be done. Some of the solutions proposed and discust were: A separate peace with Germany by Congressional resolution; a new treaty; a temporary *modus vivendi* to be arranged with Germany by the President; or a return of the Treaty to the Senate with the understanding that President Wilson would accept ratification with a single reservation holding over the League of Nations issue until after the elections.

On May 27, 1920, President Wilson vetoed the Knox peace resolution which had been recently passed by both Houses of Congress. This resolution repealed the declarations of war with Germany and Austria and provided for a resumption of commercial and diplomatic relations with those countries. The President, in taking this action,

[25] The *World* (New York).

deliberately placed upon his own shoulders for the third time the weight of responsibility for keeping the nation in a technical state of war. He declared in his message to the House that the Knox resolution was "a complete surrender of the rights of the United States so far as the German Government is concerned" and "an ineffaceable stain upon the gallantry and honor of the United States."

An attempt was made on May 28, in the House, to pass this resolution over the President's veto, but this failed, the vote being 219 to 152, thus lacking twenty-nine votes of the necessary two-thirds to override the veto.

President Wilson sent to Congress on May 24, a request to be given the power to accept, on behalf of the United States, a mandate for Armenia. The Supreme Council in Paris had asked the President to fix the boundaries of the State of Armenia and had at the same time offered the mandate for that State to the United States. In reply to the President's request, the Senate Foreign Relations Committee approved three days later the following resolution:

"Resolved, That the Congress hereby respectfully declines to grant to the Executive the power to accept a mandate over Armenia as requested in the message of the President of May 24, 1920," which was adopted by the Senate on June 1 by a vote of 52 to 23.

On the debit side in accounts of this war, the world found that it had to set down in dead from all causes, battle and disease, a few tens of millions; in crippled, perhaps 20,000,000; in homes destroyed, 1,000,000; in money loss, $120,000,000,000; besides anarchic conditions with disrupted industries over the most of Europe and parts of Asia and Africa. The war, besides the inevitable halting of the producing capabilities of the nations, had left behind it a universal disinclination, apparently, on the part of Labor to take up again the tools compulsorily laid aside in the hour of danger. It had left, as well to already overtaxed statesmen the dangerous task of preserving during the adjustment of new boundaries and the imposing of penalties, the friendly relations aroused among the Allied nations in the heat of the conflict. The menace of Bolshevism, the most embarrassing legacy of the World War, primed with all the accessories of a renewed universal struggle, was also to be placed on the debit side.

On the credit side, however, it had vivid and lasting demonstration that liberty is so prized among men that no sacrifices are regarded as too great to save it, new proof that man is a moral being and that he reacts to moral ideals. There had also sprung up a greater sense of fraternity among different races—brothers of the soul who had fought together for the same ideal. The losses, therefore, were in material things; the gains in spiritualities. While the world had been impoverished in temporal goods, it had grown richer in others; a jewel had been found in the mire of war. A generation capable of performing such prodigies of genius and valor as this war had brought into the light of day, had proclaimed to distant generations that man was master of his fate; that not far distant was the day when the work of the military beast in human government would have disappeared and men would sit lost in wonder that it had survived so late.[26]

[26] Principal Sources: *The Outlook*, The *Evening Post*, The *Times*, The *Tribune*, *The Literary Digest*, New York; Associated Press dispatches.

THE COVENANT OF THE LEAGUE OF NATIONS AND THE PEACE TREATIES

The story of the labors of the Peace Conference, and of the signing of the several Treaties, has been fully told in the preceding pages of this volume. The following list of the names of the plenipotentiaries who signed the Treaty with Germany, it is believed, will lend an additional interest to this work:

UNITED STATES. President Wilson, Secretary of State Robert Lansing, Mr. Henry White (Ambassador to France), Colonel E. M. House and General Tasker H. Bliss;

GREAT BRITAIN. Premier Lloyd George, Mr. Bonar Law, Viscount Milner, Mr. A. J. Balfour;

CANADA. Sir. George E. Foster, Mr. C. J. Doherty;

AUSTRALIA. Mr. W. H. Hughes and Sir Joseph Coo`.;

SOUTH AFRICA. General Louis Botha and Lieut.-General J. C. Smuts;

NEW ZEALAND. Mr. W. F. Massey;

INDIA. Mr. E. S. Montagu and the Maharaja of Bikaner;

FRANCE. Mr. Georges Clémenceau, M. Pichon, M. L. L. Klotz, Mr. André Tardieu, and Mr. Jules Cambon;

ITALY. Mr. Tittoni, Mr. Scialoja Marconi, Mr. Maggiorino, Mr. Ferrario, and The Marquis Imperiali;

JAPAN. Marquis Saionji, Baron Makino, Viscount Chinda, Mr. K. Matsui, and Mr. H. Ijuin;

BELGIUM. Mr. Hymans, Mr. Van der Henvel, and Mr. Vandervelde;

BOLIVIA. Mr. Ismael Moetes;

BRAZIL. Mr. Epitacio Pessoa, Mr. Pandia Calogeras, and Mr. Raul Fernandes;

CUBA. Mr. A. S. de Bustamante;

CZECHO-SLOVAKIA. Mr. Charles Kramar and Mr. E. Benes;

ECUADOR. Mr. Dorn y De Alsua;

GREECE. Mr. E. Venizelos and Mr. N. Politis;

GUATEMALA. Mr. Joaquin Mendez;

HAITI. Mr. Tertullien Guilbaud;

HEDJAZ. Mr. Rustem Haidar and Mr. Abdul Hadi Aouni;

HONDRAS. Dr. Policarpo Bonilla;

LIBERIA. Mr. C. D. B. King;

NICARAGUA. Mr. Salvador Chamorro;

PANAMA. Mr. Antonio Burgas;

PERU. Mr. Carlos G. Candamo;

POLAND. Mr. R. Dmowski and Mr. Ignace Paderewski;

PORTGAL. Dr. Alfonso Costa and Mr. Augusto Soares;

RUMANIA. Mr. J. J. C. Bratiano and General C. Coanda;

SIAM. Prince Charoon and Prince T. Prabando;

URUGUAY. Mr. Juan A. Buero;

YUGO-SLAVIA. Mr. N. P. Pachitch, Mr. A. Trumbitch, and Mr. M. R. Vesnich;

GERMANY. Herr Herman Muller (Foreign Minister), and Herr Bell, Minister of Communications and Chief of the Colonial Office.

China refused to sign with the allies as she was dissatisfied with the arrangement made for the future of Shantung.

The Treaty was ratified by Germany on July 9th; by Italy on October 7th; by Great Britain on October 10th; by New Zealand on September 2d; by Canada on September 11th; by South Africa, September 12th; by Australia, October 2d; by France, October 13th; by Japan, October 30th; by Belgium, October 13th; by Uruguay, October 24th; by Czecho-Slovakia, November 10th; and by Poland, October 30th, all in the year 1919.

SUMMARY OF THE COVENANT OF
THE LEAGUE OF NATIONS

The HIGH CONTRACTING PARTIES, in order to promote international cooperation and to achieve international peace and security by the acceptance of obligations not to resort to war, by the prescription of open, just, and honorable relations between nations, by the firm establishment of the understandings of international law as the actual rule of conduct among Governments, and by the maintenance of justice and a scrupulous respect for all treaty obligations in the dealings of organized peoples 'with one another, agree to this Covenant of the League of Nations.

Article I. The original members of the League shall be those of the signatories which are named in the annex to this Covenant and also such of those other States named in the annex as shall accede without reservation to this Covenant. Such accession shall be effected by a declaration deposited with the secretariat within two months of the coming into force of the Covenant. Notice thereof shall be sent to all other members of the League. Any fully self-governing State, Dominion, or Colony not named in the annex may become a member of the League if its admission is agreed to by two-thirds of the Assembly, provided that it shall give effective guaranties of its sincere intention to observe its international obligations, and shall accept such regulations as may be prescribed by the League in regard to its military, naval, and air forces and armaments. Any member of the League may, after two years' notice of its intention so to do, withdraw from the League, provided that all its international obligations and all its obligations under this Covenant shall have been fulfilled at the time of its withdrawal.

Article II. The action of the League under this Covenant shall be effected through the instrumentality of an Assembly and of a Council, with a permanent secretariat.

Article III. The Assembly shall consist of representatives of the members of the League. The Assembly shall meet at stated intervals and from time to time as occasion may require, at the seat of the League or at such other place as may be decided upon. The Assembly may deal at its meetings with any matter within the sphere of action of the League or affecting the peace of the world. At meetings of the Assembly each member of the League shall have one vote, and may have not more than three representatives.

Article IV. The Council shall consist of representatives of the principal Allied and Associated Powers, together with representatives of four other members of the League. These four members of the League shall be selected by the Assembly from time to time in its discretion. Until the appointment of the representatives of the four members of the League first selected by the Assembly, representatives of Belgium, Brazil, Greece, and Spain shall be members of the Council. With the approval of the majority of the Assembly, the Council may name additional members of the League whose representatives shall always be members of the Council; the Council with like approval may increase the number of members of the League to be selected by the Assembly for representation on the Council. The Council shall meet from time to time as occasion may require, and at least once a year, at the seat of the League, or at such other place as may be decided upon. The Council may deal at its meetings with any matter within the sphere of action of the League, or affecting the peace of the world. Any member of the League not represented on the Council shall be invited to send a representative to sit as a member at any meeting of the Council during the consideration of matters specially affecting the interests of that member of the League. At meetings of the Council each member of the League represented on the Council shall have one vote, and may have not more than one representative..

Article V. Except where otherwise expressly provided in this Covenant or by the terms of the present Treaty, decisions at any meeting of the Assembly or of the Council shall require the agreement of all the members of the League represented at the meeting. All matters of procedure at meetings of the Assembly or of the Council, including the appointment of committees to investigate particular matters, shall be regulated by the Assembly or by the Council, and may be decided by a majority of the members of the League represented at the meeting. The first meeting of the Assembly and the first meeting of the Council shall be summoned by the President of the United States of America.

Article VI. The permanent secretariat shall be established at the seat of the League.

Article VII. The seat of the League is established at Geneva. The Council may at any time decide that the seat of the League shall be established elsewhere. All positions under or in connection with the League, including the secretariat, shall be open equally to men and women.

Article VIII. The members of the League recognize that the maintenance of peace requires the reduction of national armaments to the lowest point consistent with national safety and the enforcement by common action of international obligations. The Council, taking account of the geographical situation and circumstances of each State, shall formulate plans for such reduction for the consideration and action of the several Governments. Such plans shall be subject to reconsideration and revision at least every ten years. After these plans shall have been adopted by the several Governments, the limits of armaments therein fixt shall not be exceeded without the concurrence of the Council. The members of the League undertake to interchange full and frank information as to the scale of their armaments, their military, naval, and air programs, and the condition of such of their industries as are adaptable to warlike purposes.

Article IX. A permanent Commission shall be constituted to advise the Council on the execution of the provisions of Articles I and VIII, and on military, naval, and air questions generally.

Article X. The members of the League undertake to respect and preserve as against external aggression the territorial integrity and existing political independence of all members of the League. In case of any such aggression or in case of any threat or danger of such aggression, the Council shall advise upon the means by which this obligation shall be fulfilled.

Article XI. Any war or threat of war, whether immediately affecting any of the members of the League or not, is hereby declared a matter of concern to the whole League, and the League shall take any action that may be deemed wise and effectual to safeguard the peace of nations. In case any such emergency should arise, the Secretary-General shall on the request of any member of the League forthwith summon a meeting of the Council. It is also declared to be the friendly right of each member of the League to bring to the attention of the Assembly or of the Council any circumstance whatever affecting international relations which threatens to disturb international peace or the good understanding between nations upon which peace depends.

Article XII. The members of the League agree that if there should arise between them any dispute likely to lead to a rupture, they will submit the matter either to arbitration or to inquiry by the Council, and they agree in no case to resort to war until three months after the award by the arbitrators or the report by the Council.

Article XIII. The members of the League agree that whenever any dispute shall arise between them which they recognize to be suitable for submission to arbitration and which can not be satisfactorily settled by diplomacy, they will submit the whole subject-matter to arbitration. Disputes as to the interpretation of a treaty, as to any question of international law, as to the existence of any fact which if established would constitute a breach of any international obligation, or as to the extent and nature of the reparation to be made for any such breach, are declared to be among those which are generally suitable for submission to arbitration. For the consideration of any such dispute the court of arbitration to which the case is referred shall be the court agreed on by the parties to the dispute or stipulated in any convention existing between them. The members of the League agree that they will carry out in full good faith any award that may be rendered and that they will not resort to war against a member of the League which complies therewith. In the event of any failure to carry out such an award, the Council shall propose what steps should be taken to give effect thereto.

Article XIV. The Council shall formulate and submit to the members of the League for adoption plans for the establishment of a Permanent Court of International Justice. The Court shall be competent to hear and determine any dispute of an international character which the parties thereto submit to it.

Article XV. If there should arise between members of the League any dispute likely to lead to a rupture, which is not submitted to arbitration as above, the members of the League agree that they will submit the matter to the Council. Any party to the dispute may effect such submission by giving notice of the existence of the dispute to the Secretary-General, who will make all necessary arrangements for a full investigation and consideration thereof. For this purpose the parties to the dispute will communicate to the Secretary-General, as promptly as possible, statements of their case with all the relevant facts and papers, and the Council may forthwith direct the publication thereof. The Council shall endeavor to effect a settlement of the dispute, and if such efforts are successful, a statement shall be made public giving such facts and explanations regarding the dispute and the terms of settlement thereof as the Council may deem appropriate. If the dispute is not thus settled, the Council, either unanimously or by a majority vote, shall make and publish a report containing a statement of the facts of the dispute and the recommendations which are deemed just and proper in regard thereto. Any member of the League represented on the Council may make public a statement of the facts of the dispute and of its conclusions regarding the same. If a report by the Council is unanimously agreed to by the members thereof other than the representatives of one or more of the parties to the dispute, the members of the League agree that they will not go to war with any party to the dispute which complies with the recommendations of the report. If the Council fails to reach a report which is unanimously agreed to by the members thereof, other than the representatives of one or more of the parties to the dispute, the members of the League reserve to themselves the right to take such action as they shall consider necessary for the maintenance of right and justice. If the dispute between the parties is claimed by one of them, and is found by the Council to arise out of a matter which by international law is solely within the domestic jurisdiction of that party, the Council shall so report, and shall make no recommendation as to its settlement. The Council may in any case under this Article refer the dispute to the Assembly. The dispute shall be so referred at the request of either party to the dispute, provided that such request be made within fourteen days after the submission of the dispute to the Council. In any case referred to the Assembly, all the provisions of this article and of Article XII relating to the action and powers of the Council shall apply to the action and powers of the Assembly, provided that a report made by the Assembly, if concurred in by the representatives of those members of the League represented on the Council and of a majority of the other members of the League, exclusive in each case of the representatives of the parties to the dispute, shall have the same force as a report by the Council concurred in by all the members thereof other than the representatives of one or more of the parties to the dispute.

Article XVI. Should any member of the League resort to war in disregard of its covenants under Articles XII, XIII, or XV, it shall *ipso facto* be deemed to have committed an act of war against all other members of the League, which hereby undertake immediately to subject it to the severance of all trade or financial relations, the prohibition of all intercourse between their nationals and the nationals of the covenant-breaking State, and the prevention of all financial, commercial, or personal intercourse between the nationals of the covenant-breaking State and the nationals of any other State, whether a member of the League or not. It shall be the duty of the Council in such case to recommend to the several Governments concerned what effective military, naval, or air force the members of the League shall severally contribute to the armed forces to be used to protect the covenants of the League. The members of the League agree, further, that they will mutually support one another in the financial and economic measures which are taken under this article, in order to minimize the loss and inconvenience resulting from the above measures, and that they will mutually support one another in resisting any special measures aimed at one of their number by the covenant-breaking State, and that they will take the necessary steps to afford passage through their territory to the forces of any of the members of the League which are cooperating to protect the covenants of the League. Any member of the League which has violated any covenant of the League may be declared to be no longer a member of the League by a vote of the Council concurred in by the representatives of all the other members of the League represented thereon.

Article XVII. In the event of a dispute between a member of the League and a State which is not a member of the League, or between States not members of the League, the State or States not members of the League shall be invited to accept the obligations of membership in the League for the purposes of such dispute upon such conditions as the Council may deem just. If such invitation is accepted, the provisions of Articles XII to XVI inclusive shall be applied with such modifications as may be deemed necessary by the Council. Upon such invitation being given, the Council shall immediately institute an inquiry into the circumstances of the dispute and recommend such action as may seem best and most effectual in the circumstances. If a State so invited shall refuse to accept the obligations of membership in the League for the purposes of such dispute, and shall resort to war against a member of the League, the provisions of Article XVI shall be applicable as against the State taking such action. If both parties to the dispute when so invited refuse to accept the obligations of membership in the

League for the purposes of such dispute, the Council may take such measures and make such recommendations as will prevent hostilities and will result in the settlement of the dispute.

Article XVIII. Every treaty or international engagement entered into hereafter by any member of the League shall be forthwith registered with the secretariat and shall as soon as possible be published by it. No such treaty or international engagement shall be binding until so registered.

Article XIX. The Assembly may from time to time advise the reconsideration by members of the League of treaties which have become inapplicable and the consideration of international conditions whose continuance might endanger the peace of the world.

Article XX. The members of the League severally agree that this Covenant is accepted as abrogating all obligations or understandings *inter se* which are inconsistent with the terms thereof, and solemnly undertake that they will not hereafter enter into any engagements inconsistent with the terms thereof. In case any member of the League shall, before becoming a member of the League, have undertaken any obligations inconsistent with the terms of this Covenant, it shall be the duty of such member to take immediate steps to procure its release from such obligations.

Article XXI. Nothing in this Covenant shall be deemed to affect the validity of international engagements such as treaties of arbitration or regional understandings like the Monroe Doctrine, for securing the maintenance of peace.

Article XXII. To those colonies and territories which as a consequence of the late war have ceased to be under the sovereignty of the States which formerly governed them and which are inhabited by peoples not yet able to stand by themselves under the strenuous conditions of the modern world, there should be applied the principle that the well-being and development of such peoples form a sacred trust of civilization, and that securities for the performance of this trust should be embodied in this Covenant. The best method of giving practical effect to this principle is that the tutelage of such peoples should be entrusted to advanced nations who by reason of their resources, their experience, or their geographical position can best undertake this responsibility, and who are willing to accept it, and that this tutelage should be exercised by them as Mandatories on behalf of the League. The character of the mandate must differ according to the stage of the development of the people, the geographical situation of the territory, its economic conditions, and other similar circumstances. Certain communities formerly belonging to the Turkish Empire have reached a stage of development where their existence as independent nations can be provisionally recognized subject to the rendering of administrative advice and assistance by a Mandatory until such time as they are able to stand alone. The wishes of these communities must be a principal consideration in the selection of the Mandatory. Other peoples, especially those of Central Africa, are at such a stage that the Mandatory must be responsible for the administration of the territory under conditions which will guarantee freedom of conscience or religion, subject only to the maintenance of public order and morals, the prohibition of abuses such as the slave trade, the arms traffic and the liquor traffic, and the prevention of the establishment of fortifications or military and naval bases and of military training of the natives for other than police purposes and the defense of territory, and will also secure equal opportunities for the trade and commerce of other members of the League. There are territories, such as Southwest Africa and certain of the South Pacific Islands, which, owing to the sparseness of their population, or their small size, or their remoteness from the centers of civilization, or their geographical contiguity to the territory of the Mandatory, and other circumstances, can be best administered under the laws of the Mandatory as integral portions of its territory, subject to the safeguards above mentioned in the interests of the indigenous population. In every case of mandate, the Mandatory shall render to the Council an annual report in reference to the territory committed to its charge. The degree of authority, control, or administration to be exercised by the Mandatory shall, if not previously agreed upon by the members of the League, be explicitly defined in each case by the Council. A permanent Commission shall be constituted to receive and examine the annual reports of the Mandatories and to advise the Council on all matters relating to the observance of the mandates.

Article XXIII. Subject to and in accordance with the provisions of international conventions existing or hereafter to be agreed upon, the members of the League—

(a) will endeavor to secure and maintain fair and humane conditions of labor for men, women and children, both in their own countries and in all countries to which their commercial and industrial relations extend, and for that purpose will establish and maintain the necessary international organizations;

(b) undertake to secure just treatment of the native inhabitants of territories under their control;

(c) will entrust the League with the general supervision over the execution of agreements with regard to the traffic in women and children, and the traffic in opium and other dangerous drugs;

(d) will entrust the League with the general supervision of the trade in arms and ammunition with the countries in which the control of this traffic is necessary in the common interest;

(e) will make provision to secure and maintain freedom of communications and of transit and equitable treatment for the commerce of all members of the League. In this connection, the special necessities of the regions devastated during the war of 1914-18 shall be borne in mind;

SECTIONAL MAPS SHOWING
PARTITION OF EUROPE
ACCORDING TO PEACE TREATIES

NEW BELGIAN-FRENCH-GERMAN FRONTIER

International Boundaries . .
International Territory } . . . .
Subject to Plebiscite . . }
Former International Boundaries

① **Moresnet** and the circles of **Eupen** and **Malmedy** ceded by Germany to Belgium.
② **Sarre Basin** internationalized, after 15 years subject to plebiscite as between Germany, France and League of Nations.
③ **Alsace-Lorraine** ceded by Germany to France.

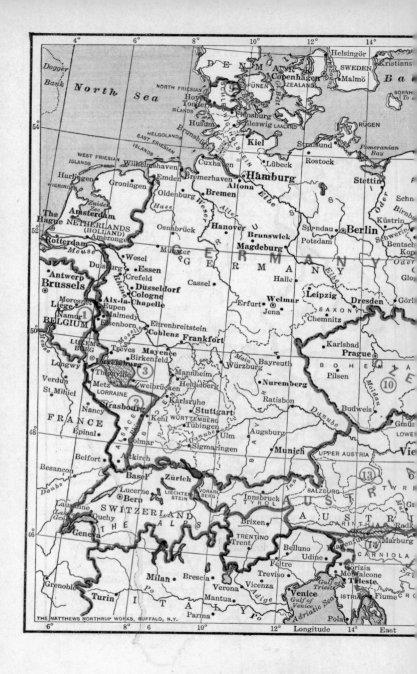

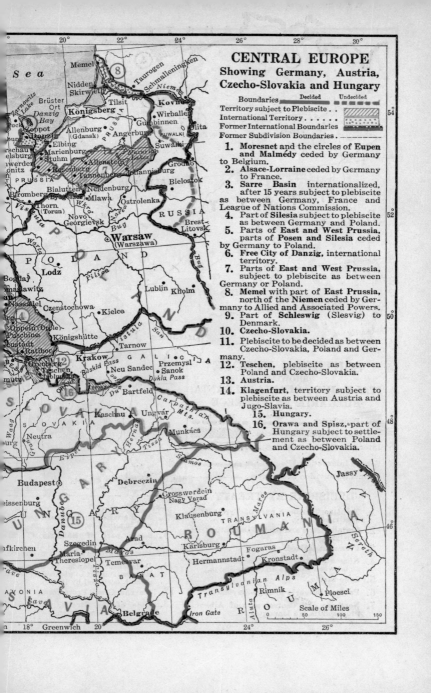

CENTRAL EUROPE

Showing Germany, Austria, Czecho-Slovakia and Hungary

Boundaries — Decided — Undecided
Territory subject to Plebiscite . .
International Territory . . . . . .
Former International Boundaries
Former Subdivision Boundaries . — — — —

1. **Moresnet** and the circles of **Eupen and Malmédy** ceded by Germany to Belgium.

2. **Alsace-Lorraine** ceded by Germany to France.

3. **Sarre Basin** internationalized, after 15 years subject to plebiscite as between Germany, France and League of Nations Commission.

4. Part of **Silesia** subject to plebiscite as between Germany and Poland.

5. Parts of **East and West Prussia**, parts of **Posen and Silesia** ceded by Germany to Poland.

6. **Free City of Danzig**, international territory.

7. Parts of **East and West Prussia**, subject to plebiscite as between Germany or Poland.

8. **Memel** with part of **East Prussia**, north of the **Niemen** ceded by Germany to Allied and Associated Powers.

9. Part of **Schleswig** (Slesvig) to Denmark.

10. **Czecho-Slovakia.**

11. Plebiscite to be decided as between Czecho-Slovakia, Poland and Germany.

12. **Teschen**, plebiscite as between Poland and Czecho-Slovakia.

13. **Austria.**

14. **Klagenfurt**, territory subject to plebiscite as between Austria and Jugo-Slavia.

15. **Hungary.**

16. **Orawa and Spisz**, part of Hungary subject to settlement as between Poland and Czecho-Slovakia.

Scale of Miles
0   50   100   150

SOUTHERN EUROPE
SHOWING
ITALY, JUGO-SLAVIA, ALBANIA, BULGARIA AND GREECE

Boundaries   **Decided**   **Undecided**

Territory subject to Plebiscite . .

International Territory . . . . .

Former International Boundaries

Former Subdivision Boundaries .

DECISIONS BY TREATY

1. **Trentino** (Southern part of Tyrol) from Austria to Italy.
2. **Gorizia, Istria** and part of **Dalmatia,** from Austria to Italy.
3. **Fiume,** undecided.
4. **Klagenfurt,** territory subject to plebiscite as between Austria and Jugo-Slavia.
5. **Jugo-Slavia.**
6. **Parts of Bulgaria** to Jugo-Slavia.
7. **Northern and Central part of Albania,** proposed Italian Mandate.

8. **Northern Epirus** (Southern part of nia), claimed by Greece.
9. **South part of Bulgaria** (Thrace Greece.
10. **Part of European Turkey** to Greece.
11. **Dodekanese Islands,** to Greece., e **Rhodes** (subject to plebiscite) and K orizo I. occupied by Italy.
12. **Smyrna,** Greek Protectorate.
13. **Zone of the Straits,** governed b Interallied Commission.

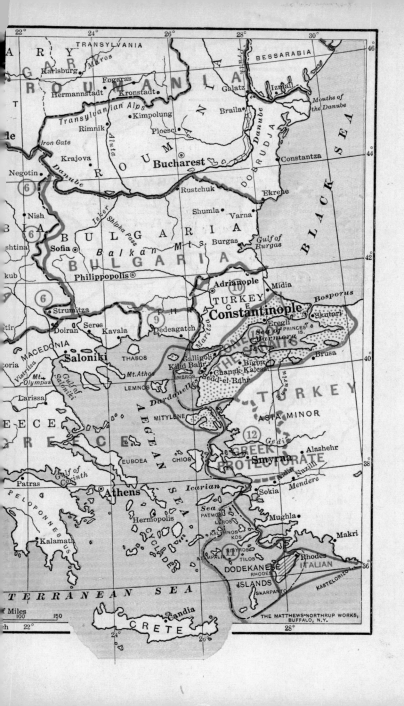

POLAND

Boundaries   Decided   Undecided
Territory subject to Plebiscite
International Territory
Former International Boundaries
Former Subdivision Boundaries

Scale of Miles
0 10 20 30 40 50   100   150

LATVIA

LITHUANIA

Memel

Nidden

Taurogen

Brüster Ort

Königsberg

PART OF

GERMANY

Tilsit

Schmalleningken

Kovno

9

Gumbinnen

Wirballen

Olita

SUWALKI

Suwalki

Osseken
Saulin
Lauenburg
Putzig
Zoppot
Danzig
(Gdansk)
Dirschau
(Tczew)
Rummelsburg
Konitz
Marienwerder
Lanken
Neustettin
Schneidemühl
Stahren
Bromberg
(Bydgoszcz)
Birnbaum
Meseritz
Posen
(Poznan)
Bentschen
Kopnitz
Lissa
Gührau
Glogau
Domaslawitz
Lorzendorf
Breslau
Nassadel
Falkenberg
Puschine
Neustadt
Leobschütz
Werndorf
Troppau
Olmütz
Brünn

Danzig
Bay

10

Elbing

Marienburg

Allenburg

Allenstein

Angerburg

Masurian Lakes

Oletzko

Johannisburg

Grodno

Bielostok

RUSSIA

8

Graudenz
Neidenburg
Tannenberg
WEST PRUSSIA
Thorn
(Torun)
Bialutten
Mlawa
Lomzha
Ostrolenka
Brest-Litovsk
(Brzesc-Litewski)

Warthe
Netze
Warthe
POSEN
Vistula
(Wisla)
Warta
Plotsk
Novo Georgievsk
Warsaw
(Warszawa)
Kalisz
Lodz
Pilica
Ivangorod
(Deblin)
Radom
Lublin
Kholm

POLAND

Wkra
Narew
Bug
Vistula
(Wisla)
Wieprz
Bug
CHOLM

1

SILESIA
Oppeln
(Opole)
4
Czestochowa
Kielce
Sandomierz
Königshütte
Bedzin
Ratibor
Oderberg
Freistadt
Jablonkow
Teschen
Orawa
Krakow
Tarnow
Przemysl
Lemberg
(Lwow)

San
Dunajec
Vistula
Poprad
Beskid Pass
Dukla Pass
Sanok
Neu Sandec

5

GALICIA

AUSTRIA

Dniester

CZECHO-SLOVAKIA

Wagg

6

Spisz

Bartfeld

Uszuk Pass

Carpathian Mts.

Munkacs

HUNGARY

1. Former Duchy of Poland.
2. Parts of East and West Prussia, parts of Posen and Silesia ceded by Germany to Poland.
3. Parts of East and West Prussia subject to plebiscite as between Germany and Poland.
4. Part of Silesia subject to plebiscite as between Germany and Poland.
5. Part of Galicia from Austria-Hungary to Poland.
6. Teschen. Plebiscite as between Poland and Czecho-Slovakia.
7. Orawa and Spisz, part of Hungary subject to settlement as between Poland and Czecho-Slovakia.
8. Part of Russia under proposal to Poland.
9. North part of Suwalki to Lithuania.
10. Free City of Danzig, international territory.

THE MATTHEWS-NORTHRUP WORKS, BUFFALO, N.Y.

For Continuation of Gallcia, see next Page.

18° Longitude East 20° from Greenwich 22°

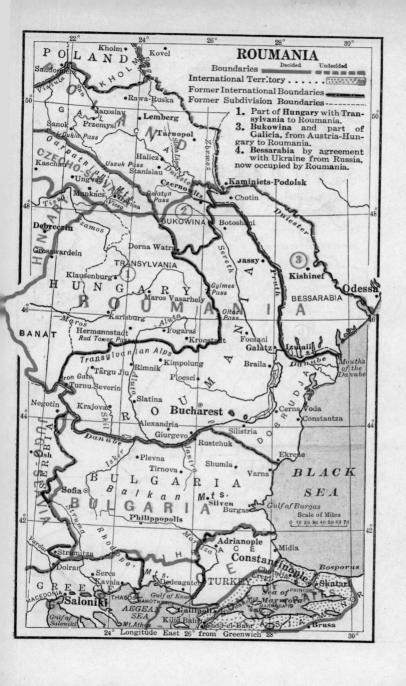

ROUMANIA

Boundaries   Decided   Undecided

International Territory . . . . . .

Former International Boundaries

Former Subdivision Boundaries - - - - - - -

1. Part of **Hungary** with **Transylvania** to Roumania.

3. **Bukowina** and part of **Galicia**, from Austria-Hungary to Roumania.

4. **Bessarabia** by agreement with Ukraine from Russia, now occupied by Roumania.

POLAND

Kholm

Kovel

Sandomierz

Vistula

San

KHOLM

Rawa-Ruska

50

GALICIA

Jaroslav

Lemberg

Sanok

Przemysl

Tarnopol

Dukla Pass

Carpathian Mts

Halicz

Seret

Zbrucz

Uszuk Pass

Stanislau

Dniester

Kaschau

CZECHO-SLOVAKIA

Ungvar

Czernowitz

Kaminiets-Podolsk

Munkács

Tisza

Visso

Delatyn Pass

48

Chotin

Dniester

Debreczin

Szamos

BUKOWINA

Botoshani

48

HUNGARY

Dorna Watra

ROUMANIA

Seret

Jassy

Prut

Kishinef

Grosswardein

TRANSYLVANIA

Maros Vasarhely

Gyimes Pass

BESSARABIA

Odessa

Klausenburg

HUNGARY

46

Karlsburg

Maros

Alata

Oltoz Pass

46

BANAT

Hermannstadt

Red Tower Pass

Fogaras

Kronstadt

Focsani

Galatz

Izmail

Transylvanian Alps

Kimpolung

Braila

Danube

Mouths of the Danube

Iron Gate

Targu Jiu

Rimnik

Ploesci

DOBRUDJA

Turnu-Severin

Aluta

Negotin

Krajova

Slatina

Cerna Voda

Constantza

44

Danube

Skit

Bucharest

44

SERBIA

Alexandria

Giurgevo

Silistria

Danube

Iron Gate

Nish

Isker

Rustchuk

Yantra

Plevna

Ekrene

Tirnova

Shumla

BULGARIA

Sofia

Varna

BLACK

Balkan Mts

SEA

42

Struma

BULGARIA

Sliven

Burgas

Gulf of Burgas

42

Philippopolis

Scale of Miles

0 10 20 30 40 50 60 70

Vardar

Maritza

Adrianople

Midia

Strumitza

THRACE

Constantinople

Bosporus

Doiran

Seres

Mts

Chatalja

Eregli

Skutari

GREECE

Kavala

Dedeagatch

TURKEY

PRINCES

MACEDONIA

THASOS

Gulf of Enos

Sea of Marmora

MARMORA ID

ANATOLIAN

Saloniki

SAMOTHRACE

Gallipoli

Brusa

Gulf of Saloniki

AEGEAN SEA

Kilid Bahr

Sedd-el-Bahr

Mt.Athos

24° Longitude East 26° from Greenwich 28°

30°

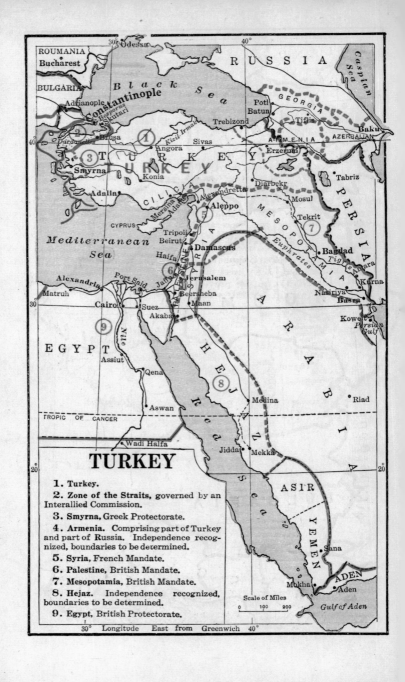

LEAGUE OF NATIONS AND TREATIES

(*f*) will endeavor to take steps in matters of international concern for the prevention and control of disease.

Article XXIV. There shall be placed under the direction of the League all international bureaus already established by general treaties if the parties to such treaties consent. All such international bureaus and all commissions for the regulation of matters of international interest hereafter constituted shall be placed under the direction of the League. In all matters of international interest which are regulated by general conventions but which are not placed under the control of international bureaus or commissions, the secretariat of the League shall, subject to the consent of the Council and if desired by the parties, collect and distribute all relevant information and shall render any other assistance which may be necessary or desirable. The Council may include as part of the expenses of the secretariat the expenses of any bureau or commission which is placed under the direction of the League.

Article XXV. The members of the League agree to encourage and promote the establishment and cooperation of duly authorized voluntary national Red Cross organizations having as purposes the improvement of health, the prevention of disease, and the mitigation of suffering throughout the world.

Article XXVI. Amendments to this Covenant will take effect when ratified by the members of the League whose representatives compose the Council and by a majority of the members of the League whose representatives compose the Assembly. No such amendment shall bind any member of the League which signifies its dissent therefrom, but in that case it shall cease to be a member of the League.

THE TREATY WITH GERMANY

The Treaty is in fifteen parts of 440 articles, in French and English texts and opens with the Covenant of the League of Nations (Part I).

Part II is devoted to the new geographical frontiers of Germany.

Part III, in 14 sections, binds Germany to accept the political changes brought about by the Treaty; establishes the two new States of Czecho-Slovakia and Poland; revises the basis of Belgian sovereignty, and alters the boundaries of Belgium; establishes new system of government in Luxemburg and the Saar basin, and restores Alsace-Lorraine to France; provides for possible additions of territory to Denmark; and binds Germany to recognize the independence of German Austria, and to accept conditions to be laid down as to States created since the Russian revolution.

By Parts II and III Germany recognizes the full sovereignty of Belgium over the contested territory of Moresnet and over part of Prussian Moresnet; she also renounces all rights over Eupen and Malmédy, the inhabitants of which are to settle the future sovereignty by plebiscite.

Luxemburg passes from the sphere of German influence.

Germany is forbidden to maintain or construct any fortifications within a distance of less than 50 kilometres from the right bank of the Rhine.

As compensation for the destruction of the coal-mines in Northern France, and as part payment toward the total reparation due for war damage, Germany cedes to France in full and absolute possession the coal-mines in the Saar basin; the government of this territory is renounced in favor of the League of Nations as trustee for fifteen years, at the end of which time the inhabitants will decide the question of sovereignty by a plebiscite.

Alsace and Lorraine are returned to France in full sovereignty and free of all public debts by the restoration of the eastern frontier of France to its full limits as it ran before the war of 1870; citizenship is regulated by detailed provisions distinguishing those who are immediately restored to full French citizenship, those who have to make formal application, and those to whom nationalization is open after three years. France is substituted for Germany as regards ownership of the railroads and rights over tramways concessions, the Rhine bridges pass to France with the obligation for their upkeep. Manufactured products of Alsace-Lorraine to a total annual amount of not more than that of the average of the preceding three years are to be admitted to Germany free of duty. For seven years (possibly ten) the port of Kehl on the right bank is to be administered with Strasburg as a single unit by a French administrator appointed and supervised by the Central Rhine Commission.

Germany acknowledges and will strictly respect the independency of Austria.

Germany recognizes the entire independence of the Czecho-Slovak State, including the autonomous territory of the Ruthenians, south of the Carpathians, and accepts the frontiers of this State as they may be determined. These in the case of the German frontier follow the old Bohemian frontier of 1914. The southwestern extremity of Upper Silesia immediately eastward of Troppau is renounced by Germany in favor of Czecho-Slovakia. Within a period of two years habitual residents over eighteen years of age will be entitled to vote for other than Czecho-Slovakian nationality. A similar option is provided for Czechs living in foreign States and desirous of gaining Czech nationality.

Germany cedes to Poland the greater part of Upper Silesia, Posen, and the province of West Prussia on the west bank of the Vistula. In the portion of Upper Silesia about Oppeln, and in the upper reaches of the River Oder as far as the old German and Austro-Silesian frontier, the inhabitants are to decide by plebiscite either for Germany or Poland. German troops and officers to be withdrawn within ten days. Workmen's and Soldiers' Councils within the area are to be dissolved, and the interim Government, except in respect of legislation and taxation, is entrusted to an International Commission of four members, one to be nominated by each of the four Powers, the United States, Great Britain, France, and Italy.

LEAGUE OF NATIONS AND TREATIES

The southern and the eastern frontiers of East Prussia facing Poland are to be fixt by plebiscites. Similar provisions in respect to the plebiscite areas in Upper Silesia concern the withdrawal of German troops and authorities, but the interim Government of the areas is placed under an International Commission of five members, appointed by the five Allied and Associated Powers with the particular duty of arranging for a fair, free, and secret vote. Prussia is assured full and equitable access to the Vistula, and provision is made for a subsequent Convention to be signed within one year between Poland, Germany, and Danzig; to assure suitable railroad, telegraphic, and telephonic communication across German territory on the right bank of the Vistula between Poland and Danzig, while Poland shall grant free passage from East Prussia into Germany.

The northeastern corner of East Prussia, about Memel, is ceded to the Associated Powers by Germany, who undertakes to accept their settlement particularly in so far as concerns the nationality of the inhabitants.

Danzig and the district immediately about it are constituted the Free City of Danzig under guarantee of the League of Nations. The actual area is to be delimited on the spot by a commission of three members, one (the President) appointed by the principal Allied Powers, one by Germany, and one by Poland. The principal Allied Powers undertake to negotiate a treaty between Poland and the Free City to effect its inclusion within the Polish customs frontier, tho with a free area in its port, and to ensure to Poland the unrestricted use of all the City's waterways, docks, and other port facilities, the control and administration of the Vistula, and the whole through railway system within the city, and postal, telegraphic, and telephonic communication between Poland and Danzig; provide against discrimination against Poles within the city; and place its foreign relations in charge of Poland.

The frontier between Germany and Denmark is to be fixt in conformity with the wishes of the population, who will vote in Northern Schleswig as a whole, and in portions of Central Schleswig by commission within ten days from the coming into force of the Treaty. The Commission is to take all steps which it thinks proper to ensure the freedom and fairness and secrecy of the vote; German and Danish technical advisers are to be chosen from the local population. Half the cost of the plebiscite is to be borne by Germany. The result of the plebiscite, which is to be decided by a majority among all adults over twenty years of age, will be immediately communicated by the Commission to the principal Allies and Associated Governments and proclaimed. If the vote result in favor of the reincorporation of this territory in the Kingdom of Denmark, the Danish Government in agreement with the Commission will be entitled to effect its occupation with their military and administrative authorities immediately after the proclamation. The plebiscite by communes in the southern section of the zone will be taken within five weeks of that in the northern parts.

The fortifications, military establishments, and harbors of the islands of Heligoland and Dune are to be destroyed, under supervision of the Allies, by German labor and at Germany's expense. They are not to be reconstructed, nor are any similar works to be constructed in the future.

Germany acknowledges, and agrees to respect as permanent and inalienable, the independence of all the territories which were part of the former Russian Empire on Aug. 1, 1914. She accepts definitely the abrogation of the Brest-Litovsk Treaties and of all Treaties, conventions and agreements entered into by her with the Maximalist Government in Russia. The Allies formally reserve the rights of Russia to obtain from Germany restitution and reparation based on the principle of the present Treaty. Germany undertakes to recognize all Treaties or agreements which may be entered into by the Allies with States now existing or coming into existence in the whole or part of the former Empire of Russia, and to recognize the frontiers as they may be determined therein.

Part IV. *German Rights and Interests outside Germany* (in 8 sections and 40 articles.) Outside Europe Germany renounces all rights, titles, and privileges as to her own or her allies' territories, and undertakes to accept whatever measures are taken by the principal Allied Powers in relation thereto.

Germany renounces in favor of the Allied Powers all her rights and titles over her overseas possessions. All movable and immovable property belonging to the German Empire or any German State pass to the Allied Government exercising authority therein. Germany undertakes to pay reparation for damage suffered by French nationals in the Cameroons or its frontier zone through the acts of German civil and military authorities and of German private individuals during the period from January 1, 1900, to August 1, 1914. Germany renounces all rights under the conventions with France of November 4, 1911, and September 28, 1912, relating to Equatorial Africa.

Germany renounces in favor of China all privileges and indemnities resulting from the Boxer protocol of 1901, all her public property other than diplomatic or consular buildings in the German concessions of Tientsin and Hankow (which China is to open to international trade) and in other Chinese territory except Shantung; agrees to restore all the astronomical instruments seized in 1900-1; renounces all claims against China or any of the Allies for the internment or repatriation of her citizens in China or for the liquidation of German interests there since Aug. 14, 1917; renounces in favor of Great Britain her state property in the British concession at Canton and of France and China jointly in the German school in the French concession at Shanghai.

China having declined to sign the Treaty, a mandate declaring the state of war with Germany to be ended was issued at Peking on Sept. 15.

All Treaties, conventions, and agreements between Germany and Siam, and all German rights in Siam, including that of extra-territoriality, ceased as from July 22, 1917; all German public property other than diplomatic and consular buildings is confiscated; and all German claims arising out of the seizure of German ships, the liquidation of German property, or the internment of German national are waived.

German rights in Liberia under the international arrangement of 1911-12 are abrogated, especially that to nominate a German receiver of customs in Liberia, and all Treaties and arrangements between Germany and Liberia are abrogated as from August 4, 1917.

In Morocco Germany, having recognized the French protectorate, renounces all her rights under the Act of Algeciras of April 6, 1906, and the Franco-German agreements of 1909 and 1911, and in all Treaties and arrangements with the Sherifian Empire.

In Egypt Germany recognizes the British protectorate proclaimed on December 18, 1914. Temporary provision for the exercise of jurisdiction by the British Consular Tribunals over German Nationals and property is made by means of decrees by the Sultan. The Egyptian Government obtains complete liberty of action in regulating the status of German nationals and the conditions under which they may establish themselves in Egypt. All German State property, including the private property of the ex-German Emperor, passes to the Egyptian Government.

Germany undertakes to recognize all arrangements which the Allied and Associated Governments may make with Turkey and Bulgaria.

German rights in Shantung, especially in respect of the territory of Kiaochow, are renounced in favor of Japan.

Part V. *Military, Naval, and Aerial Clauses.* Before March 31, 1920, the German Army must be reduced to not more than seven divisions of infantry and three divisions of cavalry with total effectives of 100,000 men, including officers and depot establishment. Officers are not to exceed 4,000. The army is to be devoted exclusively to maintenance of order in Germany and the control of frontiers. The divisions must not be grouped under more than two army corps headquarters staffs. The Great German General Staff and all similar organizations must be finally dissolved. The total administration strength of the war ministry must not exceed 300, to be included in the maximum number of 4,000 officers. Customs officers, forest guards, and coast guards are not to exceed the number functioning in 1913 and the gendarmerie and police may only be increased to an extent corresponding to the increase of population since 1913.

Until Germany is admitted a member of the League of Nations, her armament may not exceed 84,000 rifles, 18,000 carbines, 792 heavy machine guns, 1,134 light machine guns, 63 medium trench mortars, 189 light trench mortars, 204 7.7-cm. guns, 84 10.5-cm. howitzers, 40,-800,000 rounds of rifle ammunition, 15,408,000 rounds of machine gun ammunition, 176,400 rounds for trench mortars, and 271,200 rounds for field artillery. After she enters the League of Nations Germany agrees to observe the decisions of its Council in the strength of armaments. The stock of munitions is to be stored only at points notified to the Governments of the principal Allies. Notification must be made of the armament of the fortified works of land and coast forts at the coming into force of the Treaty, and these must remain the maximum number of pieces; their stock of ammunition must be reduced within two months to 1,500 rounds per piece of 10.5-cm. or under, and 500 rounds per piece of higher calibre. The manufacture of war material is to take place only at factories and arsenals approved by the principal Allies; all others to be closed down within three months of the coming into force of the Treaty. Arms, munitions, and material in excess of the permitted amount to be surrendered to the Allies within two months. Importation of arms of any sort into Germany is forbidden. The use of asphyxiating and poison gases and all analogous liquids being forbidden, their manufacture within or importation into Germany is forbidden. The manufacture or import of tanks and armoured cars is also forbidden. Germany is to disclose within three months the nature and mode of manufacture of all explosives and chemicals used by her during the war.

Conscription is to be abolished in Germany. The number of military schools is to be reduced to a minimum and all institutions in excess are to be abolished. Schools, universities, societies of discharged soldiers, shooting or touring clubs must not occupy themselves with military matters or have any connection with the ministries of war. Germany is to send no military, naval, or air mission to foreign countries, and the Allies agree not to enrol any Germans in any of their war services.

All fortified works within fifty kilometers of the east bank of the Rhine are to be dismantled.

German naval forces in commission are to be reduced within two months to six battleships (*Deutschland* or *Lothringen* type), six light cruisers, 12 destroyers, and 12 torpedo boats. No submarines are to be included, and the further building of submarines even for commerce is forbidden. All existing submarines and docks are to be handed over to the Allies, and those not able to proceed to Allied ports are to be destroyed. Other warships must be placed in reserve or devoted to commerce. The total personnel of the German navy, including administration and land defense, must not exceed 1,500.

All surface warships not in German ports at the signing of the Treaty cease to belong to Germany, who finally surrenders the vessels interned in compliance with the armistice. The breaking-up of all German surface warships under construction must begin immediately. German auxiliary cruisers and fleet auxiliaries will be disarmed and treated as merchant ships.

The personnel of the German navy is to be entirely voluntarily recruited, officers, and warrant officers to engage for a minimum of twenty-five years and petty officers and men for twelve years. No officer or man in the mercantile marine is to receive any training in the navy.

To ensure free passage into the Baltic, Germany undertakes to erect no fortification in the area between lat. 55° 27' N. and 54° N., and long. 9° E. and 16° E. Existing fortifications in this area are to be destroyed. Germany will place at the disposal of the Allies all hydrographical information concerning the channels between the Baltic and the North Sea. Other coast defenses except Heligoland may be retained, but no new fortification constructed, and the present armaments are not to be exceeded. The stock of ammunition for the guns is to be reduced to a maximum of 1,500 rounds per piece for calibres of 4.1 in. and under, and 500 rounds per piece of higher calibres. During three months after the peace Germany can use the wireless telegraphy stations, at Nauen, Hanover, and Berlin under supervision of the Allies, but for commercial purposes only; she may not during that period build big-powered stations in her own territory or that of Austria, Hungary, Bulgaria, or Turkey.

No military or naval air forces are to be retained by Germany; no dirigible may be kept; all military and naval aircraft and material is to be handed over to the principal Allies within three months.

Part VI. *Prisoners of War and Graves.* Repatriation of prisoners of war and interned civilians to take place as soon and as rapidly as possible after the Treaty. It will be carried out by a commission composed of representatives of the Allies and of the German Government, with sub-commissions composed of representatives of the individual Powers and Germany to regulate the details. The cost of repatriation of German prisoners is to be borne by the German Government. Those under sentence for offenses against discipline committed before May 1, 1919, are to be repatriated without regard to the completion of their sentence, but this does not apply in the case of offenses other than those against discipline. Prisoners who do not desire to be repatriated may be excluded, but the Allies reserve the right to repatriate them, to take them to a neutral country, or to allow them to remain. All repatriation of Germans is conditioned on the immediate release of any allied subjects remaining in Germany. Facility is to be accorded to Commissions of Inquiry to collect information as to missing prisoners of war. Germany also undertakes to impose penalties upon any official or private person who have concealed the presence of any Allied nationals. The German Government is to restore all property belonging to Allied prisoners.

The Allies and the German Government are to respect and maintain the graves of all soldiers and sailors buried in their territories.

Part VII. *Penalties.* The Allied and Associated Powers publicly arraign William II of Hohenzollern, formerly German Emperor, for a supreme offense against international morality and the sanctity of treaties. A special tribunal will be constituted to try the accused, thereby assuring him the guaranties essential to the right of defense. It will be composed of five judges, one appointed by each of the following Powers; namely, the United States of America, Great Britain, France, Italy, and Japan.

Military tribunals are to be set up by the Allies to try persons accused of acts of violation of the laws and customs of war, and the German Government is to hand over all persons so accused. Similar tribunals are to be set up by any particular Allied Power against whose nationals criminal acts have been committed. The accused are to be entitled to name their own counsel, and the German Government is to undertake to furnish all documents and information the production of which may be necessary.

Part VIII. *Reparation.* Germany accepts responsibility of herself and her Allies for causing all the loss to which the Allies and their nationals were subjected ''as a consequence of the war imposed upon them by the aggression of Germany and her Allies.''

The total obligation of Germany to pay is to be determined and notified to her after a fair hearing, and not later than May 1, 1921, by an Inter-Allied Reparation Commission, which will concurrently draw up a schedule for securing the payment of the entire obligation within a period of thirty years from May 1, 1921. If Germany has failed to discharge the debt within the period, any unpaid balance may, at the discretion of the Commission, be postponed for settlement to subsequent years or otherwise handled.

The commission shall consist of five voting members, one of whom shall be appointed each by the United States, Great Britain, France, and Italy. The fifth delegate will be appointed by Belgium, except (1) when questions affecting Japanese interests are concerned, when he shall be a delegate appointed by Japan; or (2) when questions relating to Austria, Hungary, or Bulgaria are under consideration, when the delegate of the Serb-Croat-Slovene State will be the fifth. The permanent bureau of the Commission will be in Paris and the first meeting held as soon as practicable after the coming into force of the Treaty. It will meet thereafter at such places and times as are convenient.

Pending the full determination of Allied claims, Germany shall pay the equivalent of 20,000,000,000 gold marks, out of which shall first be met the expenses of the armies of occupation and such supplies of food and raw material as the Allies may judge essential to enable Germany to meet her obligations.

To facilitate the immediate restoration of the economic life of the allied and associated countries, the Commission will take from Germany by way of security a first instalment of gold bearer bonds free of all taxes and interest. In addition to bonds for 20,000,000,000 marks payable not later than May 1, 1921, for the purpose of Article 235, there will also be issued forthwith a further 40,000,000,000 marks gold bearer bonds bearing 2½ per cent. interest between 1921 and 1926, and thereafter 5 per cent. with a 1 per cent. sinking fund payment beginning in 1926, and an undertaking to deliver 40,000,-000,000 marks gold bearing interest at 5 per cent. under terms to be fixt by the Commission.

Interest on Germany's debt shall be 5 per cent. unless otherwise determined by the Commission.

Germany agrees to the direct application of her economic resources to reparation. She recognizes the right of the Allies to the replacement ton for ton and class for class of all merchant ships and fishing boats lost or damaged in the war. She will deliver within two months of the coming into operation of the Treaty all German merchant ships of 1,600 tons gross and upwards; one half (in tonnage) of ships between 1,000 and 1,600 tons gross; and one quarter (in tonnage) of her steam trawlers and other fishing boats. The obligation includes ships building in Germany or on German Government or private account in foreign shipyards; also shipping transferred to neutral flags during the war, and not more than 20 per cent of her river fleet. Germany agrees ''as an additional part of reparation'' to build merchant ships for the account of the Allies to the amount not exceeding 200,000 tons gross annually during the next five years.

Germany undertakes in part satisfaction of her obligations to devote her economic resources directly to the physical restoration of the invaded areas. The Allies may file lists of animals, machinery, equipment, tools, and like articles of a commercial character, which have been seized, consumed, or destroyed by Germany, and which they desire to have replaced by similar animals and articles from Germany; also reconstruction materials, bricks, tiles, wood, window-glass, lime, cement, etc., machinery, heating apparatus, furniture, and like articles which it is desired to have produced and manufactured in Germany and delivered, to permit of the restoration of the invaded areas. The Commission will consider Germany's ability to meet the demands after hearing evidence of her domestic needs.

Germany accords to the delivery of coal and its derivatives:

To France: 7,000,000 tons of coal per year for ten years.

To Belgium: 8,000,000 tons per year for ten years.

To Italy: 77,000,000 tons in ten years by varying instalments.

To Luxemburg (if directed) a quantity equal to the pre-war consumption of German coal in the State.

France is also to receive for ten years, on account of her destroyed mines, an amount (not exceeding 20,000,000 tons in any of the first five years or 8,000,000 tons in any of the later five years) representing the difference between the production of her minefields before the war and during the restoration period. It is understood that all due diligence will be exercised in restoring the destroyed mines.

Germany is also to deliver to France during each of these years 35,000 tons of benzol, 50,000 tons of coal tar, and 30,000 tons of sulphate of ammonia.

Germany accords to the Reparation Commission an option on 50 per cent. of her dyestuffs and chemical drugs, to be executed within sixty days of the coming into force of the Treaty.

Germany renounces her own right and that of her nation in her submarine cables, but the value of those privately owned will be credited in the reparation account.

Germany undertakes to hand over and restore:

To the French Government: the trophies, archives, historical souvenirs or works of art carried away in 1870-71, and in the last war, especially flags and political papers.

To the King of the Hedjaz, the original Koran of the Caliph Othman, removed from Medina by the Turks and stated to have been presented to the ex-Emperor William II.

To Great Britain: the skull of the Sultan Mkwawa taken from German East Africa to Germany.

To the University of Louvain: manuscripts, incunabula, printed books, maps, and objects of collection corresponding to those destroyed in the Library of Louvain.

To Belgium: the leaves of the triptych of the Mystic Lamb painted by the Van Eyck brothers, formerly in the church of St. Bavon at Ghent (from Berlin Museum); and the leaves of the triptych of the Last Supper painted by Dierick Bouts, formerly in the church of St. Peter at Louvain (two from Berlin Museum, and two in the old Pinokothek at Munich).

Part IX. The cost of reparation and other costs arising under the Treaty will be a first charge on the assets of the German Empire and States. Until May 21, 1921, Germany may not export or dispose of any gold without the assent of the Reparation Commission.

The total cost of the Allied armies of occupation is to be paid by Germany.

Germany is to deliver to the Allies all sums deposited in Germany by Turkey and Austria-Hungary as financial support, extended by her to them during the war, and to transfer to the Allies all claims against Austria-Hungary, Turkey, or Bulgaria, in connection with agreements made during the war. She confirms the renunciation of the Treaties of Bucharest and Brest-Litovsk.

Part X. *Customs Regulations, Duties, and Restrictions.* Germany generally undertakes not to discriminate directly or indirectly against or between the trade of the Allies.

Postal and telegraphic conventions are renewed, Germany undertaking not to refuse her consent to special arrangements concluded by the new States.

Part XI. Aircraft of the Allies is to have full liberty of passage over and landing in German territory; equal treatment with German planes as to use of German aerodromes; and most-favored-nation treatment as to internal commercial air traffic. Germany accepts Allied certificates of nationality.

Part XII. Germany is required to grant freedom of transit and full national treatment to persons, goods, vessels, building stock, etc., to or from Allied States passing through German territory. Goods in transit are to be free of customs duties and rates of transport are to be reasonable. International transport is to be expedited particularly for perishable goods.

The following rivers are declared international:

The Elbe from its confluence with the Vltava (Moldau), and the Vltava from Prague.

The Oder from its confluence with the Oppa.

The Niemen from Grodno.

The Danube from Ulm.

And all navigable parts of these river-systems which naturally provide more than one State with access to the sea.

Lateral canals and channels are also declared international, and the same condition will apply to a Rhine-Danube navigable waterway should it be hereafter constructed within twenty-five years.

On the international waterways, the nationals' property and flags of all Powers shall be treated on a footing of perfect equality; nevertheless, German vessels shall not be entitled to carry passengers or goods by regular services between the ports of any Allied Power without special authority.

Within three months from the date notified to her, Germany is to cede a proportion of her tugs and vessels remaining after the deduction of those surrendered by way of restitution; she is also to cede materials, of all kinds necessary, for the allied utilization of the river-systems, the amount to be determined by an arbitrator nominated by the United States of America.

The Kiel Canal is to remain free and open to vessels of commerce and of war of all nations at peace with Germany, on terms of entire equality. Subjects, goods, and ships of all States are to be treated on terms of equality; charges are to be limited to those necessary to the upkeep of the canal, which is to be maintained by Germany, who may not undertake any works of a nature to impede navigation on the canal or its approaches. In case of violation of these conditions or disputes as to their interpretation, any interested Power can appeal to the jurisdiction established by the League of Nations.

Part XIII is devoted to Labor's Charter under the League of Nations.

Part XIV. As a guaranty for the execution of the present Treaty by Germany, the German territory situated to the west of the Rhine together with the bridgeheads will be occupied by Allied and Associated troops for a period of fifteen years from the coming into force of the present Treaty. If the conditions of the Treaty are faithfully carried out by Germany, the occupation will be successively withdrawn:

(1) At the end of five years, from the bridgehead of Cologne;

(2) At the end of ten years from the bridgehead of Coblenz;

(3) At the end of fifteen years from the bridgeheads of Mainz and Kehl, with the surrounding territory.

If the guaranties against unprovoked aggression by Germany are not considered sufficient, the evacuations may be delayed to the extent regarded as necessary for the purpose of obtaining the required guaranties. If before the expiration of fifteen years Germany complies with all the undertakings of the Treaty, the occupying forces will be withdrawn immediately.

As a guaranty for the abrogation of all Treaties entered into by

Germany with the Maximalist Government in Russia and in order to ensure the restoration of peace and good government in the Baltic Provinces and Lithuania, all German troops at present in these territories shall return within the frontiers of Germany as soon as the five principal Allies shall think the moment suitable, having regard to the internal situation of these territories.

Part XV. *Miscellaneous.*—Germany agrees to recognize the full validity of any Treaties of peace and additional conventions to be concluded by the Allies with the Powers allied with Germany, to agree to the decisions to be taken as to the territories formerly parts of Austria-Hungary, Bulgaria, and Turkey, and to recognize the new States in the frontiers fixt for them.

THE TREATY WITH AUSTRIA

Large portions of this Treaty are identical with that signed with Germany, and other portions vary only to meet the necessary alterations of circumstances. There is an introduction which notes that the war originated in the declaration made against Serbia by the former Austro-Hungarian Government, that the former Austro-Hungarian Government has ceased to exist, and that the Czecho-Slovak and the Serb-Croat-Slovene States have been recognized.

Part I. The League of Nations Covenant, as in the German Treaty.

Part II. The future Austrian Frontiers, summarized as follows:

(1) *Northern Frontiers.* The existing administrative boundaries formerly separating the provinces of Bohemia and Moravia from those of Upper and Lower Austria. These boundaries will be subjected to certain minor rectifications.

(2) *Western and Northwestern Frontiers.* The existing frontier to be maintained.

(3) *Western Frontiers.* No change in these frontiers.

(4) *Southern Frontiers.* With Italy a line starting from the Col de Reschen, and following in general the watershed between the basins of the Inn and the Drave to the north and the Adige, Piave, and the Tagliamento to the south.

In the eastern part the line, passing just east of Bleiburg, crosses the Drave just above its confluence with the Lavant, and thence will pass north of the Drave so as to leave to the Serb-Croat-Slovene State Marburg and Radkersburg, just to the north of which latter place it will join the Hungarian frontier.

(5) *Eastern Frontier.* No alteration is made in the Treaty of Peace with regard to the former frontier between Austria and Hungary.

Part III. The High Contracting Parties recognize and accept the frontiers of Bulgaria, Greece, Hungary, Poland, Rumania, the Serb-Croat-Slovene State, and the Czecho-Slovak State, as at present determined, or as they may be ultimately determined, and Austria renounces in favor of the principal Allied and Associated Powers all her rights and titles over territories formerly belonging to her which, tho outside the new frontiers of Austria, have not at present been assigned to any State undertaking to accept the settlement to be made in regard to these territories.

Italy. A special convention will determine the terms of repayment, in Austrian currency, of the special war expenditure advanced by the territory transferred to Italy to the former Austro-Hungarian Monarchy during the war. The Italian Government is substituted in all the rights which the Austrian State possest over all the railways in the territories transferred to Italy. Italy is to have free use of the waters of Lake Raibl.

Serb-Croat-Slovene State. A commission consisting of seven members, of whom five shall be nominated by the principal Allied Powers and one each by the Serb-Croat-Slovene State and Austria, shall be constituted within fifteen days from the coming into force of the Treaty to trace the new frontier line.

The inhabitants of the Klagenfurt area will be called upon to indicate by plebiscite the State to which they wish to belong. For the purpose of the vote the area will be divided into two zones, one to be occupied by Serb troops and officials, the other by Austrians. If the vote in the Senate administered area, which will be taken first, is in favor of the Serb State, a plebiscite will follow in the second area; if, however, the first zone votes for Austria, no vote will be taken in the second zone and the whole area will remain Austrian.

The Serb-Croat-Slovene State accepts all those provisions that may be deemed necessary by the principal Allies to protect the interests of racial, linguistic or religious minorities within its borders.

Czecho-Slovak State. The new boundaries with Austria are to be delimited by a field commission of seven members constituted as in the case of the Serb State, and Czecho-Slovakia also agrees to provisions for the protection of minorities within her borders.

Rumania. The Roumanian article similar to that applied to the Serb-Croat-Slovene State and Czecho-Slovakia is inserted here. It was to this that Rumania also desired to make reservations, and in consequence declined in the first instance to sign the Treaty.

Part IV. Austria renounces all rights, titles, and privileges, as to her own or Allies' territories outside Europe, and undertakes to accept whatever measures are taken by the principal Allies in relation thereto. She recognizes the British Protectorate over Egypt, undertakes not to interfere in Morocco, renounces her Boxer indemnities and other concessions in China, and recognizes that all agreements between herself and Siam, including the right of extraterritoriality, are abrogated.

Part V. Conscription is abolished in Austria, whose total military forces are not to exceed 30,000 men, including officers and depot troops. Demobilization to this extent must be completed by three months after the Treaty.

All Austro-Hungarian warships, including submarines and all

vessels of the Danube Flotilla, are declared to be finally surrendered to the principal Allied and Associated Powers. Auxiliary cruisers, etc., to the number of twenty-one, are to be disarmed and treated as merchant ships.

All warships (including submarines) now under construction in ports which belong or have belonged to Austria-Hungary to be broken up. Articles and materials arising therefrom may not be used except for industrial purposes, and may not be sold to foreign countries.

The construction or acquisition of any submarine, even for commercial purposes, is forbidden.

All naval arms, ammunition, and other war material belonging to Austria-Hungary at the date of the armistice are to be surrendered to the Allies.

The armed forces of Austria must not include any military or naval air forces. The entire *personnel* of the air forces in Austria is to be demobilized within two months.

The manufacture of aircraft and parts of aircraft is forbidden for six months.

All military and naval aircraft (including dirigible and aeronautical material) are to be delivered to the Allied and Associated Governments within three months.

Part VI. *Prisoners of War and Graves.* Conditions as in German Treaty.

Part VII. *Penalties.* There is no article in the Austrian Treaty corresponding to that of the German Treaty, which arraigns the ex-Kaiser William II. Austria, however, is required to hand over for trial, before military tribunals to be set up by the Allies, persons accused of acts of violation of the laws and customs of war; and the other provisions of this part of the German Treaty also apply.

Part VIII. The responsibility of Austria and her allies for the war is affirmed; and the Allies recognize that the resources of Austria are not adequate to make complete reparation for the loss and damage caused to them. The Allies, however, require Austria to make compensation up to a point determined by the Inter-Allied Reparation Commission, which is set up under the Treaty with Germany. Modifications to meet the case of Austria are provided.

Austria is required to pay in the course of 1919-1920 and the first four months of 1921 a ''reasonable'' sum, out of which the expenses of the armies of occupation subsequent to the armistice of Nov. 3, 1918, shall first be met and payment made for supplies of food and raw material judged by the principal Allies to be essential to enable Austria to meet her obligations for reparation.

Austria is also required to make restitution of cash, animals, objects of every nature and securities, seized in the war.

Austria undertakes to surrender to the respective Allies all records, documents, objects of antiquity and of art, and all scientific and bibliographical material taken away from the invaded territories.

She will also cede all records, documents, and historical material possest by public institutions bearing on the history of her ceded territories which have been removed during the last ten years. So far as concerns Italy, the period affected shall be extended to the date of the proclamation of the Kingdom in 1861. The new States arising out of the former Austro-Hungarian Monarchy undertake on their part to hand over documents, dating from a period not exceeding twenty years, which have a direct bearing on the history of Austria.

Part IX. *Financial Clauses.* In general these clauses follow the similar provisions of the German Treaty, as to priority of charges on the assets and revenues of Austria, payment of the costs of the armies of occupation, and of reparation.

Austria is to have free access to the Adriatic with rights to freedom of transit over territories and in ports severed from former Austro-Hungary. Austria is to allow Czecho-Slovakia to run its own trains over sections of railway leading to Fiume and Trieste through Austrian territory. The rights of Czecho-Slovakia in this connection are specified, and limited. The conditions are to be determined by a convention, and any points of difference are to be decided by an arbitrator nominated by Great Britain.

THE TREATY WITH BULGARIA

Part I contains the Covenant of the League of Nations.

Part II. The future frontiers of Bulgaria.

On the north the frontier with Rumania remains unchanged.

On the west, the frontier with the Serb-Croat-Slovene State for the most part follows the line of the old frontier with Serbia. Small portions of territory are ceded to the Serb-Croat-Slovene State, of which the most important is the town of Strumnitza and the surrounding district.

A modification is introduced into the southern frontier with territories to be subsequently attributed by the Principal Allied and Associated Powers, and the new boundary follows a line which may be drawn roughly from a point about eight miles southwest of Bashmakli to Kilkik, passing close to Ardabashi and Daridere, which remain in Bulgarian territory and crossing the Kartal Dagh and the Tokatjik Dagh.

On the southeast line a slight modification, taking in a small piece of Turkish territory northwest of Mustafa Pasha, is introduced. The Black Sea forms, as before, the eastern frontier.

Bulgaria thus loses her Thracian seaboard as well as her portion of territory in the Strumnitza district.

Part III. Bulgaria recognizes the Serb-Croat-Slovene State, in whose favor she renounces the territories situated outside the frontiers of Bulgaria as constituted by the Treaty. The new frontier is to be delimited by a commission of seven to be nominated within fifteen days of the coming into force of the Treaty.

Bulgaria renounces in favor of Greece the territories recognized by the present Treaty as forming part of Greece.

Territories in Thrace formerly belonging to Bulgaria and at present not assigned to any State are delivered by Bulgaria to the principal Allies with the undertaking to accept their settlement in regard to them; the principal Allies undertake, on the other hand, to ensure economic outlets for Bulgaria to the Ægean Sea under conditions to be fixt later.

Part IV. The military terms fix the total number of Bulgarian army effectives at 20,000, including officers; their sole function is to maintain internal order and control frontiers, and no military forces other than these are to be raised. The army is to be recruited on a voluntary basis. The number of Customs, forestry, or police officials armed with rifles are not to exceed 10,000, so that the total number of rifles in use in Bulgaria shall not exceed 30,000. The proportion of officers of all kinds is not to exceed one-twentieth and of non-commissioned officers one-fifteenth of the total effectives. Only one military school for the recruitment of officers may be maintained in Bulgaria. Within three months of the coming into force of the Treaty, Bulgaria must hand over to the Allies any surplus of armaments and munitions beyond those fixt in the Treaty. The number and calibre of guns constituting the fixt normal armament of fortified places existing at present in Bulgaria will constitute the maximum allowed. Ammunition for these guns will be reduced to the rate of 15,000 rounds per gun of the caliber of 105 mm., and 500 rounds for a gun of higher caliber. No new fortifications may be constructed, no poison gas or liquid fire manufactured or imported, nor any tanks or armored cars. The manufacture of war munitions may only be carried on in one factory, controlled by and belonging to the State, with strictly limited output.

Inter-Allied Commissions of Control will be appointed by the principal Allies to secure the execution of the military, naval, and air clauses. The Bulgarian Government must furnish these commissions of control with all information and documents required.

Part V. *Prisoners of War and Graves.* This section, which otherwise corresponds with that of the Austrian Treaty, provides for an Inter-Allied Commission of Inquiry into offenses against the laws of war committed by the Bulgarian authorities, and to search for non-repatriated nationals of the Allies and their Associates.

Part VI. *Penalties.* As in the Austrian Treaty.

Part VII. *Reparation.* The Allies recognize that the resources of Bulgaria are insufficient to provide adequate reparation and fix the amount to be paid at 2,250,000,000 francs in gold to be discharged by a series of half-yearly payments beginning on July 1, 1920. The first two payments will represent interest at the rate of 2 per cent. per annum on the total sum; subsequent payments will include interest at 5 per cent. on the total capital sum outstanding and the provision of sinking fund to extinguish the total amount on January 1, 1958. Bulgaria has power at any time to make immediate payments in reduction of the total sum due over and above the half-yearly payments; she recognizes the transfer to the Allies of any financial claims her late Allies may have against her, and the Allies agree not to require any payment in respect to those claims which have been taken into account in fixing the amount of the financial reparation to be made.

Bulgaria will return to Greece, Rumania, and the Serb-Croat-Slovene State all the records, archives, and articles of archæological, historical, or artistic interest taken away during the war, and live-stock in restitution for the animals taken away during the war. In special compensation for the destruction of coal-mines on Serbian territory, Bulgaria will deliver to the Serb-Croat-Slovene State during five years from the coming into force of the Treaty 50,000 tons of coal a year from the State mines at Pernik, provided these deliveries are sanctioned by an Inter-Allied Commission. This commission must be satisfied that the economic life of Bulgaria is not unduly interfered with; it will be established at Sofia as soon as possible, and will consist of three members, one each to be nominated by Great Britain, France and Italy. Bulgaria will be represented by a commissioner without the right to vote. The commission will lay down a list of the taxes, revenues, concessions, and monopolies by which the sums required can be raised in Bulgaria. In case of default by Bulgaria, the commission will be entitled to assume full control of the collection of taxes.

Part VIII. *Financial Clauses.* Bulgaria is required to make the following payments in the following order of priority:

(i) Cost of military ocupation.

(ii) The service of such part of the external Ottoman public debt as a commission appointed for the purpose may attribute to Bulgaria.

(iii) The cost of reparation as prescribed by the present Treaty.

Part X. *Aerial Navigation.* This section is identical with that of the Austrian Treaty.

Part XI. *Ports, Waterways, and Railways.* Almost exactly as in the Austrian Treaty.

THE TREATY WITH TURKEY

Part I contains the Covenant of the League of Nations.

Part II. The boundaries of Turkey. The frontier of Turkey in Europe is approximately that of the Chatalja lines, the northern half of these lines being, however, advanced in a northwesterly direction so as to include within the boundries of Turkey the whole area of Lake Derkos, which is a reservoir for the supply of water to Constantinople. The boundaries of Turkey in Asia remain the same, except as regards the southern frontier, which, together with the new frontier in Europe and the boundary of the Greek administrative zone round Smyrna, is shown approximately on the attached map.

Provision is also made in the Treaty for a possible modification of the present frontier between Turkey and the independent State of Armenia—*viz.* the former Russo-Turkish frontier in this region—by reference to the arbitration of the President of the United States regarding the new boundary for Armenia in the vilayets of Trebizond, Erzerum, Van, and Bitlis.

Part III. Political clauses. Subject to the provisions of the Treaty the parties agree to the maintenance of Turkish sovereignty over Constantinople, but a reservation is made that if Turkey fails to observe the provisions of the Treaty or of supplementary Treaties or conventions, particularly as regards the protection of minorities, the Allied Powers may modify the above provisions, and Turkey agrees to accept any dispositions which may be made in this connection.

The navigation of the Straits, including the Dardanelles, the Sea of Marmora, and the Bosporus, is to be open in future both in peace and war to every vessel of commerce or of war, and to military and commercial aircraft without distinction of flag. These waters are not to be subject to blockade, and no belligerent right is to be exercised nor any act of hostility committed within them unless in pursuance of a decision of the Council of the League of Nations.

The Commission of the Straits is composed of representatives appointed respectively by the United States of America (if and when that Government is willing to participate), the British Empire, France, Italy, Japan, Russia (if and when Russia becomes a member of the League of Nations), Greece, Rumania, and Bulgaria (if and when Bulgaria becomes a member of the League of Nations).

Each power is to appoint one representative, but the representatives of the United States, the British Empire, France, Italy, Japan, and Russia have two votes each, and the representatives of the other Powers one vote each.

The Commission is charged with the execution and control of any works, etc. necessary for navigation. In the case of threats to the freedom of passage of the Straits special provision is made for appeal by the Commission to the representatives at Constantinople of Great Britain, France, and Italy, which Powers under the military provisions of the Treaty provide forces for the occupation of the zone of the Straits. The representatives will concert with the naval and military commanders of the Allied forces the necessary measures, whether the threat comes from within or without the zone of the Straits.

Turkey accepts in advance a scheme of local autonomy for the predominantly Kurdish areas east of the Euphrates, south of the southern frontier of Armenia as eventually fixt, and north of the southern frontier of Turkey to be drafted by a Commission composed of British, French, and Italian representatives sitting at Constantinople. This scheme is to protect the rights of Assyro-Chaldeans and other racial or religious minorities within the above area, and with this object provision is also made for a possible rectification of the Turkish frontier where that frontier coincides with that of Persia.

Secondly, the Treaty provides for an appeal for complete independence within a stated time to the Council of the League of Nations by the Kurdish peoples within the above area, and for the grant of such independence by Turkey if recommended by the Council. In that event the Kurds inhabiting that part of Kurdistan which has hitherto been included in the Mosul Vilayet are to be allowed, if they so desire, to adhere to the independent Kurdish State.

The Turkish Government agrees to transfer to the Greek Government the exercise of her rights of sovereignty over a special area extending a certain distance round the city of Smyrna. In witness of Turkish sovereignty the Turkish flag is to be flown on one of the forts outside Smyrna.

The Greek Government is to be responsible for the administration of the area, may keep troops there to maintain order, may include the area in the Greek Customs system, and is to establish a local Parliament on the basis of a scheme of proportional representation of minorities, which is to be submitted to the Council of the League of Nations, and only to come into force after approval by a majority of the Council. The elections may be postponed for a limited period to allow the return of inhabitants banished or deported by the Turkish authorities.

Special provisions are included regarding the protection of minorities, the suspension of compulsory military service, freedom of commerce and transit, the use of the Port of Smyrna by Turkey, and the salt mines of Phocœa. After five years the local Parliament may ask the Council of the League of Nations for the incorporation of the area in the kingdom of Greece, and the Council may impose a plebiscite.

Turkey renounces in favor of Greece practically all of her rights and titles over Turkish territory in Europe, as well as over Imbros, Tenedos, Lemnos, Samothrace, Mitylene, Samos, Nikaria, and Chios, and certain other islands in the Ægean.

In the zone of the Straits the Greek Government accept practically the same obligations as are imposed in Turkey. Provision is made for a separate Treaty to be signed by Greece protecting racial, linguistic, and religious minorities in her new territories, particularly at Adrianople, and safeguarding freedom of transit and equitable treatment of the commerce of other nations. Greece also assumes certain financial obligations.

Turkey recognizes Armenia as a free and independent State, and agrees to accept the arbitration of the President of the United States of America upon the question of the frontier between Turkey and Armenia in the vilayets of Erzerum, Trebizond, Van, and Bitlis, and upon Armenia's access to the sea.

Provision is made for the obligations and rights which may pass to Armenia as the result of the award of the President, giving former Turkish territory to her; for the eventual delimitation of the Armenian frontiers in Turkey as a result of the arbitration and of the Armenian frontiers with Georgia and Azerbaijan, failing direct agreement on the subject by the three States; and for a separate Treaty to be signed by Armenia protecting racial, linguistic, and religious minorities and safeguarding freedom of transit and equitable treatment for the commerce of other nations.

Syria and Mesopotamia are provisionally recognized by the high contracting parties as independent States, in accordance with article 22 of the Covenant of the League of Nations, subject to the tendering of administrative advice and assistance by a mandatory until they are able to stand alone. The boundaries of the States and the selection of mandatories will be fixt by the principal Allied Powers. By the application of the provisions of article 22 of the Covenant the administration of Palestine is also entrusted to a mandatory. The selection of the mandatory and the determination of the frontiers of Palestine will be made by the principal Allied Powers.

The declaration originally made on November 2, 1917, by the British Government and adopted by the other Allied Governments in favor of a national home for the Jewish people in Palestine is reaffirmed, and its terms cited in the Treaty.

Turkey, in accordance with the action already taken by the Allied Powers, recognize the Hedjaz as a free and Independent State and transfers to the Hedjaz her sovereign rights over territory outside the boundaries of the former Turkish Empire and within the boundaries of the Hedjaz as ultimately fixt.

In view of the sacred character of the cities and holy places of Mecca and Medina in the eyes of all Moslems, the King of the Hedjaz undertakes to ensure free and easy access thereto of Moslems of every country desiring to go there on pilgrimages and for other religious objects, and respect for pious foundations.

Turkey renounces all rights and titles over Egypt and Cyprus as from November, 1914, and recognizes the Protectorate proclaimed by Great Britain over Egypt on December 18, 1914.

Turkey recognizes the French Protectorate in Morocco and over Tunis.

Turkey also renounces in favor of Italy all rights and titles over the Dodecanese now in the occupation of Italy and also over the Island of Castellorizzo.

Special provision is made for Turkey's acceptance of a scheme of judicial reform (on the lines either of a mixed or unified system) to be drafted by the principal Allied Powers with the assistance of technical experts of the other capitulatory Powers, Allied or neutral. This scheme shall replace the present capitulatory system in judicial matters in Turkey.

Part IV. Turkey is to assure full and complete protection of life and liberty to all inhabitants of Turkey without distinction of birth, nationality, language, race, or religion. Special provision is made for the annulment of forcible conversions to Islam during the war and for the search and delivery under the protection of mixed commissions appointed by the League of Nations of all persons in Turkey, of whatever race or religion, carried off, interned, or placed in captivity during the war.

Turkey agrees to certain measures of restitution and reparation controlled by mixed arbitral commissions appointed by the League of Nations in favor of subjects of non-Turkish race who have suffered during the war. These commissions will have power generally to arrange for carrying out works of reconstruction, the removal of undesirable persons from different localities, the disposal of property belonging to members of a community who have died or disappeared during the war without leaving heirs, and for the cancellation of forced sales of property during the war. The measures necessary to guarantee the execution of this chapter of the Treaty are to be decided upon by the principal Allied Powers in consultation with the Council of the League of Nations.

Part V. *Military Classes.* Recruiting on a voluntary and nonracial, non-religious long-service basis is to be established. Turkey will be allowed to maintain the following armed land force:—

1. Gendarmerie, 35,000 men.

2. Special elements intended for the reinforcement of the gendarmerie in case of serious trouble, 15,000 men.

3. The Sultan's bodyguard, 700 men.

An Inter-Allied commission which will be responsible for the control and organization of the Turkish armed forces.

Armament and material of war are limited to the amount considered necessary for the new armed force.

For the purpose of guaranteeing the freedom of the Straits all works, fortifications, and batteries are to be demolished within a zone extending 20 kilos, inland from the coasts of the Sea of Marmora and the Straits, and comprising the islands of the Sea of Marmora, also the islands of Lemnos, Imbros, Tenedos, and Mitylene.

The naval clauses provide for the surrender of all Turkish warships with the exception of a few small lightly armed vessels, which may be retained for police and fishery duties. Turkey is forbidden to construct or acquire any surface warships other than those required to replace the units allowed for police and fishery duties, and also forbidden to [construct] or acquire any submarine even for commercial purposes. No military or naval air forces are to be maintained by Turkey.

Part VI. Turkish prisoners of war and interned civilians are to be repatriated without delay at the cost of the Turkish Government. All repatriation is conditional upon the immediate release of any Allied subjects still in Turkey. The Turkish Government is to afford facilities to commissions of inquiry in collecting information in regard to missing prisoners of war, in imposing penalties on Turkish officials who have concealed Allied nationals, and in establishing criminal acts committed by Turks against Allied nationals.

The Turkish Government is to restore all property belonging to Allied prisoners.

The Turkish Government is to transfer to the British, French, and Italian Governments respectively right of ownership over the ground in Turkey in which are situated the graves of their soldiers and sailors and over the land required for cemeteries or for providing access to cemeteries. The Greek Government undertakes to fulfil the same obligation so far as concerns the portion of the zone of the Straits placed under its sovereignty.

The land will include in particular certain areas in the Gallipoli peninsula.

Part VII. *Penalties*. Military tribunals are to be set up by the Allies to try persons accused of acts of violation of the laws and customs of war, and the Turkish Government is to hand over all persons so accused. The Turkish Government is to undertake to furnish all documents and information the production of which may be necessary.

The Turkish Government undertakes to surrender to the Allies persons responsible for the massacres committed during the war on the territory of the former Turkish empire, the Allies reserving the right to designate the tribunal to try such persons or to bring the accused before a tribunal of the League of Nations competent to deal with the said massacres if such a tribunal has been created by the League in sufficient time.

All the resources of Turkey except revenues ceded or hypothecated to the services of the Ottoman Public Debt are to be employed as need arises effecting the following payments set forth in order of priority:—

(1) Ordinary expenses of the Allied forces of occupation after the entry into force of the Treaty.

(2) Expenses of the Allied forces of occupation since the 30th October in the territories remaining Turkish, and expenses of occupation in the territories detached from Turkey to the advantage of a Power other than that which has supported such expenses of occupation.

(3) Indemnities due on account of claims of the Allied Powers for reparation for damages suffered by their nationals.

The Turkish Government agrees to the financial indemnification of all the losses or damages suffered by the civilian nationals of the Allied Powers during the war and up to the entry into force of the Treaty.

PERSONAL SKETCHES
THE TREATY OF PEACE
AND A
CHRONOLOGY OF THE WAR

Part III

A CHRONOLOGY OF THE WAR

(Based on *The Literary Digest's* Weekly Record of Current Events)

June 28, 1914—May 27, 1920

GREAT BRITAIN AND GERMANY IN PEACE TIMES

In the upper picture are shown Edward VII and the Kaiser riding in
Berlin; in the lower George V and the Kaiser riding in London

A CHRONOLOGY OF THE WAR

(Based on *The Literary Digest's* Weekly Record of Current Events)
June 28, 1914—May 27, 1920

THE EVENTS OF 1914

JUNE AND JULY

OUTBREAK OF THE AUSTRO-SERBIAN WAR —FUTILE EFFORTS BY THE GREAT POWERS TO AVERT FURTHER WAR

June 28. The Archduke Francis Ferdinand, heir to the throne of Austria-Hungary, and his morganatic wife, the Duchess of Hohenberg, assassinated in Serajevo, Bosnia, by a Serbian Student named Gavrio Prinzip.

July 23. Austria sends an ultimatum to Serbia.

July 24. Serbia's request for an extension of time to consider ultimatum refused.

July 25. Serbia concedes all Austria's demands save Austrian participation in investigation of Archduke's murder, and asks for Hague mediation on that point.

July 26. Efforts for peace begun by London, Paris, and St. Petersburg; Sir Edward Grey aiming to secure non-interference by other Powers.

July 28. Austria declares war on Serbia.

July 29. Austrian force attacks Belgrade; mobilization begins in Russia, Germany, and France; British First Fleet leaves Portland under sealed orders.

July 30. Germany sends ultimatum to Russia, demanding mobilization cease within twenty-four hours.

July 31. Negotiations by telegraph with Kaiser, by Czar and King George, fail to get a peaceful solution of quarrel; Germany, with the exception of Bavaria, declares martial law; stock markets all over world, including New York, close doors.

AUGUST

INVASION OF BELGIUM—BATTLE OF TANNENBURG—ALSACE-LORRAINE INVADED BY THE FRENCH

Aug. 1. Emperor Francis Joseph orders general mobilization; Germany declares war on Russia; French Cabinet orders general mobilization.

Aug. 2. German troops enter Luxemburg and demand free passage across Belgium, which is refused; German troops invade Belgium from Aix-la-Chapelle.

Aug. 3. Belgium appeals to England for aid.

Aug. 4. Great Britain demands that Germany observe Belgian neutrality; Berlin refuses and Great Britain declares war on Germany; France declares that state of war exists with Germany; German troops attack Liége.

Aug. 5. Austria declares war on Russia; Montenegro declares war on Austria; Belgium declares war on Germany; one German army crosses Alsatian border near Belfort, another enters France east of Nancy; Kitchener goes into British Cabinet as Secretary of State for War.

Aug. 6. Italy notifies Great Britain she will remain neutral; Serbia declares war on Germany; Austrians repulsed by Serbians; French troops enter Alsace; British light cruiser *Amphion* sunk by a mine.

Aug. 7. Liége falls into German hands; French troops enter Altkirch in Alsace.

Aug. 8. French troops enter Mulhausen; next day German forces oblige French to evacuate town and return to Altkirch.

Aug. 11. Germans under Kluck advance toward Brussels; army of Moselle faces French near Longwy; French invasion of Alsace checked beyond Mulhausen; Russians occupy border towns in East Prussia; Serbians take Serajevo.

Aug. 12. Great Britain declares war on Austria-Hungary; Germans seize Belgian town of Huy between Liége and Namur and overcome Belgians at Haelen.

Aug. 15. Japan sends ultimatum to Germany; French gain passes in Vosges; Russian proclamation issued of self-government for Poland.

Aug. 16. British Expeditionary Force lands on Continent.

Aug. 17. Belgian Government moves from Brussels to Antwerp; German artillery overcomes Tirlemont.

Aug. 20. Van of the German army reaches Brussels; Belgian army retreats on Antwerp; Louvain entered by Germans; hostilities begin in German Southwest Africa.

Aug. 21. Germans enter Brussels; attack on Namur begins.

Aug. 23. Namur falls, and Germans move on toward Mons; French and British move northward in Belgium against right wing of Germans; Germans occupy Lunéville in Lorraine.

Aug. 24. Zeppelin bombs fall on Antwerp; second day of battle of Mons; retreat of British begins.

Aug. 25. Russians within eighty miles of Lemberg.

Aug. 26. Germans burn Louvain; battle of Le Cateau between British and Germans.

Aug. 27. Japan blockades Kiaochow.

Aug. 28. Allies in retreat toward Paris; Longwy surrenders to Crown Prince; Russians advance on Lemberg; Germans lose three cruisers in battle off Heligoland. *Mainz, Köln* and *Ariadne;* first day of battle of Nancy or Grand Couronné.

Aug. 30. Amiens taken by Germans; Laon and La Fére surrender to Germans.

429

Aug. 31. Hindenburg defeats Russians in Masurian Lakes in battle called Tannenberg.

SEPTEMBER

BATTLES OF MARNE AND AISNE— RUSSIANS TAKE LEMBERG

Sept. 1. Germans under Kluck reach Compiègne, forty miles from Paris.

Sept. 2. Kluck when north of Chantilly, turns abruptly southeast, toward center of Allied line; Malines bombarded.

Sept. 3. French Government transferred to Bordeaux; British cross the Marne near Lagny; Germans reach Marne; Lemberg occupied by Russians.

Sept. 4. Germans cross Marne; Kluck's right at Senlis.

Sept. 5. End of the Allied retreat; Great Britain, France and Russia sign agreement that none of three shall make peace without concurrence of others.

Sept. 6. First day of the battle of the Marne.

Sept. 7. Germans take Maubeuge; German retreat across Marne begins; Maunoury forces back Kluck; end of battle of Nancy.

Sept. 8. German forces driven across Marne.

Sept. 9. Critical day of the Marne; Foch makes successful thrust at La Fère Champenoise.

Sept. 10. Germans driven back by Foch and battle of Marne ends; Russians victorious at Rawa Ruska.

Sept. 12. Germans occupy positions on Aisne.

Sept. 13. French regain Soissons; battle of the Aisne begins.

Sept. 19. Reims bombarded and cathedral takes fire.

Sept. 20. French occupy a line through Roye and Péronne; Hindenburg follows Russians.

Sept. 21. Jaroslaw taken by Russians.

Sept. 22. Germans gain heights of Craonne and take Bétheny, near Reims; Russians invest Przemysl; German submarine *U-9* sinks British cruisers, *Hogue*, *Cressy*, and *Aboukir* in North Sea.

Sept. 23. Hindenburg forces Russians across Niemen; Saint Mihiel with bridge-head taken by Germans.

Sept. 24. Allies take Péronne; Russians take Soldau in East Prussia.

Sept. 26. Germans capture Saint-Quentin; Malines bombarded for the third time.

Sept. 27. Allied attack eastward from Péronne forced back on Albert.

Sept. 28. Siege of Antwerp begins.

Sept. 30. Japanese begin bombardment of Kiaochow.

OCTOBER

RACE TO THE SEA—THE BATTLE OF FLANDERS — ANTWERP FALLS — LODZ, WARSAW, AND PRZEMYSL

Oct. 1. Forts at Antwerp fall.

Oct. 2. Fighting about Augustovo ends in German defeat.

Oct. 3. Russians take Tarnow.

Oct. 5. Belgian seat of government removed from Antwerp to Ostend.

Oct. 6. Germans capture Camp-de-Romains, near Saint-Mihiel.

Oct. 7. Inner fortifications of Antwerp under bombardment; Germans take Douai; German reinforcements check advances of Russians; Japanese seize Caroline Islands.

Oct. 8. British aeroplanes visit Dusseldorf and Cologne.

Oct. 9. Antwerp falls.

Oct. 12. Boers in Cape Province mutiny and martial law proclaimed in Union of South Africa.

Oct. 13. Belgian Government removes from Ostend to Havre.

Oct. 15. Formal entry of Germans into Antwerp and Ostend.

Oct. 16. Allied north wing retakes Armentières; Japanese cruiser sunk in Kiaochow Bay; British cruiser *Hawke* sunk by German submarine *U-9*.

Oct. 18. Belgians join Allied north wing; Yser battle begun; in battle of Vistula, Russian reinforcements outflank German left; another force attacks German right and turns tide.

Oct. 19. British gunboats bombard Germans on Belgian shore driving them back from Nieuport; Serbian army surrounds Serajevo.

Oct. 20. Belgian army forms tip of Allied north wing, extended northwest from Ypres through Dixmude to Channel at Nieuport.

Oct. 24. Rebel Boers under Maritz crusht in South Africa.

Oct. 25. Tip of the Allied north wing pushed back north of Dunkirk by Germans crossing Yser; in east, Lodz and Radom retaken by Russians.

Oct. 27. British Superdreadnought *Audacious* torpedoed.

Oct. 29. Turkish cruiser bombards Theodosia, in Crimea; Odessa also bombarded and vessels sunk in harbor.

Oct. 30. Belgian army destroys dikes, flooding lower Yser, and driving out Germans.

Oct. 31. Allies gain west bank of Yser and all crossings; begins land bombardment of Tsing-tau, Kiaochow.

NOVEMBER

BATTLE OF FLANDERS CONTINUED— THORN AND THE CARPATHIANS —CORONEL NAVAL BATTLE

Nov. 1. Russian army east of Vistula; Turks bombard Sebastopol; naval engagement occurs off Coronel on Chile coast; British lose cruisers *Monmouth* and *Good Hope;* cruisers *Glasgow* and *Otranto* severely damaged; of five German cruisers attacking *Scharnhorst, Gneisenau,* and *Nurnberg* arrive at Valparaiso.

Nov. 5. England and France declare war on Turkey.

Nov. 7. Tsing-tau capitulates.

Nov. 10. German cruiser *Emden* caught and destroyed by Australian cruiser *Sydney* off Cocos, or Keeling Islands.

Nov. 11. Germans cross Yser and capture Dixmude; Przemysl reinvested by Russians; British torpedo-boat *Niger,* in harbor at Deal, sunk by raiding submarine; Botha defeats rebels in South Africa in decisive engagement; British engage Turks near Bassora at head of Persian Gulf.

Nov. 12. Russians capture Johannisburg; Germans advance into Poland; Turks capture El Arish, Egypt.

Nov. 19. German advance blocked within 40 miles of Warsaw.

Nov. 20. Russians occupy Koprikeni.

Nov. 21. Russians capture Gumbinnen; Austrians evacuate Sandec; Turks evacuate Bassora.

Nov. 23. German line at Kalisz and Thorn falls into Russian trap.

Nov. 24. British warships bombard German naval base at Zeebrugge.

Nov. 25. Russian forces attempt invasion of Hungary over Carpathians.

Nov. 26. Austrians defending Krakow defeated at Brzesko; British predreadnought *Bulwark* blows up and sinks in Thames.

Nov. 29. Russians seize Czernowitz.

Nov. 30. Belgrade taken by Austrians.

DECEMBER

MOLTKE SUPERSEDED—BATTLES OF VISTULA AND FALKLAND ISLANDS

Dec. 1. De Wet captured in South Africa.

Dec. 5. German attack at Ypres resisted; Germans take Lodz.

Dec. 7. British squadron arrives at Falkland Islands.

Dec. 8. Serbians after a six-day battle regain Valjevo and Ushitza; British gain control of junction of Tigris and Euphrates; Beyers, rebel Boer leader, killed; British squadron under Sturdee defeats German squadron under Von Spee in South Atlantic off Falkland Islands and sinks German vessels all but the *Dresden*.

Dec. 9. French Government return to Paris from Bordeaux.

Dec. 10. Falkenhayn succeeds Moltke as head of German General Staff.

Dec. 13. Turkish battleship *Messudich* sunk in Dardanelles by British submarine; Allies blockade Dardanelles.

Dec. 14. Serbians recapture Belgrade.

Dec. 16. Scarborough, Hartlepool, and Whitby, English towns, bombarded by German squadron, 48 killed, 85 wounded.

Dec. 17. Britain declares protectorate over Egypt.

Dec. 18. Germans capture Lowicz; France acknowledges Britain's protectorate over Egypt; Prince Hussein Kemal, uncle of deposed Khedive, appointed Sultan.

Dec. 21. German invaders of Poland driven across border.

Dec. 24. German air-raid on England.

Dec. 25. Eight British ships, with hydro-aeroplanes, raid Cuxhaven.

Dec. 30. Germans withdraw from Bzura.

Dec. 31. Turks invade Russian Caucasus, advancing on Kars and Ardahan.

THE EVENTS OF 1915

JANUARY

SECOND BATTLE OF SOISSONS

Jan. 1. British warship *Formidable* torpedoed and sunk in English Channel with 500 men.

Jan. 3, 4. French capture Steinbach in Alsace.

Jan. 14. North of Soissons, Germans capture heights of Vregny.

Jan. 15. Russians take Kirlibaba Pass in Carpathians.

Jan. 17-18. French advance to within ten miles of Metz.

Jan. 19. German aircraft raid Norfolk coast towns in England, killing four persons.

Jan. 24. In an attempt to raid English coast, German squadron routed by coast patrol; German cruiser *Blücher* sunk with 762 men; twelve hundred Boer rebels under Maritz in Bechuanaland repulsed; Turks beaten back near El Kantara when on road to Suez Canal.

Jan. 30. Russians overwhelm Turks at Tabriz in Caucasus.

FEBRUARY

DARDANELLE FORTS STORMED—WAR-ZONE DECREES BY GERMANY AND ENGLAND

Feb. 2. Turks attempting to cross Suez Canal repulsed; four outer forts of Dardanelles shelled by Anglo-French fleet.

Feb. 3. Austrians evacuate Tarnow.

Feb. 4. Germany proclaims a war-zone around British Isles.

Feb. 8. Turks in flight from Suez Canal; Cyprus formally annexed to British Empire.

Feb. 10. United States Government protests to Germany against decree of a marine war-zone.

Feb. 12. Thirty-four British aircraft raid Belgian coast.

Feb. 18. Germany's reply to our protest against marine war-zone decree states original plan must be enforced.

Feb. 24. Germans storm and take Przasnysz with 10,000 prisoners.

Feb. 25. Allied fleet silences all forts at entrance to Dardanelles.

Feb. 26. Russians enter fortress of Przasnysz.

MARCH

NEUVE CHAPELLE—RUSSIANS NEAR HUNGARIAN PLAIN

March 3. Stanislau in Austrian hands.

March 10. British troops take Neuve Chapelle.

March 14. German cruiser *Dresden* sunk by British off Juan Fernandez Island.

March 18. In Dardanelles British battleships *Irresistible* and *Ocean* and French battleship *Bouvet* sunk by mines; British *Inflexible* and French *Gaulois* disabled.

March 22. Przemysl falls.
March 23. Russians gain Lupkow Pass.
March 25. Turks defeated at Aradabil in Caucasus by Russians; Kurds massacre Christian residents at Urmia.
March 26. French occupy Hartmannsweilerkopf, in Alsace.
March 28. British ship *Falaba* sunk by German submarine.

APRIL

ZEPPELIN RAIDS—SECOND BATTLE OF YPRES

April 12. Russians reach Szolyva, 20 miles within Hungarian border.
April 14. Zeppelin raid on England.
April 17. Second battle of Ypres begins; Germans use poison-gas.
April 18. British gain three miles near Ypres; Russians evacuate Tarnow.
April 19. Fighting toward Ypres continues; Germans gain by use of asphyxiating gases; Hindenburg takes command of Austro-German forces.
April 20. Surrender of Keetmanshoop in German Southwest Africa.
April 25. Allied troops landed on Gallipoli.
April 26. Germans gain Hartmannsweilerkopf, in Alsace; French cruiser *Léon Gambetta* sunk in Ionian Sea by Austrian submarine.
April 28. Russian Black Sea squadron bombards Turkish forces within the Bosporus.
April 29. Germans advance east from Tilsit, seventy miles into Russian territory, beyond Schaul.
April 30. A Zeppelin raids Ipswich; Bernstorff warns Americans, in newspaper advertisement, to avoid entering war-zone on ships of Allies.

MAY

BATTLE OF THE DUNAJEC—SINKING OF "LUSITANIA"—ITALIANS CROSS THE ISONZO

May 1. American oil-steamer *Gulflight* torpedoed off Scilly Isles, no warning given.
May 2. Austro-Germans gain a victory near Tarnow.
May 3. Germans gain in onslaughts near Ypres, asphyxiating gases used.
May 5. Austro-Germans recapture Tarnow.
May 7. Cunard liner *Lusitania* torpedoed without warning off Kinsale, Ireland, and sinks in fifteen minutes, with loss of 1,152 lives.
May 9. Germans break through Allied line on Poelcappelle road.
May 10. Note to United States from German Foreign Office expresses regret for losses on *Lusitania*, but directs attention to Germany's warning, and places blame on Great Britain.
May 13. Bucharest reports Russians in occupation of Czernowitz, Bukowina.
May 16. Allies shatter two miles of German lines north of Arras; Athens reports Allies silenced Turkish fortifications at Kilhid-Bahr, on European side of Dardanelles.

May 20. Italian Chamber of Deputies confers full war-powers on Government, by a vote of 407 to 74.
May 22. Mobilization orders issued in Italy.
May 23. War declared on Austria by Italy.
May 24. Hostilities along Adriatic begin.
May 25. Coalition Cabinet formed in Great Britain; Balfour First Lord of Admiralty.
May 26. American steamship *Nebraskan*, flying American flag, blown up off Irish coast.
May 27. Italians cross Isonzo near Gorizia; British battleship *Majestic* torpedoed and sunk in Dardanelles.
May 28. Italians occupy Grado, on Gulf of Trieste.
May 30. Germany says England's violations of international procedure compelled Germany to consider *Lusitania* hostile craft.
May 31. Italian advance through Trentino reaches Mt. Zugno; Zeppelins make raid on London, dropping bombs on suburbs, killing four.

JUNE

PRZEMYSL AND LEMBERG RECOVERED BY TEUTONIC FORCES

June 2. Przemysl retaken by Germans; English gunboat flotilla on Tigris secures surrender Kut-el-Amara.
June 4. Italians take Monte Nero, on upper Isonzo; Austro-German forces advance from Przemysl on Lemberg.
June 6. Russian warship and three German transports reported torpedoed or mined in Baltic, near Riga.
June 7. British aviator destroys Zeppelin in a duel 6,000 feet above the ground.
June 8. Austro-German advance in Galicia crosses Dniester taking Stanislau.
June 9. Allies capture Neuville-St. Vaast, near Arras; Italians take Monfalcone; Germans in Poland forced back along Baltic from above Libau.
June 10. Germans in Galicia driven across Dniester; Russians occupy Caucasus between Lake Van and Ourza.
June 12. In Trentino Italians reach Rovereto and Mori; Italian aviators destroy arsenal at Pola.
June 14. Throughout Greece, save in Macedonia, election results return Venizelos, strengthening war party.
June 15. French aircraft bombard Karlsruhe, killing and wounding over 200.
June 16. Zeppelins raid British coast, killing 16 and injuring 40; twenty-five lost in raid of June 6.
June 20. In Trieste region Italians capture heights of Pliava; Germans cut Lemberg's railroad communications.
June 21. French win "labyrinth" trenches north of Neuville-St. Vaast.
June 22. Austro-Germans enter Lemberg.
June 26. Halicz taken by Austro-Germans.
June 27. Zeppelin hangars at Friedrichshafen shelled by French aviators.

A CHRONOLOGY OF THE WAR

June 29. Ngaundere, in Kamerun, occupied by British.

JULY

GREAT GERMAN DRIVE INTO RUSSIA TOWARD BREST-LITOVSK BEGINS AND VISTULA CROSSED

July 1. Mackensen advances northward between Bug and Vistula; forces concentrated in this advance number 2,000,000 men.

July 3. Italians gain ten miles in three days in Carnic Alps.

July 8. German forces in German Southwest Africa surrender unconditionally to Botha.

July 11. German cruiser *Königsberg* destroyed by British monitors in German East Africa.

July 12. Italians execute cavalry raid to within three miles of Trieste.

July 14. Germans capture Przasnysz, 50 miles from Warsaw.

July 15. Russians decide to abandon Warsaw.

July 16. Germans advance on Riga, occupying Courland; from Przasnysz descend Narew toward Warsaw.

July 17. Italian Alpini capture Venerdolol and Brizce Passes, 10,000 feet high.

July 18. Italian cruiser *Guiseppe Garibaldi* sunk by Austrian submarine.

July 19. Fifty-nine Turkish sailing vessels, laden with war-munitions sunk by Russian destroyers.

July 20. Germany claims total occupation of Courland.

July 21. Germans invest Ivangorod.

July 24. Germans cross Vistula toward the Bug.

July 25. British occupy Kut-el-Amara on Tigris.

July 28. Pope Benedict issues appeal for peace.

July 31. Below's forces capture Mitau, south of Riga.

AUGUST

IVANGOROD AND WARSAW FALL—EDITH CAVELL ARRESTED—ACHI BABA ATTACKED

Aug. 4. Ivangorod falls.

Aug. 5. German forces storm last barriers of Warsaw and enter city; Edith Cavell arrested in Brussels.

Aug. 6. Russians evacuate whole line of Vistula, with single exception of Novogeorgievsk; British land at Suvla Bay and attack Achi Baba, Gallipoli.

Aug. 8. Italians retire from Gorizia.

Aug. 10. Air-raid on east coast of England; Teutonic advance beyond the Vistula begins.

Aug. 13. More Allied troops land at Suvla Burnu, on Gallipoli, and take up positions five miles inland; desperate two-days' battle follows.

Aug. 16. Eichorn takes outer fortifications of Kovno; *Royal Edmund*, British transport from Dardanelles, sunk in Ægean Sea, nearly 1,000 soldiers lost.

Aug. 17. Kovno falls, threatening all railway-lines between Grodno, Vilna, Brest-Litovsk, Dvinsk, and Petrograd.

Aug. 19. Novogeorgievsk, great Russian fortress at confluence of Narew and Vistula, taken by Germans; White Star-liner *Arabic* sunk in eleven minutes by torpedo.

Aug. 21. Great Britain declares cotton absolute contraband; Bulgaria mobilizing 150,000 troops on Turkish frontier.

Aug. 22. Germans take Ossowiec southwest of Grodno.

Aug. 25. Half-mile gain for Allies on Gallipoli; fleet of 62 aviators drop bombs on German munition factories north of Lorraine border; Brest-Litovsk taken by Mackensen's army; Russians evacuate fortress of Olita, 30 miles south of Kovno.

Aug. 26. Russian War Office orders call up 2,000,000 more men.

Aug. 28. Lipsk, 20 miles west of Grodno, captured by Germans; in Galicia Russians retreating along 125-mile front.

Aug. 31. James Archibald, an American, discovered at Falmouth transporting official dispatches from Bernstorff, German Ambassador in United States, to German Government; dispatches seized and Archibald released; Pégoud, French airman who first looped the loop in a flying-machine, killed in action.

SEPTEMBER

AUTUMN ALLIED OFFENSIVE IN FRANCE—VILNA AND KIEF EVACUATED

Sept. 2. Russian army evacuates Grodno.

Sept. 6. Forty French aeroplanes bombard Saarbrucken, in Rheinish Prussia; Czar takes command of the Russian army in place of the Grand Duke Nicholas; Joffre visits Italian front.

Sept. 7. Zeppelins raid towns on east coast of England, killing 13 and wounding 43.

Sept. 8. Grand Duke Nicholas transferred from chief command of Russian army to viceroyalty of Caucasus; Zeppelins drop bombs over center of London, 26 persons killed and 86 injured; Austro-Germans take fortress of Dubno.

Sept. 9. Lansing requests Austro-Hungarian Government to recall Ambassador Dumba, because of his interference with munition industries in United States.

Sept. 11. Belgian Relief Committee reports expenditure of $80,000,000 since its organization.

Sept. 15. Official statements in British Parliament place army enlistments at 3,000,000 since beginning, with 800,000 engaged in making munitions; Hindenburg threatens Jacobstadt; Mackensen captures Pinsk, completing advance of nearly 100 miles since fall of Brest-Litovsk.

Sept. 16. Hindenburg flanks Vilna and Dvinsk.

Sept. 17. Vilna invested on three sides; Allies present joint note to Bulgaria demanding to know her intentions.

Sept. 19. Evacuation of Vilna completed and Kief being evacuated.

Sept. 20. Mobilization of all military forces of Bulgaria ordered for the purpose of "armed neutrality"; reports reach Washington that 500,000 Armenians have been slaughtered by Turks and Kurds.

Sept. 21. Russians retreating from Vilna.

Sept. 22. French aeroplane squadron flies from Nancy to Stuttgart where bombs are dropt.

Sept. 24. British warships bombard Zeebrugge; Russians retake Lutsk.

Sept. 25. Allied offensive on 15-mile front in Champagne, gains of two and three miles made by French; similar gains by British in Artois region including capture of Souchez.

Sept. 26. Turks recapture part of positions at Anafarta, on Gallipoli.

Sept. 28. British concentrate about Loos, northeast of Lens, take German trenches and bomb-proof shelters with second-line trenches and attack third line; Germans under Linsingen recapture Lutsk; Falkenhayn visits Eastern front; Turks driven from Tigris back on Bagdad.

OCTOBER

CONQUEST OF SERBIA—BULGARIA IN THE WAR—EDITH CAVELL EXECUTED

Oct. 1. Austrians enter Montenegro; Bulgarian troops move on Serbian frontier.

Oct. 3. Allied troops land at Saloniki.

Oct. 4. Russia sends ultimatum to Bulgaria.

Oct. 5. Artillery heavily engaged north and east of Arras and in Champagne and Argonne; German Ambassador sends note to Lansing expressing German regret for sinking *Arabic* and disavowal of act of submarine commander.

Oct. 6. French capture Champagne village of Tahure and hills north of town; Bulgaria sends ultimatum to Serbia, demanding territory ceded after Balkan war; Allied envoys at Sofia request passports; Greeks evince popular enthusiasm for Allies, greeting with cheers 70,000 French troops landed at Saloniki; Austro-German force of 400,000 attacks Serbia from north and west; Allied troops at Saloniki hurried northward to assist Serbia; two Russian cruisers bombard Varna, Bulgarian Black Sea port.

Oct. 8. Bulgarian Minister at Nish receives passports.

Oct. 9. Berlin reports occupation of Belgrade; Serbian capital removed to Ishtib.

Oct. 10. Germans in occupation of Belgrade.

Oct. 13. Zeppelins bombard London, killing 8 and wounding 34 civilians; London reports capture of main trench of "Hohenzollern Redoubt."

Oct. 14. Germans take Pozarevac and advance down Morava Valley.

Oct. 15. Great Britain declares war

on Bulgaria; Hartmannsweilerkopf, in Vosges, retaken by French; French aeroplanes bombard Metz; official figures show British casualties at Dardanelles up to October 9 to be 96,899, of whom 1,185 officers. Australian casualties amounting to 29,121; Edith Cavell, English nurse, put to death by Germans in Brussels.

Oct. 18. General Sir Ian Hamilton, in command at Dardanelles, relieved by Major-General Monro who won distinction at Marne and Aisne; Italian offensive develops near Gorizia.

Oct. 20. Allied warships bombard Bulgarian coast.

Oct. 22. Combining land and sea attacks, Russians begin flank movement from west on Germans before Riga.

Oct. 24. Aeroplane attack on Venice.

Oct. 26. On Serbo-Roumanian front, Austro-Germans and Bulgars only 20 miles apart; brigade of British troops leave Saloniki for Doiran to prepare advance on Strumitsa, in concert with French troops.

Oct. 27. Union of Bulgarian and German forces announced.

Oct. 31. Berlin announces capture of Kragujevatz in Serbia with heights south of town; end of German offensive against Dvinsk and Riga.

NOVEMBER

BRITISH TAKE AND LOSE CTESIPHON— SERBIANS RETREAT TO SKUTARI

Nov. 1. Germans occupy Chachak, in Morava Valley, Serbia.

Nov. 4. Germans and Bulgars advance upon Nish from Kragujevatz; French and Italian vessels sunk off Algerian coast by German submarines.

Nov. 8. Italian liner *Ancona*, carrying 422 passengers and crew of 60, sunk in Mediterranean by submarine flying Austrian flag; American indictments involving heavy penalties found against six Germans, of whom Lieutenant Fay is one.

Nov. 9. London reports two U-boats in Mediterranean sunk and third captured.

Nov. 10. More British troops landed at Saloniki.

Nov. 15. Kitchener reported arrived in Ægean.

Nov. 17. Austrian aeroplanes bombard Verona, Vicenza, and Grado.

Nov. 18. Monro, in command at Dardanelles, advises withdrawal of Allied forces.

Nov. 19. Serbians driven from last strip of Old Serbian territory.

Nov. 22. British forces in Mesopotamia capture Ctesiphon.

Nov. 24. Serbian Government retires to Skutari; Germans evacuating Mitau; heavy assault by Turks on Gallipoli.

Nov. 25. Bulgarians push on to Monastir, while German forces descend Vardar; Townshend's British force attacking within ten miles of Bagdad.

Nov. 27. Berlin declares last of Serbian army in western Serbia driven into Albania and Montenegro.

Nov. 28. Turkish War Office claims

retreat of Townshend's forces from Ctesiphon down Tigris.

DECEMBER

BOY-ED AND VON PAPEN RECALLED—
FIELD-MARSHAL FRENCH
RETIRES

Dec. 1. Russians capture Czernowitz; Monastir surrenders to Bulgarians.

Dec. 2. Verdict guilty rendered against Karl Buenz and three other Hamburg-American officials in United States District Court, on charge of conspiring to defraud United States; sentenced to one and one-half years' imprisonment; siege of Kut-el-Amara begun by Turks.

Dec. 3. Immediate recall of Captain Boy-Ed and Captain von Papen, of German Embassy, demanded by United States Government.

Dec. 4. Steamship *Oscar II* chartered by Henry Ford, sails for Europe with 83 peace missionaries.

Dec. 8. Part of Serbian army reaches Epirus, in Greece.

Dec. 11. At Kut-el-Amara British repulse fierce attacks; Russians drive Persian rebels out of Hamadan.

Dec. 12. Retreating Allies pass into Greece.

Dec. 15. Field-marshal Sir John French resigns as commander of British forces in France, and Sir Douglas Haig appointed to succeed him.

Dec. 17. Paul König of Hamburg-American line, and two alleged confederates arrested by United States Government, charged with having started a plot to wreck Welland Canal.

Dec. 19. French air-raiders drop fifty bombs on Metz.

Dec. 21. British troops in Suvla Bay and Anzac regions of Gallipoli withdraw.

Dec. 28. First trip made from Tromsö, Norway, to Alexandrovsk, new Arctic Russian port, just completed; this harbor being open entire year, solves Russian transportation problem.

Dec. 30. P. and O. liner *Persia* sunk in Mediterranean.

THE EVENTS OF 1916

JANUARY

GALLIPOLI EVACUATED—ZEPPELIN
RAIDS—TOWNSHEND IN
RETREAT

Jan. 1. New Russian drive from Pripet to Roumanian frontier; heights above Czernowitz taken and a German counter-drive at Tarnopol repulsed.

Jan. 2. Main part Townshend's forces retreats down Tigris after repulse from Ctesiphon.

Jan. 5. British casualties September 25 to October 8, during battle of Loos, officially announced as 59,666.

Jan. 8. Allies report effective bombardment at Arras, Berry-au-Bac, and near Saint-Mihiel; Constantinople claims 10,000 British in Kut completely surrounded.

Jan. 9. Gallipoli completely evacuated by Allies.

Jan. 10. *King Edward VII,* finest of England's predreadnoughts, strikes a mine and sinks; Bernstorff forwards to his Government terms settlement for *Lusitania* case, as agreed by President and Lansing and indorced by German Ambassador.

Jan. 13. French occupy Corfu; Vienna announces capture of Cetinje, and first occupation of the capital by an enemy in history of Montenegro.

Jan. 20. Kaiser Wilhelm arrives in Belgrade; Turks driven to forts of Erzerum.

Jan. 22. Austrians seize Montenegrin ports of Antivari and Dulcigno.

Jan. 23. Skutari, capital of Albania, captured by Austrians; two raids on Kentish coast of England by German aeroplanes; twenty-four French aeroplanes raid Metz and 130 bombs dropt on barracks and railway stations.

Jan. 25. Germans shell and destroy Nieuport cathedral; President rejects note from Germany with proposals toward settlement of *Lusitania* controversy.

Jan. 29. Turks driven out of hills north of Erzerum; Paris raided by Zeppelins, 24 killed and 30 injured.

Jan. 31. Zeppelins raid English districts in Suffolk, Norfolk, Derbyshire. Leicestershire, Lincolnshire, and Staffordshire, over 200 bombs dropt, resulting in 54 deaths and 67 injuries.

FEBRUARY

FALL OF ERZERUM—BATTLE OF
VERDUN BEGUN

Feb. 1. General Smith-Dorrien announces gradual extension Uganda railway through British East Africa entire coast-line of Kamerun clear of German control; *Appam,* British passenger-liner in West African trade, given up as lost, enters Hampton Roads under German prize-crew of 22.

Feb. 3. Proposal by Germany in settlement of *Lusitania* received by President.

Feb. 9. Two German airplanes fly over Kent, England, dropping bombs near Ramsgate and Broadstairs; renewal of Russian offensive on Volhynia, and Eastern Galicia.

Feb. 15. Ezerum, great Armenian fortress falls into hands of Russians.

Feb. 16. Russians in possession of Erzerum.

Feb. 17. Reports from Erzerum declare Turks left all heavy artillery behind, amounting to over 200 big guns; Russian warships bombarding coast-line west of Trebizond, next Russian objective.

Feb. 21. Zeppelin brought down in flames, a Fokker airplane and three other German airplanes shot down; beginning of great battle for Verdun.

Feb. 23. Crown Prince declared in possession six and a quarter miles of French trenches to a depth of a mile and seven-eighths north of Verdun.

Feb. 25. Pétain arrives at Verdun; Germany claims 10,000 prisoners; Paris estimates German Verdun losses at 150,000;; Petrograd reports Kermanshah, on road to Bagdad, successfully stormed and captured.

Feb. 26. Berlin reports capture Fort Douaumont, northeastern corner of Verdun defense, four miles from Verdun proper; French auxiliary cruiser *La Provence*, formerly passenger-ship of French line for New York, sunk in Mediterranean.

Feb. 27. *Persia's* sister ship, *Maloja*, strikes mine midway between Dover and Folkestone and sinks in thirty minutes with loss of 155 lives.

Feb. 28. German attack at Verdun shifts to southeast and west; Côte de Talu and whole of "Meuse peninsula" cleared of French, Berlin claims; thirty miles west of Verdun, in Champagne, new German attack gains mile of French trenches; Petrograd declares Turks evacuating Trebizond.

MARCH

PÉTAIN CHECKS THE GERMANS AT VERDUN—THE SINKING OF THE "SUSSEX"

March 1. Turks continue retreat west of Erzerum and toward Bitlis.

March 2. German assault on Verdun revived in fierce drive on Fresnes in Woevre district and about Le Mort Homme (Dead Man's Hill), and Côte de l'Oie (Goose Hill); Aix-la-Chapelle reports arrival of 220 hospital-trains of German wounded from Verdun; Bitlis, 110 miles south of Erzerum, taken by Russians.

March 3. Germans take village of Douaumont; French Ministry of Marine announces 4,000 aboard transport *La Provence*, sunk in Mediterranean on February 26, number of survivors about 700.

March 5. Zeppelin raid over east coast England results in 12 killed and 33 injured; Berlin announces arrival of *Möwe* safe "in a home-port," with $250,000 in gold and 199 prisoners taken from fifteen allied vessels.

March 6. At close of fourteenth day at Verdun, Crown Prince launches first attack from northwest, on front between Béthincourt and Forges; Forges taken.

March 7. Germans take Fresnes, west of Meuse, gaining footholds on both sides of Goose Hill, penetrating Crows' Wood (Bois des Corbeaux) to west, and capturing "Hill 265"; French still hold summit of Goose Hill; "Hill 265" gained by attack in force with 12,000 men; Russians continue advance toward Trebizond.

March 9. East and southeast of Douaumont plateau French report Germans apparently unable to follow up successes.

March 10. Douaumont attack continued with an assault to west; Russian fleet bombarding Varna, Bulgaria, and have sunk eight Turkish steamers in Black Sea.

March 11. Again attacking Vaux, Germans secure foothold in village, and advance upon slopes of fortress; northwest of Reims Germans take nearly a mile of French trenches.

March 12. Paris declares Germans already lost 200,000 men at Verdun.

March 15. Italian airmen drop bombs on Trieste.

March 16. Dutch passenger-liner *Tubantia*, of Holland-Lloyd, sunk by mine or torpedo when only a few hours out from Amsterdam; Tirpitz, German Minister of Marine, resigns; Admiral von Cappele made Minister in his place.

March 17. Liverpool reports Brazilian Government seized 42 German ships interned in Brazilian ports.

March 18. Dutch Rotterdam-Lloyd liner *Palembang* sunk near Galloper Light, off coast of Essex, England.

March 19. Russian troops enter Ispahan, ancient capital of Persia, 250 miles southeast of Kermanshah; four German seaplanes raid coast of England from Dover to Margate, killing nine persons and wounding thirty-one.

March 20. Sixty-five Allied airplanes bombard German seaplane and submarine base at Zeebrugge returning safely; violent offensive launched against Germans and Austrians at three points on Russian front in Riga-Dvinsk sector.

March 21. Germans gain possession of Avocourt Wood, supported by heavy artillery and liquid-fire.

March 22. Germans gain another foothold on Malancourt-Avocourt line; Germans gain foothold on Haucourt Hill, southwest of Malancourt; Russians penetrate German line at Jacobstadt; new Russian offensive extends from Riga front to Roumanian border, distance of 800 miles; bombardment of Gorizia continues.

March 23. German blows at Verdun extended westward into Argonne sector; Petrograd reports steady advance of Russians in Dvinsk region.

March 24. Channel steamship *Sussex* struck by torpedo, or mine, as she approaches Dieppe from Folkestone; ship makes port with assistance.

March 26. Five British seaplanes convoyed by light cruisers and destroyers, cross North Sea and raid German coast.

March 28. North of Pinsk, Russians drive Germans across Oginsky Canal; President requests Ambassador Gerard, Berlin, call attention of German Foreign Office to cases of *Sussex* and *Englishman*.

March 29. British now hold 80 miles of Western Front, or about one-fourth of whole.

March 30. Following 12-day lull at Douaumont activities recommenced; French claim seven German aeroplanes brought down by anti-aircraft guns;

A CHRONOLOGY OF THE WAR

Russians in Caucasus defeat Turks in region of Kara Malachkan, on direct road to Bagdad; Captain Hans Tauscher, husband of opera star, Mme. Johanna Gadski, arrested charged with having set on foot military enterprise to blow up Welland Canal.

March 31. Malancourt, on west bank of Meuse, evacuated by French; British War Office announces raid by five Zeppelins, during which about ninety bombs dropt in eastern counties and along northeast coast; one airship, the L-15, mortally hit, falls into Thames estuary, off Kentish coast; seventeen survivors of crew of forty surrender.

APRIL

BATTLES FOR VAUX AND DOUAUMONT— FALL OF TREBIZOND—IRISH REBELLION—TOWNSHEND'S SURRENDER

April 1. German attack at Verdun shifted to village of Vaux where French troops driven out; vigorous protest forwarded to Germany by spanish Government over torpedoing of *Sussex.*

April 2. Two more Zeppelin attacks on England.

April 3. Battle of Vaux still rages; French claim part of village and most of Caillette Wood.

April 4. German attempts to break through at Douaumont frustrated; Germans hurl wave-attacks south of village; in East Africa, Smuts reports Allied forces capture German mountain stronghold.

April 5. German attack at Verdun again shifted to west of Meuse; village of Haucourt taken, but Béthincourt remains in French hands; to west French advance, taking large part of woods north of Avocourt; British relief force, with Gorringe in command, seeking rescue of Townshend at Kut-el-Amara, ascends Tigris and captures Felahie, driving Turks back; Canadian Finance Minister announces that force raised in the Dominion for overseas service now equals 300,000.

April 9. Russians reported at Trebizond in force and attack on port begun.

April 10. On southern frontier of German East Africa. Portuguese troops occupy Kionga, taken from Portugal by Germany in 1894.

April 17. Trebizond taken by Russians in combined land and sea attack; on German submarine sunk by the French, of which captain and crew are captured, is found documentary evidence of torpedoing of the *Sussex;* Captain Franz von Papen, former military attaché to German Embassy indicted by Federal grand jury on charge of having engaged in a military enterprise to destroy Welland Canal.

April 18. Russian army pushing westward from Erzerum captures high mountain range at Ashkala;

Wolf von Igle, assistant of von Papen, arrested in New York.

April 19. President dispatches note to Germany firmly stating conviction of United States that Germany has been culpable in *U*-boat violations of international law; declaring that, unless Germany will immediately abandon her submarine campaign United States must sever diplomatic relations.

April 20. Large flotilla of transports, arriving at Marseilles, brings Russian soldiers to support of French; transports understood to have made 10,250-mile journey from Vladivostok.

April 21. Sir Roger Casement's arrest near an Irish port announced.

April 22. Paris declares that, up to date, Germans made use of 30 divisions of troops, amounting roughly to 450,000 men, in Verdun struggle.

April 24. Revolution in Ireland began in Dublin.

April 27. Dublin revolution spreads, and all Ireland placed under military law; in Mesopotamia, daring attempt made to send relief-ship up Tigris to British at Kut-el-Amara, but vessel runs aground and is destroyed.

April 28. Third contingent of, Russian troops arrives at Marseilles; fire rages in Dublin, while Post Office, Stephen's Green, and other parts of city in hands of members of Sinn Fein, with sniping prevalent; after holding out against Turks for 143 days, Townshend compelled, through exhaustion of supplies, to surrender his force of 9,000 officers and men at Kut-el-Amara.

April 30. "Irish Republic," after an existence of 120 hours, overthrown, with unconditional surrender of leaders; Gerard leaves Berlin to confer with Kaiser at front on submarine situation.

MAY

SECOND PHASE OF BATTLE OF VERDUN — THE NAVAL BATTLE OFF JUTLAND—ITALIANS BEFORE GORIZIA

May 1. French offensive, launched southeast of Fort Douaumont; remnants of Sinn Fein organization in Ireland surrender unconditionally, making over 1,000 prisoners taken.

May 2. Five Zeppelins raid northeast coast of England.

May 3. Four leaders in Dublin uprising court-martialed, convicted of treason, and shot in Tower of London.

May 4. Another contingent of Russian troops disembarks at Marseilles.

May 7. Pétain, hero of Verdun, promoted to command of armies between Soissons and Verdun.

May 8. Russian operations against Turks reported successful at Erzingan and Diabekr.

May 10. Lansing announces receipt of note from Germany admitting *U*-boat commander sank *Sussex*, and promising indemnity and punishment of commander.

May 15. Trial of Casement for high treason begins in London.

May 16. British compulsion bill, providing military service for all males, married or single, between ages of 18 and 41, passes final reading in House of Commons, vote 250 to 35; at trial of Casement for treason, shown that Germany sent Russian rifles and other supplies into Ireland.

May 18. Three Germans ships, *Kolga, Hera,* and *Bianca,* sunk in Baltic by British submarines.

May 19. Germans west of Meuse occupy French positions along Haucourt-Esnes road.

May 22. French recapture all but northern part of Fort Douaumont, held ninety days by Germans; Townshend and staff deported to Prinkipo, Prince's Island, in sea of Marmora.

May 25. Fort Douaumont retaken by Germans through aid of Bavarian divisions.

May 26. Three more towns in German East Africa captured.

May 27. Gallieni, who helped check advance of Kluck on Paris at beginning of war, dies in Paris.

May 28. German losses before Verdun reckoned by French at 300,000; remnant of Serbian army, between 80,-000 and 100,000, men recuperating at Corfu, transferred to Saloniki.

May 31. British squadron cruising in North Sea, off Jutland, west coast of Denmark, encounters German fleet and engages in great naval battle lasting twelve hours; German navy never again came out to fight.

JUNE

RUSSIA'S NEW OFFENSIVE—KITCHENER'S DEATH—SECOND BATTLE OF YPRES—REVOLT OF ARABIA

June 4. Allies take over control Saloniki, replacing Greek police and establish martial law.

June 5. Russia begins long-awaited offensive; Kitchener lost with entire staff on cruiser *Hampshire* which struck by mine or torpedo sank off West Orkney Islands, while Kitchener was on way to Russia.

June 7. Berlin reports Fort Vaux taken; in midst of heavy artillery-fighting about Ypres, Germans penetrate Hooge.

June 8. Russians capture Lutsk.

June 10. Brusiloff occupies Buczacz, on west bank of Styrpa, strategical gateway to Bukowina; official announcement states cruiser *Hampshire,* in sinking of which Kitchener and staff were lost, was destroyed by a mine, and sank in ten minutes.

June 11. Town and fortress of Dubno fall before Russian advance, which gives Russia complete possession of Volhynian triangle.

June 12. In Trentino important units of Austrian force withdrawn to meet Russians on Eastern Front.

June 17. Two German armies go to aid of Austrians in region of Stochod and Styr rivers.

June 18. Czernowitz, capital of Bukowina, falls to Russians; Moltke,

formerly German Chief of Staff, dies suddenly of heart-disease while attending a memorial service for von der Golz in Reichstag.

June 19. Between Lutzk and Vladimir-Volynski, Austrians break through Russian sector.

June 22. French report aviators bombed German cities, Trèves, Karsruhe, and Mulheim, in reprisal for raids on Bar-le-Duc and Lunéville; Radautz, in southern Bukowina, falls to Russians, giving control of about one-half of Roumania's western frontier; revolt of Arabs against Turkish rule, Arabs taking Mekka, Jedda, and Taif; Sherif of Mekka besieging Medina.

June 23. Germans take Thiaumont field-work; whole of Crownland of Bukowina passes to Russians; Austrians retreating into foothills of Carpathians.

June 24. Sergeant Victor Chapman, son John Jay Chapman, New York, member American flying corps in service of France on Western Front, killed in air-battle over Verdun.

June 26. Italians begin recover ground lost to Austrian invaders; Asiago retaken and troops penetrate to outskirts of Arsiero.

June 27. Total of prisoners captured by Russians since advance began 199,354; Austrian army in flight in Italy.

June 28. German forces under Lingingen occupy Limewka.

June 29. Russians battle toward Kolomea, taking 10,506 prisoners and three lines of trenches; Casement found guilty and condemned to hang.

JULY

BATTLE OF SOMME BEGUN—BRUSILOFF'S SUCCESSES AGAINST AUSTRIA

July 1. British and French offensive started on both sides Somme in Picardy along front 25 miles near Montauban advance made of five miles; Mametz, Serre, Contalmaison, Dompierre, and Fay taken, while British close in about Fricourt; Austrian troops fall back on Stanislau.

July 2. British take Fricourt and Curlu village with nearly 10,000 prisoners; on Yser, British monitors shell Germans between Lombaertzyde and Nieuport; west of Kolomea Russians advance, taking 2,000 prisoners; in Africa Belgians advance along Kagera River and take Biaramulo, southwest of Victoria Nyanza.

July 3. Allies advance on Somme; French lines reach within three miles of Péronne; British take La Boisselle, with 4,300 prisoners.

July 4. French offensive captured Estrees, Barleux and Belloy-en-Santerre; Germans take Thiaumont again after six assaults.

July 6. Brusiloff's army advances toward Kovel; Austrian force west of Kolomea driven back five miles; Lloyd George appointed Secretary for War, to succeed Kitchener.

July 8. Hardecourt falls to French

while British occupy position in Trones Wood; Russians twenty-five miles from Kovel.

July 9. As sequel to Jutland battle, two hundred British vessels from Petrograd and Cronstadt came through Baltic for British trade.

July 10. British under Smuts occupy Taanga, port in East Africa; Arab rebels take Kinfuda on Red Sea.

July 11. British take German line on Somme on eight-mile front with 7,500 prisoners.

July 14. Aircraft raid Padua in Italy, dropping bombs and killing two persons

July 15. Arabian province of Hejas declares its independence.

July 16. Anglo-French advance brings troops to mile from Combles; High Wood taken, as well as outskirts of Martinpuich, Pozières, and other points close to German third line.

July 18. Belgian troops reach Victoria Nyanza, and defeat German forces.

July 21. In Lemberg drive Czar's forces cross Styr and advance to gates of Berestetchko; Russian thirteen-mile advance reported from Caucasus.

July 23. British infantry capture outworks of Pozières, and make gain on Bapaume road; Russians held at the Stokhod.

July 24. British gain ground in High Wood, and occupy part of Pozières; Italians take Monte Cimone and summit of Mount Stradone; Russians rout Turks in Caucasus, closing in on three sides of Erzingan.

July 25. Erzingan falls to Russian attack; Grand Duke Nicholas thus clears whole of Armenia of Turks.

July 26. Occupation of Pozières completed by Allies.

July 28. Longueval passes into British control, along with rest of Delville Wood; Capt. Charles Fryatt, recently honored for exploits in war against submarines, and later captured by Germans, shot by them for attempting to ram a German submarine.

July 29. Three Zeppelins raid east coast of England, dropping thirty-two bombs in Norfolk, Yorkshire, and Lincolnshire.

July 30. Heavy engagement between Delville Wood and Somme, resulting in advance of British; in Caucasus, Russians pushing on toward Sivas and Kharput.

July 31. General Kaledine obtains full control Stokhod River, and Russians reach Graberki and Sereth; Arab force takes town and fort at Yembo.

AUGUST

ITALIANS TAKE GORIZIA—RUSSIANS ADVANCE FURTHER—ROUMANIA IN THE WAR

Aug. 3. All German and Austrian armies on Eastern Front put under supreme command Hindenburg; Casement hanged in Pentonville Prison, London; at Verdun, French troops reoccupy Fleury, taking trenches at Thiaumont and slopes of Hill 320.

Aug. 4. Loss of two Italian submarines officially announced.

Aug. 5. More than mile German second-line trenches near Pozières taken by British.

Aug. 6. Russians take west bank Sereth; British forces, by a counterattack, put to flight Turks who threatened them from Romani.

Aug. 7. Italians take Austrian positions in Tofana sector; on lower Isonzo take nearly whole of Hill 85; Botha arrives in German East Africa to see close of Allied campaign against Germans.

Aug. 8. Italy takes bridge-head at Gorizia and two mountain defenses.

Aug. 9. At Verdun Germans drive French from greater part of Thiaumont, in addition making progress in Fleury; Russian forces within eight miles of Stanislau; Italians take Gorizia, with 10,000 prisoners; assisted by bombardment from fleet in sector of Monfalcone, also capture Monte Sabotino and Podgora; on east bank of Isonzo, take Monte San Michele; from seven to ten Zeppelins take part in air-raids on east coast counties of Great Britain.

Aug. 10. Fourth contingent Russian troops landed at Brest for service on Western Front.

Aug. 11. Russians take Stanislau; Austrians in retreat toward Haliez; Italians drive toward Trieste proceeds with capture of Doberdo plateau.

Aug. 12. Cadorna's troops take Oppacchiesella; army now six miles south of Gorizia.

Aug. 15. Russians take Jablonitza at pass into Carpathians; Italians reach suburbs of Tolmino.

Aug. 16. Allied army nearer Combles and Berny; in Carpathians Russians capture Vorokhta and Ardzemoy.

Aug. 18. Submarine *Deutschland* arrives from America at Bremen.

Aug. 19. Thiépval ridge taken and important hill near Pozières, with half a mile of trenches beyond Martinpuich; last defender forced out of Maurepas; French take Fleury; Austrian admiralty announces aero-bombardment of Venice.

Aug. 21. Terrific battle in progress in Balkans along 150 mile front.

Aug. 22. First contingent of 80,000 Russians disembarks at Saloniki to join reorganized Serbian army.

Aug. 23. British victory reported south of Thiépval in Somme district; on right bank of Meuse.

Aug. 24. In Zeppelin raid, London outskirts reached; eight killed and thirty-three injured.

Aug. 25. British advance on Somme, pushing beyond Delville Wood; Russians resume advance in Caucasus; Turks evacuating Bitlis; Mush recaptured and west of Lake Van Russians pursue Moslems toward Mosul; in German East Africa, Kilossa reported fallen into British hands.

Aug. 26. British aviators raid German airship sheds near Namur; Roumania declares war on Austria-Hungary; Germany declares war on Roumania; first fighting between Austrians and Roumanians reported; Bulgars take all but one of Greek forts surrounding Kavala; occupation this port gives Bulgaria opening on Ægean; thirty million dollars worth of interned German ships seized by Italians.

Aug. 31. Roumanians, invading Bulgaria, capture Rustchuk.

SEPTEMBER

ALLIED SUCCESSES ON SOMME—
ROUMANIANS CHECKED—
GREECE IN THE WAR

Sept. 1. Allied fleet arrives at Piræus.

Sept. 2. Allied fleet seizes seven Teutonic ships at Piræus; Hermannstadt, in Hungary, falls to Roumanian invaders; German Zeppelins visit England, dropping many bombs over east coast cities; one raider over London brought down in flames in open country.

Sept. 3. In sudden drive toward Combles British and French take three towns, parts of two more, and about 3,000 prisoners; Bulgarian forces invade Dobrudja.

Sept. 5. Bulgarian forces press into Roumania; bridge-head of Turtukai taken, as well as important railroad town of Dobric; Constanza, Roumania's only important seaport, bombarded by German naval aeroplanes.

Sept. 7. Tutrakan, considered gate to Bucharest, taken by German and Bulgar forces.

Sept. 8. Roumanians take Orsova at Iron Gates of Danube.

Sept. 9. Roumanians take Olah Toplitza and five other towns, indicating advance of thirty miles; Roumanians cross Danube near Orsova and take Negotin.

Sept. 10. Germans take Silistria, second Roumanian fortress in Dobrudja.

Sept. 11. Roumanians driving ahead into Transylvania following retreating Austrians; Bulgar troops in Dobrudja retake practically all territory Roumania forced Bulgaria to cede after second Balkan War.

Sept. 12. French now located on Péronne-Bapaume-Béthune road.

Sept. 13. French take Bouchavesnes, all of l'Abbé Wood, and German trench-system north of village; group of seaplanes bombard Venice.

Sept. 14. Nearly all approaches to Combles in hands of Allies; squadron of aeroplanes raid Trieste, dropping five tons of explosives on shipyards.

Sept. 15. British take Flers, Martinpuich, High Wood, Courcelette, and almost all of Bouleaux Wood; Bucharest admits Roumanian retreat in Dobrudja; in Transylvania, Roumanian advance continues with occupation of Bogata, Barscaolt, and Octerna, on middle Aluta, forty miles from frontier; Sarrail's Allied offensive in Macedonia pushes Bulgars back to within fifteen miles of border; Italian troops resume drive on Trieste.

Sept. 16. Berlin gets report of great victory in which Roumanian army in Dobrudja smashed; Serbians, French, and Russian forces drive back Bulgarian right wing further into Macedonia, approaching Florina.

Sept. 18. French push to within 200 yards of Combles; Italian advances pass Oppachiasella; German East African forces reported routed.

Sept. 19. Serbian troops in pursuit of retreating Bulgars cross frontier; in Transylvania Teutons repulse Roumanians south of Hatzog.

Sept. 20. Russian troops within few hundred yards of railway-station of Halicz; Roumanians win over Bulgars and Teutons near Enigea, in Dobrudja.

Sept. 21. Italians take up new position east of Gorizia; London reports Russo-Roumanian forces win Dobrudja battle over Mackensen; for six days fighting rages from ten miles south of Constanza to Cernavoda, on Danube; revolution in Crete reported from Athens; revolutionists said to have established provisional government.

Sept. 22. French enter outskirts of Combles; pro-Ally revolt in Greece spreads to Epirus and Macedonia.

Sept. 24. Kiffin Y. Rockwell, American aviator with French flying corps, killed in air-battle with German machine on Alsace frontier; French aviators, in flights of 500 miles, drop bombs on Krupp works at Essen.

Sept. 25. Combles completely cut off; along six-mile front between Combles and Martinpuich, more than mile of German trenches fall into British hands; Allied forces advance nearer Monastir; another success for Arab rebels announced from Cairo.

Sept. 26. Combles taken by British and French troops entering from opposite sides; British also take Thiépval and Gueudecourt, three miles from Bapaume; Vulcan Pass and Szurduk Pass, in Transylvanian Alps, evacuated by Teutons; German aeroplane squadron bombards Bucharest; former Premier Venizelos arrives in Crete and announces plan of a provisional government.

Sept. 27. Berlin reports capture of Vulcan Pass in Transylvania; Mackensen's forces in counter-attack win victory over Roumanians; London says Greece decided to enter Entente.

Sept. 28. Since beginning of Somme drive, French have recaptured 78 miles of territory, with approximately 40,000 German prisoners; British reach top of Thiépval Ridge, dominating Ancre Valley.

Sept. 29. Roumanians defeated in battle around Hermannstadt.

Sept. 30. Allies report gains along Somme, German trenches south of Eaucourt l'Abbaye occupied; Falkenhayn drives Roumanians back near Hermannstadt.

A CHRONOLOGY OF THE WAR

OCTOBER

DOUAUMONT RECOVERED—SOMME SUC-
CESSES AND ITALIAN GAINS—
ROUMANIAN REVERSES

Oct. 1. British take Eaucourt l'Abbaye; tanks used to great advantage;
Russians resume advance on Lemberg.

Oct. 2. Roumanian army crosses
Danube and invades Bulgaria; Zeppelins raid London; one of aircraft
brought down in flames.

Oct. 3. Austrian monitors in Danube
cut pontoon-bridge by which Roumanians entered Bulgaria; Berlin admits
withdrawal in Transylvania.

Oct. 4. Austro-German troops under
Mackensen cut off attempted Roumanian invasion of Bulgaria; in
Dobrudja, Russo-Roumanian forces
take Amzacea.

Oct. 5. Russians beat back Turkish
forces from west of Trebizond into interior; Cunard liner *Franconia*, sunk
in Mediterranean by submarine.

Oct. 7. Le Sars taken, and British
and French within two and one-half
miles of Bapaume; Italians take a
peak 6,187 feet high northwest of
Trent; British capture five villages in
drive on Seres; German war-submarine
U-53 arrives at Newport, R. I.

Oct. 8. British complete occupation of Le Sars; German submarine
U-53, which visited Newport. R. I.,
and another torpedoed six steamships
off Nantucket.

Oct. 9. Bucharest admits evacuating
Kronstadt.

Oct. 10. London admits Roumanian
defeat been turned into rout.

Oct. 12. Foch continues encircling of
Sailly-Saillisel, north of Somme;
Italian forces push nearer Trieste; in
western Macedonia Allied forces continue push toward Monastir.

Oct. 15. Norman Prince, American
aviator, flying in service of France
dies as result of injuries.

Oct. 17. Allied forces seize remaining
three ships of Greek fleet, as well as
railway-station at Piræus, landing
1,000 marines.

Oct. 18. Sailly-Saillisel falls to
French; with 300 French marines surrounding Royal Palace, and populace
in uproar, Athens reported in worst
situation since beginning of disturbances.

Oct. 19. French at outskirts of
Péronne; great 300-mile battle continues unabated from Pinsk marshes
to Roumanian frontier.

Oct. 20. Mob riots reported from
Athens.

Oct. 21. Mackensen smashes Roumanian left wing in Dobrudja offensive and reaches coast, advancing
on Black Sea port of Constanza;
Italian forces in Dolomites rout Austrians.

Oct. 23. Constanza, Roumania's chief
port on the Black Sea, captured by
Bulgaro-Teuton invaders; Teuton
troops approaching Cernavoda.

Oct. 24. At Verdun French retake
village and fort of Douaumont, Thiaumont, Haudromont quarries, La Caillette Wood, Damloup battery, and

trenches along four-mile front to
depth of two miles; forces under Mackensen drive Roumanians back from
Constanza to Tzara Murat.

Oct. 25. Cernavoda falls to Mackensen's army; Falkenhayn's army storms
Vulcan Pass.

Oct. 26. Roumanian forces in retreat
in Dobrudja destroy bridge over
Danube at Cernavoda.

Oct. 28. Captain Boelke, Germany's
greatest aviator, killed during a battle
on Western Front.

Oct. 30. German *U*-boat attacks and
sinks two British vessels with Americans among crews.

Oct. 31. Under French commander,
Berthelot, Roumanians win a victory
over Falkenhayn, driving Teutons
back across Roumanian border.

NOVEMBER

FURTHER ROUMANIAN REVERSES—
VAUX AND MONASTIR RECOVERED
—GREAT AIR-BATTLES

Nov. 1. South of Red Tower Pass
Teutons penetrate twelve miles into
Roumania.

Nov. 2. Berlin admits evacuating Fort
Vaux; Roumanians push Teutons
back.

Nov. 5. French drive Germans from
positions on Bapaume road; almost
all of Saillisel, which adjoins Sailly,
taken by Allies; at Verdun Allies add
all of Vaux and all of Damloup villages to gains; near Somme, high
ground near Butte de Warlecourt occupied by Allies; in joint manifesto by Emperors of Germany and
Austria, ancient Kingdom of Poland
revived and Polish autonomy re-
established.

Nov. 9. Roumanian forces operating
in Dobrudja, with new Russian reinforcements, retake Hirsova, on Danube,
driving back Mackensen.

Nov. 10. First general air-battle of
war by large squadrons of airplanes;
forty-two British, French and German
aircraft reported brought down; Allied airmen disposed of twenty-five
German machines and lost seventeen;
German casualties from beginning of
war compiled by London from German official lists, set at 3,755,693; of
this total 910,234 killed; 30,000 Belgians deported by Germans; all males
between seventeen and thirty sent away
in cattle-cars; Pope protests and State
Department, Washington, makes rep-
resentations to Berlin.

Nov. 12. British and French aviators
raid steel-works at Volkingen, in
Rhine Province, northwest of Saar-
bruck.

Nov. 13. After two days of fighting,
Serbians and French push Bulgars
back seven miles southeast of Monastir.

Nov. 15. Berlin admits Teutonic lines
outflanked by Serbians and French on
way to Monastir.

Nov. 16. Roumanians reported retreating along Transylvania front, pursued by Falkenhayn; Allied army under Sarrail reported only four miles
from Monastir.

Nov. 17. Guynemer brings down twenty-first machine; inner forts of Monastir fall to Serbians and French; German invaders of Roumania push into Wallachian plain; French aviator bombarded Munich, went over Alps, and landed near Venice, 435 miles from his starting-place on Western Front.

Nov. 18. Allies take Monastir.

Nov. 21. Francis Joseph, Emperor of Austria and King of Hungary, dies at Schönbrunn, near Vienna, at eighty-six; had ruled for sixty-eight years; succeeded by his grand-nephew, Archduke Charles.

Nov. 22. Teutonic envoys to Greece leave Athens for Kavala, in accordance with Allied demand; White Star Steamship *Britannic* in use as a hospital ship, sunk by mine in Ægean, with loss of fifty lives.

Nov. 23. Roumanian army retires to Alt Valley, 90 miles from Bucharest, leaving 10,000 square miles in Teutonic hands; Allied troops advance north of Monastir, taking Dobromir.

Nov. 24. Orsova and Turnu-Severin taken from Roumanians; all Wallachia believed lost.

Nov. 25. British naval planes invade Bavaria, dropping 2,000 pounds of bombs on blast-furnaces at Dillingen; Falkenhayn defeats Roumanian army in Alt Valley while Mackensen closes in at the rear; Greek provisional government, headed by Venizelos, declares war on Germany and Bulgaria.

Nov. 27. Roumanians driven from Alt Valley; Alexandria falls to Teutons with grain-supplies and entire Roumanian bank of the Danube.

Nov. 28. Roumanian Government leaves Bucharest for Jassy.

DECEMBER
BUCHAREST TAKEN—PEACE PROPOSALS FROM GERMANY

Dec. 2. Fifty miles to north of Bucharest Falkenhayn cuts through first Roumanian army, capturing headquarters; truce arranged in Athens between troops of Allies and Royalists.

Dec. 3. Premier Trepoff informs Russian Duma that by official agreement of Allies, made in 1915, Russia is to have Dardanelles and Constantinople at end of war.

Dec. 5. British Cabinet crisis brought to head by resignation of Premier Asquith; Unionist leader, Bonar Law, summoned by King and asked to form Cabinet, but declines.

Dec. 6. Central Powers take Bucharest; Lloyd George announced as new British Premier.

Dec. 7. Roumanians retreat along 125-mile front through Wallachia.

Dec. 10. Berlin reports arrival of merchant-submarine *Deutschland* at Bremen, after a nineteen-day trip to United States carrying a $2,000,000 cargo.

Dec. 12. Central Powers present note for Entente containing peace proposals.

Dec. 13. Nivelle, commander of French at Verdun, appointed commander of French armies of the north and northeast.

Dec. 15. French at Verdun drive Germans back for two miles along seven-mile front; Vacherauville, Louvemont, Chambrettes Farm, and forts of Hardaumont and Bézonvaux taken; Greek king grants latest Entente demands; Russian Duma unanimously votes categorical refusal to entertain any German peace proposals at present time.

Dec. 20. Wilson sends notes to all belligerents, asking them present terms on which they will consider peace.

Dec. 21. Wilson's peace-note welcomed by Central Powers.

Dec. 24. Pope Benedict praises Wilson peace-note, as do Scandinavian countries; King of England states war must be fought out.

Dec. 26. German reply to Wilson's peace-note proposes an immediate peace-conference, but does not state Germany's terms.

THE EVENTS OF 1917

JANUARY
BRITISH SUCCESSES ON THE TIGRIS AND IN PALESTINE

Jan. 1. Total losses British since start Somme offensive given as 520,-017.

Jan. 2. Prisoners captured by Allies on all fronts in 1916 total 582,723.

Jan. 4. Haig now commands largest army Great Britain ever levied—nearly 2,000,000 trained and officered men.

Jan. 8. Russians lose battle of Sereth; Focsani falls into Teutonic hands.

Jan. 11. British crossed border from Egypt and take Raffa in Palestine; Turkish trenches northeast of Kut-el-Amara taken.

Jan. 17. Definite announcement Greek Government accepted Allies' ultimatum unconditionally.

Jan. 21. British take over part of French front in Somme sector; British drive Turks out of positions on right bank of Tigris, near Kut.

Jan. 22. Dispatches from Ottawa state Canada has sent to date, 434,-539 men to the front; in message to Senate, Wilson outlines peace plans.

Jan. 26. Turkish first-line trenches southwest of Kut-el-Amara, with portions of second line, taken by British.

Jan. 27. Paris reports Guynemer brought down five enemy aeros in three days, bringing his total to thirty; seven hundred thousand inhabitants of invaded regions of northern France reported under enforced labor for Germans.

A CHRONOLOGY OF THE WAR

FEBRUARY

UNRESTRICTED SUBMARINE WARFARE
BEGUN—KUT-EL-AMARA RECOVERED
—ZIMMERMANN'S NOTE AND
BERNSTORFF'S PASSPORTS
GIVEN

Feb. 1. Port of New York closed to all outgoing vessels upon Washington's receipt of German note, announcing intensified submarine warfare.

Feb. 2. Number of transatlantic liners, including American liner *St. Louis*, held up in New York in face of German warning; Wilson addresses joint session of Congress, and announces Bernstorff given passport, and recall of Gerard from Germany as result of Teutonic submarine warfare.

Feb. 4. Daniels orders reserve force of Atlantic fleet ready for immediate service.

Feb. 5. Naval authorities at Manila seize twenty-three German vessels in harbor, taking crews ashore; customs officials, examining captured boats, report every one received extensive damage, apparently at hands of crews.

Feb. 6. Tonnage of vessels sunk by German *U*-boats from February 1 to date reported to exceed 86,344 tons; forty-five vessels sunk since greater submarine warfare inaugurated, including number of neutral boats.

Feb. 11. Gerard reaches Zurich, Switzerland.

Feb. 13. Largest naval appropriation in history of country passes Congress; calls for the expenditure of more than $368,000,000 and is passed by vote of 353 to 23.

Feb. 17. British tighten hold on Kut-el-Amara, taking fortifications on Tigris, with 2,000 prisoners, and much war-material.

Feb. 18. Warning from German Government reaches Washington to effect that arming of American merchantmen will be regarded as a warlike move.

Feb. 24. German line gives way on both sides of Ancre before British artillery; seven Dutch vessels which left Falmouth with a German "reasonable assurance of safety," reported torpedoed almost immediately after leaving harbor; three sunk, four badly damaged; Dutch Government and people reported aroused to highest pitch.

Feb. 25. In fog Teutons effect what was said to be greatest retirement on Western Front in two years; yield about three miles in the Ancre sector to the Allies; British cross Tigris and take four lines of Turkish trenches.

Feb. 26. Germans still falling back on Ancre, giving up to British nearly twenty-five square miles of ground; British only two miles from Bapaume; Kut-el-Amara falls before British advance, opening again road to Bagdad; Cunard liner *Laconia* sunk; three Americans lose lives; Wilson asks Congress for authority to arm outgoing American liners.

Feb. 27. British met Turks in battle about fifteen miles northwest of Kut-el-Amara.

Feb. 28. Gommecourt, Tilloy, and Puisieux-au-Mont taken by Allies; fleeing Turkish army in Mesopotamia reported hemmed in by British thirty miles from Kut-el-Amara; Washington hears Germany through Zimmermann, Foreign Minister, suggested to Mexico and Japan an alliance by which war was to be made on the United States, if it did not remain neutral.

MARCH

GREAT GERMAN RETREAT IN WEST—
FALL OF BAGDAD—REVOLUTION
IN RUSSIA

March 1. Bill to empower Wilson to arm merchant ships passed by House, 403 to 13.

March 2. German army retires on a front of fourteen miles to depth of from two to three miles and British push forward; German Admiralty announces no warning will be given by submarines to any ship bound forbidden area of Atlantic.

March 3. Russians capture Hamadan, Persian city near Turkish border; Zimmermann admits he attempted to ally Mexico and Japan against the United States.

March 4. British army takes over French lines for twenty-five miles southward on Somme; continued filibuster, led by Senator La Follette, prevents vote on Armed Ship Bill and Congress adjourns without passing measure; Wilson tells country Senate has "tied his hands" and made defense of American rights on sea impossible.

March 7. Percentage of submarine destruction for week dropt from 1.04 per cent. of ships entering British ports in first two weeks of February to 0.46 per cent. in week ending March 4.

March 8. British cavalry within fourteen miles of Bagdad; Russian center now forty miles beyond Hamadan; Turks in general retreat all along line; Count von Zeppelin, inventor of dirigible balloon, dies at Charlottenburg, aged seventy-eight.

March 9. Wilson decides to arm American merchantmen at once and to supply them with naval gunners, without waiting for authority from Congress; issues call for extra session of Congress April 16 "to consider all matters collateral to defense of our merchant marine."

March 11. Bagdad falls; Turkish army defending city completely outmaneuvered and out-fought by British in three days' battle; cavalry advancing beyond Bagdad; tabulation of authenticated records of men killed, wounded, and missing in European war received Washington show, among military proper, 4,441,200 dead, 2,598,500 wounded, and 2,564,500 missing; civilian dead and wounded, especially on Russian and Balkan fronts, estimated at 400,000 more, bringing total war loss to over ten million; Entente's losses 6,318,400, those of Central Powers 3,384,800.

March 12. British campaign against German forces in German East Africa virtually ended; Wilson formally announces to all nations except Germany his decision to arm American merchantmen against illegal assault.

March 14. British advance thirty miles beyond Bagdad; China severs diplomatic relations with Germany.

March 15. Revolution in Russia reported and declared a complete success; members of Duma, led by President Rozdianko, refused to dissolve session when ordered to do so by Czar's ukase; Czar abdicated for himself and his son; new revolutionary Provisional Government pledges itself to conduct war vigorously.

March 16. Government Russia vested in Council of Ministers, chosen from Duma; Great Britain, France, and Russia recognize Provisional Government.

March 17. Extended German retreat to Hindenburg line begins on West Front; French and British armies advance without resistance from two to four miles on front of thirty-five; Zeppelin L-39 shot down near Compiègne, forty-five miles from Paris; Captain Guynemer brings down three German aeroplanes, raising his total to thirty-four.

March 18. Péronne occupied by Allies; German retreat continues on front of hundred miles, to depth of twelve; French take Noyon and Nesle; Germans evacuate entire Noyon salient and fall back to Hindenburg line, twenty-five miles to rear of former positions; three American steamships, *City of Memphis, Illinois,* and *Vigilancia* sunk by German submarines; vessels manned entirely by Americans and twenty-two men missing; *Vigilancia* sunk unwarned.

March 19. British and French continue to advance on a one-hundred-mile front; two hundred and fifty towns and villages occupied; 1,300 square miles rewon by Entente since retreat begun.

March 20. German armies in retreat devastated whole country on line of retreat; Washington officials of opinion that state of war exists between Germany and United States in spite of technicality of armed neutrality.

March 21. Wilson calls special session Congress for April 2, two weeks in advance of date originally set.

March 22. American oil-tanker *Healdton,* unarmed and bound to Holland through safety zone prescribed by Berlin, sunk unwarned with loss of twenty American lives; German Admiralty announces return of commerce-raider *Möwe* to German port after second cruise in Atlantic; *Möwe* captured thirty-five steamers and five sailing-ships, aggregating more than 123,100 tons.

March 23. Germans flood city of La Fère; Czar reaches palace at Tsarkoe Selo, where kept under guard.

March 24. United States withdraws from Belgium; Brand Whitlock,

American Minister, recalled to Havre, and American members of Belgium Relief Commission turn work over to Dutch; naval officers, inspecting German ships seized in our ports, find machinery so damaged it will be impossible to send them to sea without extensive repairs which may take from three to nine months; Cardinal Mercier awarded Grand Prize for "the greatest and finest acts of devotion."

March 26. Liner *St. Louis,* first armed American ship to pass through barred zone, arrives safely in British port.

March 28. Nivelle begins offensive south of Laon, drives wedge into German lines between Oise and Aisne.

March 29. In a speech before Reichstag, Bethmann-Holweg places responsibility for war upon United States; British troops near Gaza rout Turkish army of 20,000 in two-days' battle, and continue advance toward Jerusalem.

March 30. The entire force of Federal Government's civilian employees, approximately 500,000, summoned to aid Secret Service in detection of persons engaged in plots against United States.

APRIL

CONGRESS DECLARES WAR—ARRAS AND AISNE BATTLES—BALFOUR, VIVIANI, AND JOFFRE IN AMERICA

April 1. British gain two miles in drive at St. Quentin on front five miles long.

April 2. Wilson asks Congress to declare state of war with Germany owing to ruthless and unrestricted submarine campaign; recommends utmost practical cooperation in counsel and action with the Entente, extension of liberal financial credit to them, mobilization all material resources of America for purpose of supplying Entente and United States with adequate munitions war, full equipment of navy, and immediate enrolment of army of 500,000 men, preferably by means of universal service, to be increased later by an additional army of equal size; announced armed American freighter *Aztec* sunk by German U-boat; Senator Lodge, Massachusetts, knocks down a pacifist who assaulted him in Senate corridor.

April 3. Roosevelt calls upon Wilson to congratulate him upon speech, and exhorts entire country to support President.

April 3. All American members of the Relief Commission leave Belgium.

April 4. Senate passes war resolution by a vote of 82 to 6.

April 5. House of Representatives passes war resolution by vote of 373 to 50; unarmed American ship *Missourian,* when returning to the United States in ballast, sunk in Mediterranean by a submarine; British and Russian armies in Mesopotamia effect junction; Russians drive the last Turkish soldiers from Persia.

April 6. Wilson signs resolution formally declaring state of war with

A CHRONOLOGY OF THE WAR

Germany; sixty alleged ringleaders in German plots this country arrested immediately after declaration war; ninety-one German vessels interned in American harbors taken over by United States; seizure amounts to approximately 629,000 tons, with a value of $148,000,000.

April 7. Greatest air-battle of war over and behind German lines during last 48 hours; Haig sent out full British air forces to scout and secure photographs behind German positions; operation was successfully performed; Germans lost 46 planes and 10 balloons, British and French 44 machines; more than eight tons of bombs dropt on German communications and supply-depots; Cuba declares war on Germany and seizes four ships interned in harbors.

April 9. Fourteen Austrian ships interned in American harbors taken over by Government; Wilson formally approves plan building a fleet of 1,000 wooden ships of from 3,000 to 3,500 tons each to meet loss of tonnage due to submarine warfare; British offensive on a twelve-mile front north and south of Arras; German positions penetrated two and three miles deep, and many important fortified points captured, including "field fortress" of Vimy Ridge.

April 10. British and Canadian troops advance two miles on entire twelve-mile front, and take 11,000 prisoners; official figures from the United States State Department report 686 neutral vessels, 19 of them American, been sunk during unrestricted submarine campaign; Brazil severs diplomatic negotiations with Germany; all estates and investments belonging to former Czar transferred to Russian Government; Roosevelt confers with Wilson and pledges support to "selective draft" measure and other features of Administration program.

April 11. Great Britain to send Commission of Foreign Secretary Balfour, Admiral de Chair, General Bridges, and Governor Bank of England to United States for conference on the war; French Commission to be headed by former Premier Viviani and Marshal Joffre, also coming; revenue bill authorizing a bond issue of $5,000,000,000 and $2,000,000,-000 in certificates of indebtedness introduced in House; Herbert C. Hoover accepts chairmanship new Food Board in United States; Argentina indorses stand taken by United States against Germany.

April 12. British pierce German lines between Vimy Ridge and Givenchy; British continue successes in vicinity of Gaza.

April 13. London cables two hospital-ships sunk in war-zone; Haig reports British "astride Hindenburg line" north of Arras.

April 14. British announce great push forward at Arras and St. Quentin; in Arras sector invest Lens on three sides; French artillery active all along front; England issues call to citizens and Allies, warning them of possible food shortage and requesting them economize on food; London

cables Maude routs Turks northeast of Bagdad; House of Representatives passes seven-billion war-loan without dissenting vote.

April 15. Nivelle launches great offensive on front twenty-five miles between Soissons and Reims; 10,000 German prisoners taken.

April 17. United States Senate unanimously passes seven-billion bond issue; House Military Committee votes 13 to 8 against selective-draft feature of Army Bill; Senate Committee approves selective-draft by vote of 10 to 7.

April 18. French resume attack on Aisne, capturing heights overlooking river on north; Germans driven out of six villages between Soissons and Reims; South of Aisne, Nivelle seizes and holds Vailly; French increase total number prisoners to 17,000.

April 19. Military authorities take over piers of North German Lloyd and Hamburg-American lines in Hoboken, New Jersey, to be used as shipping-base; Germans throw 240,000 fresh troops against Nivelle without checking advance; French troops gain in Champagne and take three villages on Aisne.

April 20. Entry of United States into war marked by religious ceremonies in London, attended by King and Queen.

April 21. Balfour and British Commission arrive in the United States.

April 23. Maude occupies Samara; Turkish forces in Palestine defeated in battle near Gaza.

April 24. Haig reports forty German airplanes brought down with loss of only two English machines; Wilson signs $7,000,000,000 Bond Bill, and United States will lend Great Britain $200,000,000 at once; French War Commission, Viviani, Joffre, and military and financial attachés, arrive in Washington.

April 25. Wilson appoints Elihu Root head of American Commission to Russia; Joffre and Viviani given immense ovation by Washington crowds; U-boat activity in week greatest since opening of submarine compaign.

April 27. In speech at Guildhall, Lloyd George says submarines can make England feel pinch, but can never starve her out, owing to fact that 3,000,000 acres of new land have been brought under cultivation for 1918; House votes down Roosevelt plan of raising a volunteer force for France by 170 to 106.

April 28. Both House and Senate pass Army Bill for raising army by selective draft; Senate, 81 to 8; House, 397 to 24; volunteer amendment is rejected by large majorities; Senate bill provides for conscription of men between ages of 21 and 27, while House fixes the limits as 21 and 40; Secretary McAdoo announces $5,000,-000,000 bond issue be known as "Liberty Loan of 1917"; British advance at every point on seven-mile front north of Scarpe; more of Chamindes-Dames plateau captured.

April 29. Pétain, defender of Verdun, appointed Chief of Staff of

445

French armies; French and British Commissions decorate tomb of Washington at Mount Vernon.

MAY

ANGLO-FRENCH OFFENSIVES IN THE WEST—THE SELECTIVE DRAFT—PERSHING SAILS—ITALIANS DRIVE TOWARD TRIESTE

May 2. Comparison of report of War Offices of the nations on Western Front shows total of 714 airplanes lost in April—366 of these German, 147 British and 201 French and Belgian; of German machines lost, 263 brought down by British airmen, 6 by anti-aircraft guns, 95 by French pilots, and 2 by Belgians.

May 3. Wilson and Balfour reach agreement on main features of Allied submarine campaign about to be launched; Hoover arrives from Europe, says submarine menace growing and that food conditions in Europe grave; Joffre and Viviani leave Washington for tour in Middle West; French sailors who escorted Viviani and Joffre to this country feted by 22,000 New Yorkers in Madison Square Garden.

May 4. Craonne stormed, giving French control of Craonne plateau; French capture 23,000 prisoners and 176 heavy guns since April 18.

May 5. French cut salient of four miles from Hindenburg line, near Laon, taking 4,300 prisoners; Joffre makes first set speech in Chicago.

May 7. Balfour cables London that French, British, and American plans for cooperation in war are completed on all essential matters; medical force of 240 about to start for England, first uniformed American troops to carry flag to West Front; Junker party in Reichstag demands Bethmann-Hollweg's resignation.

May 9. War Revenue Bill, reported to House, means $3,800,000,000 yearly in taxes in addition to recent bond issue; million people line Fifth Avenue to cheer Joffre and Viviani in New York; British, chiefly Canadians, attack Bavarians holding Fresnoy and retake all lost ground west of village.

May 10. Joffre given enthusiastic reception at special gala performance at the Metropolitan Opera House, New York; during day he unveils statue Lafayette in Brooklyn and is presented with gold replica of Statue of Liberty in Central Park.

May 11. British troops on southwestern outskirts Lens meet three terrific counter-attacks, in two of which liquid fire used to prepare the way for German advance; Balfour and British Commission received with enthusiasm by people New York City; Joffre spends day at West Point.

May 14. Kerensky, Russian Minister of Justice, declares "as affairs are going now, it will be impossible to save the country."

May 16. On two-mile front, from Gavrelle to Scarpe, Hindenburg hurls massed attack against French and British with troops fresh from Russian front; attack repelled after fierce

battle; squadron American torpedoboat destroyers reached Queenstown May 4, and at once began patrol duty on seas; announced that after first of month no naturalized German may go within half a mile of any State armory without a special permit; Russian Government and Radicals reach agreement, and reconstruction of Cabinet begun; Miliukoff, Foreign Minister, resigns from Cabinet.

May 17. United States Senate passes the Army Draft Bill, 65 to 8; Bullecourt in hands of British.

May 18. Sea-battle in Adriatic on May 14, in which cruisers, destroyers, submarines, and airplanes representing five nations engaged; British, French, and Italian craft drove off Austrian squadron; Wilson signs the Army Bill calling upon 10,000,000 Americans to register on June 5, from which number the first increment of 500,000 men to be chosen for the army; President rejects Roosevelt's offer to raise volunteer force; Wilson directs expeditionary force of 25,000 regular troops, under Pershing, to proceed to France "at as early a date as practicable."

May 20. Pershing and staff sail for France unknown to public.

May 23. First detachment United States engineers, under Maj. William Barclay Parsons, engineer of first New York subway, reaches London; King George and Queen Mary welcome surgeons and nurses at Buckingham Palace; War Revenue Bill passes the House by a vote of 329 to 76.

May 24. Italian forces on Carso take 9,000 prisoners in drive toward Trieste.

May 29. Italian drive toward Trieste continues successfully; since May 14 more than 23,000 Austrian prisoners and 36 guns captured.

May 31. Emperor Charles of Austria, at the opening of Reichsrath, gives a pledge of reform and conciliation toward "all who abandon intention to threaten us."

JUNE

MESSINES RIDGE CAPTURED—AMERICAN MISSION TO RUSSIA—LIBERTY LOAN OVER-SUBSCRIBED

June 4. Alexieff, commander-in-chief of Russian armies, resigns and Brusiloff appointed to succeed him.

June 5. Armed merchantman *Mongolia* engages in second fight with submarines off Irish coast.

June 7. British carry Messines Ridge in Wytschaete salient overlooking Ypres which was held for two years by Germans; offensive preceded by terrific mine-explosions heard in London; territory five miles long and three miles deep captured.

June 8. Pershing with 57 aids, 50 privates, and a large clerical force reach London; one hundred American aviators, first of American fighting forces, reach France; British troops strengthen position on captured ridge; two hundred girl-students of Petrograd Technical Institute enrolled in regiment of women that will fight under same conditions as men

June 9. Balfour reaches London and enthusiastically declares visit to United States will remain "epoch in history of two great English-speaking nations."

June 12. Senate approves Espionage Bill, giving Government control of all exports, to prevent supplies reaching Germany through neutral countries; British extend gains east and northeast Messines, capturing Gaspard; King Constantine I of Greece abdicates in favor of second son, Prince Alexander; American Mission, headed by Elihu Root, reaches Petrograd.

June 13. Pershing reaches Paris where is met and enthusiastically welcomed by Joffre, Ambassador Sharp, and vast crowds; American troops assigned to position on battle-front under Pétain.

June 15. Wilson signs War Budget and Espionage Bills, thus making immediately available $3,340,000,000 for war-machinery; British troops at Arras and south of Ypres victorious on seven-mile front, completing occupation of old first-line trenches of Germans near the Lys; first Liberty Loan subscription closed; $2,000,000,000 asked for, $3,035,000,000 subscribed. (See June 22.)

June 20. Canadian troops capture a nest of trenches which been Germans' chief place shelter between the Canadian lines and Lens.

June 22. Total amount subscribed to Liberty Loan is $3,035,226,850, more than 4,000,000 persons participated; Elihu Root makes first public appearance in Russia at large gathering in Petrograd, and, outlining causes which induced America enter the war, declares she will fight "until world is made safe for democracy."

June 26. First American troops reach France; Canadian troops occupy La Coulotte, south of Lens.

June 27. British Admiralty report shows falling off in submarine sinkings.

June 28. Debate in lower Austrian House discloses strong peace sentiment; Brazil revokes decree of neutrality, which is tantamount declaration of war.

June 29. Greek Government breaks off diplomatic relations with Germany, Austria-Hungary, Bulgaria, and Turkey.

JULY

BETHMANN-HOLLWEG RESIGNS — RUSSIA'S LAST OFFENSIVE FAILS— KERENSKY PREMIER—ENTENTE GAINS IN THE WEST

July 2. French recapture all ground lost to Germans on Chemin-des-Dames, east of Cerny; Minister of War Kerensky, in person, leads victorious Russian advance; conspiracy to destroy shipping on Great Lakes, thereby delaying organization of American armies, disclosed.

July 3. Major-General Scott reaches southwestern battle-front in time to witness beginning of Russian offensive;

American destroyers, convoying transports with troops to France, fight off a fleet of submarines, sinking one.

July 4. France celebrates Fourth of July and gives ovation to American troops in Paris about to leave for training behind battle-front; London joins in observing day and American flag flies over House of Parliament.

July 9. "No-annexation, no-indemnity" speech made by Erzberger in Reichstag; Wilson issues a proclamation drafting State troops into United States Army on August 5, and declaring them discharged from old militia status on that date.

July 10. Russian army captures Halicz, considered key to Lemberg.

July 11. Germans drive back British on Belgian coast to Yser, capturing 1,250 prisoners.

July 12. Russian troops under Korniloff capture Kalusz.

July 14. House passes Aviation Bill which provides $640,000,000 for construction aerial fleet; Kaiser appoints Dr. Georg Michaelis, Prussian Under-Secretary, to succeed Bethmann-Hollweg as Chancellor.

July 16. Reichstag party-leaders, after conference with Hindenburg and Ludendorff, declare they stand for peace without indemnities or territorial acquisition.

July 17. French, in a sweeping attack, regain positions captured by the Germans in their drive of June 29 on left bank of Meuse, in Verdun region; King George announces name of royal house of England hereafter be House of Windsor, instead of House of Saxe-Coburg Gotha.

July 20. Russian regiments throw down arms and leave trenches, with result Germans pierce wide front east of Lemberg; Premier Lvoff resigns and Kerensky appointed Premier in place; Pershing leaves Paris for a long tour British battlefront with Haig; draft day in the United States results in registry of 9,700,000 for service in first army of conscription to be sent to Europe.

July 23. Disorganization and demoralization among Russian troops admitted in official dispatches from Petrograd; Tarnopol reported in hands Germans.

July 24. Petrograd reports entire units Provisional army return to trenches and absolutely decline to obey orders.

July 26. Austro-German troops press victory in Galicia over demoralized Russian forces; Petrograd concedes most of heavy Russian artillery been lost.

July 27. Reports from Vienna state Russians evacuating Czernowitz, capital of Bukowina.

July 28. German aircraft raid Paris for first time in year and half; only two bombs are dropt; Ruzsky and Gurko summoned to Petrograd take charge of troops in Galicia for purpose of making stand against Germans.

July 29. Kerensky goes to front, to endeavor to reorganize Russian armies with aid of old leaders.

July 31. In greatest offensive of war British and French tear out German first line, and a portion of second and third over front more than twenty miles in Flanders; ten towns and 3,500 men are taken; German forces still pressing forward in Galicia.

AUGUST

PASSCHENDAELE RIDGE—ITALIAN DRIVE ON ISONZO—AMERICANS IN TRAINING IN FRANCE

Aug. 1. In Flanders battle 5,000 German prisoners taken; Emperor William issues address to German people declaring he is not animated by spirit of conquest, but fighting "in defense of a strong, free empire."

Aug. 2. Brusiloff resigns as Commander-in-Chief of Russian armies and Korniloff appointed to supreme command; Kaiser summons practically every leader of prominence in army and navy to war conference at Brussels.

Aug. 3. Czernowitz, capital of Bukowina, which has changed hands ten times during war, again in possession Archduke Joseph.

Aug. 5. Canadian troops in new drive on Lens.

Aug. 9. Roosevelt issues vigorous statement in which demands German-American press be muzzled at once, that laws be framed forbidding printing of newspapers here in German, or languages of other hostile countries.

Aug. 10. Renewal great battle in Flanders; Haig captures practically all German positions east and southeast of Ypres.

Aug. 12. Battle on large scale raging along Roumanian front.

Aug. 15. Secret removal of former Emperor Nicholas and family from palace of Tsarskoe Selo; royal prisoners on way to Tobolsk, in Siberia; London issues text of Pope's appeal to belligerent nations.

Aug. 16. Germans report successful bombardment of the cathedral of St. Quentin.

Aug. 19. Deposed Czar Nicholas with wife and children, arrive at Tobolsk, 1,500 miles from Petrograd.

Aug. 20. French overwhelm Germans on eleven-mile front north of Verdun, while Italians take 7,600 prisoners in big drive for Trieste.

Aug. 21. Pershing and several of staff officers witness battle of Verdun; 3,000 more prisoners taken by Italians in drive along Isonzo.

Aug. 22. British penetrate German lines for third of a mile in Ypres sector, taking positions for mile along Ypres-Menin road.

Aug. 23. Germans reported to have launched fierce campaign to reach Petrograd and force Russian peace; famous Chasseurs Alpins, known as "Blue Devils of France," assigned as companions-in-arms of American troops whom they will instruct in art of modern war; Canadian troops now

on edge of city of Lens; Italians capture Monte Santo and continue drive along Isonzo; Austrians removing everything of value from Trieste; American airmen taking part in battle Verdun.

Aug. 28. Austrian high command orders civilian population to evacuate Trieste; fugitives seek refuge in interior Austria; Wilson replies to Pope's peace message, declaring his terms are impossible, and stating that object of America is to "free world of the menace of Kaiser, without desire for reprisal on German people."

Aug. 30. Pershing moves from Paris headquarters to region in eastern France turned over by French Government for mobilization and training American troops.

SEPTEMBER

RIGA FALLS—LUXBURG'S DISPATCHES PUBLISHED—CIVIL WAR IN RUSSIA

Sept. 1. French strike hard blow on Aisne front.

Sept. 3. Riga falls to German troops; Austrian losses in Italian thrust toward Trieste estimated at 125,000 men.

Sept. 6. House passes War Bond Bill, totaling $11,538,945,460; includes $4,000,000,000 in new loans to Allies and $2,000,000,000 for War-Savings Certificates; amount of second Liberty Loan $3,000,000,000.

Sept. 8. Luxburg's Argentina dispatches, *"spurlos versenkt"* (sink without trace), published.

Sept. 10. Kerensky deposes Korniloff as rebel, and establishes martial law in Petrograd; Senate passes War Tax Bill by a vote 69 to 4.

Sept. 11. Civil war begins in Russia.

Sept. 12. Steamship *Minnehaha*, of Atlantic Transport Line, sunk by submarine, fifty lives lost.

Sept. 13. Petrograd announces collapse of revolt of Korniloff.

Sept. 14. London announces success British navy in engagements in which eight German submarines sunk in open battles; Italian forces again take summit San Gabriele after three weeks' fighting.

Sept. 15. Russian revolt ends with arrest Korniloff, with Lokomski his chief aid, and two subordinate commanders.

Sept. 16 Kerensky, as President, declares Russia a republic.

Sept. 20. British in Flanders cut a mile into German line on front of eight miles and take 2,000 prisoners.

Sept. 25. Captain George Guynemer, French aviator, killed.

Sept. 26. Report of British Admiralty shows smallest *U*-boat toll since February last; Soukhomlinoff, former Russian Minister of War, found guilty of high treason and sentenced to hard labor for life.

Sept. 30. Italians capture heights south of Podlaca in Isonzo sector.

A CHRONOLOGY OF THE WAR

OCTOBER

BATTLE OF CAPORETTO — HERTLING MADE CHANCELLOR—ANGLO-FRENCH PROGRESS IN THE WEST

Oct. 1. Greatest attack on London by German airplanes since war began; battle lasted two hours and a half.

Oct. 3. Week's record of submarine sinkings again lowered.

Oct. 6. Russia approaching civil war.

Oct. 9. Lansing makes public series cipher telegrams between German Government and Bernstorff, in 1916, which shows Germany used United States as base for military operations against Canada in 1916, and plotted wholesale sabotage in munitions factories throughout United States; British capture Poelcapelle, while French take St. Jean de Mangelare and Veldhoek.

Oct. 10. Dr. Michaelis, German Chancellor, announces at sitting of Reichstag that peace is impossible "so long as Germany's enemies demand any German soil or endeavor drive wedge between people and Emperor"; mutiny in German navy occurred at Wilhelmshaven, involving four battleships.

Oct. 11. Franz von Papen, formerly German military attaché, with sixteen other men indicted by New York grand jury for complicity in bomb plots.

Oct. 12. Capelle. German Minister of Marine, resigns as result recent mutiny in German fleet.

Oct. 13. German forces landed on Oesel and Dago islands, thus completing conquest of Gulf of Riga, and menacing Petrograd.

Oct. 18. Naval battle, during which Russian battleship *Slava* is sunk in Gulf of Riga.

Oct. 20. Eleven Zeppelins attacked London, killing 27 and injuring 53; met by French planes, result four Zeppelins driven to earth; nine neutral merchantmen and a convoy of two destroyers sunk in North Sea by German raiders.

Oct. 22. German force landed on mainland of Esthonia.

Oct. 24. British Admiralty reports increase in losses by mine and submarine; French forces on Aisne deal heavy blow to enemy, inflicting serious casualties and capturing 8,000 prisoners; fresh German forces, operating with Austrians, launch big offensive against Italy.

Oct. 25. Decisive victory of French north of Aisne secured to Allies high plateau dominating Fort Malmaison, real key of ridge between Aisne and Ailette, while capture of village Chavignon brings French within six miles of Laon; German-Austrian Carporetto drive begun; tremendous character of the blow Germany aiming at Italy becoming apparent; twenty full divisions, numbering 320,-000 men, together with a large force artillery, engaged; Berlin reports that 10,000 prisoners taken, including divisional and brigade staffs; German drive extends on twenty-five-mile front from Tolmino to Carso.

Oct. 26. Italian disaster increasing; Germans captured 30,000 prisoners and 300 guns; Italians reported evacuating Bainsizza plateau; Cadorna's gains lost.

Oct. 27. French section Flanders line drives forward on front almost three miles to a depth of one and a third miles; reports from Berlin place number of Italian prisoners taken by Germans at 65 000, and guns captured at more than 500; second Liberty Loan overwhelming success; subscriptions more than $5,000,000,000, and subscribers more than 10,000,000; more American troops reach trenches.

Oct. 28. Belgians, attacking in conjunction with French, capture whole Merckem peninsula, a few miles from Dixmude.

Oct. 29. Tremendous German-Austro drive into Italy continues over sixty-five-mile front; Cadorna falling back toward Tagliamento; extent of defeat grows; three enormous wedges driven into Italian lines and enemy reported bringing up more troops; Italian forces preparing to make a stand on Tagliamento.

Oct. 30. British under Haig drive forward half a mile into outskirts of Passchendaele, near end of last ridge that separates British from plain of Flanders; Berlin reports French artillery - fire on Chemin - des - Dames "reaches powerful proportions; Hertling appointed Chancellor to succeed Michaelis; Austro-German forces occupy Udine.

Oct. 31. Italian armies in retreat with German forces well within gun range of the Tagliamento; foe now holds 1,000 square miles of Italian territory and a total of 120,000 Italian prisoners and 1,000 guns; Allies rushing plans to aid Italy.

NOVEMBER

BOLSHEVIKI IN POWER—CLÉMENCEAU MADE PREMIER OF FRANCE— THE CAMBRIA AND MALMAISON BATTLES

Nov. 1. British and French reinforcements arrive on Italian front, 30,000 available within four or five days; main part Cadorna's armies crossed Tagliamento in good order; British forces in Palestine occupy Beersheba and capture 1,800 prisoners.

Nov. 2. Germans begin retreat from Chemin-des-Dames east of Soissons; German forces rushed to Trentino.

Nov. 3. Three Americans killed, five wounded, and eleven captured during a German raid on a trench held by American infantry; in sharp battle in Kattegat British destroyers sink German auxiliary cruiser *Marie* and ten armed patrol vessels; Germans evacuate whole section on Aisne on front of thirteen miles; during battle of Malmaison French aviators fought 611 aerial engagements, bringing down sixteen airplanes and destroying three captive balloons.

Nov. 4. Lloyd George arrives Paris on way to Italy; Craonne, Ailles, Cerny, and Courtecon now occupied by French.

Nov. 5. Austro-German forces cross Tagliamento and proceed westward.

Nov. 6. Passchendaele, dominating plain of Flanders, taken by Canadian forces in brilliant dash; Italians forced to abandon entire line along Tagliamento.

Nov. 7. New revolutionary movement begun in Russia; _U_-boat toll for week lowest since announcement of unrestricted warfare; Secretary McAdoo announces subscriptions to second Liberty Loan amounted to $4,617,532,-300, in which 9,400,000 men and women participated.

Nov. 8. Capture Gaza by British; Petrograd dispatches announce city in complete control of Bolshevik (Maximalist) forces; Kerensky denounced as traitor and his arrest ordered; in official proclamation Council of Workmen's and Soldiers' Delegates constitutes itself Government of Russia.

Nov. 9. Cadorna removed as Commander-in-Chief and assigned as Italian representative in inter-Allied Commission; Diaz succeeds Cadorna; Revolutionary Committee takes over all Government offices in Moscow; Nikolai Lenine, Bolshevik leader, announces plan to offer an immediate armistice of three months, during which "elected delegates of all nations will settle question of peace"; army is appealed to, to protect 'the revolution against "imperialistic attempts until the new Government obtains a democratic peace"; all Cabinet Ministers are arrested at Winter Palace after its surrender and confined in fortress of St. Peter and Paul; entire Turkish army in Palestine retreating to north.

Nov. 10. Italians, with British and French allies, establish themselves in new positions on lower Piave; British in Palestine occupy Ascalon.

Nov. 11. Italian resistance to German invasion stiffens all along front; Kerensky reported marching on capital with 200,000 men.

Nov. 12. British forces operating against Turks reach point thirty miles Jerusalem; American forces on Eastern Front in France have first experience with gas-shells.

Nov. 13. Clémenceau succeeds Ribot as French Premier; American aviators take part in bombing expeditions over German lines.

Nov. 14. Korniloff's capture Kremlin, in Moscow; British Government faces crisis as result of Lloyd George's Paris speech; Premier meets situation by a statement in House Commons; Washington reports Wilson will support plans for perfect coordination between nations; _U_-boat losses for past week lowest yet reported; British army in Palestine advances seven miles, threatening Jaffa and railway to Jerusalem; Turkish forces in Mesopotamia driven from thirty to fifty miles north of Tekrit by Maude's troops; British now 100 miles south of Mosul; forces of Crown Prince Rupprecht defeated in desperate attempt to recapture Passchendaele.

Nov. 15. Georges Clémenceau accepts invitation from President Poincaré to form a new French Cabinet.

Nov. 16. Venice being evacuated, population having been reduced from 160,000 to 20,000; Kerensky said to have fled in disguise; loss of life since beginning of Russian insurrection estimated from 2,000 to 5,000; Kerensky's forces, which advanced thirty-five miles from Gatchina to Tsarskoe Selo are defeated; driving the Turks before them, British reach point on railroad thirty-five miles northwest of Jerusalem.

Nov. 17. Large area lower Piave flooded by engineers to prevent a Teutonic advance on Venice.

Nov. 18. British occupy Jaffe.

Nov. 19. Nine more Americans dead at the front, two killed in the fighting, two accidentally, four by illness, and one by suicide; on Asiago plateau Italians start an offensive; at Zenson and Figare attempts to cross Piave repulsed in battle during which enemy lose 3,000 men in killed and captured; Maude, in command of British forces Mesopotamia, dies after brief illness.

Nov. 20. In St. Quentin region smashing blow delivered against enemy on a thirty-five-mile front; Lloyd George asking United States to rush troops and shipping; Fayolle, noted French general, placed in command French forces in Italy and leaves Paris for front; the exodus of enemy aliens from Washington begins.

Nov. 21. Council of the People's Commissaries in Russia has offered an armistice on all fronts in order to treat for immediate peace; American troops are proceeding to Europe in stream which promises that by July Pershing will have at command the million Americans for whom Lloyd George has appealed; Clémenceau scores a notable victory House of Deputies, when he appeals for prosecution of war with all the resources and power of France; British troops within five miles of Jerusalem and rapidly closing in; British drive smashes Hindenburg line in an attack extending over thirty-two miles with Cambrai the objective; surprize attack led by tanks opened way for advance of infantry and cavalry through wire entanglements; at one point German line was penetrated more than five miles; cavalry charged batteries, sabered gunners, and held positions until relieved by infantry; operations led by Byng, in command of Third Army.

Nov. 22. Kerensky's troops surrender; Ukrainian Government has sent an army of 150,000 against Kaledine and Cossacks; Byng's troops holding all positions captured and consolidates them.

Nov. 23. For first time since war began, England celebrates Byng's victory in old-fashioned way by ringing bel's; Secretary Baker states "there are more American troops now actually in Europe than we expected to have there at this time," and that the rate at which troops are being sent over is being constantly accelerated; Ludendorff starts for Eastern Front with a large staff in connection with peace offer of Russian Bolsheviki.

A CHRONOLOGY OF THE WAR

Nov. 25. Italians holding line on Asiago plateau against furious Austro-German attacks; French and British troops in considerable numbers in Italy tho not on battle-lines.

Nov. 26. French War Cross conferred upon fifteen Americans for gallantry in the German raid of November 2.

Nov. 27. Within twenty-four hours Italians smashed German's first and second defense lines between Brenta and Piave.

Nov. 28. Italians definitely defeat enemy's efforts to break line on upper Piave.

DECEMBER

BYNG REPULSED BEFORE CAMBRAI—JERUSALEM FALLS—RUSSIA SIGNS ARMISTICE WITH CENTRAL POWERS

Dec. 1. By fierce fighting British succeed in regaining nearly a mile of front lost near Gouzeaucourt; captured orders and maps show enemy's intention was to deliver an encircling attack; German commander-in-chief on Russian front notifies Bolsheviki of readiness to open peace negotiations.

Dec. 2. Germans in most desperate fighting endeavor to recapture ground taken by British west and south of Cambrai; British had had no chance to dig in and struggle reported to have been fierce hand-to-hand conflict in the open; Berlin claims capture of 100 cannon with 6,000 prisoners.

Dec. 3. Many American engineers and workmen caught in German encircling movement at Cambrai dropt their shovels to fight the Germans and some killed; an actual armistice goes into operation in sections of Russo-German front, and fraternizing begins.

Dec. 4. German counter-offensive in West ends.

Dec. 6. London reports retirement of British from untenable positions in Cambrai sector was not discovered by Germans until following day; Berlin War Office announces suspension of hostilities along the entire Russian front for a period of ten days, during which negotiations for armistice be concluded; Paris dispatches state large force of Austro-Germans attacking Italians on a ten-mile front from Monte Sisemol north and east; Berlin reports capture of 11,000 prisoners and 60 guns.

Dec. 7. United States declares war on Austria, Senate passing resolution 74 to 0, and House 361 to 1, negative vote being cast by Socialist.

Dec. 10. Japanese troops have landed at Vladivostok to protect valuable supplies; city of Jerusalem surrendered to British; for first time since days of Crusaders city in hands of Christian troops.

Dec. 13. Negotiations to conclude armistice to replace existing truce of Germany with Russia begins at headquarters of Prince Leopold.

Dec. 14. Trotzky, Bolshevik Foreign Minister, declares that if armistice is signed for Eastern Front at Brest-Litovsk Russian delegates are empowered to enter into peace negotiations.

Dec. 16. Formal announcement made by Berlin that armistice between Russia and Germany is signed; Russia thus violates her pledge to Allies not to make seperate peace.

Dec. 18. London dispatch tells of air-raid over city in which sixteen to twenty large German Gothas took part.

Dec. 20. Counter-revolution in South Russia spreading northward and struggle increasing in intensity; Ukraine Rada, which opposes Lenine and his followers, declares Ukraine a democratic republic and rejects ultimatum from the Bolshevik Government.

Dec. 21. Ukraine has joined Cossacks and Bolshevik Government has given Rada forty-eight hours in which to reconsider; mobs in Petrograd said to be sacking homes of rich; in desperate attacks Italians win back much of ground lost in region of Monte Asolone.

Dec. 23. At Brest-Litovsk peace delegates begin session; Emperor William informs his Government he contemplates going to Brest-Litovsk if agreement is reached, in which case he will endeavor to "assemble all the sovereigns of Europe in a peace conference similar to that which followed the Napoleonic wars"; in a succession of brilliant attacks Italians dislodge enemy from great part of Monte Asolone.

Dec. 24. German forces which crossed Piave driven back with severe losses; in Christmas message to troops Kaiser declares battles of 1917 prove that "the Lord is the avowed ally of the German people, and that for those who do not want peace it must be compelled with the iron fist."

Dec. 26. Wilson, by proclamation, takes possession all nation's railroads with auxiliary water-lines, elevators, warehouses, and all other equipment.

Dec. 27. One of largest air-raids attempted on Italian front defeated and nearly half of German fleet of twenty-five aeroplanes destroyed; British and Italian machines engaged enemy at close quarters.

Dec. 28. Trotzky says if Allies refuse join in negotiations within ten days, Russia be forced to conclude a separate peace.

Dec. 29. Thirteen persons killed and sixty injured when open city of Padua in northern Italy bombarded by enemy.

Dec. 31. Ukrainian and Cossack forces in battle on southwestern front defeat Bolshevik troops, taking 400 prisoners and capturing 8 big guns and 328 machine-guns.

THE EVENTS OF 1918

JANUARY

WILSON'S FOURTEEN POINTS SPEECH—
PEACE NEGOTIATIONS AT BREST-
LITOVSK

Jan. 2. Germany demands Russia turn over to her Poland, Courland, Esthonia, and Lithuania.

Jan. 3. Trotzky declares Russian workers will not consent to German terms.

Jan. 4. Growing disposition among Russians to recognize Lenine.

Jan. 5. Trotzky, accompanied by Russian delegates, on way to Brest-Litovsk to resume peace negotiations with Germany.

Jan. 7. Serious quarrel in Crown Council of Germany, internal situation is acute, due to Russian peace fiasco.

Jan. 8. Before Congress in joint session Wilson in famous Fourteen Points speech enunciates war plans and peace program of United States and tenders to Russia assistance and sympathy.

Jan. 9. Spirited artillery battle on banks of Brenta, and a heavy bombardment along Piave; French in a raid penetrate German defenses east of St. Mihiel for nearly a mile; aircraft during December put out of commission 76 German machines, 23 of which fell within French lines, and 18 were destroyed over enemy territory; French losses, 19 planes.

Jan. 10. Secret service agents discover extensive movement to organize German sabotage in United States; thirty Germans and some Scandinavians arrested; owing to losses by sinking of ships and crop failures United States plans to release for export an additional 90,000,000 bushels of wheat to aid Allies.

Jan. 11. Full text Wilson's address to Congress reaches Paris; Germans withdraw general peace terms, made public at Brest-Litovsk conference on Christmas.

Jan. 12. Chamber of Deputies places stamp of approval on war aims of Allies as stated by Lloyd George and Wilson by indorsing them by a vote of 395 to 145.

Jan. 17. In mutiny among submarine crews at German naval base at Kiel, thirty-eight officers are killed.

Jan. 20. Strikes spreading throughout Austria; Rome reports heavy losses of Austrian airplanes on Italian front, 42 having been destroyed during last fortnight; British naval forces bombard Ostend; in an action at entrance of Dardanelles between British and Turkish forces Turkish cruiser *Midullu*, formerly German *Breslau*, sunk, and the *Sultan Yavuz Selim*, formerly the German *Goeben*, beached; British lost monitor *Raglan* and a small monitor.

Jan. 22. Because of desertion of 160,000 Turkish troops between Constantinople and Palestine, Falkenhayn abandons plan to reorganize Turkish army for offensive against British in Palestine; two British steamships sunk in Mediterranean by which 718 lives lost; submarine sinkings held at a low point during week.

Jan. 26. Wilson, in a proclamation, calls for a more intensive effort to save food to supply Allies.

Jan. 29. Italian forces renew offensive east of Asiago; Clémenceau presides at first meeting of Supreme War Council at Versailles; Great Britain, France, Italy, and the United States represented.

Jan. 30. Monte di Val Bella and Col del Rosso fall to the Italians; operations on the Asiago resulted in capture of 2,600 prisoners, six guns, and one hundred machine-guns; Secretary Baker announces American troops in action in France.

Jan. 31. Paris reports systematic German air-raid on city during which twenty were killed and fifty injured; four squadrons of Germans dropt 28,000 pounds of bombs; thirty French planes rose to meet them and for two hours a spectacular battle raged; two hospitals struck and several buildings burned.

FEBRUARY

AFTER PEACE WITH RUSSIA GERMAN
MILITARY AGGRESSIONS ARE
RESUMED

Feb. 1. Bolshevik forces capture Odessa, with a population of 450,000, and Orenburg, the headquarters of Cossacks.

Feb. 2. Italians report enemy losses reaching as high as 50 per cent. of men engaged during a week west of Brenta, where Allies won notable successes; result is ascribed to unity of action of Italian, French, and British batteries.

Feb. 5. British transport *Tuscania*, with 2,179 United States troops on board, torpedoed and sunk off north coast of Ireland; 1,912 survivors landed in Ireland; 159 American soldiers lost.

Feb. 6. Two American aviators accompanying a French escadrille on a bombing expedition encounter enemy squadron of eight planes; general engagement ensues above clouds and one American sends German plane to ground; Bonar Law announces German *U-boats* have slain 14,120 non-combatant British men, women and children.

Feb. 8. Jellicoe declares he believes by August the submarine menace will have ended.

Feb. 9. Text of Kaiser's birthday message pleads for home unity and urges that all other issues be put aside for triumph on battlefield; peace treaty between Central Powers and Ukraine has been signed.

Feb. 11. Bolshevik Government withdraws from war with the Central Empires, and orders demobilization; no formal treaty of peace is signed, however; Roumania's situation

A CHRONOLOGY OF THE WAR

now critical; Wilson appears unexpectedly before Congress and reads a message in reply to speech of Chancellor Hertling.

Feb. 12. American dead as the result sinking of *Tuscania* reported to number 159; bodies of 145 have been buried along coast; British Government refuses to recognize treaty of peace between Ukraine and Central Powers.

Feb. 13. Roumania has defied Central Powers and will "survive or perish with the Entente cause."

Feb. 14. American artillery take an important part in French raid between Tahure and Butte du Mesnil.

Feb. 15. Trotzky declares Russia has withdrawn from war.

Feb. 19. Lloyd George in House of Commons, asks for immediate continuation of supreme control over every other issue of war.

Feb. 20. Heavy firing reported in Champagne, where American infantry recently took part in French advance; Germans are driven back in a raid on American lines.

Feb. 21. British Government instructed agent at Kief to make declaration that Great Britain will not recognize any peace in the East which involves Poland without consultation with Poland; German troops advancing on a front extending from shores of Esthonia to southern border of Volhynia; Minsk, most eastern point attained, been entered, and in south fortress of Rovno taken.

Feb. 22. Peace treaty between Ukraine and Germany ratified; peace negotiations with Roumania begun at Castle Bufftea, near Bucharest; Jericho occupied by British forces with little opposition.

Feb. 23. German vanguard reaches Walk, in Livonia, 90 miles northeast of Riga; Wilson issues proclamation that fixes price of 1918 wheat—which must be sold in the market before June 1, 1919—at from $2 to $2.28.

Feb. 24. Bolshevik leaders accept German peace conditions, which include relinquishment of all claim to 160,000 square miles of Russian territory, payment of $1,500,000,000 indemnity, and occupation of Petrograd by Germans.

Feb. 26. Details of raid of American and French troops in Chemin-des-Dames sector tell of hand-to-hand fighting in a German dugout where the entire enemy party was captured; Americans chased Germans out of other shelters and pursued them beyond the objectives, their rash enthusiasm causing some French criticism; German Chancellor in "peace" address before Reichstag defended campaign against Russia as merely to enable Germany to obtain fruits of peace with Ukraine.

Feb. 27. Hoffman, in command of German invading army, Russia, announces advance will continue until a peace treaty is signed and carried out on lines laid down by Germany.

MARCH

LUDENDORFF BEGINS GREAT DRIVE—
AMERICAN TROOPS IN RAIDS ON
EASTERN FRENCH FRONT—
PERSHING OFF TO FOCH

March 1. Many American casualties resulted from an enemy raid in salient north of Toul; raid successfully repulsed; dispatch from Venice states 45 air-attacks been made on Venice up to February 26, when in a night raid lasting three hours 300 bombs were dropt.

March 2. Berlin announces occupation of Kief; German raid on line in Chemin-des-Dames sector repulsed, some Americans killed and several slightly wounded.

March 3. Petrograd dispatch announces signing of peace treaty with Germany, Bolshevik delegates accepting all terms, fearing new demands.

March 5. German attack on the trenches held by American forces in Lorraine repulsed; Germans continue to advance in Russia; Narva, one hundred miles southwest of Petrograd, captured and troops advancing on capital.

March 6. Preliminary peace treaty been signed by Roumania and the Central Powers under terms of which Roumania cedes province of Dobrudja as far as Danube to Central Powers, and undertakes to further transport of German troops through Moldavia and Bessarabia to Odessa; Petrograd being abandoned by Bolshevik Government and Moscow proclaimed capital of Russia.

March 7. United States will sell all German property in this country, beginning with Hamburg-American and the North German Lloyd steamship piers in Hoboken; American troops now holding more than eight miles of trenches on battle-front in France.

March 8. First complete unit of American air-service appeared in field and for the first time in war American observation balloon, fully manned and protected by Americans, was sent up.

March 10. Secretary of War Baker arrives in France and proceeds to Paris; American troops on Lorraine front resist heavy concentrated bombardment, enemy firing almost a hundred gas-shells into American battery position; more than fifty French war-crosses distributed among American troops along Chemin-des-Dames for gallant part men played in eleven engagements.

March 11. First wholly American raid made in sector north of Toul, and surprize of Germans complete; Americans penetrated enemy's first and second lines, inflicting casualties in killed and wounded and returning to their own lines safely with booty in supplies and munitions.

March 12. American detachment successfully carried out surprize attack on German trenches south of Richecourt; Americans east of Lunéville again raid German positions; going far beyond their objective they engage in hand-to-hand fighting, using automatic pistols and rifles; American forces made important raid on German lines in Toul sector; enemy fled upon approach of Americans; American artillery completely destroyed 200 German gas-projectors discovered through a photograph taken over German lines.

March 15. Moscow conference votes to support the Lenine treaty with Germany and her allies by 453 to 30.

March 16. Senate passes without division Daylight-Saving Bill as amended by House.

March 17. Washington states American troops being sent to France faster than any previous time since war began; Secretary Baker's promise of half a million men in Europe early this year being fulfilled; British aerial attacks on German towns causing panics and many persons leaving Rhine cities for Central Germany or Switzerland.

March 18. Seven more Americans been cited by French commander for Croix de Guerre in recognition of bravery while under fire in Lunéville sector; Supreme War Council of Allies issued a statement condemning German political crimes against Russian and Roumanian peoples and refusing to recognize Germany's peace treaties with those countries.

March 19. War Department announces casualties among American Expeditionary Forces as 1,925, divided as follows: Killed in action, 154; killed or prisoner, 1; killed by accident, 145; died of disease, 683; lost at sea, 237; suicide, 11; unknown cause, 14; died of wounds, 37; executed, 1; civilians, 7; gassed, 6; total deaths, 1,296; wounded, 594; captured, 21; missing, 14.

March 21. Long-heralded grand offensive of Germans launched soon after dawn by enormous masses of Kaiser's troops against British front in France; at nightfall greatest battle of the war, in its scope and number of men engaged, was raging with unabated fury; after an intense bombardment, a powerful infantry-attack was launched on a front of more than fifty miles, extending from the Oise, near La Fère, to Sensée, about Croisilles; captured maps, indicating intentions of Germans, show that on no part of long front did they attain their objectives.

March 22. Great drive continued along nearly the entirely fifty-mile front, British slowly withdrawing; Kaiser at front with Hindenburg and Ludendorff and directing operations; casualties among Germans, who are attacking in huge masses, declared to be appalling, entire ground at points of attack being covered with enemy dead.

March 23. First stage of great battle finished with Germans claiming advantage all along the line from Monchy, near Arras, to La Fère; casualties in the three day's fighting estimated at 150,000 German and 100,000 British; British retiring to prepared positions in the region from which Germans retreated previous spring; tremendous artillery-fire was heard in London, 180 miles away; Haig reports British taken up new positions and "are heavily engaged with the enemy."

March 24. One-half of territory in France wrested from Germans in 1916 again in their hands, as result of four days' fighting.

March 25. Battle continued all day on wide fronts south of Péronne and south and north of Bapaume; the enemy occupying Bapaume and Nesle; south of Péronne German troops were driven back; heavy loses inflicted on enemy by artillery and low-flying airplanes.

March 26. Force of German offensive not yet checked; fighting continued with undiminished violence along the front comprising Braysur-Somme, Chauainet, Roye, and Noyon; Pershing reported two American regiments of railway-engineers in battle with British on March 25 and 26.

March 27. Germans take Albert and British forces are prest back on both banks of Somme, but holding their line; in counter-attack British recapture Moriancourt and Chinilly; Germans attacking in great strength gain a foothold in Ablainville; at all other points infantry are beaten off with great loss; Amsterdam reports enormously long ambulance-trains passing through Belgium with German wounded.

March 28. Eighth day of German offensive results in tremendous attacks being stopt, while French win a brilliant victory in south; fierce fighting reported south of Scarpe, and south of Somme; British maintain positions; French troops in counter-attack with bayonet driving Germans out of Courtemanche, Mesnil-St. Georges, and Assainvillers; long-range gun bombarding Paris a product of Krupp works at Essen.

March 29. On ninth day of great battle German drive brought to practical halt; captured documents reveal that objective of German attack astride the Scarpe was capture of Vimy Ridge and Arras; battle at Montdidier continued. Germans, notwithstanding fierce counter-attacks, unable to eject French from village; 75 persons killed and 90 wounded, mostly women and children, when a shell fired by German long-range gun fell on a church in Paris on Good Friday; Clémenceau, on return from front, tells a gathering of Deputies that "come what may, the foe will not break through"; Pershing calls on Foch and in his own name and that of the United States asks that American troops be engaged in present battle, and offers "all that we have."

March 30. Sharp fighting resumed on seventy miles of front during day, but Haig reports British position remains intact; citing the great battle as main reason for it. Lloyd George announces Foch been placed in command of Allied armies on Western Front.

March 31. French Government acceded to request Pershing and American troops will fight side by side with British and French in Picardy; in brilliant operations Canadian cavalry and British infantry recapture Moreuil.

APRIL

FOCH MADE GENERALISSIMO—ARMENTIÈRES, KEMMEL HILL AND THE ZEEBRUGGE EXPLOIT

April 1. Battle maintained on whole front north of Montdidier with new attacks against Grivesnes repulsed; by brilliant counter-attacks Hangarden-Santerre recaptured; French estimates place foe's losses during eleven-day offensive at between 275,000 and 300,000 men.

April 2. Offensive still further slackened.

April 4. American forces now occupy a sector on Meuse Heights south of Verdun; fifteen more Americans cited by French for gallantry in action; during last Allied raid on Coblenz 26 persons killed and 100 wounded; in last raid on Trèves 60 killed and hundreds injured; in raid on Cologne a troop-train struck and caused 248 deaths, half of which were of soldiers bound for Picardy front.

April 5. Battle on a thirty-mile front from Grivesnes, north of Albert, continued through night.

April 6. Bombardment Paris by long-range guns resumed; three persons wounded; before large and enthusiastic audience in Baltimore, Wilson declares nation stands united for a war to victory and use of "force to the utmost".

April 9. On eleven-mile front from Givenchy to La Bassée Germans drive in line held by British and Portuguese to a depth of four miles at one or two points; Richebourg-St. Vaast and Laventie taken by enemy.

April 10. British reports first American troops arrive on British line and greeted enthusiastically; dispatch from Amsterdam states German troops at Limburg, Prussia, mutiny as they are about to start for France; under terms of peace treaty Russia loses 780,000 square kilometers of territory and 56,000,000 inhabitants, 32 per cent. of the population of the country; German attacks now extend for more than 150 miles; north of Armentières enemy presses on to Wytschaete-Messines Ridge and Ploegsteert; south of Armentières German force is established on left bank of Lys, east of Estaires, and in neighborhood of Bac St. Maur; British maintain position between Estaires and Givenchy.

April 11. Romanof family suffering want on allowance of $200 a month; letter of Emperor Charles of Austria, written to brother-in-law, Prince Sixtus de Bourbon, made public, in which Emperor acknowledges just claims of France to Alsace-Lorraine, and offers to support France's claim, as well as declaring that Belgium should be re-established; heavy fighting in progress on northern end battle-front; north of Armentières determined attack develops and British withdraw from Armentières, which is full of gas.

April 12. French and American troops drive enemy out of foothold gained in Apremont Forest; Americans take 22 prisoners belonging to six different units; Haig, in order to British troops, states that "Every position must be held to the last man. There must be no retirement. With our backs to the wall, and believing in the justice of our cause, each one of us must fight to the end."

April 13. German advance checked on ten-mile front. British holding line of railroad from Armentières to Hazebrouck.

April 14. British and French agreed in conferring upon Foch title of Commander-in-Chief of Allied Armies in France; violent attack by four German companies on American position on Meuse north of St. Mihiel repulsed successfully in fierce hand-to-hand fighting.

April 15. Neuve-Église lost by British; fierce fighting north of Merville, Germans being driven back with great loss.

April 16. Germans make important gains in drive for Channel ports; Bailleul taken and drive extended two miles beyond that point; Wytschaete and Spanbroekmolen also occupied; at nearest point Germans now only thirty miles from coast; situation considered most critical since war began; enemy attack renewed in strength on front from Meteren to Wytschaete; approaching under cover of a mist German forces took both positions after prolonged struggle; Meteren recaptured by British; heavy artillery action reported south of Montdidier; French make progress in Noyon sector; heights of Wytschaete stormed and Bailleul taken by Germans; situation extremely critical.

April 17. Greek and British troops crossed Struma River on eastern flank of Macedonian front and occupied seven towns; British withdraw from east of Ypres to new line.

April 18. Checked on northern side of salient below Ypres, Germans shift attack, west of La Bassée and Givenchy; ten divisions hurled against British on a ten-mile front; at end of day British line remained intact; attacks against British position south of Kemmel repulsed.

April 19. American and French troops raid German line on Meuse; hostile movement south of Kemmel successfully repulsed; French position greatly improved through engagements in Hangard district; Italian regiments in France form right wing of Allied armies; Reims now nothing but pile smoking ruins; during the week Germans fired more than 100,000 shells into the heart of city.

April 21. In sharp fighting American sector northwest of Toul Germans, with picked troops, penetrated as far as Seicheprey, a mile and a quarter behind the front; driven out by a counter-attack of the Americans with no gain; American loss placed at more than 200; enemy loss estimated at from 300 to 500; Americans armed with short shot-guns, which sprayed buckshot over advancing troops, seriously breaking down German morale; Paris reports bombardment by the long-range gun continues; since March 23, 118 persons killed and 230 injured; attempt by enemy to advance northeast of Ypres stopt by British artillery.

April 22. Baron von Richthofen, leader of German fliers with eighty air victories to credit in Berlin, brought down behind British lines and buried with military honors.

April 23. In a daring effort to block channel at Zeebrugge, German submarine, two old cruisers loaded with cement sunk, operations carried on under concentrated fire of enemy; British cruiser *Vindictive* ran gauntlet of mines and submarines and a heavy gunfire and landed sailors and machine-guns; an old British submarine, filled with explosives, ran up alongside mole and blown up; two destroyers made their way inside mole where they blew up lock-gates; similar enterprise at Ostend not so successful.

April 25. British and French forced to withdraw from positions between Bailleul and Wytschaete.

April 26. German forces capture summit of Mount Kemmel which dominates entire northern side of salient; isolated and surrounded, French troops on summit fought until overwhelmed by force of numbers.

April 27. British press state the crisis in Flanders is more perilous than any that has hitherto arisen; Paris dispatch states eleven American ambulance men won War Cross by gallant services during battle now in progress.

April 28. Ypres still held by British, but foe gained a footing in outskirts of Locre; serious anti-German demonstrations occurred in Austria.

April 30. Total American casualty list in France to date: Killed in action, 588; died of wounds, disease or accident, 1,311; from other causes, 95; missing in action, 93; severely wounded number 555; British official report states that successful counterattacks drove enemy from ground gained in neighborhood of Locre, whole village now being in hands of the Allies.

MAY

THE GERMAN DRIVE SOUTH TO THE MARNE—AMERICANS AT CANTIGNY

May 1. German attack hurled against Americans who occupy a short sector west of Villers-Bretonneux; attack repulsed, the Germans leaving many dead; American loss reported "rather severe"; Gavril Prinzip, assassin of Archduke Francis Ferdinand and his wife, died in fortress near Prague of tuberculosis.

May 2. Germans establish military rule in Kief.

May 4. Washington reports "overwhelming success" of third Liberty Loan campaign at midnight, when it was indicated that the subscriptions will amount to more than $3,867,-000,000.

May 5. Emperor Charles, the Austrian Chief of Staff, and several high German and Austrian officials, reached Italian front.

May 7. Clémenceau, returning from the front, declares American troops are continuing to arrive in force; believes Entente forces invincible.

May 9. Large German patrol attempted to rush American positions on Picardy front, but frustrated; total losses of Allied and neutral ships due to submarine warfare during April approximately one-half those during April of last year; last year figures were 634,685 tons, while in April, 1918, tonnage lost was 381,631.

May 10. Operations designed to close ports of Ostend and Zeebrugge completed when obsolete cruiser *Vindictive*, filled with concrete, sunk between piers at entrance of Ostend harbor.

May 13. Big ammunition-dump in Cantigny fired by American artillery and at same time two fires started in Montdidier followed by numerous explosions; enemy activity reported increasing along Italian front.

May 16. Opening of offensive on Italian front developed with Italian troops taking lead; troops of new American army arriving within zone of British forces in northern France; air-fighting on tremendous scale on Western Front with American aviators participating; Wilson arrives in New York and reviews Red Cross parade which inaugurated $100,000,-000 drive; Washington announces subscriptions to third Liberty Loan reached $4,170,019,650.

May 18. In an address at Metropolitan Opera House, New York, Wilson announces no limit will be placed on number of men that will be sent to France to "win the war worthily."

May 23. Unprecedented aerial activity on battle-front and behind German lines; Mannheim again attacked, a chlorine factory being set on fire; on May 21 bombs dropt on four of enemy's large airdromes near Ghent and Tournai, and billets near Armentières, Bapaume, and Bray; enemy aircraft been particularly active in Picardy, on American front, bombing villages in the rear of the lines and killing number of women and children.

May 27. Italians launched important offensive northwest of Trent, capturing 870 prisoners and 12 guns, and taking summit of Monte Zignolon and spur east of pass; Great German offensive resumed on practically entire front; terrific blows struck in Flanders and on Aisne; attack began 3.30 in morning at Berry-au-Bac, and same time attacks made on French on right and left along high ground traversed by Chemin-des-Dames; in British sector attack supported by tanks; on left enemy pushed back British to second line of defense; in neighborhood of Dickebusch Lake enemy succeeded in penetrating for short distance into French positions; battle continued throughout day with extreme violence on front of forty miles.

May 28. Offensive made rapid progress during day in Aisne sector and at night continued apparently unchecked; numerous towns taken by storm and Berlin claims capture of 15,000 prisoners; French and British retiring steadily; continuous pressure maintained all day against British troops on Aisne front and severe fighting continues on entire British sector, and second-line positions maintained until late hour; at end of day weight of enemy troops carried them across Aisne to west of British sector; west of Montdidier Americans, supported by British tanks, brilliantly occupied salient along front of two kilometers and strongly fortified village of Cantigny, capturing 170 prisoners and material; in an attack on village of Cantigny Americans gained all objectives, capturing 145 Germans, including two officers; American losses slight and only two men reported missing.

May 29. Enormous number of fresh troops thrown into German lines extends and widens drive on Aisne front, pushing point of new salient five miles farther south, making maximum penetration of enemy for the three days seventeen and one-half miles; Soissons, after stubborn resistance and fighting in streets, evacuated by French; southeast of city battle extended to Belleu, Septmonts, Ambrief, and Charcise; troops covering Reims withdrawn behind Aisne Canal; German attack made over front approximately thirty miles wide and at least 240,-000 men employed.

May 30. In center, about seven miles north of Marne, French reserves, aided by American troops, check German thrust toward Château-Thierry; another attack on American positions at Cantigny hurled back by artillery-fire.

May 31. Enemy pushing forward with strongly augmented forces, reaches Marne; despite vigorous counter-attacks enemy passed Oulchy-la-Ville and Oulchy-le-Château; United States transport *President Lincoln* sunk by German *U*-boat on her way to this country; vessel was struck by three torpedoes and remained afloat only eighteen minutes; twenty-three of crew, including three officers, missing; German *U*-boats been operating off coast of United States; northwest of Toul American troops raid German lines on 500-yard front, penetrating positions for 500 yards; defensive works and dugouts destroyed.

JUNE

AUSTRIANS DEFEATED ON THE PIAVE—
AMERICAN MARINES TAKE BELLEAU
WOOD—BEAURICHES AND VAUX

June 1. Germans occupy front on Marne thirteen miles wide, forming apex of V-shaped salient between Château-Thierry and Verneuil; situation admitted critical.

June 2. Thirty-eight officers and men

of American Expeditionary Force cited for gallantry in action; enemy reached outskirts of forest of Retz, surrounding Villers-Cotterets, forming one of principal defenses of approach to Paris by Ourcq Valley; Germans again bomb group of hospitals that were attacked on May 19.

June 3. Foch brought his reserve force into field; to north of Aisne, Mont Choisy was recaptured for fifth time by French.

June 5. Marines finally beat off desperate attacks of enemy at Belleau Wood; wiped out enemy patrol, and charged and captured enemy positions, taking machine-guns and many prisoners; other American troops penetrated enemy positions in Picardy and Lorraine.

June 6. French official report on American operations at Château-Thierry stated "courage of Americans beyond all praise"; attack by French and American troops on point of German salient nearest to Paris, west of Château-Thierry, drove back invaders nearly mile on front of two miles; attack between Ourcq and Marne carried out by French and Americans advanced French line in region of Veuil-ly-le-Poterie and Bouresches.

June 7. French and Americans capture villages of Veuilly-la-Poterie and Bouresches, both points of great strategical value which fought over most bitterly for several days; Bligny, between Marne and Reims, captured; American troops gained ground on front of Torcy, Belleau, and Bouresches, west of Château-Thierry; further advances by American troops near Château-Thierry.

June 8. First mention of American forces in official German reports.

June 9. Unsuccessful attacks by enemy northwest of Château-Thierry.

June 10. Marines at daybreak again attack German lines, penetrating two-thirds of mile on 600-yard front in Belleau Wood northwest of Château-Thierry; French Government issues statement in which it says that "with strong will and irresistible activity American troops continue absolutely to dominate adversaries they oppose"; German offensive between Montdidier and Noyon marked by aerial operations on tremendous scale.

June 13. German advance practically ceased.

June 15. German drive for Paris effectively checked; enemy driven out of Coeuvres-et-Valsery, south of Aisne; Austrians opened great offensive on front from Asiago Plateau to sea, distance of 90 miles.

June 16. On long battle-line in Italy terrific fighting still in progress, all ground yielded under weight of first grand rush by French, British, and Italians recovered with exception of few places on Piave River; enemy infantry passed to right bank of Piave; end of six days desperate fighting marked by complete arrest of German offensive.

June 7. Proof that Austrian offensive

broken down shown by fact that Italians with British and French Allies aggressive along 100-mile battle-front from southeast of Trent to Adriatic Sea.

June 18. Violence of great Italian battle diminished in vital mountain sectors but increased along Piave.

June 19. An assault by large units of German shock-troops been concentrated on western side of Reims between Vrigny and Ormes met by heavy French fire and unable to make progress; Turkish troops sack American hospital at Tabriz and seize American and British consulates; American patrols crossed Marne east of Château-Thierry establishing contact with enemy; American artillery east and west of Château-Thierry deluged enemy with shells for several hours; Austrian troops had to cross Piave in perilous position; river swollen to flood, many bridges swept away, cutting off supplies of food and ammunition, troops penned on flat ground terribly cut up by Italian artillery and Allied airplanes.

June 21. For first time Italian airmen had as companions "daring American pilots"; American forces rushed enemy's positions without artillery preparation; midnight American artillery poured an avalanche of projectiles into wood east of Château-Thierry where host of German troops and material had been located by aerial photographs; American troops forming Rainbow division, cited by French General for fine military qualities and services.

June 22. More than 900,000 American troops have left for Europe; record five months ahead of program.

June 23. Greatest of Austria's armies falling back across Piave in confusion; losses in one week's fighting estimated at 200,000.

June 24. American troops capture northwestern part Belleau Wood; Austrian rout appears complete; an official message announces evacuation by enemy of Montello Plateau and right bank of Piave.

June 25. Further advances were made by American troops in Château-Thierry region.

June 26. Complete recapture of all Italian arms, artillery and material reported; one Austrian report admits loss of 20,000 by drowning in Piave; Americans extend their line northwest of Belleau Wood; new positions give United States Marines possession of virtually all of Belleau Wood dominating ridge beyond.

June 27. Reports of murder of Emperor Nicholas in Ekaterinburg persist in Moskow; Clémenceau visits American unit that fought at Belleau Wood and expresses warm appreciation.

June 28. British in north and French in south deliver smashing blows against surprized Germans, winning large area of ground.

June 29. First American troops landed in Italy; British report states that since June 1, 1,040 airplanes and 71 observation-balloons reported

downed on all battle-fronts and in Allied raids on Germany; on Western Front 781 airplanes reported downed.

JULY

FOCH'S GREAT COUNTER-OFFENSIVE IN THE MARNE SALIENT, AMERICANS MAKING 30 PER CENT. OF HIS FORCE

July 2. American units in night attack capture village of Vaux, close to Château-Thierry; production of snips in the United States during June broke all records, steel and wooden ships delivered to Shipping Board totaling 280,140 deadweight tons; steel ships totaled 262,900 tons; up to and including June 30, 1,019,115 American troops left for France; during the month of June an average of 9,212 American soldiers left for France every day.

July 4. Australian troops, assisted by American infantry and some tanks, drove against enemy lines east of Amiens over four-mile front, capturing villages of Hamel and Vaire and Hamel Woods, together with 1,500 prisoners; as fitting celebration of Independence Day 54 steel and 41 wooden vessels launched in United States shipyards; before gathering of diplomats and representatives of foreign nations at tomb of Washington at Mount Vernon, Wilson declares there can be but one issue to war—a final settlement; five American aviators attached to Italian army decorated with Italian War Cross by King Victor Emmanuel.

July 5. Czecho-Slovaks win in great battle with Bolsheviks 250 miles west of Irkutsk; Czecho-Slovaks now said to be in control of 3,000 miles of Siberia.

July 6. General Count von Mirbach, German Ambassador to Russia, assassinated in Moscow.

July 7. Italians occupy right bank of new Piave and fortify themselves on vast tract of land recaptured.

July 8. French forces launch attack southwest of Soissons.

July 9. Reports that Kuhlmann, German Foreign Minister, resigned are confirmed.

July 10. In fight north of Château-Thierry Lieut. Quentin Roosevelt brought down his first German airplane; rapid strides being made by French, British, and Italian forces in Albania, offensive being pushed on front of sixty miles; town of Berat occupied by Italian forces and French allies; British monitors reported assisted French and Italian troops in reaching Fiere.

July 13. British statement on aerial operations announces that in one year on Western Front Royal Air Force has accounted for 3,233 enemy airplanes, while naval airmen shot down 623, a total of 3,856.

July 15. American and British troops occupy whole of Murman coast in northern Russia; German Marne offensive resumed after violent artillery preparation at 4.30 A.M., striking on both sides of Reims; American forces holding western side of Marne salient meet ons.aught gallantly; just east of Château-Thierry German advance checked by Americans who, in counterattack after Germans crossed river, took 1,500 prisoners, including complete brigade staff; Germans driven back to original positions; German long-range guns resume bombardment of Paris.

July 17. Quentin Roosevelt killed when his airplane was brought down in flames during fight south of Reims on July 14.

July 18. Foch strikes Crown Prince's right flank vital blow; French and Americans, closely cooperating, fight their way six miles along Aisne, reaching outskirts of Soissons; south of Soissons Allied troops reach Rozières, driving Germans back eight miles from their starting point; advance so rapid that cavalry thrown into action; French report French and American forces taking more than twenty villages, several thousand prisoners, and quantity of war material; Pershing's report states that in American sector on Marne enemy entirely driven from south bank; Americans in Marne salient comprise 30 per cent. of Entente force.

July 19. In great Allied counteroffensive French and American troops push on about two miles and hold advanced positions despite counterattack; Paris reports 17,000 prisoners and 360 guns taken; Scottish troops capture village of Meteren, taking 300 prisoners and number of machine-guns; Australians push forward south of Meteren; American troops cooperating with French between Aisne and Marne, penetrate enemy's lines to depth of several miles.

July 20. Germans begin retreat across Marne; 20,000 prisoners and 400 guns captured; whole south bank of the Marne held by Allied forces; as a result of operations in Meteren sector British line been advanced on front of about 4,000 yards and Meteren and Le Waton are now held by British troops; between Aisne and Ourcq; French in conjunction with Greek and Italian troops make further advance in Albania, capturing Meran and Mount Tizee; Nicholas Romanof, former Czar of Russia, declared executed on July 16.

July 21. Entire property of Nicholas Romanof, his wife, and mother, as well as all other members of royal house, including deposits in foreign banks, been forfeited to Russian Republic; Pershing states prisoners captured by American troops during battle on Marne total 17,000, with 560 guns; Americans continue advance.

July 22. Powerful counter-attacks by Germans between Marne and Ourcq met by Franco-American troops, who increased their gains, advancing northeast and taking village of Epieds; Pershing reports fresh successes between Aisne and Marne.

July 23. Violent engagements reported between Marne and Reims; in local engagement north of Montdidier French captured Mailly-Raineval, Sauvillers, and Aubvillers.

July 25. French report capture of Oulchy-la-Ville, Hill 141, village of Coincy, and most of Tournelle Wood; Pershing reports continued American advance with capture of southern half of Forest of Fère.

July 27. Arrival of force of American troops reported on Italian front.

July 28. French have crossed Ourcq and penetrated into Fère-en-Tardenois.

July 30. Americans beat Germans back nearly two miles north of Fère-en-Tardenois in terrific fighting; Franco-American advance captured tremendous stores of German ammunition abandoned in hasty retreat; Field-Marshal von Eichhorn and his adjutant, Captain von Dressler, killed by bomb in Kief.

July 31. Czecho-Slovaks, in a surprise attack, capture large railway-bridge at Syzran in the Volga region.

AUGUST

GERMAN DEFEAT IN ALBERT-MONT-DIDIER SALIENT—SOISSONS AND FISMES TAKEN

Aug. 1. Mangin's French-American army advances on twelve-mile front on west side of Champagne salient, taking Cramoiselle, Meunière Wood, and Cierges.

Aug. 2. French reports note fall of Soissons, crossing of the Crise, and taking of Coulonges, Goussancourt Villers - Agron, Ville-en - Tardenois, Gueux, and Thillois.

Aug. 3. Pershing awarded Grand Cross of Legion of Honor by French Government; First Army Corps, commanded by Major-General Hunter Liggett, occupied center of Allied forces which drove in the German salient on Marne.

Aug. 4. German retreat of six miles on ten-mile front between Montdidier and Moreuil near Amiens; Fismes taken by Allies, whose forces reach Vesle to east and cross river in several places; Aisne crossed between Soissons and Benizel, and French make further gains northwest of Rheims; Pershing reports Germans driven in confusion beyond the Vesle, 8,400 prisoners and 133 guns taken by American troops alone.

Aug. 6. Premier Clémenceau announces Allied counter-offensive wiped out German salient between Soissons and Reims and resulted in capture of more than 35,000 prisoners and 700 guns; Foch made Marshal of France and Pétain receives Military Medal.

Aug. 7. Franco-American troops cross Vesle.

Aug. 8. Submarine sinkings for July officially stated to be less than for June; in new offensive in Picardy, between Braches and Morlancourt, British troops, assisted on south by French forces, sweep forward for an average gain of five miles; ten thousand prisoners and 100 guns reported captured.

Aug. 9. Fresh blows bring Allied extreme penetration in Picardy to fourteen miles; number of prisoners officially reported 17,000, and between 200 and 300 guns taken; in Lys Valley British troops advance on ten-mile front on maximum depth of four miles; on Vesle, American troops capture Fismette; Rome reports squadron of Italian airplanes, commanded by Capt. Gabriele d'Annunzio, has flown over Vienna and dropt manifestoes.

Aug. 10. Picardy offensive gains maximum of six miles, Montdidier, Lihons, and Proyart falling to Allies; American troops participate in capture of Chipilly "the most serious reverse of the war," is pan-German *Deutsche Zeitung's* description of first day of Picardy Allied offensive.

Aug. 15. Canadian troops take Damery and Parvillers, northwest of Roye; total number of prisoners captured by British Fourth Army since morning of August 8, 21,844; in same period prisoners taken by French First Army amount to 8,500, making total of 30,344 German prisoners captured in the operations of Allied armies on Montdidier-Albert front; first contingent of American troops "is now arriving at Vladivostok"; the unit consists of the Twenty-seventh Regular Infantry Regiment.

Aug. 17. General March, Chief of Staff, announces overseas shipments of men total more than 1,450,000.

Aug. 21. Czecho-Slovak forces completely in control of railway from Baku to Ural Mountains; northwest of Soissons French take Lassigny and advance over front of 15 miles, piercing German lines to maximum depth of five miles; British capture villages of Beaucourt, Bucquoy, Ablainzeville, Moyenneville, Achiet-le-Petit, and Courcelles.

Aug. 22. French forces advance seven miles between Aisne and region north of Soissons; Albert captured by British troops.

Aug. 23. British take nine towns on front of more than thirty miles; several thousand prisoners taken; cross Oise River, eight miles east of Noyon.

Aug. 24. Bray, Thiepval, and four other villages captured by British; American troops west of Fismes sector advance as far as Reims-Soissons road.

Aug. 25. Against fresh German troops British forces capture fourteen villages, including Contalmaison, Martinpuich, Le Sars, and Mametz; British airplanes bombed Karlsruhe on August 23; nine persons killed and six injured.

Aug. 27. French troops capture Roye and advance two miles beyond.

Aug. 29. Noyon falls in new French advance; French troops cross Ailette at several points near Campagne; British troops take Bapaume and close in on Péronne; north of Soissons American forces drive Germans out of Juvigny.

Aug. 31. Fierce fighting east of Arras brings British again into Bullecourt; south of Bapaume Gueudecourt is captured; American forces with Mangin's army north of Soissons advance eastward in vicinity of Juvigny and Bois de Beaumont.

SEPTEMBER

SWITCH LINE TAKEN, ST. MIHIEL RECOVERED, HINDENBURG LINE BROKEN AT TUNNEL—BULGARIA SURRENDERS—PALESTINE RECOVERED

Sept. 1. Australian troops take Péronne with 2,000 prisoners; other English forces capture Bouchavesne, four miles north of Péronne, and Rancourt, five miles north; American troops fight for first time on Belgian soil, capturing Voormezeele.

Sept. 2. British forces break through Quéant-Drocourt line, or "switch line"; Neuve-Eglise captured; American troops who captured Voormezeele advance eastward in pursuit of German rear-guard; north of Soissons United States troops reach Terney-Sorny and cross St. Quentin-Soissons road.

Sept. 3. Czecho-Slovaks recognized by United States as belligerent nation; driving on toward Cambrai, British forces capture fourteen villages and 10,000 prisoners; Quéant, point of juncture between Drocourt-Quéant switch and Hindenburg line, taken.

Sept. 4. German forces retreat on front of twenty miles north of Vesle, followed by French and American troops; north of Péronne British troops make progress on front of fifteen miles, forcing passage of Canal du Nord.

Sept. 5. French win thirty towns along Ailette; with cooperation of Americans ground gained to east of Coucy-le-Château; London reports total of 465 German airplanes destroyed and 200 disabled since start of offensive on August 8.

Sept. 6. Ham and Chauny, on road to southern part of Hindenburg line at La Fère, captured by French; heights dominating Aisne captured and held by French and Americans.

Sept. 12. Registration-day for United States new selective draft passes without disorder, with indications that 13,-000,000 mark will be surpassed; first American army under own command, assisted by French, attacks salient of St. Mihiel; an extreme gain of five miles and capture of 8,000 prisoners and of half a dozen towns at end of first day's operations.

Sept. 13. American troops wipe out St. Mihiel salient, reaching line of Norroy, Jaulny, Xammes, St. Benoit, Hattonville, Hannonville, and Herbeuville.

Sept. 14. American troops gain mile on new front east of St. Mihiel; total prisoners officially reported 20,-000.

Sept. 15. American forces advance two to three miles on thirty-three-mile front; fortress-guns of Metz come into action against them; American patrols approaching Pagny on west bank of Moselle; Maissemy, northwest of St. Quentin, falls to British, together with trench-system to east and southeast.

Sept. 16. Renewal of German *U*-boat activities in American waters by attack on steamship ninety miles from coast, in-bound in ballast, with ninety-six wounded Canadian officers on board.

Sept. 17. Serbian and French troops continue offensive in Macedonia, progressing more than five miles; three thousand prisoners and twenty-four guns captured.

Sept. 18. Clémenceau declares in an address to French Senate: "We will fight until the hour when the enemy comes to understand that bargaining between crime and right is no longer possible"; British and French advance on twenty-two-mile front north and south of St. Quentin; British cross Hindenburg line at Villeret and Gouzeaucourt; French troops reach western outskirts of Francilly-Selency, three miles west of St. Quentin; 6,000 prisoners are captured by British; American First Army completes occupation of line in St. Mihiel sector running parallel with Hindenburg line; Serbian, French, and Greek troops advance an average of ten miles on a front of twenty miles in Macedonia.

Sept. 19. Bulgarian troops, driven back through mountains region of Rojden and Balettes Massif, reported in flight across Cerna River; forty-five villages fallen to Serbian troops, operating with French and Greek detachments; British and French forces in Palestine attack on front of sixteen miles between Rafat and sea and push forward twelve miles; more than 3,000 prisoners, many guns, and large quantities of material among booty.

Sept. 20. Mœuvres, seven miles west of Cambrai, recaptured by British; northwest of St. Quentin, Haig's troops advance line more than mile; bombardment of American hospitals, with loss of eight American wounded; Metz forts and batteries under fire from American guns.

Sept. 22. Serbian troops, pressing Bulgarian and German troops in central Macedonia; Turkish army operating in Palestine between Jordan and Mediterranean virtually wiped out by British and Allied forces, 18,000 prisoners, 120 guns, four airplanes, and large quantity of transport in hands of pursuing forces; Arab forces of King of Hejaz cooperated to eastward by destroying bridges and tearing up railroad lines near Derat.

Sept. 23. French hold west bank of the Oise for more than half distance from La Fère to Moy; Italian troops in Macedonia advance more than seven miles and take sixteen villages; British and Greek airmen bomb Constantinople and drop thousands of leaflets; British freighter arriving in ballast at "an Atlantic port" reports attack by torpedo and shellfire while 800 miles from United States coast, September 13; *U*-boat continued firing for one hour and twenty-four minutes; another steamship, belonging to United States Shipping Board, reports an encounter with *U*-boat on September 19, 500 miles off American coast; London reports 25,000 Turkish prisoners and 260 guns captured in advance of British armies northward through Palestine; having seized passages of the Jordan at Jisred-Dameer, last avenue of escape open to enemy west of the river closed by British troops; Seventh and Eighth Turkish armies virtually ceased to exist, entire transport captured.

Sept. 24. British cavalry capture port of Haifa, together with Acre and Es-Salt; British and French attacking on adjacent fronts, totaling about seven miles west of St. Quentin, capture 1,300 prisoners and four towns; Allied lines now less than three miles from St. Quentin; French cavalry operating with Serbians capture Prilep, northeast of Monastir; Greek and French troops operating on British left reported at Gurinchet, few miles west of the Vardar; thus far more than 11,000 prisoners and 140 guns been counted, in addition to immense stores of material.

Sept. 25. Admiral von Hintze assures Reichstag that, despite repeated rejection of peace offers from Central Powers, Germany maintains readiness for peace; Bulgarians retreating on total front of 130 miles; more than 45,000 prisoners and 265 guns been taken by British in Palestine.

Sept. 26. First American Army delivered an attack in Argonne between Meuse and Aisne rivers on front of twenty miles smashing through Hindenburg line for average gain of seven miles and capturing 5,000 prisoners; two divisions take German trenches and strong points northwest of St. Quentin and 1,500 prisoners; British extending occupation about Sea of Galilee and Fourth Turkish Army virtually surrounded; British and Greek troops invade Bulgaria from Doiran region, forcing way over Belashitza mountain range.

Sept. 27. Wilson opens fourth Liberty Loan campaign with a speech in Metropolitan Opera House in New York in which outlines plan for League of Nations to be formed at Peace Conference; British pierce Hindenburg line at several points; Haig carries Cambrai defenses, Americans aiding, and takes 6,000 prisoners; American troops capture outer defenses of Hindenburg system southwest of Le Catelet; proposal from Bulgarian Government for armistice of forty-eight hours, with view making peace; offer causes intense excitement in Germany; British forces on Macedonian front capture Strumitza.

Sept. 28. Replying to Bulgarian request for armistice, Great Britain insists upon unequivocal submission; Americans reached Kreimhilde line in Argonne at Brieulles and advance to Exermount; French and Americans push onward in Champagne and take German railway base; Belgian and British capture Poelcappelle and 4,000 prisoners; capture of Fort Malmaison, one of strongholds southeast of (Laon; Haig reports capture of more than 10,000 prisoners, 200 guns, and ten villages; Allenby takes 5,000 more Turkish prisoners and captures 350 guns; up to date 50,000 prisoners been taken by British; Bulgarian crisis produces panic on Berlin Stock Exchange.

Sept. 29. Haig reports air-force co-operated in every phase of operations; enemy troops bombed and machine-gunned from extremely low heights and heavy casualties inflicted; Pershing's army in Argonne sweeping all barriers aside; in three days United States troops cut through defenses that had stood four years; capture of Dixmude by Belgians, over 5,500 prisoners and 100 guns captured; forces under Haig, including Americans, make notable advance and are now at edge of Cambrai; American troops capture Bellicourt and Nauroy on St. Quentin Canal at tunnel; Americans on Champagne captured Brieulles-sur-Meuse and Romagne on Kreimhilde line.

Sept. 30. Outskirts of Cambrai and two villages near St. Quentin won by British; Belgians entered Roulers, and British to south close to Menin; 30,-000 Czechs, Poles, and Silesians gathered near Troppau, Austria, and declarerd in favor of foundation of a Czecho-Slovak State and Czecho-Polish solidarity; force of 10,000 Turks surrender to British in Palestine; Bulgaria surrendered unconditionally to Allies, hostilities ceasing officially at noon; armistice signed with full consent of King Ferdinand.

OCTOBER

DAMASCUS FALLS — THE MEUSE-ARGONNE BATTLE——GERMANS ASK FOR AN ARMISTICE

Oct. 2. Allenby's forces occupy Damascus, taking over 7,000 prisoners; Germans evacuating Lille; St. Quentin in hands of French; two thousand prisoners taken between Ves'e and Aisne; whole Hindenburg system below Bellicourt tunnel now in British and American hands.

Oct. 3. American, British, and Italian warships destroy Austrian naval base and warships at Durazzo; appointment of Prince Maximilian of Baden as Chancellor announced; Rome reports Italians have occupied Fieri and Berat; from September 18, Allenby has taken 71,000 men and 350 guns, and King Hussein's Arabs report 8,000 additional prisoners; gains made by French armies operating from St. Quentin to the Argonne closed only avenue of escape for Germans on the west side of Argonne Forest; Germans evacuate Armentières and Lens; British and Belgian troops capture villages in neighborhood of Roulers.

Oct. 4. 1,800,000 American troops now abroad; American troops join Gouraud's army in strong thrust north

of Somme-Py in Argonne; Americans are astride Kriemhilde line, last organized defense-system between them and Belgian border; British now well to east of Lens.

Oct. 5. Austro-Hungarian minister at Stockholm charged to request Swedish Government to transmit to Wilson proposal to conclude general armistice with him and his Allies; immediate suspension of hostilities proposed in Reichstag by Prince Maximilian, new Chancellor; German retreat before Gouraud perceptibly quickening; Fort Brimont captured by French troops; French and Americans make gains of two or three miles during attack on a 30-mile front between Meuse and Champagne; Berthelot's army crosses Aisne Canal at new points; preceding their withdrawal, Germans set fire to Douai and many villages near Cambrai; in Belgian offensive 10,500 prisoners and 350 guns taken; entire Flanders ridge won in first forty-eight hours.

Oct. 6. Indescribable panic on Berlin Stock Exchange October 5; Amsterdam forwards text of Germany's peace note to Wilson; Franco-Americans under Gouraud make eight-mile gain near Reims.

Oct. 7. Franco-American troops take St. Étienne on Arnes; three tremendous blows dealt foe in France; British, French, and Americans tear away last defenses of Hindenburg line on twenty-mile front between Cambrai and St. Quentin, advancing an average distance of three miles, with maximum penetration of five miles; Pershing's army, including French units, assaults on seven-mile front east of Meuse above Verdun, gaining two miles; Gouraud's army, in which many Americans are incorporated, attack on a front of four or five miles from Machault, north of St. Étienne, and advance two miles; Haig, with American aid, captures Brancourt and Premont; Allies still moving forward everywhere; American "lost" battalion in Argonne Forest rescued virtually intact; last shells fall upon Reims on October 4.

Oct. 9. Haig reports Hindenburg system cleared on a thirty-five-mile front between Scarpe and Oise; American First Army made victorious attack on the whole twenty-five-mile front from center of the Argonne Forest to several miles east of Meuse; First British Army captures Ramillies and Cambrai and crosses Scheldt Canal.

Oct. 10. Dublin mail-boat *Leinster* torpedoed while making trip to Holyhead; report says 400 persons perished; French and British warships enter Beirut, chief seaport of Syria; Ludendorff suffers a physical collapse and relinquishes command of German army; Haig announces capture of Le Cateau, fifteen miles southeast of Cambrai.

Oct. 11. Austria-Hungary and Turkey inform Germany they will accept Wilson's peace terms; Kaiser summons sovereigns of all German federal states for consultation before answering Wilson's note; American First Army advances five miles, clearing Argonne Forest and taking 1,000 more prisoners, making total capture since October 8, about 7,000; Germans abandon positions north of Suippe and Arnes on a forty-mile front; Grandpré occupied, bringing Allies about two miles from railroad center of Vouziers; additional reports show Chemin-des-Dames being evacuated under blows from Italian and French units; Craonne and La Fère, on the Oise, half surrounded; American "Wildcat" Division on front of Haig's offensive, captures Vaux-Andigny and St. Souplet.

Oct. 12. Germany's reply to Wilson, offering to accept peace terms, published in Berlin; rumors of Kaiser's abdication also published; British within one mile of Douai; Gouraud captures Vouziers.

Oct. 13. Foch's forces wrests Laon, La Fère, and major part of the St. Gobain Massif from enemy.

Oct. 14. Enemy driven back five miles on twenty-mile front east of Ypres by new Allied blow in Flanders; French, British, and Belgian troops drive wedge deeper in enemy's positions, covering naval bases of Zeebrugge and Ostend; the armies sweep forward to within four miles of Courtrai; Roulers captured; in Champagne enemy continues flight north and east; Gouraud's army crosses Aisne along wide front and is within twenty-five miles of Mezières, on Franco-Belgian frontier; Germany's peace note delivered at State Department in Washington; in a prompt reply Wilson leaves all questions of armistice to military advisers of Powers arrayed against Germany; United States Senate breaks all precedents by vigorously applauding Wilson's reply to Germany's peace note.

Oct. 15. Durazzo, Austrian naval base in Albania, taken by Italian forces; British warships reported entering Ostend; Allied forces drive six miles deeper into enemy's Flanders line; over 10,000 men and 100 guns taken in this drive; Allies sweep forward on whole 200-mile line; British within three miles of Lille and capture four villages; on Picardy-Champagne line more than dozen villages and additional thousands of prisoners taken by Pétain's men; Americans redouble attacks and widen breach in Brunhilde line, capturing four villages northwest of Argonne Forest; Gouraud resumes attacks, crossing Aisne and taking Olizy and Fermes, west of Grandpré.

Oct. 16. Wilson's reply caused panic in Berlin banking circles; Hungarian independence declared by Magyar Parliament; Americans capture Grandpré, base of German operations in Champagne; British army patrols enter Lille.

Oct. 17. Ostend taken by Allied naval and land forces and King Albert and Queen Elizabeth enter city; Bruges entered by Belgian patrols; Zeebrugge

abandoned and Belgian coast practically cleared of enemy; Haig announces occupation of Douai; on three-mile front from Le Cateau to Bohain British and American troops hurl Germans back two miles and take 3,000 prisoners; on Argonne front, Pershing's men advance another mile in region of Grandpré; on arriving at Atlantic port army-transport *Amphion* reported two-hours' running fight with submarine 800 miles off Atlantic coast; steps for organization of Austria on federalized basis proclaimed by Emperor Karl.

Oct. 18. French capture Thielt, west of Ghent; Zeebrugge and Bruges occupied by Allied troops; British take Tourcoing and Roubaix; new Anglo-American thrust southeast of Cambrai causes Germans to retreat rapidly; British now astride Douai-Denain road, four miles southeast of Douai; on Champagne front Americans and French strengthen grip on west end of Kriemhilde line at Grandpré; Pershing's men advance about mile beyond Romagne and capture Bantheville.

Oct. 19. Wilson rejects Austrian peace plea; German newspapers suggest abdication of Kaiser and Crown Prince; German evacuation of Brussels begins.

Oct. 21. Revolution in Sofia; more than 3,000 killed in street fights between Bolshevik laborers and troops and police.

Oct. 22. British enter western suburbs of Valenciennes.

Oct. 25. French patrols cross Danube into Roumania on northwestern frontier; east of Meuse Americans drive enemy from eastern ridge of Bois d'Ormont; west of the Meuse, in region of Grandpré, straighten out lines and capture important ridges; since October 23, 8,400 prisoners and over 100 cannon captured in section.

Oct. 28. British and Italian forces advance four miles beyond Piave and take 7,000 Austro-Hungarians; in four days armies taken more than 16,000.

Oct. 29. Allies drive forward west of Piave, taking heights of Alano; over 21,000 prisoners taken in five days; American troops held in reserve fighting zone.

Oct. 30. Diaz's men advance six miles, reaching foe's great base of Vittorio, twelve miles beyond Piave.

Oct. 31. American troops advance north of Grandpré and occupy Bellejoyeuse Farm and southern edges of Bois des Loges; capture of entire Turkish force opposing British on Tigris announced in London; prisoners estimated at 7,000; Turkey surrenders, armistice taking effect at noon; conditions include free passage of Dardanelles; Italian troops sweep northward fifteen miles through Venetian Alps and reach Ponte nell' Alpi; through capture of mountain pass of Vadal, retreat of fifteen Austrian divisions operating between Brenta and Piave cut off; east of Piave enemy completely routed.

NOVEMBER

SEDAN, MAUBEUGE AND MONS TAKEN—
ARMISTICE SIGNED, KAISER ABDI-
CATES, AND REVOLUTION IN
GERMANY

Nov. 1. Austria-Hungary splits up into a group of independent States; Emperor Charles said to have left Vienna and Count Tisza shot dead by soldier; Austrians in utter rout on east half of battle-line; seventy-three divisions said to have mutinied and quit battlefield; American troops land at Pola; conference of Allied representatives at Versailles agrees on armistice terms.

Nov. 3. French and Americans sweep ahead on fifty-mile front-line above Verdun; Argonne region cleared and additional prisoners and stores captured; Belgians advance and reach approaches to Ghent; since offensive began on July 15, Allied armies captured 362,355 men, including 7,990 officers, 6,217 cannon, 38,622 machine-guns, and 3,907 mine-throwers; in offensive on Sedan front, American aviators bring down 124 enemy airplanes, losing 20 machines; Emperor William addresses to German Chancellor decree avowing firm determination to cooperate in full development of new laws which deprive him of autocratic power; Rome announces capture of Trent and Trieste, whole regiments of Austrians surrendering; Italian cavalry enter Udine, fifty miles beyond Piave.

Nov. 4. Before November 3 some 300,000 Austrians and not less than 5,000 guns captured by Italian armies; Americans start new attack against enemy's line east Meuse; Pershing's flank and Gouraud's army force Germans to fall back behind Ardennes Canal to Le Chesne; American First Army passes beyond Stenay and now striking for Sedan; advance within a mile and quarter of Beaumont; further west troops reach Vernieres, about ten miles northeast of Vouziers; Pershing has occupied about forty villages in territory reconquered from Germans.

Nov. 5. Germans retreating on seventy-five-mile front from Scheldt to Aisne; Allies cross Franco-Belgian frontier between Valenciennes and Bavay, eight miles west of Maubeuge; Americans take Liny-devant-Dun and Milly-devant-Dun, east of Meuse, and occupy hills on east bank of river; American fliers bomb Mouzon and Raucourt on Verdun front; German Government informed by Secretary Lansing that Foch authorized by United States and Allies to communicate terms of armistice to its official representatives.

Nov. 6. Americans push forward three miles; now engaged within sight of Sedan; German armistice delegation reaches Allies lines.

Nov. 7. General revolt of German navy, men becoming complete masters at Kiel, Wilhelmshaven, Heligoland, Borkam, and Cuxhaven; great part of Schleswig in hands of revolutionists; 20,000 deserters from army march

through streets of Berlin; serious riots break out in Hamburg and Lubeck; red flag hoisted at Warnemunde, seaport of northern Germany, and Rostock on Baltic; chaos in Austria; Pershing reports Rainbow Division and units of First Division entering suburbs of Sedan; entire region between Meuse and the Bar liberated by First American Army in cooperation with French.

Nov. 8. German delegates reach Foch's headquarters near Senlis; text of Allies conditions read and delivered to them; they asked cessation of fighting, which is refused, and given seventy-two hours in which to accept or reject terms; Munich Diet passed decree deposing Wittelsbach dynasty and republic proclaimed in Bavaria; Hamburg completely in hands of revolutionists; Bremen, Schwerin, and Tilsit join in movement and form Soldiers' Councils, which have already control of Bremerhaven and Cuxhaven; red flags hoisted on ships in several ports; German Socialists demand abdication of Emperor William and renunciation of throne by Crown Prince.

Nov. 9. Berlin messages report abdication of Kaiser and renunciation of throne by Crown Prince; Emperor's son-in-law, Duke of Brunswick, and heir abdicates; rebellions in Hanover, Cologne, Brunswick, and Magdeburg announced; French troops cross Meuse between Mezières and Sedan; Pétain's cavalry sweep over Belgian boundary near Chimay-Guise road; railroad center of Hirson captured and Mezières and Mohon surrounded; Haig announces capture of Maubeuge, last important French fortress in hands of Germans; Americans hold both banks of river from Verdun to Sedan.

Nov. 10. Pershing reports considerable gains by First and Second American Armies along line between Meuse and Moselle; on American left Gouraud's men cross Meuse on wide front between Mezières and Sedan and pursue retreating Germans, while French astride Belgian boundary capture Charleville and continue rout of enemy; British and Canadians advance on Mons; people's government instituted in Berlin; Friedrich Ebert takes Chancellorship; similar revolutions in all parts of Germany; severe fighting in Berlin; many persons killed and wounded before officers of garrison surrendered; Hohenzollern dynasty overthrown and Herr Ebert charged with formation of new government; crews of dreadnoughts in Kiel Harbor join revolutionists.

Nov. 11. Day of the signing of armistice near Senlis; on Sedan front thousands of American heavy guns fired parting shot to Germans at exactly 11 o'clock; Germans hurled few shells into Verdun just before the hour; Haig reports capture of Mons; at cessation of hostilities British had reached general line of Franco-Belgian frontier, east of Avesnes, Jeumont and Sivry, and four miles east of Mons, Chievres, Lessines, and Grammant; revolution

A CHRONOLOGY OF THE WAR

progressing steadily throughout Germany; Hindenburg placed himself and German army at disposition of new government "in order to avoid chaos"; garrisons along Dutch frontier in revolt; Potsdam and Doeberitz garrisons in hands of new authorities; fourteen of twenty-six states, including four kingdoms, reported securely in hands of Reds; Wurttemburg declared republic, king stating he will not oppose will of people; Hamburg, Bremen, and Lübeck ruled by Socialists, and power of rulers gone from Grand Duchies of Oldenburg, Baden, Hesse, Mecklenburg-Schwerin, and Mecklenburg-Strelitz; Kaiser departs from Spa for Holland and held up near Eysden awaiting decision of Dutch Government; 2.45 A.M. Washington announces armistice signed and hostilities will cease at eleven o'clock, November 11; sirens and bells started peace celebrations in all parts of United States and Canada; at 10 A.M. President issues proclamation announcing signing of armistice; duration of armistice shall be thirty days, with option to extend.

Nov. 13. Holland decides to permit Kaiser to remain on Dutch soil on same terms of internment as other high officers of German army; he takes name of Count William Hohenzollern; Emperor Charles of Austria issues proclamation declaring that, "with unalterable love of my peoples," he will not be hindrance to their free development.

Nov. 14. Former Crown Prince is interned in Holland.

Nov. 15. New German Government appeals to Wilson to hurry peace negotiations; American Third Army, designated "Army of Occupation," is marching to occupy position on Rhine.

Nov. 18. Entrance of American troops into Briey, heart of Lorraine iron-fields.

Nov. 20. French troops reach left bank of the Rhine and American troops, cooperating with Pétain, pushing forward into Luxemburg and Germany; entrance of Pétain into Metz; King Albert makes entry into Antwerp amid great popular rejoicing; twenty German submarines surrender to Rear-Admiral Tyrwhitt thirty miles off Harwich.

Nov. 21. Surrender of nine German battleships, five battle-cruisers, seven light cruisers, and fifty destroyers of German High Seas Fleet takes place; nineteen more submarines surrender to British squadron.

Nov. 22. Twenty more German submarines surrender, making total thus far handed over 59; King Albert makes triumphant entry into Brussels accompanied by Queen Elizabeth and their children.

Nov. 23. Allied warships enter Black Sea and visit various ports.

Nov. 26. More than 1,500,000 prisoners of various nationalities released by Germans.

Nov. 27. Cardinal Mercier, Primate of Belgium, declares that forty-nine Belgian priests were tortured and put to death by Germans during the occupation.

Nov. 28. Official announcement made in London that during the war Great Britain actually lost nearly 1,000,000 men, killed or dead through other causes.

Nov. 29. Approximately 200 German submarines destroyed during the war; Premier Lloyd George states that British Government has been advised by greatest jurists in kingdom that former German Emperor was guilty of an indictable offense for which he ought to be held responsible.

DECEMBER

WILSON GOES TO EUROPE—ENTENTE FORCES OCCUPY THE RHINE

Dec. 2. Wilson declares he is going to Europe because Allies, having accepted his Fourteen Points as peace principles, desire his personal counsel in their interpretation and application.

Dec. 3. Senator Knox, former Secretary of State, introduces resolution declaring Peace Conference should defer to some future time project for general League of Nations.

Dec. 4. Count William Hohenzollern refuses to be interviewed by an Associated Press correspondent; Wilson and party sail for France on the *George Washington*.

Dec. 6. Crown Prince formally renounced all his rights of succession; an official statement in London gives British merchant tonnage losses from beginning of war to October 31 as 9,031,-828; new construction in the United Kingdom during same period was 4,342,296 tons and 530,000 tons purchased abroad; enemy tonnage captured was 716,520, making net loss 3,443,012 tons.

Dec. 11. Lloyd George tells a meeting at Bristol Allied war-bill against Germany is $120,000,000,000 and Germany "should pay to utmost of her capacity."

Dec. 12. British troops hold all great bridges across Rhine at Cologne; conditions in Petrograd "beyond human power to grasp."

Dec. 13. Mackensen and staff interned in Hungary; Wilson arrives at Brest and starts for Paris; Pershing reports American army marching into Germany has come to stand on Rhine.

Dec. 14. President and Mrs. Wilson enter Paris, received by Poincaré, Clémenceau, and other eminent Frenchmen.

Dec. 15. Wilson lays a wreath on tomb of Lafayette; three great Rhine bridge-heads provided by armistice occupied by advanced Allied forces—British at Cologne, Americans at Coblenz, and French at Mainz (Mayence).

Dec. 16. American Third Army, which now occupies more than 4,500 square miles in Germany, takes possession of fortress of Ehrenbreitstein, opposite Coblenz.

Dec. 20. To October 25 total German casualties were 6,066,679, of whom 4,750,000 were Prussians.

Dec. 22. Russian war casualties totaled 9,150,000 men, according to telegram from Petrograd; of these 1,700,000 killed; disabled men numbered 1,450,000, while 3,500,000 other soldiers wounded; Russians taken prisoner totaled 2,500,000.

Dec. 26. Spartacan forces, under leadership Liebknecht,, seize Prussian War Ministry; ten dreadnoughts returning from duty overseas enter New York Harbor and are reviewed by Secretary Daniels.

Dec. 27. British general elections give Lloyd George a majority of 237 or 329, counting 46 Unionists; 72 Sinn-Feiners, none of whom are expected to take seats, were returned from Ireland; Wilson, in London staying at Buckingham Palace, replying to welcoming address of King George at State Banquet, says that substantial agreements on question of peace terms have been reached by Allied leaders.

THE EVENTS OF 1919

JANUARY

PEACE CONFERENCE ASSEMBLES IN PARIS—LEAGUE OF NATIONS COVENANT ADOPTED

Jan. 8. Theodore Roosevelt buried on hillside in Oyster Bay cemetery in presence of nation's leaders.

Jan. 10. Government forces in complete control of inner section of Berlin.

Jan. 12. Luxemburg proclaimed republic; Grand Duchess goes to nearby château.

Jan. 17. Dr. Liebknecht and Rosa Luxemburg, Spartacan leaders, killed in Berlin.

Jan. 18. Paris Peace Conference opened on Quai d'Orsay in Clock Hall.

Jan. 24. By vote of 52 to 18 Senate passes bill appropriating $100,000,000 for famine relief in Europe; House passed measure short time before vote of 272 to 43.

Jan. 25. Peace Conference unanimously adopts a resolution to create League of Nations.

Jan. 30. Great colonial Powers, notably Great Britain and France, have accepted in principle American proposal that League of Nations exercise supervision over German colonies and allot their administration to mandatary Powers; Republican leaders in United States Senate continue attacks on attitude of President regarding colony question; Knox and Lodge look upon internationalization plan as "a stupendous and preposterous undertaking."

FEBRUARY

STRIKES AND RIOTS IN BERLIN—EISNER ASSASSINATED—WILSON COMES HOME

Feb. 11. German National Assembly elects Friedrich Ebert President of German State by vote of 277 out of 379 votes.

Feb. 12. Ebert in speech accepting Presidency, denounces Allied armistice terms and declares that "we shall combat domination by force to the utmost from whatever direction it may come."

Feb. 13. Twenty thousand store employees in Berlin strike for higher wages; everywhere throughout empire strikes of the workers are being met by counter-strikes of doctors and other professional classes; state of siege declared at Hamburg, until people of city surrender all arms.

Feb. 14. League of Nations plan read to plenary session of Peace Conference by Wilson.

Feb. 15. Wilson sails from Brest for Boston; in a cable message to Congress, requests that debate on League of Nations plan be postponed until after his arrival.

Feb. 18. Senator Borah, a leading opponent of League, declines to meet President to discuss League; Italian delegates notify Peace Conference they will not accept proposal that conflicting claims of Italians and Jugo-Slavs in Dalmatia be arbitrated; under Jugo-Slavs proposal Wilson was to have been arbitrator.

Feb. 19. Senator Miles Poindexter, of Washington, opens attack on World League in United States Senate; Representative Fess, of Ohio, delivers a speech in opposition to League in House of Representatives; peace parleys in Paris temporarily hampered by attempt on life of Clémenceau, head of the Conference.

Feb. 21. Kurt Eisner, Premier of Bavaria, shot dead in Munich by Count Arco Valley, a member of the nobility; Herr Auer, Bavarian Minister of the Interior, shot from public gallery Diet Building at Munich; Deputy Osel killed and two other officials seriously wounded in general firing that accompanied assassination of Auer.

Feb. 23. Wilson arrives in Boston aboard *George Washington*.

Feb. 26. Wilson speaks in defense of League of Nations before members of Senate and House Foreign Affairs Committees at after-dinner conference in White House; London watching "with intense interest" Wilson's Campaign to win support for the League.

Feb. 27. Former German Kaiser has appealed to German revolutionary government for money and was advanced $150,000; proportion of wealth to which he is still entitled personally is said to be $18,750,000.

Feb. 28. Lodge, of Massachusetts, attacking constitution of League of Nations in the Senate, demands a "binding and shackling peace" with enemy as the first move; draft of the League of Nations received in Germany as meaning little less than ruin for Germans.

MARCH

REPARATION TERMS AND THE TRIAL OF THE KAISER

March 3. Peace Conference Committee on Reparation estimates that $120,-000,000,000 is amount which enemy countries ought to pay Allied and Associated Powers; France asks an immediate payment of $5,000,000,000.

March 5. At meeting of German Cabinet, attended by party leaders and delegates of ship-owners, was unanimously agreed that Germany will not submit to coercion by the Entente Powers.

March 10. Supreme Council has unanimously agreed that Germany's military force shall be limited to 100,-000 volunteers serving twelve years.

March 12. Peace Conference's Commission on Waterways recommends that Rhine and Kiel Canal be thrown open to all nations in peace times; War Council agrees to limit German navy to six battleships, five cruisers, twelve 800-ton destroyers, and twenty-six smaller destroyers.

March 14. Wilson arrives in Paris shortly after noon and confers with Premiers Lloyd George and Clémenceau.

March 20. Virtually all Ukraine now in hands of Bolsheviki.

March 21. Italian delegation to Peace Conference unanimously decides to withdraw unless Fiume is assigned to Italy contemporaneously with conclusion of peace; Ukrainian troops besieging Lemberg entered that city after five days of hard fighting.

March 25. Greatest crowd in history of New York City, estimated at 2,000,000, lines Fifth Avenue to welcome home Twenty-seventh Division, formerly New York National Guards Division.

March 28. Allied troops in Russia, on both Siberian and Archangel fronts, now number 369,465.

APRIL

GERMAN PROTESTS AS TO PEACE TERMS —THE CASE OF FIUME

April 10. League of Nations commission adopts section excepting Monroe Doctrine from any of provisions of document; League of Nations is to have supervision over Saar Valley for fifteen years, after which plebiscite will be taken to determine wishes of inhabitants regarding future form of government.

April 14. Peace Conference decides that Germany must pay 100,000,000,-000 gold marks (about $25,000,000,-000) for losses and damage caused by war; 20,000,000,000 marks of which must be paid in two years, 40,000,-000,000 in thirty years, and 40,000,-000,000 when a commission shall determine; about 55 per cent. goes to France, between 20 and 30 per cent. to Great Britain, and between 2 and 5 per cent. to United States.

April 15. Indisputable evidence of massacre by Bolsheviki of more than 2,000 civilians in and near town of Osa been obtained by representatives of Red Cross, who have just returned from section, according to report from Omsk.

April 16. Conditions laid down in Treaty of Peace denounced by German press; complete anarchy reigns in Munich.

April 17. First German ship to enter New York Harbor since United States went into the war comes into port; she is Hamburg-American liner *Kaiserin Augusta Victoria*, which has been turned over to United States to bring back American troops.

April 22. Allies will not consent that peace conditions be submitted to a plebiscite.

April 23. Ural Cossack troops, acting with Siberian forces under Admiral Kolchak begins offensive in southeastern Russia.

April 27. A revised text of League of Nations covenant was made public.

April 28. Council of Four provides in Peace Treaty for prosecution and trial of former Emperor William; revised form of covenant of League of Nations is adopted by Conference without a dissenting voice.

April 29. Main German Peace Delegation arrives at Versailles.

MAY

GERMAN DELEGATES GET PEACE TERMS AT VERSAILLES—KOLCHAK'S SUCCESSES AGAINST THE BOLSHEVIKI

May 1. First meeting between Peace Conference and German plenipotentiaries takes place at Versailles.

May 7. Allied and Associated Powers and German plenipotentaries meet at Versailles and Germans hear Entente peace terms and make protest.

May 9. Omsk Russian Government issues a statement indicating that all details of its establishment are completed.

May 11. Six members of German Peace Mission leave for Berlin to discuss peace situation with Government where violent opposition to treaty exists.

May 13. Philipp Scheidemann, German Chancellor, in a speech before National Assembly in Berlin, urges Germans reject Peace Treaty.

May 14. Austrian Peace Delegates reach Paris.

May 15. Body of Edith Cavell, English nurse executed by Germans at Brussels, interred in Norwich, after an impressive memorial service in Westminster Abbey; Brockdorff-Rantzau, head German peace delegation, reported by Berlin as saying Peace Treaty can not be signed because impossible to fulfil terms; Samara, an important city on Volga, captured by troops of Kolchak.

May 16. German Government states Government unalterably opposed to signing the Peace Treaty in present form.

May 18. German war losses given as 2,050,460 dead, 4,207,028 wounded, and 615,922 prisoners, in figures published in Berlin.

May 19. General Denikine, conducting operations of an anti-Bolshevik army on Volga, announces capture of 10,-000 prisoners and 28 guns.

May 23. Allied and Associated Council rejects Germany's plea for clemency, declaring her share of burdens growing out of war based on her ability to carry it and not on her deserts; Bolsheviki begin evacuation of Moscow.

May 26. Council of Four decide to recognize any non-Bolshevik government in Russia that agrees to convene National Assembly and respect the frontiers determined by League of Nations.

May 27. Council of Four and Japan offer Kolchak money and supplies to maintain all-Russian Government, on condition he will hold elections for a constituent assembly.

May 28. Secretary Glass reports fifth war loan total was $5,249,908,300, loan being oversubscribed $749,908,-300; total number of subscribers given as 12,000,000; all arrangements completed for blockading Germany in case German delegates refuse to sign Peace Treaty; if Germany does not sign, will be given seventy-two hours' notice of termination of armistice, on expiration of which period British, French, and Americans will advance into Germany.

May 29. German delegation's counter-proposals to the Peace Treaty delivered to the secretariat of Peace Conference.

May 30. Bolsheviki before quitting Riga shot thirty persons in central prison.

May 31. German delegation been notified by Allies that no more notes regarding terms will be received by Peace Conference.

JUNE

KNOX'S ANTI-LEAGUE RESOLUTION—
SINKING OF THE GERMAN
WARSHIPS

June 2. Austria's peace terms handed to her delegates.

June 10. Resolution is introduced in United States Senate by Senator Knox, which, if adopted, would place that body on record as in favor of immediate peace with Germany, as considering that war-aims of United States exprest in war-declaration had been accomplished, and as deferring consideration of League of Nations until later, when American people shall have had time to pass on it.

June 21. The Germans scuttle their fleet interned at Scapa Flow.

June 24. Allies advance on North Dwina.

June 25. President Ebert issues a proclamation to the German people announcing the completion of peace and urging them to bend their efforts to the fulfillment of its terms.

June 27. President Wilson announces before leaving Paris that he proposes to submit to the United States Senate a treaty carrying out arrangements whereby the United States and Great Britain will come to the assistance of France in case she is menaced by Germany.

June 28. War with Germany ends with the signing of the Treaty of Peace by plenipotentiaries representing Germany and the delegates of twenty-six of Allied and Associated Governments.

June 29. President Wilson sails for home on the *George Washington*.

JULY

RATIFICATION OF PEACE TREATY BY
GERMANY AND GREAT BRITAIN

July 9. The German National Assembly adopts resolution ratifying Peace Treaty.

July 10. President Ebert signs bill ratifying Peace Treaty and document is dispatched to Versailles.

July 12. Premier Clémenceau officially notifies German Peace delegation of the raising of the German blockade.

July 14. Great peace celebrations in France.

July 18. General Pershing receives the freedom of the City and a sword of honor at the Guildhall, London.

July 19. Great Britain celebrates the coming of peace with the greatest procession in her history in London; the parade headed by Pershing.

July 20. The peace conditions of Allied and Associated Powers are placed in the hands of the Austrians.

July 21. The British House of Commons ratifies the Peace Treaty with Germany.

July 23. Mutiny of Russian troops on Onega front, No. Russia.

July 26. Mutiny of Russian troops on Waga front, No. Russia.

July 30. Marshal Foch created a Field Marshal by King George V. and receives freedom of City and a sword of honor at the Guildhall, London.

AUGUST

KNOX'S DEMAND FOR A SEPARATE
PEACE WITH GERMANY

Aug. 1. German National Assembly approves new German constitution.

Aug. 2. Bela Kun overthrown at Buda Pest.

Aug. 8. Belgian Chamber of Deputies unanimously ratifies Peace Treaty.

Aug. 29. Senator Knox, of Pennsylvania, declares in Senate that the only safe way to deal with the Peace Treaty is to reject it altogether and negotiate a separate pact with Germany.

SEPTEMBER

PERSHING MADE A FULL GENERAL—
HIS WELCOME HOME—D'ANNUNZIO
AT FIUME

Sept. 2. Supreme Council of Peace Conference decides to send note to German Government demanding suppression of article in new German Constitution providing for the representation of Austria in the German Reichstag; Senate passes a bill, giving General Pershing permanent rank of General.

A CHRONOLOGY OF THE WAR

Sept. 10. Peace Treaty is reported to the United States Senate with four reservations and forty-five amendments; Dr. Karl Renner, head of Austrian delegation to the Peace Conference, signs the Treaty of Peace; great parade takes place in New York of the First Division, headed by General Pershing, Cardinal Mercier witnessing the parade.

Sept. 11. The Bratiano cabinet in Roumania falls.

Sept. 12. Turkey, in reply to President Wilson's demand, declares that measures will be taken for the maintenance of order.

Sept. 13. Denikine's forces win important victory over Bolsheviki; nine thousand Bolsheviki taken prisoners and many guns captured; President Wilson reviews the Pacific Fleet at Seattle.

Sept. 14. According to official information reaching London, Admiral Kolchak in pursuing his offensive against the Bolsheviki has broken their front in three places; the League to Enforce Peace makes public an appeal to the Senate to ratify the Treaty of Peace "without amendment and without delay."

Sept. 15. Gabriele d'Annunzio, supported by an armed force, occupies Fiume and proclaims its union with Italy; the Serbian Ministry, headed by Premier Davidovitch, resigns, as a protest against certain terms in the Peace Treaty.

Sept. 17. A report from Budapest says the Roumanian Army has begun to withdraw from that city.

Sept. 18. Communists of Westphalia, the Prussian province lying between Hanover and the Rhine region, planning revolution under the leadership of the Russian Bolsheviki; on the Ukrainian front the Bolsheviki forced General Petlura out of Dadomysl; General Pershing, in the Chamber of the House of Representatives with the members of both Houses of Congress assembled, receives formal thanks on behalf of the nation for the services he and his officers and men rendered in France; Roland Rohlfs, in a Curtiss *Wasp* tri-plane, equipped with a 400 horse-power motor, breaks all altitude records by ascending to a height of 34,610 feet, from Roosevelt field at Mineola, New York.

Sept. 19. Peace Treaty handed to Bulgarian plenipotentiaries in Paris; a *Soviet* Government proclamation published at Petrograd declares a state of siege in Moscow in consequence of the operations of Cossack troops south of that city.

Sept. 20. The *Soviet* of Petrograd has empowered the people's commissary to begin peace negotiations with the Allies on the basis of conditions fixt by the Allied Powers.

Sept. 21. The Polish Army achieved a complete victory over the Bolsheviki after a ten-day battle on the Dvina River; Gabriele d'Annunzio, holding the city of Fiume with 20,-000 men, according to a dispatch from Fiume, refuses to surrender;

the Belgian Ambassador at The Hague has been withdrawn and the Dutch Ambassador at Brussels has also been recalled. The rupture is said to have been caused over the demand for a revision of the Scheldt River treaty.

Sept. 22. King Albert and Queen Elizabeth of Belgium board the transport *George Washington* for the United States; Germany agrees to annul Article 61 of her Constitution, providing for Austrian representation in the German Reichstag.

Sept. 23. Premier Paderewski of Poland appears before the Supreme Council in Paris and demands that Galicia be assigned to Poland; Russian *Soviet* Government makes a peace offer to Ukraine, on the basis of recognition of the independence of Ukraine if that nation will maintain neutrality in the *Soviet* struggle against Admiral Kolchak and General Denikine; Tommaso Tittoni, Italian Foreign Minister, resigns because of the Fiume incident; in the first test in the Peace Treaty fight the Senate by a vote of 43 to 40 decides that its program shall be directed by Senator Lodge, chairman of the Foreign Relations Committee and leader of the reservationists.

Sept. 24. Red troops are reported to have captured Tomsk, 500 miles east of Omsk, the seat of the all-Russian Government; an encounter takes place in Saarbrück between German *bourgeoisie* and French soldiers, many persons on both sides being wounded.

Sept. 25. "Reservationist" Senators serve notice on President Wilson that Peace Treaty will be defeated unless a reservation to Article X is adopted; Secretary Daniels announces the receipt of a cablegram from Admiral Knapp, commanding the naval forces in foreign waters, to the effect that American sailors have been landed in the Fiume region and have seized Trau on the lower Dalmatian coast; cables from Rome relating to the Fiume situation include reports that civil war in Italy seems imminent.

Sept. 26. Viscount Grey, successor of Lord Reading as British Ambassador to the United States, arrives in New York from England; eight German liners, including the former Hamburg-American steamer *Imperator*, second largest ship in the world, are assigned to the United States by the Inter-Allied Shipping Commission; President Wilson abandons his speaking tour and returns to Washington, owing to illness, brought on by nervous and physical exhaustion.

Sept. 27. London announces that the British evacuation of Archangel has been completed; the Supreme Council decides to send Germany a note demanding the evacuation of Lithuania by German troops under drastic penalties for non-compliance; the Supreme Council of the Peace Conference decides on the appointment of a commission to study the question of the repatriation of the German and Austrian prisoners in Siberia.

Sept. 28. A plebiscite held to determine the future government and the economical policy of the Duchy of Luxemburg, returned a majority in favor of the retention of Grand Duchess Charlotte as ruler and for a customs union with France; President Wilson reaches Washington and will devote most of the week to complete rest.

Sept. 29. A resolution demanding that Fiume be made an Italian city is passed by the Italian Chamber of Deputies.

Sept. 30. Troops from the British Fleet of the Black Sea have been landed in Odessa.

OCTOBER

PEACE PRELIMINARIES—VISIT OF KING AND QUEEN OF BELGIUM—COAST TO COAST AIR RACE

Oct. 2. The French Chamber of Deputies ratifies the German Peace Treaty by a vote of 372 to 53; King Albert and Queen Elizabeth of Belgium land in New York for their American visit; dispatch from Rome says that the Italian steamship *Epiro*, with 200 Italian troops and some American officers on board, was fired upon by Jugo-Slav regular troops; the Turkish cabinet, headed by Gamad Ferid Pacha, Grand Vizier and Minister of Foreign Affairs, resigns, says a report from Constantinople.

Oct. 3. The National Legislative Assembly of Guatemala ratifies the treaty with Germany; leaders in the Peace Treaty fight have decided that as a "last ditch" defense they will require that the reservations adopted must be submitted to the Allies and approved by them before American ratification of the Treaty becomes effective.

Oct. 5. The German Government issues an order suppressing all public meetings of strikers in order to block any designs of the radicals to carry out their revolutionary plans.

Oct. 6. United States ships at Spalato have been withdrawn, and American food supplies are being removed from the city; a new Cabinet is formed in Turkey, according to reports from Paris, headed by Ali Riza Pacha, as Grand Vizier.

Oct. 7. King Victor Emanuel of Italy ratifies the German and Austrian treaties by royal decree.

Oct. 8. Forty-seven airplanes start from Roosevelt Field, Mineola, New York, in a coast to coast air race. Simultaneously a number of contestants start from San Francisco.

Oct. 10. King George completes Great Britain's ratification by signing the Peace Treaty; the Supreme Council at Paris grants the Bulgarian plenipotentiaries an extension of ten days in which to comment on the draft of the Peace Treaty; the Italian Government has agreed to the creation of a buffer state, comprising Fiume and the adjacent coast territory southward, as a solution of the Adriatic problem.

Oct. 11. The French Senate ratifies the Peace Treaty with Germany and also the Franco-American and Franco British Defense Treaties; report from Rio de Janeiro says that though Brazil has not yet ratified the Peace Treaty, its ports have been reopened to German shipping; Lieutenant Melville W. Maynard first to cross continent in the transcontinental air race, flying 2,701 miles in less than 25 flying hours. His total elapsed time was three days, three hours and 37 minutes.

Oct. 12. The state of war in France and Algiers is declared ended and the censorship lifted, by two Presidential decrees; Kijuro Shadehara, former vice-Foreign Minister, is appointed Japanese Ambassador to the United States.

Oct. 13. A nation-wide campaign in favor of the League of Nations opens in the city of London under the Presidency of Sir Horace B. Marshal, Lord Mayor; wireless message from General Denikine claims further victories against the Bolsheviki in the Orel and Kief regions.

Oct. 14. The Allies ask Germany to join in a blockade of Soviet Russia. President Poincaré of France signs a decree of general demobilization, effective upon "the cessation of hostilities"; Leon Bourgeois has been appointed to represent France in the League of Nations Council.

Oct. 15. The Clémenceau ministry is sustained in the French Chamber of Deputies by a vote of 324 to 132; contingent of 2,200 regular troops leave Camp Dix for Silesia, where they will do police duty during the plebiscite to determine whether the province will join Poland or remain under German sovereignty; formal custody of five of the eight former German passenger ships, title to which is now a subject of diplomatic discussion between the United States and Great Britain, is transferred from the War Department to the United States Shipping Board; Capture of the important city of Orel by General Denikine's army is claimed by Denikine and admitted in an official statement of the Russian Soviet; the Northwestern Russian Army of General Yudenitch has pushed 35 miles beyond Yamburg, which was recently captured, and is within 50 miles of Petrograd.

Oct. 16. The Shantung amendment, giving the German concessions to China instead of Japan, is defeated in the Senate by a vote of 55 to 35; the House of Representatives of Uruguay approves the Peace Treaty; the text of the note of the Supreme Council inviting Germany to participate in the blockade of Russia is published in Berlin, and shows that Sweden, Norway, Denmark, Holland, Finland, Spain, Switzerland, Mexico, Chili, Argentina, Colombia and Venezuela have also been invited to take part in the blockade; American participation in northern Russian hostilities and around Archangel has resulted in a total of 553 casualties, according to a complete record given out by the War Department; the House passes the bill urged by the State Department, extending for one year after the declaration of peace, the war-time control over the issuance of passports to aliens desiring to enter the United States; the German authorities begin carrying out the evacuation of first and second zones of Schleswig, complying with the Peace Treaty conditions; the Supreme Council decides to send a representative to Budapest to deal with new complications in the situation there growing out of complaints as to the military tactics of the Roumanians; General Ludendorff is reported to have refused to appear before the parliamentary Commission investigating the responsibility of German leaders in the war; German government hands to Marshal Foch its reply to the demands of the Allies concerning the evacuation of the Baltic Provinces; Captain d'Annunzio, whose forces are now holding the city of Fiume, sends a message to Premier Clemenceau asking that the latter take the initiative in securing a declaration from the Allied Governments making Fiume a free port; the army of General Yudenitch is 25 miles from Petrograd, which is being evacuated by the Bolsheviki; a wireless report announces that the Don Cossack troops have captured 9,000 Bolsheviki in the vicinity of Veroneza, recently occupied by General Denikine after hard fighting.

Oct. 17. The Austrian National Assembly ratifies the Peace Treaty of St. Germain, by a vote without debate; the last two of the four amendments to the Peace Treaty are voted down in the Senate, and ratification of the Peace Treaty without textual amendments is now conceded to be certain. It is, however, considered equally certain that reservations will be adopted.

Oct. 18. The Peace Conference decides to leave the settlement of the Fiume question to direct negotiations between Italy and Jugo-Slavia; the City Council of Vienna adopts resolutions asking American assistance for that city so it may be able to exist through the winter; Lieutenant Melville W. Maynard lands at Roosevelt Field, Long Island, being the first to complete the round trip transcontinental flight.

Oct. 20. Greek troops are advancing to occupy western Thrace, says a Salonica dispatch, in harmony with the terms of the Allies; the Bolsheviki forces in Petrograd, assailed by the Russian Northwestern Army under General Yudenitch and isolated from the world, are said to be preparing for a seige; the troops of General Denikine drive the Bolsheviki from Kief, which they had temporarily occupied.

Oct. 21. French ratification of the Peace Treaty is completed when the State seal is affixed to the document; the committee appointed by the German Government to investigate the responsibility of the German officials for the war, holds its first session in Berlin.

Oct. 22. The Senate passes the bill

extending war-time restrictions on passports for one year so as to exclude radicals and other undesirable aliens from the country; ten reservations to the Peace Treaty are adopted by the Senate Foreign Relations Committee. They provide that the United States shall assume no obligation to preserve the territorial integrity of other countries without the action of Congress.

Oct. 23. By a vote of 185 to 113 the British Government's alien bill is defeated in the House of Commons; Arthur J. Balfour has resigned as Foreign Secretary and Lord Curzon has been appointed to succeed him; Bela Kun, former dictator in Hungary during the Communist régime escapes from the internment camp at Vienna and goes to Italy, where he is reported to be promoting a revolutionary movement; four additional reservations to the Peace Treaty are adopted by the foreign Relations Committee, making the total so far adopted fourteen; the Supreme Council of the Peace Conference sends a note to Bucharest stating that the Council is ready to consider a modification of the clauses of the St. Germain treaty with Austria, guaranteeing protection to racial and religious minorities, as soon as the Roumanian Government is ready to sign the Treaty.

Oct. 26. President Carl Seitz of the Austrian Republic signs the Treaty of Peace, which completes its acceptance by Austria.

Oct. 27. By a vote of 40 to 38 the United States Senate rejects the Johnson amendment to the Peace Treaty which would have given the United States an equal voice with the British Empire in the League Assembly; Tokio dispatch says that the Japanese Privy Council, which advises the Emperor on important matters of state, approves the Peace Treaty; it is announced in the House of Commons that a reorganization of the British War Cabinet has been effected, by which the body has been converted into a Peace Cabinet; the British Chancellor of the Exchequer presents to the House of Commons revised estimates showing that the British national deficit is approximately two and one half billion dollars.

Oct. 28. According to dispatches from Paris, the recent elections to the new Communal Council for Fiume resulted in an overwhelming victory for the party that desires Fiume annexed to Italy.

Oct. 29. The Supreme Council takes up the consideration of reported violations of the Peace Treaty by the Germans; the International Labor Conference of the League of Nations begins its session at Washington. Delegates from more than 30 countries, representing all of the world's major nationalities, are in attendance; uprisings are said to have occurred throughout the Ukraine against the forces of General Denikine and large bodies of troops of General Petlura and General Makhno are joining the Red army. The insurgents are said to have taken many towns south of the Dnieper.

Oct. 30. Peace Treaty ratified by Japan, which country thus becomes the fourth of the principal Allied and associate powers to take official action on the Treaty. The other countries that have ratified are Italy on October 7, Great Britain on October 10, and France on October 21; the British Government's financial policy is sustained by the House of Commons by the overwhelming majority of 355; Germany in her reply to the Entente declines to participate in a blockade of Soviet Russia, stating that she does not believe the blockade would achieve the desired purpose; General Denikine has recaptured Orel from the Bolsheviki.

Oct. 31. The transport *President Grant* arrives in Brest with 5,000 American troops for the Army of Occupation, who will be assigned to duty at Coblenz.

NOVEMBER

PEACE PRELIMINARIES—CLEMENCEAU'S FAREWELL—SENATE REJECTS PEACE TREATY

Nov. 2. The town of Krasnaia Gorka, a strong Bolshevik position on the Gulf of Finland, has capitulated to General Yudenitch.

Nov. 4. Premier Clémenceau gives France his farewell message in a speech for the Government party at Strasbourg, Alsace, on the eve of his contemplated retirement from political life; Japan, in reply to a note from the American Government sent last September regarding conditions in Siberia, expresses a willingness to cooperate with the American authorities; the Finnish Government informs General Yudenitch that it is unable to grant his request to cooperate with him for the deliverance of Petrograd.

Nov. 6. Senator Knox of Pennsylvania, offers a treaty reservation in the Senate giving the United States "complete liberty of action in carrying out the recommendations and obligations resulting from membership in the League"; according to revised figures announced by the French Budget Committee, France's war expenses amount to $31,800,000,000, exclusive of pensions and losses in the devastated regions.

Nov. 7. The Senate adopts the "Preamble" to the Lodge slate of reservations, now known as reservation number one. This requires the assent of three of the four principal Allied Powers to the Senate's reservations before American ratification becomes effective.

Nov. 8. A semi-official message reaching Copenhagen from Prague announces that the Czecho-Slovak National Assembly adopts both the Versailles and the St. Germain treaties; the Brazilian Chamber of Deputies approves the Versailles Peace Treaty without discussion or amendment.

Nov. 11. The Brazilian Senate ratifies the Peace Treaty, and President Pessoa affixes his signature.

Nov. 12. The members of American Deligation to the Peace Conference notify the Supreme Council that they will depart from France during the first days of December; reports from Upper Silesia indicate that the results of the municipal elections there were most favorable to the Poles, who secured a majority of the votes throughout the province; the Entente has granted a credit of 60,-000,000 to Austria which will be utilized principally for the purchase of raw materials.

Nov. 13. The United States Senate by a vote of 46 to 33 adopts the Foreign Relation Committee's reservation on Article 10. Under this the United States assumes no obligation to preserve the territorial integrity or political independence of any other country or to interfere in controversies between nations; the return of American dead buried in the outlying cemeteries of France has been authorized by the French Government and the work of disinterment has been ordered by the War Department; Franklin D'Olier, of Pennsylvania, former Lieutenant Colonel in the American Expeditionary Forces, is chosen to be the first national commander of the American Legion; the Senate of Paraguay approves the adhesion of that country to the League of Nations and to the International Labor Organization; the Rumanian troops begin evacuating Budapest; a message from Omsk says that the evacuation of that city by the Allied missions is carried out according to the program that had been adopted; between Nov. 6 and 10 the Reds captured four entire regiments of Admiral Kolchak's troops and two divisional staffs.

Nov. 14. Finland has decided to aid General Yudenitch with 30,000 volunteers in a new attempt to take Petrograd within the next few weeks; the Bolsheviki have captured Yamburg, 68 miles southwest of Petrograd.

Nov. 15. Gabriel D'Annunzio heads a new expedition to Zara on the Dalmatian coast, receiving an enthusiastic welcome from the Italians there who had been awaiting his coming; the United States Senate for the first time in its history, applies cloture rule, the measure being adopted in connection with its action on the Peace Treaty.

Nov. 16. General Yudenitch has resigned the command of the Russian Northwest Army. General Laidoner, Commander in Chief of the Esthonian Army, has succeeded him.

Nov. 17. The Belgian Cabinet under Premier Telacroix tenders its resignation; the latest returns from the recent election in Italy indicate that Premier Nitti has doubtless been re-elected by a large majority; D'Annunzio's latest exploit in the capture of Zara appears to have made him master of the entire Dalmatian coast; President Wilson states that he will pigeon-hole the treaty if the Lodge program of reservations goes through unchanged; a message from Omsk says that that city is evacuated by the ministers, the military staff and the missions which still remained there. Admiral Kolchak, head of the government, remains with his armies. The Bolsheviki occupy points on both the railway lines, approximately 100 miles west of Omsk.

Nov. 18. By a vote of 55 to 38 the Senate adopts a reservation providing that the United States shall not be bound by any action of the League of Nations in which any nation or its dependencies cast more than one vote; the Prince of Wales reaches New York City for several days' visit as the guest of the city; official dispatches received at the State Department confirm Bolsheviki claims, recently made, of the capture of Omsk by Bolsheviks on November 15.

Nov. 19. The Senate rejects the Peace Treaty, with or without the Lodge reservations, on three overwhelming votes, and then adjourns the present session; 20,000 troops of General Yudenitch's northwestern army have gone over to the Bolsheviki.

Nov. 21. The Supreme Council decides to give Poland a mandate over Eastern Galicia, under the League of Nations for 25 years; the Supreme Council approves the text of an agreement granting political suzerainty over the Spitzbergen archipelago to Norway; the Bolsheviki bombarded Omsk for several hours. Between the periods of the bombardment, fire broke out in the town which is reported to have been half destroyed.

Nov. 22. The Prince of Wales ends his American visit and sails for home; the State Department renews its request to the French Government for the return of bodies of American soldiers buried in France; General Denikine claims to have broken through the Red lines between Orel and Tambov, southeast of Moscow, and to have annihilated 50,000 Bolshevik troops.

Nov. 23. A Serbian division 12,000 strong has been concentrated at Spalato on the Dalmatian coast, ready to oppose Gabriele d'Annunzio if he approaches that city.

Nov. 24. Tomasso Tittoni, Italian Foreign Minister, resigns, and Vitario Scialoia, Minister without portfolio, is named to succeed him; France declines to permit the United States to return the American dead until January 1, 1922.

Nov. 25. The Supreme Council sends Germany a note asking an explanation of the delay in the signing of the protocol, relative to the carrying out of the terms of the Armistice.

Nov. 27. The Peace Treaty with Bulgaria is signed in Paris.

Nov. 28. The Supreme Council adopts the British suggestion for partition of the German war-fleet, under which Great Britain receives 70 per cent of the total tonnage; France, 10 per cent; Italy, 10 per cent; Japan 8 per cent, and the United States, 2 per cent. Lady Astor, the American wife of Viscount Astor, is elected to Parliament from the Sutton Division of

Plymouth in the balloting of November 15. She is the first woman to hold a seat in the British Parliament.

Nov. 29. The Supreme Council decides that France is to have ten of the German submarines because during the war she was unable to build to the extent of the other Allies; the Omsk army continues to retreat on a wide front.

Nov. 30. An armistice providing for the immediate evacuation of Lithuania by the Germans has been signed by Germany and Lithuania; eleven generals and a thousand other officers of the army of Admiral Kolchak, and 39,000 troops, were captured by the Bolsheviki at Omsk; the Council of Ministers of the Kolchak Government have resigned at Irkutsk; a dispatch from Warsaw to Paris confirms the news that the Polish Army has formed a junction with the army of General Denikin.

DECEMBER

PEACE PRELIMINARIES—SIXTY-SIXTH CONGRESS—ENGLAND TO AUSTRALIA FLIGHT

Dec. 1. The Sixty-sixth Congress convenes and prepares for the immediate consideration of pressing international and domestic problems.

Dec. 2. According to advices from Berlin, Germany's opposition to signing the protocol is due to the attitude of the United States Senate toward the Treaty of Peace; President Wilson presents his annual message to Congress; twelve million dollars from the United States Treasury was contributed this year for relief of the undernourished children of Europe, principally in Poland and Czecho-Slovakia.

Dec. 3. The Supreme Council extends to December 8 the time allowed Roumania in which to reply to the latest Allied note. This is in the nature of an ultimatum to Roumania, so far as signing the Treaty is concerned; the head of the German delegation in Paris states that Germany is willing to sign the agreement putting the Peace Treaty into effect if certain clauses objectionable to her are eliminated; the Supreme Council addresses a note to Germany, protesting against an increase of Germany's armament contrary to the provisions of the Peace Treaty.

Dec. 4. The Supreme Council extends an invitation to Hungary to send Hungarian plenipotentiaries to Neuilly to conclude peace between the Allied nations and Hungary; all war-claims against our Government in France are to be settled for the maximum sum of $3,600,000, under an agreement between the War Department and the French Government.

Dec. 5. The plenipotentiaries of Jugo-Slavia sign the Bulgarian Treaty and also the financial annexes to the Austrian Treaty; the Supreme Council approves treaty provisions regulating the frontier between Poland and Czecho-Slovakia, which places western Galicia within the boundaries of Poland; the Supreme Council takes up the consideration of immediate measures to remedy the financial difficulties of various countries; the countries to be aided include former enemy nations, particularly Austria.

Dec. 6. The Supreme Council drafts a note demanding that Germany sign the protocol providing for the carrying out of the peace terms; the Bolshevik forces continue to gain against the Siberians. Their latest success is the occupation of Barabinsk, not far from Omsk, the Siberians offering no resistance.

Dec. 7. The Supreme Council notifies Dr. Carl Renner, Austrian Chancellor, that it is willing to receive him personally and hear his appeal for aid for his country; Gustav Noske, German Minister of Defense, states that he will recommend to his Government a refusal to sign the protocol; the actual war-cost of the United States Navy was $2,982,000,000, according to the annual report of the Secretary of the Navy.

Dec. 8. The Supreme Council delivers to the German delegation notes which contain certain modifications of the terms of the protocol to which Germany objects. Among other things it is agreed to consider the economic effects on Germany of indemnities required for the sinking of the warships in the Scapa Flow; a peace-time Regular Army of 300,000 men and 18,000 officers is decided on by the House military sub-committee.

Dec. 9. A new all-Russian Government is formed at Irkutsk by Admiral Kolchak under the Premiership of V. Pepeliayev; the chief members of the American peace delegation leave Paris to return to the United States; the Supreme Council decides on the principles on which light German warships will be divided among the smaller Powers for coast-defense purposes. It has also been decided that the destruction of such German ships as shall be destroyed is to be carried out by the Powers to which they are allotted; Turkey's gold reserves, now in Berlin, shall be transferred to Paris, the Supreme Council decides.

Dec. 10. General Conada, former Roumanian Premier, signs the Austrian and Bulgarian treaties for Roumania; Capt. Ross Smith, Australian aviator, arrives in Port Darwin, Australia, by airplane from England, thus winning a prize of 10,000 pounds sterling offered for the first aviator to make the flight; the Norwegian Parliamentary Nobel Committee decides not to award the Nobel peace prizes for 1918 and 1919; two Jugo-Slav army corps are reported to be moving toward Dalmatia and northern Albania. The Servian Government explains that this movement is a precautionary measure against any Italian attempt to occupy these sections; the Bolsheviki begin a new offensive on the Narva front. All attacks are said to have been repulsed with heavy losses to the Bolsheviki.

Dec. 11. The German reply to the Supreme Council's note demanding the signing of the peace protocol is received in Paris.

Dec. 12. A Moscow official dispatch announces the capture by the Bolsheviki, of Kharkov, in southern Russia, one of the bases of General Denikin.

Dec. 13. General Denikin captures 2,850 Bolsheviki and a number of cannon and machine guns in cavalry raids near Kamyshin; the city of Poltava, about seventy-five miles southwest of Kharkof, is captured by the Bolsheviki.

Dec. 14. Germany in her note replying to the Allied demand that she sign the protocol expresses a willingness to make reparation for the sinking of the German warships at Scapa Flow; in a statement issued at the White House, it is made clear that the President will make no compromise, and does not intend to withdraw the Treaty and resubmit it, but intends to let the responsibility "rest on the Republican Senators"; a report from Fiume says Gabrielle d'Annunzio has decided to hand over the command of that city to regular troops under General Caviglia, former Minister of War.

Dec. 15. The Siberian Army continues to retreat before the Bolsheviki. The Bolsheviki are said to have advanced about 217 miles from Omsk.

Dec. 16. The capture by the Bolsheviki of Novo Nikolavesk on the Trans-Siberian Railroad, 390 miles east of Omsk, is reported in Moscow. It is said that more than five thousand prisoners, many guns, and several generals of the Kolchak army were taken by the Soviet troops.

Dec. 17. The Supreme Council decides that it will be necessary to furnish relief to Austria in the amount of $70,000,000 for the purchase of food; a message by wireless received in London from Moscow reports the alleged capture of Kief and the occupation of Kupiansk, southeast of Kharkof, by the Bolsheviki.

Dec. 18. Premier Lloyd George states in the House of Commons that the Allies have decided to make peace with Turkey at the earliest possible moment, without the participation of the United States; a new turn in the Fiume situation is brought about by opposition to the withdrawal of Captain d'Annunzio's forces which may block acceptance of proposals of General Badoglio, Italian Chief of Staff, to assume command at Fiume; Amanullah Khan, reigning Amir of Afghanistan, issues a manifesto of independence.

Dec. 19. An unsuccessful attempt is made in Dublin to assassinate Viscount French, Lord Lieutenant of Ireland. One of the attacking party is killed, and a detective in Viscount French's car is wounded; General Denikin has gained an important victory in the Volga Valley, according to information from Helsingfors, and is said to have taken 10,250 prisoners and considerable equipment.

Dec. 20. The first section of the German Commission entrusted with preparations for putting the Peace Treaty into effect arrives in Paris.

Dec. 21. The second section of the German mission reaches Paris; the

Italian Chamber of Deputies adopts an order expressing confidence in the Government and upholding Premier Nitti's Cabinet.

Dec. 23. The Supreme Council answers the German note of December 15 and suggests that if it is discovered that errors had been made in the estimate of floating-dock material in the possession of Germany, upon which demands had been based for reparation for the sinking of the Scapa Flow fleet, such demands will be proportionately reduced; law officers of the Crown at a recent conference with French and Belgian law officers have made out a case against the former German Emperor and framed an indictment; the French Chamber of Deputies votes confidence in the Government, 458 to 75. The vote also carried approval of Premier Clemenceau's program.

Dec. 24. Japan's representative in the Supreme Council objects to the form of mandates under which that country is to have charge of the former German colonies in the Pacific; owing to doubts regarding the first plebiscite at Fiume, another has been taken, which resulted in 75 per cent of the votes being cast in favor of the Italian Government's proposals relative to the future occupation of the city, under which Fiume is to decide its own fate.

Dec. 27. Removal and shipment home of bodies of American soldiers buried in those parts of France not included in the battlefields and advance areas have been approved by the French Minister of the Interior.

Dec. 29. Sir William Osler, world-famous physician, dies at his home in Oxford, England, at the age of seventy.

Dec. 30. All points in connection with the signature of the protocol have been settled, except that relating to naval material; Count Apponyi, heading the Hungarian Peace delegation, indicates that the Hungarian Government will make a fight for restoration of some of the territory taken away from it, when the delegation goes to Paris; Viscount Grey, after three months of service in Washington as British Ambassador, leaves the capital for England to report to his Government.

THE EVENTS OF 1920

JANUARY

PEACE PRELIMINARIES—THE LEAGUE OF NATIONS—ADMIRAL SIMS AND THE NAVY DEPARTMENT

Jan. 1. According to estimates by the British War Office, Germany's armed forces total nearly a million men, which, under the terms of the Peace Treaty, must be reduced to 100,000 men by March 31; dispatches received in Vienna from Sofia state that Bulgaria has been declared under martial law.

Jan. 2. The possibility of a Bolshevik move upon the East is causing alarm in Great Britain. The collapse of Admiral Kolchak and the precarious position of General Denikin leaves the door to India open to the "Red" army; Turkey appoints a delegation to make peace with the Allies.

Jan. 3. The French Government grants permission for the removal to the United States of the bodies of 20,000 American soldiers buried in France.

Jan. 4. Budapest advices state that the high court which has been trying Bela Kun, former Communist dictator of Hungary, found evidence to show him guilty of 236 murders, nineteen robberies, and the use of 197,000,000 crowns for Communist propaganda in Vienna alone.

Jan. 7. It is decided that representatives of the United States will not be present during the exchange of ratifications of the Peace Treaty; the Hungarian peace delegation, numbering about sixty, and headed by Count Apponyi, arrives in Paris.

Jan. 8. President Wilson in a letter to the chairman of the Jackson-day banquet indicates his opposition to Peace-Treaty reservations and advocates that the question of ratification be submitted to a vote of the people at the next election; William J. Bryan in his address at the Jackson-day banquet opposes President Wilson's proposal to submit the question of ratification to a referendum, and urges a compromise; the Supreme Council has refused a request of the German Government to modify the German frontier lines as they are stipulated in the Peace Treaty.

Jan. 8. Cero de San Miguel, a small volcano near Cordoba, Mexico, breaks into violent eruption, resulting in two hundred deaths; Great Britain, France, and the United States propose to grant complete sovereignty to Fiume under the League of Nations.

Jan. 9. The Bolsheviki have captured Krasnoyarsk, eastern Siberia.

Jan. 10. Ratifications of the Treaty of Versailles are exchanged in Paris, and Peace between Germany, France, Great Britain, and the other Allied and associated Powers, with the exception of the United States, becomes effective; formal notice is served on Germany by the United States, in connection with the exchange of ratifications in Paris, that the conditions of the armistice still govern relations between the United States and Germany; a Bolshevik Moscow wireless dispatch to London says Admiral Kolchak has been arrested in Irkutsk by Colonel Pepeliayev, who has ordered him to hand over control of all affairs.

Jan. 11. A resolution is passed at a public meeting of the new Fatherland League in Berlin, urging the Germans to turn the former Kaiser over to the Allies for trial; Raymond Poincaré, President of the French Republic, is elected Senator for the Department of the Meuse by a vote of 742 out of 772 votes cast; the Democrats in the Senate decide to disregard President Wilson's plea to the Democratic leaders at the Jackson-day dinner to make the Peace Treaty the issue at the Presidential election.

Jan. 12. President Wilson issues a call for the first meeting of the Council of the League of Nations to convene at Paris, January 16; the Bolsheviki claim the capture of 25,400 prisoners on the southern front between December 21 and January 9.

Jan. 13. Representatives of twenty-six national organizations appeal to President Wilson, Senator Lodge, and Senator Hitchcock for immediate ratification of the Peace Treaty; the blockade against Germany in the Baltic is lifted as a result of the signing of the Peace Treaty; the Allies complete the list of persons they will ask Germany to surrender as guilty of crimes against the rules of warfare. It includes 880 persons; the United States Government refuses to accept any part of the indemnity to be paid by Germany for the destruction of the German Fleet at Scapa Flow, because it objects in principle to the settlement made by the Supreme Council; withdrawal of the American forces from Siberia is authorized by President Wilson, and the movement of troops will begin at once; the House by a vote of 183 to 123 adopts a resolution calling upon Secretary of War Baker to furnish complete information regarding the awards of the Distinguished Service Medals.

Jan. 14. Italy accepts the project for an agreement on the Adriatic question. It has also been handed to the Jugo-Slavs; eminent citizens of nine nations address memorials to their governments directing attention to impending bankruptcy and anarchy in Europe. They urge the calling of an economic conference of the leading nations of the world, including Germany and Austria.

Jan. 15. The Supreme Council drafts a note to the Dutch Government asking for the extradition of the former German Emperor; Sir Oliver Lodge arrives in New York for a lecture tour in America.

Jan. 16. The League of Nations is formally launched by the Executive Council of the League in Paris. Representatives of France, Great Britain, Italy, Japan, Belgium, Spain, Greece, Portugal and Brazil are present; Paul Deschanel, President of the French Chamber of Deputies, is nominated for the Presidency, thus defeating Premier Clemenceau; according to dispatches received in Basle, Odessa, the chief port of Russia on the Black Sea, has been occupied by the Bolsheviki.

Jan. 17. Rear-Admiral Sims, testifying before the Senate Committee investigating naval awards, charges that the fighting forces of the United States Navy were seriously handicapped in doing their share toward defeating Germany, through inefficiency in the Navy Department that prolonged the war; Paul Deschanel is elected President of the French Republic by 734 of the 889 members of the National Assembly voting. His majority was the largest since the election of Louis Adolphe Thiers, the first President after the fall of the Empire, who was chosen unanimously.

Jan. 18. Premier Clemenceau and members of his Cabinet resign.

Jan. 19. Dr. Karl Renner, Austrian Chancellor, informs the Foreign Affairs Committee of the Assembly that an offensive and defensive alliance has been concluded at Prague between Austria and Czecho-Slovakia; at a mass-meeting in Constantinople protests are voiced against the reported intention of the Peace Conference to dismember the Turkish Empire and to internationalize Constantinople; the Senate Naval Affairs Committee orders an inquiry into the charges made by Admiral Sims regarding the inefficiency of the Navy Department during the war.

Jan. 21. Assistant Commissioner of Police Redmond, of Dublin, is shot by an assassin and instantly killed in Harcourt Street, one of Dublin's main thoroughfares.

Jan. 22. The recently formed cabinet of Premier Millerand receives a vote of confidence by the Deputies. The vote is considered a moral defeat for the Government, however, as more than three hundred deputies abstained from voting.

Jan. 23. The Dutch Government delivers a note to the Peace Conference unqualifiedly refusing to surrender William Hohenzollern, former German Emperor, for trial.

Jan. 24. Former British Premier H. H. Asquith formally accepts the invitation of the Liberals of Paisley to stand as their candidate for Parliament; this is considered as an event of the first importance in England.

Jan. 25. German troops begin the evacuation of Upper Silesia, in accordance with the terms of the Peace Treaty which require that the movement begin fifteen days after its ratification.

Jan. 26. Hungary submits a memorandum to the Entente plenipotentiaries, declaring that the military clauses in the Treaty drawn up for Hungary are not acceptable. It is asserted that the army of 35,000 men allowed by the Treaty is not sufficient to maintain order; the movement of the American Expeditionary Forces out of Siberia began January 17.

Jan. 27. The second meeting of the Council of the League of Nations will take place in London, probably on February 10; General Denikin and his staff have taken refuge on board a British vessel at Constantinople.

Jan. 29. Germany sends a note to the Allies asking the revision of the extradition clauses of the Versailles Treaty; Premier Millerand of France calls upon General Janin, commanding the Czecho-Slovak forces in Siberia, to explain his action in handing over Admiral Kolchak to the Siberian revolutionary forces and to take measures for his release; General Yudenich, commander of the Russian Northwest Army, has been placed under arrest.

Jan. 30. The Cabinet of Premier

Millerand of France is given a vote of confidence in the Chamber of Deputies, 510 to 70; Georges Gaston Quien, accused of betraying Edith Cavell to the Germans, is sentenced to twenty years' imprisonment; advices from Montreal say that since the armistice more than a thousand enemy aliens have been deported from Canada; a demonstration participated in by five thousand persons takes place at Hanover, Germany, in protest against the extradition of former Emperor William.

Jan. 31. A committee of counselors has been named in Great Britain to decide the official date of the ending of the war. It is declared that thousands of pounds are involved in legal proceedings which have been held up pending an authoritative decision on the point; the Japanese Embassy at Washington is officially informed that the Japanese Government has invited China to enter upon negotiations for the return of German rights in Shantung to China.

FEBRUARY

PEACE PRELIMINARIES—OPENING SESSION OF THE LEAGUE OF NATIONS

Feb. 1. Viscount Grey, British Ambassador to the United States, writes a letter to the London *Times* favorable to the Treaty reservations, now under consideration in the United States Senate; a bill backed by sixty-five members is introduced in the French Chamber of Deputies which would give women civil, political, and economic equality with men.

Feb. 2. The Council of Ambassadors in Paris issues a formal denial of rumors that the Allies will promote or recognize the restoration of the Hapsburg dynasty in Hungary.

Feb. 3. The Allies hand the list of Germans accused of war-crimes to the German representative in Paris, with a demand for their extradition. The list contains eight hundred names, headed by former Crown Prince Frederick William; the American dollar rises to the greatest premium in history. Sterling falls to about $3.33, francs to about seven cents, lire to a little over five cents, and the German mark to 1.09 cents.

Feb. 4. Kurt von Lersner, head of the German Peace Delegation in Paris, resigns rather than transmit to his Government the list of 896 Germans whose extradition is demanded by the Allies.

Feb. 5. President Wilson virtually serves informal notice on the British Government of his displeasure over the letter of Viscount Grey published in the London *Times* declaring Britain favorable to the Lodge reservations; at the conclusion of a session of the German cabinet, correspondents are informed that the Ministers are unanimous in declaring that the surrender of the men demanded by the Allies is an utter physical impossibility; the completion of the record of casualties of the American Expeditionary Forces in the war shows that 34,844 men were killed in action, including 382

at sea; 13,960 died of wounds; 23,-738 died of disease; and 5,102 died from accident or other causes. The wounded in action numbered 215,423.

Feb. 7. President Wilson instructs the Democratic Senators to oppose Republican proposals for a reservation on Article X. The President, however, announced that he would favor certain specific reservations.

Feb. 9. The treaty by which Norway is given sovereignty over Spitzbergen is signed at Paris, Hugh C. Wallace, the American Ambassador at Paris, signing for the United States.

Feb. 10. A majority of the Republicans assure Senator Lodge they will support any modifications of the original reservations he will accept; Frederick Wilhelm, former Crown Prince of Germany, cables President Wilson that he will surrender to the Allies, suggesting that he be made the victim rather than the men whose extradition is demanded.

Feb. 11. Senator Hitchcock, leader of the Administration forces, rejects compromise overtures from the Republicans on the Peace Treaty, involving a compromise reservation to Article X retaining the principle of the Lodge reservation; Admiral Kolchak has been executed by his own troops to prevent his rescue by White troops moving in the direction of Irkutsk for that purpose; the latest information received in Constantinople from Odessa says the Bolshevik army is now in control of the latter city; the opening session of the Council of the League of Nations meets at St. James's Palace, London. No American representative was present.

Feb. 12. The Hungarian peace delegation hands the secretary of the Peace Conference a memorandum outlining the desires of Hungary. It insists upon maintenance of historical Hungary and asks for a plebiscite in the disputed districts; the German Army is still 400,000 strong, according to a report reaching Paris. In addition there are 100,000 policing forces, officers and non-commissioned officers. Germany is also reported well supplied with tanks, machine guns, and airplanes.

Feb. 13. The Democrats in the Senate formally present to the Republicans a written pledge, signed by twenty-eight Senators, to vote for the bipartisan conference reservation on Article X, as a compromise to obtain ratification of the Treaty; the League of Nations Council at its meeting in St. James's Palace, London, decides to call an international financial conference at the earliest possible moment to study the financial crisis and look for means of remedying it; Switzerland is admitted to membership in the League; German doctors at Brunsbuettel on the Baltic Canal vote not to go on board ships flying flags of nations which were parties to the demand for the extradition of Germans accused of war-crimes; Robert Lansing resigns as Secretary of State at the request of President Wilson. The resignation takes place "at once"; the Bolshevik commander at Odessa threatens to open fire on the British warships if they remain in the harbor there for more than three days; Admiral Kolchak and one of his ministers, Pepeliayev, were shot at Irkutsk on February 7.

Feb. 14. Germany reopens her Embassy in London, which has been closed since 1914; the Norwegian Cabinet decides to ask the consent of Parliament for Norwegian participation in the League of Nations; discussion of the question of Holland's entrance into the League of Nations is opened in the Dutch Parliament.

Feb. 15. N. W. Rowell, Acting Secretary of State for External Affairs in Canada, declares that his country will never consent to ratification of the Peace Treaty by the United States if the Lenroot reservation is adopted which would deprive Canada of her independent voting power in the League of Nations; agreement is reached by the Supreme Allied Council to permit the Sultan to maintain his court in Constantinople; Hugh C. Wallace, the American Ambassador, delivers to the French Foreign Office a memorandum from President Wilson in which the President said he could not approve of Premier Lloyd George's proposed settlement of the Adriatic question; a Moscow communication reaching Warsaw announces that Bolshevik detachments have passed the Bessarabian frontier, and crossed the Dneister River, taking many prisoners.

Feb. 16. An official decree is issued by the Italian Government ratifying the Peace Treaty with Bulgaria.

Feb. 17. Joseph Caillaux, former French Premier, is placed on trial before the Senate, charged with conspiracy against his country in time of war; Senator Hitchcock, Administration leader, declares the Democrats have abandoned completely their efforts to obtain ratification, and that rather than permit the Treaty to be ratified with reservations dictated by Senator Lodge they are prepared to join with the "irreconcilables" and vote against ratification; though both the White House and the State Department denied that President Wilson's note on the Adriatic question contained a threat to "withdraw from European affairs." it is now said to be admitted in official circles that the President had served notice he would consider withdrawing the German Treaty from the Senate and had also intimated that he would withdraw the French Treaty if the Lloyd George settlement of the Adriatic question were adopted; the reply of the Allied Supreme Council to President Wilson's Adriatic note is handed to Ambassador Davis in London.

Feb. 18. Paul Deschanel becomes the tenth President of the French Republic, succeeding Raymond Poincaré; President Wilson receives the reply of the Allied Premiers to his note threatening withdrawal from European affairs unless the Adriatic question is settled as agreed among the Powers last December.

Feb. 19. An international financial conference under the auspices of the League of Nations will be held in March either at Brussels or at The Hague; martial law is proclaimed in the Sarre region on account of disturbances taking place there; the national debt of Germany is expected to reach $51,000,000 by the end of March; President Wilson sends to the State Department a reply to the Entente Premier's note on the Adriatic question.

Feb. 20. The Second Chamber of the Dutch Parliament approves Holland's entrance into the League of Nations; Rear-Admiral Robert E. Peary, discoverer of the North Pole, dies in Washington at the age of sixty-four; universal military training as a part of the future military policy of the United States is approved in principle by the House Military Committee; the Bolsheviki capture Archangel.

Feb. 21. In the course of three test votes in the Senate, four additional Democratic Senators break from the Administration leadership on the Peace Treaty and vote to adopt the original Lodge Reservation on withdrawal from the League of Nations; Admiral Nicholas Horthy, Commander-in-Chief of the Hungarian Army, is reported to have been made Regent of Hungary by the National Assembly.

Feb. 22. The Republic of France presents 6,000 "certificates of gratitude" to relatives and friends of soldiers who died in defense of France's frontiers.

Feb. 23. Final settlement of the Adriatic question is to be placed in the form of a boundary treaty for ultimate submission to the American Senate for ratification; the final documents of the Hungarian reply to the Allied peace terms are presented to the Secretary of the Peace Conference in Paris.

Feb. 25. Bainbridge Colby, former Republican and Progressive, is appointed Secretary of State by President Wilson to succeed Robert Lansing; Mr. Herbert H. Asquith, former British Premier, is reelected to Parliament from Paisley; President Wilson's second note of the month on the Adriatic problem is received and delivered to the Allied Peace Council in London.

Feb. 26. The United States Senate readopts the Lodge reservation on mandates by a vote of 68 to 4. This is the first time since the Treaty was submitted to the Senate that a reservation has received more than the two-thirds votes necessary for the ratification; President Wilson's last note on the Adriatic question is made public. In it the President stands firm on his "threat" to consider taking America out of European affairs and refusing to join the League of Nations.

Feb. 27. The Entente Premiers accept the President's proposal that the Adriatic question be settled by negotiations between the Italian and Jugo-Slav Governments; Major R. W. Shroeder makes a new altitude record in an airplane at Dayton, Ohio, reaching an elevation of 36,020 feet.

Feb. 28. President Wilson signs the transportation act providing for the return of the railroads to private control March 1.

Feb. 29. Premier Nitti of Italy and Anton Trumbitch, Jugo-Slav Foreign Minister, hold a conference in London to discuss the Adriatic problem. This follows the proposal of the Allied Premiers to President Wilson; a siege of Fiume has begun with a stringent blockade against commodities, including foodstuffs. Its purpose is to compel the surrender of D'Annunzio.

MARCH

PEACE PRELIMINARIES—COUP D'ETAT IN GERMANY—SENATE AND THE PEACE TREATY

March 1. Private operation of the country's railroads is resumed one minute after midnight after twenty-six months of government operation.

March 2. The Senate readopts the original Lodge reservations on domestic questions and the Monroe Doctrine by large majorities; the Supreme Council decides that Turkey shall have no navy; Germany is to be permitted to float an international loan in neutral European countries and South America, and, if possible, in the United States, according to a decision of the Supreme Council.

March 4. The Senate by a vote of 48 to 21 readopts the original Lodge reservation on Shantung amended to eliminate mention of China or Japan; the Senate also by a vote of 55 to 14 adopts a reservation providing that no person not appointed by Congress shall represent the United States in any body established by the Peace Treaty. A final proposal for a compromise on a reservation to Article X is submitted to President Wilson by the Democratic leaders; it becomes known that by the Treaty now being completed by the Conference of foreign Ministers and Ambassadors, Turkey has virtually been stript of all territory in Europe.

March 5. President Wilson is formally asked by the Democratic Senators to decide whether the Peace Treaty shall be ratified with the reservations that are now being adopted by the Senate or whether the Administration followers shall again defeat ratification; the Dutch Government for the second time refuses to deliver the former German Emperor to the Allies for trial.

March 6. A report reaching London from Helsingfors says the Bolsheviki have begun a new attack on Finland.

March 7. President Wilson in his latest note to the British and French Premiers on the Adriatic question reiterates his willingness to approve "a mutual agreement between the Italian and Jugo-Slav governments reached without prejudice to the territorial or other interests of any third nation," but insists that such agreement must be in harmony with the principles laid down in the Anglo-French-American memorandum of December 9; a report from Berlin to London says large forces of Bolsheviki open an offensive against the Poles on both sides of the Pripet region.

March 8. President Wilson refuses to discuss with Democratic Senators reservations to Article X on which they hoped a compromise was possible; stubborn fighting is reported from the Polish front, where the Bolsheviki have just launched a new drive.

March 9. The Senate approves the Lenroot reservation providing that the United States, except in cases where Congress has consented, assumes no obligation resulting from any decision of the League of Nations unless such decision is reached by a vote in which the United States is represented equally with any other member of the League.

March 10. The Republicans in the Senate withdraw their offer of a compromise on the Article X reservation submitted to the Democrats. More than one-half of the Democratic Senators announce that they will ratify the Treaty with the Lodge reservations; the chief training-school cadets at Grosslichterfelde, Prussia, through which most of the officers of the Germany Army passed, is closed in accordance with the terms of the Peace Treaty; Jugo-Slav officials rejoice at the attitude taken by President Wilson in his latest note on the Adriatic.

March 12. Senator Lodge makes a final offer of compromise on a reservation to Article X in the Senate. It is immediately opposed by Democratic Senators; a new Hungarian peace treaty is definitely agreed upon by the Peace Conference.

March 11. The Syrian Congress at Damascus declares Syria to be an independent state; the moderate forces in British labor win a decisive and highly important victory when the Trades Union Congress decides by a vote of 3,870,000 to 1,050,000 against the use of direct action or a general strike to force the nationalization of the coal-mines; Hjalmar Branting is named Premier in Sweden. He is the first Socialist to hold this office in that country.

March 13. The Government of Friedrich Ebert, the Socialist President of the German Republic, is overthrown by a military *coup d'état*. The National Assembly is dissolved, and Dr. Wolfgang Kapp, one of the founders of the Fatherland party, ousts Gustav Bauer, the Chancellor and himself takes that office. General Baron von Leuttwitz is appointed Commander-in-Chief of the Army; the Allied Supreme Council is called in extraordinary session to consider protective measures as the result of the overthrow of the Ebert Government by monarchist leaders in Berlin.

March 14. President Ebert, of the old Government, calls upon the Socialists and working classes generally to stand by the old Government and to use the strike weapon so that the counter-revolution may be promptly supprest.

March 15. Emir Feisal, the eldest son of King Hussein of Hedjaz, is declared king of Syria with Palestine as a part of the kingdom. Mesopotamia is also reported to have declared its independence, wtih Emir Abysmal, third son of King Hussein, as king; the counter-revolution in Germany appears to have reached an end; the Senate adopts the Lodge compromise reservation to Article X. The reservation as adopted provides, in effect, that the United States shall assume no obligation to preserve the territorial integrity or political independence of any other country by the employment of its military or naval forces unless Congress shall so provide by act or joint resolution.

March 16. Republican Senate leaders are making tentative plans for a separate peace with Germany, in case the Peace Treaty fails of ratification.

March 17. Chancellor Kapp, head of the new Government at Berlin, has resigned in favor of President Ebert; a report from Constantinople says the Allied forces under Gen. Sir George F. Milne, of the British Army, occupy the Turkish capital. The Allies issue a proclamation saying that the occupation is provisional and for the purpose of compelling the Ottoman Empire to fulfill treaty terms and end the reign of disorder; according to a report from Berlin, Dr. Kapp has fled Berlin; a royal decree is issued in Holland, saying the place to be allotted to former Emperor William of Germany as his residence will form part of the Province of Utrecht and that it will be fixt later by the Government.

March 18. The Senate adopts the fourteen Lodge reservations to the Peace Treaty, and in addition a reservation approving self-determination for Ireland; a peace-time Army of 299,000 enlisted men and 17,800 officers is approved by the House in passing the Army Reorganization Bill by a vote of 246 to 92.

March 19. The Senate by a vote of 49 to 35 refuses to ratify the Peace Treaty and sends it back to President Wilson; the Lord Mayor of Cork is shot dead by an assassin who entered his residence and escaped in an automobile.

March 20. According to official dispatches received at the Finnish Legation in Washington, the Bolsheviki have started an offensive against Finland, using the Murman Railroad as a base.

March 21. The London Air Ministry announces that the 5,300-mile airplane race across Africa from Cairo to the Cape is won by Colonel Van Rybzvo'd in a Vozrtrekker machine; a Bolshevik communication received in London claims that in the direction of Novorossisk the "Reds" have captured 6,000 prisoners and 20 guns and in the region of Ekaterinodar they have taken 15,000 prisoners, a large number of guns, and much booty.

March 22. A Warsaw dispatch says the Bolsheviki have launched repeated attacks along various parts of the Polish front, considered by the military authorities to be preliminary to the long-heralded general spring offensive.

March 23. The Supreme Council decides to offer the protection of the League of Nations to an independent Armenia, which would comprise Russian Armenia and certain territories taken from Turkey; the Dutch Premier reads to Parliament a royal decree by which the island of Wieringen is granted to the former German Crown Prince as a place of residence "without prejudice to future arrangements"; the House passes the Naval Appropriation Bill, carrying approximately $425,000,000, and it now goes to the Senate; the Polish Army takes the offensive against the Bolsheviki in the Baltic region and captures several thousand prisoners.

March 24. Democratic Senators suggest to President Wilson the ratification of the Peace Treaty with a single reservation providing for the decision of the United States on the League of Nations Covenant after the Presidential election, as a basis on which he may resubmit the Treaty to the Senate; dispatches from Beirut to Constantinople announce that Emir Feisal, the recently proclaimed King of Syria, has given the French until April 6 to leave Syria and the Arabs have ordered the British out of Palestine; Mrs. Humphrey Ward, the noted English author, dies in a London hospital. She was born in Tasmania, June 11, 1851.

March 25. The Bolsheviki have commenced the long-planned spring attack by launching a drive against the Polish line at scattered points along a front of approximately four hundred miles.

March 26. It is reported from Constantinople that the south Russian anti-"Red" volunteer army has virtually disappeared. General Denikin, the anti-Bolshevik leader in southern Russia, and his general staff have been at Novorossisk since March 14 with an army of about six thousand.

March 27. 3,500 three-inch field guns have been found by the Inter-Allied Commission in the vicinity of Berlin and altogether 12,000 of these guns have been discovered throughout Germany, as well as 6,000 airplanes intact; Odessa, the great Russian port on the Black Sea, is occupied by Ukrainians, according to information received by the Ukrainian mission in Paris; Novorossisk, the last base in southern Russia under control of General Denikin, is captured by the Russian Bolsheviki.

March 29. German army troops to the number of 10,000 have invaded the Ruhr valley. France called the attention of the Allies to what is described as a gross violation of the Peace Treaty, and urged that action be taken.

March 30. Allied powers have accepted Holland's last note regarding the former Kaiser, in which the Dutch refuse to surrender him, but promise to guard him carefully; President Wilson in his latest note to the Allies demands the expulsion of the Turk from Constantinople and from Europe.

March 31. A resolution declaring the war with Germany at an end is reported to the House by the Committee on Foreign Affairs. The resolution gives Germany forty-five days in which to notify the United States that she also considers peace established; by a vote of 348 to 94 the Government's Irish Home Rule Bill passes the second reading in the House of Commons. The bill now goes to the committee stage before the third and final reading.

APRIL

PEACE PRELIMINARIES—FRENCH OCCUPY GERMAN TOWNS

April 1. The Supreme Council asks the League of Nations to accept a mandate for Armenia; a special meeting has been called to consider the offer.

April 3. The American Commission, headed by Major-General Harbord, appointed by President Wilson to study conditions in the former Turkish Empire, report that it would require from 25,000 to 200,000 American troops the first year to hold the mandate for Armenia, that it would be five years before the mandate would be self-supporting, and that the cost to this Government would be $757,350,000; the German Government makes a formal demand upon France for permission to take up arms against the Ruhr Communists.

April 4. Advices that German troops are pouring into the Ruhr district with full government authority and in violation of the Treaty cause the French Government to issue orders for troops to cross the Rhine and occupy Darmstadt, Frankfort, Hamburg, and Hanau.

April 5. Some detachments of the French troops have already begun an advance for the occupation of Frankfort. The French Government issues a note defining its position in the present crisis; administration Leader Hitchcock says President Wilson will send the Peace Treaty back to the Senate for a second time "when he vetoes the Peace resolution or when Congress fails to pass a resolution over his veto."

April 6. An official communication issued in Paris says the military operation contemplated by the French against Frankfort and Darmstadt has been completed, as has also that of Hanau, previously evacuated by the German troops.

April 8. After a full discussion of the Franco-German incident by the Cabinet Council in London, an authoritative statement is issued to the effect that France acted entirely on her own initiative in deciding to occupy German towns; that Great Britain, the United States, Italy, and Belgium were all opposed to the plan, and that France's action has caused a delicate situation; at a council of Belgian Ministers in Brussels, held under the presidency of the King, it was decided to inform the French Government that the Belgian Government is ready to associate itself with France and to send a detachment of the French in the occupation to cooperate with the French in the occupation of the Ruhr region.

April 9. The German Government hands Premier Millerand a note declaring that Germany will hold France responsible for all damages and casualties growing out of the occupation of the Rhine cities; the House passes the Knox Resolution, declaring a state of peace with Germany and repealing all the special war-legislation. Twenty-two Democrats join the Republicans in voting for the resolution.

April 11. Great Britain replies to the French note on the Ruhr occupation reaffirming the determination to enforce the Versailles Treaty, but in cooperation with the other Allies; the withdrawal of all German troops no longer needed in the Ruhr district is begun.

April 13. A Warsaw dispatch reports a victory for the Poles over the Bolsheviki on the southeastern front.

April 14. President Wilson presides over the first Cabinet meeting held at his call since September 2, 1919; Ludwig C. A. K. Martens, self-styled Ambassador of the Russian Soviet Government to the United States, is found by the Senate Foreign Relations Committee to be an alien enemy.

April 19. Sir Auckland Geddes, recently appointed British Ambassador to the United States to succeed Viscount Grey, arrives in New York from Southampton; the House Appropriations Committee estimates the total loss to the Government growing out of Federal control of the railroads at about $1,375,000,000.

April 20. Russia and Germany sign a treaty in Berlin for the exchange of war prisoners, of whom 200,000 are still in Germany. The treaty is practically the same as that signed by Great Britain and Russia.

April 22. President Wilson, in a letter read to the Democratic State convention at Wichita, Kan., declares the issue to be put forward must be the duty of America to follow up victory by establishing a League of Nations; Joseph Caillaux, former Premier of France and twice Minister of Finance is convicted of "commerce and correspondence with the enemy"; sentenced to three years' imprisonment, five years' forced residence to be selected by the Minister of the Interior, and ten years' loss of political rights, the latter clause carrying with it the inability to vote or to hold office.

April 24. Premier Nitti, of Italy, and Anton Trumbitch, the Jugo-Slav Foreign Minister, accept President Wilson's settlement of the Adriatic problem, making Fiume a buffer state, with no continuity of territory between Fiume and Italy. Plebiscites will decide the disposition of the islands in dispute.

April 25. The Supreme Council asks President Wilson to fix the boundaries of the new state of Armenia, and officially offers the mandate for Armenia to the United States Government; France is given a mandate for Syria, and Great Britain is made mandatary for Palestine, which is established as the homeland of the Jews; the indemnity to be paid by Germany is tentatively fixed at an annual payment of 3,000,000,000 marks, figured at the pre-war exchange-rate, for thirty years. This will make a total of about $22,000,000,000.

April 30. A new peace resolution providing for a separate peace with Germany and Austria is reported to the Senate by Senator Lodge, chairman of the Foreign Relations Committee. The measure requests President Wilson to negotiate peace treaties with Germany and Austria and also repeals the declarations of war against Germany and Austria, repeals war-time legislation, and retains to the United States all former German and Austrian property taken over by the Alien Property Custodian or other government agencies until all claims of American nationals against Germany and Austria shall be satisfied.

MAY

TURKS RECEIVE PEACE TREATY—PRESIDENT
WILSON VETOES KNOX RESOLUTION—
SENATE FAILS TO RATIFY PEACE
TREATY

May 11. The Turkish Peace delegation receives the Peace Treaty at Paris; the Treaty, among other things, provides for permanent occupation of Constantinople by Allied troops, awards Thrace to Greece, and stipulates that the Turks shall recognize Armenia's independence and accept the arbitration of the President of the United States as to the frontier.

May 12. News is received in Paris that a settlement of the Adriatic question has been reached between Jugo-Slav and Italian delegates at Pallanza. It is said the Italian delegates agreed that Italy should recognize the "Wilson line" as the frontier between Italy and Jugo-Slavia; also that Fiume be placed under Italian sovereignty, but that the League of Nations should control the port.

May 15. The Senate by a vote of 43

to 38 passes the Knox resolution repealing the declarations of war with Germany and Austria and providing for a resumption of commercial and diplomatic relations with those countries.

May 19. German war-criminals on the list recently presented the Government by the Allies are summoned by the chief imperial public prosecutor to appear before the Supreme Court at Leipzig between June 7 and June 20, says a report from Berlin; According to what is perhaps the first concise statement of France's war-losses, 1,400,000 of that country's soldiers were killed, 800,000 maimed, and 300,000 wounded, out of the 8,000,000 mobilized. Of material losses 600,000 houses were destroyed, 75,000,000 acres of arable land laid waste and 3,000 miles of railroad and 25,000 miles of highways were completely destroyed.

May 21. The House by a vote of 228 to 139 adopts the Knox peace resolution as a substitute for the original peace mesure passed by the House; eighteen Democrats broke away from the Administration leadership and voted for the resolution.

May 24. President Wilson in a special message to Congress urges American acceptance of a mandate over Armenia.

May 27. The Senate Foreign Relations Committee by a vote of 11 to 4 adopts a resolution refusing the request of President Wilson that he be authorized to accept for the United States a mandate over Armenia; President Wilson vetoes the Knox Peace resolution recently passed by Congress; the President in his veto message declared that if peace were established through the resolution the purpose for which the United States entered the war would not be attained; the Senate by a vote of 62 to 12 opposes the Armenian mandate and by a vote of 52 to 23 adopts the Foreign Relations Committee's resolution refusing the consent of Congress for President Wilson to accept the mandate.

INDEX

THE CLEAN-UP OF REIMS

This street is the Rue Chanzy, one of the many streets in Reims, which, by early summer in 1919, had been cleaned up, as here shown, to the extent of making the roadway free of rubbish, and so passable for vehicles. Most parts of the city still showed destruction of buildings similar to what is seen here

INDEX

INDEX

Belgium
  destruction of Termonde, I, 321-324.
  devastation of, I, 351-353.
  Edith Cavell's death, 363-371.
  flight for Ostend, I, 302-304.
  German advance in, I, 266 267.
  Germany's declaration of war
    against I, 169-173.
  German departure from, II, 3.
  Haelen battle, I, 290-292.
  Louvain, destruction of, I, 293-297.
  Namur's siege and fall, I, 302-314.
  refugees in, VI, 137-140.
  relief work in, I, 373-374.
  roads through, from Germany to
    France, I, 245-248.
  stories of atrocities, I, 353-362.
  strength of her army, I, 309-310.
  the German crossing of its frontiers,
    I, 256-257.
  the fall of Liége, I, 257-264.
  the massacre at Tamines, I, 319-320.
  Tirlemont bombarded, I, 292-297.
  visit of king and queen to United
    States, X, 377.
  Zeebrugge and other cities occupied,
    VI, 126-145.
Belgrade, bombardment of, I, 87-88;
  VIII, 263-266.
Belleau Wood, marines at, V, 132-135,
  167.
Belloc, Hilaire, I, XV; II, 94; 103.
  as to the battle of Marne, II, 66-68.
Berlin, welcome of, to returning soldiers, VI, 375-376.
Bernhardi, Gen. Fredk. Von, at the
  first Marne battle, II, 112-113.
  in defense, V, 222.
  on the western front, V, 75.
  on world power or downfall, I, 16.
Bernstorff, Count J. Von, German ambassador to the United States, I, 220.
  German note on Arabic case deliv-
    ered by, IX, 281.
  on the sinking of the Lusitania, IX,
    251.
  passport sent to, by United States,
    IV, 10.
Berthelot, Gen'l, west of Reims, V, 214;
  VI, 33.
Bethmann-Hollweg, Theodore, German
  Chancellor, author of, "scrap of paper" phrase, I, 177-181.
  as to peace, IV, 313.
  his military necessity speech, I, 255.
  his fall, IV, 194-197.
  his "Woe to the Statesmen" speech,
    VII, 272-274.
  proposes plan to Reichstag, IV, 314-
    316.
  sketch of, X, 209-212.
Beyers, and the Transvaal rebellion,
  IX, 184-186.
Birdwood, Gen. Sir. W. R., sketch of,
  X, 92.
Bismarck Archipelago taken by the
  British, IX, 180.
Bismarck, the yoke he placed on
  France in 1870, X, 327.
Bissing, Gen. von, his command in Bel-
  gium and his death, I, 375.
Bliss, Gen. T. H., X, 92.
Blücher, sinking of the, in the Dogger
  Banks battle, X, 31-33.
Boehm, Gen'l, in the Marne salient, V,
  261.

Boelke, Capt., aviator, IV, 282.
  his exploits, IV, 278.
Boer rebellion, the, suppressed by Gen.
  Botha, IX, 181-186.
Boillot, Georges, aviator, exploits, IV,
  273-274.
Bolsheviki, make peace for Russia with
  Germany, IV, 323-351.
  rise of the, in central Russia, VII,
    310, 320-330.
  Russia's frightful sufferings under
    the, VII, 378-384.
Bordeaux, French government returns
  from, II, 274.
Borden, Sir Robert L., sketch of, X,
  212.
Bosnia and Herzegovina, annexation of,
  as cause of the war, I, 118-122.
Botha, Gen. Louis, conquers German
  southeast Africa, IX, 186-193.
  in German East Africa, IX, 197.
  sketch of, X, 212.
  suppressed the Boer Rebellion, IX,
    181-186.
Boulogne, as a German goal, II, 195-
  201.
  airplanes efforts to take, from, II,
    199-201.
Bouresches, marines at, V, 132-133.
Bovoeric Gen., IX, 130-132.
  sent home, IX, 292-293.
Boy-ed. Capt., and the sinking of the
  Lusitania, IX, 252.
Brazil declares war on Germany, I,
  223-224.
  in the peace conference, X, 298.
Bremen, a submarine, fate of, IX, 313-
  314.
Breshkovskaya, Catherine, her release
  from Siberia, VII, 283-284.
Breslau, the warship, VIII, 11-12.
  the, made over to Turkey, I, 198.
  the, reported sunk, X, 39.
Brest-Litovsk, fall of, VII, 161.
  peace of, between Germany and Rus-
    sia.
  the treaty of, with Russia VII, 332-
    353.
  with Roumania, VII, 349.
  with Ukraine, VII, 335-339.
Briand, Aristide, sketch of, X, 213-214.
Brindisi, IX, 10.
British, and the Battle of Jutland, X,
  61-84.
  aids in clearing Belgium, VI, 126-148.
  at the battle of Armentières, V, 61-
    94.
  at Kemmel Hill, V, 106-109.
  at Passchendaele Ridge, IV, 199-220.
  Bismarck Archipelago IX, 180.
  defeated by Germans off Coronel, X,
    18-26.
  defeat the Germans at Falkland
    Islands, X, 26-30.
  in the Albert Montdidier salient, V,
    296-333.
  in Ludendorff-Arras drive, V, 36-60.
  issues war zone decree, IX, 235-247.
  occupy Rhine at Cologne, VI, 366-
    370.
  reinforce the Italians, IX, 113.
  strike of in Picardy, VI, 46-47.
  submarine activity of, in the Bal-
    tic, IX, 298.
  submarines of, in the Baltic, IX,
    231-233.

487

INDEX

Château Thierry, American troops at, V, 129-141.
Americans at, V, 228-231.
Americans drive Germans back from, V, 220-224.
First American division at, I, 41.
German purpose at, V, 215.
Chemin des Dames, Lorraine, American raids from, 357-360.
Britain's counter thrust at, IV, 189-192.
German attempts at, IV, 175-178.
Chile, her attitude in the war, I, 225-226.
China, declares war on Germany, I, 230.
Christmas, the first at the front, II, 258-262.
Churchill, Winston, statement of, as to the British navy, X, 3-6.
Clancy, William, at Vimy Ridge, III, 358-359.
Clemenceau, Premier, as to Ludendorff, V, 31.
made premier, IV, 260-261.
sketch of, X, 215-220.
visits London, VI, 379.
wounded, X, 302.
Coblenz, Americans at, VI, 363-365.
Colored troops with Gouraud east of Reims, V, 218.
Columbian, sinking of, IX, 316-317.
Compeigne, battle near, II, 38.
Ludendorff's drive for, V, 150-163.
Zeppelin shot down at, IV, 304.
Conference, The Peace, opening of, X, 297.
representatives at, X, 297-298.
Congress of Berlin, the, I, 66; 119-120.
Constantine, king of Greece, his pro-German attitude in Greece, I, 196-198.
his fall, VIII, 322-324.
Constantinople, Allies in, VI, 255-256.
railroad from, to Bagdad, VIII, 3-14.
to go to Russia, VII, 248-249.
Corfu, island of, taken by the Entente, VIII, 282.
Coronel, battle of, X, 18-26.
Cossacks, in the defense of Warsaw, VII, 81-82.
Coucy Castle blown up by the Germans, III, 341-342.
Couronné, The Grand, Castlenau at, I, 281.
battle of, I, 283-285; II, 65-76.
Courtrai, entered, VI, 129.
Cradock, Admiral Sir Christopher, at the battle off Coronel, X, 18-26.
Cressy, sinking of the, IX, 212-215.
Crown Prince, armies of, flanked, VI, 74.
an offensive by the, in the Argonne, III, 8-10.
defeat in the Marne salient, V, 289.
his flight to Holland, VI, 304-310.
interview with, VI, 316-319.
of Germany, retreat of, II, 101-103.
plight of army of, V, 266.
siege of Verdun by army of, III, 71-153.
Ctesiphon, British retreat from, VIII, 67-72.
Cuba, declares war on Germany, I, 221-222.
Cyprus, annexed by Great Britain, VIII, 32-33.

Czecho-Slovaks, rise in Siberia to aid the Entente, VII, 362-363.
operation of, in Siberia, VII, 375-378.
Czernin, Count, as to Germany's desperate condition in 1917, IV, 316-318.
on Brest-Litovsk peace treaty, IV, 340-341.
opportunity for peace, IV, 349-350.
Czernowitz, taken by the Russians, VII, 214-215; 221-222.
Dacia, case of the, IX, 301-303.
Damascus, fall of, VIII, 228.
D'Annunzio, Gabriele, IX, 140.
his coup at Fiume, X, 378-382.
Dardanelles, Allies submarines in, IX, 304-305.
the allied navies attempt to force them, VIII, 76-93.
Darfu, war in, VIII, 30-32.
Davis, Richard Harding, cited, I, 300-302.
Dead Man's Hill, Americans at, VI, 54-55.
Declaration of war by, Germany against Russia, I, 157-166.
Allies against Turkey, I, 198-204.
between Germany and France, I, 167-169.
Brazil against Germany, I, 223-225.
Bulgaria against Serbia, I, 195.
China against Germany, I, 230.
Cuba and Panama against Germany, I, 221-222.
Germany against Belgium, I, 169-173.
Germany against Portugal, I, 209-213.
Great Britain against Germany, I, 173-181.
Greece against Germany, I, 229.
Haiti against Germany, I, 233.
Indians, New York against Germany, I, 233.
Italy against Germany, I, 215-217.
Italy against Austria, I, 205-209.
Japan against Germany, I, 185-187.
Liberia against Germany, I, 231.
Roumania against Austria, I, 213-215.
Russia against Bulgaria, I, 192-195.
Siam against Germany, I, 230.
The United States against Germany, I, 217-221.
United States against Austria, I, 231.
Degoutte, Gen'l, at battle of Marne, V, 234-260.
on Americans in the Marne salient, V, 294.
Delcassé, Théophile, French foreign minister, Fashoda, I, 129.
sketch of, X, 220.
Denikin, General, leader of Don Cossacks, comes to aid of Russia against the Bolsheviki, VII, 388-392.
Dernburg, Dr. Bernhard, and the sinking of the Lusitania, IX, 252.
D'Esperey, Gen. Franchet, at the first Marne battle, II, 95.
defeats Bulgarians, VI, 34-36.
sketch of, X, 104-105.
Deutschland, German submarine, her arrival in America, IX, 307-310.
second arrival of, in America, IX, 319.

489

INDEX

INDEX

Germany
  loses the Switch Line, V, 336-342.
  loss of, in the second Marne battle,
    V, 249-250.
  losses of, IV, 239-245.
  losses of, V, 249-250.
  many bids for peace, IV, 309-340.
  necessity of, to make sacrifices, IV,
    204.
  on the defensive, III, 239-240.
  peace bids of, with a new offensive
    as the alternative, IV, 352-368.
  plans of, in Asia Minor, VIII, 3-14.
  preliminary activity in 1918, IV, 356-
    370.
  price of peace in Russia, IV, 26-39;
    323-351.
  President Wilson's speech asking
    Congress to declare war on, IV,
    27-32.
  preparations of United States for
    war with, IV, 40-59.
  realizing her defeat, VI, 116.
  resources of, at beginning of the
    war, I, 139-151.
  responsibility of, for forcing the
    war, I, 104.
  retirement from the Marne, II, 98-
    103.
  retreat from Chemin des Dames, IV,
    192.
  rejected by senate, X, 393.
  seeks peace, V, 388, 389, 392.
  sends troops from Russia to France,
    VII, 359.
  sends forces into Galicia, VII, 61.
  sinks three more American ships,
    IV, 21-22.
  spies of, in United States, IV, 8-59.
  the armistice with Russia, IV, 248.
  treaty with prolonged controversy
    over, X, 360-394.
Ghent, King Albert enters, VI, 141-
    142.
  Gibbon, Percival, cited, IX, 81.
  its liberation, VI, 140-142.
Gibbs, Philip, cited, II, 28-31, 50, 224,
    225; III, 47, 328, 329, 335, 336,
    351, 353; IV, 328; VI, 94, 187-
    189; 370-371.
Giolitti, Signor, Italian Prime Minister,
    statement of, as to war in 1913, I,
    79-80.
Givenchy, attacks near, V, 86-87.
Gneisenau, sinking of the, at Falkland
    Islands, X, 26-30.
  the, at the battle off Coronel, X, 18-
    26.
Goeben, the, driven on a beach, X, 39.
  made over to Turkey, I, 198.
  the, warship, VIII, 11-12.
Gommecourt taken, III, 318.
Good Hope, sinking of the, X, 21-24.
Goltz Von der, his work in Turkey,
    VIII, 5, 18.
  his death, VIII, 152-153.
Gorizia, effects of attack on, IX, 47-
    49.
  fall of, IX, 64-70.
Goschen, Sir Edward, British Am-
    bassador to Germany, his account,
    the "scrap of paper" episode, I, 176-
    181.
Gough, Gen'l Sir H., his failure in the
    Amiens drive, V, 9-14.
Gouraud, advancing, VI, 57-59.
  captures Berry-au-Bac, VI, 102.

  east of Reims, V, 214, 216-220.
  enters Sedan, VI, 184.
  his advance, VI, 105-107.
  in Champagne, drive to Sedan, VI,
    42-67.
Gouzeaucourt, gains at, VI, 4.
Graham, Stephen, cited, VII, 170-172.
Grandpré, in ruins, VI, 172.
Great Britain, at first battle of Ypres,
    II, 232-240.
  achievements of, IV, 250-259.
  at the Marne battle, II, 88-89.
  annexes Cyprus, VIII, 32-33.
  and the Turks on the Suez Canal,
    15-27.
  at battle of Messines Ridge, IV, 163-
    174.
  bombards the Bulgarian coast, VIII,
    271.
  conquers Palestine, VIII, 204-226.
  forces moved north, II, 160-165.
  forced into the war, I, 103.
  Gen. Byng's Cambrai thrust, IV, 221-
    233.
  her colonial forces, II, 168.
  her declaration of war against Ger-
    many, I, 175-181.
  her effort to prevent war between
    Germany and Russia, I, 158-165.
  her fleet sails under sealed orders,
    I, 75.
  her operations at Gallipoli, VIII, 94-
    137.
  her attempt to force the Dardanelles,
    VIII 76-93.
  her reply to German peace propos-
    als, IV, 5-6.
  inactivity of, III, 158-160; 163-164.
  loses Kut, VIII, 157-167.
  position on the Persian Gulf, IV,
    56-64.
  resources of, at the beginning of the
    war, I, 139-151.
  sailing and arrival of her expedi-
    tionary force, II, 8-15.
  takes Bagdad, VIII, 187-195.
  takes Jersualem, VIII, 215-221.
  work done by navy of, I, 53-55.
  withdrawal of, from Gallipoli, VIII,
    133-137.
Greece, declares war on Germany, I,
    229.
  her early attitude in the war, I,
    196-198.
  invasion of, by Bulgaria gets into
    the war, VIII, 300, 301, 313.
Greene, Maj-Gen., F. V., I, 8.
  cited, I, 28; XIV
Grey, Sir Edward (now Viscount), an-
    nouncement by, I, 74.
  Ambassador from Great Britain, X,
    386.
  his effort to avert war, I, 174-175.
  on the ultimatum to Serbia, I, 72.
  protesting to Germany against vio-
    lation Belgian neutrality, I, 171-
    173.
  sketch of, X, 234-236.
Gröener, General, succeeds Ludendorff,
    VI, 162-163.
Gulflight, sinking of the, IX, 248.
Gumbinnen, battle of, VII, 16-18.
Guynemer George, airman, at Verdun,
    III, 105.
  his exploits, IV, 265-268.
  his death, IV, 288-290.
Haelen, battle of, I, 290-292.

INDEX

HISTORY OF THE WORLD WAR